# American Social Leaders

FO... ...IAL TAXATION

VOTES FOR WOMEN

# American Social Leaders

William McGuire and Leslie Wheeler

Editors
**Amy Lewis**
**Paula McGuire**

Consulting Editors
**Gary Gerstle**
The Catholic University of America

**James M. McPherson**
Princeton University

**ABC-CLIO**

Santa Barbara, California
Denver, Colorado
Oxford, England

**Library of Congress Cataloging-in-Publication Data**

McGuire, William, 1917–
    American social leaders : from colonial times to the present /
  William McGuire and Leslie Wheeler ; editors, Amy Lewis, Paula
  McGuire, consulting editors, Gary Gerstle, James M. McPherson.
      p.  cm.—(Biographies of American leaders)
    Includes bibliographical references.
    1. Social reformers—United States—Biography—Dictionaries.
  I. Wheeler, Leslie, 1945–  .  II. Series.
  HN65.M38  1993    303.48′4′092273—dc20     93-3991
  [B]

ISBN 0-87436-633-X (alk. paper)

99 98 97 96 95 94 93      10 9 8 7 6 5 4 3 2 1 (cloth)


BIOGRAPHIES OF AMERICAN LEADERS


Developed by Visual Education Corp., Princeton, New Jersey

ABC-CLIO, Inc.
130 Cremona Drive, P.O. Box 1911
Santa Barbara, California 93116-1911


This book is printed on acid-free paper ∞.
Manufactured in the United States of America

# Contents

## Biographical Profiles, 3

# List of American Social Leaders

# Preface

*American Social Leaders: From Colonial Times to the Present* is a biographical reference work containing 350 profiles of American men and women who have been leaders of the social and intellectual movements that have significantly affected American life and thought since the country was first settled by colonists. Each of the 350 profiles strives to balance an account of a leader's career with an assessment of his or her most important contributions to public life.

As in *American Political Leaders,* our double task as consulting editors has been to aid in the identification of social leaders included in this book and to review carefully each profile submitted by the two authors, William McGuire and Leslie Wheeler.

Compiling an appropriate list of social leaders has been a challenging task, for the universe of such individuals is virtually limitless. The number and variety of social movements that have flourished in this country have probably exceeded that of any other nation on earth. The first group of leaders includes Americans who have thrown themselves into movements for democracy, good government, and human rights; for working-class justice, educational reform, and self-help; for religious redemption, temperance, and moral purity; for racial, ethnic, and sexual equality; for international peace, physical fitness, and environmental protection; and for many more causes. Leaders selected from these social movements alone could easily have filled the space available in this volume. We have tried to pick those individuals whose movements and leadership were, in our estimation, most important. We have also tried to include a selection of leaders representing the full range of social movements so that readers would learn of the remarkable breadth of social activism in American history. Finally, we have made a special effort to be up-to-date: readers will find in this volume an ample selection of individuals from the twentieth-century movements for civil rights, American Indian rights, feminism, gay rights, consumer protection, and Protestant evangelicalism.

A second group of social leaders whose biographies appear in the following pages achieved distinction because of the influence of their ideas rather than their actual leadership of reform movements. These individuals, who might be termed "public intellectuals," were leading figures in American philosophy, economics, anthropology, education, sociology, history, physics, psychology, medicine, and other scholarly disciplines. They are included because their reputations extended well beyond the university community and because their beliefs were important in shaping public policy and public opinion, and, sometimes, in inspiring social movements. Hannah Arendt; Franz Boas; John Dewey; Albert Einstein; Milton Friedman; Robert, Helen, and Staughton Lynd; Margaret Mead; and Frederick Jackson Turner are among those intellectuals who qualify as social leaders.

A third, and small, group of social leaders comprises individuals who exercised their influence through journalism: as publishers of newspapers and magazines, as journalists or critics, and, in a few instances, as photographers or cartoonists. We chose only those publishers, like William Randolph Hearst, Joseph Pulitzer, and Henry Luce, widely known to the public as the creators of new styles of journalism and as individuals with strong opinions on issues of the day. In selecting journalists and critics, we have used a broader standard. We have sought to include not only those like Walter Lippman, Martha Gellhorn, and Edward R. Murrow, whose political commentary reached millions, but also those who exercised enormous influence over smaller, but politically significant, reading publics. W. E. B. Du Bois, Randolph Bourne, Louis Adamic, William Buckley, Gloria Steinem, Irving Howe, and Garry Wills are among those chosen in this way.

A fourth, and quite different, group of social leaders is also represented—those who converted their success as inventors, industrialists, and philanthropists into popular influence. There have been many such individuals in American history—enough, arguably, to fill an entire volume. Here, we have included only those who achieved enormous fame and whose public statements carried unusual weight. Thomas Edison, Henry Ford, and Andrew Carnegie are among those so chosen.

The inclusion of public intellectuals, journalists, and select industrialists and inventors gives this volume an uncommonly wide reach. The volume also includes living social leaders. No other volume has such coverage, making *American Social Leaders* uniquely valuable and up-to-date as a one-volume biographical resource.

We think that a variety of users, including high school students, college students, and adults who are not in school, will find much valuable information in the pages that follow. Those readers who allow themselves time to browse will become acquainted with a large number of talented, energetic, and concerned Americans. In the process, they will come to appreciate the role of social leaders and their ideas, organizations, and activities in enriching, challenging, and often changing American society.

Gary Gerstle
James M. McPherson

# Editors' Note

The profiles included in this volume aim to provide the student or general reader with biographical and historical information to place the subjects within a particular social movement. Significant events in American history are described and important terms are defined Cross-references have been provided to connect people and events and provide historical context. Each profile contains a brief bibliography for further reference, and the reader is urged to consult a library for additional materials. Black-and-white portraits illustrate many of the subjects.

A User's Guide follows, illustrating the special features of the profiles.

Editorial development of the book was provided by Visual Education Corporation of Princeton, New Jersey. The editors wish to acknowledge Dale Anderson and Richard Lidz, for their editorial advice; Kim Nir, for special editorial assistance and fact-checking; Linda Biemiller, for copyediting; Cindy Feldner, for keying and proofreading; and Susan Hormuth, for picture research.

Amy Lewis
Paula McGuire

# User's Guide to Entry Format

Below is a description of the entry format used in this book; the format is illustrated on the facing page.

*Headnote:* The headnote contains the following parts:

Entry Name: Profiles are arranged alphabetically by the last name of the subject profiled. The subject's full name is used in the heading, including any middle name(s). If the subject was commonly known by initials (H. L. Mencken), a nickname (Mother Jones), or a shortened version of his or her given name (Woody Guthrie), this form is included in the text of the profile. Some profiles are presented as a "multiple entry" that lists two or more members of the same family in the order of the appearance within the entry.

Date of Birth/Death: If the exact date of birth or death is unknown, it is preceded by the abbreviation "ca."

Occupation(s): The most significant occupations of the subject's life, and/or the social movements in which he or she was involved, are listed in alphabetical order.

*Summary of Subject's Significance:* The first paragraph gives a concise description of the subject's contributions to American society.

*Cross-References:* To aid the reader's use of the volume, a simple cross-reference system has been devised. Within the profiles, the printing of names in SMALL CAPITALS indicates a cross-reference, of which there are two kinds. The first is a name printed in small capitals, which indicates that the subject mentioned has a profile that will be found in its alphabetical position. The second kind of cross-reference features a name in small capitals preceded by the word "see." This indicates that the reader may turn to that profile for an explanation of a term or an event just mentioned.

*Bibliography:* Each profile concludes with a brief bibliography listing sources for further reference (including, in some cases, works by the individual profiled). The author, title, and date or dates of publication are included for each source. Sources are in alphabetical order by the last name of the author. Works by the same author are organized chronologically by year of publication. The reader is encouraged to consult a library for additional materials.

*Headnote*

# Meredith, James Howard

(June 25, 1933–   )
Civil Rights Activist

*Summary of Subject's Significance*

James Meredith's application to the University of Mississippi in 1961 sparked a violent crisis that opened the way to the desegregation of the university and eventually of the state at large.

J. H. Meredith (as he was christened) was born and raised near Kosciusko, in central Mississippi, one of ten children of Moses and Roxie Meredith, who owned a large farm. After attending local segregated schools he went to St. Petersburg, Florida, where an uncle lived, and finished high school, again at a segregated institution. Looking toward a good education, in 1951 Meredith enlisted in the U.S. Air Force (at which time he expanded J. H. to James Howard).

Meredith spent nine years in the air force and was discharged a staff sergeant in summer 1960. During his service he had earned credits for college-level courses by correspondence. While he had his sights on the University of Mississippi, he had a wife and child, and realistically he decided to begin by entering Jackson State, a black college.

Meredith discussed his intentions with MEDGAR EVERS, the state field secretary for the National Association for the Advancement of Colored People (NAACP; see JOEL E. SPINGARN). Evers agreed that *Cross-Reference* the association's legal defense and education fund could help Meredith with his effort to transfer to the University of Mississippi. His application was submitted on January 31, 1961. Nearly two years passed before Meredith's registration on October 1, 1962. Both the university and the state of Mississippi interposed resistance—political, legal, and finally, on Governor Ross R. Barnett's part, physical. A federal court order and the presence of federal troops brought the crisis to an end, but not before the campus was the scene of violence, rioting, and two deaths. Calm returned to the university, though troops remained, and Meredith graduated in August 1963. The attention this controversy attracted in the media made Meredith's name well known and raised national consciousness of the civil rights struggle.

During 1964 and 1965, Meredith was at the University of Ibadan, Nigeria, taking graduate courses in economics. He returned to the United States the following year to enroll in the college of law at Columbia University but interrupted his studies in 1966 to take part, with STOKELY CARMICHAEL and others, in a "March Against Fear" from Memphis to Jackson, the aim of which was to encourage voter registration. Segregationists shot at the marchers and wounded both leaders. Meredith, despite the lingering effects of his injuries, continued at Columbia and earned his law degree in 1968. *Cross-Reference*

In later years Meredith lectured at American and African colleges and undertook various business ventures, including stockbroking and property investments in New York. After returning to Mississippi, in 1972 he ran unsuccessfully on the Republican ticket for the U.S. Senate against James Eastland. Despite his prominent role in the civil rights movement, Meredith was a political conservative at heart, and in 1989 he joined the staff of Senator Jesse Helms, of North Carolina. For two years he devoted his time to an intensive study of American social policies from the eighteenth century to the present. Meredith then returned to Jackson to write a book and engage in local politics.

**BIBLIOGRAPHY**

Lord, Walter, *The Past That Would Not Die,* 1965; Meredith, James H., *Three Years in Mississippi,* 1965. *Bibliography*

# American Social Leaders

# Abernathy, Ralph David

(March 11, 1926–April 17, 1990)
Civil Rights Leader

The Baptist clergyman Ralph Abernathy was MARTIN LUTHER KING, JR.'s closest coworker during the civil rights movement of the 1950s and 1960s and the leader of the Southern Christian Leadership Conference (SCLC) after King's death.

The tenth of twelve children and the youngest of seven sons, Ralph Abernathy was born near Linden, in western Alabama. His father made a success of his large farm and was the leader of the black community—indeed, the first black person to serve on a jury in the county. Ralph graduated from high school in time to enter the U.S. Army and serve in Germany as World War II was ending. He was ordained a Baptist minister at the age of twenty-two and only thereafter, in 1950, graduated from Alabama State College, a black institution in Montgomery.

While Abernathy was doing graduate work in sociology at Atlanta University, he met Martin Luther King, Jr., who was preaching at his father's church, Ebenezer Baptist. After earning his M.A. in 1951, Abernathy took the pulpit at First Baptist Church, in Montgomery, where King arrived as pastor of the Dexter Avenue Baptist Church in 1954.

When ROSA PARKS was arrested for refusing to give up her bus seat to a white passenger in December 1955, Abernathy called on the black community to boycott the buses. He and King formed the Montgomery Improvement Association to coordinate the action, with King as president and Abernathy as his second in com-

National Archives

mand. After a year of the boycott the bus company agreed to end segregated seating. A month later, King and Abernathy joined black church leaders from other southern states in Atlanta and formed the SCLC, under King's presidency, to lead nonviolent resistance to segregation. While Abernathy (who was elected SCLC's secretary-treasurer) was in Atlanta, his house and church in Montgomery were firebombed. The house was damaged but his family members were unhurt; the church burned down and was rebuilt.

In 1961, at King's urging, Abernathy became pastor of the West Hunter Street Baptist Church in Atlanta, which was near the SCLC offices, and he was named vice president of the SCLC. During the years of the civil rights struggle, he was with King at many of the historic occasions: the brutal assault on the Freedom Riders (see JAMES FARMER) at Montgomery in May 1961; the march on Washington and King's "I Have a Dream" speech in August 1963; the violent events at St. Augustine, Florida, in spring 1964, and the award of the Nobel Prize for Peace in Oslo, Norway, that fall; the march from Selma to Montgomery in spring 1965. Abernathy complemented his friend's intellectual and philosophical qualities with a sense of humor and a common touch.

Late in 1967, King began to plan the Poor People's Campaign, designed to unite poor Americans, regardless of race, in a descent on Washington that would bring their concerns to the very door of the federal government. In

April 1968, however, he and Abernathy had gone to Memphis, Tennessee, to support a strike of underpaid garbage collectors. On April 4, 1968, King was shot by a sniper and died shortly afterward, with Abernathy at his side.

The SCLC leaders accepted Abernathy as King's choice to succeed him as president. A few days later, Abernathy led a demonstration in support of the sanitation workers, which included marchers who had flown in from around the country. The strikers succeeded in reaching a settlement with the Memphis city government.

Abernathy carried on with the Poor People's Campaign. In May, motorcades of jobless and poor began arriving in Washington, where a campground near the Lincoln Memorial had been made available for a month by the National Park Service. Abernathy called it Resurrection City. He presented demands for job assurances and aid for the unemployed to members of Congress; the demands eventually brought a few gains in government policy. The campaign was pronounced a disaster, however: facilities were inadequate, and there was trouble with violence and crime. When the people in Resurrection City overstayed the permit for the encampment, Abernathy and some of his aides were sentenced to three weeks in jail.

Abernathy championed other civil rights causes: the boycott by California grape-pickers led by CESAR CHAVEZ, and the antiwar People's Coalition for Peace and Justice in 1971. He continued to lead the SCLC until 1977, when he unsuccessfully stood for a seat in the U.S. House of Representatives. After resigning the SCLC presidency, he devoted himself to his pastorate at the West Hunter Street Baptist Church, to lecturing on civil rights, and to writing his life story, which he completed just a year before his death.

BIBLIOGRAPHY

Abernathy, Ralph, *And the Walls Came Tumbling Down*, 1989; D'Emilio, John, *The Civil Rights Struggle: Leaders in Profile*, 1979; Garrow, David J., *Bearing the Cross: Martin Luther King, Jr., and the Southern Christian Leadership Conference*, 1986; Viorst, Milton, *Fire in the Streets: America in the Sixties*, 1979.

# Adamic, Louis

(March 23, 1899–September 4, 1951)
Author, Journalist

Slovene American author Louis Adamic explored the immigrant experience in America in his novels and autobiographical works of nonfiction.

The son of peasant parents, Louis Adamic was born in the village of Blato in Slovenia, which was then part of Austria-Hungary. He attended the gymnasium in Ljubljana, Slovenia, but was expelled for playing a prank. In 1913, at age fourteen, he immigrated to the United States. In New York City, Adamic worked for a time at the office of a Slovenia-language newspaper and later at a variety of odd jobs. In 1916 he enlisted in the army, and two years later became a naturalized citizen.

Harboring literary ambitions, during the 1920s Adamic began translating Serbian, Croatian, and Slovenian stories into English. Most of his translations were published in a magazine, *Living Age*. In 1928 the well-known journalist and social critic H. L. MENCKEN accepted an article by Adamic, entitled "The Yugoslav Speech in America," for publication in the *American Mercury*. Adamic wrote other articles for the *American Mercury*, many of them autobiographical. Becoming interested in the 1910 bombing of the *Los Angeles Times* building during a strike at the newspaper, Adamic wrote his first book, *Dynamite* (1931), a study of labor violence in America.

In his second book, *Laughing in the Jungle* (1932), Adamic returned to autobiography, writing of his childhood and early years as an immigrant. Also in 1932, Adamic won a Guggenheim Fellowship for fiction with the sponsorship of such major literary figures as Sinclair Lewis, Carl Sandburg, and Mencken. He used it to revisit his homeland, where he spent a year gathering material for a third book, *The Native's Return* (1934). This book, about life in Yugoslavia, became a best-seller and established Adamic's reputation. However, the book also involved Adamic in controversy in both the United States and Yugoslavia, because to some people it appeared to endorse communism.

Adamic followed *The Native's Return* with two novels: *Grandsons* (1935), a saga about a Slovenian family that comes to America; and *Cradle of Life* (1936), also dealing with the immigrant experience in America. His next and one of his most important books, *My America* (1938), was a collection of impressions, again reflecting Adamic's immigrant background, and conveyed through letters, diary entries, articles, and character sketches.

In 1940 Adamic became editor of *Common Ground*, a quarterly that sought to promote racial tolerance and to examine the complicated racial and cultural problems of contemporary American society. By this time, Adamic's interest in the lives of immigrants

and the problems of acculturation they experienced had intensified. He wrote another extremely popular book, *From Many Lands* (1940), as well as numerous articles, and he lectured on the subject.

While filled with ethnic pride, Adamic was highly enthusiastic about American democracy. In his book *Two-Way Passage* (1941), he proposed that European Americans be returned to their homelands to take to Europe "in person—the American Revolution, the American Experience." This idea so impressed President Franklin D. Roosevelt that on January 13, 1942, he invited Adamic to a meeting at the White House, along with the British leader Winston Churchill. Adamic later wrote a detailed account of the meeting in *Dinner at the White House* (1946), which included a comment that Churchill's policy toward Greece was influenced by his ties to a British bank with Greek interests. In 1947 Winston Churchill took issue with the comment and successfully sued Adamic for libel.

During the late 1930s and early 1940s, Adamic had watched events in Yugoslavia with growing concern. In 1943 he published *My Native Land*, a book which sought to arouse American sympathy and support by explaining Yugoslavia's past history, along with its current crises. Adamic also generated controversy by speaking out in favor of Marshal Tito's faction of the Yugoslav underground movement. In 1944 Tito awarded Adamic the Yugoslavian Order of National Unity.

Although active in rallying foreign-born Americans behind the war effort during World War II, in the postwar years Adamic was often identified as a communist and a subversive. In the election of 1948 he backed the leftward-leaning Progressive party candidate, Henry Wallace, yet tended to keep his distance from American Marxists. When Tito broke with Soviet leader Joseph Stalin in 1948, Adamic sided with Tito, thereby arousing the anger of Soviet communists. The following year, Adamic returned from a six-month visit to Yugoslavia even more a partisan of Tito. His last book, *The Eagle and the Roots*, published posthumously in 1952, was in large part a laudatory biography of Tito, and portrayed Yugoslavia as a democracy stubbornly resisting Soviet communism. Despite conjecture that Soviet agents were responsible, Adamic's death at Riegelsville, New Jersey, in September 1951, was ruled an apparent suicide.

**BIBLIOGRAPHY**

Christian, Henry A., *Louis Adamic: A Checklist*, 1971; McWilliams, Carey, "Louis Adamic, American," *Nation*, September 22, 1951; Raditsa, Bogdan, "My Memories of Louis Adamic," *American Mercury*, December 1951.

# Addams, Jane

(September 6, 1860–May 21, 1935)
Peace Activist, Reformer

Jane Addams, one of the country's most outstanding humanitarians and a leader of Progressive reform, is best known for the establishment of Hull House in Chicago, which was one of the first social welfare settlement houses in the United States, and her efforts for world peace.

Addams was born in Cedarville, Illinois. After graduating from Rockford College (then the Rockford Female Seminary) at the top of her class in 1881, she entered the Woman's Medical College of Pennsylvania the same year. Also that year her father died, and only months later, she was forced to withdraw from medical school because of ill health. In 1883 she made her first trip to Europe. What she saw and learned abroad convinced her to devote her life to helping the poor.

On a trip to Europe in 1888, Addams told her friend and traveling companion, Ellen Gates Starr, that she wanted to purchase a house in a poor neighborhood so that she and other

The Nobel Foundation

middle-class college-educated women could share what they had learned with those less fortunate. Starr took up the idea enthusiastically. They visited Toynbee Hall, a welfare settlement house that had been founded in London's East End four years earlier. They agreed it was a perfect model for what was needed in the United States.

Addams and Starr purchased the run-down old Hull mansion in a poor Chicago neighborhood composed of Eastern European immigrants. In 1889 the two women moved in and began offering instruction in sanitation, hygiene, English, and other subjects. Cultural events, including art exhibits, poetry readings, concerts, and theatrical events, were also offered.

Although Hull House was founded by both Addams and Starr, Addams was the one who took the leading role. Under her guidance, Hull House became a political as well as a social center, "a spearhead of reform" (to use one historian's phrase). To her credit, Jane Addams assembled an extraordinary constellation of people who gathered at and learned from Hull House. These included such social reformers as ALICE HAMILTON, FLORENCE KELLEY, and JULIA LATHROP, as well as JOHN DEWEY, CLARENCE DARROW, and UPTON SINCLAIR.

Addams became one of the nation's most prominent Progressives, helping to organize campaigns for child labor reform, the implementation of the nation's first juvenile court system, trade unions, public schools, public sanitation codes, building codes, and public parks and playgrounds. The success of Hull House soon outstripped Addams's ability to support it by herself, and she had to raise money from wealthy Chicagoans.

Hull House was such a success that it served as an inspiration and model for similar centers across the United States. Addams also used it as a training ground for other middle-class women she attracted to social work through her speeches, articles, and books. In *The Spirit of Youth and the City Streets* (1909), she addressed the generational conflicts between immigrants and their children, with unusual sensitivity for the time. In *Twenty Years at Hull House* (1910), she told the story of the Hull House settlement center, and she addressed the problem of prostitution in *A New Conscience and an Ancient Evil* (1912).

In addition to her social work at Hull House, Addams campaigned for Prohibition, woman suffrage, and, in 1912, the Progressive party. A staunch pacifist, she had written about the need to end war in *Newer Ideals of Peace* (1907). She became chairman of the Woman's Peace Party when World War I began, and president of the International Congress of Women. She even traveled to Europe in 1915 in a vain attempt to facilitate a negotiated settlement to the war. When the United States entered the war in 1917, she suffered considerable ostracism for her refusal to support the war effort and for her defense of German immigrants who were being persecuted because of their origins.

After the war ended, Addams worked on Herbert Hoover's war relief staff, helping to feed the starving in Europe. In 1919 she was elected president of the Women's International League for Peace and Freedom, a position she held for the rest of her life, and in 1920 she helped to found the American Civil Liberties Union (see ROGER BALDWIN). In 1931 she was awarded the Nobel Prize for Peace "as the right spokesman for all the peace-loving women of the world," sharing the prize with NICHOLAS MURRAY BUTLER.

Addams died of cancer in her seventy-fifth year. As a tireless worker striving to improve social conditions and to enrich the lives of both the poor and those who served them, especially women, Addams was at the cutting edge of reform during her time. In a sense she invented the vocation of social work, opening the eyes of her country to the fundamental needs of its citizens.

**BIBLIOGRAPHY**

Addams, Jane, *Twenty Years at Hull House,* 1910, and *The Second Twenty Years at Hull House,* 1930; Davis, Allen F., *Spearheads for Reform,* 1985; Lasch, Christopher, *The New Radicalism in America,* 1986.

## Agassiz, Jean Louis Rodolphe

(May 28, 1807–December 14, 1873)
Educator, Naturalist

Swiss-born Louis Agassiz won renown in America as a teacher, founder of Harvard's Museum of Comparative Zoology, and popularizer of natural science. Although Agassiz steadfastly opposed Darwin's theory of evolution, his actual work lent support to it.

Born a minister's son in the Swiss canton of Fribourg, Louis Agassiz studied at the universities of Zurich and Heidelberg before earning his Ph.D. at the University of Erlangen in 1829 and a medical degree at the University of Munich in 1830. Preferring natural science to medicine, Agassiz went to Paris to study under naturalist Georges Cuvier. Agassiz also met in Paris the explorer and geographer Alexander Humboldt, who helped him to begin his teaching career in Neuchâtel in 1832.

During the next decade, Agassiz produced a five-volume classification of fossil fishes that aroused great interest in this area of study and brought a new degree of order to the zoological past. Although he was not the first to observe the effects of glaciation in scratched and polished rocks and in the shape of the earth in certain parts of Europe, his extensive investigations did much to advance the theory that during a so-called ice age, large parts of Europe had been covered by glaciers.

The American phase of his career began in 1846, when Agassiz was invited to lecture in Boston. These and subsequent lectures in other eastern cities were such huge successes that in 1848 Agassiz was offered the chair of natural history at the newly organized Lawrence Scientific School at Harvard. Agassiz enthusiastically accepted the professorship and set out to promote the study of the natural history of his new home.

In 1855 Agassiz began a ten-volume work, *Contributions to the Natural History of the United States*. Four volumes were published, but the work proved too difficult for both lay readers and scientists, who additionally were becoming concerned with Darwin's theories.

Agassiz rejected these theories himself, remaining convinced that animal life had been formed according to divine plan. Nevertheless, he continued to amass raw data that others would cite in support of evolution. Agassiz's work ranged from studies of glaciers in North America to marine biology. In 1859, thanks largely to his efforts, the Museum of Comparative Zoology was established at Harvard. Agassiz served as curator of this museum until his death.

Although he made extensive field trips to Brazil in 1865 and to the Western United States in 1868 and 1871, it was as a teacher and lecturer that Agassiz made his most important contribution. In his classes Agassiz emphasized the direct study of nature, discouraging the use of books except for detailed research. As he was fond of saying: "If you study nature in books, when you go out-of-doors you cannot find her"; and "Strive to interpret what really exists." His skillful teaching, combined with his obvious passion for his subject, made Agassiz's classes so popular that RALPH WALDO EMERSON complained that "something should be done to check the rush towards natural history."

In addition to ensuring that Harvard became a center for natural history research and studies, Agassiz was concerned with the teaching of the subject in the lower schools. He urged a better method that replaced rote memorization with hands-on contact with the natural materials being studied, and argued the value of training in natural history for any kind of mental work.

To promote better teaching of natural history, Agassiz established in 1873 the Anderson School of Natural History on Penikese Island off the Massachusetts coast. The school did not survive his death later that year, but Agassiz's inspired methods of teaching did. His influence was so pervasive that during the latter part of the nineteenth century, every notable teacher of natural history had either been a pupil of Agassiz himself or of one of his students.

**BIBLIOGRAPHY**

Agassiz, Elizabeth Cary (ed.), *Louis Agassiz, His Life and Correspondence*, 2 vols., 1885; Lurie, Edward, *Louis Agassiz: A Life in Science*, 1960.

# Alcott, Amos Bronson

(November 29, 1799–March 4, 1888)
Educator, Transcendentalist

Bronson Alcott pioneered child-centered education and is considered a forerunner of JOHN DEWEY. As a Transcendentalist, he joined many reform efforts of the time and started the experimental Temple School and a utopian community called Fruitlands. He was the father of novelist Louisa May Alcott.

Alcott was born near Wolcott, Connecticut, the eldest of eight children. He was himself largely self-educated and taught school in rural Connecticut in the early 1820s, in Boston from 1828 to 1830, and in Germantown, Pennsylvania, from 1831 to 1833.

In this period, he developed his new educational philosophy. At a time when learning was by rote and discipline by the rod, Alcott attracted attention with a revolutionary educational program that tried to achieve balanced growth of mind, body, and spirit. He argued that study was a pleasurable end in itself rather than a means. In addition to study, he included recreation; rather than memorization, he promoted reading from books in a student library. He absolutely disapproved of corporal punishment. His rejection of traditional religion grew even more radical when he developed an interest in Transcendental philosophy (see RALPH WALDO EMERSON) while in Germantown. Through his reading of Plato and other philosophers, Alcott came to believe that people have innate ideas that come not through the senses or from reasoning, but directly from God. For moral education, then, he employed a question and answer method intended to help students articulate the ethical ideas that he was sure they all possessed innately.

In 1834 Alcott returned to Boston to found what was to become his most controversial educational experiment, the Temple School. With ELIZABETH PEABODY serving as his assistant, Alcott put his new program into practice. Although Peabody's *The Record of a School* aroused interest in Alcott's methods, his own *Conversations with Children on the Gospels*, in two volumes (1836–1837), brought him under sharp attack because he promoted independent thought about religious matters. Two Boston newspapers condemned as blasphemous and obscene Alcott's description of childbirth as a process involving God. Enrollment at the school declined sharply, and Alcott finally had to close it in 1839 when most of the parents of his remaining pupils objected to his admitting an African American girl as a student.

In 1840 Alcott, his wife (the former Abigail May, whom he had married in 1830), and their growing family moved to Concord, Massachusetts, so that he could be close to Emerson and other Transcendentalists. Although Alcott, along with other members of this group, believed that true reform came from within the individual, he also joined in many of the reform movements of the day, including abolition, temperance, and vegetarianism. Indeed, his efforts to support his family by farming in Concord suffered because he was always leaving to attend reform meetings.

In 1842 Alcott went to England to visit a group of Englishmen who admired his educational ideas and had founded a school called Alcott House near London. He returned to America with three of his English disciples—Henry Wright, Charles Lane, and Lane's son William—and together with them started Fruitlands, a utopian community like those that were springing up all over America during these years. Located near Harvard, Massachusetts, Fruitlands was based on strict vegetarian principles. Even the eating of vegetables was limited to those Alcott called the "aspiring vegetables," because they grew upward toward the heavens. But since Alcott and the other men were more interested in discussing philosophy and attending reform meetings than in farming, the community only lasted from June 1843 until January 1844. Thereafter, Alcott traveled around the country giving informal lectures, or "conversations," that were popular, though not especially remunerative.

From 1859 to 1865 Alcott served as superintendent of Concord's dozen schools. He added singing and calisthenics to the curriculum and called for the introduction of other innovations like dancing, hours of directed conversation, and a course of reading aloud. He also formed what may have been the first parent-teacher association. Three annual reports he wrote during this period reflect his advanced views of education.

In 1879, after the huge success of his daughter Louisa May Alcott's novel *Little Women* (1868) had made the family financially secure, Alcott started the Concord Summer School of Philosophy and Literature in his home. The informal school served as a center for the discussion of Transcendentalism and educational theory. Alcott directed it until 1882 when he was stricken with paralysis, from which he never fully recovered; he died six years later. Although Alcott published a number of books, much of his work is not considered particularly readable. As a result, later generations have found it difficult to understand his ideas or the extent of his acknowledged influence on the Transcendentalists.

**BIBLIOGRAPHY**

Alcott, Bronson, *Essays on Education*, 1960; Bedell, Madelon, *The Alcotts, Biography of a Family*, 1980; Dahlstrand, F. C., *Amos Bronson Alcott, an Intellectual Biography*, 1982.

# Alger, Horatio

(January 13, 1832–July 18, 1899)
Author

Horatio Alger's stories of boys who rose from rags to riches by virtue and hard work made him one of the most popular writers of the late nineteenth century. The "Alger hero" he created suggested to Americans of his generation and long afterward that economic opportunity was available to all.

Born the son of a Unitarian minister in Revere, Massachusetts, Alger graduated from Harvard in 1852. After a brief visit to Europe and three years' work as a newspaperman, he gave in to his father's wish that he become a minister and entered Harvard Divinity School, receiving his degree in 1860. Alger then spent a year in Paris, and in 1864 was ordained a minister of a Unitarian church in Brewster, Massachusetts. Two years later he resigned and moved to New York City.

In New York, Alger came to know the Newsboys' Lodging House, founded by the philanthropist CHARLES LORING BRACE as a home for orphans and runaway boys. He developed a lasting friendship with the superintendent of the institution, Charles O'Connor, and spent most of his time there. Alger also became good friends with many of the boys, including a Chinese orphan, Ah Wing, whose accidental death was a great blow to the writer.

Before Alger came to the Newsboys' Lodging House, he had written several unsuccessful books, such as *Bertha's Christmas Vision* (1856). Now, inspired by the stories the boys told him of their lives, he produced a string of best-sellers, beginning with *Ragged Dick* (1867) and followed by *Fame and Fortune* (1868), *Luck and Pluck* (1869), *Sink or Swim* (1870), and *Tattered Tom* (1871). Among them, Alger's books sold more than 20,000,000 copies, with most of the royalties going to the Newsboys' Lodging House.

In a typical Alger story, a poor but virtuous boy comes to a big city, usually New York, where he struggles to make his way against overwhelming odds. After enduring many hardships, he performs a heroic deed that brings him to the attention of a wealthy patron and his fortune is assured. For example, Ragged Dick saves from drowning the son of a wealthy man, who rewards him generously.

Before Alger, American writers like COTTON MATHER and Benjamin Franklin had presented

Library of Congress

virtue and industry as the keys to success. But Alger was one of the first to address himself specifically to boys and to use fiction to convey his message. His stories appealed strongly to boys, because they were first and foremost tales of adventure. The stories were also set in locales like New York City, San Francisco, and the South Seas that were likely to appeal to young boys living on farms and in small towns, who themselves longed to escape to the city and make their fortunes.

Writing so rapidly that he once completed a book in two weeks, Alger produced some 119 novels. The speed with which he wrote is evident in the novels' flimsy plots, wooden characterization, and stilted dialogue. Although he dreamed of writing a serious adult novel, Alger lacked the ability to do so. Besides fiction, Alger wrote juvenile biographies of a number of Americans who had overcome poverty to become famous leaders. These biographies included *Abraham Lincoln, the Backwoods Boy* (1883) and *From Canal Boy to President* (1881), the story of James Garfield.

The rags-to-riches theme of Alger's books was used to reinforce the prevailing business philosophy of late–nineteenth-century America. This philosophy held that anyone could rise to the top by working hard. It also held that government intervention in the economic system would get in the way of progress because it would give some an unfair advantage over others.

Alger's popularity extended well beyond his lifetime. Through his books, he helped establish one of the most powerful and pervasive myths in American life—that any individual, however humble his or her beginnings, could become president or a millionaire by dint of hard work and good deeds. Thanks to him, the term "Alger hero" entered the American language and the legend embodied by this hero became the basis of the "American Dream" of success through individual effort.

**BIBLIOGRAPHY**

Mayes, Herbert R., *Alger,* 1928; Tebbel, John, *From Rags to Riches: Horatio Alger and the American Dream,* 1963.

# Alinsky, Saul David

(January 30, 1909–June 12, 1972)
Community Activist

Saul Alinsky devoted his life to fighting poverty by helping communities of the urban poor organize to address their demands.

Saul David Alinsky was born in the slums of Chicago, the only child of orthodox Jewish parents from Russia. His father was a tailor. His father and mother divorced when Saul was thirteen, and the boy moved with his father to Los Angeles and periodically visited his mother in Chicago. After graduating from Hollywood High School in 1926, he entered the University of Chicago. His major was archaeology, which he combined with sociology. Already interested in social causes, he organized a group of students who drove down to southern Illinois with truckloads of provisions to help coal miners who were at odds with JOHN L. LEWIS, head of the United Mine Workers.

Graduating in 1930, in the teeth of the Great Depression, Alinsky saw that prospects in archaeology were unpromising and stayed on at the University of Chicago to do graduate work in criminology, with a fellowship. His doctoral subject was a study of the gangster Al Capone's crime syndicate, and he befriended the gang members and spent two years taking notes on their talk and stories. Having decided against scholarship, Alinsky took a job with the Illinois Division of Criminology, working with delinquent youths. In 1933 he was hired as a criminologist for the Illinois State Penitentiary at

Joliet, where he acquired an insight into the causes of criminal behavior: "poor housing, discrimination, economic insecurity, unemployment, and disease," he told an interviewer later in life.

During the 1930s, even before he made a career of social activism, Alinsky spent his free time helping to raise funds for the International Brigade in the Spanish Civil War, the Newspaper Guild, and southern sharecroppers. In 1938 he took on as a full-time project the Back of the Yards neighborhood in Chicago, a slum area next to the stockyards that was controlled by the meat-packing companies. Its poor were mainly Irish. To channel their demands for better jobs, schools, and housing, Alinsky organized the slum residents into the Back of the Yards Council, which won the support of the Roman Catholic clergy, some of the Democratic party, and the labor unions. By such means as boycotts, rent strikes, and picket lines, the people pressured the private and public elites—the packing companies, government bureaucrats—into reforms that made the area a decent neighborhood. Alinsky's credo was based on three tenets: organize, show people what they can do, and trust them.

In 1940, with financial backing from the Chicago philanthropist Marshall Field III and support from Catholic church leaders, Alinsky established the Industrial Areas Foundation

(IAF) as a base for advice and help to troubled communities interested in organizing. During the World War II years he was a consultant to the U.S. government on questions of labor and finance. Resuming his community work for the IAF, he antagonized those in power and was periodically arrested. While in jail, he wrote *Reveille for Radicals* (1947), a manifesto of his radical views rooted in his experiences with IAF. He also wrote a biography of his early adversary and later exemplar, John L. Lewis, in 1949.

Alinsky, supported during the late 1950s by a coalition of churchmen and businessmen, formed the Organization for the Southwest Community in an impoverished area of Chicago. He first worked with poor blacks in 1960, when he assembled the Woodlawn Organization in a blighted area near the University of Chicago to help local residents deal particularly with housing and sanitation problems. Elsewhere in his home city he helped create the Northwest Community Organization.

In 1965 Alinsky went to Rochester, New York, to organize poor blacks in their fight for greater job opportunities at Eastman Kodak Corporation, the city's principal employer. The organization, named FIGHT, standing for "Freedom, Independence, God, Honor—Today," won concessions in the hiring and training of African Americans and recognition of FIGHT as the black community's representative in dealing with the city government regarding education, housing, and such matters. Alinsky fostered similar organizations in Detroit, Buffalo, Syracuse, and other cities. He turned much of his attention later to helping organize white middle-class communities, which were losing power and had become alienated from neighboring black groups.

Federal programs aimed at fighting poverty earned slight praise from Alinsky, who told an interviewer that they would "only institutionalize the old city hall and social work approach at a time when traditional approaches will not do." Another journalist wrote that Alinsky "cannot be bought; he cannot be intimidated; and he breaks all the rules."

Alinsky retired in his sixties to Carmel, California, where he died of a heart attack.

**BIBLIOGRAPHY**

Alinsky, Saul, *Rules for Radicals: A Pragmatic Primer for Realistic Radicals,* 1971; Finks, P. David, *The Radical Vision of Saul Alinsky,* 1984; Horwitt, Sanford D., *Let Them Call Me Rebel: Saul Alinsky, His Life and Legacy,* 1989; Terkel, Studs, *Hard Times,* 1970.

# Allen, Richard

(February 14, 1760–March 26, 1831)
Abolitionist, Religious Leader

Founder and first bishop of the African Methodist Episcopal Church and a critic of slavery and other forms of discrimination, Richard Allen was one of the most influential African American leaders of the postrevolutionary era.

Born a slave in Philadelphia, Allen was sold, along with his family, to a farmer near Dover, Delaware. With his master's permission, he taught himself to read and write and joined the Methodist Church in 1777, becoming licensed to preach in 1782. Two years later, Allen attended the first general conference of the Methodist Church in Baltimore. He converted his master and purchased freedom for himself and his family, returning with them to Philadelphia in 1786.

In Philadelphia, Allen preached to both African Americans and whites at the St. George Methodist Church. When many more African Americans began coming to the services, drawn by Allen's preaching, church officials made them sit in a separate part of the building, first along the sides, then in the gallery. One Sunday, while Allen was preaching, two African Americans, Absalom Jones and William White, were pulled from their knees while at prayer and told to go to the gallery. The entire African American congregation left the church in protest. In 1787 Allen established an independent organization, the Free African Society, that was the first of its kind. The organization held religious services, extended mutual aid to members, set standards of moral conduct, and called for an end to slavery.

Out of this organization came an independent church, the Bethel Church, established in 1794, with Allen as deacon and later elder of the first African Methodist Episcopal (AME) congregation. Other AME congregations were established in Baltimore; Wilmington, Delaware; and other cities. In 1816 sixteen AME congregations met in Philadelphia for the official founding of the African Methodist Episcopal church. Allen was ordained the new church's first bishop.

Allen's concern with the uplift of his race also led him in 1795 to found a day school for sixty students. In 1804 he organized a "Society of Free People of Color for Promoting the Instruction and School Education of Children of African Descent." Earlier in 1797, Allen had helped to start a black Masonic lodge in Philadelphia.

As a recognized leader of the city's African American community, Allen on several occasions mobilized this community for the civic good. During the yellow fever epidemic of 1793, he organized African Americans to serve as nurses and undertakers. Later, during the War of 1812, he and two other leaders recruited 2,500 African Americans to build adequate defenses for the city.

In 1799 and 1800 Allen led the African American community in petitioning the state legislature for the immediate abolition of slavery. In 1800 a similar petition was also sent to Congress. With the founding of the American Colonization Society in 1817, Allen helped organize a convention of 3,000 African Americans to oppose the society's plan of sending free African Americans back to Africa. In an 1827 letter to *Freedom's Journal*, the first African American newspaper in the United States, Allen declared: "This land which we have watered with our tears our blood, is now our mother country; & we are well satisfied to stay where wisdom abounds, & the gospel is free."

Nevertheless, Allen later took part in a movement to resettle African Americans in Canada. In 1830, the year before he died, Allen signed a call for the "First Annual Convention of the People of Colour" to discuss means of improving the lot of African Americans in the United States and of establishing a settlement in Canada. The conventions were held periodically from 1831 until the Civil War, despite criticism from other African American leaders, who disapproved of the convention movement.

Meanwhile, the AME church grew in size and influence, expanding to 20,000 members by the time of the Civil War. It served as a model for other African American organizations developed later in the century to promote solidarity and provide self-help.

**BIBLIOGRAPHY**

Allen, Richard, *The Life, Experience, and Gospel Labors of the Rt. Rev. Richard Allen, Written By Himself,* 1793; George, Carol V. R., *Segregated Sabbaths: Richard Allen and the Emergence of Independent Black Churches 1760–1840,* 1973.

# Altgeld, John Peter

(December 30, 1847–March 12, 1902)
Reformer

John Peter Altgeld, the outspoken reform governor of Illinois in the 1890s, was accused of being an anarchist and a Red for his actions in defending workers in labor disputes and against the corrupt use of power and wealth in government.

Born in Nieder Selters, Nassau, Germany, Altgeld came to the United States with his parents in 1848. He grew up on a farm in Ohio, where he had to work hard and had little time for school. After serving as a private in the Union army from 1864 to 1865, Altgeld taught school in Missouri, worked as a law clerk, and was admitted to the Missouri bar in 1871. Three years later, he was elected state's attorney for An-

Library of Congress

drew County, but resigned this position when he moved to Chicago in 1875. There he established a law practice and made a fortune in real estate speculation, while becoming active in Democratic politics. After an unsuccessful bid for a congressional seat on the Democratic ticket in 1884, Altgeld was elected judge of the Superior Court of Cook County (Chicago) in 1886 and became chief justice four years later. In 1892 he was elected the first Democratic governor of the state since the Civil War.

Shortly after his inauguration in June 1893, Altgeld stirred up bitter controversy with his pardon of three anarchists who had been convicted of complicity in the Haymarket Square riot of 1886. Together with five other anarchists and socialists (of whom four had been hanged

and one had committed suicide), these men had been found guilty of conspiracy to instigate the man who threw a bomb that killed seven policemen at a labor rally. Altgeld maintained that the men had not been given a fair trial. In the storm that followed, Altgeld himself was accused of being an anarchist and a dangerous radical.

Undaunted, Altgeld proceeded with a reform program. In 1884 he had published *Our Penal Machinery and Its Victims,* expressing his view that the poor lacked equal opportunity before the law. He now revamped the state penal system, providing for more humane treatment of prisoners, a new parole system, and a streamlined criminal court procedure. He also modernized the University of Illinois and helped secure legislation providing for better working conditions and protecting woman and child labor. After Illinois's first factory law had been passed, Altgeld appointed FLORENCE KELLEY as the state factory inspector. His appointment of another prominent social worker, JULIA LATHROP, to the Illinois Board of Charities led to improvements in the state-run poorhouses, where in the past the young, the old, the sick, and the insane had often been lumped together in the same institutions.

Altgeld's position in the Pullman strike of 1894 again brought him under sharp attack. Workers at the Illinois-based Pullman

Company went on strike to protest wage cuts. The head of the American Railway Union, EUGENE V. DEBS, offered to arbitrate the strike, but when this was refused, he ordered a boycott of all trains using Pullman cars. The railroads retaliated by firing employees who took part in the boycott, and as whole crews quit in protest, the railroads ground to a halt. Altgeld was, nevertheless, able to keep the trains running in Illinois. He strongly protested President Grover Cleveland's action in sending in federal troops to break the strike and restore order.

Convinced that under the federal system state governments should be allowed to solve their own problems without interference, Altgeld demanded that the president withdraw the troops. The president refused, and Altgeld's critics again charged him with being an anarchist.

In the wake of the Pullman strike, Altgeld became increasingly outspoken in his support of organized labor and his attacks on the power and wealth of large corporations. As the election of 1896 approached, he came out in favor of free silver, or replacing gold dollars with cheaper silver coinage in order to boost the economy. He might well have been the Democratic candidate for the presidency if it were not for his foreign birth. He did, however, play an important role in drawing up the Democratic platform with its call not only for free silver, but for "the passage of such laws as may be necessary to protect [labor] in all its rights." With Altgeld's blessing, William Jennings Bryan became the Democratic nominee, while Altgeld ran for a second term as governor. Both Bryan and Altgeld lost their respective bids for office, though Altgeld ran ahead of Bryan.

Although Altgeld was also defeated when he ran for mayor of Chicago in 1899, he remained a force in national Democratic politics, calling for public ownership of utilities and opposing anti-immigration legislation. In 1901 he entered a law partnership with the reformist attorney CLARENCE DARROW, but his activities were cut short by his death a year later. In his dying words, Altgeld expressed the hope that social justice would ultimately triumph.

---

**BIBLIOGRAPHY**

Barnard, Harry, *"Eagle Forgotten": The Life of John Peter Altgeld,* 1962; Christman, H. M. (ed.), *Writings and Addresses of John Peter Altgeld,* 1960; Lindsey, A., *Pullman Strike,* 1942.

## Ames, Jessie Daniel

(November 2, 1883–February 21, 1972)
Civil Rights Activist, Suffragist

A Southern pioneer in both the feminist and the civil rights movements, Jessie Ames courageously fought for the abolition of lynching and led interracial organizations that furthered progressive aims.

Jessie Ames was of Texas origin: born in Palestine, in the eastern part of Texas, and raised in nearby Overton and then in Georgetown, near Austin. Her father, from Buffalo, New York, worked as a railroad station master and telegrapher; her mother, from Indiana, had been a schoolteacher. As a child, Jessie Daniel heard from the family's kitchen help about a lynching in another town, an experience that influenced her lifelong dedication to the abolition of lynching. She graduated from Southwestern University, in Georgetown, and in 1905 married Roger Post Ames, an army medical officer thirteen years her senior. The marriage was an unhappy one. Her husband worked in Central America, and Jessie Ames visited him occasionally while living with her family in Texas. He died of black water fever, a form of malaria, in 1914, and Jessie Ames was left with three children to raise. For a time, she and her widowed mother ran a local telephone company.

Jessie Ames was discovering feminism, and in 1916, with her mother's encouragement, she organized a county suffrage association. Elected treasurer of the Texas Equal Suffrage Association in 1918, she worked to make Texas the first southern state to ratify the Nineteenth Amendment of the Constitution, which established that the right to vote should not be denied or abridged on account of sex. A year later Ames became the founding president of the Texas League of Women Voters (LWV), and in 1923 she represented the national LWV at the Pan-American Congress. She was a delegate to the national Democratic party conventions of 1920, 1924, and 1928. Determined to enlist newly enfranchised women behind progressive social goals, she organized and presided over the Texas branch of the American Association of University Women and was active in the Committee on Prisons and Prison Labor and the Federation of Women's Clubs.

Ames began to see the limitations of the women's movement in an era when the Ku Klux Klan dominated politics. African American women were excluded from many organizational activities, and attention to racial oppression was ruled out. Ames nevertheless persisted. In 1924 she became field secretary for the Commission on Interracial Cooperation (CIC), which had been founded in 1919 to deal with racial tension in the South, and in 1929 she became director of the CIC's woman's committee at its headquarters in Atlanta, Georgia. The next year she took a further and braver step—she founded the Association of Southern Women for the Prevention of Lynching (ASWPL), an organization of enfranchised white women, which eventually enlisted 40,000 members. When Ames learned of a threatened lynching, often from friendly law officers, she used her network to reach ASWPL members in the county. In this way the Association drew upon the social and moral force of white women

to forestall mob violence. The ASWPL challenged the justification often given for lynching: the defense of white womanhood. Jessie Ames compiled statistics showing that only 29 percent of lynch victims had been accused of rape or other crimes against white women. Opposition to her work arose not only from Klansmen but also from members of the Women's National Association for the Preservation of the White Race, who charged that the ASWPL was "defending criminal Negro men at the expense of innocent white girls."

When the CIC founder and director Will Alexander became head of the Farm Security Administration in 1937, Ames ran the Commission, strengthened local interracial committees, and established a monthly journal, *The Southern Frontier*, to inform such groups of developments in race relations.

A federal antilynching law in 1940 did not win Ames's support, because she expected that, though the bill might pass the House, Southern senators would eventually defeat it. From May 1939 to May 1940, for the first time since records had been maintained, no lynchings occurred. Cases of lynching thereafter decreased, but not altogether. An average of three lynchings per year took place in the decade of the 1940s, and from 1951 to 1985 ten lynching deaths occurred in the entire country.

In 1943 the ASWPL and the CIC were absorbed in the new Southern Regional Council, and Ames withdrew from national activity and moved to Tryon, in the Blue Ridge Mountains of North Carolina. She was active in Democratic politics and social work for the Methodist Church. In 1968, crippled by arthritis, she went back to Texas and lived in a nursing home in Austin, where, two years before her death at age eighty-eight, honors were paid her as a pioneer feminist and civil rights activist.

**BIBLIOGRAPHY**

Ames, Jessie Daniel, *Southern Women Look at Lynching*, 1937; Hall, Jacquelyn Dowd, *Revolt Against Chivalry: Jessie Daniel Ames and the Women's Campaign Against Lynching*, 1979.

# Anthony, Susan Brownell

(February 15, 1820–March 13, 1906)
Reformer

Hailed as "the Napoleon of the woman's rights movement," Susan B. Anthony led the fight for woman suffrage for more than fifty years, bringing to the cause superb organizational abilities, boundless energy, and single-minded determination.

Susan B. Anthony was born in Adams, Massachusetts, into a reform-minded Quaker family. The family moved, and she attended local schools in Battenville, New York, then studied for four months at a Quaker boarding school for girls near Philadelphia. Anthony then taught at several New York schools, becoming head of the female department of the Canajoharie Academy in 1846. Here she joined the temperance movement and made her first public address as president of the local Daughters of Temperance.

Courtesy of the New-York Historical Society, New York City

In 1850 Anthony left teaching to help on her father's farm near Rochester, New York, while continuing her temperance work. In 1851, through AMELIA BLOOMER, a fellow temperance worker, she met ELIZABETH CADY STANTON, who three years earlier had called the first woman's rights convention in Seneca Falls, New York. The two women became good friends, but despite Stanton's urging, Anthony at first held back from joining the woman's rights movement. In 1852, however, when Anthony was denied permission to speak at a Sons of Temperance meeting, she and other female delegates walked out and founded the Woman's State Temperance Society of New York, with Stanton as president. That same year, Anthony attended her first woman's rights convention in Syracuse, New York, and was committed to the cause from then on. She began wearing the Bloomer costume of a short dress and trousers (see AMELIA BLOOMER), but gave it up after a year because of the ridicule it provoked. More importantly, Anthony was the chief organizer of a series of state and national women's rights conventions held in New York State in the years before the Civil War. She and Stanton also embarked on a county-by-county petition campaign to lobby the New York legislature for an improved married women's property law, which was finally passed in 1860. In addition, Anthony served as a state agent for the American Anti-Slavery Society and worked to secure equal pay for women teachers.

During the Civil War, Anthony and Stanton organized the Women's National Loyal League, backing the emancipation of the slaves. After the war, Anthony helped form the American Equal Rights Association to press for both woman and black suffrage. To her dismay, many former abolitionist colleagues insisted that it was "the Negro's hour" and that women should wait until African American males had won the vote before advancing their own cause. Nevertheless, Anthony and Stanton went to Kansas to campaign for a state woman suffrage amendment. While there, they received support from an eccentric financier and Democrat, George

Francis Train, and accepted his offer to finance a woman suffrage paper.

In January 1868 Anthony published the first issue of *The Revolution,* running articles on labor problems and trade unions, as well as campaigning against the Fifteenth Amendment, which proposed giving black males the vote (but denying it to women). But when Train cut back on his financial support, the paper went heavily into debt, and in 1870 Anthony was forced to sell it. She spent the next six years making lyceum lecture tours in order to pay back the debts.

Meanwhile, in 1869 Anthony and Stanton formed the National Woman Suffrage Association (NWSA) to work for a Sixteenth Amendment, giving women the vote. Stanton was elected president of the new organization, while Anthony was a member of the executive committee and later vice president at large. Later that year, a more conservative group of women, led by LUCY STONE and JULIA WARD HOWE, formed a rival national suffrage organization, the American Woman Suffrage Association (AWSA), which opposed a federal suffrage amendment, urging instead a state-by-state approach.

Anthony devoted the rest of her long life to the cause of woman suffrage. Besides working for a federal amendment, she took part in numerous state campaigns, including ones in California, Michigan, and South Dakota. In 1872, after concluding that nothing in the Constitution specifically prohibited women from voting, Anthony registered and voted in Rochester. She was arrested, tried, and ordered to pay a $100 fine, but when she refused to pay the fine, it was never collected. In the late 1870s, with the help of Stanton and other feminists, Anthony began work on a history of the movement. The first of what was to be a six-volume series, entitled the *History of Woman Suffrage,* appeared in 1881.

When the National and the American woman suffrage associations were finally united as the National American Woman Suffrage Association (NAWSA) in 1890, Anthony became vice president of the new organization. She succeeded Stanton as president in 1892. In 1895 Anthony made her first tour of the South, urging equality for African Americans in white churches and schools as well as black churches. As a living symbol of the woman's rights movement, Anthony drew large crowds wherever she went. In 1900, at the age of eighty, she resigned from the presidency of NAWSA but continued to work for the cause; that same year, she helped to open the University of Rochester to women.

Having earlier helped to organize the International Council of Women (1888), Anthony in 1904 joined with CARRIE CHAPMAN CATT in founding the International Woman Suffrage Association in Berlin and became its honorary president. In February 1906, Anthony made her last speech at a woman suffrage convention in Baltimore, leaving as her message for the future: "Failure is impossible." A month later, she died in Rochester at the age of eighty-six. In 1920 the goal to which she had dedicated her life was finally achieved with the passage of the Nineteenth Amendment.

**BIBLIOGRAPHY**

Barry, Kathleen, *Susan B. Anthony: A Biography of a Singular Feminist,* 1988; Dubois, Ellen C., *Feminism and Suffrage: The Emergence of an Independent Suffrage Movement in America, 1848–1869,* 1978.

# Arendt, Hannah

(October 14, 1906–December 4, 1975)
Philosopher, Political Scientist

Hannah Arendt, who came to the United States from her native Germany as a refugee, became a political theorist of exceptional learning and incisive intelligence and depth. Her books analyzing contemporary political currents influenced numerous intellectuals in this country and in Europe.

Arendt was born in Hanover, Germany, and grew up in Königsberg, East Prussia, her parents' home city. Her parents, Paul Arendt and Martha Cohn, were middle-class German Jews. After taking her B.A. at the University of Königsberg, Hannah Arendt went to Heidelberg University for graduate study under the philosophers Martin Heidegger (with whom she had a brief love affair) and Karl Jaspers. She earned her Ph.D. in 1928 for a dissertation on "The Concept of Love in [St.] Augustine." The same year she married Günther Stern, a Marxist student of philosophy, who took her to Frankfurt and introduced her to HERBERT MARCUSE and others in the Marxist circle. (Years later she and Stern had a friendly divorce.) When Adolf Hitler took power in 1933, Arendt left for Paris, where she studied and worked for an agency that helped locate Jewish orphans in Palestine. In 1940 she was married again, to Heinrich Blücher, a working-class German who had been a communist. (In America he taught art history.)

Later that year, shortly before the Nazis overran France, Arendt and her husband found a new refuge in the United States. She hoped for a teaching appointment and meanwhile worked briefly for the Conference on Jewish Relations and began to publish articles on political and philosophical themes in such journals as the *Partisan Review*, edited by WILLIAM PHILLIPS and PHILIP RAHV. From 1946 to 1948, when she was editor in chief of Schocken Books, she was responsible for publishing works such as the diaries of Franz Kafka. For four years Arendt served as executive secretary for Jewish Cultural Reconstruction, Inc., which collected and sought to preserve Jewish documents that the Nazis had looted.

In 1951, the year after she became an American citizen, Arendt published the book she had been researching and writing for years, *The Origins of Totalitarianism*, in which she argued that both communism and National Socialism (Nazism) were totalitarian systems of rule in which the state had amassed complete political power and rendered individual citizens powerless and vulnerable to manipulation. She delineated in unprecedented detail the circumstances of modern life that gave rise to such systems and the conditions necessary for their perpetuation. In the process, she tried to make political and historical sense of the terror of Nazism and communism, specifically of the crimes committed by Hitler against European Jews and by Stalin against the millions of Soviet citizens he suspected of disloyalty.

Arendt's reputation as a scholar and writer was now established. She was awarded a Guggenheim fellowship in 1952 and the next year was invited to lecture to the Christian Gauss Seminars in Criticism at Princeton University. Other academic appointments followed: as visiting scholar at the University of Chicago, the University of California at Berkeley, and Brooklyn College, and then again teaching at Princeton, as the first woman to have the rank of full professor. For the last eight years of her life Arendt was a professor at the New School for Social Research in New York City.

In 1958 Arendt published *The Human Condition*, based on her lectures at Chicago. Examining Marxism in its various aspects, she dwelled on its relation to work and action. The book gave a picture of what a world of free people—working, acting, and making—could be like. Arendt's most controversial work was *Eichmann in Jerusalem: A Report on the*

*Banality of Evil* (1963). *The New Yorker* had sent her to Israel to cover the trial of Adolf Eichmann, who had been an officer in Nazi Germany responsible for the deaths of many Jews. After the war he had escaped to Argentina, where Israeli secret service men had kidnapped him and flown him to Jerusalem for the trial, after which he was hanged. In five articles in the magazine, she wrote that it was simplistic to pin the guilt entirely on Eichmann, giving him a power beyond his capacity. Others were responsible, many other Germans, other Europeans, and even the Jews, who had accepted the Nazi evil actively or passively. Some critics were uncomfortable with her insistence that rather ordinary people were responsible for a great deal of Nazi evil. Rather than accept her theory about the "banality of evil," they preferred to see Eichmann and other Nazi officials as monstrous and extreme personalities.

At the time of her death, Arendt was writing *The Life of the Mind,* a work to be in three parts, "Thinking," "Willing," and "Judging," of which only the first two parts were published in 1978.

**BIBLIOGRAPHY**

Arendt, Hannah, *Between Past and Future,* 1961, *On Revolution,* 1963, and *Crises of the Republic,* 1973; May, Derwent, *Hannah Arendt,* 1986; Young-Bruehl, Elisabeth, *Hannah Arendt: Politics, Conscience, Evil,* 1982.

# Armstrong, Samuel Chapman

(January 30, 1839–May 11, 1893)
Educator

As the founder of Hampton Institute, Samuel Chapman Armstrong made an important contribution to the education of both African Americans and American Indians. His school served as a model for others, including Tuskegee Institute, started by his most famous pupil, the African American leader BOOKER T. WASHINGTON.

Samuel Armstrong was born on the island of Maui, Hawaii, to missionary parents. Shortly after his birth, the family moved to Honolulu, where Armstrong enjoyed a vigorous outdoor

Library of Congress

life as part of a large family and with many Hawaiian children as playmates. He attended the Royal School at Punahou, which became Oahu College, and after two years of undergraduate study enrolled as a junior at Williams College in Massachusetts in 1860.

During the Civil War Armstrong fought bravely at Gettysburg and was made a colonel, then left the war a brevet brigadier general. He assumed command of the Ninth Regiment, United States Colored Troops, which had an outstanding service record. Armstrong then became an agent for the Freedmen's Bureau, formed to aid the former slaves. In March 1866 Armstrong took charge of a large encampment of African Americans in and around the village of Hampton, Virginia.

At Hampton, Armstrong became concerned with educating the freedmen. He felt it was important for them to receive a practical education that would enable them to become gainfully employed. His headquarters were on an estate with an old mansion and 159 acres, and it was an ideal setting for an industrial school. In 1867 Armstrong convinced the American Missionary Association to purchase the estate, and he helped to raise money for the school. The Hampton Normal and Industrial Institute opened in 1868.

In addition to training in industrial arts, Hampton offered a curriculum that included humanities, natural sciences, and mathematics. Under Armstrong's leadership, the school also stressed character building as a means of uplift for African Americans. While Armstrong was not completely opposed to direct action to secure equal rights, he felt that blacks must first demonstrate that they were worthy of equality. This philosophy made a strong impression upon students like Booker T. Washington, who enrolled at Hampton in 1872 and for whom Armstrong served as a kind of substitute father. Besides Washington, many other aspiring young African Americans were attracted by the program at Hampton, and by 1878 the school had an enrollment of 500.

Several years later, Hampton also had an enrollment of 150 American Indians. Armstrong traveled west to visit reservation schools and became involved in furthering civil rights and education for Indians. His belief that their academic success at Hampton would make them good leaders at home came to be challenged later when cultural clashes became evident.

Armstrong died at the age of fifty-four as the result of a stroke and was buried with military honors at Hampton Institute.

A gifted leader, Armstrong left behind a school that was widely respected by African Americans and American Indians alike because of its combination of general education with vocational training. His other important legacy was the idea that the key to the advancement of African Americans lay in self-discipline, thrift, and hard work—an idea that would be promoted by Booker T. Washington.

**BIBLIOGRAPHY**

Peabody, F. A., *Education for Life,* 1913; Talbot, E. A., *Samuel Chapman Armstrong,* 1904.

# Baker, Ella Jo

(December 13, 1903–December 13, 1986)
Civil Rights Leader

Ella Baker, a founder of the Student Nonviolent Coordinating Committee (SNCC), saw the need for young African Americans to work together and independently of the adult establishment for their civil rights. For over sixty years she was active in a range of social causes.

Ella Baker (she dropped the "Jo") was born in Norfolk, Virginia, a "port of call" for her father, Blake Baker, who was a waiter for one of the shipping lines on the Norfolk-Washington service. When Ella was eight, her mother, Georgianna, moved the family to her parents' farm near Littleton, in eastern North Carolina, where they had worked as slaves. Ella was witness to the mutual caring of the black community, observing how her grandfather, a part-time preacher, made sacrifices to help his neighbors.

Wanting Ella to be educated well, her mother sent her to high school and college at Shaw University, an old Baptist institution for blacks in Raleigh. After graduating in 1927, Ella Baker hoped to study sociology at the University of Chicago, but economic realities prevailed and she went to New York and worked as a waitress and a factory hand. In time, thanks to her education, the writer George Schuyler took her on the staff of *Negro National News*.

In 1932, during the Great Depression, Baker helped form the Young Negroes Cooperative League and as its national director organized consumer cooperatives. The Works Progress Administration (WPA), set up under the New Deal, hired her to lecture and write on consumer affairs. Six years later, Baker began a long connection with the National Association for the Advancement of Colored People (NAACP; see JOEL SPINGARN). Starting as a member, she was made a field organizer and, in 1943, national director of the NAACP branches. She traveled around the South at considerable risk, visiting black communities and recruiting members. In 1946 Baker took a leave from the NAACP in order to raise a niece, though she also admitted to feeling disappointment that the Association was not achieving its best possibilities. She remained an NAACP member, however, while working for the New York Cancer Society, and in 1954 she became president of the New York City chapter of the NAACP and concerned herself with desegregation in the public schools.

Ella Baker returned south in 1958, recruited by her friend BAYARD RUSTIN to be executive secretary of the Southern Christian Leadership Conference (SCLC; see RALPH D. ABERNATHY and MARTIN LUTHER KING, JR.). In 1960 she organized the Nonviolent Resistance to Segregation Leadership Conference at her alma mater in Raleigh, attended by some 300 leaders of students taking part in sit-ins. The aim was to improve communication between activist students, and the outcome was the founding of SNCC (pronounced "Snick"). Baker left the SCLC, which she had come to see as overly cautious and male-dominated with no role for the young, and took a job with the Young Men's Christian Association (YMCA) in Atlanta while running the SNCC office. Soon afterward she was in Mississippi, helping to register black citizens to vote. In 1964, having helped found the Mississippi Freedom Democratic Party (see STOKELY CARMICHAEL and FANNIE LOU HAMER), she was the keynote speaker at its convention and set up its Washington office. (The Party's delegates were not seated at the Democratic convention that year, though some of its leaders were elected to office in the state.) Baker's next job was with the Southern Conference Educational Fund, involved in the ongoing struggle for desegregation.

Baker urged young African Americans to work independently and broaden their social outlook, to make the sit-ins more than symbolic protests. With her eye on economic issues, she asked, "What's the use of integrating lunch counters when blacks can't afford to sit down to buy a hamburger?" She foresaw that the young would be the chief fighters in the struggle for equality. Besides protesting against segregation, SNCC volunteers organized literacy programs, voter registration drives, and health-care clinics for rural blacks.

In 1972, after Baker returned to New York, she joined groups working for freedom in South Africa and Zimbabwe (formerly Rhodesia) and made herself available as a consultant to community organizations. She died at home on her eighty-third birthday, not as well known as other civil rights leaders because she was a woman in a company of male clergymen who saw women as followers rather than leaders.

**BIBLIOGRAPHY**

King, Mary, *Freedom Song*, 1987.

# Baker, Ray Stannard

(April 17, 1870–July 12, 1946)
Author, Reform Journalist

Ray Stannard Baker, who grew up on the frontier and wrote about rural American life, was also an outstanding reporter who joined the muckrakers in exposing corruption and inequality, and became a spokesperson for the Progressive Era.

Baker, whose forebears had distinguished themselves in both the American Revolution and the Civil War, was born in Lansing, Michigan, the son of a land agent and the oldest of six brothers. The family moved to St. Croix Falls, in northwestern Wisconsin, when Baker was five. The boy grew up influenced by the hard life of the frontier and, in contrast, by the cultural attainments of his parents, who were both college graduates. Baker earned a B.S. degree from Michigan Agricultural College in East Lansing in 1889. He worked for his father for three years and then entered law school at the University of Michigan. Preferring journalism to law, Baker left the university in June 1892 and landed a job as a reporter on the *Chicago News-Record.* Almost at once he was covering such events as Coxey's army of the jobless, which reached Washington in May 1894 (see JACOB S. COXEY), and in the same year the Pullman strike in Chicago, led by EUGENE V. DEBS, perhaps Baker's first encounters with social injustice. In 1896 he married Jessie Irene Beal, the daughter of his former botany professor. They became parents of four children.

In 1898 Baker joined the staff of *McClure's* in New York (see SAMUEL S. MCCLURE). The magazine was changing the world of journalism with its high-quality content and its crusading writers, who included IDA M. TARBELL and LINCOLN STEFFENS. Along with them, Baker soon took part in the social reform muckraking movement, investigating forms of corruption in American life. He wrote about such matters as J. P. Morgan and the United States Steel Corporation (1901); the violence used by the United Mine Workers against nonunion workers in the anthracite coal strike in Pennsylvania (1902); the lives of garment workers in New York City (1904); and the abuses by railroad trusts (1905). The series of articles on trust abuses brought Baker to the attention of President Theodore Roosevelt, who asked Baker's advice in designing a system of regulations for the railroads (Hepburn Bill, 1905–1906). Roosevelt attacked muckraking in 1906, however, thus ending a warm association between him and Baker.

Baker and some of his colleagues at *McClure's* resigned in 1906 to take over *The American Magazine.* Baker was seeking a broader, more spiritual answer to the corruption in American life and was attracted briefly to socialism and the social gospel movement (see WALTER RAUSCHENBUSCH). At this time, under the pseudonym David Grayson, he also began writing a series of "adventures in contentment," which were philosophical sketches about country life. Later published in book form in nine volumes between 1907 and 1942, though without great critical acclaim, Baker's "adventures" had huge popularity and heavily outweighed Baker's recognition as a reform journalist.

Baker also continued to write about problems in the United States, including a series on race relations ("Following the Color Line," 1908). In 1912 he at first supported the reform candidate, Robert M. La Follette, for president. Then, instead of supporting Theodore Roosevelt's Bull Moose candidacy, which destroyed La Follette's bid for the presidency, Baker backed Woodrow Wilson. Baker became a firm champion of Wilson's policies and ideas, advocating U.S. entry into World War I in 1917 and serving as director of the American delegation's press bureau at the Paris Peace Conference. Among his several works on Wilson is a monumental authorized—and fairly uncritical—biography, in eight volumes, written from 1927 to 1939: *Woodrow Wilson: Life and Letters*, which was awarded the Pulitzer Prize in 1940.

During his last years, Baker wrote two autobiographical volumes, *Native American* (1941) and *American Chronicle* (1945). He died of heart disease in Amherst, Massachusetts, at age seventy-six.

Some people considered Baker a mere popularizer—overly optimistic and not critical enough about social conditions in the United States—however, Baker left a legacy of fine reportage and a dedication to seeking a better life for people in all walks.

**BIBLIOGRAPHY**

Baker, R. S., *Woodrow Wilson and World Settlement*, 3 vols., 1922; Bannister, R. C., Jr., *Ray Stannard Baker: The Mind and Thought of a Progressive*, 1966; Semonche, J. E., *Ray Stannard Baker: A Quest for Democracy in Modern America*, 1969; Wilson, H. W., *McClure's Magazine and the Muckrakers*, 1970.

# Balch, Emily Greene

(January 8, 1867–January 9, 1961)
Economist, Peace Activist, Social Reformer

Emily Balch, a lifelong dissenter, was a leader of the pacifist movement the world over and winner of the Nobel Prize for Peace in 1946.

Born in Jamaica Plain, a suburb of Boston, in a family with old New England antecedents, Emily Balch was influenced by the pastor of the family's Unitarian church, at the age of ten, to pledge her life to "the service of goodness." She entered Bryn Mawr College in 1886, a member of the first graduating class. Awarded Bryn Mawr's first European Fellowship, she spent a year in Paris studying the French system of relief for the poor. A monograph, *Public Assistance of the Poor in France* (1893), reported her research. She became a social worker in Boston; helped to found Denison House, an early settlement house; and joined the Federal Labor Union, part of the American Federation of Labor (see WILLIAM GREEN and JOHN L. LEWIS).

Balch decided, however, that she could do more good as a teacher of economics, and studied at Harvard (at its Annex, the forerunner of Radcliffe College) and the University of Chicago, then at the University of Berlin. In 1896 she joined the faculty of Wellesley College as an assistant in economics and, having advanced step-by-step, in 1913 was a professor and head of the departments of sociology and economics. Her courses included discussion and readings in socialism, immigration, labor affairs, women's role in the economy, and the work of thinkers such as Karl Marx and THORSTEIN VEBLEN. One of her students has recalled Balch's emphasis on "clearing one's mind of class and race prejudice."

While teaching, Balch was active in a variety of social causes. From 1904 to 1906 she used a leave (half unpaid) to study immigration by living in Slavic communities in the United States and traveling to the regions of Austria-Hungary where many of the immigrants originated; in 1910 she published *Our Slavic Fellow Citizens*, which helped to correct the racist views of people who wanted to limit immigration. Meanwhile, Balch had declared herself a socialist. (In 1921 she became a member of the Society of Friends, or Quakers.)

When World War I broke out, Balch took an uncompromising pacifist stand. In 1915 she accompanied JANE ADDAMS to the International

Congress of Women at The Hague, which discussed peaceful solutions of the conflict. Returning home, she devoted herself to the peace movement and helped found the Woman's Peace Party and the broadly based Emergency Peace Federation. Because of Balch's defense of conscientious objectors, participation in demonstrations, liberal articles in magazines, and activity in the Committee Against Militarism (forerunner of the American Civil Liberties Union; see ROGER BALDWIN), Wellesley College dismissed her in 1918.

At the second International Congress of Women in 1919, Balch joined in founding the Women's International League for Peace and Freedom (WILPF) and served for several years as its secretary-treasurer at its headquarters in Geneva, Switzerland. She worked with the WILPF for the rest of her life, often through the League of Nations on such issues as drug control and disarmament. She represented the WILPF on a commission appointed by President Herbert Hoover to investigate conditions in American-occupied Haiti, and wrote most of its report, *Occupied Haiti* (1927), urging an end to the occupation (which came about in 1934).

Distressed by Adolf Hitler's persecution of German Jews during the 1930s, Balch helped many refugees to resettle in the United States. During World War II, which she reluctantly supported, with her customary compassion she helped to relocate Japanese-Americans who had been interned in camps.

In 1946 Balch became the second American woman to be awarded the Nobel Prize for Peace, which she shared with John Mott, an international Young Men's Christian Association (YMCA) leader. Illness prevented her from attending the ceremonies, but in 1948 she went to Norway and belatedly delivered her Nobel lecture, "Toward Human Unity or Beyond Nationalism." She donated the prize, $17,000, to the WILPF and related causes. Balch continued to be active in WILPF affairs to the end of her life. She died the day after her ninety-fourth birthday.

**BIBLIOGRAPHY**

Randall, M. M., *Improper Bostonian: Emily Greene Balch*, 1964, and (ed.), *Beyond Nationalism: The Social Thought of Emily Greene Balch*, 1971.

# Baldwin, Roger Nash

(January 21, 1884–August 26, 1981)
Civil Liberties Leader

Roger Baldwin was the principal founder of the American Civil Liberties Union (ACLU) and its director for thirty years.

Roger Baldwin was born in Wellesley, Massachusetts, in a family that was Yankee, aristocratic, and Unitarian. He attended public schools and earned an A.B. in 1904 and an M.A. in anthropology in 1905, both from Harvard. For the next three years he taught sociology at Washington University in St. Louis while working at a settlement house. His social work led to three years of service as chief probation officer of the city's juvenile court. Baldwin's work with youth gave him a national reputation. His book *Juvenile Courts and Probation*, with Bernard Flexner, became a standard text.

In 1909 Baldwin attended a lecture by EMMA GOLDMAN, the anarchist, which he called "a turning point in my life.... Here was a vision of the end of poverty and injustice by free association of those who worked, by the abolition of privilege and by the organized power of the exploited." While serving as the secretary of the Civic League of St. Louis, Baldwin got his "first impulse to civil liberties" when he encountered police refusal to license a hall for Goldman and later for the birth-control advocate MARGARET SANGER.

When the United States entered World War I in 1917, Baldwin came to New York City and with Norman Thomas founded the National Civil Liberties Bureau, an arm of the American Union Against Militarism. The bureau defended draft resisters and conscientious objectors— "the first nonpartisan defense of the principles of the Bill of Rights of a countrywide character," in Baldwin's words. The next year, he himself was convicted and given a year in jail for refusing to be drafted.

Released after serving nine months, Baldwin spent a year as a blue-collar worker, roaming the country, hopping on freight trains, taking lowly jobs in factories and restaurants. He joined the Industrial Workers of the World (IWW) Cooks and Waiters Union (see WILLIAM D. HAYWOOD) and in 1919 took part in the Pittsburgh steel strike as a prounion spy.

In 1920 Baldwin was back in New York City, where he took the lead in founding the ACLU, along with JANE ADDAMS, HELEN KELLER, JOHN DEWEY, CLARENCE DARROW, Norman Thomas, and Morris Ernst, as well as two conservative lawyers, Albert DeSiver and Walter Nelles. Baldwin was made director and served for thirty years, during which he was the central figure in every major civil liberties case in the country. For him the courts were the tool in enforcing the freedoms guaranteed by the Bill of Rights, and he worked untiringly to preserve those rights.

Under Baldwin's direction, often with volunteer lawyers of professional distinction, the

ACLU

ACLU participated in the Scopes "monkey trial" in Tennessee (1925), in which a teacher was tried and convicted of teaching evolution contrary to state law; the Sacco-Vanzetti case (1920s), in which two Italian anarchists were convicted of murder and eventually put to death in the electric chair, more because of their political views, many people believed, than because of the evidence; the campaign to lift the ban on James Joyce's novel *Ulysses* (1933); and *Brown* v. *Board of Education,* a school desegregation case (1954). The ACLU fought Mayor Frank Hague's interference with union organizing in Jersey City (1930s); obtained free-press rights for the Jehovah's Witnesses (1940s); fought the government's confinement of Japanese-Americans in camps during World War II; and defended the free-speech rights of such conservative organizations and individuals as the Ku Klux Klan, the German-American Bund, and Henry Ford.

The ACLU policy called for staunch defense of the liberties of everyone regardless of their political views, and it readily lent its services to socialists, communists, and other left-wing organizations and causes. Baldwin himself belonged to no political party, though before World War II his political sympathies lay with the left. In 1940, however, the ACLU board, urged by Baldwin, adopted a "loyalty" resolution that barred from membership on the board or the staff any "member of a political organization which supports totalitarian dictatorship in any country." On this basis the board voted to remove ELIZABETH GURLEY FLYNN, a member of the American Communist party. Baldwin broke his long personal friendship with Flynn, who had been in the IWW with him. Later, explaining the action, Baldwin said that "feeling ran high when the Nazi-Soviet pact exploded the myth that the Communists were a democratic ally." Some critics suggested that government pressure had been a factor in the Flynn incident. (Twenty-six years later, the expulsion of Flynn was repudiated when the ACLU board voted to drop wording that barred sympathizers of communist, fascist, or other totalitarian ideas from membership.) What seemed another inconsistency in 1940 was Baldwin's agreement with other members of the ACLU that because of the threat of Nazism war service was admissible. He also opposed the ACLU's going to court in defense of draft resisters during the Vietnam War.

At the invitation of General Douglas MacArthur, Baldwin went to Japan to advise on a civil rights policy under the occupation, and he was also a consultant on civil liberties in the American zone of occupied Germany. After he retired from the ACLU in 1950, he worked with the United Nations on questions of civil liberty. Throughout his long career, Baldwin was active in many liberal organizations, and in the American Political Science Association and the National Audubon Society. In later life, he spent winters teaching the law of civil liberties at the University of Puerto Rico.

Baldwin was married twice, both times to reformers. His first wife, Madeline Z. Doty, whom he married in 1919, was an advocate of prison reform. They were divorced in 1935, and the next year he married Evelyn Preston, a woman of means who was interested in the labor movement, with whom he enjoyed an affluent life-style. They had one daughter, Helen, active as a feminist, who predeceased her father. Baldwin died in 1981 at a hospital near his home in Oakland, New Jersey, at the age of ninety-seven. In an editorial, the *New York Times* observed that "He leaves two legacies: more spacious liberty and the duty to keep fighting for it."

### BIBLIOGRAPHY

Baldwin, Roger, *The Prospects of Freedom*, 1952, and *A New Slavery: The Communist Betrayal of Human Rights*, 1953; Lamson, Peggy, *Roger Baldwin, Founder of the American Civil Liberties Union*, 1976; Walker, Samuel, *In Defense of American Liberties*, 1990.

# Bancroft, George

(October 3, 1800–January 17, 1891)
Historian

George Bancroft spent some forty years writing his ten-volume *History of the United States*, the result of prodigious scholarship and a bias for the democratic point of view (which he believed he presented "objectively"). It has been a key document for the understanding of a past era of the country.

George Bancroft was born in Worcester, Massachusetts, the son of Aaron Bancroft, a Unitarian minister who wrote a biography of George Washington, and Lucretia Chandler. He entered Phillips Exeter Academy, in Exeter, New Hampshire, at age eleven, and Harvard University at age thirteen, graduating at seventeen. After a year at Harvard Divinity School, he went to Germany to study at the University of Göttingen, where he earned Ph.D. and M.A. degrees in 1820. For two more years Bancroft traveled and studied in Berlin, Weimar, Heidelberg, Paris, London, and Rome. Along the way he met such famous men as Alexander von Humboldt, Georg Wilhelm Friedrich Hegel, Johann Wolfgang von Goethe, Marquis de Lafayette, and Lord Byron, associations that provided the young traveler with an exceptionally broad experience.

In 1822 Bancroft returned to Harvard for a year as a tutor of Greek, while preaching in churches around Boston. With J. G. Cogswell he founded the experimental Round Hill School in Northampton, Massachusetts, in 1823. Four years later he married Sarah H. Dwight. Bancroft was a failure as a teacher, partly because the attitudes and mannerisms he had picked up abroad irritated his students and friends, and in 1830 he sold his interest to Cogswell and began writing for the *North American Review*. He displayed an unusual breadth of scholarly political knowledge and a sympathy for the Democratic party and popular causes. He set to writing his ten-volume *History of the United States,* which began publication in 1834. Written from the point of view of Jacksonian democracy, the *History* was from its first volume widely acclaimed by both scholars and the public.

Bancroft's wife died in 1837, leaving him with three young children. Later that year he accepted an appointment by President Martin Van Buren as Collector of the Port of Boston. Soon afterward he married Mrs. Elizabeth Davis Bliss, a widow with two children; she bore him a daughter. In 1844 Bancroft ran unsuccessfully for governor of Massachusetts, but in recognition of his help at the Democratic convention that nominated James K. Polk for the presidency that year, Polk named him secretary of the navy. In summer 1845 he was the official eulogist of the late Andrew Jackson.

In 1846 Bancroft was appointed minister to Great Britain. He thus gained an opportunity to continue research for his *History,* two more volumes of which had appeared meanwhile. Again he had a notably rich experience abroad, meeting European historians and having access to valuable archives. His three years in London also strengthened his American attitudes and convictions on the eve of the 1848 democratic uprisings in Europe.

Having returned to the United States, Bancroft spent the years 1849 to 1867 chiefly writing the remaining volumes of the *History.* During the Civil War he opposed slavery and a divided union and strongly supported President Abraham Lincoln in his conduct of the war. In 1866 Bancroft delivered the memorial address for Lincoln before Congress. When President Andrew Johnson offered him the post of minister to Prussia in 1867, he accepted. He remained in Berlin until 1874, accomplishing important diplomatic work. Using European archives and consulting German scholars, he finished the tenth and final volume of the *History.* In his remaining years Bancroft lived in Washington during winters, resuming political friendships, preparing a revised "centenary edition" of the *History* (1876), and writing other works, including a two-volume history of the U.S. Constitution and biographies of Presidents Lincoln and Van Buren. When Bancroft died in Washington in 1891, President Benjamin Harrison ordered flags in the capital to be flown at half-mast.

As a historian Bancroft wrote prose that, while often high-flown and rhetorical, displayed his scholarship and worldly experience and the unusual depth of his sources. His style is considered outmoded now, as is his method of paraphrasing documents instead of presenting them verbatim, but his collections of source materials, still available, are admirable.

**BIBLIOGRAPHY**

Brooks, Van Wyck, *The Flowering of New England,* 1936; DeWolfe Howe, M. A., *The Life and Letters of George Bancroft,* 1908.

# Banks, Dennis James

(April 12, 1932–   )
American Indian Activist

Dennis Banks, a dedicated worker for American Indian rights, helped found the American Indian Movement (AIM) to protect traditional Indian ways and protest against discrimination and poor treatment by the government.

Dennis Banks was born on the Leech Lake Indian Reservation, in north-central Minnesota, to poor parents of the Anishinabe (Ojibwa or Chippewa) people. His original name was Nowacumig, meaning "Standing Outside." At the age of five, he was taken from his parents and sent to boarding schools run by the U.S. Bureau of Indian Affairs in North and South Dakota and finally to a military school at Pipestone, Minnesota. During the years away from his family and people he lost his native language.

In 1953, Banks enlisted in the U.S. Air Force and after training as an aerial photographer was sent to Japan and Korea. Upon his discharge in 1959, he returned to Leech Lake and worked off and on as a laborer. Unable to find a steady job, he drifted from one midwestern city to another, struggling with a drinking problem. In March 1966 he was arrested on a burglary charge and sent to prison. He made use of his time to study and read, and he never again used alcohol. As he has said, while in prison, like other persons of color, he learned the importance of fighting for the identity of his people.

Upon his release in May 1968, Banks worked briefly as a minority recruiter for the Honeywell Company in Minneapolis. In July, taking heart from the civil rights struggle, he and three other Indian men founded AIM. Chapters were soon formed on reservations and in cities around the country. AIM pledged, among other goals, to fight racial discrimination in housing, health care, and employment; abuse of Indian treaty rights to land and natural resources; and brutal police treatment of Indians during arrests.

In fall 1969, Banks and other AIM leaders organized the "Indians of All Tribes" occupation of the federal prison on Alcatraz Island, in San Francisco Bay, which had been abandoned since 1963. AIM's position was that surplus federal property should be returned to Indian control. The takeover, which lasted until June 1971, attracted national attention to the AIM cause. In fall 1972, AIM organized the "Trail of Broken Treaties," a motorcade some 4 miles long that traveled from the West Coast to Washington, D.C., where Banks and other AIM leaders expected to meet with government officials and discuss a twenty-point agenda, including the restoration of Indians' treaty-making powers. When the officials refused to meet, the demonstrators seized the offices of the Bureau of Indian Affairs and occupied them for several days.

Banks was invited by the Lakota people to Custer, South Dakota, in February 1973, to lead a protest against the lenient sentence of a white man who had murdered an Indian, and a violent confrontation broke out between police and protesters. Charges were filed against Banks, but he was not immediately arrested. Soon afterward, AIM called for the occupation of the nearby village of Wounded Knee, where in 1890 U.S. cavalry had massacred some 200 Sioux men, women, and children. Under Banks's leadership, several hundred mostly young men and women, from the Sioux and from other nations, held Wounded Knee for seventy-one days against a siege force of police, U.S. marshals, FBI agents, and vigilantes. After a negotiated surrender, Banks and others were arrested and tried. He was later acquitted of the Wounded Knee charges but convicted of assault at Custer. In August 1973, when he was elected national director of AIM, the organization pledged to campaign for repeal of the inadequate Indian Reorganization Act of 1934 and for the dismantling of the Bureau of Indian Affairs.

To avoid imprisonment, Banks and his wife, Kamook, an Oglala Sioux, went underground and eventually to California, where he was granted amnesty by Governor Jerry Brown. From 1976 to 1983 he studied at the University of California at Davis and served as chancellor of the nearby D-Q University, an Indian-controlled institution. In 1978 he organized the first "spiritual run" of Indians from Davis to Los Angeles and "The Longest Walk" of at times 30,000 Indians from San Francisco to Washington. The walk, 3,600 miles, sparked a halt to proposed legislation that would have abrogated Indian treaties with the government.

In early 1983, after Governor Brown left office and his successor, George Deukmejian, threatened extradition, Banks was given sanctuary by the Onondaga Nation at its reservation near Syracuse, New York. After more than a year of restricted life, he decided to surrender in South Dakota and served eighteen months in a state penitentiary, where he did voluntary social work among the inmates. Upon parole, he went to Oglala, near Wounded Knee, and founded Loneman Industries, associated with the Honeywell Company, to train and employ Indians in the area.

Banks later moved to Kentucky and worked to halt grave robbers digging for artifacts at Indian grave sites. In order to raise funds for AIM, he continued to lead sacred runs by Indians and other people, one of the longest being a 7,000-mile run from London to Moscow in 1990.

**BIBLIOGRAPHY**

Churchill, Ward, *Agents of Repression: The FBI's Secret War against the Black Panther Party and the American Indian Movement,* 1988; Matthiessen, Peter, *In the Spirit of Crazy Horse,* 1983, new edition, 1991.

# Barnard, Henry

(January 24, 1811–July 5, 1900)
Educational Reformer

Henry Barnard was a leader, along with HORACE MANN, of the movement to reform the public school system in mid–nineteenth-century America.

Born in Hartford, Connecticut, Barnard attended the Monson (Massachusetts) Academy and the Hopkins Grammar School in Hartford, before entering Yale in 1826. After graduation, he studied law privately and then at Yale; he was admitted to the Connecticut bar in 1835.

Two years later, Barnard was elected to the Connecticut General Assembly. He served three consecutive terms and in 1838 successfully sponsored a bill for the improvement of the common schools that provided for a state board of commissioners and a secretary chosen by them. After some hesitation, Barnard gave up his law practice and his position in the legislature to become the new secretary of education.

When Barnard took office, Connecticut's schools were suffering from decentralization and inadequate funding. The result was that many school houses had fallen into a state of disrepair, equipment was sparse, and teachers were poorly trained.

To arouse public support for education, Barnard addressed public meetings, set up schools for teachers, and founded and edited the *Connecticut Common School Journal.* But after four years' service, Barnard, a Whig, was voted out of office when the Democrats came to power in 1842.

Barnard next went to Rhode Island, where he helped to found the Rhode Island Institute of Instruction and to secure the passage of a school act. In 1849, with the return of the Whigs to power in Connecticut, Barnard went back to his native state, serving as principal of the state's first normal school at New Britain, and also as superintendent of schools.

Barnard was chancellor of the University of Wisconsin from 1858 to 1860 and president of St. John's College in Annapolis, Maryland, from 1866 to 1867. In 1867 he became the first U.S. commissioner of education, fulfilling the duties of this post with only partial success until 1870.

More effective as an author than as an administrator, Barnard began publishing the *American Journal of Education* in 1855. This encyclopedic work dealing with every phase of public education ran to thirty-two volumes of over 800 pages each, which appeared at irregular intervals until 1882. Barnard also republished sections from this work in his fifty-two-volume *Library of Education.*

In his writings, Barnard emphasized the importance of professionalism in education. He advocated teacher training and the eventual creation of a unified, national public education system. Along with Horace Mann, he believed that public education would help overcome poverty and crime. To this end, he laid particular stress on moral education.

**BIBLIOGRAPHY**

Cremin, Lawrence, *American Education: The National Experience, 1783–1876,* 1980; Katz, Michael B., *Bureaucracy and Schools: The Illusion of Educational Change in America,* 1971.

# Barton, Clarissa Harlowe

(December 25, 1821–April 12, 1912)
Nurse, Reformer

As nurse, humanitarian, and president of the American Red Cross, Clara Barton devoted many years of her life to aiding soldiers during wartime and to providing large-scale disaster relief during peacetime.

Born in North Oxford, Massachusetts, Clara Barton had her first nursing experience when, beginning at age eleven, she took care of an ailing older brother for two years. She taught school at the age of eighteen, and then opened one of the first free public schools in New Jersey at Bordentown (pupils usually paid fees at that time). Two years later, in 1854, she became copyist in the U.S. Patent Office.

With the outbreak of the Civil War, Clara Barton began aiding soldiers of the Sixth Massachusetts Regiment who had been wounded during a riot in Baltimore and were without adequate provisions while camped in Washington. Advertising in a Massachusetts paper, she was able to secure bandages, medicines, and clothing, which she then distributed to the soldiers. Barton later traveled by mule through Virginia, Maryland, and South Carolina, handing out supplies, providing first aid, and preparing soup and coffee for the Union troops. She sometimes worked under fire, and on at least one occasion had to wring the blood from her skirts.

For her heroic and humanitarian service, Barton became known as the Angel of the Battlefield. She acted entirely on her own, having no connection with the U.S. Sanitary Commission, which was the largest volunteer agency providing medical facilities to the Union army. Barton held only one official position when she briefly served as acting head nurse with the Army of the James in 1864. The war over, Barton headed a search for missing soldiers, identifying more than 90 percent of the graves of Union soldiers at the Confederate prison at Andersonville, Georgia; she also lectured extensively throughout the country. Finally, exhausted, she went to Europe to recuperate in 1869. There Barton learned of the International Committee of the Red Cross, founded in 1863 at a convention in Geneva, Switzerland, to provide relief to wounded soldiers. By 1864 eleven nations had ratified the Geneva Treaty, giving neutral status to wounded soldiers of future wars, as well as to ambulances and first-aid personnel of combatant nations. During the Franco-Prussian War of 1870 to 1871, Barton herself participated in Red Cross relief work. In 1877, after her return to America, she embarked on a five-year campaign to get the U.S. government to ratify the Geneva Treaty and to set up an American Red Cross organization. By stressing the need for organized relief for victims of disasters such as droughts, fires, and floods, she was ultimately successful. In 1881 the American Association of the Red Cross was formed with Barton as its president, and one year later President Chester A. Arthur signed the Geneva Treaty.

During Barton's twenty-three-year presidency, the organization provided relief for twenty-one disasters, both at home and abroad. It did so without aid from the government, relying instead on voluntary contributions, as was Barton's wish. She also saw that the American Red Cross concerned itself with rehabilitation as well as relief. For example, after the Galveston hurricane of 1900, the organization provided 1.5 million strawberry plants to needy

American Red Cross/National Archives

farmers so they could begin making a living again.

During the Spanish-American War of 1898, Barton at the age of seventy-seven again took to the field, riding mule wagons under the hot tropical sun of Cuba to provide aid to American troops and Cuban refugees. Nevertheless, she came under criticism from both within and without the organization by those who felt she should have managed operations from her desk in Washington. There were also rumors—never substantiated—of fiscal impropriety. Barton did, however, resist establishing the Red Cross on an impersonal, businesslike basis with formal accounting practices, and with authority delegated to her various associates. The latter eventually launched a successful revolt, and in 1904 Barton resigned as president of the Red Cross.

Barton spent her remaining years at her home in Glen Echo, Maryland, where she had moved in 1897. Still vigorous, she made occasional public appearances, carried on an extensive correspondence, and in 1906 founded the National First Aid Association of America in Boston. A lifelong feminist, Barton was friendly with the leaders of the women's rights movement, supporting their drives for the vote and for equal pay for equal work. She died in Glen Echo at the age of ninety-one.

**BIBLIOGRAPHY**

Barton, Clara, *History of the Red Cross,* 1882, and *The Red Cross in Peace and War,* 1899; Stevenson, A., and F. Giacoia, *Clara Barton, Founder of the American Red Cross,* 1982.

# Beard, Charles Austin

(November 27, 1874–September 1, 1948)

# Beard, Mary Ritter

(August 5, 1876–August 14, 1958)
Historians

Charles and Mary Beard's influential works on the history of the United States were among the first to stress the role of impersonal economic forces in shaping the nation's politics and culture. Their separate careers were distinguished by a broad range of social concerns.

Both Beards were Indiana natives and both had Quaker antecedents. Charles Austin Beard was born on a farm near Knightstown, east of Indianapolis. His father, William Henry Harrison Beard, was a prosperous businessman, interested in banking and real estate as well as farming. An agnostic, he sent his two sons to a Quaker school and bought them the local newspaper to edit as youths. Charles went to DePauw University, where a professor of political science, James R. Weaver, introduced him to the social ideas of John Ruskin, Karl Marx, Walter Bagehot, and Lester Frank Ward. During a summer in Chicago young Beard investigated JANE ADDAMS's Hull House, heard orations by JOHN PETER ALTGELD and William Jennings Bryan at the Democratic National Convention, and first viewed city poverty. After DePauw, he went to Oxford University to study English constitutional history. Beard's interest in the labor movement, socialism, and reform was awakened, and in 1899, with Walter Vrooman, an American socialist of means, he founded Ruskin Hall, a workers' school (now Ruskin College).

After returning to the United States, Beard had a year of graduate study at Cornell University during which, in March 1900, he married his college sweetheart, Mary Ritter. He returned with Mary to Ruskin Hall, where as secretary he wrote articles for the school's journal and gave speeches to working-class audiences in the industrial centers, while his wife worked in the woman suffrage movement. Beard's first book appeared in 1901: *The Industrial Revolution*, an introduction for working-class readers.

Mary Ritter Beard had been born in Indianapolis, one of six children in a well-to-do lawyer's family. She graduated from DePauw in 1897 and taught German until her marriage. When she and her husband returned from Oxford in 1902, both undertook graduate studies at Columbia University. Charles Beard received his Ph.D. in 1904 and was appointed to the Columbia faculty; Mary withdrew from graduate school to raise their two children and to work as a dedicated suffragist. She edited a publication of the Woman Suffrage League and was active in the Women's Trade Union League. The first collaboration of the Beards, in 1914, was *American Citizenship*. The previous year Charles had published what RICHARD HOFSTADTER called "the most controversial historical work of his generation," *An Economic Interpretation of the Constitution of the United States*, in which he theorized that the Founding Fathers had looked after their own immediate economic interests when they wrote the Constitution.

At Columbia, Beard had allied himself with the promoters of the "New History," James Harvey Robinson and Harry Elmer Barnes, and had embraced the antiformalist ideas of the historian Frederick Jackson Turner, who urged the study of the vital forces that lay behind institutions. In the controversy over Beard's book, orthodox conservatives were aroused and students rallied to his defense. His eloquence and wit as a lecturer and his unpretentious and friendly manner made him a favorite on the Columbia campus. In 1917, however, Beard resigned his professorship on the issue of academic freedom. The university's trustees and its president, NICHOLAS MURRAY BUTLER, wanted to suppress any faculty criticism of American participation in the war. Though Beard supported the war effort, he could not tolerate the dismissal of professors who opposed the war. In a strong letter of resignation, Beard protested the domination of the university by trustees "who have no standing in the world of education, who are reactionary and visionless in politics, narrow and medieval in religion."

For more than twenty years Beard had no regular academic appointment. He was, however, far from idle. In 1918, with Robinson, JOHN DEWEY, Alvin S. Johnson, and THORSTEIN VEBLEN, he organized the New School for Social Research. For five years he was director of the New York Training School for Public Service. In 1922, with his wife, he was in Tokyo as adviser to the Institute of Municipal Research, which was planning a greater Tokyo, and he returned after the 1923 earthquake to advise on the rebuilding of the city. From 1927 to 1928 he was in Yugoslavia to advise on problems of the federation, but Serbian oppression of other nationalities persisted and he gave up that mission. Home in Connecticut, he started a notably successful dairy farm. In 1939 Beard returned to Columbia as a visiting professor; the next year, he was appointed to a chair of American history at Johns Hopkins University.

During the two decades of absence from the academic world, Charles Beard wrote many articles and almost sixty books, including collaborations with his wife. In 1921 they published their *History of the United States,* and, in 1927, their two-volume *Rise of American Civilization,* a best-seller which became a classic. Stressing the theme of economic determinism against a panorama of historical and cultural detail, the work posits a recurring conflict between agriculture and business, province and metropolis. Two sequels followed: *America in Midpassage* (1939) and *The American Spirit* (1943).

In his last decade Beard spent much energy attacking President Franklin D. Roosevelt and the New Deal and pursuing an isolationist view of World War II. He endorsed the platform of the antiwar America First Committee but withheld from joining it when he began to see it as a forum for "native fascists." In *The Republic* (1943), he revised his opinion of the Founding Fathers, seeing them as patriots with a concern for national unity and constitutional government. In his last two books, *American Foreign Policy in the Making, 1932–1940* (1946), and *President Roosevelt and the Coming of the War, 1941* (1948), Beard produced some 900 pages of polemics aiming to prove that Roosevelt had deceived the American public and had provoked the Japanese into attacking Pearl Harbor.

Amidst her collaborations with her husband, Mary Beard pioneered the field of women's studies. In 1934 she published a fifty-page syllabus for the first women's studies program. Her five-year struggle to found a World Center for Women's Archives, though unsuccessful, brought scholarly attention to the contributions of women throughout history.

One more joint effort had come from the Beards: *The Basic History of the United States* (1944). Mary Beard, who throughout her career had allied herself with the most radical wing of the women's rights movement, published her best-known work, *Woman as Force in History,* in 1946. After her husband's death in 1948, she continued writing and published a memoir, *The Making of Charles A. Beard,* in 1955. Mary Beard died in Phoenix, Arizona, in 1958.

**BIBLIOGRAPHY**

Beale, Howard K. (ed.), *Charles A. Beard: An Appraisal,* 1955; Borning, Bernard C., *The Political and Social Thought of Charles A. Beard,* 1962; Goldman, Eric, *Rendezvous with Destiny,* 1978; Hofstadter, Richard, *The Progressive Historians,* 1968.

# Beecher, Catharine

(September 6, 1800–May 12, 1878)
Educator, Reformer

A proponent of women's education and the author of the widely read *Treatise on Domestic Economy*, Catharine Beecher served as a self-appointed counselor to nineteenth-century American women, urging them to wield their moral influence as wives, mothers, and teachers, while at the same time accepting their social and political subordination.

Beecher was born in East Hampton, New York, the oldest of the eight surviving children of the well-known Congregational minister, Lyman Beecher, and his wife, Roxana (Foote) Beecher. She was educated at the private school her mother operated in the Beecher home, then briefly at Miss Sarah Pierce's School in Litchfield, Connecticut, where the family had moved.

In 1822 Beecher, then a schoolteacher in New London, Connecticut, became engaged to a brilliant young mathematics professor at Yale, Alexander Metcalf Fisher. When Fisher died in a shipwreck the next year, Beecher underwent an emotional and intellectual crisis that led to her decision to become an educator of women.

In 1823 Beecher and her sister Mary opened a girls' school in Hartford, Connecticut. Later incorporated as the Hartford Female Seminary, the school became one of the leading institutions of its kind in New England with its advanced curriculum and superior teaching. In an essay on female education, published in 1827, Beecher made the novel proposal that schools for women be endowed. Later she came to believe that women, as the moral leaders within the lives of families, were especially capable of performing the role of teacher.

But the work of running the school took its toll on Beecher. In 1831, on the verge of collapse, she resigned from her position and moved to Cincinnati, where her father had become president of the Lane Theological Seminary, and where she opened another school, the Western Female Institute. Beecher also published several elementary textbooks and took an active part in the local temperance movement. But she shied away from involvement in the growing abolitionist movement. In *An Essay on Slavery and Abolitionism, with Reference to the Duty of American Females* (1837), written in response to the abolitionist leader Angelina Grimke, Beecher maintained that any activity "which throws woman into the attitude of a combatant, either for herself or others," did not fall within "her appropriate sphere."

Teaching, on the other hand, did fall within women's appropriate sphere, and after financial difficulties and poor health forced Beecher to give up her school in 1837, she devoted herself to writing and lecturing on the need for trained women teachers in the West. She helped raise money and oversaw the selection and placement of women teachers in the West for the Board of National Popular Education, started in Cleveland for this purpose.

In 1852 Beecher founded the American Woman's Educational Association to work for the establishment of endowed, nondenominational women's normal schools in the West, where local young women could receive teacher training. Thanks to her efforts, such institutions were started in Milwaukee, Wisconsin; Dubuque, Iowa; and Quincy, Illinois; but they all—except the Milwaukee Normal Institute (later Milwaukee-Downer College), whose development Beecher personally oversaw—proved short-lived.

It was as an author rather than as a founder of schools that Beecher had the greatest impact. In 1841 Beecher published *A Treatise on Domestic Economy,* an advice book that established her reputation as a "household divinity" throughout the country. The book went through numerous editions, including the highly popular *The American Woman's Home* (1869), which Beecher wrote in collaboration with one of her sisters, HARRIET BEECHER STOWE.

In *A Treatise*, Beecher not only provided much useful advice on household matters but also advanced the idea that domesticity was both a scientific and sacred vocation that women should prepare for in the same way that men prepared for careers outside the home. She counseled her readers to be thrifty and industrious housewives who placed their families' comfort over elegance and fashion, and to be careful mothers, who took seriously their responsibility for molding the minds of their children. In Beecher's view, because of their capacity for self-sacrifice women were uniquely qualified to teach children, whether within or outside the home. And as mothers and teachers, women had an important role to play in shaping the national morality.

Beecher's conviction that women should not participate in politics made her an early and vigorous opponent of the woman suffrage movement. She did, however, advocate women's economic independence, and spent the remaining three decades of her life writing and lecturing on this subject, as well as on her ideas about women's domestic and moral responsibilities.

**BIBLIOGRAPHY**

Rugoff, Milton, *The Beechers: An American Family in the Nineteenth Century*, 1982; Sklar, Kathryn Kish, *Catharine Beecher: A Study in American Domesticity*, 1973.

# Beecher, Henry Ward

(June 24, 1813–March 8, 1887)
Reformer, Religious Leader

Henry Ward Beecher was among the most influential ministers in nineteenth-century America. For nearly forty years, people crowded Beecher's church in Brooklyn to hear his preaching on public issues and church doctrine. According to his sister, HARRIET BEECHER STOWE, Beecher had "the misfortune of a popularity which is perfectly phenomenal."

Beecher was born in Litchfield, Connecticut, the son of LYMAN BEECHER, a leading Congregational

Library of Congress

minister. After graduating from Amherst College in 1834, he completed his education at the Lane Theological Seminary in Cincinnati, Ohio, and was ordained in 1837. As a minister, Beecher rejected the stern Calvinist God of his father in favor of a loving God.

In July 1839 Beecher became the pastor of the Second Presbyterian Church in Indianapolis, Indiana. During his eight years in Indianapolis he used a highly emotional preaching style that earned him a large following. The national reputation he began to acquire at this time was enhanced by the publication in 1844 of *Seven Lectures to Young Men* on the subject of character building.

Beecher moved to New York in 1847 to become the minister of the newly established Plymouth Church, a small Congregational church in Brooklyn. His ability to attract large audiences quickly surpassed the capacity of the church, and, when it burned down, a new one with a large semicircular gallery capable of holding several thousand people was built to take its place. Beecher never wrote out his sermons, but they were taken down stenographically, printed in pamphlet form, and widely circulated. Beecher was also an extremely popular public lecturer and a frequent contributor to the *Independent*, a Congregationalist journal, and later to the *Christian Union*.

Beecher's antislavery lectures and sermons made him a recognized leader of the movement. He was against the spread of slavery, but felt that it should not be interfered with where it already existed. In 1856 he encouraged antislavery settlers to immigrate to Kansas to ensure that it remained a free state, and he raised money to ship Sharps rifles, nicknamed "Beecher's Bibles," to help these settlers in their fight against proslavery forces from Missouri.

Beecher supported the Republican presidential candidates John C. Frémont in 1856 and Abraham Lincoln in 1860. With the outbreak of the Civil War, Beecher supported the North but criticized Lincoln for waiting to issue the Emancipation Proclamation. In 1863 Beecher traveled to England to present the Northern case before hostile audiences. After the war, Beecher endorsed President Andrew Johnson's moderate Reconstruction plan. In the widely circulated "Cleveland Letter" of 1866, he called for prompt readmission to the Union of the former Confederate states and an end to military government in the South.

In the postwar years, Beecher also gave his support to the woman suffrage movement. He believed that the franchise was a natural right and objected to any interference with it.

In 1874 a scandal titillated the nation and tarnished Beecher's reputation when a good friend, Theodore Tilton, accused him of committing adultery with Tilton's wife, Elizabeth. Tilton took his complaint to court, suing Beecher for $100,000 in damages. The six-month, highly publicized trial ended in a hung jury. Later, a special committee of the Congregational Church Association declared Beecher innocent of the charges against him.

In the 1880s, Beecher also came under attack for his evolutionary views. Although he rejected a literal interpretation of the Bible in favor of Darwin's theory of evolution, Beecher retained his belief in miracles. Nevertheless, his views, published in *Evolution and Religion* (1885), were so controversial that Beecher resigned from the Association of Congregational Ministers in 1882, against its protest. He continued to write, lecture, and preach at Plymouth Church with his customary energy until his death five years later.

**BIBLIOGRAPHY**

Abbott, L., *Henry Ward Beecher,* 1980; Clark, C., *Henry Ward Beecher: Spokesman for Middle Class America,* 1978; Elsmer, J. S., *Henry Ward Beecher: The Indiana Years, 1837–1847,* 1973; McLoughlin, W. G., *The Meaning of Henry Ward Beecher,* 1970; Rugoff, M., *The Beechers,* 1981.

# Beecher, Lyman

(October 12, 1775–January 10, 1863)
Educator, Religious Leader

Clergyman and educator Lyman Beecher was one of the most important religious figures in America in the nineteenth century. Preaching a less strict form of Calvinism, he helped promote revivals in the Congregational churches of New England and bring evangelical religion to the West.

Born in New Haven, Connecticut, Lyman Beecher was the son and grandson of blacksmiths. Entering Yale College at the age of 18, he came under the influence of Timothy Dwight, the college president and a well-known minister. After studying for the ministry under Dwight, Beecher in 1799 became pastor of the Presbyterian Church at East Hampton, Long Island, New York. During the eleven years he preached there, Beecher received much positive notice, especially for a sermon against drinking. In 1810 he accepted a call to become pastor of the Congregational Church in Litchfield, Connecticut, then a center of wealth and culture.

Beecher subscribed to what became known as the New School of Presbyterianism. Rather than stressing predestination, he emphasized the freedom of the human will to turn away from sin and accept God. By preaching this more hopeful message twice on Sunday and at meetings during the week, he drew a large following. In 1813 Beecher founded the Connecticut Society for the Reform of Morals. The group initiated a crusade to wipe out breaking of the Sabbath, profane language, and drinking. Beecher was particularly concerned with the latter evil. Six sermons he preached against intemperance in 1825 found wide circulation when published; they were even translated into several languages.

His reputation now extending throughout New England, Beecher in 1826 was chosen to head the new Hanover Street Church in Boston, which was started to combat the growth of Unitarianism. There Beecher met with such success that he was compared to JONATHAN EDWARDS, leader of the First Great Awakening in New England in the 1700s. However, some violently anti-Catholic sermons of Beecher's inadvertently led to a Boston mob attacking a convent in 1831.

The following year, Beecher seized the opportunity to bring religion to the West by becoming president of the Lane Theological Seminary in Cincinnati, Ohio, as well as pastor of the city's Second Presbyterian Church. But soon after his arrival, Beecher ran into trouble with Cincinnati's Old School Presbyterians, who were angered by his New School beliefs. Charged with heresy, he was brought to trial before church courts and councils. The case dragged on for three years before it was finally withdrawn. It had the effect of hastening the split in the Presbyterian Church in the United States into Old and New School branches in 1837 and 1838. In 1843 Beecher resigned from his pulpit to form the Walnut Street Church for New School Presbyterians.

Beecher also had difficulties at Lane Seminary over the question of slavery. When students led by the radical abolitionist THEODORE WELD held a series of debates on slavery in 1834, the trustees passed a resolution forbidding all discussion of the subject. No abolitionist himself, Beecher had supported the debates initially, because he believed in freedom of speech, but now he backed the trustees' action. As a result, many of the students departed for Oberlin College in Ohio (see CHARLES GRANDISON FINNEY), which soon became a center of abolitionist agitation.

While Beecher was president of Lane Seminary, several of his sons received their religious training there. One son, HENRY WARD BEECHER, went on to become one of the most popular ministers of late–nineteenth-century

America. One of Beecher's daughters, HARRIET BEECHER STOWE, won fame as the author of the antislavery novel *Uncle Tom's Cabin,* based on information gathered while she was living in Cincinnati. Still another daughter, CATHARINE BEECHER, was influential as an educator and author of advice books for women.

Retiring as president of the Lane Seminary in 1850, Beecher returned to the East the following year to prepare his theological works for publication. These were published in three volumes in 1852 and 1853. Beecher spent his last years living with his son Henry in Brooklyn, New York, where he died.

**BIBLIOGRAPHY**

Beecher, Lyman, and B. Cross (ed.), *The Autobiography of Lyman Beecher,* 1961; Caskey, M., *Chariot of Fire: Religion and the Beecher Family,* 1978; Henry, S. C., *Unvanquished Puritan: A Portrait of Lyman Beecher,* 1973; Rugoff, Milton, *The Beechers: An American Family in the Nineteenth Century,* 1982.

# Bellamy, Edward

(March 26, 1850–May 22, 1898)
Author, Reformer

Edward Bellamy attracted a huge following with his utopian novel, *Looking Backward* (1888).

Bellamy was born in Chicopee Falls, Massachusetts, where he lived for most of his life. In 1868 he traveled to Europe, where he was appalled by the poverty and suffering in the urban slums of Germany. Back in the United States, Bellamy became a lawyer but found the field did not meet his standards of justice. Switching to journalism, he joined the staff of the New York *Evening Post* in 1871, moved on to the *Springfield Union,* and then with his brother founded the Springfield *Daily News* in 1880.

Two years later, Bellamy quit journalism to devote himself to writing short stories and novels. Among his early works was a historical novel about Shays's Rebellion (see DANIEL SHAYS), titled *The Duke of Stockbridge* and serialized in 1879. The concern with social problems evident in that novel eventually led Bellamy to write his best-known book, *Looking Backward: 2000–1887.*

The novel's hero, Julian West, falls asleep in 1887 and wakes up in 2000 to discover that the poverty and suffering of late–nineteenth-century industrial America have been replaced by a perfect society. The government owns the means of production, employing all people between the ages of twenty-one and forty-five. All members of society share equally in the nation's wealth. This new society brings out the best rather than the worst in people; in it, the selfishness, greed, and cutthroat competition of capitalism have

Library of Congress

given way to a cooperative spirit that enables people to live together in peace and harmony. Their lives are also made easier and more pleasant by numerous gadgets, foreshadowing inventions like radio, motion pictures, and television. Bellamy called his system "Nationalism."

*Looking Backward* was an enormous success, selling almost a million copies, and it is still in print today in various editions. "Nationalist" clubs were formed across the country to discuss his ideas. The overwhelmingly favorable response persuaded Bellamy that his Nationalist system could be achieved in a timely and peaceful manner without the class warfare of Marxian socialism. In 1891 he moved to Boston and began publishing a weekly, the *New Nation,* which laid out a concrete program of reform. Bellamy and his followers supported the Populists in the election of 1892, because of their call for measures like nationalization of the railroads and municipal ownership of util-

ities. But soon afterward, the Nationalist movement went into a decline, and Bellamy himself had to spend more and more time responding to growing criticism of his ideas. He stopped publication of his weekly and, despite poor health, devoted his last years to writing a sequel to *Looking Backward.* Called *Equality* and published in 1897, the book was much less successful. Although the formal movement sparked by *Looking Backward* was short-lived, the book had a powerful impact, inspiring large numbers of reformers to take on the cause of reform.

**BIBLIOGRAPHY**

Bowman, Sylvia E., *Year 2000: A Critical Biography of Edward Bellamy,* 1958; Bowman, Sylvia E., et al., *Edward Bellamy Abroad: An American Prophet's Influence,* 1962.

# Benedict, Ruth Fulton

(June 5, 1887–September 17, 1948)
Anthropologist, Social Activist

Ruth Benedict's anthropological studies of American Indian societies laid much of the basis for studies in culture and personality. She used her scientific work to oppose racial discrimination and racist theories.

Ruth Fulton was born in New York City, the elder of two daughters of Frederick Samuel Fulton, a surgeon, and Bertrice Joanna Shattuck. When she was two her father died. She suffered from partial deafness from the time she was a baby. Ruth spent much of her childhood with her Shattuck relatives on a farm in New York State and later lived in Buffalo where her mother worked as a teacher.

Ruth Fulton entered Vassar College when she was eighteen and began to favor humanistic ideas in place of her family's conventional

religion. Graduating in 1909, she spent a year abroad, did social work in Buffalo, and taught in schools for girls in California, where the varied Asian population groups attracted her interest. In June 1914 she married a biochemist, Stanley Rossiter Benedict, and thereafter lived mainly in New York City.

Homemaking was unfulfilling for Ruth Benedict, and she tried her hand at writing poetry, detective stories, and historical biographies and then at modern dance and social work. In 1919 curiosity sent her to lectures at the New School for Social Research, and she was stirred by Elsie Clews Parsons, an anthropologist studying American Indians, and Alexander Goldenweiser, a cultural sociologist. Thus Benedict, in 1921, began graduate study at Columbia University under the pioneering anthropologist FRANZ BOAS, who persuaded her to start on her dissertation immediately. She undertook a study of American Indian religion, working from documentary sources. For *The Concept of the Guardian Spirit in North America* she earned a Ph.D. in 1923.

From 1923 until 1931, when not serving as an untenured lecturer at Columbia and editor of the *Journal of American Folklore,* Benedict pursued fieldwork in the Southwest. In spite of her deafness, interpreters helped her obtain rich material on the Pima of southern Arizona and the Cochiti and Zuñi of New Mexico (see ALFONSO ORTIZ). She published *Tales of the Cochiti Indians* (1931) and *Zuñi Mythology* (1935).

During the 1920s Benedict was influenced by the linguist and anthropologist Edward Sapir, who introduced her to the work of Sigmund Freud, C. G. Jung, and other psychologists; and by MARGARET MEAD, at first her student and then her colleague and closest friend. Benedict developed the theory of configuration: a culture followed a basic psychological pattern formed over generations. Possibly from Jung she took the concept of psychological types, noting that a society's behavior was comparable to the fixed behavior of an individual. The theory was elucidated in her most famous book, *Patterns of Culture* (1934), whose closing words call for accepting "the coexisting and equally valid patterns of life which mankind has accepted for itself from the raw materials of existence."

In 1931 Benedict was appointed an assistant professor at Columbia and took over much of her mentor Boas's teaching. She was sympathetic as well to his intense bias against racism and prejudice, borne out by her book *Race: Science and Politics* (1940) and a widely circulated pamphlet written with Gene Weltfish, *Races of Mankind* (1943).

In the late 1930s Benedict spoke out for cultural diversity in the public schools. During World War II, she was one of several anthropologists recruited by the Office of War Information to study the "national character" of foreign societies. As head of the Basic Analysis Section of the Bureau of Overseas Intelligence, she supervised research bringing anthropological methods to bear on findings from documentary sources and interviews with immigrants and refugees. The material was made available to government agencies for policy planning and action—in effect, for propaganda, morale building, and "psychological warfare." Benedict's subjects included Thailand, Burma, Romania, the Netherlands, and finally Japan. From the last grew her book *The Chrysanthemum and the Sword* (1946), which delineated the complexities of Japanese character.

Returning to Columbia after the war, Benedict received a grant from the Office of Naval Research to carry on a project, with Margaret Mead, continuing their research on contemporary cultures. In spring 1948, she became a full professor, and she and Gene Weltfish were honored by the Southern Conference for Human Welfare for their writings against racial and religious prejudice. After a summer traveling in Europe for the research project and lecturing at a United Nations Educational, Scientific, and Cultural Organization (UNESCO) conference on child rearing, Benedict suffered a fatal heart attack soon after arriving home.

**BIBLIOGRAPHY**

Caffrey, Margaret M., *Ruth Benedict: A Stranger in This Land,* 1989; Mead, Margaret, *An Anthropologist at Work: Writings of Ruth Benedict,* 1959, and *Ruth Benedict: A Biography,* 1974; Modell, Judith S., *Ruth Benedict: Patterns of a Life,* 1983.

# Bethune, Mary Jane McLeod

(July 10, 1875–May 18, 1955)
Civil Rights Activist, Educator

Mary McLeod Bethune had the zeal of a missionary for achieving social, economic, and educational opportunities for black Americans, and particularly for black women. Living and working in the segregated South, she displayed courage and astuteness in dealing with realities and winning through to her goals.

Mary Jane McLeod was born in Mayesville, in central South Carolina, fifteenth in a family of seventeen children. Her parents, freed slaves, acquired a few acres that were planted with cotton and rice and were worked by the entire family. Mary Jane was able to attend a Presbyterian mission school and did well enough to receive a scholarship to a seminary for girls in Concord, North Carolina. Having completed the equivalent of two years of college, she received another scholarship that enabled her to attend the Moody Bible Institute in Chicago for a year. A deeply religious Presbyterian, McLeod was eager to go to Africa as a missionary, but the Presbyterian Mission Board assigned only white missionaries to Africa. From 1895 to 1898 she taught at mission schools in Georgia and South Carolina. In 1898 she married Albertus L. Bethune, also a schoolteacher; their only child, Albert, was born in 1899. Her strong devotion to teaching created problems in her marriage, and her husband left her.

For four years Mary Bethune taught at a Presbyterian mission school in Palatka, Florida. In 1904 she founded the Daytona Normal and Industrial Institute in what is now Daytona Beach, Florida, starting, as she wrote, with "five girls, a small cabin, and $1.50." They used charcoal for pencils and mashed elderberries for ink. In the South of that time, there was inadequate provision for the education of black youths, in particular of young women, and Bethune's school provided a much needed opportunity. An effective fund-raiser, she solicited from local people as well as northerners, both black and white. The Institute, though emphasizing religion, character development, and vocational training, added courses in education and nursing. In 1929, it was merged with the Cookman Institute, a school for young men, becoming Bethune-Cookman College. Under Bethune's presidency, it became an accredited junior college and, in 1948, a four-year liberal arts college. It is now integrated.

During the 1920s, Bethune set up schools for the children of black workers in the turpentine camps and, despite threats from the Ku Klux Klan, organized black voter registration efforts in her part of the state.

In those years, Bethune served as president of the National Association of Colored Women and led fund raising toward acquiring the home of FREDERICK DOUGLASS as its headquarters in Washington, D.C. In 1927 she was the only black woman at a meeting of the National Council of Women of the United States, where she met Eleanor Roosevelt, who became a personal friend. Bethune was appointed to presidential commissions under Calvin Coolidge, Herbert Hoover, and Franklin D. Roosevelt. In 1935 Roosevelt named her to the National Advisory Committee of the National Youth Administration (NYA), which was set up under the New Deal to help young people find jobs and acquire education. Subsequently she was appointed director of NYA's Division of Negro Affairs. Though Bethune's responsibility was to ensure that black youths participated in NYA programs, she was only partially successful in getting equal appropriations for black activities. She managed, nevertheless, to get a special black college fund established, through which her office arranged help for blacks unable to receive NYA aid through regular channels.

Bethune's most significant work was in behalf of black women, thousands of whom she enlisted in the struggle for civil and women's rights. In 1935 she founded and became president of the National Council of Negro Women (NCNW), which united several dozen organizations and addressed women's concerns on a variety of fronts. During World War II the NCNW worked for the integration of black women in the Women's Army Corps (WAC) and led a war bond drive to finance a Liberty ship named for the abolitionist HARRIET TUBMAN. Bethune helped form the Federal Council on Negro Affairs, popularly called the Black Cabinet, which worked for equable benefits for blacks from the federal government. She published newspaper columns and numerous articles, particularly on black history and culture, that grew out of her activities as the long-time president of the Association for the Study of Negro Life and History and as vice president of the National Association for the Advancement of Colored People (NAACP; see JOEL E. SPINGARN) and the National Urban League.

In 1935 Mary Bethune received the Spingarn Medal from the NAACP for her notable contributions toward the advancement of black Americans. During the New Deal years Bethune conferred with President Roosevelt several times a year. She reported those meetings in an article, "My Secret Talks with FDR," in *Ebony*, April 1949. In that year she returned to Daytona Beach, where she continued an active life until her death from a heart attack at age seventy-nine. In 1974 a statue of Mary McLeod Bethune was dedicated in Lincoln Park, in Washington, near the statue of Abraham Lincoln dedicated in 1876 by President Ulysses S. Grant and Frederick Douglass.

**BIBLIOGRAPHY**

Holt, Rackham, *Mary McLeod Bethune*, 1964; Peare, Catherine O., *Mary McLeod Bethune*, 1951.

# Bettelheim, Bruno

(August 28, 1903–March 13, 1990)
Psychologist

Bruno Bettelheim was a pioneer in treating psychological problems of children and adolescents, and his methods were major contributions to pediatric therapy. His theories, often considered provocative, won him adversaries as well as admirers.

Bruno Bettelheim was born in Vienna, Austria, to assimilated upper-middle-class Jewish parents. As an adolescent during World War I, he lived through a time of social and economic chaos, with food shortages, widespread anti-Semitism, and political upheaval. In 1917 he joined a youth organization, the Jung Wandervögel (Young Wanderers, in English), whose members' interests included socialist politics and human relations. Bettelheim first heard of psychoanalysis from an older youth, Otto Fenichel (who later became a famous psychoanalyst), and began to read the work of Sigmund Freud, the founder of psychoanalysis. After graduating from a gymnasium (high school), he went into the family business and married. He was also doing graduate work at the University of Vienna in philosophy, psychology, and art history. In the late 1920s, because of problems in his marriage, Bettelheim decided to give psychoanalysis a try; he began working with Richard Sterba, a well-known psychoanalyst.

Bettelheim received a Ph.D. in psychology at the University of Vienna, but he had no formal training as a psychoanalyst, though he spent several years in analysis with Sterba. He became interested in the treatment of autism, a disorder in which a child withdraws into a private world, communicating with others little or not at all. He and his first wife, who was working in a school directed by Anna Freud, took a troubled child into their home and observed the progress the child made in a warm environment.

When the Nazis annexed Austria in 1938, Bettelheim was arrested because of his Jewish identity and his activity in the resistance movement against the fascist government of Austria. He spent nearly two years confined in the concentration camps at Dachau and Buchenwald, Germany. After being released through the intercession of American friends, he immigrated to the United States. He was a research associate with the Progressive Education Association at the University of Chicago for two years; he then taught psychology at Rockford College in northern Illinois. In 1944 Bettelheim began teaching at the University of Chicago and simultaneously was appointed head of the Sonia Shankman Orthogenic School, a laboratory school at the university that is devoted to children with severe emotional disorders who have not responded to usual types of psychotherapy.

Bettelheim's experience of the cruelty in the concentration camps gave him insights into the human personality. Rather than using a rigid and impersonal approach, he introduced unorthodox ways of treating disturbed children and adolescents: warm, humane treatment that respected the dignity of the individual. He stated that 85 percent of his patients made a full recovery, a claim that some specialists criticized.

Bettelheim was a prolific writer of articles and books that grew out of his work. *Love Is Not Enough* (1950) and *Truants from Life* (1955) are classics of psychoanalytic literature on education and child care. In *The Informed Heart* (1960), considered his most profound and important book, he showed how the impact of even the least significant detail of the environment could alter personality for good or ill. *The Empty Fortress* (1967), expressly on autism, focused on the relationship of parent and child.

Bettelheim retired as director of the Shankman School in 1973 and, continuing to be active as a writer, moved to California with his second wife, Gertrud Weinfeld, who died in 1984. In 1990 he moved to a retirement home near Washington, D.C. Apparently feeling desperate because of reverses in his health, family life, and work, he committed suicide.

**BIBLIOGRAPHY**

Bettelheim, Bruno, *Symbolic Wounds,* 1954, *A Home for the Heart,* 1974, *The Uses of Enchantment,* 1976, and *Freud's Vienna and Other Essays,* 1990; Cohler, Bertram J., and Jacqueline Sanders, *International Journal of Psycho-Analysis,* vol. 72, 1991.

# Blackwell, Alice Stone

(September 14, 1857–March 15, 1950)
Suffragist

Alice Stone Blackwell was a prominent suffragist who in later life espoused many humanitarian causes and became increasingly radical.

Born in Orange, New Jersey, Alice Stone Blackwell grew up in a household where the women's rights movement was of paramount importance. Both her father, Henry Brown Blackwell, and her mother, LUCY STONE, were active suffragists, while her aunt, ELIZABETH BLACKWELL, was the first woman to receive a medical degree in America. Another aunt,

ANTOINETTE BROWN BLACK-WELL, was the first woman to be ordained a minister in the United States.

After years of frequent moves, the family settled in 1869 in the Boston suburb of Dorchester, where they established the American Woman Suffrage Association and a suffragist paper, the *Woman's Journal.* In 1881 Alice entered the recently established Boston University, one of two women in a class of twenty-six men. Previously shy and insecure, she now shone as a student, becoming class president and graduating Phi Beta Kappa. After graduation in 1885, she began writing for the *Woman's Journal,* and two years later she began editing the *Women's Column,* a collection of suffrage news items supplied free of charge to newspapers all over the country. Eventually she assumed total charge of the *Woman's Journal.*

In 1890 Blackwell was instrumental in bringing about the merger of the two rival national suffrage organizations into the National American Woman Suffrage Association. She became the recording secretary of the new organization, holding this position for nearly twenty years and generally working behind the scenes in an advisory capacity.

In 1893 Blackwell began to pursue a wider variety of reform interests. Over the next years she joined such organizations as the Women's Christian Temperance Union, the Anti-Vivisection Society, the National Association for the Advancement of Colored People (NAACP; see JOEL E. SPINGARN), and the American Peace Society. Influenced by a young Armenian divinity student, Johannes Chatschumian, she took up the cause of needy Armenian refugees; also, outraged by the op-

Library of Congress

pression of the Russian people under Czarist rule, she helped form an organization called the Friends of Russian Freedom.

Retiring from the *Woman's Journal* shortly before the ratification of the Nineteenth Amendment in 1920, giving women the vote, Blackwell became involved in politics. She was a founding member of the Massachusetts League of Women Voters and supported the Progressive candidate, Robert M. La Follette, for president in 1924. In the reactionary atmosphere of the 1920s, she grew more and more radical, campaigning against the deportation of suspected foreign-born radicals under the Espionage Act and supporting the defense of Sacco and Vanzetti, Italian immigrants with anarchist views who were accused of murder and robbery in Massachusetts. Blackwell also pushed to have black students admitted to Boston University, where she served on the board of trustees. Frail and gray-haired, she was a regular fixture at protest meetings in Boston throughout the decade.

In 1930 Blackwell finally completed a biography of her mother, *Lucy Stone: Pioneer in Woman's Rights,* upon which she had labored lovingly for forty years. In the last two decades of her life she went blind and lost most of her savings through the dishonesty of her business agent. Supported by an annuity fund set up by friends, she lived until the age of ninety-two.

**BIBLIOGRAPHY**

Flexner, Eleanor, *Century of Struggle: The Woman's Rights Movement in the United States,* 1959, rev.,

1975; Hays, Elinor Rice, *Morning Star: A Biography of Lucy Stone*, 1961; Kraditor, Aileen S., *The Ideas of the Woman Suffrage Movement*, *1890–1920*, 1965; Merrill, Marlene Deahl, *Growing Up in Boston's Gilded Age: The Journal of Alice Stone Blackwell, 1872–1874*, 1990.

# Blackwell, Antoinette Louisa Brown

(May 20, 1825–November 5, 1921)
Feminist, Religious Leader

Antoinette Brown Blackwell was the first American woman to be ordained as a minister of a recognized denomination. An author and lecturer as well, she was active in the woman suffrage and temperance movements.

Antoinette Brown was born in Henrietta, New York, an area that was swept by waves of religious enthusiasm, and she joined the Congregational church at an early age. She attended Monroe County Academy, the first public high school in the state.

In 1846, with her family's support, Antoinette Brown enrolled at Oberlin College in Ohio, which was the first coeducational college in the country (see CHARLES GRANDISON FINNEY). Here she became close friends with the feminist and abolitionist LUCY STONE, who was to be her sister-in-law. Graduating in 1847 from the nondegree literary course, she decided to pursue theological studies at Oberlin against the objections of her family and the college faculty. Although Brown completed the three-year theological course, she was denied a student license to preach because of her sex and was not allowed to graduate officially in 1850. (In 1878 Oberlin finally granted her an honorary A.M. and in 1908 an honorary D.D.)

Upon leaving Oberlin, Brown lectured on woman's rights, abolition, and temperance. She was a delegate to the World Temperance Convention in New York City in 1853 but as a woman was not allowed to speak. She was occasionally invited to preach at liberal Unitarian churches, but most clergymen were opposed to her.

Finally, on September 15, 1853, Brown was ordained as minister of the First Congregational Church in Butler, New York. She left her position after a year, however, when she discovered that her views were too liberal for the orthodox Calvinist congregation. Ultimately Brown became a Unitarian, and in 1855 she went to New York City to work among the poor. She described her experiences in a series of articles for the *New York Tribune*, which were later published in book form as *Shadows of Our Social System* (1856).

In 1856 Antoinette Brown married Samuel Charles Blackwell, a businessman and brother of pioneer doctors ELIZABETH BLACKWELL and EMILY BLACKWELL and of Henry Brown Blackwell, who had married Brown's friend from Oberlin, Lucy Stone. Settling in New Jersey, the couple had five daughters. While raising her family, Antoinette Blackwell kept up with her intellectual and theological studies, which bore fruit in such books as *The Sexes Throughout Nature* (1875), *The Physical Basis of Immortality* (1876), and *The Philosophy of Individuality* (1893). A moderate feminist, she believed that men and women were equal but that they did not share the same feelings and attitudes. Blackwell further believed that every woman ought to have an occupation. While advocating equality in marriage, she strongly opposed divorce for religious reasons.

Her husband suffering financial reverses, Blackwell returned to the lecture platform in 1878. She was also active in the American Woman Suffrage Association and other women's organizations and contributed to Lucy Stone's *Woman's Journal.* After her husband's death in 1901, Blackwell settled in Elizabeth, New Jersey, where she helped found All Souls' Unitarian Church. In 1920, when women finally won their right to vote, she went to the polls, though ill and nearly blind. She died a year later at the age of ninety-six.

**BIBLIOGRAPHY**

Cazden, E., *Antoinette Brown Blackwell,* 1983; Hersh, Blanche G., *The Slavery of Sex: Feminist-Abolitionists in America,* 1978.

## Blackwell, Elizabeth

(February 3, 1821–May 31, 1910)

## Blackwell, Emily

(October 8, 1826–September 7, 1910)
Physicians, Reformers

Elizabeth Blackwell was the first woman to receive a medical degree in the United States or Europe. Together with her sister, Emily, also a pioneer physician, she did much to open the medical profession to women.

Elizabeth and Emily Blackwell were born in England. Their father, Samuel Blackwell, was an abolitionist and man of liberal views who believed that women should be educated equally with men. The two sisters were not the only members of the family to distinguish themselves. Sisters Anna and Ellen became writers. Brothers Henry and Samuel were both reformers who married other reformers. Henry wed abolitionist and feminist LUCY STONE; Samuel married minister and suffragist ANTOINETTE BROWN BLACKWELL.

In 1832, when Elizabeth was eleven and Emily six, the family immigrated to America, settling first in New York City and then, in 1838, in Cincinnati, where their father hoped for better prospects for his sugar-refining business. His death shortly after the move left the family heavily in debt and made it necessary for Elizabeth to help support the family. She did so by teaching in the boarding school the Blackwells opened in their home, and then in the town of Henderson, Kentucky.

Finding teaching not to her liking, Elizabeth cast about for another profession and decided upon medicine after a woman friend who was dying of cancer said she would have been spared a great deal of agony if she could have been treated by a female physician. While teaching music in North and South Carolina, Elizabeth studied privately under two physicians who were brothers, John and Samuel Dickson. In 1847 she went to Philadelphia, where with the help of several liberal Quaker physicians she sought admission to medical schools in Philadelphia and New York City. Having been turned down by all of these, plus Harvard and Yale, she applied to a number of smaller schools in rural areas.

In October 1847 Elizabeth Blackwell was finally accepted by Geneva Medical College (later Hobart) in upstate New York—not because the faculty was particularly liberal, but because the all-male student body voted unanimously to admit her. Graduating in 1849, she became the first woman to receive a degree from a regular medical college. She then went to Europe to obtain clinical training. While studying at La Maternité, the major lying-in hospital in Paris, she contracted ophthalmia. Blind in one eye as a result, she abandoned her goal of becoming a surgeon. She also studied briefly at St. Bartholomew's Hospital in London.

Upon her return to America in 1851, Blackwell settled in New York City and struggled to establish a medical practice. She was refused a position at the city's hospitals and dispensaries and was cold-shouldered by her male colleagues. Even landladies spurned her, reluctant to rent office space to a "female physician" (at the time this term was synonymous with "abortionist"). In desperation, she bought a house she could barely afford and, until she could develop a practice, began giving a series of lectures on good hygiene for women. Later published as *The Laws of Life, with Special Reference to the Physical Education of Girls* (1852), the lectures appealed to liberal Quaker women, who became her first patients. With their support, in 1853 she opened a small dispensary to give medical care to poor women. Three years later she was joined by her sister Emily and another woman physician, Marie Zakrzewska, and in 1857 expanded the dispensary into a hospital, the still-existing New York Infirmary for Women and Children. The hospital was unique in being an all-female institution, where women received medical care from physicians of their own sex.

In 1859 Elizabeth Blackwell began planning a medical college for women. These plans temporarily were suspended because of the Civil War, during which she figured prominently in the Women's Central Association of Relief, helping to select and train nurses for the Union army. In 1868, however, she realized her goal with the opening of the Women's Medical College of the New York Infirmary. In keeping with her determination to provide women with a medical education equal to that of men, the college had entrance examinations, a three-year graded curriculum, and plenty of opportunities for clinical experience. It trained hundreds of women physicians before merging with the Cornell University Medical College

after that institution opened its doors to women in 1899.

Leaving Emily to run the hospital and medical school in 1869, Elizabeth Blackwell returned to England, where she remained for the rest of her life. She established a private practice in London, founded the National Health Society to promote hygiene, supported other women doctors, and taught gynecology. In 1876 she retired to a seaside house in Hastings because of poor health.

In the last three decades of her life, Elizabeth Blackwell wrote several books on moral reform, an early interest. She argued in behalf of sex education for young people and against prostitution and the "double standard" in sexual relations. While continuing to stress the importance of hygiene and proper sanitation, she rejected such medical advances as vaccination and animal experimentation. She died at Hastings at the age of eighty-nine.

Emily Blackwell grew up in the same liberal family atmosphere as Elizabeth but was more influenced by her older sister's example than by her father. Deciding to become a doctor like Elizabeth, Emily taught school in Henderson, Kentucky, and then in Cincinnati to raise money for her medical education. After being turned down by eleven medical schools, including Elizabeth's alma mater, Geneva College, she was finally accepted by Rush Medical College in Chicago in 1852. The next year, the school succumbed to pressure from the State Medical Society for admitting a woman and closed its doors to her. Fortunately, Emily was able to complete her second year of study at the Medical College of Western Reserve University in Cleveland, graduating with honors in 1854.

Emily Blackwell, like Elizabeth, got her clinical training abroad, studying in Edinburgh, London, Paris, Berlin, and Dresden. Returning to the United States in 1856, she helped her sister and Marie Zakrzewska open the New York Infirmary for Women and Children, which she ran single-handedly for a period in 1859 while her sister was away in England (Marie Zakrzewska had moved to Boston). Emily proved such an able manager that larger quarters were soon needed, and in 1860, a year after Elizabeth's return, the sisters moved the hospital into a bigger house.

With the establishment of the medical school in 1868, Emily Blackwell became professor of obstetrics and diseases of women (later gynecology), assuming full responsibility for both the college and the infirmary after her sister's departure for England in 1869. For the next thirty years she pursued this work. Under her expert guidance, the college expanded its facilities and maintained high professional standards. That it closed in 1899 was due to Emily's belief, which Elizabeth shared, that women should be educated together with men. So when the Cornell University Medical College in New York admitted women students on an equal basis with men, Emily decided that a separate school was no longer needed and arranged for her students to transfer to Cornell.

She continued to work at the hospital until her retirement in 1900. Ten years later, she died in Maine of enterocolitis, having survived her older sister by only three months.

Although their early careers were closely linked, Elizabeth and Emily Blackwell followed different, but complementary, paths. While Elizabeth Blackwell achieved distinction as a medical pioneer and social reformer, Emily is best remembered as a practicing physician and medical educator, carrying on the work her sister had begun.

**BIBLIOGRAPHY**

Hays, Elinor R., *Those Extraordinary Blackwells*, 1967; Morantz-Sanchez, Regina, *Sympathy and Science: Women Physicians in American Medicine*, 1985; Sahli, N., *Elizabeth Blackwell, M.D., (1821–1910); A Biography*, 1974.

# Block, Herbert Lawrence

(October 13, 1909–   )
Cartoonist

Herbert Block is one of the foremost editorial cartoonists in the country. Using the pen name "Herblock," he has provided trenchant commentary on the national and international political scene for more than half a century and in the process received numerous awards for service to civil liberties, education, and journalism.

Born in Chicago, Block won a Chicago Art Institute scholarship at age twelve and attended evening art classes. After graduation from high school, he attended Lake Forest College, leaving after two years to become a cartoonist in 1929 with the Chicago *Daily News*. At this time, he adopted the pen name "Herblock" by combining his first and last names into one word. In 1933 he joined the Cleveland office of the Newspaper Enterprise Association (NEA), a feature service. While with the NEA he earned a reputation as a political cartoonist with strong opinions. In 1942 Block won the Pulitzer Prize for cartooning for his work the previous year. The following year, Block joined the army. While stationed in Florida and New York, he drew cartoons for the army's Information and Education Division.

Upon his discharge in 1946, Block became the editorial cartoonist for the *Washington Post*. At the *Post* he continued to distinguish himself for the political sophistication, technical simplicity, and clever wording of his cartoons. Block won the Heywood Broun Award of the American Newspaper Guild for outstanding journalistic achievement in 1948 and in 1950, and he published his first book, *The Herblock Book*, containing about 400 of his best-known cartoons, in 1952. Two years later, he won his second Pulitzer Prize for a cartoon based on the death of the Russian leader, Joseph Stalin. It showed Death as a grim reaper leading Stalin and holding the communist's bloody sickle with the caption, "You were always a great friend of mine, Joseph." In a later cartoon, Block showed the leaders of the Kremlin happily examining a map of China with the caption, "Five Hundred Million of Them—All Expendable." Block was the first to label the anticommunist hysteria of the 1950s "McCarthyism," and his cartoons helped lead to Senator Joe McCarthy's downfall.

Syndicated in more than 200 newspapers, Block's cartoons have generally expressed a liberal viewpoint in their emphasis on basic human rights, civil liberties, and democratic principles. In the 1950s and 1960s Block's cartoons reflected his sympathy with the civil rights movement. He also emerged as a strong critic of American involvement in Vietnam.

In 1966 Block designed the U.S. postage stamp commemorating the 175th anniversary of the Bill of Rights. In 1979 Block received a third Pulitzer Prize for cartooning. Among the recent awards he has received are the World Hunger Media Award (1984), the Elijah Lovejoy award for freedom of the press (1986), the Franklin Roosevelt Freedom medal (1987), and the Good Guy award of the Women's National Political Caucus (1989).

Taken together, Block's eight books of cartoons constitute a comic and often biting record of the major personalities and events of the last fifty years.

**BIBLIOGRAPHY**

Block, Herbert, *Herblock's Special for Today*, 1958, *Straight Herblock*, 1964, *The Herblock Gallery*, 1968, *Herblock State of the Union*, 1972, *Herblock On All Fronts*, 1980, and *Herblock At Large*, 1987; Deur, Lynne, *Political Cartoonists*, 1972.

# Bloomer, Amelia Jenks

(May 27, 1818–December 30, 1894)
Editor, Reformer

Best known for the costume named after her, Amelia Bloomer advanced the causes of women's rights and temperance through her work as a pioneering woman newspaper editor and as a lecturer.

Born in Homer, New York, Amelia Jenks taught school briefly before marrying Dexter Bloomer, a Quaker newspaper editor and antislavery reformer, in 1840. The couple settled in Seneca Falls, New York, where with her husband's encouragement Bloomer began to write articles for his paper and for a local temperance journal. In 1848 she attended but took no active part in the first major women's rights convention at Seneca Falls. That same year, Bloomer helped to start a Ladies' Temperance Society, and in January 1849 she began publishing the *Lily*. Although initially limited to temperance, the paper soon became the first in the country to devote itself to women's issues. It was also the first American newspaper that was completely owned, published, and edited by a woman. Many of the paper's articles on women's rights were written by the feminist leader ELIZABETH CADY STANTON, under the pen name of "Sunflower." In 1850 Bloomer's introduction of Stanton to SUSAN B. ANTHONY marked the beginning of their historic partnership.

Early in 1851, Bloomer attracted national notoriety by her defense in the *Lily* of the costume that was to take its name from her. Elizabeth Smith Miller, daughter of the reformer GERRIT SMITH, had worn full Turkish pantaloons with a short skirt on a visit to Stanton, who then decided to adopt the outfit as a less cumbersome and more healthy alternative to the voluminous skirts and tightly laced stays worn by women at the time. Bloomer herself wore the costume for the next eight years, abandoning it after she decided it was taking attention away from more important aspects of the women's rights movement.

Library of Congress

In 1852 Bloomer made her debut as a lecturer at a temperance meeting in Rochester, where she supported a proposal to make drunkenness grounds for divorce in New York State. The following year, she embarked on a speaking tour of the state with Anthony and other feminist leaders and took part in national antislavery, temperance, and women's rights conventions in New York City.

At the end of 1853 Bloomer and her husband moved to Mount Vernon, Ohio, where he edited and was part owner of a reform paper, the *Western Home Visitor.* Bloomer continued to edit the *Lily,* which by this time had a circulation of over 6,000, and lectured on temperance and women's rights throughout Ohio and Indiana. Adhering to their feminist principles, she and her husband hired women typesetters for their papers and refused to fire them when the male staff threatened a strike.

In 1855, after moving to Council Bluffs, Iowa, Bloomer sold the *Lily* because of her new home's poor rail connections and lack of good printing facilities. Nevertheless, she kept up her interest in the cause the paper had supported, helping to organize local temperance organizations and becoming president of the Iowa Woman Suffrage Society in 1871. She also continued to contribute vigorously written reform-minded articles to newspapers and journals.

**BIBLIOGRAPHY**

Bloomer, D. C., *Life and Writings of Amelia Bloomer,* 1895; Gurko, Miriam, *The Ladies of Seneca Falls: The Birth of the Woman's Rights Movement,* 1976; Stanton, Elizabeth C., et al., *History of Woman Suffrage,* vols. I–III, 1881–1886; Thorp, Margaret Farrand, *Female Persuasion,* 1949.

# Boas, Franz

(July 9, 1858–December 21, 1942)
Anthropologist

Franz Boas, who led in forming an American science of anthropology, was a scholar of broad learning, concerned with all aspects of humanity and its culture. He exposed the fallacies in Nazi racial theories and defended democracy and freedom of thought, inculcating his principles in students who became distinguished anthropologists.

Boas was born in Minden, Westphalia, in western Germany. His father, Meier Boas, was a well-to-do merchant; his mother, Sophie Meyer, was an intellectual much interested in science. His secondary education embraced natural science, literature, history, and music, and in university (he attended Heidelberg, Bonn, and Kiel) he specialized in mathematics, physics, and finally geography. Like many students in German universities of those days, he did his share of carousing and dueling—and a duel was often the result of an anti-Semitic slur (Boas was Jewish). Boas got his doctorate at Kiel with a dissertation on the color of ocean water.

After a year of military service, Boas went to Berlin, where he came under the influence of two important anthropologists, Rudolf Virchow and Adolf Bastian. As a project, in summer 1883 he joined an expedition to Baffin Land (now Baffin Island), in the Arctic off northeast Canada, intending to study Eskimo migration routes. He spent a year there, observing Eskimo life and resolving to find out what determines human behavior. Thus he became an anthropologist.

Boas spent some months in the United States looking into possible academic appointments before returning to Berlin to work under Bastian, lecture at the university, and write up the results of his Eskimo studies. While he qualified for a German university appointment, instead he came to the United States and worked as an editor of the magazine *Science* in New York. From 1889 to 1892 he was an instructor of anthropology at the newly chartered Clark University, in Massachusetts (see G. STANLEY HALL). During the next four years he did anthropological work at the Chicago World's Fair and the American Museum of Natural History, in New York City. In 1896 he was appointed a lecturer at Columbia University and three years later became a full professor, meanwhile continuing his connection with the museum. Boas spent the remaining thirty-seven years of his career at Columbia. He had become an American citizen in 1891.

Boas concentrated his scientific work on the Indians of the Northwest Coast of British Columbia, and particularly on the Kwakiutl tribe of Vancouver Island. He had reconnoitered the coastal area when he came to America in 1887 and subsequently made many field trips, collecting folklore for linguistic analysis and cultural study. His publications on the Kwakiutl are classics of anthropological research. In 1897 Boas extended the scope of his work by launching the Jesup North Pacific Expedition, which over some thirty years investigated the aboriginal peoples of the entire northwest area and neighboring Siberia. During 1910 to 1912, Boas spent time in Mexico directing archaeological work on pre-Columbian sites and studying obscure tribes.

In 1911 the first volume of the *Handbook of American Indian Languages* appeared, under Boas's editorship. It set forth his view that every language arose from a unique cultural experience and could be analyzed only in terms of that experience. The science of descriptive linguistics developed from Boas's approach, which emphasized rigorous discipline in fieldwork and analysis. Boas published another major work that year, *Changes in Bodily Form of Descendants of Immigrants,* a report for the United States Immigration Commission. Boas used biometric methods to show that the head forms of American-born children were significantly unlike those of their immigrant parents. He thereby proved that the environment profoundly affected physical features and other characteristics thought to be inherited. His third important contribution in 1911 was *The Mind of Primitive Man*, which challenged assumptions that racial mental ability and cultural achievement were correlated and taught that human differences are the consequence of the various cultures in which people are born and brought up.

In the area of race Boas made his most telling contribution. In 1931, addressing the American Association for the Advancement of Science as its president, he stated, "There is no reason to believe that one race is by nature so much more intelligent . . . or emotionally more stable than others that the difference would materially influence its culture." Through his writings, graduate teaching (MARGARET MEAD and RUTH BENEDICT were his students), and professional activities, Boas mounted a vigorous and ultimately successful assault on these racist ideas and the substantial body of intellectual work they had inspired. Retiring from teaching in 1936, Boas said, "What we know as race is largely a matter of environment. There is no such thing as pure race. All European races are mixtures of many stocks . . . Germany has one of the most-mixed stocks in Europe." He authorized the underground circulation in Germany of a pamphlet he wrote on the race question.

When Boas died suddenly of a heart attack, he was working on a study of the relation between physical and mental development and taking an active part in politics to defend intellectual freedom and democratic equality.

**BIBLIOGRAPHY**

Boas, Franz, *Race, Language, and Culture*, 1940, and *Race and Democratic Society*, 1945; Degler, Carl N., *In Search of Human Nature: The Decline and Revival of Darwinism in American Social Thought*, 1991; Herskovitz, Melville J., *Franz Boas*, 1953; Marshall, Hyatt, *Franz Boas, Social Activist*, 1990; Stocking, George W., Jr. (ed.), *A Franz Boas Reader*, 1974.

# Bond, Julian

(January 14, 1940–  )
Civil Rights Leader, Politician

Julian Bond, an activist and dedicated organization worker during the years of the civil rights movement, served for twenty years as an effective member of the Georgia State Assembly and subsequently as a lecturer and college professor.

The descendant of a freed slave, Julian Bond was born in Nashville, Tennessee, to parents who both had graduate degrees. His father, Horace Mann Bond, was president of Lincoln University, near Philadelphia, and, later, dean of the School of Education at Atlanta University (Georgia). Julian's mother, Julia Anges Washington, was a college librarian. Young Bond was educated at the George School, a Quaker-run prep school at Newtown, Pennsylvania, where he was the only African American student.

The Quaker atmosphere of the George School encouraged Bond's interest in pacifism and nonviolent activism. He moved to Atlanta with his family in 1957 and entered Morehouse College (part of Atlanta University), where one of his professors was MARTIN LUTHER KING, JR. While in college, Bond wrote and published poetry, was an intern for *Time* magazine, and was a cofounder of the Committee on Appeal for Human Rights (COHAR), a civil rights group that organized the first sit-in at the Atlanta City Hall, during which Bond was arrested for the first time. This and other nonviolent protests organized by COHAR over three years led to the integration of Atlanta's movie theaters, lunch counters, and parks. On Easter weekend 1960, Bond joined with many other students in the South to form the Student Nonviolent Coordinating Committee (SNCC; see ELLA BAKER), and became its communications director, editing the SNCC newsletter, *The Student Voice,* and working in voter registration drives in rural Georgia, Alabama, Mississippi, and Arkansas. He left Morehouse College short of graduation in 1961 and worked as a reporter and managing editor for the Atlanta *Inquirer,* a weekly paper founded by Morehouse students and faculty to give the black protest movement a voice. (He married Alice Clapton in that year. They have several children.) In 1971 Bond returned to Morehouse and graduated with an A.B. degree in English, a step which no doubt helped to develop his outstanding abilities at writing and public speaking.

Bond was elected from an Atlanta district in 1965 to a one-year term in the Georgia House of Representatives in a special election following the court-ordered reapportionment of the legislature, but the house voted not to seat him because of his outspoken opposition to American participation in the Vietnam War. In 1966 he won a second election, and again the House of Representatives voted to bar him from membership. He won a third election, for a two-year term, in November 1966, and the following month the United States Supreme Court ruled unanimously that the Georgia legislature had violated Bond's rights in refusing him his seat. He was sworn in as a member of the Georgia House on January 9, 1967.

Bond was elected to the Georgia State Senate in 1974 and served six two-year terms. During his time in the Georgia General Assembly, Bond sponsored more than sixty bills that became law, including a statewide program to provide low-interest home loans for low-income citizens. In 1986 he was defeated by a former SNCC ally, JOHN R. LEWIS. Political observers suggested that the white minority bloc vote supported Lewis because he was believed to be less militant than Bond.

At the Democratic National Convention in Chicago in 1968, Bond led the Georgia Loyal National Delegation, an insurgent group that succeeded in unseating the handpicked regulars, and he was nominated for vice president. Because he was seven years younger than the legal age, Bond withdrew his name.

Since leaving the political arena, Bond has served as president of the Southern Poverty Law Center and the Institute for Southern Studies. He has sat on the boards of many service organizations, including the National Association for the Advancement of Colored People (NAACP; see JOEL E. SPINGARN) and the American Civil Liberties Union (ACLU; see ROGER BALDWIN). For the 1990 to 1991 academic year he was a visiting professor at Harvard University and American University.

**BIBLIOGRAPHY**

Bond, Julian, *A Time to Speak, a Time to Act,* 1972; Bond, Julian, with Adolph Reed, Jr., "The Assault on Equality," *The Nation,* December 9, 1991; Carson, Clayborne, *In Struggle: SNCC and the Black Awakening of the 1960s,* 1981.

# Bonnin, Gertrude Simmons

(February 22, 1876–January 26, 1938)
American Indian Leader

Throughout her life, Pan-Indian activist and writer Gertrude Bonnin, or Zitkala-Sa, fought for American Indian self-determination and the preservation of an Indian culture.

Born on the Yankton Sioux reservation in South Dakota to a Sioux mother and a white father, Gertrude Simmons early left home against the wishes of her mother, who wanted her to stay in the tribe. She went to a mission school in Wabash, Indiana, graduated at nineteen, and entered Earlham College, in Richmond, Indiana. Simmons was a good student, but she found living in white society difficult.

Leaving college after two years because of illness, Simmons taught at the Carlisle Indian School, in Carlisle, Pennsylvania, from 1897 to 1899. She studied violin briefly at the New England Conservatory of Music and traveled to Paris with the Carlisle Indian Band in 1900. The next year she published *Old Indian Legends,* and her writings about Indian life began to appear in national magazines.

Simmons found work as a clerk in the Bureau of Indian Affairs at Standing Rock (New Mexico) Indian Reservation. There she met and married Raymond Talesfase Bonnin, a Sioux, in 1902. They had a son in 1903 and worked at other reservations in Utah until 1916.

The Bonnins joined the Society of American Indians (SAI), founded in 1911 for the purpose of improving the lives of Indians and preserving

National Archives

their culture. Gertrude Bonnin became secretary of the SAI in 1916, and her family moved to Washington, D.C.

Though the SAI fell apart, Bonnin, or Zitkala-Sa (meaning "Red Bird"), as she was also known, persevered in keeping alive a Pan-Indian movement in the 1920s through the National Council of American Indians, which she founded in 1926, and the Indian Welfare Committee of the General Federation of Women's Clubs. She was instrumental in focusing on tribal religious and land issues and in finding ways to get public support. In 1924 she helped investigate government abuses of Indians in Oklahoma and wrote the resulting report, *Oklahoma's Poor Rich Indians: An Orgy of Graft and Exploitation of the Five Civilized Tribes—Legalized Robbery.* In the same year Bonnin worked to get out the Indian vote for the Curtis Bill granting citizenship to all Indians.

For the last twenty years of her life, Bonnin worked out of Washington—often returning to participate in tribal affairs in South Dakota—to promote cultural pluralism. She hoped to guarantee the right of self-determination to Indian peoples through the establishment and preservation of strong tribal identities and the maintenance of their lands as cultural homelands. Along the way she clashed with President Franklin D. Roosevelt's Indian commissioner, John Collier, who had formerly been an ally on

Indian affairs and who now resented her advice. As a result she was overly critical of his enlightened Indian Reorganization Act passed by Congress in 1934.

Nonetheless, until her death Bonnin continued to work for the recognition of Indian cultures and values through lectures and correspondence. She died in Washington at the age of sixty-one and was buried in Arlington National Cemetery.

In addition to *Old Indian Legends,* Bonnin wrote *American Indian Stories* and innumerable articles and composed an opera, *Sun Dance,* in collaboration with William F. Hanson. Her important correspondence with the Bureau of Indian Affairs is preserved in the National Archives.

**BIBLIOGRAPHY**

Bonnin, Gertrude S., *American Indian Stories,* rep., 1985; Gridley, M. E., *American Indian Women,* 1974; Hertzberg, Hazel, *The Search for an Indian Identity: Modern Pan-Indian Movements,* 1971.

## Bourne, Randolph Silliman

(May 30, 1886–December 22, 1918)
Author, Reformer

Randolph Bourne's early death cut off a career of exceptional promise as an uncompromising critic of American politics, society, and educational policy.

Randolph Bourne was born in Bloomfield, New Jersey, the eldest of four children in a modest middle-class family. A difficult birth left him with facial deformities, and an attack of spinal tuberculosis at the age of four made him a stunted hunchback. After a private school education Bourne earned his living for several years working for a producer of player-piano rolls. While Bourne attended Columbia University, from 1909 to 1913—his teachers included CHARLES BEARD and JOHN DEWEY—he wrote idealistic essays about his hopes for youth, which were published as *Youth and Life.* A fellowship from the university enabled Bourne to spend a year in Europe on the eve of the outbreak of war, traveling and observing cultural conditions, about which he turned in a report notable for its acute, clear prose in the tradition of HENRY DAVID THOREAU. In 1914 he became an editor of the newly founded *The New Republic.* His articles on educational reform, influenced by the theories of Dewey, attracted wide attention and led to two books on progressive education, *The Gary Schools* (1916) and *Education and Living* (1917).

Bourne fell in with the young radical group that frequented the Liberal Club in Greenwich Village, where he lived. He vehemently opposed America's entry into World War I and wrote strongly pacifist articles for the *Masses* and *Seven Arts,* both of which the government suspended in 1917. Despite the humanitarian character of Bourne's articles of protest, *The New Republic* declined to publish them. Bourne refused to compromise his principles and lived in poverty, devoting his time to an iconoclastic work analyzing and fiercely indicting the government. He died in the influenza epidemic of 1918, neglected, though he had given eloquent voice to the attitudes and opinions of a suppressed American minority during the war. As his posthumously published works began to appear, however, his reputation revived. His *Untimely Papers,* edited by James Oppenheim, came out in 1919; *The History of a Literary Radical*, edited by Van Wyck Brooks, appeared in 1920. He is today recognized as one of the significant reformist critics in philosophy, politics, education, and literature and was one of the first exponents of what would later become known as cultural pluralism.

**BIBLIOGRAPHY**

Blake, Casey Nelson, *Beloved Community*, 1990; Clayton, Bruce, *Forgotten Prophet: The Life of Randolph Bourne*, 1984; Moreau, John A., *Randolph Bourne, Legend and Reality*, 1966; Vitelli, James R., *Randolph Bourne*, 1981.

## Bowditch, Henry Ingersoll

(August 9, 1808–January 14, 1892)
Abolitionist, Physician

Physician by profession and abolitionist by conviction, Henry Ingersoll Bowditch assisted runaway slaves in the North and helped establish an ambulance unit during the Civil War. A leader in the field of public health, he served on the Massachusetts State Board of Health and wrote a history of preventive medicine.

Born in Salem, Massachusetts, Bowditch was a son of the prominent mathematician and astronomer, Nathaniel Bowditch. He graduated from Harvard in 1828 and, after some uncertainty, entered the Harvard Medical School, earning his M.D. in 1832. He served as an intern at the Massachusetts General Hospital. In 1832 Bowditch traveled to Paris, where he studied under the famous French physician Pierre Charles Alexandre Louis. During a brief stay in England, he attended the funeral of English abolitionist leader William Wilberforce.

Returning to Boston in 1834, Bowditch established a medical practice and, stirred by WILLIAM LLOYD GARRISON's angry attacks on slavery, became an ardent abolitionist. In 1842

Library of Congress

Bowditch's abolitionist sentiments led him to take part in the so-called Latimer case. George Latimer, an escaped slave, was arrested in Boston and faced being returned to his owner. Together with William F. Channing and Frederick S. Cabot, Bowditch formed the Latimer Committee to aid the runaway. The three published a newspaper three times a week for over six months to publicize the case. The committee also helped organize a huge Latimer Petition that was sent to John Quincy Adams in the House of Representatives. Although the House refused to hear the petition, it served to link the right of petition with the cause of runaway slaves. Bowditch and Latimer's other sponsors saw that he avoided reenslavement by getting his owner to sign a deed of emancipation in exchange for $400. The Latimer case represented the first public defiance of the Fugitive Slave Act.

Afterward, Bowditch assisted other runaway slaves and worked to foster antislavery sentiment in the North. He offered to serve the army as a doctor in 1862, but was horrified by the treatment of the wounded, arguing for the institution of an ambulance corps. His pleas became louder when his own son, Nathaniel, died in the war in 1863. Bowditch wrote *A Brief Plea for an Ambulance System for the Army of the United States; as drawn from the Extra Sufferings of the Late Lieut. Bowditch and a Wounded Comrade.* This pamphlet so aroused public opinion that in 1864 an ambulance corps was established.

Otherwise, Bowditch's greatest medical service was in the field of public health. He served on the Massachusetts State Board of Health, established in 1869, only the second organization of its kind in the country, and on the National Board of Health, started in 1879. In 1877 Bowditch published *Public Hygiene in America,* which had an important influence on the public health movement in the United States. Two years later he became president of the American Medical Association. From 1880 until the end of his life, he suffered declining health.

**BIBLIOGRAPHY**

Bowditch, Vincent Yardley, *Life and Correspondence of Henry Ingersoll Bowditch,* 1902; Filler, Louis, *The Crusade Against Slavery,* 1960.

# Brace, Charles Loring

(June 19, 1826–August 11, 1890)
Philanthropist, Reformer

Charles Loring Brace was a reformer who pioneered in child welfare work. He helped found the Children's Aid Society, serving as its executive secretary for more than thirty years.

Charles Loring Brace was born in Litchfield, Connecticut, into a long-established New England family. In his younger years he was taught by his father, a teacher at an academy for young women. In 1842 Brace entered Yale, graduating with honors four years later. After a brief period of teaching school, he enrolled in the Yale Divinity School, where he came under the influence of Horace Bushnell, a Congregational minister with a strong liberal bent. Deciding that a conventional ministry was not for him, Brace moved to New York City in 1848. While continuing his theological studies, he began working among the city's poor and preaching to them on Sundays. In 1850 Brace departed for Britain and the Continent, studying for a time in Germany and traveling in Hungary. He was imprisoned there as a supporter of the Hungarian independence move-

ment and released a month later, after vigorous appeals from the American envoy.

Brace returned to the United States in 1852, having made a commitment to work among the poor. He again took up residence in New York City, serving as a visitor and occasional preacher to the inmates of the city prison and hospital on Blackwell's Island, and as a helper at a mission in the Five Point district, a notorious slum. He also helped organize Sunday meetings for boys in various poor districts. In the course of this work, Brace was struck by "the immense numbers of boys and girls floating and drifting about our streets with hardly any assignable home or occupation, who continually swelled the multitude of criminals, prostitutes and vagrants."

Deciding that existing institutions were inadequate to help these children, Brace was instrumental in founding the Children's Aid Society in 1853. He was appointed the society's executive secretary, a post he held for the rest of his life. Brace put a great deal of time and effort into recruiting children from the slums into the society's programs and enlisting the financial help of wealthy benefactors. Under his guidance, the society established inexpensive lodging houses for homeless children with jobs, as well as industrial schools to train them in basic skills. It also ran night schools, sanitariums, and summer camps.

Brace's pet project was the placing of poor city children with foster families in rural areas and small towns, where he believed they would grow up free from the corrupting influences of the city. Placing-out, as this practice was called, had been in existence for centuries, but as the first charitable organization in America to make widespread and systematic use of the practice, the Children's Aid Society significantly influenced child welfare policy for the next half century. During this period, it placed nearly 100,000 slum children. The emphasis in placing-out, as in the society's other programs, was to help children help themselves.

Though his work for the society consumed most of his time, Brace managed to support other causes. He was strongly against slavery, and while he never became an abolitionist, he backed the Free-Soil party (see GERRIT SMITH) and later the Republican party. During the Civil War, he wrote newspaper articles advocating emancipation as a war measure.

Brace also contributed to the literature of philanthropy with *The Dangerous Classes of New York, And Twenty Years' Work Among Them* (1872), which made his reputation as a world authority on the subject, and *Gesta Christi; or, a History of Humane Progress under Christianity* (1882), which helped spur the Social Gospel movement (see WALTER RAUSCHENBUSCH) by maintaining that Christianity had been a moving force behind progress in the past and would continue to be so. One of the few clergymen of his times to be untroubled by Charles Darwin's theory of evolution, Brace regarded it as a "law of progress" leading to humanity's spiritual advancement.

Brace's philanthropic work combined with his outgoing personality brought him a large circle of distinguished friends in the United States and abroad, including RALPH WALDO EMERSON, HENRY WARD BEECHER, Charles Darwin, and British philosopher John Stuart Mill. While on a health-seeking trip to Europe, Brace died in Campfer, Switzerland, at the age of sixty-four.

**BIBLIOGRAPHY**

Hawes, Joseph M., *Children in Urban Society*, 1971; Mennel, Robert M., *Thorns and Thistles: Juvenile Delinquents in the United States, 1825–1940*, 1972; Wheeler, Leslie, "The Orphan Trains," *American History Illustrated*, December 1983.

# Brady, Mathew B.

(ca. 1823–January 15, 1896)
Photographer

Mathew Brady's monumental photographic record of the Civil War for the first time made immediate and graphic to a civilian population the horrors of war.

Born in Warren County, New York, Brady took up drawing on the advice of an artist friend. The painter-inventor Samuel F. B. Morse taught him how to take daguerreotypes, an early photographic process used chiefly for portraits. In 1844 Brady opened his own studio in New York City, where he soon attracted a large and distinguished clientele. He won awards for his work at the annual exhibits of the American Institute from 1844 to 1848, and in 1849 became the first daguerreotypist to receive a gold medal.

In 1845 Brady had hit upon the plan of making daguerreotypes of all the famous Americans of his day in order to preserve their faces for posterity. The collection included such national giants as Henry Clay, Daniel Webster, John C. Calhoun, and later Abraham Lincoln, who sat for Brady in a remarkable series of portraits. In 1850 Brady held an exhibition of these portraits and published a book called *Gallery of Illustrious Americans.* A year later, Brady exhibited a collection of forty-eight portraits at the Crystal Palace Exhibition in London, winning a medal. While in London, Brady learned of the wet-plate photographic process and began to use it in his work. Two years later, Brady also won a medal at the New York World's Fair.

When the Civil War broke out in 1861, Brady, who was by now a world-renowned and wealthy photographer, decided to invest his entire fortune of $100,000 in making a photographic record of the war. In 1855 an Englishman named Robert Fenton had photographed soldiers and campsites during the Crimean War, but no one had ever attempted war coverage on a large scale. Together with Alexander Gardner, who managed the Washington office and served as his chief cameraman, Brady hired and equipped teams of photographers to accompany the Union armies. Brady's teams photographed nearly every phase of the war. Although the wet-plate process prohibited taking photographs of battle action, Brady's cameramen were able to document a battle's carnage a day or more after the fighting was over. While he didn't do any of the actual photography himself, Brady was on the scene supervising his crews after such battles as Bull Run in 1861, Antietam and Fredericksburg in 1862, and Petersburg in 1864. Brady also bought, traded, or borrowed the work of other photographers not on his payroll to add to his collection.

Published in woodcut copies in weekly magazines and exhibited at his galleries in New York and Washington, where thousands came to view them, Brady's photographs had a powerful and immediate impact. Now for the first time, the American public could see for themselves the awful slaughter and destruction wrought by the war. As *Humphreys Journal* noted in October 1861, "The public are indebted to Brady, of Broadway, for numerous excellent views of 'grim-visaged' war." Later, in 1862, a *New York Times* reporter commented about Brady's photographs of the corpse-strewn battlefield at Antietam: "Mr. Brady has done something to bring home to us the terrible reality and earnestness of war. If he has not brought bodies and laid them in our door-yards and along streets, he has done something very like it."

The massive project turned out to be a financial disaster, however. Obsessed with being the one and only complete photographic historian of the war, Brady not only threw all his resources into the effort but also stopped paying his bills until, his credit exhausted, he had to declare bankruptcy. He was forced to give up his New York studio and sell his negatives. In 1875, thanks to the intervention of a politician friend, the government purchased about 2,000 of Brady's 3,500 war pictures for $25,000. Unable to regain the reputation of his early career, Brady spent his remaining years in relative poverty and obscurity.

**BIBLIOGRAPHY**

Commager, Henry Steele (ed.), *Photographic History of the Civil War,* 5 vols., 1957; Horan, James D., *Mathew Brady,* 1955; Kunhardt, Dorothy Meserve, and Philip B. Kunhardt, Jr., *Mathew Brady and His World,* 1977.

# Brandeis, Louis Dembitz

(November 13, 1856–October 5, 1941)
Associate Justice of the Supreme Court, Reformer

Throughout a long public career, first as a "people's attorney" and then as an associate justice on the U.S. Supreme Court, Louis Brandeis made significant contributions in the areas of progressive reform, social legislation, and liberal interpretation of the law.

Brandeis was born in Louisville, Kentucky, into a cultured German Jewish family that had immigrated to America from Prague during the revolutions of 1848. He attended local schools and graduated from high school at age fifteen. In 1875, without having first earned an undergraduate degree, Brandeis entered Harvard Law School, where he achieved an outstanding academic record.

After practicing law briefly in St. Louis, he returned to Boston and formed a legal partnership with a Harvard classmate. Their practice was so successful that by the 1890s Brandeis had become financially independent and was able to devote himself to a variety of reform causes. In this work he served as an unpaid counsel, and he even reimbursed his law firm for the time that otherwise would have gone to fee-paying clients. Because he did not charge a fee, Brandeis became known as the "people's attorney."

Like other Progressives, Brandeis was concerned that the gigantic trusts, which by this time were a dominant force in American business, curtailed individual opportunity and threatened political democracy. Beginning his efforts on the local level, Brandeis in 1900 formed the Public Franchise League to work against monopolies in Boston transportation and other public utilities. He succeeded in getting the Boston gas industry to institute a plan developed in London in which the company both reduced utility rates and raised the dividends paid to stockholders.

On the state level, Brandeis investigated the inefficiencies and waste of industrial life insurance. As a remedy, he created Savings Bank Life Insurance, an inexpensive form of insurance sold at savings banks to low-income wage earners, which was adopted in Massachusetts (1907) and later in Connecticut and New York and which Brandeis regarded as his most important reform. He also fought a ten-year (1905–1914) battle against the New Haven Railroad's attempt to secure a monopoly on transportation in New England. Based on this experience, Brandeis wrote a series of articles for *Harper's Weekly* called "Breaking the Money Trust," which were later collected and published as *Other People's Money—And How the Bankers Use It* (1914). In the articles, Brandeis exposed the enormous power wielded by bankers in corporate America and called for reforms aimed at protecting investors and consumers. The Progressive senator from Wisconsin, Robert M. La Follette, hailed this work.

Also during these years, Brandeis took up the cause of labor. In 1908 in the case of *Muller* v. *Oregon,* he argued successfully before the U.S. Supreme Court in behalf of an Oregon law limiting the working day for women laundry workers to ten hours. Brandeis believed in a "living law" that went beyond legal precedents and addressed changing conditions. In what became known as the Brandeis brief, he marshaled a vast amount of economic and sociological evidence to prove that working long hours was harmful not only to the health of workers but to society as a whole. Two years later, Brandeis was called upon to mediate a long, drawn-out strike in the New York garment industry, which he settled with such innovations as the preferential union shop, in which union membership was favored but not required, and an arbitration mechanism within the industry.

Brandeis's involvement with the predominantly Jewish garment workers, combined with a meeting with Jacob de Haas, a leading Zionist editor, drew him to Zionism. He soon assumed a leadership role in the American movement to establish a Jewish homeland in Palestine, and though he resigned his official position when he was appointed to the Supreme Court, he continued to be active in the movement on an informal basis for the rest of his life.

Conservation was another cause that engaged Brandeis during this period. He played an important role in the congressional investigation prompted by Chief Forester Gifford Pinchot's discovery that Richard Ballinger, the secretary of the interior, had agreed to lease Alaskan mineral lands to private business interests. Although Ballinger was found not guilty, sharp questioning by Brandeis revealed that he had no concern for conservation. After Ballinger's resignation, his successor adopted conservation policies based on Brandeis's recommendations.

In 1912 Brandeis met Woodrow Wilson and was influential in shaping his New Freedom presidential program. Though denied an official position in Wilson's administration, he continued to serve as an informal adviser to the president, helping to draft such important legislation as the Clayton Antitrust Act and the Federal Trade Commission Act (both in 1914).

In 1916 Wilson nominated Brandeis to be an associate justice on the U.S. Supreme Court. Given Brandeis's reputation as a "radical" in some circles and the fact that he was the first Jew to be nominated to the Court, the nomination sparked fierce opposition. But after a four-month battle, he was confirmed by the Senate and commenced a distinguished twenty-three-year career on the bench. As a Supreme Court justice, Brandeis became well known for his dissenting opinions, in which he supported the right of state governments and Congress to take bold actions in the face of social and economic changes and gave the individual freedoms guaranteed by the Bill of Rights, notably freedom of speech, a more liberal interpretation. Although his views went against those of the majority on the Court at the time, they were later accepted as the law of the land.

Brandeis generally supported the New Deal of President Franklin Roosevelt. Yet he joined the Court in its unanimous decision holding the National Industrial Recovery Act unconstitutional on the grounds that it sought to regulate intrastate rather than interstate commerce. Other reforms, such as the truth-in-securities legislation, a program of conservation, and laws setting minimum wages and unemployment insurance and guaranteeing collective bargaining, were in keeping with the lifelong thrust of Brandeis's personal efforts.

In 1939, feeling that he could no longer meet his own high standards of performance, Brandeis resigned from the Court. He died in Washington, D.C., two years later at the age of eighty-four.

**BIBLIOGRAPHY**

Dawson, Nelson L., *Louis D. Brandeis, Felix Frankfurter, and the New Deal*, 1980; Gal, Allon, *Brandeis of Boston*, 1980; Paper, Lewis, *Brandeis*, 1983; Strum, Philippa, *Louis D. Brandeis: Justice for the People*, 1984.

# Bridges, Alfred Bryant Renton

(July 28, 1901–March 30, 1990)
Labor Leader

Harry Bridges was a leading figure in America's twentieth-century labor movement. He organized the West Coast longshoremen in the 1930s and continued to direct union strikes and strategies that bettered the lives of the rank and file of maritime workers.

Alf Bridges, as he was called in his youth, was born in Melbourne, Australia, to Irish parents whose families on both sides had been involved in the Irish independence cause. His father, Alfred Earnest Bridges, was a well-to-do realtor of Conservative politics; an uncle, Renton, a Labor party supporter, had more influence on young Alfred. The family was Roman Catholic, and young Bridges went through a parochial high school, then clerked in a shop and worked briefly in his father's business. Collecting rents from poor people in the Melbourne slums gave him a close look at the effects of poverty. The adventure novels of Jack London made him eager for the seafaring life, and he shipped out on sailing vessels around the Pacific for five years.

In 1920 Harry Bridges (he got the nickname from American shipmates) sailed into the port of San Francisco and left the ship after an argument with the captain over his mistreatment of the crew. He knocked around in western oil fields and in Mexico, where he was impressed by the government's effective laws protecting workers. He went back to sea and, coming into New Orleans during a maritime strike in 1921, jumped ship and joined the picket line. After concluding that the moderate American Federation of Labor (AFL; see WILLIAM GREEN and JOHN L. LEWIS) had let the strikers down, Bridges joined the Industrial Workers of the World (IWW; see WILLIAM D. HAYWOOD) as an organizer. That year he applied for American citizenship but let the application run out because, he once said, he was too broke to pay the fee.

In 1922 Bridges began working as a dock worker in San Francisco. Two years later, having left the IWW, he tried to organize a local of the International Longshoreman's Association (ILA), an AFL union. He succeeded in 1933. The next year, as chairman of the Joint Maritime Strike Committee, Bridges mounted a strike for recognition by Pacific shippers and got sailor crews and teamsters to join. On July 5 the police attacked the picket line, killing two men and wounding a hundred, and the governor of California declared the port under martial law. The general strike that followed was virtually industry-wide. In arbitration, the longshoremen won most demands—a thirty-hour week, better wages, and time and a half for overtime. The strike was one of several across the nation in 1934 that revitalized the American labor movement and brought great pressure on President Franklin D. Roosevelt and the Democratic party to push through Congress legislation favorable to American workers.

In 1935 Bridges united seven unions in the Maritime Federation of the Pacific, extending his influence as far as Hawaii. He reorganized the ILA locals in 1937 as the International Longshoremen's and Warehousemen's Union (ILWU) and, after winning a four-month strike, took the ILWU into the Congress of Industrial Organizations (CIO; see JOHN L. LEWIS). Bridges was then elected ILWU's first president and a member of the CIO executive board.

The charge of Communist party membership was periodically made against Bridges, possibly because he was a fierce critic of exploitative capitalism and made no secret of his approval of some Soviet achievements and his opposition to fascism. During the late 1930s he opposed shipping scrap metal to Japan and loading armaments for Nazi Germany and Fascist Italy. In 1938, when deportation hearings were called against Bridges, the secretary of labor, Frances Perkins, got them postponed on technical grounds, and he was judicially cleared of Communist affiliation. In 1940, when the House of Representatives voted to deport him, the bill died in committee. Another effort launched in 1941 went through appeal during the World War II years, when Bridges was supporting the war effort and pledging no strikes "for the duration" as long as union security was preserved. In 1945 the Supreme Court invalidated the deportation order, and Bridges became a United States citizen.

Those who knew Bridges have said that, with his independent mind, he would have been an unlikely member of any party requiring disciplined "toeing the line." And as he said late in life, as an alien and a union leader he would have been a fool to join the party. He did support many of the Communist party's political policies in the 1940s, but he did not allow his political sympathies to interfere with the practice of democracy in his union.

With the war won, Bridges led major strikes of the ILWU in 1948 (West Coast) and 1949 (Hawaii). The Communist charge persisted: in 1949 a federal grand jury indicted him for perjury in denying at his citizenship hearing that he had been a party member. He was cleared of all charges in 1955. In 1960 he signed a contract with shippers to reduce labor costs through better productivity by accepting automation (containers) in return for wage hikes and pension guarantees. In 1970 he was appointed a member of the San Francisco Port Authority and the next year, when the membership voted for a strike that closed Pacific ports for months, he reluctantly agreed for democracy's sake. After Bridges died of emphysema at age eighty-eight, the mayor of San Francisco praised his "courage and devotion to principle" and ordered city flags flown at half-staff.

**BIBLIOGRAPHY**

Dunlap, Carol, *California People*, 1982; Larrowe, Charles P., *Harry Bridges: The Rise and Fall of Radical Labor in the U.S.*, 1972; Nelson, Bruce, *Workers on the Waterfront: Seamen, Longshoremen, and Unionism in the 1930s*, 1988.

# Brown, Helen Gurley

(February 18, 1922–    )
Editor, Writer

Through her books and her editorship of *Cosmopolitan*, Helen Gurley Brown has fashioned an influential image of a "new woman"—glamorous, sexually active, single, and economically ambitious. This identity, Brown has insisted, offers young women a more satisfying life than "dour" feminism or homemaking.

Born in Green Forest, a small town in the Ozark Mountains of Arkansas, Helen Gurley was the daughter of two schoolteachers. As a child of the Great Depression she had a fear of economic insecurity: she gave dancing lessons to other children to earn pocket money. When she was ten her father died in an elevator accident, and her mother moved with Helen and her sister Mary to Los Angeles. Helen Gurley was valedictorian of her high school class. After business school she held a series of secretarial jobs, while helping to support her mother and her sister (who had had polio). She has said she was motivated to excel by her handicaps: "being flat-chested, pale, acne-skinned, terrified." In 1948 she became executive secretary to Don Belding, chairman of an advertising agency, Foote, Cone & Belding, who recognized her literary talent and promoted her to a copywriting job. Gurley went on to become one of the highest-paid advertising copywriters in the country and one of the few listed in *Who's Who in American Women.*

In 1959 Helen Gurley married David Brown, a movie producer with Twentieth Century-Fox. He too was impressed by her writing and urged her to do a book for and about the single woman, entitled (his suggestion) *Sex and the Single Girl.* She wrote it on weekends over a year. Published in 1962, *Sex and the Single Girl* was on best-seller lists for several years. It has been published in twenty-eight countries and translated into sixteen languages. Warner Brothers paid $200,000 to use the title for a movie starring Natalie Wood and Tony Curtis. Helen Gurley Brown described her book as "not a study on how to get married but on how to stay single—in superlative style. . . . I think I've shared a common experience with millions of unmarried girls and have been able to express it so that people will say, 'Yes, this is how it really is.'"

In 1965 the magazine *Cosmopolitan,* for years catering to the housewife, was losing circulation and advertising income. Its publishers, the Hearst Corporation, decided to focus *Cosmopolitan* on the problems and interests of the younger working woman and, recognizing Helen Gurley Brown's expertise, appointed her editor in chief. Under her guidance the magazine's sales and advertising rose spectacularly, from under 800,000 to nearly 3 million. It now

*Cosmopolitan*

has twenty-three foreign editions. Brown slants the magazine to working women between ages eighteen and thirty-four and includes articles on health, beauty, careers, and relationships. The feminist writer BETTY FRIEDAN criticized the new *Cosmopolitan* as debasing to women, fostering "an immature teenage-level sexual fantasy." Brown's supporters point out that she has provided an honest guide to self-improvement for unmarried women in an era of sexual permissiveness. Brown describes herself as "a health nut, a feminist, an irredeemable but contented workaholic and passionately interested in the relationship between men and women."

The Hearst Corporation in 1986 established the Helen Gurley Brown Research Professorship at the Medill School of Journalism at Northwestern University. Brown has been inducted into the Publisher's Hall of Fame, which has honored such leaders as HENRY R. LUCE, the founder of *Time,* and De Witt Wallace, the founder of *Readers Digest.*

**BIBLIOGRAPHY**

Brown, Helen Gurley, *Sex and the Single Girl,* 1962, *Sex and the Office,* 1964, and *Helen Gurley Brown's Single Girl's Cookbook,* 1969.

# Brown, John

(May 9, 1800–December 2, 1859)
Abolitionist

Boston Athenaeum

A militant abolitionist, John Brown believed that slavery must be overthrown by force. In 1859 he led a raid against the town of Harpers Ferry, Virginia, which perhaps more than any other single event polarized the North and South and led directly to the outbreak of the Civil War.

John Brown was born in Torrington, Connecticut, into a deeply religious, God-fearing family with Puritan ancestry. His father was an early abolitionist and an agent on the Underground Railroad (see HARRIET TUBMAN), who plied different trades and moved frequently. John Brown spent most of his boyhood in Hudson, Ohio. He had little formal schooling and worked as a tanner for his father. In 1820 he married Dianthe Lusk, who bore him seven children. She suffered from mental illness, as had Brown's mother and several maternal relatives—facts which later raised questions about Brown's sanity and that of his sons. After his first wife's death, Brown married sixteen-year-old Mary Ann Day, by whom he had thirteen children.

In 1825 Brown moved his family to Richmond, Pennsylvania. He opened a tannery there, and his barn became a station on the Underground Railroad. Ten years later, after the failure of his tannery, he returned to Ohio, engaging in a number of businesses including sheep raising and wool dealing that plunged him into debt and finally bankruptcy. In 1846 he moved to Springfield, Massachusetts, and opened a wool-grading business that like his earlier ventures ended disastrously.

Throughout these years, Brown's hatred of slavery intensified. While living in Ohio, he had protested the segregation of blacks in the Congregational church he attended, and in 1848 he published an essay, "Sambo's Mistakes," criticizing African Americans for "tamely submitting" to oppression by whites instead of "nobly resisting." In 1849 Brown moved to North Elba, New York, in the Adirondack Mountains, where the wealthy abolitionist GERRIT SMITH had set aside 200 acres for an African American settlement. Offering to teach the settlers farming, Brown lived in complete equality among them. By 1851, however, he was back in Ohio, trying to run a farm and plagued by financial difficulties. Nevertheless, that same year, in Springfield, Massachusetts, Brown managed to organize a group of free blacks to assist fugitive slaves.

In 1855 Brown went to Kansas to help establish it as a free state, bringing with him a wagon loaded with weapons and ammunition for the free-soil fight. Settling near Osawatomie, he soon became known as Osawatomie Brown. In May 1856 clashes between the Free-Soilers and the "Border Ruffians," as the proslavery forces were called, reached a climax when a proslavery band burned and sacked the antislavery stronghold of Lawrence. On the night of May 24, Brown, vowing revenge, led a group that included four of his sons and two associates to Pottawatomie Creek, where they killed five proslavery men.

In the months that followed, "Captain" John Brown, as he was now known, led a series of cattle rustling raids against proslavery settlers. In retaliation, a force of 400 Border Ruffians attacked Osawatomie and burned it to the ground. Brown was wounded and his son Frederick was killed in the fighting. That fall (1856) Brown and most of his family moved to the East. Visiting Boston in January 1857, Brown met such leading abolitionists as THOMAS WENTWORTH HIGGINSON and SAMUEL GRIDLEY HOWE. They agreed to help him get rifles and money to continue the war in Kansas.

Returning to Kansas late in 1857, Brown found both sides inclined to settle their differences peacefully. He then began recruiting young men for an invasion of the South aimed at freeing the slaves and inciting a revolt. Brown was convinced that God had chosen him to lead this "holy" war against slavery. When they learned of his plans, Howe, Higginson, Gerrit Smith, and three other men formed the "Secret Six" to help Brown in his new venture with guns and money. In May 1858 Brown called a meeting of his black and white supporters at Chatham in Ontario, Canada. He described his plan to establish a free state in the Appalachian Mountains, from which he could launch raids against slaveowners and free their slaves. Though scantily attended, the meeting adopted a provisional constitution for Brown's proposed state and chose him as commander in chief.

The next month, Brown was back in Kansas under the name of Shubel Morgan. Late in 1858, he launched a raid into Missouri, in which a planter was killed and eleven slaves were freed. Thanks to extensive help from antislavery sympathizers, Brown was able to convey the slaves safely to Canada.

In the summer of 1859, Brown decided on a plan to seize the federal arsenal at Harpers Ferry, Virginia. Renting a farmhouse in nearby Maryland, he was joined by sixteen whites, including three of his sons, and five black men. On October 16 Brown and his band seized the town and armory, freeing a few slaves and taking several white hostages. When news of the raid got out, local militia and a company of U.S. Marines under the command of Robert E. Lee arrived. Refusing to flee into the mountains, Brown and his men holed up in the engine-house of the armory, which they defended until it was overpowered. Two of Brown's sons died in the fighting, and Brown himself was wounded. In all, ten of Brown's original band were killed.

Taken to prison at Charlestown, Virginia, Brown was put on trial for treason. His dignified bearing during his trial won him much sympathy in the North. But after efforts to prove him insane failed, he was convicted and then hanged on December 2, 1859. To northerners who hated slavery he became a martyr. Southerners, on the other hand, saw Brown as the monstrous leader of a violent northern conspiracy to overthrow the South. About a year and a half later, the Civil War began. As they marched to battle, Union troops sang: "John Brown's body lies a-mouldering in the grave. But his soul is marching on."

**BIBLIOGRAPHY**

Boyer, Richard O., *The Legend of John Brown: A Biography and History,* 1973; Lorenz, Graham, *John Brown: A Cry for Freedom,* 1980; Oates, Stephen B., *To Purge This Land with Blood,* 1970; Villard, Oswald Garrison, *John Brown, 1800–1859: A Biography Fifty Years After,* 1910.

# Brownmiller, Susan

(February 15, 1935–   )
Author, Feminist

Susan Brownmiller published the most comprehensive study of rape ever undertaken, which has brought this grave social problem to the closer attention of the feminist movement, the police, social workers, and the public at large.

Born in the Flatbush section of Brooklyn, New York, Susan Brownmiller discovered that her birthday was the 115th anniversary of the birth of the woman-suffrage leader SUSAN B. ANTHONY—a coincidence (including their given names) that proved to be important to her even in childhood. Her father was a clothing salesman of moderate means; her mother was a secretary who was independent-minded, a trait she passed on to her daughter. Brownmiller went to Cornell University in 1952, intending to study law. At a time when college students were being called the Silent Generation because of their indifference to social problems, Brownmiller was drawn to radicalism and joined the Students for Peace and the Cornell chapter of the National Association for the Advancement of Colored People (NAACP; see JOEL E. SPINGARN).

After three years, Brownmiller left Cornell to study acting in New York City. She got fewer parts than rejections and began to look for a radical cause that she could identify with. She studied briefly at the Jefferson School of Social Science with the American Marxist historian Herbert Aptheker, who guided her toward new philosophical insights that later influenced how she thought about the abuse of women. During the mid-1960s Brownmiller spent two summers as a civil rights worker in Mississippi. Having set her sights on journalism, she reported and wrote television news, joined the staff of the *Village Voice*, and then as a freelance writer made a name with interview articles in the *New York Times Magazine* on public figures such as Senator Eugene McCarthy and Congresswoman Shirley Chisholm.

In the late 1960s, Brownmiller discovered her radical cause in the women's liberation movement. She was a founder of the New York Radical Feminists (NYRF) in 1968, and in March 1970 she published a forceful article on the movement, "Sisterhood Is Powerful," in the *New York Times Magazine*. The NYRF picketed the Miss America Pageant in Atlantic City, New Jersey, and, because they thought it to be "one of the most demeaning magazines toward women," staged a sit-in at the offices of the *Ladies Home Journal.* In 1971 Brownmiller organized a conference on rape that was a milestone in militant feminism and made her aware that the subject demanded careful research.

Rape, statistics showed, had become the fastest-growing violent crime in the country. Brownmiller's studies, involving four years of research and interviews, led to her comprehensive and influential book *Against Our Will: Men, Women and Rape* (1975), which became a best-seller and is still in print. Examining rape as a weapon to subjugate women in the male-female power relationship, Brownmiller's book cast a spotlight on this serious social problem. She wrote that rape should be dealt with through reform of police procedures and the law and through building up women's physical defenses against sexual attack. She herself trained in karate and counseled on antirape techniques. She has led in denouncing pornographic magazines and films that brutalize and dehumanize women.

Brownmiller has continued her career as a writer, lecturer, and teacher campaigning against the abuse of women. In 1989 she published a critically praised novel, *Waverly Place,* based on the Steinberg-Nussbaum case, in which a man regularly beat and mistreated his wife and adopted children.

**BIBLIOGRAPHY**
Brownmiller, Susan, *Femininity,* 1984.

# Bruner, Joseph

(September 20, 1872–January 13, 1957)
Indian Rights Leader

Joseph Bruner, though successful as a businessman in the white society of Oklahoma, devoted himself to American Indian organizations—serving Indians not only in his state, but throughout the United States.

Bruner was born on his parents' allotment in what is now the city of Tulsa, Oklahoma. Ark-Tah-Yah-Cho-Chee, his Indian name, means "Lightning Bolt of the Deer Clan." His parents, John Bruner and Lucy Fife, were of the Creek Nation, one of the Five Civilized Tribes from the southeastern states, which in the 1820s were allotted lands in what was called Indian Territory. The Creeks who followed the "Trail of Tears" and settled in the Tulsa area were from the vicinity of Tulsey (now Tallassee), Alabama, which is how Tulsa got its name. Joseph Bruner was said to have been the first male child born in Tulsa, then called Lockerbroker.

Bruner knew no English until he went to the Creek National School and briefly to Bacone College, an Indian institution at Muskogee founded by Baptists. For a spell he was a cowboy, and in 1893 he married Marguerite Elma Dart, of Shawnee ancestry. Settling in the town of Sapulpa, near Tulsa, Bruner acquired a reputation as an interpreter of both Creek and Euchee. He had a real estate and insurance business and, having become knowledgeable about the laws affecting Indian titles and inheritances, often helped fellow Indians with oil deals. He was called the "Creek Land Man." In time Bruner went into farming and acquired oil property.

The Creek Nation's headquarters were and are at the Council House, in Okmulgee, south of Sapulpa. The legislature is bicameral, with a house of kings and a house of warriors, in which Bruner served beginning in his teens. In 1905 he played a leading part at the Sequoyah Convention at Muskogee, at which several hundred representatives of the Five Tribes met to write a constitution for the state of Sequoyah which they—vainly—hoped would be established in the Indian Territory.

In the 1930s Bruner took up the cause of a Creek claim, filed in 1904, seeking more than a million dollars to compensate for losses when the federal government, concerned about the Creeks' Confederate bias during the Civil War, made them move from Indian Territory to Kansas. Bruner went to Washington to rally support. (In 1947 the government offered half the claimed amount, which the Creek Council refused.)

In 1924 Bruner led in forming the Society of American Indians. When John Collier became commissioner of the Bureau of Indian Affairs in April 1933, Bruner at first favored his appointment, having been impressed by his sympathy for Indian causes. The passage the next year of the Indian Reorganization Act, however, brought a negative reaction from many Indians, who believed that the act, which restored to the tribes the rights to self-government and cultural autonomy that the federal government had previously stripped away, worked to their disadvantage. At a meeting at Muskogee, Collier faced opposition from representatives of the Five Civilized Tribes, under Bruner's leadership. Bruner and his followers favored assimilation and feared that the act would bring segregation, rule out the work of missionaries, tie up oil and mineral rights, and imperil their individual claims to property. Bruner favored continuing the work of CARLOS MONTEZUMA, who, he said, preferred for Indians to adopt white civilization.

In 1935 Bruner formed a stronger organization, the American Indian Federation (AIF), representing tribes all over the United States. As president and the power behind the AIF, Bruner set up as a lobbyist in Washington. Testifying before the House Indian Affairs Committee, he charged that Collier's ideas tended toward communism and atheism and that he should be removed. Collier served as commissioner until 1945, working amicably and constructively with Indian organizations.

Bruner, however, continued his attacks on Collier and the Bureau of Indian Affairs. In 1936, at a convention of the AIF in Salt Lake City, literature offered to the delegates included Nazi pamphlets, and subsequently there was suspicion of AIF links with the America First Committee and the German-American Bund.

Bruner remained AIF president until late in life. When he died at age eighty-four he was praised in Oklahoma newspapers as a champion of traditional tribal customs, an advocate of education for Indians, and an opponent of discrimination of any kind.

**BIBLIOGRAPHY**

Philp, K. R., *John Collier's Crusade for Indian Reform*, 1977.

# Bryant, William Cullen

(November 3, 1794–June 12, 1878)
Abolitionist, Editor, Poet

Famous as a nature poet (he was sometimes called the American Wordsworth), William Cullen Bryant was for many years editor of the New York *Evening Post*. His editorials helped to form an American conscience against slavery and to build support of the Union cause in the Civil War.

Born in the village of Cummington, in western Massachusetts, Bryant was the son of Peter Bryant, a physician of intellectual interests, and Sarah Snell, both of whose families dated back to the settlement of New England. In his childhood Bryant was delicate and nervous, but his parents raised him to be a robust, active boy who liked to roam the countryside. His mother taught him the alphabet when he was sixteen months old, and he benefited from his father's excellent library. Having mastered Latin and Greek with private teachers, he entered Williams College at the age of fifteen. After a year he left to study on his own, hoping to attend Yale University. His father's means could not afford Yale, however, and he went to nearby Worthington to read law for three unhappy years.

As a boy Bryant had hoped for the gift of poetry, and early on he produced some worthy efforts. At seventeen, disappointed that he could not go to Yale, he wrote what proved to be his most famous poem, "Thanatopsis," which he hid in his desk. Five years later his father found the manuscript of that and the lyric "To a Waterfowl" and, unknown to the poet, sent them to Richard Henry Dana, Sr., editor of the *North American Review*, where they appeared in 1817. Bryant's literary reputation was made. Meanwhile he had discovered William Wordsworth's poetry, which influenced his own work.

Admitted to the bar in 1815, Bryant set up a practice in Great Barrington, where he married Frances Fairchild in 1821. Though he did well as a lawyer he was discontented, and in 1825 he went to New York as coeditor of the *New York Review and Athenaeum Magazine*. Continuing to write and publish poetry, Bryant was by now recognized as the country's leading poet. His earnings nevertheless were inadequate for himself and his family, and he was on the point of resuming a law practice when, in 1826, he was hired as assistant editor of the New York *Evening Post*, which became his life. By 1833 he was the paper's editor, owned a one-third share, and no longer had financial worries.

In his eloquent editorials, Bryant backed free trade, Andrew Jackson for the presidency, and the right of working men to form unions. He made his paper famous for its literary style, though he himself wrote little poetry during these years. Bryant took his family to Europe for an extended visit in 1834 and returned hurriedly to New York in 1836 when he got word that the paper was in trouble. He devoted several years to putting the *Evening Post* back on its feet, editorially and financially, and became an important spokesman for the views of the Democratic party.

Early on, Bryant spoke out against slavery and was opposed to all compromise over the issue. By 1856 he had broken with the Democratic party and turned to the Radical Republicans, becoming a supporter of JOHN BROWN and Abraham Lincoln. When the South seceded, Bryant firmly rejected concession and urged active prosecution of the Civil War and the abolition of slavery. Only after the war did Bryant turn from his radical position to back President Andrew Johnson's moderate reconstruction policy. He deplored the impeachment proceedings against Johnson in 1868.

With the coming of Ulysses S. Grant's administration the following year, Bryant began to withdraw from the management of the *Evening Post*. He was still grief-stricken over the death of his wife in 1865, and as consolation began a translation of all of Homer, which he finished in 1871. Besides keeping his hand in at the *Evening Post*, Bryant continued to speak and work for social causes and traveled again to Europe. He died following an accidental fall in 1878.

While the *Evening Post* never had the importance or wide appeal of the *New York Tribune* of the time, its editorial pages had a dedication, moral commitment, and refinement far ahead of other papers of the day. Bryant was more scholarly and knowledgeable than most editors, and his writing for the paper was distinguished, setting standards that sometimes cost him readers but maintained his liberal influence on other opinion makers. His journalism, like his poetry, had a purity, accuracy, and meditative quality typical of the New England tradition that had formed him.

**BIBLIOGRAPHY**

McDowell, T. (ed.), *William Cullen Bryant: Representative Selections*, 1935; Peckham, H. H., *Gotham Yankee: A Biography of William Cullen Bryant*, 1950.

# Buckley, William Frank, Jr.

(November 24, 1925–   )
Author, Editor, Political Activist

William F. Buckley, Jr., has been called the nation's leading conservative and the founder of modern American conservatism. The journal he established, the *National Review*, has set a moral and literary standard of excellence for the American right.

Bill Buckley was born in New York City, the sixth of ten children of a wealthy Texas oilman whose properties were chiefly in Latin America. His mother was Aloise Steiner, from New Orleans. Both families had a tradition of devout Catholicism and conservatism. Young Buckley was educated at Catholic private schools abroad and at the exclusive Millbrook School, in New York, near the family estate in Sharon, Connecticut. He learned Spanish in his youth, thanks to a Mexican nursemaid and study at the University of Mexico. From 1944 to 1946 he went through officer training in the U.S. Army, became a second lieutenant, and was briefly assigned to duty in the United States.

Having entered Yale University in 1946, Buckley majored in economics, history, and political science and made a mark on the debating team and as chairman (that is, editor) of the Yale *Daily News*. He got his B.A. with honors in 1950, married Pat Taylor from Vancouver, British Columbia, Canada, and returned to Yale to teach Spanish. During that year Buckley completed his first book, *God and Man at Yale: The Superstitions of Academic Freedom* (1951), which presented the conservative and pro-Christian point of view that characterized Buckley's creed. He saw Yale as a center of antireligious and socialist teachings and urged the dismissal of professors who advocated such attitudes. His conviction that the Catholic religion and opposition to communism had to be linked was, according to one observer, an inheritance from his father's view of the pre-1920 Mexican Revolution.

After a year as a CIA undercover agent in Mexico City, Buckley joined the staff of a monthly called *American Mercury*. When the magazine took on an anti-Semitic tone, Buckley resigned and free-lanced as a writer, producing with his brother-in-law L. Brent Bozell a book entitled *McCarthy and His Enemies*, which supported Senator Joseph R. McCarthy's allegations that the U.S. government had been infiltrated by communist agents.

In fall 1955 Buckley founded the *National Review*, a biweekly journal of political and literary opinion, which became the most influential voice of the conservative segment of the public. Buckley, as editor in chief, brought in right-wing writers such as Russell Kirk, James Burnham, MAX EASTMAN, and Whittaker Chambers, as well as promising young writers not necessarily identified with conservatism, such as Joan Didion, GARRY WILLS, and Renata Adler. The *Review*, aiming at respectability, steered away from whatever might be considered fascist or anti-Semitic. In 1960 Buckley launched an attack in its pages on the fanatically anticommunist John Birch Society, on the ground that it ill-served the national interest. That year he helped found Young Americans for Freedom (YAF), to organize and train young conservatives.

Buckley ran for mayor of New York City in 1965 on the ticket of the Conservative party, which had been founded a few years earlier. The party lacked the strength to bring Buckley more than 15 percent of the vote, though in 1970 Bill Buckley's older brother James was elected to the U.S. Senate as the Conservative candidate.

After the defeat in the mayoralty election, Buckley began a weekly television interview program, *Firing Line*, on which a vast range of personalities have been guests. Buckley's wit, sharp tongue, and urbanity made him a popular national figure. He has lectured at the New School for Social Research and served on the advisory board of the United States Information Agency and the U.S. delegation to the United Nations General Assembly.

Buckley has strongly supported Republican platforms and administrations, though not with utter consistency. He objected to President Richard M. Nixon's recognition of China and softening toward the Soviet Union, and after the Watergate scandal he advocated Nixon's resignation. He also found President Gerald R. Ford too soft toward the Soviets. President Jimmy Carter's treaty recognizing Panama's eventual sovereignty over the Canal Zone met with Buckley's approval. President Ronald Reagan's administration had his backing, though in the Iran/Contra episode he was unable to defend Oliver North and John Poindexter, maintaining that their insubordination had brought on the scandal. In the 1980s some observers noted a mellowing, a relaxing of some of Buckley's conservative strictures.

In the 1970s Buckley had begun turning out a series of spy novels, the hero of which is an upper-echelon man not unlike himself, dedicated to fighting communism. He has also written books about his exploits as an ocean-going sailboat captain.

**BIBLIOGRAPHY**

Buckley, William F., Jr., *Gratitude: Reflections on What We Owe to Our Country*, 1990; Judis, John B., *William F. Buckley, Jr.: Patron Saint of the Conservatives*, 1988; Winchell, Mark R., *William F. Buckley, Jr.*, 1984.

# Bunche, Ralph Johnson

(August 7, 1904–December 9, 1971)
Government/United Nations Official

As a high official of the United Nations for twenty-five years, Ralph Bunche led peacekeeping efforts in troubled areas of the world. He was awarded the Nobel Prize for Peace in 1950, the first person of African descent to win that honor.

Ralph Bunche, whose ancestry included American Indians and a grandfather who was a slave, was born in Detroit, Michigan, the son of Fred Bunche, a barber, and Olive Agnes Johnson, a musician. Both parents died when he was twelve, and he was brought up in Los Angeles by his maternal grandmother, Lucy Johnson, whom he described as the strongest woman he ever knew. He was valedictorian of his high school class and a sports champion. Bunche won an athletic scholarship to the University of California at Los Angeles and supplemented it with income from menial jobs. He graduated *summa cum laude* in 1927, having been a star three-sports athlete and a debater during his college career.

United Nations

After receiving an M.A. in political science at Harvard University, Bunche began teaching at Howard University in Washington and by 1937 was a full professor. He took a leave of absence for graduate study at Harvard and earned a Ph.D. in 1934 for a dissertation on French colonial administration in West Africa, where he did fieldwork. Postdoctoral studies in anthropology followed at Northwestern University, the London School of Economics, and the University of Cape Town, South Africa. In 1936 Bunche was codirector of the Institute of Race Relations at Swarthmore College, and from 1938 to 1940 he collaborated on field studies with the Swedish sociologist Gunnar Myrdal for the latter's path-breaking study of race relations, *An American Dilemma* (1944).

Bunche left Howard University in 1941 to join the War Department as an analyst for Africa and the Far East for the Office of the Coordinator of Information, later the Office of

Strategic Services. For the joint chiefs of staff he wrote reports of strategic military importance on colonial areas. In 1944 he moved to the Department of State as a specialist in the Division of Territorial Studies, where he was in a position to correct ingrained misconceptions about the peoples of the Third World. He was the first African American to hold the rank of chief in the Department of State.

By 1944 Bunche was in the mainstream of planning for what would become the United Nations (UN). He was a member of the U.S. delegation at both the Dumbarton Oaks Conference, held in Washington in 1944 to plan the organization, and the San Francisco Conference (held in 1945), where the UN and its charter came into being. Bunche was mainly responsible for that document's sections on trusteeship and, in 1946, Trygve Lie, the first secretary-general of the UN, asked for Bunche's services. Bunche became the director of the Department of Trusteeship and Information From Non-Self-Governing Territories.

When Israel declared its statehood in May 1948, after the UN had approved a plan to partition the British mandate of Palestine into an Arab state and a Jewish state, the surrounding Arab nations invaded. Bunche, who had been appointed secretary of the UN Palestine Commission, was in the midst of unfolding events. At his request, the UN Security Council ordered an armed force to oversee the partition, under the command of Count Folke Bernadotte, of Sweden. When Bernadotte was assassinated, Bunche succeeded him as acting mediator; in 1949, using objectivity, energy, patience, and wisdom, Bunche brought about a cease-fire and armistice. He received the 1950 Nobel Prize for Peace. As a Nobel spokesman said, "The outcome was a victory for the ideas of the United Nations, but . . . it was one individual's efforts that made victory possible."

During the rest of his career, Bunche worked to make the UN an effective peacekeeping body. In 1955 he became under secretary for special political affairs, and from 1967 until his retirement in 1971 he was an under secretary–general. In 1956, during a crisis over the Suez Canal arising after a conflict between Israel and Egypt, Bunche directed a neutral peacekeeping force and enabled the canal to reopen. In 1960 he was sent to the newly independent nation of Congo (now Zaire), preventing the government's collapse. He established a peacekeeping force in Cyprus in 1964, and the next year was in charge of monitoring a cease-fire between India and Pakistan.

Bunche joined MARTIN LUTHER KING, JR., on civil rights marches in Selma and Montgomery, Alabama, and agreed with King that the tremendous funds expended on the Vietnam War should instead be spent to fight racism and poverty. In his last years he was an adviser to the UN secretary-general, U Thant. He died at the age of sixty-seven, of diabetes and heart disease, leaving his wife, whom he had met and married in college, and three children.

**BIBLIOGRAPHY**

Bunche, Ralph, *The Political Status of the Negro in the Age of FDR*, 1973; Cornell, Jean G., *Ralph Bunche: Champion of Peace*, 1976; Johnson, A. D., *The Value of Responsibility: The Story of Ralph Bunche*, 1978.

# Burbank, Luther

(March 7, 1849–April 11, 1926)
Horticulturist

Horticulturist Luther Burbank used Darwinian principles to produce over 800 new varieties of plants. While Burbank's work won him praise from the scientific community, it also brought him blame from religious fundamentalists who objected to his tampering with nature.

Born in Lancaster, Massachusetts, Burbank grew up on a farm. This background influenced his work, as did his reading of Charles Darwin's *Variation of Animals and Plants Under Domestication*, which he discovered at the local library. In 1868 when he was twenty-one, Burbank purchased a 17-acre farm at Lunenberg, Massachusetts, where he began his first experiments with plant variation. He used the profits from one of his successful creations, the Burbank, or Idaho, potato, to move to California in 1875, setting up a nursery garden and greenhouse on a 4-acre plot in Santa Rosa.

Over the next fifty years, Burbank conducted experiments with thousands of different kinds of plants. Recognizing the importance of environment as well as heredity to plant production, he sought to provide the best soil and other conditions conducive to growth. But his greatest success came through modifications of the heredity of different plants.

Though ignorant of genetic principles, since Gregor Mendel's work in this area had yet to be rediscovered, Burbank was able to develop better varieties of plants by applying the Darwinian principles of selection and preservation. Through the technique of hybridization, or the cross-pollinating of different plant varieties, he produced seed from which he grew new plants. He then ruthlessly selected for preservation those plants with desirable variations and discarded all the rest. The results of Burbank's experiments included stoneless prunes, thornless blackberries, new varieties of flowers like the giant Shasta daisy, improved vegetables, and a type of spineless cactus suitable for feeding cattle in arid regions.

Besides winning gold medals for a number of his "new creations," Burbank received from the Carnegie Institution in 1905 a $10,000-a-year grant with the understanding that the institution could record his scientific data. Neither party was apparently satisfied with the arrangement, and the grant was withdrawn after five years. Throughout, Burbank's aim was to produce better plant varieties, not to prove scientific theories or make discoveries.

Extending his ideas about plants to people, Burbank wrote *Training of the Human Plant* (1907), a pamphlet focusing on the role of environment in human development and calling for an educational program designed to foster productive, socially aware adults. Burbank also described his work with plants in the twelve-volume series *Luther Burbank: His Methods and Discoveries and Their Practical Application*, completed in 1915; and in the eight-volume *How Plants Are Trained to Work for Man*.

During his lifetime, Burbank's reputation suffered somewhat from exaggerated accounts of his creations that led some to suspect him of fakery. He also came under attack from fundamentalist religious leaders when he expressed opinions that went against their beliefs. But through his practical application of evolutionary principles, Burbank created new varieties of plants that were economically important and spurred the development of scientific plant breeding.

**BIBLIOGRAPHY**

Beeson, Emma Burbank, *The Early Life and Letters of Luther Burbank*, 1927; Burbank, Luther, *Partner of Nature*, 1939.

# Burns, Arthur Frank

(April 27, 1904–June 26, 1987)
Economist, Presidential Adviser

A prominent economist in public service for more than thirty years, Arthur F. Burns brought to the federal government both a staunch fiscal conservatism and a commitment to a New Deal role for government in the promotion of economic prosperity.

Arthur F. Burns was born in Stanislau, Austria-Hungary, in the region of Galicia, now part of the Ukraine. He was the son of Nathan Burnseig and Sarah Juran. When he was ten the family immigrated to the United States and settled in Bayonne, New Jersey. A teacher suggested that the boy shorten his name. He was a good student and in high school was a talented debater. He learned his father's trade, house painting, but was drawn toward an intellectual career and entered Columbia College in New York City on a scholarship in 1921. Burns worked his way through college with a variety of jobs and occasionally sold articles on business to the *Herald Tribune*. He chose economics as his major after considering law, architecture, and dramatic criticism, and earned both A.B. and M.A. degrees in 1925, with Phi Beta Kappa honors. While studying for his Ph.D. at Columbia, Burns became a protégé of Wesley Clair Mitchell, a founder of the National Bureau of Economic Research and a critic of orthodox economics. He worked with Mitchell at the Bureau, which published his dissertation, *Production Trends in the United States since 1870,* in 1934, the year he received his Ph.D. Meanwhile Burns had become an instructor of economics at Rutgers University, in New Jersey, and by 1943 had advanced to full professor. Columbia University appointed him a professor in 1945; he was given the John Bates Clark chair in 1959.

Burns's career was threefold: he was an academic, an economics research scholar, and a public servant. At the National Bureau of Economic Research (1948–1953), he served as director of research and as president and produced important studies. In 1953 President Dwight Eisenhower, who had known Burns at Columbia, appointed him his chief economic adviser to the alarm of some Republicans who had expected him, as a Democrat (who voted for Eisenhower), to be a New Deal economist. To spur recovery he recommended tax cuts and easier credit policies, which created a notable boom in 1955. Having left the government during Eisenhower's second term, he still advised the president unofficially, and blamed the rocky economy of the late 1950s on excessive taxes and irregular fiscal policies. In 1961 Burns became the only conservative member of President John F. Kennedy's Advisory Committee on Labor-Management Policy. During Lyndon B. Johnson's presidency he advocated reduced government spending because he dreaded inflation, which hurt "the poor, the elderly, the less educated—those in our society most in need of shelter from economic adversity." He proposed a curb on costly domestic expenditures during the Vietnam War, which he opposed.

In 1969 President Richard Nixon, long a friend, appointed Burns to a new cabinet-grade post, that of counsellor to the president on a broad range of legislative and executive matters. Later in the year, Nixon nominated him as chairman of the seven-member Board of Governors of the Federal Reserve System. The appointment was approved by Democrats and Republicans alike.

Burns became a far more visible and influential chairman than his predecessors had been. Inflation became an acute national problem during Burns's chairmanship, especially after the Arab oil-producing countries began, in 1973, to raise significantly the price of their precious commodity. Inflation was a problem that Burns had long worried about, and the monetary weapons that the Federal Reserve placed at his disposal made him a key player in government efforts to control spiraling prices.

During President Jimmy Carter's administration, Burns joined the conservative American Enterprise Institute, but he later returned to the capital as an adviser to President Ronald Reagan, who appointed him ambassador to West Germany from 1981 to 1985.

Arthur Burns had married Helen Bernstein in 1930; they had two sons, a lawyer and an economist. Burns died at the age of eighty-three after undergoing triple-bypass heart surgery.

## BIBLIOGRAPHY

Burns, Arthur F., *The Frontiers of Economic Knowledge*, 1954, *Prosperity without Inflation*, 1957, and *The Management of Prosperity*, 1966; Tuch, Hans N., *Arthur Burns and the Successor Generation*, 1988.

# Butler, Nicholas Murray

(April 2, 1862–December 7, 1947)
Educator, Peace Activist

In his long career, Nicholas "Miraculous" Butler led in developing Columbia College into one of the world's principal universities, of which he was president for half of his lifetime. He also was prominent on the American political scene and in the movement for international peace and disarmament.

Nicholas Murray Butler, a New Jersey native, was born in Elizabeth, the eldest of five children, and grew up in Paterson, where his father had a textile business. Butler graduated from high school at the age of thirteen and studied privately until he was sixteen, when he entered Columbia College, in New York City,

Library of Congress

intending to go into law. The college's president, Frederick A. P. Barnard, persuaded Butler to go instead into education, a neglected field. He worked his way through Columbia and upon graduating in 1882 with honors won a three-year fellowship that enabled him to do graduate work for two years (he received his Ph.D. in 1884) and to spend a year at the universities of Paris and Berlin.

Butler returned to Columbia in 1885 as an assistant in philosophy and five years later became a professor and dean of the newly created faculty of philosophy. He was a force in making Columbia a university emphasizing graduate study, in moving the institution from mid-town New York to Morningside Heights, and in introducing summer and extension courses. He led in organizing a program of training courses for public-school teachers, which became affiliated with Columbia in 1893 as the Teachers College. In 1902 Butler became president of Columbia, a post he held for more than forty years. He founded the schools of journalism and of medicine, and by 1911 Columbia was the world's largest university. He recruited distinguished faculty members—such as JOHN DEWEY and CHARLES BEARD—but often ruled his faculty like an autocrat, resulting in dismissals and resignations, particularly during World War I, when he fired professors who opposed the draft.

A lifelong Republican, Butler was a frequent adviser to presidents, and in 1912 he replaced the late James S. Sherman as vice presidential candidate on the Republican ticket, which lost to the Democratic ticket headed by Woodrow Wilson. In 1920 and again in 1928 he unsuccessfully sought his party's presidential nomination. Butler as a conservative favored limited government controlled by an elite. He opposed the income tax, the child labor amendment, Prohibition, taxing the wealthy, and militarism.

Butler's career in the international peace movement was distinguished if ambivalent. In 1910 he encouraged Andrew Carnegie to establish the Carnegie Endowment for International Peace, with a $10 million fund, and he took a leading part in its work. He published *The Basis of Durable Peace* in 1917, proposing a postwar international organization based on international law. Yet he supported American involvement in World War I and had reservations about the League of Nations as a peacekeeping body. He helped bring about the Kellogg-Briand Pact in 1927. Aristide Briand, the French foreign minister, proposed to Frank Kellogg, the American secretary of state, a bilateral renunciation of war, and at Butler's behest Kellogg urged that all nations join the plan. Though sixty-two nations eventually ratified the pact, it never proved effective. Butler argued that economic nationalism was a major threat to peace and proposed an economic union of European nations; however, he approved of colonialism and opposed Philippine independence.

In 1931 Butler was awarded the Nobel Prize for Peace jointly with JANE ADDAMS. In World War II, he attacked isolationists and urged the United States to join an international peacekeeping organization, which proved to be the United Nations. Butler died in December 1947, six months after Dwight D. Eisenhower was chosen as his successor as president of Columbia University.

**BIBLIOGRAPHY**

Butler, Nicholas Murray, *Looking Forward,* 1932, *Across the Busy Years,* 1939–1940, and *The World Today,* 1946; Whittemore, Richard, *Nicholas Murray Butler and Public Education,* 1970.

# Cable, George Washington

(October 12, 1844–January 31, 1925)
Author

As the author of novels and stories dealing with his native city, New Orleans, George Washington Cable was one of America's foremost regional writers. Throughout his life, Cable advocated equal rights for African Americans.

Cable was born in New Orleans, the son of a New England mother and a father who came from a long line of Virginia slaveowners. With his father's death, Cable, aged fourteen, took over the family's support. During the Civil War he enlisted in the 4th Mississippi Cavalry and, though twice wounded, served till the end of the war. While recuperating from a bout of malaria, he began writing columns for the New Orleans *Picayune,* and in 1869 he was hired as a reporter for the paper. He was soon dropped, however, when he refused to cover theatrical performances because to do so went against his religious beliefs. Cable then found work as an accountant and correspondence clerk for a local company of cotton merchants. Rising at 4 A.M., he continued the program of self-education he had started at camp during the war. After mastering French, he began delving among old records in the city archives and was fascinated by the romantic stories he found there. With the encouragement of Edward King, a literary scout who was making a tour of the South for *Scribner's Monthly,* Cable sent material to the magazine, and in 1873 his first story, "'Sieur George," was published.

Six years later, Cable's first book, a collection of seven stories entitled *Old Creole Days,* appeared. He followed it with several novels which made his literary reputation. Among them were *Madame Delphine* (1881), *The Grandissimes* (1884), *Dr. Sevier* (1885), *John March, Southerner* (1894), and *Gideon's Band* (1914). He also wrote historical nonfiction, which included such books as *The Creoles of Louisiana* (1884) and *Strange True Stories of Louisiana* (1889).

In his writing, Cable recaptured the colorful world of the Creoles, the French-speaking natives of New Orleans, in the antebellum period. Yet he did so with a realism that was new to southern fiction. Cable had come to view as morally wrong both slavery and the postwar efforts to deny African Americans equal rights, and he implicitly condemned the oppression of African Americans in his fiction. He also wrote essays and lectured in the hopes of advancing African American rights. Two collections of his social essays were published as *The Silent South* (1885) and *The Negro Question* (1888).

Cable's social views aroused much resentment in the South, where the editor of the Atlanta *Constitution* accused him of advocating a mingling of the races. Partly to escape the abuse that was heaped upon him in his own region and partly to be closer to his literary market, Cable moved with his family to Northampton, Massachusetts, in 1885. At Northampton he started the Home-Culture Clubs, later known as the Northampton People's Institute, with a gift from a friend, the business leader and philanthropist ANDREW CARNEGIE. He also embarked on reading tours of the entire country, sometimes in the company of fellow local colorist Mark Twain.

In his later years, Cable continued to write novels about his native city. He died in St. Petersburg, Florida, at the age of eighty.

**BIBLIOGRAPHY**

Bikle, Lucy L. Cable, *George W. Cable, His Life and Letters,* 1928; Turner, Arlin, *George W. Cable: A Biography,* 1956.

# Cabrini, Frances Xavier

(July 15, 1850–December 22, 1917)
Religious Leader

Saint Frances Xavier Cabrini, better known as Mother Cabrini, became known as the saint of immigrants for her work in establishing orphanages, nurseries, hospitals, and schools for Italian immigrants throughout the United States and in Latin America.

Maria Francesca Cabrini was born at Sant' Angelo Lodigiano in Lombardy, Italy. At age thirteen, she went to study with the Daughters of the Sacred Heart in nearby Arluno, receiving her schoolteacher's license five years later. A pious girl who took annual vows of chastity from the time she was eleven, she applied for admission to the Daughters of the Sacred Heart but was refused because of her frail health. She taught school at the neighboring village of Vidardo until 1874. At the urging of her spiritual adviser, Monsignor Antonio Serrati, she went to work at a small orphanage, the House of Providence, in Codogno. Taking religious vows in 1877, she was made directress of the orphanage; after its closing in 1880, she formed a new religious order, the Missionary Sisters of the Sacred Heart. By the end of seven years, the order had established seven convents.

Though Mother Cabrini had planned to establish a convent in China, Pope Leo XIII persuaded her to minister to Italian immigrants in the Americas instead. On March 31, 1889, Mother Cabrini, along with six sisters, arrived in New York, determined to do what she could to aid the city's 40,000 Italian immigrants, most of whom lived in slums. Undaunted by the fact that no preparations had been made for her arrival by the archbishop of New York, she managed to start a day school for Italian children and, soon afterward, an orphanage and a novitiate.

During the next decade, Mother Cabrini went on to establish orphanages, nurseries, hospitals, and schools in such cities as Chicago, Denver, Seattle, and Los Angeles. She also started schools and other charitable establishments in Nicaragua, Argentina, and Brazil, and in France and England. For the most part, though not exclusively, these charitable foundations were for the benefit of Italian immigrants. In 1909 Mother Cabrini took U.S. citizenship. She was named superior general of her order for life in 1910. By 1917 it had grown to include sixty-five charitable houses and about 1,500 daughters.

Mother Cabrini died at the age of sixty-seven. She was canonized nearly thirty years later, in 1946, the first American citizen to become a saint.

**BIBLIOGRAPHY**

A Benedictine of Stanbrook Abbey, *Frances Xavier Cabrini*, 1944; Martindale, Cyril C., *Life of Mother Francesca Saverio Cabrini*, 1931; Maynard, Theodore, *Too Small a World: The Life of Francesca Cabrini*, 1945; Vian, Nello, *Mother Cabrini*, 1938.

# Calderone, Mary Steichen

(July 1, 1904–  )
Physician, Sex Educator

D r. Mary Calderone has been one of the most effective crusaders for a mature and responsible approach to the treatment of sexual education in the public schools. She came to public attention in the 1950s as medical director of the Planned Parenthood Federation of America.

Mary Steichen was born in New York City, the elder daughter of the renowned photographer Edward Steichen, and Clara Smith. She spent her early years in Paris, where her father was studying art, and attended Vassar College, majoring in chemistry. After graduating in 1925, she decided on a stage career and studied for three years in New York. During that period she married another actor, W. Lon Martin, and had two daughters. Concluding that both her dramatic career and her marriage were failures, she divorced her husband, went through psychoanalysis, and took vocational tests that pointed her toward medicine as a profession. The death of her elder daughter from pneumonia at the age of eight brought on a deep emotional crisis, but Mary persevered with her studies and earned her M.D. at the University of Rochester in 1939. She interned at Bellevue Hospital and took a master's degree in public health at Columbia University, where she met and married Frank Calderone, M.D. Their marriage produced two more daughters. (Dr. Frank Calderone later became chief administrative officer of the World Health Organization.)

Dr. Mary Calderone worked in public health for several years, and in 1953 she became medical director of the Planned Parenthood Federation of America (see ALAN GUTTMACHER). In her lectures to physicians and public health workers, she insisted on the need for family planning as a public health measure. She was aware of the inquiries pouring into Planned Parenthood's offices, not only about birth control but about sexual problems in general. Letters begging for information about impotence, frigidity, and homosexuality underlined the predicament of numerous people troubled by sexual ignorance. Out of Calderone's concern and that of colleagues in her field grew the Sex Information and Education Council of the United States (SIECUS), founded in January 1965 with Calderone as executive director. The aim of SIECUS was to establish human sexuality as a health entity, and in so doing to help teachers, therapists, and other professionals with information about sex education. Calderone, lecturing around the country on such topics as homosexual rights, sex for the handicapped and elderly, abortion, pornography (which she did not deplore), and masturbation, became a controversial figure, condemned by such groups as the John Birch Society, which called her "an aging sexual libertine." As the result of Calderone's pioneer work, grade schools and high schools throughout the country have introduced courses in sex education with the guidance of SIECUS. Her books have had a broad impact: notably, *Family Book About Sexuality,* with Eric Johnson (1981), and *Talking with Your Child about Sex,* with James W. Ramey (1982). She has received thirty awards and honorary degrees from professional groups and institutions.

After retiring from SIECUS in 1982, Calderone continued to be active and held several academic appointments, including a lectureship in sexuality at New York University (1982–1988). She contributed an article to the *New York Times* Op-Ed page, September 16, 1989, writing as a Quaker to defend the right of an imperfect fetus not to be born.

**BIBLIOGRAPHY**

Calderone, Mary (ed.), *Abortion in the United States,* 1958.

# Carmichael, Stokely

(June 29, 1941–  )
Civil Rights Leader

Stokely Carmichael, a notably effective leader of the Student Nonviolent Coordinating Committee (SNCC; see ELLA BAKER), brought the concept of Black Power into the civil rights struggle.

Stokely Carmichael was born in Port of Spain, Trinidad—then part of the British West Indies, now part of the Republic of Trinidad and Tobago. When he was two, his father, a carpenter, immigrated with his wife and daughters to New York, leaving Stokely in the care of his grandmother. The boy received a sound education at the Tranquility Boys School, which, following the British pattern, emphasized white culture. Yet in Trinidad there was integration of a sort: members of the predominant black population held important posts in government, business, and schools.

When Stokely was eleven he joined his family in New York, living first in Harlem and then in the Bronx. He found that, unlike Trinidad, the United States gave African Americans little consequence in society. His "British" education, however, prepared him for acceptance in the high-ranking Bronx High School of Science. He entered Howard University, in Washington, D.C., and graduated with an A.B. in philosophy in 1964.

Carmichael had been radicalized in high school, when on television he saw sit-ins by black students in the South. He joined the Congress of Racial Equality (CORE; see JAMES FARMER), and while at Howard became a Freedom Rider, participating in the integrated bus rides into the South that CORE organized to confront segregation in interstate travel. Joining demonstrations in Mississippi, he was frequently arrested and beaten. After graduating from Howard, Carmichael became an organizer for SNCC, whose integrated membership registered voters, taught rural blacks to read and write, and opened clinics. In Lowndes County, in eastern Mississippi, which had an African American majority, Carmichael led a SNCC team that increased registered black voters from 70 to 26,000, outnumbering white voters.

In 1966 the violent white resistance to civil rights protests in the South, in combination with the many beatings he personally had suffered, impelled Carmichael to abandon his commitments to nonviolence and integration. Carmichael organized a separate black party, the Lowndes County Freedom Organization, and chose as its "logo" a ferocious black panther. He favored a militant approach to the civil rights struggle, emphasizing black freedom rather than integrated nonviolent cooperation. In May 1966 Carmichael was elected chairman of SNCC, succeeding JOHN R. LEWIS. Soon afterward, he joined JAMES MEREDITH's "March Against Fear" down a Mississippi highway, shouting "Black Power!" to the black farmers along the roadside.

The Black Power concept became Carmichael's personal mission, signifying political power, the organizing of black people for liberation by "any means necessary"—a viewpoint in which he agreed with MALCOLM X. Lecturing widely in this country and abroad, he dropped nonviolence as a principle of SNCC, believing that the social system could not be turned around unless there was the threat of violence and disorder.

In 1967 Carmichael broke with SNCC, joined the Black Panther Party, founded by HUEY NEWTON and others, and became its prime minister. The Panthers, strongest in northern cities, offered the most revolutionary message to young urban blacks, rejecting middle-class values, demanding discipline, and issuing calls for revolutionary and (if necessary) violent change. In a more positive aspect, the Black Panthers protected blacks against police harassment, organized antidrug clinics, and set up lunch programs in the schools. When in

1969 the Panthers, under their minister of information, ELDRIDGE CLEAVER, opted for cooperation with white radical groups, Carmichael resigned from the party and left the country.

With his wife, the South African singer Miriam Makeba, Carmichael established residence in the small nation of Guinea-Bissau, a former Portuguese colony in West Africa, and adopted the name Kwame Toure. He occasionally revisits the United States to lecture on African culture as the logical extension of Black Power and to promote his African Peoples Revolutionary Party.

**BIBLIOGRAPHY**

Carmichael, Stokely, *Black Power*, 1967; Carson, Clayborne, *In Struggle: SNCC and the Black Awakening*, 1981; Weisbrot, Robert, *Freedom Bound: A History of America's Civil Rights Movement*, 1990.

# Carnegie, Andrew

(November 25, 1835–August 11, 1919)
Industrialist, Philanthropist

Andrew Carnegie rose from poverty to become one of the richest men in the world by gaining virtual control of the U.S. steel industry. He was also notable as a philanthropist, who gave millions of dollars to advance education, establish public libraries, and promote world peace.

Carnegie was born in Dunfermline, Scotland. His father, a handloom weaver, was impoverished by the introduction of power looms. In 1848 he immigrated with his family to the United States. They settled in Pittsburgh, Pennsylvania, where young Andrew found work as a bobbin boy in a textile mill at a salary of $1.20 a week. A year later, he got a job as a messenger in a telegraph office, and he began his rise from "rags to riches." Learning telegraphy himself, Carnegie became one of the

Courtesy of the New-York Historical Society, New York City

first operators in the country to be able to take messages by sound. He so impressed Thomas A. Scott of the Pennsylvania Railroad that Scott hired him to be his personal clerk and telegraph operator. Again Carnegie did such a good job that six years after joining the railroad, he was named superintendent of the Pittsburgh division. Then in 1861, when Scott was appointed assistant secretary of war, Carnegie became superintendent of the eastern military and telegraph lines. During the Civil War he helped coordinate rail transportation for the Union army and organized the army's telegraphic system.

Already during these years, Carnegie, with advice and loans from Scott, had begun to invest in telegraph, oil, iron, bridge, and railroad companies. In 1865, though offered the post of assistant general superintendent on the Pennsylvania Railroad, he resigned and devoted himself to his other business interests. Within a few years, he had an annual income of $50,000 and was considering retiring and taking up a scholarly life. Deciding not to retire at this time, Carnegie nevertheless frequented intellectual as well as business circles in New York City, where he lived after 1867.

When the depression of 1873 struck and properties were cheap, Carnegie used almost all of his money to invest in steel. He hired the best people in steel technology and plant management and introduced the Bessemer process and other innovations. In this way, he was able to produce a higher quality of steel at a lower price than his competitors. He also kept production costs, wages, and salaries down and maintained complete control over his enterprise, in order to plow profits back into it.

During the next thirty years, U.S. steel production increased until the nation surpassed Great Britain as the foremost steel producer in the world, thanks largely to Carnegie. He steadily expanded his holdings by lease or purchase, in 1888 acquiring the important steel works at Homestead, Pennsylvania. Four years later, however, Carnegie's reputation as an employer was damaged by a bloody strike at the Homestead plant. The strike revealed Carnegie's plans to destroy the iron and steel workers' union, and the event raised a public outcry. Otherwise, the decade of the 1890s was a time of even greater growth for Carnegie steel. Already Carnegie had begun the process of vertical integration, by which he came to control raw materials, transportation, and distribution within the steel industry. Now he took advantage of the depression of 1893 to 1897 to acquire the rich iron deposits of the Mesabi Range in Minnesota and to purchase the Pittsburgh, Shenango, and Lake Erie Railroad connecting the steel-producing center with the Northwest water routes. By 1900 the Carnegie Steel Company, organized a year earlier with a capital of $350 million, controlled the bulk of U.S. steel production.

In 1901 Carnegie sold the company to interests that formed the United States Steel Corporation, and he dedicated the rest of his life to philanthropy. As early as 1868, Carnegie had written himself a memorandum declaring that "the amassing of wealth is one of the worst species of idolatry—no idol more debasing than the worship of money." A year later he made his first gift—public baths given to his birthplace of Dunfermline, Scotland. Twenty years afterward, in 1889, Carnegie published an article entitled "Wealth" in the *North American Review*. In this article, which became known as "The Gospel of Wealth," Carnegie stated his belief that the accumulation of capital was necessary to human progress. He further maintained that rich men had a moral obligation to distribute their money for the public good with the same energy and systematic thoughtfulness they had used to acquire it.

Putting into practice his own gospel of wealth, Carnegie made benefactions totaling about $350 million. This money provided for thousands of public libraries and church organs and helped advance both higher education and the cause of peace. Carnegie endowed the Carnegie Institute of Pittsburgh (1895), the Carnegie Trust for the Universities of Scotland (1901), and the Carnegie Institute of Washington (1902). He also helped establish the schools that are now part of Carnegie Mellon University and contributed generously to such southern black schools as Hampton and Tuskegee institutes. In 1905 he started the first pension fund for college and university professors. In 1911 the Carnegie Corporation of New York was created to handle the distribution of Carnegie's money for educational and research purposes.

In the interests of world peace, Carnegie established the Carnegie Endowment for International Peace (1910) and gave money for the construction of three "temples of peace": The Hague Peace Palace in the Netherlands, a Central American Court of Justice in Costa Rica, and the Pan American Union Building in Washington, D.C. His optimism shattered by the outbreak of World War I in 1914, Carnegie died five years later at the age of eighty-three.

In addition to "Wealth," Carnegie wrote numerous articles on business and public affairs. His best-known books include *Democracy Triumphant* (1886), *The Empire of Business* (1902), and his *Autobiography* (1920).

**BIBLIOGRAPHY**

Hacker, Louis M., *The World of Andrew Carnegie: 1865–1901,* 1968; Leichtman, R. B., *Carnegie Returns,* 1983; Swetnam, George, *Andrew Carnegie,* 1980.

# Carnegie, Dale

(November 24, 1888–November 1, 1955)
Author, Educator, Lecturer

Dale Carnegie's courses in public speaking and personality development have helped countless people overcome neurotic handicaps and become self-confident and at ease in social contacts.

Dale Carnegie was born in Maryville, in the northwest corner of Missouri, one of two sons of a farmer, James William Carnagey (Dale changed the spelling of his last name when he was a young adult). The family moved to a farm near Warrensburg, in central Missouri, where young Carnegie grew up. Encouraged by a touring lecturer for the Chautauqua movement, which brought speakers on many topics to small towns across America, he developed a gift for public speaking in Sunday school, at civic events, and on the high school debating team. Carnegie attended the State Teachers College in Warrensburg, practicing recitations as he rode his horse in from the farm. He graduated in 1908 and went to work for the International Correspondence School, but having sold only one course he became a salesman for a meat-packing firm.

Having saved up for further study, Carnegie headed for New York in 1911. A detour into acting was not successful, and he got a job at the 125th Street YMCA teaching night classes in public speaking. Carnegie made a hit and was soon on his own, earning $500 a week, with an office in Times Square and a staff of instructors. His methods, which he improvised as he went along, helped people to overcome their fears of public speaking. In 1916 he attracted much attention when he rented Carnegie Hall for a lecture. (The story goes that, at this time, thinking of the philanthropist ANDREW CARNEGIE, he changed the spelling of his name.)

A stint in the army interrupted Carnegie's career. After his discharge, he became business manager for the author LOWELL THOMAS, who lectured with a slide show about the war hero Lawrence of Arabia. Touring abroad, Carnegie met and married a French countess, Lolita Baucaire. In the 1920s he revived his classes and published a textbook, *Public Speaking: A Practical Course for Business Men* (1926). He contracted with big companies such as Westinghouse to train their executives. Carnegie's interest in prominent men led him to write *Lincoln, the Unknown* (1932) and *Little-Known Facts About Well-Known People* (1943).

Carnegie's most famous book was *How to Win Friends and Influence People* (1936). The book offered commonsense advice on speech and presenting oneself that was summed up by one reviewer as, "Smile, be friendly, never argue or find fault, or tell a person he is wrong." Carnegie's simple formula for success became an overnight best-seller, and he was in demand for radio shows, lectures, and magazine articles. The book has sold nearly 5 million copies and has been translated into some thirty languages. Spurred by its success, Carnegie founded the Carnegie Institute for Effective Speaking and Human Relations, with branches throughout the United States, Canada, South America, and Europe.

In 1944 Carnegie (whose first marriage had ended in divorce) married Dorothy Prince Vanderpool, who became his business partner and helped him start public-speaking classes for women. She wrote *How to Help Your Husband Get Ahead in His Social and Business Life* (1953).

Carnegie's last book was *How to Stop Worrying and Start Living* (1948). That it was less successful than his earlier books is attributed to the postwar public's stronger interest in "self-help" books based on psychiatric techniques. He died at his home in Forest Hills, New York, at age sixty-six, four years after the birth of his daughter and only child, Donna Dale.

**BIBLIOGRAPHY**

Huber, Richard, *The American Idea of Success*, 1971; Longgood, William, *Talking Your Way to Success: The Story of the Dale Carnegie Course*, 1962; Meyer, Donald, *The Positive Thinkers*, 1965.

## Carson, Rachel

(May 27, 1907–April 14, 1964)
Author, Scientist

Rachel Carson was a noted biologist and ecology writer whose books played a major role in launching the modern environmental movement.

Carson was born in Springdale, Pennsylvania. She graduated from Pennsylvania College for Women (now Chatham College) in 1929 with a degree in zoology and received her M.A. from Johns Hopkins University in 1932. From 1931 until 1936 she worked as a laboratory assistant in zoology at the University of Maryland and did postgraduate work during the summer at the Marine Biological Laboratory in Woods Hole, Massachusetts, on Cape Cod.

Carson became an aquatic biologist with the U.S. Bureau of Fisheries in 1936. Part of her work consisted of writing scripts for radio broadcasts about marine life. After one of her revised scripts was published in the *Atlantic Monthly* in 1937, she was invited to turn it into a book. *Under the Sea-Wind: A Naturalist's*

*Picture of Ocean Life* (1941) exhibited a sensitive style and thorough knowledge of sea life.

Carson continued to write and edit conservation pamphlets at the U.S. Bureau of Fisheries and to publish articles. In 1947 she became editor in chief of the publications of the Bureau of Fisheries, later renamed the U.S. Fish and Wildlife Service. Four years later her second book, *The Sea Around Us* (1951), won critical acclaim and became a best-seller after excerpts were published in *The New Yorker* and the *Yale Review*. There was no doubt after this book's success that Carson was someone uniquely capable of and qualified for making complex scientific subjects such as the interrelationship of marine plant and animal life understandable and appealing to a wide audience. *Under the Sea-Wind* was reissued and also became a best-seller, and Carson retired from her government position. She moved to West Southport, Maine, and, with the help of a

Guggenheim Foundation fellowship, began an ecological study of the American Atlantic coastal shore. The results of her investigation were published in *The Edge of the Sea* (1955).

Carson's third book, *Silent Spring* (1962), also serialized in *The New Yorker*, became much more than a best-seller. *Silent Spring* touched off a controversy that led to a fundamental shift in the public's attitudes toward the use of pesticides such as DDT. In *Silent Spring* Carson managed to correct the prevalent belief that the indiscriminate use of pesticides created no harmful effects upon wildlife other than upon the insects they were designed to kill. "For the first time in history," she wrote, "every human being is now subjected to contact with dangerous chemicals, from the moment of conception until death."

With the publication of *Silent Spring* Carson discovered herself at the center of a national controversy. The public became outraged over the reckless use of toxic chemicals and the lack of scientific and regulatory control of the country's natural resources, while representatives of the chemical industry ridiculed her work. A federal commission appointed by President John F. Kennedy to investigate the matter confirmed Carson's warning that pesticides posed a serious potential health hazard.

The well-documented and challenging information Carson so urgently presented in *Silent Spring* provided the spark that launched the ecology movement in the United States. Today, Americans are acutely aware of many of the possible dangers to their environment and, thanks to the example provided by Rachel Carson, have begun to demand protection for the world around them.

Elected to the American Academy of Arts and Letters, Carson was also the first woman to be awarded the Audubon Medal. She died in 1964 at the age of fifty-six.

**BIBLIOGRAPHY**

Brooks, P., *The House of Life: Rachel Carson at Work,* 1972; Graham, F., Jr., *Since Silent Spring,* 1970.

## Carter, William Hodding, Jr.

(February 3, 1907–April 4, 1972)
Journalist

H odding Carter, who was born and lived nearly all his life in the Deep South, was an outspoken opponent of racial segregation and bigotry. His editorials won him a Pulitzer Prize in 1946.

Carter was born in Hammond, Louisiana, near New Orleans, and spent much of his youth close to the Mississippi River. Two childhood memories stayed with him: as a six-year-old, seeing a yelling gang of white boys chasing a frightened black youngster; and some years later encountering the hanging black body of a lynching victim. He went north for his college education: to Bowdoin College, in Maine (B.A., 1927) and to Columbia University's school of journalism (B.Litt., 1928). After a year of teaching at Tulane University, Carter held down newspaper jobs in New Orleans and in Jackson, Mississippi. In 1932, six months after he married Betty Werlein, he was fired by the Associated Press bureau chief in Jackson for "insubordination." On a shoestring, he and his wife started their own paper, the *Daily Courant*, in Hammond. Carter's main target was the political boss and demagogue Senator Huey P. Long.

In 1935, after Long was assassinated, the Carters moved to Greenville, Mississippi, in the bottom land between the Yazoo and Mississippi rivers known as the Delta. Carter once said he moved there because Mississippi offered "the best fight in sight." For more than thirty years he was editor and publisher of the paper he founded in Greenville, the *Delta Democrat-Times*. Carter's target now became Senator Theodore Bilbo, who, he felt, was making the name of Mississippi "synonymous with every evil prejudice that besets our democracy."

For several years Carter was away from Greenville, but the *Democrat-Times* continued under his guidance. In 1939 he was awarded a Nieman fellowship at Harvard, a grant to newspapermen for a year of study. Carter then served a few months on the staff of the progressive paper *PM*, in New York, before he was called up for duty with his National Guard artillery unit. While at a training camp he lost the sight of his right eye in an accident. He continued his army service nonetheless and was assigned to duty in Cairo, to launch and edit the Middle East editions of the army publications *Stars and Stripes* and *Yank*. In 1945, discharged as a major in Intelligence, Carter went back to Greenville to resume his fight against bigotry—not only against Bilbo, but also against the white supremacists Senator James Eastland, Congressman John Rankin, and others.

In 1946 Carter received a Pulitzer award for his editorials on intolerance—notably, one that asked for fairness for the Nisei (Japanese American) soldiers returning from World War II—and in the same year he started another newspaper in Greenwood, Mississippi, the *Morning Star*, which received countrywide notice for a story on a group of white men arrested for beating a Negro to death. He wrote books of fiction and nonfiction about the country he knew, including the novel *The Winds of Fear* (1944), about interracial tensions in a fictional Southern town, and the autobiographical *First Person Rural* (1963). Carter, who had lost the sight of his remaining eye, died at the age of sixty-five in his home at Greenville, having lived to witness, to a degree, the social changes that he had fought for.

**BIBLIOGRAPHY**

Carter, Hodding, *Lower Mississippi*, 1942; Carter, Hodding, with Anthony Rogosin, *Gulf Coast Country*, 1951; Kneebone, John T., *Southern Liberal Journalists and the Issue of Race, 1920–1944*, 1985.

# Carver, George Washington

(ca. 1864–January 4, 1943)
Botanist, Educator

George Washington Carver devoted his life to research primarily to benefit agriculture in the South—and in particular the situation of black farmers. He was famous for discovering numerous ways of using agricultural products. Above all, he was a symbol of accomplishment for young African Americans before desegregation.

"Carver's George," as he was first called, was born in slavery on a farm at Diamond Grove, in the Ozarks of southwest Missouri. Who his father was is not known. Moses Carver had purchased Mary, George's mother, as a helper and companion for his wife Susan. Mary bore four children, two daughters who died and two sons, Jim and George. Slave raiders kidnapped the infant George and his mother. It is said that she was sold down South and that the baby was ransomed by Moses Carver in exchange for a race horse.

In December 1865, after the ratification of the Thirteenth Amendment, abolishing slavery, George and his brother Jim remained on the Carver farm. George got some education and showed a gift for tending plants. In his teens, he left the Carvers in search of education.

Carver attended a school for blacks in the county seat, Neosho, where he began calling himself George Carver, and then a high school in Min-

Library of Congress

neapolis, Kansas, where he took a middle initial, W, to avoid confusion at the post office. When asked if it stood for Washington, he said, "Why not?" He made a living doing domestic work and taking in washing, and graduated in 1885. After a college in Highland, Kansas, rejected him because of his race, he tried farming for two years in western Kansas, but the extremes of weather on the prairie discouraged his efforts. Carver moved to central Iowa, where, with the help of a white Baptist minister and his wife, he was admitted to Simpson College, in Indianola, in 1890, the college's second black student.

Carver wanted to become an artist, and his paintings were admired, but his art teacher persuaded him to study horticulture under her father, a professor at the Iowa State College of Agriculture, at Ames. Carver transferred there—becoming the college's first black student—and earned a B.S. in 1894 and an M.S. in 1896. He worked as an assistant botanist at an agricultural experiment station, and his experiments in cross-fertilization won praise from the station's director.

Carver's reputation had spread, and soon after receiving his M.S. he was invited by BOOKER T. WASHINGTON to come to Tuskegee Institute, in Macon County, Alabama, as director of agricultural studies. He spent the rest of his life at Tuskegee, though originally he had hoped to return to painting as his profession. For the first nineteen years, Carver worked under the thumb of the autocratic Washington, who found fault with Carver's unsystematic methods and shortcomings as an administrator. At the time, Carver was doing some of his most important work. Having been shocked by the poverty and discouragement of black farmers in the country around Tuskegee, he felt his mission was to develop methods of agriculture that would help them. He taught more effective and cheaper methods of fertilizing, for example. In view of the widespread illiteracy, he organized a Farmers Institute, at which he lectured, and traveled around the county in a wagon (later an auto) fitted out to demonstrate new techniques. He encouraged three crops that could be alternated with cotton: cow peas, an acceptable food for people as well as farm animals and a crop that added nitrogen to the soil; sweet potatoes, which could be stored for winter use; and, above all, peanuts, a cheap source of protein that also replenished nutrients in the soil.

Carver became famous as the "Peanut Man" after he testified before the House Ways and Means Committee, in 1921, insisting that protective tariffs were necessary to back the peanut industry. He displayed a variety of products he had made from peanuts—milk, breakfast food, livestock feed, and others. He claimed eventually that he had produced more than 300 such products, though few were commercially feasible and the peanut industry did not prosper greatly on their account.

Carver took out patents on few of his many discoveries. He kept slight records, and was vague when asked about formulas. A daily reader of the Bible, he attributed his successes to "Mr. Creator." In his late years he became a celebrity, visited by other celebrities but hampered by Jim Crow laws restricting blacks in society when he traveled to lecture and went north to receive honors. He was above all, in his lifetime, a symbol of potential for young African Americans. Shortly after his death in 1943, Senator Harry S Truman introduced a bill to create the George Washington Carver National Monument near his birthplace at Diamond Grove.

**BIBLIOGRAPHY**

Elliott, Lawrence, *George Washington Carver, The Man Who Overcame*, 1966; Holt, Rackham, *George Washington Carver: An American Biography*, 1963; McMurray, Linda, *George Washington Carver*, 1981.

# Catt, Carrie Lane Chapman

(January 9, 1859–March 9, 1947)
Suffragist

Carrie Chapman Catt was one of the leading fighters for the passage of the Nineteenth Amendment, which gave women the vote in 1920.

Born near Ripon, Wisconsin, Carrie Lane grew up self-reliant and independent on a farm near Charles City, Iowa. She graduated from the local high school in three years, earning her B.S. from Iowa State College in 1880. She then served as principal of the Mason City, Iowa, high school and two years later was appointed superintendent of schools. In 1885 she married Leo Chapman, owner and editor of the *Mason City Republican*, of which she became assistant editor. After his death a year later, she returned to Charles City, where she soon became active in suffrage work. In 1887 she joined the Iowa Suffrage Association and in 1890 attended her first national suffrage convention as a state delegate. Also in 1890, she married George William Catt, a civil engineer who supported woman suffrage. Before their marriage the couple drew up a contract stating that she would have four months of each year to work for suffrage. The Catts settled in New York City.

A superb organizer as well as a first-rate public speaker, Catt rose rapidly in the suffrage ranks. In 1895 she became chair of the committee administering the fieldwork of the National American Woman Suffrage Association (NAWSA). Catt worked hard to put the suffrage organization on what she called a "sound organizational basis." Her abilities so impressed SUSAN B. ANTHONY that when Anthony retired from the presidency of the NAWSA in 1900 she chose Catt, rather than her close friend Anna Howard Shaw, to be her successor. Shaw, however, became president when Catt was forced by her husband's poor health to resign as president in 1904. Catt left Shaw a well-structured and financially sound nationwide organization. George Catt's death in 1905 at the age of forty-five left his wife financially independent for the rest of her life.

For the next several years, Catt focused her energies on the world scene, helping to found and serving as head of an International Woman

Suffrage Alliance, working on campaigns in New York City and State, and finally founding a Woman Suffrage party and leading a campaign in 1913 and 1914 for a state suffrage referendum. Though the measure went down in defeat, Catt's brilliant handling of the campaign brought her to the attention of national suffrage leaders, who in 1915 drafted her to serve again as president of the NAWSA.

When Catt again took office, the national movement was badly divided. Under the leadership of ALICE PAUL, a militant group had emerged. This group, which eventually became the Woman's party, concentrated its efforts on securing a federal suffrage amendment and believed that the Democrats (as the party in power) should be held responsible for failure to pass the amendment. Catt rejected this strategy, not wishing to alienate long-time Democratic supporters of the vote for women and believing it unwise to limit the effort to the federal level. Instead, in what she dubbed the "Winning Plan," Catt proposed combining work for a federal amendment with action on the state level. Unless more states gave women the vote, Catt believed that ratification of a federal amendment had little chance of success. Her plan was adopted by the NAWSA as its official policy in 1916.

When the United States entered World War I in 1917, Catt was faced with a dilemma: Should she follow her pacifist convictions (earlier, Catt had helped JANE ADDAMS found the Woman's Peace party), or should she give priority to her commitment to suffrage? Opting for the latter course, Catt served on the Woman's Committee of the Council of National Defense and urged women to take part in the war effort while continuing to work for suffrage. Her po-

sition helped win President Woodrow Wilson's support for a federal suffrage amendment, and a string of state suffrage victories in 1917 and 1918 further advanced the cause.

After the federal amendment had passed the House and the Senate in May and June of 1919, respectively, Catt oversaw the grueling, fourteen-month-long battle for ratification. She spent two tense months in Tennessee, the last state needed for ratification, but in the end her efforts were rewarded when the legislature passed the amendment by a margin of just one vote, and the Nineteenth Amendment became law in the summer of 1920.

After this—her greatest triumph—Catt went on to help found the League of Women Voters. She also resumed her work for world peace, campaigning for the League of Nations and helping to organize a conference for peace and disarmament.

Catt had shared her home since her husband's death with her good friend Mary Garrett Hay, in New York City, on a farm near Ossining, New York, and finally in New Rochelle, New York, where Hay died in 1928. Catt's final work was for the Women's Centennial Exposition, 1840–1940. She died of a heart attack at age eighty-eight.

### BIBLIOGRAPHY

Anthony, Susan B., and Ida H. Harper (eds.), *History of Woman Suffrage*, vols. 4–6, 1902–1922; Catt, Carrie Chapman, and Nettie Rogers Shuler, *Woman Suffrage and Politics*, 1923; Flexner, Eleanor, *Century of Struggle: The Woman's Rights Movement in the United States*, 1972, rev., 1975.

# Channing, William Ellery

(April 7, 1780–October 2, 1842)
Reformer, Religious Leader

On the base of William Ellery Channing's statue in the Boston Public Garden are inscribed the words: "He breathed into theology a humane spirit."

His appeal for tolerance and humanitarianism in religion made him the recognized head of the Unitarian movement, and in his views on education, slavery, war, and social questions he was ahead of his time.

William Ellery Channing was born in Newport, Rhode Island, third of ten children in a family with New England forebears on both sides. His father, William, was an attorney general of Rhode Island; his mother, Lucy Ellery, was the daughter of a signer of the Declaration of Independence, William Ellery. When young William was thirteen his father died, leaving the family in financial straits. In order to attend Harvard College, Channing lived with relatives, and he was described as overly studious to the detriment of his health. Having graduated at eighteen, he spent a year and a half as a tutor to the Randolph family of Richmond, Virginia, where he first encountered Negro slavery. Returning north in weakened health, he studied theology at home and at Harvard. (Barely 5 feet tall and weighing less than 100 pounds, he was in delicate health all his life.) Channing was ordained minister of the Federal Street Congregational Church in Boston, a position he held until his death. In 1814 he married a wealthy cousin, Ruth Gibbs, but he refused to draw on her income. They had four children, two of whom died in infancy.

Channing was a leader among Congregationalists in the turn away from Calvinism, with its severe doctrines emphasizing the depravity of humanity. In 1819 he preached a controversial sermon in Baltimore, defending the liberal view and the gospel of love, which became the platform of the Unitarian church. Known as "the apostle of Unitarianism," Channing in 1825 led the formation of the American Unitarian Association, with 125 churches.

A minister has to be a moral leader, Channing held, who convinces his congregation to accept the responsibilities of Christianity—to work through self-improvement toward the perfection of society. Accordingly, he took part in most of the reform movements of his time. He proposed that the government set aside funds from selling public lands to support education, and he advocated adult education and the ideas of HORACE MANN. The cities of the United States could be international centers of civilization, he taught, if citizen leaders would accept their responsibilities for the welfare of the poor. Intemperance as a vice is the community's responsibility rather than the victim's, and improved living conditions could do more to solve the problem than prohibitive laws. In 1816 Channing preached a sermon against war which led to the organization of the Massachusetts Peace Society at his house.

From 1821 to 1823 Channing, with his wife, traveled abroad for his health. In England he met and was influenced by literary personages such as William Wordsworth and Samuel Taylor Coleridge. Coleridge wrote of him, "He has the love of wisdom and the wisdom of love." Later, perhaps inspired by his travels, Channing published essays on Napoleon (whom he despised as a warmaker), John Milton, and the French quietist theologian François Fénelon. Channing's own influence on American literature was direct. RALPH WALDO EMERSON, Henry Wadsworth Longfellow, and other New England writers who were involved with the Unitarian movement were indebted to Channing.

On another trip abroad, in 1830, this time to the West Indies for his wife's health, Channing again encountered slavery. Three important works of Channing dealt with the slavery question: *Slavery* (1835), *The Abolitionist* (1836), and *Duty of the Free States* (1842), in the last of which he argued that the free states should leave the Union if Texas were annexed as a slave state. He did not join the abolitionists, whose tactics he thought inadmissibly violent; even so, his antislavery sermons and writings brought protests from some members of his congregation. In his last public address, in August 1842, on the eighth anniversary of the abolition of slavery in the British Empire, he said, "Slavery does all that lies in human power to unmake men, to rob them of their humanity. . . . Here is the master evil." Appealing to reason and conscience, Channing helped pave the way for emancipation.

Channing died at the age of sixty-two in Bennington, Vermont, of typhoid fever contracted while traveling in New England.

**BIBLIOGRAPHY**

Mendelsohn, Jack, *Channing, the Reluctant Radical,* 1971; Patterson, R. L., *The Philosophy of William Ellery Channing,* rep., 1972; Rice, M. H., *Federal Street Pastor,* 1961.

# Chavez, Cesar Estrada

(March 31, 1927–April 23, 1993)
Labor Union Leader

Cesar Chavez organized California grape pickers into the first effective and enduring migrant worker union in American history.

Chavez was born into a Mexican American family in Yuma, Arizona. Because his parents were migrant farm workers, Chavez received only a minimal amount of formal education while growing up in a long series of farm labor camps in California and Arizona. He dropped out of school in the seventh grade in order to work full-time in the fields harvesting various crops.

In 1945 Chavez joined the U.S. Navy and saw ac-

Library of Congress

tion in the Pacific. After his discharge in 1947, he returned to the life of a migrant farm worker. In 1952 he was introduced to Fred Ross, an agent of the community organizer SAUL ALINSKY. Ross had been sent to southern California to recruit local talent to staff a self-help Community Service Organization. At first as a volunteer, and then as a paid staff member at the Community Service Organization (CSO) office in San Jose, California, Chavez led voter registration drives; helped Mexican Americans and Mexican migrant farm workers in coping with immigration problems; and organized CSO chapters in other cities.

In addition to learning how to recruit and train local volunteer leaders while working for the CSO, Chavez gained a profound insight into the fact that community organizers could not expect to be appreciated by the people they helped. And yet he believed that "whatever you do, and no matter what reasons you may give to others, you do it because you want to see it done, or maybe because you want power." Another reality he came to understand: the lot of the migrant worker has always been a particularly tough one, and one that Americans have found it convenient to ignore because so many of the workers are immigrants.

Chavez became general director of the CSO in 1958, but this did not prevent him from growing increasingly dissatisfied as the CSO attracted more and more middle-class liberals and fewer and fewer poor farm workers. When the CSO leadership refused to support his vision of creating a farm workers union in 1962, he resigned and founded the National Farm Workers Association (NFWA).

Within three years, Chavez had enrolled 1,700 families in the NFWA. This enabled the NFWA to negotiate pay raises from two local growers in Delano, in the San Joaquin Valley, but Chavez felt it was still far too small an organization to risk confrontation with the large growers. Nevertheless, when another farm workers union affiliated with the AFL-CIO (see WILLIAM GREEN and JOHN L. LEWIS) went on strike in September 1965 for higher wages, the NFWA membership voted to join them.

Previous efforts to mount farm worker strikes had always failed for two basic reasons: the workers did not have enough money to outlast the growers, and the growers could easily replace the striking workers with imported Mexican farm workers. Agricultural workers, moreover, were not covered by the National Labor Relations Act and thus had fewer organizational rights than their industrial counterparts. To help overcome these weaknesses, Chavez, as the leader of the new combined United Farm Workers (UFW) union,

shrewdly sought out the assistance of other labor unions and liberal politicians across America. Furthermore, he drew considerable inspiration from the civil rights movement, then in full swing.

The nonviolent campaign Chavez organized and the publicity provided by his middle-class liberal and AFL-CIO labor union allies succeeded in forcing many of the wine grape growers to capitulate within a year. The table grape growers, who won a court battle that allowed them to import Mexican farm workers, proved much more obstinate. Unable to stop them from harvesting their grapes and shipping them out of the state for sale, Chavez resorted to implementing a national boycott of all California table grapes. Beginning in 1965, the grape strike went on for five years.

UFW representatives fanned out across the nation in a superbly organized drive for support that involved church meetings, rallies, marches, sing-ins, and a bilingual traveling theatrical group. These tactics proved so successful that national consumption of California table grapes dropped by an estimated 20 percent.

During this period Chavez gained national stature as a labor union spokesman. The skill he employed in his public statements is illustrated in the following extract of testimony he offered during a Senate subcommittee appearance:

> What farm workers in our country are asking for is the opportunity to earn a living, and not charity. I hope everyone here today agrees that a man who works on a farm is made just like a factory worker, that his children like to eat just as much as a factory worker's, and that his wife does not like to live in a substandard house. Well, if farm workers are equal, they deserve the same protection of the law that other men enjoy.

The economic hardship the boycott imposed upon the growers slowly eroded their opposition to recognizing and negotiating with the UFW. On April 1, 1970, the United Farm Workers Organizing Committee and David Freedman & Co and the Wonder Palms Ranch signed the nation's first table grape labor contract. The three-year agreement provided for a wage increase, provision for health insurance, and regulations prohibiting the use of certain pesticides.

Following this victory and, in March 1977, the settlement of a jurisdictional dispute with the Teamsters Union over which types of farm workers the two different unions could attempt to recruit, the UFW concluded agreements with the other large table grape growers. It then began the long process of winning the right to represent farm workers in negotiating with the growers of numerous other crops.

Cesar Chavez died in his sleep on April 23, 1993 in San Luis, Arizona, at the home of family friends. He was 66 years old.

**BIBLIOGRAPHY**

Dunne, John Gregory, *Delano: The Story of the California Grape Strike,* 1967; Garver, Susan, and Paula McGuire, *Coming to North America: From Mexico, Cuba, and Puerto Rico,* 1981; Matthiessen, Peter, *Sal Si Puedes,* 1969; Terzian, James P., and Kathryn Cramer, *Mighty Hard Road,* 1970.

# Child, Lydia Maria Francis

(February 11, 1802–October 20, 1880)
Author, Reformer

Lydia Maria Child wrote *An Appeal in Favor of That Class of Americans Called Africans* (1833), an early and important antislavery book that attracted a number of prominent people to the movement, while costing Child much of her popular readership.

Lydia Maria Francis was born in Medford, Massachusetts. Although her formal education went no further than attendance at a local girls' school, she was an avid reader and in 1824, at the age of twenty-two, published her first novel, *Hobomok,* the controversial story of a marriage between a white woman and a Pequot Indian man. The novel had considerable success and was followed by a collection of stories and a second novel. In 1825 she also began publishing *Juvenile Miscellany,* a bimonthly educational magazine for children that was the first of its kind in America.

The young author next wrote *The Frugal Housewife* (1829), a compendium of practical suggestions about household management that was aimed at women of moderate means. The book went into thirty-three editions in America and many editions abroad. After it came two other books about women's work and three volumes of biographical essays for a series called the Ladies' Family Library, which were hailed by the prestigious *North American Review.*

At the peak of her popularity, her career took a sharp turn in another direction. In 1828 Lydia Maria Francis had married David Lee Child, a lawyer and reform-minded editor who helped WILLIAM LLOYD GARRISON found the New England Anti-Slavery Society. Converted to the cause by her husband and Garrison, Lydia Maria Child published *An Appeal in Favor of That Class of Americans Called Africans* in 1833. The book traced the history of slavery from ancient times, detailed its evils, and called for the immediate emancipation of the nation's slaves.

*An Appeal* came out at a time when feelings against African Americans and abolitionists ran high. A horrified public stopped buying Lydia Maria Child's books. Nevertheless, the book helped persuade WILLIAM ELLERY CHANNING, WENDELL PHILLIPS, and THOMAS WENTWORTH HIGGINSON to join the abolitionist movement. Child joined the Boston Female Anti-Slavery Society in 1834. She published, among other antislavery works, an anthology called *The Oasis*

(1834), as well as her most popular romantic novel, *Philothea*, but she and her husband failed to prosper financially.

In 1840 when the abolitionist movement split apart, Child sided with the more radical faction led by Garrison; a year later, she moved to New York to become the editor of the American Anti-Slavery Society's official organ, the *National Anti-Slavery Standard*, whose readership soon surpassed that of Garrison's *The Liberator*. In 1843 she resigned from the editorship and withdrew from the American Anti-Slavery Society after sharp disagreement with Garrison over his "no union with slaveholders" position. For the next sixteen years Child devoted her energies to writing journalistic pieces, children's literature, and other books directed toward a popular audience.

Then in 1859, fired by the abolitionist JOHN BROWN's raid on Harpers Ferry, Virginia, she wrote to him in prison, offering her services as a nurse. This brought an angry letter from the wife of a Virginia senator, to which Child replied with an eloquent assault on the restriction of free speech and use of violence against abolitionists. Picked up by the New York *Tri-bune* and later reprinted by the American Anti-Slavery Society in pamphlet form, the correspondence sold over 3 million copies. In 1860 Child published three more antislavery pamphlets and after emancipation compiled *The Freedmen's Book*, an instructional anthology for and about African Americans, which was distributed free of charge by the Freedmen's Aid Society.

In her remaining years, Child wrote *An Appeal for the Indians* (1868) and articles for various periodicals on such subjects as civil service reform and the eight-hour day for workers. A supporter of woman's rights in principle, she nevertheless was critical of the organized suffrage movement. Child died in 1880 at the age of seventy-eight.

**BIBLIOGRAPHY**

Baer, Helene C., *The Heart Is Like Heaven*, 1964; Holland, P. G., M. Meltzer, and F. Krasno (eds.), *Selected Letters of Lydia Maria Child*, 1982; Meltzer, Milton, *Tongue of Flame*, 1965.

# Chomsky, Avram Noam

(December 7, 1928–   )
Linguist, Political Activist

Noam Chomsky has been a leading dissident intellectual who has applied a critical mind to problems of language and intelligence and to questions of national policy and international peace.

Noam Chomsky was born in Philadelphia, the older son of a professor of Hebrew at Dropsie College who had emigrated from Russia in 1913. As a boy, Chomsky was sent to an experimental progressive school. In childhood he displayed linguistic precocity: at ten he was able to read his father's edition of a Hebrew grammar of the thirteenth century. The experimental school paid slight attention to marks, and it was only when Chomsky attended a public high school that he realized he was a good student.

In 1945 Chomsky enrolled at the University of Pennsylvania while living at home and teaching at a Hebrew school. During his first two years he studied philosophy and Arabic with some interest, but he was more involved with socialism and Zionism, in particular the events in Palestine that were leading to the establishment of the state of Israel. He considered dropping out of college and going to Palestine to join a kibbutz and promote Arab-Jewish cooperation in a socialist framework.

At this point, Chomsky came under the influence of Zellig Harris, a professor of linguistics at the university, whose interests were close to his. Harris enabled Chomsky to work in an unconventional way, abandoning the normal curriculum and taking graduate courses in linguistics, philosophy, mathematics, and Hebrew. He earned a B.A. in 1949 (the year he married) and an M.A. in 1951, with a thesis on "Morphophonemics of Modern Hebrew." Chomsky received a fellowship for graduate study at Harvard University, with a stipend that relieved him of having to get a job. His Ph.D. in linguistics, however, was granted by the University of Pennsylvania in 1955, for a thesis on "Transformational Analysis." That year he became an assistant professor at the Massachusetts Institute of Technology (MIT), and in 1961, a full professor.

During 1953 Chomsky lived in an Israeli kibbutz for a few months. He found the life hard but, as he told an interviewer, "I liked it very much in many ways," and he considered settling there. However, he was troubled by the ideological conformity and the exclusionary attitudes toward Arabs and Oriental Jews (immigrants from North African and Asian countries). The appointment at MIT confirmed his decision not to live in Israel. More recently, he has taken a stand against Israeli settlement in the occupied territories.

As a rule, Chomsky has tended to avoid sectarian limitations. His career has been wide-

Donna Coveny/MIT

ranging and his literary output in all areas has been extraordinarily prolific. His highly technical scholarly work, challenging traditional views of how language develops, is considered to have revolutionized the study of linguistics. Language, he has taught, is generated through an inborn ability in the individual. Once generated, language is liable to infinite creative variation. Chomsky's theorizing draws on mathematics and even on classical philosophical thought.

Chomsky's protest against the Vietnam War made him a hero to the New Left and drew him ever deeper into radical politics, though while advocating protest he also has defended the freedom of the individual will. Chomsky has aimed to expose much of U.S. policy as a mask for irresponsible power and unjustified privilege, and he has insisted that the so-called free press promotes a futile conformity in American intellectual life. A noteworthy statement of his views is an extended essay, "The Responsibility of Intellectuals," in his book *American Power and the New Mandarins* (1969). He has spoken out in protest of American policy and action in Southeast Asia, Central America, the Near East, and East Timor.

**BIBLIOGRAPHY**

Chomsky, Noam, *Language and Problems of Knowledge,* 1987; Peck, James (ed.), *The Chomsky Reader,* 1987; Salkie, Raphael, *The Chomsky Update: Linguistics and Politics,* 1990.

# Clark, Kenneth Bancroft

(July 24, 1914–   )
Educator, Social Activist

Kenneth B. Clark has been a pioneer in the civil rights movement. His research contributed to the U.S. Supreme Court's 1954 ruling against "separate but equal" doctrine in education, and he has led in advocating integrated schools in northern cities as well as in the South.

Born in the Panama Canal Zone, Kenneth B. Clark was the son of a cargo superintendent for the United Fruit Company, Arthur Bancroft Clark, of West Indian origin. His mother, born Miriam Hanson, from Jamaica, choosing to educate her children in the United States, left in 1919 for New York with Kenneth and a younger daughter. Her husband, unwilling to be subjected to the racial prejudice of American life, stayed behind. Miriam Clark settled in Harlem and worked as a seamstress in the garment district. She became one of the first black shop stewards for the International Ladies Garment Workers Union (ILGWU). Harlem was then an integrated community, though by the time Kenneth Clark finished the eighth grade black students were in the majority, and counselors were advising them to attend a vocational high school. His mother protested, and he went to an academic high school.

Kenneth Clark went on to Howard University, in Washington, D.C., and majored in psychology. He had courses in political science with Dr. RALPH BUNCHE, who became a role model for him. After earning his B.A. and M.S. degrees Clark taught at Howard for a year, and in 1938 began graduate work at Columbia University, toward a Ph.D. in experimental psychology (1940). While at Howard, he married Mamie Phipps, from Arkansas, and she joined him at Columbia and also earned her Ph.D. in psychology. Clark and Bunche were on a research team under direction of the Swedish economist Gunnar Myrdal, for a project, supported by the Carnegie Corporation, which produced Myrdal's important two-volume work *An American Dilemma: The Negro Problem and Modern Democracy* (1944).

In 1942, after serving as a social science analyst for the U.S. Office of War Information, studying the morale of the black population, Clark became an instructor in psychology at the College of the City of New York. (He became a full professor in 1960, having been the first African American to have a permanent appointment at a city college.) In 1946 the Clarks founded the Northside Testing and Consultation Center, a nonprofit organization in Harlem, whose professional staff used psychotherapy to help emotionally disturbed youngsters. Later, renamed the Northside Center for Child Development, the organization shifted its emphasis to transforming the negative self-image that society imposed on black children. "We . . . had to try to develop in the parents and the children the strength to attempt to change the social pathology around them—to work at problems of injustice and inequity," Clark told an interviewer.

Kenneth and Mamie Clark's clinical work led to studies, reported in scientific journals, showing how segregation affects black children's self-esteem. In one test, African American children were asked to choose between white and brown dolls when given instructions such as "Give me the doll that looks bad" and "Give me the doll that is a nice color." Most children, the Clarks reported, showed a preference for the white doll rather than the brown doll, thus demonstrating their feeling that society prefers white people.

In 1951 Kenneth Clark began to work with the National Association for the Advancement of Colored People (NAACP; see JOEL E. SPINGARN) on school segregation cases. When test cases (known as *Brown* v. *Board of Education*) were appealed to the U.S. Supreme Court, the NAACP presented documentation, prepared by Clark and other social scientists, entitled "The Effects of Segregation and the Consequences of Desegregation: A Social Science Statement." It was the first time that a nonlegal brief on the social and psychological aspects of a constitutional issue had been submitted to the Supreme Court.

The Court, in a unanimous decision on May 17, 1954, overturned the "separate but equal" doctrine and held that segregation deprived the students in question of the equal protection of the Fourteenth Amendment. Among other authorities (including Myrdal's study), the Court cited a 1950 article of Clark's on the effect of discrimination on personality development. His book *Prejudice and Your Child* (1955) describes the effects of segregation upon white as well as black children.

Clark's concern also turned to the quality of education, the competence of teachers, and the problems of delinquency and crime. In 1962, aided by federal funds, Clark established Harlem Youth Opportunities Unlimited (HARYOU), which began a study of juvenile delinquency in Harlem. In his recommendations Clark proposed such strategies as preschool classes and after-school study centers, with community participation. In 1964 HARYOU was taken over by political rivals and allowed to founder. Clark's experience, however, led to another book, *Dark Ghetto: Dilemmas of Social Power* (1965).

In 1967 Clark became president of the Metropolitan Applied Research Center (MARC), which designed an academic achievement program for the children of the District of Columbia, more than 90 percent of whom were black, and most of whom were poor. Owing to a passive public, the plan was defeated, though most MARC projects were successful.

Clark closed MARC in 1975, the year he retired from City College. He and his family established a consulting firm that dealt with clients in government, business, education, and organizations seeking advice on affirmative-action programs and other aspects of race relations. Kenneth Clark has consistently advised against all-black public schools, colleges, dormitories, and clubs, a stand that earned him early opposition from Black Power supporters (see STOKELY CARMICHAEL and ELIJAH MUHAMMAD). In January 1991 in a letter to the *New York Times*, Clark pointed out that separate schools for black students violate the Supreme Court's historic decision of 1954.

**BIBLIOGRAPHY**

Clark, Kenneth, *The Pathos of Power*, 1974; Clark, Kenneth, with Jeannette Hopkins, *A Relevant War Against Poverty*, 1968; Clark, Kenneth (ed.), with Talcott Parsons, *The Negro American*, 1966.

# Clay, Cassius Marcellus

(October 19, 1810–July 22, 1903)
Abolitionist

Kentucky abolitionist Cassius Marcellus Clay stirred up controversy in his native state by campaigning for emancipation and publishing an antislavery newspaper. An avowed racist, Clay generally attacked slavery on economic rather than on moral grounds, anticipating arguments that would later be made by another southern abolitionist, HINTON HELPER.

The son of a wealthy slaveowner and a distant cousin of the famous political leader Henry Clay, Cassius Clay was born at White Hall, the family estate in Madison County, Kentucky. Educated at the local schools and privately, he went to the North for college, graduating from Yale in 1832. While at Yale, Clay heard noted abolitionist WILLIAM LLOYD GARRISON speak. Clay was impressed with Garrison and also with the northern system of free labor.

Elected to the Kentucky legislature in 1835, Clay was at first moderate on the slavery question. Then in his campaign for reelection in 1840, he pushed for a state law to restrict the importation of slaves, blaming the South's economic stagnation on its system of unfree, unpaid labor. This argument especially appealed to the state's small farmers and artisans. Clay won the restriction but lost the election. In 1844 Clay freed his own slaves and denounced the annexation of Texas as a scheme to extend slavery.

In 1845 Clay began publishing an abolitionist newspaper, *The True American*, in Lexington, Kentucky. Foreseeing trouble because Lexington was in the heart of the state's slave-owning area, he kept cannons and rifles in his office. Nevertheless, Clay's proslavery opponents managed to break into the newspaper office while Clay was away. They seized his equipment and shipped it across the river to Cincinnati, Ohio, which was a free state. Clay later moved his paper, having changed its name to the *Examiner*, to Louisville, Kentucky.

Although he was against the annexation of Texas, Clay served as a volunteer in the Mexican War, in which he was taken prisoner and later released. In 1849 he ran an unsuccessful race for governor of Kentucky. In the 1850s Clay became a Republican and a close friend of Abraham Lincoln. He hoped Lincoln would give him a cabinet post after Lincoln was elected president in 1860. Instead Lincoln made Clay minister to Russia, a post in which he served from 1863 to 1869. Before leaving for Russia, Clay fought briefly in the Civil War and argued for the abolition of slavery in the seceded states. As minister to Russia, Clay helped maintain friendly relations between Russia and the United States and played a role in the purchase of Alaska.

After the war, Clay broke with the Republicans over their Reconstruction policy, supporting Democrat Samuel J. Tilden in the election of 1876. A violent man, who during his lifetime had fought a number of duels, Clay spent his last years barricaded in his house in Kentucky. He died at the age of ninety-two.

**BIBLIOGRAPHY**

Clay, Cassius Marcellus, *The Life of Cassius Marcellus Clay: Memoirs, Writings and Speeches*, 1886; Filler, Louis, *The Crusade Against Slavery*, 1960; Ritchie, W., *The Public Career of Cassius Marcellus Clay*, 1974.

# Cleaver, Leroy Eldridge, Jr.

(August 31, 1935–   )
Civil Rights Leader

Eldridge Cleaver led a life of transformations: youthful years of crime and imprisonment; a decade as a famous black activist, writer, and wandering exile; and the last quarter century as a conservative fundamentalist Christian.

Born in a village called Wabbaseka in eastern Arkansas, Eldridge Cleaver was one of six children of a troubled, violent marriage. His father, Leroy, a waiter and occasional piano-player, regularly beat his wife and children. Working as a dining-car waiter, Leroy Cleaver moved the family to the slums of Phoenix, Arizona, then to Los Angeles. The father abandoned the family; the mother, originally a schoolteacher, worked as a janitor.

Cleaver spent his youth in prisons. Between the ages of twelve and eighteen he was in a series of reform schools, for petty theft and for selling marijuana. During one confinement he had a brief conversion to Roman Catholicism. When in 1953 he was arrested again on a drug charge, he was sentenced to the California state prison at Soledad for two and a half years. There he completed high school and read widely, particularly the political classics, including Voltaire, Marx, and W. E. B. Du Bois. Released, he went back to the marijuana trade and added more violent crimes. A conviction for assault with intent to kill brought him eight years in San Quentin and Folsom state prisons.

The long imprisonment brought Cleaver to new realizations. "I admitted that I had gone astray . . . from being a human being. . . . My pride as a man . . . seemed to collapse. . . . That is why I started to write. To save myself," he wrote in *Soul on Ice* (1968), the book that made his reputation. Cleaver discovered the Black Muslim faith (see MALCOLM X) and, though it was forbidden, became a minister to other inmates. *Ramparts* magazine began to publish Cleaver's writings, and its publishers worked for his parole, which was granted in 1966.

In San Francisco, Cleaver worked on the *Ramparts* staff, was in demand as a lecturer, and started a social center for black youth. There in February 1967 he met HUEY NEWTON, cofounder of the Black Panthers, a group that aimed to protect blacks from police intimida-

Library of Congress

tion. He joined the Black Panthers, became the minister of information for the group, and later that year married Kathleen Neal, who had been active in the Student Nonviolent Coordinating Committee (SNCC; see ELLA BAKER). During 1968 Cleaver ran for the U.S. presidency on the ticket of the Peace and Freedom party, a black and white coalition. Because of a run-in with the Oakland police, however, Cleaver was charged with breaking parole, returned to prison, and released on a writ of habeas corpus. In November, he jumped bail and left for Cuba with his wife, then moved to Algiers (where a son was born). He made visits to North Korea (where a daughter was born), Moscow, and African countries, and eventually was granted asylum in Paris.

In 1975 Cleaver returned to the United States, pleaded guilty to old charges, and was placed on probation again. Declaring himself a born-again Christian, he published *Soul on Fire* (1976) about his conversion and was involved successively with BILLY GRAHAM, the Unification Church ("Moonies"), Mormonism, his own "Cleaver Crusade," and a Christian-Islamic sect he led, called Christlam. As a political right-winger he ran unsuccessfully for Congress and the U.S. Senate. In the late 1980s, in straits, he was arrested for cocaine possession and burglary.

**BIBLIOGRAPHY**

Scheer, Robert (ed.), *Eldridge Cleaver: Post-Prison Writings and Speeches*, 1969; Weisbrot, Robert, *Freedom Bound: A History of America's Civil Rights Movement*, 1990.

# Cloud, Henry Roe

(December 28, 1886–February 9, 1950)
American Indian Leader, Educator

Though ordained as a minister, Henry Roe Cloud focused his career on American Indian education and government administration. Under the New Deal he worked effectively to improve educational opportunities for Indian youth.

Henry Cloud was born to Winnebago parents in a tepee on the reservation in eastern Nebraska. His birth name, Wonah'ilayhunka, means "War Chief." He went to Indian mission schools until he was a teenager, when through the interest of a clergyman he was sent to the Mount Hermon School, near Northfield, Massachusetts. Later he met a missionary couple, the Reverend and Mrs. Walter C. Roe, who adopted him and encouraged him to go to Yale University. He was the first American Indian to earn degrees at Yale: an A.B. in 1910, and an M.A in 1914. Between the two degrees he studied at Oberlin College and at the Auburn Theological Seminary, in New York State, where he was ordained a Presbyterian minister in 1913, having added Roe to his name.

Cloud was chairman of a delegation of Winnebago who met with President William Howard Taft in 1912 and 1913. His forte, however, was in education, and the next year he was on a commission to survey the education of Indians. Under the aegis of his adoptive parents, he founded the Roe Indian Institute at Wichita, Kansas, in 1915, and was its president for thirteen years. The institute emphasized training for leadership, rather than the vocational approach of other schools. In 1923 Cloud served on the President's Committee of One Hundred, set up to review federal policy regarding Indians. In the late 1920s Cloud was on the staff of still another survey, by the Brookings Institution, and was joint author of its report to the Department of the Interior, which cast light on the poverty and wretchedness of reservation life and strongly challenged the Dawes General Allotment Act of 1887 depriving tribes of millions of acres of their land. The report had an evident effect in Washington.

Cloud was appointed a regional representative in the Bureau of Indian Affairs in 1931, and two years later President Franklin D. Roosevelt made him superintendent of the Haskell Institute, in Lawrence, Kansas, the country's largest Indian school. The appointment of Cloud, an American Indian, was indicative of the New Deal's enlightened policy of appointing Indian administrators whenever possible, as put into effect by the newly appointed head of the Bureau of Indian Affairs, John Collier. Cloud's concern to develop leaders was somewhat dampened by the vocational emphasis of the Haskell Institute's program, and he left in 1936 to join the Bureau of Indian Affairs as supervisor of Indian education, a post which allowed him greater freedom in implementing his reform programs.

Cloud's last post was as superintendent of Indian agencies in Oregon, where he encouraged the recording of family histories for Northwest Coast Indians as a basis for dividing a court settlement of $16 million, awarded to redress illegal confiscation of Indian land by early settlers.

Cloud had married Elizabeth Bender, a part-Chippewa, in 1916, and she worked with him in managing the American Indian Institute (the original Roe Institute). After Cloud's death, she continued to be involved in the National Congress of American Indians and for eight years was national chairman of Indian welfare for the General Federation of Women's Clubs.

**BIBLIOGRAPHY**

Dockstader, Frederick J., *Great North American Indians: Profiles in Life and Leadership*, 1977.

# Coffin, William Sloane, Jr.

(June 1, 1924–   )
Clergyman, Social Activist

As a Yale chaplain and then as minister of New York's prestigious Riverside Church, the Reverend William Sloane Coffin, Jr., became a leading critic of American foreign policy and an advocate of America's downtrodden.

Coffin was born in New York City, one of three children of an executive of the furniture company W. & J. Sloane. His mother was Catherine Butterfield. When young Coffin was nine his father died and his mother moved the family to Carmel, California. He showed promise as a pianist, and at age fourteen he was taken to Paris to study with a famous teacher, Nadia Boulanger. With the outbreak of World War II he came back and entered Phillips Andover Academy, in Andover, Massachusetts. Coffin studied for a year at the Yale University school of music and then went into the U.S. Army, where he was commissioned in the infantry.

Coffin's first duty was as a liaison officer with the French army. After an intensive course in Russian, he was assigned as a liaison officer with the Soviet army. At the war's end he was assigned to work at an internment camp in Germany for anti-Stalinist Russian soldiers who, he learned, were to be turned over to the Soviet army for transport to the USSR—a fate they were unaware of. Some of the soldiers committed suicide when they discovered where the boxcars they were boarding would take them. Coffin cannot forget his involuntary part in the operation. In a memoir, he spoke of his lifelong "burden of guilt," which influenced career decisions he later made.

Back at Yale in 1947, Coffin completed his B.A., majoring in government. He was named to a post in the Central Intelligence Agency (CIA) but decided instead to enroll at Union Theological Seminary. After a year he took the CIA appointment and was sent to Germany for three years in a project training anti-Soviet Russians for undercover work in the Soviet Union, an assignment that slightly allayed his guilt. He completed his preparation for the ministry at Yale University Divinity School with a B.D. in 1956 and, ordained a Presbyterian pastor, served year-long chaplaincies at Phillips Andover and at Williams College.

From 1958 to 1976, while Coffin was chaplain at Yale, he was deep into social activism that often took him away from the campus. In the summer of 1960, for Operation Crossroads Africa, he took a group of students to Guinea, in West Africa, to build a community center. For some years he was an adviser to the U.S. Peace Corps and director of a training center in Puerto Rico. In the 1960s Coffin joined the Freedom Riders to challenge segregation in the South (see JAMES FARMER) and was arrested several times for leading protests.

Having been a cofounder of Clergy and Laity Concerned about Vietnam, in 1967 Coffin opened his chapel at Yale as sanctuary for young men refusing service in the armed forces. That year, during an antiwar demonstration that he and Dr. BENJAMIN SPOCK organized in Boston, many young conscientious objectors turned in their draft cards. Coffin delivered the cards to the Department of Justice, which refused them. The next year he and Spock were convicted of conspiracy to abet disobeying the Selective Service Act, a charge that was later dropped. Coffin went to Hanoi, North Vietnam, in 1972, one of a "committee of liaison," to escort home three released prisoners of war.

Coffin resigned from Yale in 1976 and a year later was chosen, from among 250 candidates, to be senior minister of the Riverside Church in New York City. The church, interdenominational though nominally Baptist, was built at the expense of John D. Rockefeller, Jr.; it is notably progressive in its concern with social programs. Coffin, while continuing his international work for arms control with Clergy and

Laity Concerned, was involved with local groups, including many black parishioners, in facing such social problems as unemployment, juvenile delinquency, and drug traffic.

At Christmas 1979, Coffin was one of four Christian ministers who traveled to Teheran at the invitation of Iran's Revolutionary Council (but at their own expense) to visit the American hostages in the American Embassy and observe that they were not mistreated. Upon returning he urged that the U.S. government adopt a more "humble [and] religious" stance toward the captors and acknowledge the justice of some of Iran's grievances against the United States.

Coffin left Riverside Church in 1989 and took the executive directorship of the national body of SANE/FREEZE, a coalition working to end the arms race. He urged the dissolution of the North Atlantic Treaty Organization (NATO) and the destruction of short-range nuclear weapons. Americans, he has said, must understand that the United States is not morally superior to every other country and has its own record of "the very evils we profess to abhor." In 1990 he left the directorship to be president of national SANE/FREEZE.

**BIBLIOGRAPHY**

Coffin, W. S., Jr., *Once to Every Man: A Memoir*, 1978; Coffin, W. S., with Morris L. Leibman, *Civil Disobedience: Aid or Hindrance to Justice?* 1972.

## Commons, John Rogers

(October 13, 1862–May 11, 1945)
Economist, Labor Historian, Reformer

An institutional economist who helped shape social policy in Wisconsin and nationally, and the editor of two monumental works on industrial and labor history, John R. Commons contributed significantly to twentieth-century reform.

Born in Hollandsburg, Ohio, John R. Commons grew up in Indiana and earned his A.B. degree from Oberlin College in Ohio (see CHARLES GRANDISON FINNEY) in 1888. He then went to the Johns Hopkins University to study under the economist RICHARD T. ELY. Leaving after three years without taking a degree, he held a series of teaching posts at Wesleyan University in Connecticut (1890–1891), Oberlin College (1891–1892), Indiana University (1892–1895), and Syracuse University (1895–1899). In each case, the instructorship ended because of Commons's radical views.

A Christian Socialist, Commons published *Social Reform and the Church* in 1894. He believed that the churches could serve as agents to achieve reform, that conflicts between competing economic groups could be resolved peacefully, and that economics ought to be studied through field research.

In 1899 Commons opened the Bureau of Economic Research in New York City to collect data on prices for the Democratic National Committee. From 1902 to 1904 he served as assistant secretary of the National Civic Federation, in which position he advocated that the joint-conference method be used to resolve labor-management disagreements.

In 1904, at the invitation of Richard T. Ely, Commons returned to the University of Wisconsin, serving as a member of the department of political economy for the next thirty years. At the time, the "Wisconsin idea," which involved close teamwork between social scientists and the government, was in full swing under Governor Robert M. La Follette. Commons advised La Follette on railroad policy and, helped by his students, wrote Wisconsin's laws for the civil service, public utilities, and workers' compensation. In 1911 Commons played a major role in creating the Wisconsin Industrial Commission and served on it for the next two years. The commission sought to resolve labor and management issues by having representatives of both labor and management develop industrial codes—a practice that Commons had long believed in.

Commons joined with Ely and others in founding the American Association for Labor Legislation in 1906. He also served from 1913 to 1915 on the United States Commission on Industrial Relations, established by President Woodrow Wilson to look into labor unrest. In 1923 Commons represented four western states that alleged that the United States Steel Corporation had engaged in price discrimination. He also served as president of the National Consumers' League (1923–1925), which promoted passage of wage and price legislation and helped establish an unemployment insurance plan for workers in the garment industry. Frequently testifying before various congressional committees in Washington, D.C., Commons was instrumental in shaping the Social Security Act of 1935. Many of the programs that he and his students had helped launch in Wisconsin became models for New Deal reforms in the 1930s.

During these years, Commons was also engaged in scholarly work. Having taken over Richard T. Ely's project of collecting documents on the history of labor, Commons and his students conducted research across the country, publishing the ten-volume *Documentary History of American Industrial Society* in 1910 and 1911. As a conceptual framework for the series, Commons employed a stage analysis of economic development, emphasiz-

ing the contributions to the evolution of the American industrial system made by retailers and the growth of markets. A similar framework informed the first two volumes of *The History of Labor in the United States*, which were published in 1918 under Commons's editorship. (His students finished two more volumes that were published after he retired in 1935.) The guiding concepts of these two works came to be known as the Wisconsin school of economics.

Commons also published two important theoretical books, *The Legal Foundations of Capitalism* (1924) and *Institutional Economics* (1934). Unlike classical economists who believed that individuals were in the grip of economic forces beyond their control, Commons stressed the means by which collective or institutional action by groups such as corporations, trade unions, and governments could regulate and enlarge individual actions. He held that such institutional action was governed not by fixed laws but by changing laws and customs, and he looked to the courts to support wage and hour laws.

After his retirement and despite the personal tragedies of the death of his wife, his children, and his sister, Commons remained a productive scholar with a loyal following of students and disciples. He spent his last years in a trailer camp in Fort Lauderdale, Florida, dying in Raleigh, North Carolina, at the age of eighty-two.

**BIBLIOGRAPHY**

Commons, John R., *Myself,* 1943, and *The Economics of Collective Action,* 1950; Harter, Lafayette G., *John R. Commons: His Assault on Laissez-Faire,* 1962.

# Comstock, Anthony

(March 7, 1844–September 15, 1915)
Reformer

Anthony Comstock was such a well-known defender of the public morality of America in the late nineteenth and early twentieth century that his name became synonymous with moralistic censorship. Besides crusading against what he considered to be obscene books and pictures, Comstock exposed swindlers and medical quacks.

Born in New Canaan, Connecticut, Comstock was brought up a strict Congregationalist and attended public schools until he was eighteen. He then worked as a store clerk, and during this period an incident occurred that affected his later life. After shooting and killing a mad dog that was running wild in the streets, Comstock went after the dog's owner, who illegally exchanged groceries for whiskey. He broke into the man's house and emptied his supply of whiskey onto the floor. Later Comstock referred to his enemies as "mad dogs," pursuing them with similar relentlessness.

During the Civil War, Comstock served in the Union army from 1863 to 1865, then worked as a clerk and salesperson in Connecticut and New York City. Inspired by the Young Men's Christian Association's (YMCA) campaign against erotic books and pictures, Comstock in 1868 secured the arrest of two New York publishers under a state antiobscenity law. He relentlessly pursued one of these publishers, Charles Conroy, who some years later severely wounded Comstock in the face with a knife.

Library of Congress

In 1871 Comstock married Margaret Hamilton. That same year, Comstock offered his services to the YMCA's Committee for the Suppression of Vice, which he had helped to organize. Two years later, he left his store job to work with the New York Society for the Suppression of Vice. Also in 1873, Comstock went to Washington to lobby (successfully) for stricter laws barring obscene material from the mails. As a special agent of the postal service, serving without pay until 1906 when he was made to accept a salary of $1,500 a year, Comstock was the chief enforcer of these so-called Comstock laws.

In 1872 and 1873 Comstock gained national attention with his drive against two sisters, VICTORIA WOODHULL and TENNESSEE CLAFLIN. These women's rights activists and free-love advocates had printed in their weekly newspaper an exposé of HENRY WARD BEECHER's alleged adultery with the wife of one of his parishioners. Comstock had the sisters arrested on the charge of using the mails to circulate immoral material. Although the case against them collapsed and brought Comstock some ridicule, his campaign against vice spread to other cities, such as Boston, which formed its own Watch and Ward Society.

Comstock was merciless in his pursuit of those he felt were a menace to the public morality. Documented cases of at least fifteen suicides relating to his hounding exist, including that of Madam Restell, a New York abortionist and dispenser of contraceptives (then illegal), whom Comstock tricked into confessing her trade and then imprisoned.

While Comstock's campaigns drew wide support in the 1870s, in the next decade they began to meet with opposition, as Comstock included in his attacks people with socialist and freethinking views like Ezra Hervey Heywood and Robert Ingersoll. The British playwright George Bernard Shaw coined the term "comstockery" to describe the assault on so-called obscene literature. Shaw himself came under attack by Comstock, who in 1905 started legal proceedings to keep Shaw's play about prostitution, *Mrs. Warren's Profession,* from being performed in New York. But the court refused to close the play.

Directing his attention to art as well as literature, Comstock in 1887 raided the Herman Knoedler Gallery in New York and appropriated photographs of French art masterpieces.

In 1906 he also took action against the Art Students' League for using nude models.

Less publicized but more praiseworthy were Comstock's exposés of mail swindlers, fraudulent banking schemes, lotteries, and medical quacks. He wrote about his work in several books and pamphlets including *Frauds Exposed* (1880), *Traps for the Young* (1883), and *Gambling Outrages* (1895).

Comstock died of pneumonia at his home in Summit, New Jersey, at age seventy-one, still an active crusader.

**BIBLIOGRAPHY**

Bennett, D. M., *Anthony Comstock: His Career of Cruelty and Crime,* 1887, rep., 1970; Broun, Heywood, and Margaret Leech, *Anthony Comstock, Roundsman of the Lord,* 1927; Trumbell, C. G., *Anthony Comstock, Fighter,* 1913.

# Conant, James Bryant

(March 26, 1893–February 11, 1978)
Diplomat, Educator, Scientist

Though James B. Conant was a scientist in several fields, as well as a diplomat, he made his most important contribution as an educator and a researcher in American education. His studies led him to warn that the millions of unemployed youths in American cities were "social dynamite."

James Bryant Conant was born in Dorchester, a suburb of Boston, Massachusetts. Conant was a precocious chemistry student at the Roxbury Latin School. He entered Harvard University at age seventeen and graduated at age twenty, *magna cum laude.* He earned his doctorate in 1916. Conant taught chemistry at Harvard for seventeen years, except for two years in the army's Chemical Warfare Service during World War I and a year in Germany in 1925 studying university teaching. In organic chemistry, he did important research on the structure of chlorophyll (the green color factor of plants) and of hemoglobin (the color factor in red corpuscles).

From 1933 to 1953 Conant was president of Harvard, though during World War II he took on other responsibilities. As a firm anti-isolationist advocating international commitments, he spoke for universal military conscription and the 1941 lend-lease bill, which allowed countries vital to American defense more credit to buy or lease war supplies. And as chairman of the Office of Scientific Research and Development he was a leading adviser on the production of the atomic bomb and witnessed its first test in the New Mexico desert in July 1945. Conant advised the American delegation to the United Nations Atomic Energy Commission in 1947, and in 1950, he had an important role in founding the National Science Foundation.

Having introduced reforms at Harvard—in admissions policies, for example, so as to admit more non-Eastern U.S. students and those of limited means; in the improvement of teacher education; and in founding the Nieman Fellowships for journalists—Conant resigned from the presidency in 1953 upon being appointed U.S. High Commissioner for West Germany. When the occupation of West Germany ended in 1955, Conant became U.S. ambassador and served for two years.

With grants from the Carnegie Corporation in 1957, Conant undertook what is considered his principal contribution: a thorough study of American public high schools and teacher education. His book *Slums and Suburbs* (1961) was a ground-breaking document on the need for upgrading the education of poor children in urban areas. Conant warned that insufficient guidance for impoverished black youths would lead to social catastrophe. In *Shaping Educational Policy* (1964), he advocated decentralizing school administration while increasing cooperation between states. He advocated busing to urban high schools in order to promote integration. He continued to call for the improvement of teacher training, which he considered then to be "scandalous." For a time Conant was chairman of the board of the Educational Testing Service, in Princeton, New Jersey.

Conant, having retired in his later years, died at age eighty-four in a New Hampshire nursing home.

---

**BIBLIOGRAPHY**

Conant, James B., *The American High School Today*, 1959, *The Education of American Teachers*, 1963, *Shaping Educational Policy*, 1964, and *My Several Lives*, 1970.

## Conwell, Russell Herman

(February 15, 1843–December 6, 1925)
Educator, Philanthropist, Religious Leader

Russell Conwell was a Baptist minister and a popular lecturer. In his famous "Acres of Diamonds" speech, he maintained that everyone could and should get rich and become a philanthropist. His lecture earned him millions of dollars, much of which he donated to Temple University.

Conwell was born in Worthington, Massachusetts, into a poor abolitionist family, whose home was a way station on the Underground Railroad (see HARRIET TUBMAN). After attending Yale briefly, Conwell served as a captain in the Union army during the Civil War. He then earned his law degree from the Albany (New York) Law School and was admitted to the bar in 1865. Thereafter, he worked as a journalist, lecturer, and lawyer, first in Minneapolis, then in Boston.

Conwell had become an atheist while in school but had turned to religion after being severely wounded in the Civil War. He was ordained a Baptist minister in 1879 and was able through his preaching to revive the run-down First Baptist Church in Lexington, Massachusetts. From 1881 until his death Conwell was minister of the Grace Baptist Church in Philadelphia. When Conwell took charge, the church was in debt and had a small congregation. Under his leadership, the church flourished; in 1891 it was able to move to a new Baptist Temple with seating for 3,000 people.

In 1884 Conwell founded what became Temple University when a young printer told him he wanted to be a minister but could not afford to go to school. Conwell agreed to teach him and six of his friends during the evening in the church basement. As the number of students increased, it was necessary to enlist the help of more teachers and rent first one small house, then another. Within four years, a chartered college for working people was established, with Conwell as its first president and a student body of 590. During Conwell's lifetime, more than 100,000 students received instruction at Temple University. Conwell also founded Samaritan Hospital in 1891.

Much in demand as a lecturer, Conwell toured the country, giving his "Acres of Diamonds" speech more than 6,000 times in fifty-five years. In it, he stated that opportunity lurks in everyone's backyard, that everyone can and ought to become wealthy and then use his or her fortune for the benefit of humanity. Conwell advised his listeners to "Keep clean, fight hard, pick your openings judiciously, and have your eyes forever fixed on the heights toward which you are headed." Like the novels of HORATIO ALGER, Conwell's lecture served to re-

inforce the myth of the "self-made man," which held that anyone could rise from rags to riches through hard work and virtuous living. His lecture was also a variant of ANDREW CARNEGIE's "Gospel of Wealth" (1889), in that he urged wealthy people to use their money for the good of humanity. Like Carnegie and the industrialist and philanthropist JOHN D. ROCKEFELLER, who was also a Baptist, Conwell acted on his beliefs, financing Temple University and other philanthropic efforts with the nearly $8 million he received in fees and royalties from the printed form of his lecture. Conwell died in Philadelphia at the age of eighty-two.

**BIBLIOGRAPHY**

Burr, Agnes Rush, *Russell H. Conwell and His Work*, 1917; Carter, Joseph C., *The "Acres of Diamonds" Man*, 1981.

# Cooper, Peter

(February 12, 1791–April 4, 1883)
Industrialist, Inventor, Philanthropist

A highly successful industrialist and inventor, Peter Cooper was an early advocate of the idea that wealth is a public trust. Acting on this belief, Cooper founded Cooper Union, an adult education institute in New York City for the working class.

According to Cooper, "The duty and pleasure of every rich man [was] to do something in a public way for the education and uplifting of the common people." He greatly influenced later philanthropists like ANDREW CARNEGIE.

Peter Cooper was born in New York City. Although largely self-educated and only barely literate, he had great manual dexterity and a remarkable knack for inventing things. At seventeen, Cooper invented a machine for joining the hubs of carriage wheels. Later, as the owner

of a glue factory, Cooper so perfected production techniques that he was able to supply virtually the entire demand for glue in America.

In 1828 Cooper used part of the fortune he had made from his glue factory to establish the Canton Iron Works in Baltimore. The next year, with iron obtained at Canton, he built the *Tom Thumb*, the first steam locomotive to be constructed in America, for the Baltimore & Ohio Railroad.

Shrewdly recognizing the need for "iron rails" that would accompany the growth of railroads, Cooper invested all his wealth in building additional iron works in New York, New Jersey, and Pennsylvania. The rolling mill he constructed at Trenton, New Jersey, became, with the help of several of his patented inventions, one of the largest iron production sites in the country. It was also the first in America to use the Bessemer process for making steel faster and more cheaply.

Cooper was always alert to the investment possibilities provided by new inventions. When banks would not finance the laying of a telegraph cable across the Atlantic, he became the president of the New York, Newfoundland & London Telegraph Company and personally provided the money to accomplish the task. He also served as president of the North American Telegraph Company, the largest owner of domestic cable telegraph lines in America.

In addition to business acumen, Cooper possessed a keen sense of social responsibility. As an alderman in New York City, he supported the creation of paid police and fire departments, an improved water supply, and small parks and squares. Cooper also served on the New York City board of education for many years. He was a staunch supporter of free public education and was against using public funds to finance parochial schools.

From 1857 to 1859, Cooper established the Cooper Union for the Advancement of Science and Art. This unique and still thriving institution fulfilled Cooper's vision of a place where access to free technical courses, public lectures, and a library would enable working-class people to improve the quality of their lives. Ever the champion of "poor toilers and producers," Cooper attacked privilege and en-

Library of Congress

dorsed efforts to make economic opportunity equally available to everyone. He was in favor of abolishing slavery, eliminating corruption in city government, establishing a civil service system, implementing government regulation of railroad rates, and adopting progressive taxation.

In his emphasis on the need for government to promote the general good and to regulate industry, Cooper anticipated the major thrusts of twentieth-century reform movements.

Cooper set forth his views in public addresses and pamphlets. Two collections of his writings are *Political and Financial Opinions of Peter Cooper* (1877) and *Ideas for a Science of Good Government* (1883).

Cooper supported the goal of the National Independent party (Greenbackers) for the introduction of paper currency. As the party's candidate for president in 1876, he polled about 82,000 of the 8.5 million votes cast. In the early 1880s, when Cooper was over ninety years of age, he became a leader of the National Anti-Monopoly League, which opposed the spread of trusts.

**BIBLIOGRAPHY**

Mack, E. C., *Peter Cooper of New York*, 1949; Nevins, Allan, *Abram S. Hewit: With Some Account of Peter Cooper*, 1935; Raymond, R. W., *Peter Cooper*, 1901.

# Coughlin, Charles Edward

(October 25, 1891–October 27, 1979)
Political Dissident, Roman Catholic Priest

Father Coughlin, known as the "radio priest" of the era of the Great Depression, turned from liberal views to bigotry as he espoused hatred of such targets as the New Deal, Jews, union labor, and communism. He was eventually silenced by the Roman Catholic church.

Coughlin was born in Hamilton, Ontario, the son of Irish parents. His father, Thomas J. Coughlin, worked as a stoker on Great Lakes ships and later as a sexton; his mother, Amelia Mahoney, was a seamstress. An only child, Coughlin grew up literally in the ambiance of the Roman Catholic church: his parents' house stood between St. Mary's Cathedral and a parish school. At twelve he began high school in Toronto at St. Michael's College, under the Basilian Fathers, an order strongly influenced by the social activism preached by Pope Leo XIII. Continuing as an undergraduate, he earned a name as an orator and debater. In 1911, having decided to join the priesthood, Coughlin entered St. Basil's Seminary, also under the Basilians, who filled him with ideals of social and economic justice.

Coughlin was ordained on June 29, 1916, and later returned to Hamilton to celebrate his first public mass in St. Mary's Cathedral in the presence of his devout mother. He was assigned to teach and coach football at Assumption College, near Windsor, Ontario, across the river from Detroit. His reputation as a speaker brought invitations to address Catholic organizations as well as secular groups in Detroit and Windsor. In 1923 he decided to leave the Basilians and work as a parish priest.

The bishop of the archdiocese of Detroit first assigned Coughlin to assist pastors of large churches in the cities, and then in 1926, to work in a parish in Royal Oak, a suburban community north of Detroit, which was expanding as auto workers moved in. The older residents, mostly Protestants, were hostile to Catholics and "foreigners," and many joined the Ku Klux Klan. When the Klan burned a fiery cross in front of the church, which was named the Shrine of the Little Flower, Coughlin searched for a way to attract sympathy and much-needed financial support. His solution was to arrange to broadcast his sermons, explaining Catholicism and criticizing the Klan, over radio station WJR in Detroit. His eloquence and commanding personality began to win him a popular response. He was said to have "one of the great speaking voices of the twentieth century." By 1930, when the Columbia Broadcasting System (CBS) opened its national network to Coughlin, he was reaching a public close to 40 million people.

Meanwhile, contributions were pouring in, and in 1928 Coughlin began building a new Shrine of the Little Flower, with a seven-story tower, a huge statue of Christ, and a splendid rectory for himself and his growing staff. The emphasis of his radio sermons had been mainly religious, but after the stock market crash of 1929, the beginning of the Great Depression, and the rise of unemployment, Coughlin turned more and more to political issues. He attacked not only communism but also Wall Street, the worship of money, international bankers, and capitalism in general. In 1932 he assailed Prohibition as the cause of crime and gangsterism and spoke as a champion of the jobless veterans of World War I. He supported the presidential candidacy of Franklin D. Roosevelt with the slogan "Roosevelt or Ruin!" and after his election strongly supported him and the New Deal; for a time they had friendly personal relations. He styled himself the advocate of the "little guy," of the ordinary American who had suffered greatly during the depression but who was powerless to alter his fate. Millions of Americans came to feel that Coughlin spoke for them.

But the New Deal moved too slowly for Coughlin. In 1934 he founded the National Union for Social Justice and began to turn against Roosevelt. In 1935 he agitated against United States membership in the World Court and influenced its rejection by the Senate. A year later he started a weekly newspaper, *Social Justice*, and joined GERALD L. K. SMITH and FRANCIS E. TOWNSEND in founding the Union party, which nominated William Lemke for the presidency. When Coughlin called Roosevelt a liar, his bishop made him apologize, though he later withdrew the apology. Meanwhile, CBS dropped the broadcasts because of their controversial nature, and Coughlin organized his own radio network.

By 1936 Coughlin's political sympathies had shifted sharply to the right. Hatred of Roosevelt became Coughlin's fixed idea. He called the New Deal a communist conspiracy leading to dictatorship, and he began to voice anti-Semitic diatribes, directed especially at Jewish financiers, in his broadcasts and in *Social Justice*, along with praise of the fascism of Hitler and Mussolini. He in turn was praised by the leaders of the pro-Nazi German American Bund, and the Christian Front, organized by Coughlin's followers in some cities, behaved like Nazi storm troopers. He lashed out against organized labor, would not employ union members, and helped HENRY FORD fight the unionization of his company.

After the outbreak of World War II in 1939, Coughlin allied himself with the isolationist faction and continued to praise the Axis powers, saying that the war had been caused by a British-Jewish-Roosevelt conspiracy. His following fell away; under pressure of the Catholic hierarchy he was forced to stop broadcasting; and *Social Justice* was barred from the mails as seditious. Coughlin remained parish priest of the Shrine of the Little Flower for twenty-four more years until pressed to retire; he then lived quietly in a wealthy Detroit suburb until he died at age eighty-eight.

**BIBLIOGRAPHY**

Brinkley, Alan, *Voices of Protest: Huey Long, Father Coughlin, and the Great Depression*, 1982; Marcus, Sheldon, *Father Coughlin: The Tumultuous Life of the Priest of the Little Flower*, 1973.

## Cox, Harvey Gallagher, Jr.

(May 19, 1929–   )
Religious Activist

Harvey Cox, a Baptist clergyman and professor of theology, has been an outspoken advocate of civil rights, liberal theology, nuclear disarmament, and world peace.

Harvey Cox was born and brought up in the suburbs west of Philadelphia, Pennsylvania. His father had a painting and wallpapering business which went under in 1940, after which he worked in a factory until his death in 1955. The family was conservative Baptist, though Harvey Cox, Sr., seldom went to church until his late years. Harvey, Jr., earned a B.A. at the University of Pennsylvania in 1951 and went on to the Yale University Divinity School. When he took a year off to be Protestant chaplain at Temple University, in Philadelphia, Cox discovered that most of the Baptist students there were black, and he got to know the black Baptist churches. After receiving his B.D. degree in 1955, Cox became director of religious activities at Oberlin College, in Ohio, where he invited MARTIN LUTHER KING, JR., to speak. The next year Cox was ordained a minister of the American Baptist Church.

From 1958 to 1962 Cox was associated with the American Baptist Home Mission Society while working toward a Ph.D. in the history and philosophy of religion at Harvard. Having completed his doctorate, Cox with his wife and two small children went to Berlin for a year as an "ecumenical fraternal worker" at the Gossner Mission in the city's eastern (communist-controlled) zone. He met with study groups and participated in a Christian-Marxist dialogue with East Germans that gave him insight into their views.

Cox's subsequent career was academic in its structure and wide-ranging in its commitments. He taught briefly at the Andover Newton Theological School, outside Boston, then joined the faculty of the Divinity School at Harvard, where in 1970 he became a full professor. His first book, *The Secular City* (1965), brought him to wide attention for his analysis of how American Christians should reconcile faith and worship with the realities of today's urban society. His prolific writings and lectures exhibit a notable breadth, tolerance, and curiosity.

In 1963 the Cox family moved into a house in Roxbury, a black neighborhood in southwest Boston. Cox was working with an inner-city ministry in the area, the Blue Hill Christian Center, that wanted, as he wrote, "to make a statement about racial integration." At the center, Cox founded the first northern chapter of the Southern Christian Leadership Conference (SCLC; see RALPH D. ABERNATHY and MARTIN LUTHER KING, JR.). A few weeks later, at the invitation of Martin Luther King, Jr., Cox and other members of the Boston SCLC went to Williamston, in eastern North Carolina, to join a nonviolent march protesting segregation. Cox and the others, along with black marchers, were arrested, jailed, and mistreated. Cox later was with King in demonstrations in Selma, Alabama, and St. Augustine, Florida. Cox named his son Martin after King and his daughter Sarah after Sarah Small, an SCLC leader in Williamston.

In later years, Cox has traveled extensively in Latin America, studying liberation theology with Catholic and Protestant leaders. He went to Rome to investigate a Catholic community called St. Paul's, in which the laity conduct the services—similar to a Baptist congregation he belongs to in Cambridge. In support of nuclear disarmament Cox visited Hiroshima, protested in Utah against the MX missile system, and led a nationwide movement to bring about a bilateral nuclear freeze.

**BIBLIOGRAPHY**

Cox, Harvey, *Just as I Am*, 1983, and *Many Mansions: A Christian's Encounter with Other Faiths*, 1988.

# Coxey, Jacob Sechler

(April 16, 1854–May 18, 1951)
Reformer

Jacob Coxey vividly dramatized the plight of the unemployed by leading a march on Washington, known as Coxey's Army, to demand relief during the depression of the mid-1890s.

Born in Selinsgrove, Pennsylvania, Jacob Coxey quit school at the age of fifteen in order to work in an iron mill. He later opened a sandstone factory in Massillon, Ohio, in 1881. Coxey joined the Greenback wing of the Democratic party, which supported the issuing of paper money without specie backing in order to increase the amount of money in circulation and help people pay their debts.

During the depression of 1893—the worst period of hard times the nation had then known—Coxey's sympathy for the large numbers of people thrown out of work led him to come up with a plan to help them. He proposed that the federal government undertake a gigantic program of road construction that would be financed by issuing $500 million in new greenbacks. This program would increase the amount of money in circulation, while providing jobs for the unemployed and relieving distress. Coxey also proposed that state and local governments be authorized to borrow federal funds, again in greenbacks, to finance public works, giving as security non–interest-bearing bonds. Coxey's plan might have attracted little attention had he not teamed up with Carl Browne, a flamboyant cartoonist and sideshow medicine man, who told him about marches of the jobless in California. Coxey then decided to make his own march on Washington.

Library of Congress

On March 25, 1894, "Coxey's Army," numbering 100 marchers, left Massillon, Ohio. The army grew to about 500 marchers and attracted a great deal of national publicity. Some people regarded it as a genuine threat, while others dismissed it as a mere curiosity.

Reaching Washington on May 1, Coxey's marchers paraded down Pennsylvania Avenue with much fanfare but were halted by police just short of the Capitol. Coxey and a few others made a rush for the Capitol steps and were arrested for walking on the lawn. Although "Coxey's Army" and other arriving "armies" remained encamped in the capital until August, Congress did nothing to help the unemployed. Coxey's plan received a brief hearing before being buried in a congressional committee.

Nevertheless, Coxey had succeeded in calling attention to the plight of the jobless in a unique way. His march may well have contributed to the ground swell of support for the Populist party that enabled it to elect six senators and seven congressmen in 1894. Running for Congress himself in the fall of 1894, Coxey won 21 percent of the vote.

Throughout the rest of his long life, General Coxey, as he was ever afterward known, was a perennial candidate for office on various tickets. He ran and was defeated for governor of Ohio in 1897, for the U.S. Congress in 1924 and 1926, for the U.S. Senate in 1916 and 1928, and for president of the United States in 1932 on the Farmer-Labor ticket. Finally in 1931, at the age of seventy-seven, Coxey won election as mayor of Massillon on the Republican ticket, but lost his bid for reelection in 1933.

Meanwhile, Coxey also continued to lobby Congress in behalf of his plan. In 1914 he led another and smaller march on Washington, in which he was able to speak from the Capitol steps. The closest his plan came to acceptance was during the recession of 1927 and 1928 when it fell only one vote short of a favorable report from a House committee. In 1944, at the age of ninety, Coxey again addressed a small audience from the Capitol steps, claiming that he was finishing the speech he had begun fifty years earlier. He died in Massillon seven years later.

Although Coxey's monetary ideas never caught on, his proposal that the government finance public works projects to relieve unemployment was incorporated into the New Deal of President Franklin D. Roosevelt during the Great Depression of the 1930s. Moreover, his tactic of marching on Washington was used by later groups of the jobless and destitute to call attention to their plight.

**BIBLIOGRAPHY**

Foner, Philip S., *History of the Labor Movement in the United States,* vol. 2, 1955; McMurry, Donald, *Coxey's Army: A Study of the Industrial Army Movement of 1894,* 1929.

# Croly, Herbert David

(January 23, 1869–May 17, 1930)
Author, Journalist, Reformer

As the author of *The Promise of American Life* (1909) and the founding editor of *The New Republic,* Herbert Croly was a major spokesperson for reform during the Progressive era.

Croly was born in New York City, the son of two prominent journalists and social activists, Jane Cunningham Croly, who wrote under the pen name of Jennie June, and David Goodman Croly. Herbert was especially influenced by his father, who believed that scientific laws could be used to manage the perfect society.

Croly's formal schooling included attendance at a private school in New York, the City College of New York, and several interrupted years at Harvard University. After his father's death in 1893, Croly edited a real estate paper, *The Record and Guide,* and served on the staff of the *Architectural Record.* That same year he suffered a nervous breakdown.

Returning to Harvard for what was a third time in 1895, Croly had as teachers the eminent philosophers WILLIAM JAMES, Josiah Royce, and George Santayana. When he left after four years of study, though without taking a degree, he went back to the staff of the *Architectural Record.* (In 1910 Harvard granted Croly a courtesy bachelor's degree.)

Croly served as the editor of the *Architectural Record* from 1900 to 1906, then left the staff to write his most famous book, *The Promise of American Life.* Published in 1909, the book soon attracted national attention.

Croly defined the "promise" of American life as "an improving popular economic condition, guaranteed by democratic political institutions" and bringing about social betterment. He believed that past efforts to realize this promise were ill-suited to a present marked by the rise of giant corporations and organized labor, as well as by the entry of the United States into world affairs. Croly wanted to revise national goals and democratic institutions by attracting able and disinterested people to serve government in the national interest. He envisioned a strong national government serving broad democratic interests and watched by independent critics; the government would control and direct the activities of corporations, redistribute income, and maintain international peace through a system of perpetual reform.

Among those who read and were influenced by Croly's book was former president Theodore Roosevelt. The two men met and corresponded and Roosevelt incorporated many of Croly's ideas into his "New Nationalism" campaign for the presidency waged from 1910 to 1912. Croly's ideas also had an impact upon the "New Freedom" of Roosevelt's opponent, Democrat Woodrow Wilson, who won the election.

In 1914 Croly extended his influence as a critic-reformer when, thanks to the generosity of Willard and Dorothy Whitney Straight, he was able to found a weekly journal called *The New Republic.* Intended for an educated, liberal readership, Croly's magazine was staffed by such distinguished journalists as WALTER LIPPMANN.

By the time the first issue of *The New Republic* appeared, war had already broken out in Europe. Croly used the journal's pages to urge President Wilson to lead the neutral nations in a world reform effort. Later he backed the entrance of the United States into World War I but parted company with Wilson over the Treaty of Versailles. His opposition to the treaty, however, lost readership for *The New Republic.*

Disillusioned by the abandonment of reform that came with President Warren G. Harding's "return to normalcy," Croly looked to third-party candidates to accomplish his program. In the election of 1924 he supported Robert M. La Follette of the Progressive party. Also during the 1920s, Croly let slip his editorial leadership of *The New Republic,* and it became more diversified in its point of view. In a few years Croly had turned his interest from politics to religion and philosophy. In 1928 he suffered a stroke and retired from *The New Republic* and moved to Santa Barbara, California. He died two years later.

**BIBLIOGRAPHY**

Forcey, Charles, *The Crossroads of Liberalism: Croly, Weyl, Lippmann and the Progressive Era, 1900–1925,* 1961; Kesselman, S., *The Modernization of American Reform,* 1979; Lasch, Christopher, *The New Radicalism in America,* 1961.

# Dana, Charles Anderson

(August 8, 1819–October 17, 1897)
Editor

As an editor successively of two great New York newspapers, the *Tribune* and the *Sun,* Charles A. Dana exerted a powerful influence on public opinion. During the Civil War, he was an important link between General Ulysses S. Grant and President Abraham Lincoln and a tenacious investigator of corruption in the army.

Charles A. Dana was born at Hinsdale, in southwest New Hampshire, of Puritan ancestry. His father kept a country store, failed in business, and turned to farming; his mother died when he was nine. As a farm boy Dana learned Latin on his own, and when he was sent to Buffalo to work in an uncle's store he read widely and learned Greek. He entered Harvard University at age twenty, having qualified by his independent study, but had to drop out two years later because his eyesight became impaired. (Twenty years afterward, Harvard gave Dana an honorary A.B.)

Fired by idealism, young Dana joined Brook Farm, an experimental enterprise in West Roxbury, Massachusetts, based on communal living (see MARGARET FULLER and RALPH WALDO EMERSON). For five years he was active at Brook Farm as a teacher of languages, a farm worker, a managing trustee, and a writer for the *Dial.* When the venture had to close in 1846 because of a devastating fire, Dana turned to journalism and, after a year on a Boston paper, became city editor of the *New York Tribune,* founded in 1841 by HORACE GREELEY, who had met him on a visit to Brook Farm.

For fifteen years Dana, eventually as managing editor, was second in command of the *Tribune.* Greeley sent him to Europe from 1848 to 1849 to cover the revolutionary movements that were beginning to challenge kings and autocrats, and Dana's intelligent, honest, and colorful dispatches to the *Tribune* and other journals brought realities home to

Americans. His experiences also helped to dispel many of his idealistic illusions and turn him toward cynicism. In spite of the *Tribune*'s demands on his time, he edited *The Household Book of Poetry* (1857), an enormously successful anthology, and, in collaboration with George Ripley, who was at both Brook Farm and the *Tribune* with him, the *New American Cyclopaedia* in fifteen volumes. As a newspaperman he had a compact, fresh, epigrammatic style. His editorials blended Whig orthodoxy with reform principles; he advocated a railway to the Pacific, the abolition of slavery, and a high protective tariff, while opposing labor unions and strikes. Upon the outbreak of the Civil War, Dana and Greeley began to draw apart. Their strong personalities clashed, and Greeley demanded Dana's resignation in March 1862.

Dana complied and shortly thereafter was recruited by Secretary of War E. M. Stanton, who sent him as a special investigator to General Grant's headquarters in Mississippi. Ostensibly he was to look into the conduct of the paymaster service, but in fact he was to report on military operations and enable President Lincoln to take stock of Grant's capabilities. Dana at once saw Grant's superior qualities and so reported. His dispatches, almost daily, brought home to the president what Dana perceived—that Grant was "the most modest, the most disinterested and the most honest man I ever knew." Dana furthermore uncovered an alarming degree of corruption and fraud among the army's quartermasters and contractors. Dana in his reports praised the bravery of the black troops fighting under Grant.

Dana was subsequently made an assistant secretary of war, serving in the Washington office and in the field in Virginia. His *Recollections of the Civil War,* published in 1898 after his death, are a valuable record of the time. He left Washington a few weeks after Appomattox, edited an unsuccessful paper in Chicago for two years, then returned east for what proved to be the most significant part of his career— the editorship and part ownership of the New York *Sun,* which he carried to the end of his life. Dana established high standards of news reporting and writing; it was said that his own simple, strong, clear style became the style of the *Sun.* He recruited famous newspapermen and put a premium on giving the news, maintaining an excellent corps of foreign correspondents, and featuring "human interest" stories, which attracted a literate class of readers. The *Sun* was known as the "newspaperman's newspaper." Dana's views, expressed in editorials and news policy, were sometimes prejudiced and hardheaded. He often seemed motivated by personal animosity. For allegations of corruption, he attacked Grant, whom he had formerly honored. Though nominally a Liberal Republican, he gave only lukewarm support to Greeley, candidate of both that party and the Democrats, who lost to Grant. When the civil service was reformed in 1883, Dana criticized it as a "German bureaucratic system." He wanted to annex Cuba and if possible Canada, and continued to be hostile to labor unions. He supported a losing candidate in every presidential election until 1896, when he came out for William McKinley and opposed William Jennings Bryan on the free-silver issue. (Bryan was in favor of the federal government replacing gold dollars with the free coinage of silver in order to help debtors and farmers.) When he died the following year at his estate near Glen Cove, Long Island, colorful obituaries appeared in all the New York papers except, as he wished, in the *Sun.*

**BIBLIOGRAPHY**

Dana, Charles A., *Eastern Journeys, Notes of Travel,* 1898, and *The Art of Newspaper Making,* 1900; Stone, Candace, *Dana and the Sun,* 1938; Wilson, J. H., *The Life of Charles A. Dana,* 1907.

# Dana, Richard Henry, Jr.

(August 1, 1815–January 6, 1882)
Author, Lawyer, Reformer

Best known as the author of *Two Years Before the Mast*, a classic account of an ocean voyage from Massachusetts to California and back, Richard Henry Dana, Jr., was also one of the most influential lawyers of his day in the cause of antislavery.

Born in Cambridge, Massachusetts, into an illustrious family, Dana entered Harvard College in 1831 but left after two years because of eye trouble. In an effort to regain his health, he set sail on a voyage around Cape Horn to California as a common sailor on the brig *Pilgrim*. Returning to Boston in 1836, Dana resumed his studies at Harvard and earned his degree a year later. He then studied law and was admitted to the bar in 1840. That same year, *Two Years Before the Mast* was published and immediately became popular. Written "to enlighten the public as to the real situation of common seamen," the book also helped to spark interest in California, which was then a province of Mexico. Dana went on to specialize in admiralty law and produced a manual, *The Seaman's Friend.*

Although Dana rejected the radical abolitionism of leaders like WILLIAM LLOYD GARRISON, he nevertheless became involved in antislavery politics, helping to found the Free-Soil party (see GERRIT SMITH) in 1848. After Congress passed the Fugitive Slave Act of 1850, Dana took part in the defense of both runaway slaves and the abolitionists who attempted to rescue them. His most famous case involved the fugitive slave Anthony Burns in 1854. Dana lost the case but won considerable sympathy for the antislavery cause.

As United States district attorney for Massachusetts during the Civil War, Dana prosecuted slave traders. He also rendered an important service to the Union cause by convincing the U.S. Supreme Court to uphold the expansion of federal authority necessary to blockade Confederate ports.

In his remaining years, Dana suffered disappointments. In 1868 he was badly defeated in his bid for Congress. Then in 1876, when he was appointed U.S. ambassador to Britain by President Ulysses S. Grant, the Senate refused to confirm his nomination. Two years later, on a trip to Europe to study international law, he died suddenly in Rome at the age of sixty-six.

**BIBLIOGRAPHY**

Gale, R. L., *Richard Henry Dana, Jr.*, 1969; Lucid, R. F. (ed.), *The Journal of Richard Henry Dana, Jr.*, 3 vols., 1968; Shapiro, S., *Richard Henry Dana, Jr. 1815–1882*, 1961.

# Darrow, Clarence Seward

(April 18, 1857–March 13, 1938)
Lawyer, Reformer

One of the most brilliant trial lawyers of his time, Clarence Darrow used his remarkable abilities in the courtroom to defend the common person in a number of celebrated cases involving labor leaders, poor people, African Americans, and a Tennessee schoolteacher who challenged the state law against teaching evolution.

Darrow was born in Kinsman, Ohio, to parents who were abolitionists. Schooled at Allegheny College in Pennsylvania and the University of Michigan Law School and trained in a Youngstown, Ohio, law office, he was admitted to the bar in 1878. Darrow practiced law in Ohio for nine years, then moved to Chicago, where he became junior law partner to JOHN PETER ALTGELD, a reformer. Darrow, Altgeld, and others tried to win amnesty for four of the eight union organizers convicted in the 1887 Haymarket riot case (four had already been hanged). When Altgeld became governor, he issued the desired pardon.

In 1894 Darrow left his job as a corporation counsel for Chicago to defend EUGENE V. DEBS and other American Railway Union leaders against contempt charges brought about as a result of the Pullman Company railroad strike. Though unsuccessful, the case gave Darrow a national reputation as a labor lawyer. He served as chief counsel to the United Mine Workers in the coal strike of 1902 and five years later won the acquittal of WILLIAM D. HAYWOOD, C. H. Moyer, and George Pettibone, officials of the Western Federation of Miners, for complicity in the assassination of former governor Frank Steunenberg of Idaho in 1905.

Library of Congress

The turning point in Darrow's career as a labor lawyer came in 1911. Defending two socialists accused of planting a bomb that killed twenty-one people, Darrow learned of his clients' guilt. He advised them to plead guilty and to request the mercy of the court on the grounds that they had not intended to hurt anyone. The case prompted labor leaders to accuse Darrow of selling the men out. In addition to this challenge to his professional integrity, Darrow's reputation was sullied when a private detective who had been caught trying to bribe a juror claimed that Darrow had put him up to it. Darrow won acquittal on the bribery charges, but his law practice was ruined.

At age fifty-four, unable to earn a living as a labor or corporate lawyer, Darrow began a third career as a criminal lawyer willing to handle unpopular cases. He worked for a fraction of his former fees but discovered a tremendous satisfaction in helping the indigent. He also established important legal precedents and raised the national consciousness about freedom of speech, civil rights, and capital punishment (which Darrow regarded as legalized murder). Only one of the fifty clients charged with murder he agreed to defend was ever sentenced to death.

In 1924 Darrow represented Richard Loeb and Nathan Leopold, Jr., the young sons of two wealthy and distinguished Chicago families, in "the crime of the century." Loeb and Leopold had murdered thirteen-year-old Bobby Franks to see if they felt remorse. They did not. Since there was no question as to their guilt, Darrow had to come up with another way to cheat the gallows. Using psychiatric evidence to prove that his clients had been temporarily insane, Darrow won for them sentences of life imprisonment instead of the death penalty. This was the first time an insanity plea had been successfully employed as a defense in a murder case in the United States.

The following year Darrow agreed to defend public schoolteacher John L. Scopes, who had violated a Tennessee law against the teaching of Darwin's theory of evolution. The Scopes "Monkey Trial" attracted tremendous national attention. While movie cameras rolled and reporters furiously scribbled notes, Darrow, an agnostic, squared off with several-time presidential candidate William Jennings Bryan, a religious fundamentalist. Technically, Darrow lost the case; Scopes was convicted and fined. But Darrow accomplished his real goal of using the trial to point out the absurdity of trying to reconcile evolutionary science with a literal belief in the biblical story of the creation.

In 1925 and 1926 Darrow scored a victory for social justice when he successfully defended an African American family in Detroit who had used force against a white mob trying to evict them from their home in a white neighborhood.

Besides handling his law practice, Darrow participated in politics as an independent Democrat, serving in the Illinois state legislature for a few years in the early 1900s. In 1934 President Franklin D. Roosevelt made Darrow chair of a board charged with judging whether or not the National Industrial Recovery Act (1933) harmed small businesses. Darrow's committee was sharply critical of the act.

The same eloquence and strong convictions that made Darrow so impressive in the courtroom made him a popular lecturer and debater on topics ranging from religion to the reform of the judicial and penal systems. Darrow also published a number of books, including a novel and an autobiography.

**BIBLIOGRAPHY**

Darrow, Clarence, *Crime, Its Cause and Treatment,* 1922, and *The Story of My Life,* 1932; Ravitz, Abe C., *Clarence Darrow and American Literary Tradition,* 1962; Tierney, Keven, *Darrow,* 1979; Weinberg, Arthur, and Lila Weinberg, *Clarence Darrow: A Sentimental Rebel,* 1980.

# Day, Dorothy

(November 8, 1897–November 29, 1980)
Reformer, Religious Leader

Dorothy Day, besides founding the Catholic Worker movement, was a prominent advocate for social justice. A nonviolent social radical and a devout Roman Catholic, Dorothy Day played a seminal role in developing the social and economic thinking of a generation of American Catholic priests and laypersons.

Day was born a Protestant in Brooklyn, New York, and raised by her sports writer father, an agnostic, to be indifferent toward religion. She grew up in the Bay Area of California and Chicago. After attending the University of Illinois for two years on a scholarship, Day moved back to New York with her family in 1916. She joined the Industrial Workers of the World (IWW, known as the Wobblies; see WILLIAM D. HAYWOOD) and for two years she worked as a reporter for *The Call,* a socialist daily newspaper, covering strikes, protests, and walkouts.

When she left *The Call* she wrote for two other radical publications, *The Masses* and *The Liberator.*

During this period Day adopted a Bohemian life-style and became an intimate member of the radical intellectual circle of socialist writers and artists centered in Greenwich Village. The birth of her daughter in 1927 from a liaison with Forster Batterham (a biologist, atheist, and anarchist) prompted her to dramatically reorient her life to conform with a long-felt need to find a spiritual foundation for human existence. Against her common-law husband's desire, Day had her baby baptized a Roman Catholic, and then entered the Catholic church herself. Although her actions terminated her relationship with Batterham, she never regretted her choice.

Day did not sacrifice her commitment to radical social ideas when she became a Catholic. She brought them with her, maintaining her radical attitudes in matters of social justice, race relations, pacifism, and conscientious objection to military service, though adhering to traditional Catholic teaching about theological issues. "When it comes to labor and politics," she once said, "I am inclined to be sympathetic to the left, but when it comes to the Catholic Church, then I am far to the right."

Through her work for *Commonweal,* a liberal Catholic magazine, she met Peter Maurin. He had a utopian vision for creating a future world that coincided with Day's hunger to combine her radical political ideas and Catholicism. They decided in 1933 to publish *The Catholic Worker,* a penny monthly newspaper for Catholics that focused on social issues. They also opened a hospice in New York to provide meals and temporary lodging for some of the Great Depression's unemployed, as well as for destitute families and derelicts. It became a prototype for Catholic hospices across the nation, some thirty of which were set up.

The early articles in *The Catholic Worker* publicized the social programs of the Catholic church and dealt with poverty and problems of unemployment. Concern for the downtrodden in society continued to dominate the publication long after the Great Depression, but it gradually became recognized just as much for its support of interracial justice, pacifism, and disarmament. Day's social policy, expressed in her actions and in *The Catholic Worker,* looked to the person rather than to mass action to transform society, but she remained committed to a vision of a radically improved world. She was sometimes arrested in demonstrations—typically in 1973 with CESAR CHAVEZ and his striking United Farm Workers.

Day's social activism frequently brought her into conflict with conservative Catholic church officials, but she was never ordered to curtail her behavior or leave the church. She liked to describe herself as a "Christian anarchist," which meant that she was often at odds with church officials but always animated by the spirit of love that she found perfectly exemplified in the life of Christ.

**BIBLIOGRAPHY**

Coles, Robert, *Dorothy Day: A Radical Devotion,* 1987; Ellesberg, Robert (ed.), *By Little and By Little: The Selected Writings of Dorothy Day,* 1983; Miller, William, *Dorothy Day: A Biography,* 1982; Piehl, Mel, *Breaking Bread: The Catholic Worker and the Origin of Catholic Radicalism in America,* 1982.

# De Bow, James Dunwoody Brownson

(July 10, 1820–February 27, 1867)
Editor, Statistician

James D. B. De Bow championed development and diversification of the southern economy many years before the Civil War; in 1846 he began publishing his *Commercial Review of the South and Southwest*, whose issues, in one scholar's words, provide "a superb window into the southern mind during the years before secession."

James D. B. De Bow was born in Charleston, South Carolina, one of two sons of a merchant from New Jersey who had lost his fortune. Orphaned as a boy, De Bow managed to get an education by desperate means, often living close to starvation. He graduated from the College of Charleston in 1843, at the head of his class, and after a year's study of law was admitted to the bar. Being a poor speaker and of unhealthy appearance, he was unsuccessful in the courtroom and turned to literary work. He contributed philosophical and political essays to the *Southern Quarterly Review* and eventually became its editor. An article he wrote in 1845 on "The Oregon Question," defending Britain's claim to the region, made him known in this country and abroad. At a convention in Memphis in 1845, where the idea of federal aid for the southern economy was discussed, De Bow decided to found a monthly magazine devoted to the economy and business activities of the South. He settled in New Orleans and published the first issue of the *Commercial Review of the South and Southwest*. The journal was a failure until the sugar planter Maunsel White befriended De Bow and loaned him funds. Within two years, *De Bow's Review*, as the journal was generally known, had the largest circulation of any magazine published in the South. De Bow got out of debt, ate red meat for the first time in his life, and took an investigative trip through New England.

In 1847, when the University of Louisiana (later Tulane University) was organized, De Bow urged that its curriculum include a course in political economy, and he persuaded Maunsel White to subsidize the professorship. De Bow was appointed to the chair, but few students applied for the course. To eke out his slim earnings from the *Review*, De Bow obtained the post of director of the Louisiana Bureau of Statistics, which conducted a state census. His work apparently was noticed in Washington: President Franklin Pierce appointed De Bow superintendent of the United States Census. A by-product of his work was his *Statistical View of the United States* (1854), in which De Bow, in an introductory essay, made constructive suggestions for the improvement of census procedures that were taken into account. His prestige benefited when he was chosen to preside over a convention in Knoxville, Tennessee, on commercial affairs.

Throughout these years and to the end of his life, De Bow continued to edit and publish his *Review*. He increasingly championed Southern nationalism, and after 1850 he welcomed contributions from supporters of secession. He defended slavery: "the negro was created essentially to be a slave," he wrote, "and he finds his highest development and destiny in that condition." He espoused Josiah C. Nott's theory of "polygenism," the idea that the human races were separate biological species.

De Bow saw an urgent need for the South to attain industrial and commercial independence from the North, though he expected that agriculture would remain predominant. Among the projects he advocated, prior to the outbreak of the Civil War, were a transcontinental railroad through the South, a canal across Central America, and direct trade with Europe. He wrote of the South's "manifest destiny" over all of the Americas to its south.

During the Civil War, while the *Review* was suspended, the Confederate government appointed De Bow its principal agent for the purchase and sale of cotton. In July 1866 he resumed publication of his journal, directing its policy toward rebuilding national unity and developing the entire nation's economy. Seven months later, having traveled north to visit his dying brother, B. F. De Bow, he fell ill and died at Elizabeth, New Jersey, leaving a wife and three children. *De Bow's Review* continued publication for a few more years under other auspices.

**BIBLIOGRAPHY**

Paskoff, Paul F., and Daniel J. Wilson, *The Cause of the South: Selections from De Bow's Review, 1846–1867,* 1958; Skipper, Otis Clark, *J. D. B. De Bow, Magazinist of the Old South,* 1958.

# Debs, Eugene Victor

(November 5, 1855–October 20, 1926)
Labor Leader, Socialist

As a union organizer and several-time presidential candidate, Eugene Debs was one of the most popular leaders of the labor and socialist movements in American history.

Debs was born in Terre Haute, Indiana, to Alsatian immigrant parents. At age fourteen he left school and went to work on the railroad, becoming a locomotive fireman. He left railroading for a clerking position but later joined the Brotherhood of Locomotive Firemen (in 1875), serving as secretary of the local lodge. Debs worked hard to build the struggling union; in 1880 he became secretary-general of the national organization and editor of the national journal, *The Locomotive Fireman's Magazine.* During this period, he also began a political career in the Democratic party, holding a post in the Terre Haute city government (1880–1884) and serving as an Indiana state legislator (1885–1887). But most of his time and energy went to the union, which thanks largely to his efforts increased its membership from 2,000 to 20,000.

Initially an opponent of strikes and a supporter of craft unionism, Debs came to believe that the labor movement would be best served by an industrial union of all workers, unskilled as well as skilled. He left his position with the Locomotive Firemen, and in 1893 formed the American Railway Union (ARU) with the aim of bringing together in one organization all railway workers. The Great Northern Railroad strike of April 1894 boosted ARU membership to 150,000.

In May 1894, against Debs's better judgment, workers at the Chicago-based Pullman Sleeping Car Company, many of whom belonged to the ARU, went on strike to protest drastic wage cuts and high rents at the company town. When all ARU members boycotted trains to which Pullman cars were attached, rail traffic from Chicago to the West Coast ground to a halt. Although Debs tried to prevent violence, President Grover Cleveland sent federal troops to Chicago, and in the riots that followed at least thirty people were killed. The courts stopped the strikers with an injunction, which Debs ignored out of the belief that the precedent thus set would destroy the labor movement. Convicted for contempt of court, he served six months in jail. The ARU collapsed, and Debs emerged from prison a changed man.

While in jail, Debs read books by EDWARD BELLAMY and other socialist authors that helped convince him that capitalism must be replaced by socialism if the American worker were ever to achieve economic justice. After supporting the Democratic and Populist candidate, William Jennings Bryan, in 1896, Debs founded the Social Democratic party of America the following year. In 1900 his party merged with a faction of the Socialist Labor party to become the Socialist party of America.

Debs was not effective as a party leader; he proved unable to mediate successfully between the right-wing, middle-class, professional branch of the party and its left-wing members. Also, Debs was frequently inconsistent in the positions he took. Though he opposed the trade unionism of SAMUEL GOMPERS, who, in turn, regarded him as a great enemy, Debs nevertheless believed that in order for socialism to advance it must work through the unions. But when it came to spreading the socialist message and winning votes, Debs was unsurpassed. With his forceful speaking style, he attacked the capitalist system and extolled the virtues of socialism.

In Debs's first presidential campaign in 1900 he won nearly 100,000 votes. He ran again in 1904, 1908, and 1912. In that election Debs polled a remarkable 901,000 votes. At 6 percent of the total, this was the highest percentage ever won by a Socialist presidential candidate in the United States.

During these years, Debs also wrote for and edited a Socialist weekly, *Appeal to Reason,* and was a popular speaker on the lecture circuit. In 1905 he took part in the founding of the Industrial Workers of the World (see WILLIAM D. HAYWOOD), a militant industrial union, but soon withdrew after he became dissatisfied with the organization's methods.

When the United States entered World War I on the side of the Allies in April 1917, the Socialist party met in St. Louis and declared itself completely opposed to the war as a fight for capitalism. Debs warmly supported this declaration, and a year later, after a number of Socialist leaders had been jailed for speaking out against the war, Debs decided to do so himself, regardless of the possible consequences. An antiwar speech he made in Ohio led to his arrest in June 1918 under the Espionage Act. Debs was tried, convicted, and sentenced to ten years in prison.

Taken first to Moundsville, West Virginia, Debs was soon transferred to the federal penitentiary at Atlanta, Georgia. While in prison, he again ran for president in the election of 1920, and again received nearly a million votes. Concerned that the elderly and ailing Debs might die in prison, President Warren G. Harding pardoned him on Christmas Day, 1921. Though Debs was released from prison, his rights as a citizen were not restored.

Debs returned to his home in Terre Haute, but failing health soon made him leave for a sanitarium near Chicago. During his confinement there, he wrote a series of articles attacking prison conditions, which were later collected and published posthumously as *Walls and Bars* (1927). In the election of 1924, Debs supported the Progressive party candidacy of Robert M. La Follette. The following year, he was made editor of a new Chicago-based Socialist weekly, the *American Appeal.* Yet Debs's health remained poor. The year after that, he died of a heart attack. At his funeral in Terre Haute, thousands came to pay tribute to one of American socialism's most popular and impassioned advocates.

**BIBLIOGRAPHY**

Egbert, D. D., and S. Persons (eds.), *Socialism and American Life,* 2 vols., 1952; Ginger, Ray, *Eugene V. Debs,* 1962; Salvatore, Nick, *Eugene V. Debs: Citizen and Socialist,* 1982.

# Delany, Martin Robison

(May 6, 1812–January 24, 1885)
Black Nationalist, Journalist, Physician

Martin Delany has been hailed as "the father of African nationalism" because of his strong racial pride and his belief that African Americans must forge their own destiny.

Delany was born in Charles Town, Virginia (now West Virginia), the son of a free black woman and a slave, who with his wife's help purchased his freedom. The family moved to Chambersburg, Pennsylvania, and in 1831, Delany moved to Pittsburgh, where he studied medicine under a local doctor and continued his regular education at a private black academy. In 1843 he began publishing the *Mystery,* the only black weekly in America. When forced to close the paper four years later because of inadequate financial support, Delany joined FREDERICK DOUGLASS as coeditor of the *North Star.* He also lectured to abolitionist audiences, working, uncomfortably, with white abolitionists. In 1850 Delany was admitted to the medical school of Harvard College but was only able to complete one of the two required terms, because white students asked the college to dismiss him and two other black students.

His experience at Harvard made Delany strongly doubt that African Americans could achieve equality within the United States. In 1852 he published *The Condition, Elevation, Emigration, and Destiny of the Colored People of the United States,* in which he recommended emigration as the answer for blacks. Two years later, Delany organized a National Emigration Convention that drew more than a hundred black men and women to Cleveland. As the head of a commission empowered by the convention to find a homeland for African Americans, Delany visited the Niger Valley in Africa in 1859 and negotiated with the Yoruba people for land to settle on.

During the Civil War, Delany helped recruit troops for the all-black regiments that were formed after President Abraham Lincoln agreed to accept such troops into the Union army. Delany further proposed the formation of a black guerrilla army to infiltrate the Confederacy. In 1865 Lincoln commissioned Delaney as a major. The war ended before the infiltration plan could go into effect.

In South Carolina after the war, Delany served as an agent of the Freedmen's Bureau and in various other positions, including trial justice in Charleston. Vigorously opposed to the political corruption he found within the local Republican party, Delany ran for lieutenant governor of the state in 1874 as an Independent Republican but was defeated. He devoted his later years to writing *Principia of Ethnology: The Origin of Races and Color* (1879), in which he stressed the role of black people in the development of world civilization. Delany died at the age of seventy-two in Xenia, Ohio, where he had moved his family at the end of Reconstruction.

**BIBLIOGRAPHY**

Litwack, Leon, *North of Slavery,* 1961, and *Been in the Storm Too Long: The Aftermath of Slavery,* 1979; Sterling, Dorothy, *The Making of an Afro-American: Martin Robison Delany,* 1971; Ullman, Victor, *Martin R. Delany, The Beginnings of Black Nationalism,* 1971.

# Deloria, Vine Victor, Jr.

(March 26, 1933–   )
American Indian Rights Leader, Author

Vine Deloria has been a leading spokesman for American Indian nationalism through his teaching, lectures, books, and organizational work. Coming from a line of Christian ministers and himself a former student of theology, he lost faith in Western religion and found it in the American Indians' tribal religions.

Deloria, of Sioux (that is, Dakota) ancestry, was born on the Pine Ridge Reservation, in southwest South Dakota, and is a member of the Standing Rock Reservation near the boundary with North Dakota. Both his father and his grandfather were Episcopal priests. The name Deloria came from a great-great-grandfather, a French fur trader named Des Lauriers, who married the daughter of a chief of the Yankton branch of the Sioux. The name was anglicized in a later generation. Vine Deloria, Jr.'s mother was Barbara Eastburn. An aunt, Ella Cara Deloria, was a scholar of the Dakota language and folklore who worked with the anthropologist FRANZ BOAS and taught in Indian schools.

Young Deloria went to reservation schools, the Kent School (in western Connecticut), and Iowa State University, where he earned a B.S. in 1958, with two years out in the U.S. Marine Corps Reserve. From 1959 to 1963, Deloria studied for the ministry at the Lutheran School of Theology, in Rock Island, Illinois, and earned a master's degree while working as a welder at a nearby factory. For a year he was on the staff

Office of Public Relations, University of Colorado at Boulder

of the United Scholarship Service, a church organization in Denver that aimed at placing American Indian students in schools. Disillusioned by its paternalistic approach, he left in 1964. He also decided against being ordained a minister.

For the next three years Deloria was in Washington as director of the National Congress of American Indians, an assignment that he found gratifying and instructive. As he grappled with a great variety of problems, he got a vivid sense of how American Indians were being exploited and victimized. The need, he decided, was greater autonomy for Indians— freedom of direct access to government agencies, not through the Bureau of Indian Affairs. Legal training, he realized, was essential for his own goals. Accordingly, Deloria enrolled in the law school of the University of Colorado and earned a J.D. degree in 1970.

Meanwhile Deloria had published his first book, *Custer Died for Your Sins: An Indian Manifesto* (1969), in which he dealt with broken treaties, genocidal wars, meddlesome missionaries, officious anthropologists, and the Bureau of Indian Affairs, and spoke for the revival of tribalism. In 1970 he published *We Talk, You Listen*, in which he continued to state his case for re-tribalization, focused on the relation of Indians to the environment, and protested white acculturation of Indians. *God Is Red* (1973) contrasts traditional Indian religion with Christianity and laments the decay of community life and the growing rootlessness of Americans in general.

During the 1970s, after teaching ethnic studies for two years at Western Washington State College, in Bellingham, Deloria divided his time between his home in Denver and an office in Washington, where he founded the Institute for the Development of Indian Law. He served as its chairman until 1976. He devoted his legal and educational services to a wide range of Indian causes, including the Native American Rights Fund, the Oglala Sioux Legal Rights Foundation, the American Indian Resource Associates at Oglala, and the National Indian Youth Council, of which he was a cofounder. In 1974 he was an expert witness at the trials of the leaders of the Wounded Knee occupation (see DENNIS BANKS), stressing the occupation's religious and historical background. He assumed the editorship of *Indians in Contemporary Society*, volume 2 of the Smithsonian Institution's *Handbook of North American Indians*.

Deloria became a professor of political science at the University of Arizona in 1978, while continuing his many outside activities. In 1991 he moved back to the University of Colorado as a professor of American Indian studies in the Center for Studies of Ethnicity and Race in America, teaching also in the departments of history, religion, and law. He lives in Boulder with his wife and family.

**BIBLIOGRAPHY**

Deloria, Vine, Jr., *Behind the Trail of Broken Treaties*, 1974, *The Indian Affair*, 1974, and (ed.), *American Indian Policy in the Twentieth Century*, 1985.

# Dewey, John

(October 20, 1859–June 1, 1952)
Educator, Philosopher

John Dewey was perhaps the most influential American thinker of his era. He was a leading exponent (along with WILLIAM JAMES) of the doctrine of pragmatism, which in Dewey's hands provided the groundwork for a program of social reform. As an educator, Dewey launched America's progressive education movement.

Dewey was born on a farm in Burlington, Vermont. Encouraged to read widely by his parents, he attended the Burlington public schools, entering the University of Vermont at the age of fifteen. After graduation in 1879, Dewey taught school for several years, first in Oil City, Pennsylvania, and later at a private academy in Vermont. During these years he published his first philosophical articles in the *Journal of Speculative Philosophy*. At the suggestion of Professor H. A. P. Torrey of the University of Vermont, Dewey decided to pursue graduate work in philosophy. In 1882 he entered the newly formed Johns Hopkins University. Here he was influenced by the pioneer child psychologist G. STANLEY HALL and by philosopher Charles S. Peirce. Awarded a doctorate in 1884, Dewey became assistant professor of philosophy at the University of Michigan, where with the exception of a year (1888–1889) at the University of Minnesota, he remained for the next decade. From 1889 on he was a full professor and chair of the philosophy department.

During his years at Michigan, Dewey published a number of articles and books on philosophy, psychology, and education. In *Psychology* (1887) Dewey maintained that the field was a natural science, not a part of metaphysics. Increasingly he began to move away from the abstract study of philosophy toward its practical applications in the realm of contemporary affairs. Eventually he adopted the pragmatism of William James, whereby ideas are evaluated in terms of their consequences. But much more than James, Dewey was concerned with using human intelligence to promote social reform. Dewey's brand of pragmatism became known as instrumentalism.

Dewey spent the next decade of his career (1894–1904) at the University of Chicago, where he served as chair of the department of philosophy, psychology, and pedagogy and won renown as an educator. In 1896 Dewey and his wife (the former Harriet Alice Chipman, whom he had married in 1886) organized the university's laboratory school, which they used to try out new methods of teaching and curricula and to test some of Dewey's more general educational principles. He believed that education ought to be intimately connected to the rest of life and that instruction ought to be combined with practical experience. He therefore abandoned the tradition of rote learning and recitation, focusing instead on problem-solving activities ("learning by doing") that encouraged children to think creatively. In 1899 he published *The School and Society*, an influential, if controversial, book setting forth his educational philosophy and based on a series of lectures given to parents at the laboratory school. He also published several other important books during this period, and from 1899 to 1900 he served as president of the American Psychological Association.

In 1905 Dewey left the University of Chicago because of differences with university president, William Rainey Harper, and assumed a joint appointment in philosophy at Columbia University in New York and in education at the university's Teachers College. He remained associated with Columbia for the rest of his life. In the course of the next three decades, Dewey achieved a worldwide reputation as America's most influential philosopher.

He developed and elaborated upon his ideas in a series of major books, including *Democ-racy and Education* (1916). Dewey believed that education could be used as a tool for social reform. He further believed that the test of a democracy was the extent to which the people likely to be affected by a particular decision have participated in making it.

In keeping with his activist philosophy, Dewey involved himself with a wide range of liberal social, political, and cultural causes and organizations. He served as president of the American Philosophical Association from 1905 to 1909 and became president of the American Association for the Advancement of Science in 1909. He helped found and served as the first president of the American Association of University Professors (AAUP) in 1915, taking part in investigations of unfair treatment of faculty members and violations of academic freedom. The following year, he became a charter member of the Teachers' Union. In 1919 Dewey was one of the founders of the New School of Social Research in New York City, which became a major center for adult education.

Dewey supported the U.S. entry into World War I, and when the war was over, he engaged in foreign travel and teaching. In 1919 he lectured in Japan and then spent the next two years traveling and lecturing in China. He traveled to Turkey (1924); to Mexico (1926), where he taught; and to the Soviet Union (1928), where he studied education. Dewey was the moving force behind the American Committee for the Outlawry of War in 1921, which was largely responsible for the Kellogg-Briand Pact of 1928. He was also a charter member of the American Civil Liberties Union, the League for Industrial Democracy, and the League for Independent Political Action. In addition, Dewey for many years headed the People's Lobby, a national organization that worked to achieve a Progressive social and political agenda.

Retiring from active teaching at Columbia in 1930, Dewey was appointed professor emeritus and served in this capacity for the rest of his life. He continued to do research and write, producing more major books as well as a steady stream of articles. Dewey also remained involved with public affairs. In 1937 and 1938 he served as chair of the commission of inquiry into the charges that Leon Trotsky had plotted to subvert the government of the Soviet Union. The commission's finding that Trotsky was innocent brought Dewey under sharp attack by American and Soviet communists. In 1939 he helped form the American Committee for Cultural Freedom. When the distinguished English philosopher Bertrand Russell was denied a teaching position at the City College of New York because of his views on sexual politics, Dewey came to Russell's defense and decried this action by the city as a violation of academic freedom.

Vigorous and productive until the end, Dewey died in New York City at the age of ninety-two. Hailed during his lifetime, Dewey left behind a philosophy aimed at solving human problems, as well as theories about learning that have shaped the progressive education movement in the United States.

**BIBLIOGRAPHY**

Bullert, Gary, *The Politics of John Dewey*, 1983; Cahn, Steven M. (ed.), *New Studies in the Philosophy of John Dewey*, 1977; Dykhuizen, George, *The Life and Mind of John Dewey*, 1973; Hook, Sidney, *John Dewey: An Intellectual Portrait*, 1971; Westbrook, Robert, *John Dewey and American Democracy*, 1991.

# Divine, Father

(ca. 1880–September 10, 1965)
Religious Leader

Father Divine's interracial Peace Mission was important in moving African American churches toward commitment to the struggle for racial justice.

The origins of the man who became famous as the black cult leader, Father Divine, are obscure. He was probably born around 1880 near Savannah, Georgia, as George Baker. He began to preach as a youth, calling himself the Messenger, and his message that God was in every person of whatever color got him a term on a chain gang. Around 1900 he moved north and worked as a gardener and a part-time Baptist preacher. Returning to Georgia, his preaching in Valdosta resulted in another jail sentence. He came back north and with his wife Peninah settled in an all-white town, Sayville, Long Island, calling himself the Reverend Major J. Devine. For his so-called Peace Mission he bought a large house, in which he gave food and lodging to members of the religious group that formed around him. By the time of the Great Depression, Major Devine was offering his growing body of adherents not only spiritual counsel but also help in securing jobs. In 1930 he took the name Father Divine. When in 1931 the Peace Mission offered free Sunday banquets at the Sayville house, attended by both black and white followers, the town had Father Divine arrested for disturbing the peace, and he was sentenced to a year in prison. The judge died suddenly three days after the trial, and Father Divine remarked, "I hated to do it." By this time many of his followers believed him to be the personification of God.

Father Divine moved the Peace Mission to Harlem in 1933. What had started as a modest communal movement grew rapidly until, in 1942 when the headquarters were transferred to Philadelphia, there were some 200 major centers, called Heavens, and many thousands of followers. Divine organized his disciples into a network of religious cooperatives based on racial equality. His inner circle, perhaps 10,000, lived communally in the Peace Mission houses, and the movement reached countless others in the ghettos.

The Mission's code banned alcohol, drugs, tobacco, and profanity, and encouraged chastity, the repayment of debts, and self-improving education. Its followers ran businesses and shared the income. During the depths of the depression the Peace Mission enterprises prospered thanks to profits brought by flourishing trade and modest living costs in the "Heavens." Cheap food and rent helped many unemployed families survive. Divine also founded a system of farm cooperatives where the urban poor who were resettled raised produce for the market. To expand into exclusive neighborhoods, white followers evaded housing covenants so that property could be bought for the membership—for example, next door to the Roosevelt family's Hyde Park mansion, a large estate where Mission people were model residents. Father Divine encouraged political activism—for civil rights, antilynching legislation, full employment, a cooperative

economy under government regulation. His leadership made active reformers of many ghetto residents previously unconcerned with politics.

Divine was far from being a mainstream civil rights leader, however. From the 1930s until his death, his ideas tended to be dramatic, even eccentric.

In 1946, after the death of his first wife, Divine chose a young white woman, Edna Rose Ritchings, as his "virgin bride." As Mother Divine she eventually became leader of the Peace Mission movement. Father Divine died in 1965, not long after sending congratulations to President Lyndon B. Johnson for urging voting rights legislation.

**BIBLIOGRAPHY**

Burnham, Kenneth E., *God Comes to America,* 1979; Harris, Sara, *Father Divine,* 1971; Weisbrot, Robert, *Father Divine and the Struggle for Racial Equality,* 1983.

# Dix, Dorothea Lynde

(April 4, 1802–July 17, 1887)
Reformer

Dorothea Dix was world-renowned for her work in behalf of the mentally ill. Born in Hampden, Maine, into difficult circumstances—her mother was an invalid and her father improvident—Dorothea Dix received her education in Boston and in Worcester, Massachusetts, while living first with her grandmother and then with her great aunt. At the age of fourteen she opened her own school in Worcester, and a few years later she ran a school for young girls in Boston. She also wrote several books for children. After developing tuberculosis and eventually suffering a total

physical breakdown, Dix gave up teaching and spent a year in England recuperating.

After her return to Boston, Dix was asked in March 1841 to teach a Sunday school class for women in the East Cambridge jail. Dix found insane women living in filthy, unheated cells. She appealed to the local court to install stoves in the women's cells and with the help of philanthropist SAMUEL GRIDLEY HOWE saw that heat was provided and the women's quarters renovated.

Imbued with the spirit of reform, Dix embarked on a study of the prevailing treatment of the mentally ill. She discovered that aside from a few model institutions like the privately run McLean Hospital in Boston, where inmates were treated humanely, most institutions housed the insane under sordid conditions, neglecting and abusing them. Dix then conducted a survey of jails, almshouses, and houses of correction in the state, recording in her notebook the shocking details of mentally ill inmates who were chained and beaten. She set forth her findings in an 1843 memorial to the Massachusetts legislature, which after weeks of heated debate finally approved funds for the expansion of the Worcester State Lunatic Hospital.

Library of Congress

Encouraged by her success, Dix carried her crusade to Rhode Island and New York, employing the same technique of an investigation of existing facilities followed by a memorial to the legislature. In both states she was successful in securing funds for new institutions. She was also responsible for the establishment of new institutions in New Jersey, Pennsylvania, and some states in the Midwest and the South. Dix's efforts were much publicized, and reformers in other areas sought her help. But though sympathetic to such causes as women's rights, public education, and abolition, she devoted her energies to the mentally ill. She did, however, become involved in prison reform, as many mentally ill people were housed in prisons. In her book *Remarks on Prisons and Prison Discipline in the United States* (1845), Dix advanced such penal reforms as the education of prisoners and the separation of various types of offenders.

Becoming convinced of the need for federal legislation to help the mentally ill, Dix in 1853 tried to get Congress to set aside 12 million acres of public land in trust and devote the income to help the insane and the vision-, hearing-, and speech-impaired. Though the bill that would have accomplished this passed both houses of Congress, it was vetoed by President Franklin Pierce.

Not long after the outbreak of the Civil War, Dix proposed to the War Department the plan of establishing a volunteer corps of women nurses. Commissioned superintendent of army nurses in June 1861, Dix at the age of fifty-nine and in poor health began the difficult task of finding nurses and procuring medical supplies. Her lack of administrative experience and her exacting requirements brought complaints from hospital personnel, and in October 1863 Dix's authority was reduced.

After the war, Dix continued her work for the mentally ill, raising money for the more than fifty hospitals that had been established as a result of her efforts. In 1881 she retired to one of the first institutions she had helped to found, the Trenton State Hospital in New Jersey. She died there at the age of eighty-five.

BIBLIOGRAPHY

Brooks, Gladys, *Three Wise Virgins*, 1957; Dain, Norman, *Concepts of Insanity in the United States, 1789–1865*, 1964; Dix, Dorothea, *On Behalf of the Insane Poor: Selected Reports*, in Rothman, David (ed.), *Poverty, U.S.A.: the Historical Record Series*, 1971; McKown, Robin, *Pioneers in Mental Health*, 1961; Marshall, Helen E., *Dorothea Dix, Forgotten Samaritan*, 1937; Wilson, Dorothy, *Stranger and Traveler: The Story of Dorothea Dix, American Reformer*, 1975.

# Donnelly, Ignatius

(November 3, 1831–January 1, 1901)
Author, Reformer

Author and spellbinding orator Ignatius Donnelly championed the cause of farmers and workers as a leader of the Farmers' Alliance and later of the Populist party, which he helped to form.

Ignatius Donnelly was born in Philadelphia and attended the public schools there. He was admitted to the bar but in 1856 gave up his practice and moved to Minnesota, where he hoped to make his fortune through land speculation. Together with an associate, he founded Nininger City, but after the Panic of 1857 destroyed land prices, he left the city and became a wheat farmer.

A highly effective public speaker, Donnelly served two terms as Republican lieutenant governor of Minnesota (1859–1863) and three terms in the U.S. House of Representatives (1863–1869). In Congress, Donnelly supported the Civil War and Radical Reconstruction. He tried unsuccessfully to get Minnesota to give the vote to its few black residents, and he pushed for the establishment of the National Bureau of Education to secure equal educational opportunities for everyone, regardless of race. Donnelly also advocated opening the western lands to immigrant settlers. Defeated for reelection to the House in 1868 and 1870, Donnelly parted company with the Republican party over the issue of a protective tariff, which he felt was being used to enrich eastern manufacturers at the expense of western farmers. In Donnelly's view, the Republican party had become too much the tool of the privileged few.

Donnelly's concern over the increasingly industrialized society of the postwar years led him to join the Liberal Republican movement in 1872. After the failure of Liberal Republicanism, Donnelly in 1873 became active in the Grange, a farmers' organization, through which he hoped to forge a political alliance between farmers and laborers. He served in the Minne-

sota state senate (1874–1878) while editing from Nininger City a weekly newspaper, the *Anti-Monopolist.* The paper advocated currency and banking reform, railroad rate regulation, and easy credit for farmers.

When the Grange movement proved unable to make political headway, Donnelly became involved with the Greenback party, which sought an increase in paper money, or greenbacks, as a means of helping cash-poor farmers. In 1878 he ran unsuccessfully for Congress as a Greenback-Democrat. He then wrote a number of very popular pseudoscientific books, including *Atlantis: The Antediluvian World* (1882), "proving" the existence of the "lost continent," and *The Great Cryptogram* (1888), advancing the theory that Francis Bacon was the true author of Shakespeare's plays. In his widely read novel, *Caesar's Column* (1889), set in New York City of the future, Donnelly presented a society controlled by a few wealthy people. This corrupt ruling class so brutalizes farmers and workers that the result is a bloody revolution, described by Donnelly in horrifying detail.

Back in politics, Donnelly again failed to win a seat in Congress in 1884 but two years later was elected to the state legislature by the newly formed Farmers' Alliance. In the legislature, Donnelly pushed for regulation of the railroads, an end to child labor, and a statewide industrial code. Elected president of the Minnesota Farmers' Alliance in 1890, he figured prominently at the Cincinnati convention of the National Farmers' Alliance in May 1891, serving as chairman of the resolutions committee and helping to form the People's, or Populist, party.

At the official founding convention of the Populist party in Omaha, Nebraska, in 1892, Donnelly wrote the party platform with a preamble that accused the wealthy few of stealing "the fruits of the toil of millions." The platform itself called for the nationalizing of banks, government ownership of the railroads, direct election of senators, and a graduated income tax. Caught up in the fever pitch of excitement that accompanied the launching of the party, Donnelly wrote a novel, *The Golden Bottle* (1892), in which a poor farmer becomes president on the Populist ticket and successfully reforms the American economy and society. In the election of 1892, the Populist presidential candidate won over a million popular votes and the party generally did well in the West. But it lost ground in Minnesota, where Donnelly was badly defeated in his bid for the governorship.

In the election of 1896, Donnelly reluctantly supported the Democratic candidate, William Jennings Bryan. After Bryan lost the election and the Populist movement began to fall apart, Donnelly, nevertheless, remained active in the party. He ran for vice president in 1900 on the ticket of the Middle-of-the-Road Populists, a splinter group. He died two months later at age sixty-nine.

**BIBLIOGRAPHY**

Goodwyn, Lawrence, *Democratic Promise: The Populist Movement in America*, 1976; Hicks, J. D., *The Populist Revolt*, 1931; Hofstader, Richard, *The Age of Reform*, 1955; Ridge, Martin, *Ignatius Donnelly: The Portrait of a Politician*, 1962.

# Douglass, Frederick

(ca. 1817–February 20, 1895)
Abolitionist, Reformer

Editor, orator, and abolitionist, Frederick Douglass was the foremost African American leader of the nineteenth century.

Frederick Douglass was born a slave in Tuckahoe, Maryland. His mother, Harriet Bailey, was black; his father was an unknown white man. He spent his childhood separated from his mother under cruel and violent conditions. In 1825 Douglass was sent to Baltimore, where he worked as a house servant and was taught to read and write by his sympathetic mistress against her husband's advice. After eight years, he was sent back to the country to work as a field hand. He tried soon to escape the harshness of this life but was caught. He was returned to Baltimore, where he worked in the shipyards as a caulker. Still determined to escape, he succeeded in 1838, using the borrowed papers of a free black sailor. After his escape he took the last name of Douglass and married Anna Murray, a free black woman he had known in Baltimore. The couple settled in New Bedford, Massachusetts, where Douglass tried to find work as a ship caulker, but racial discrimination forced him to become a day laborer instead.

A major turning point in Douglass's life occurred in 1841 when he was unexpectedly called upon to speak at an abolitionist meeting held in Nantucket, Massachusetts. Douglass so impressed abolitionist leader WILLIAM LLOYD GARRISON that Garrison asked him to become an agent for the Massachusetts Anti-Slavery Society. Douglass soon became one of the abolitionist movement's star orators. Because of his eloquence and poise on the platform, listeners sometimes questioned whether Douglass could have been a slave. To prove the truth of what he said, Douglass in 1845 published an account of his experiences under slavery, *Narrative of the Life of Frederick Douglass*. (Together with two later autobiographies, *My Bondage and My Free-*

*dom* [1855] and *The Life and Times of Frederick Douglass* [1881], the series is considered one of the best examples of a slave narrative and a classic American autobiography.) But since it contained much factual information, Douglass ran the risk of being recaptured. To avoid this fate, he embarked on a lecture tour of the British Isles, lasting nearly two years.

Upon Douglass's return to the United States in 1847, his friends raised the money to buy his freedom. They also provided him with financial backing to start his own abolitionist newspaper, the *North Star,* which he published from Rochester, New York, for the next seventeen years. Along with Garrison's *The Liberator,* the *North Star* became a leading organ of the abolitionist movement. In its pages, Douglass also supported vocational education for African Americans and urged members of his race to lead upright lives. In addition, he tried, unsuccessfully as it turned out, to start an industrial school for young black students. Unlike the later African American leader BOOKER T. WASHINGTON, who had similar views on economics and character-building, Douglass was outspoken in condemning racial discrimination wherever it occurred.

At the same time, Douglass's fellow feeling for other human beings, whether white or black, male or female, led him to take part in reform movements that were not aimed specifically at black people. In 1848 he attended the meeting at Seneca Falls, New York, that marked the official beginning of the woman's rights movement, and he remained a supporter of woman suffrage throughout his life. Convinced that alcohol consumption resulted in poverty and vice, Douglass also addressed a

Library of Congress

meeting of the New York State Temperance convention in Rochester in 1852.

In the early 1850s, Douglass broke with Garrison over the issue of moral suasion versus political action to end slavery. Having become convinced that political action was necessary, Douglass supported the Free Soil party and after 1856 the newly formed Republican party. Although on friendly terms with the militant abolitionist JOHN BROWN, Douglass declined to join in Brown's raid on Harpers Ferry, Virginia, in 1859, because he believed it was doomed to failure. After Brown's capture, Douglass fled to Canada for several months, fearing that he might be seized as an accomplice, since he had known of the plot in advance and had helped raise money for it.

Douglass welcomed the coming of the Civil War, which to him was a crusade for freedom. He urged President Abraham Lincoln to free the slaves as a war measure and to let African Americans fight in the Union army. After the Emancipation Proclamation of 1863, Douglass became a recruiting agent for two black Massachusetts regiments. Among the first to enlist were his two oldest sons.

During Reconstruction, Douglass continued to work for black equality, urging that the freedmen be given civil rights and the vote. In the 1870s Douglass moved to Washington, D.C., where he edited the *New National Era,* a weekly paper designed to offer moral support to the freedmen, and became president of the ill-starred Freedmen's Bank, which soon failed. A loyal supporter of the Republican party, Douglass was rewarded by President Rutherford B. Hayes in 1877 with an appointment as marshal of the District of Columbia. Although the post was a minor one and Hayes removed its ceremonial functions, Douglass, as the first African American to hold this office, considered his appointment a victory for his race. In 1881 President James A. Garfield appointed Douglass recorder of deeds for the District of Columbia—another first for African Americans.

While holding public office, Douglass continued to speak out against the growing movement towards segregation, disenfranchisement, and finally the lynching of African Americans. Yet he retained his faith that African Americans would one day occupy an equal place in American society. This faith was reflected in his 1884 marriage to a white woman, Helen Pitts, who had worked in the recorder's office as his secretary. (Douglass's first wife had died two years before.) To critics who objected, Douglass remarked that his first wife "was the color of my mother, and the second, the color of my father."

In 1889 Douglass received another government appointment as minister-resident and consul general to the Republic of Haiti, a post he held for two years. Active until the end, Douglass died suddenly at the age of seventy-eight, after attending a woman suffrage convention in Washington, D.C.

**BIBLIOGRAPHY**

Blight, David W., *Frederick Douglass' Civil War: Keeping Faith in Jubilee*, 1989; Douglass, Frederick, *Narrative of the Life of Frederick Douglass*, 1845, rep., 1991, *My Bondage and Freedom*, 1855, and *Life and Times of Frederick Douglass*, 1881; Foner, Philip S., *Frederick Douglass*, 1960, and (ed.), *The Life and Writings of Frederick Douglass*, 4 vols., 1950–1955; McFeely, William, *Frederick Douglass*, 1991.

# Dow, Neal

(March 20, 1804–October 2, 1897)
Prohibitionist

Father of the "Maine Law" of 1851, the first state law to prohibit the sale of alcoholic beverages, Neal Dow was the most important nineteenth-century prohibitionist.

Born in Portland, Maine, Neal Dow was raised a devout Quaker. He received his education at local private schools and at the Friends' Academy at New Bedford, Massachusetts. Afterward Dow joined his father in his tannery business and became wealthy.

Dow's Quaker background, his parents' interest in reform, and what he observed of the evils of drink in the workplace all drew him into the new temperance movement. He became active in the temperance program of the Maine Charitable Mechanics' Association and appealed to the self-interest of fellow business-men by pointing out that drunken workers were not good workers, and that intemperance contributed to poverty.

In 1834 Dow was the delegate of the Portland Young Men's Temperance Society to the state convention that established the Maine Temperance Society to fight hard liquor. Becoming convinced that abstinence from all alcoholic beverages, including wine and beer, was necessary, he withdrew from this organization to help form in 1838 the Maine Temperance Union, which had as its goal total abstinence. Dow and his coworkers in the movement now began to press for a statewide prohibition law. In 1846 they were able to persuade the Maine legislature to pass a law banning the sale of beverage alcohol by the drink.

Though limited in its enforcement provisions, this was the first statewide prohibition law in the country.

Dow then turned to politics to achieve his goal of a stricter prohibition law. In 1851 he was elected mayor of Portland, and that same year convinced the legislature to pass the "Maine Law" of 1851, which forbade the manufacture and sale of all alcohol, except for medicinal purposes. The new law became famous throughout the country, inspiring most states in the Northeast and the Midwest to pass similar laws in the next few years. It also established Dow's reputation as an international leader of the prohibition movement. He embarked on extensive speaking tours of the North and in 1853 served as president of the World's Temperance Convention in New York City.

Reelected mayor in 1855, Dow became convinced of the need for an even tougher enforcement measure and that year won the Intensified Maine Law, which provided for imprisonment for first offenders. Yet an antiprohibition riot in Portland, in which one rioter was killed by the police acting on Mayor Dow's orders, led to the law's repeal a year later. A number of other states soon followed suit by repealing their unpopular prohibition laws.

Defeated at home, Dow traveled to Great Britain to lecture about prohibition in 1856. Two years later, he was elected to the Maine legislature and helped to pass a weak prohibition law. With the outbreak of the Civil War, Dow, who was a staunch abolitionist as well as a prohibitionist, became colonel of the 13th Regiment of Maine Volunteers. Promoted to brigadier general, he was captured by Confederate troops near Port Hudson, Louisiana, in 1863, and after being imprisoned for over a year was released.

After the war, Dow resumed prohibitionist activities on a full-time basis. He made two more speaking trips to Great Britain, and addressed the new temperance groups in America that were the offshoot of the Women's Crusade of 1873 and 1874. In this crusade, groups of women were able to shut down hundreds of saloons in the Midwest. As prohibition grew into a national movement, so did Dow's popularity as a leader and lecturer. In 1880 he ran for president on the Prohibition ticket, winning 10,305 votes.

Thanks largely to the efforts of FRANCES WILLARD, president of the Women's Christian Temperance Union, Dow was hailed as one of the saints of the movement. In 1884, when he was eighty, Dow took part in a successful campaign for a prohibition amendment to the Maine state constitution. He died in Portland at the age of ninety-three. His autobiography, *The Reminiscences of Neal Dow: Recollections of Eighty Years* (1898), was published after his death.

**BIBLIOGRAPHY**

Byrne, F. L., *Prophet of Prohibition: Neal Dow and His Crusade*, 1961.

# Dubinsky, David

(February 22, 1892–September 17, 1982)
Labor Leader

David Dubinsky, child of a Russian ghetto, became the president and a driving force of one of the great American trade unions. As a believer in democratic socialism, he became a political leader of national prominence and a founder of the American Labor and the Liberal parties.

Dubinsky was born David Dobnievski in Brest-Litovsk, in what was then Russian Poland (today it is in Belarus, on the Polish border), and grew up in Lodz, an industrial city in central Poland. At primary school he was taught to read and write in Yiddish, Polish, and Russian, and at thirteen he was taken out of school and put to work in his father's bakery. At fifteen, having become a master baker, he was elected secretary of a bakery union local. When he joined a strike he was arrested and jailed, but he was released ten days later thanks to a bribe. A year later, when he attended a meeting of a dissident Jewish socialist group, the Bund, he was again arrested by the Russian authorities and banished to Siberia. On the way he was held in Warsaw and Moscow prisons, where he encountered mature political prisoners who contributed to his education. He managed to escape from a Siberian gulag and make his way to Lodz where, under a false name, he baked by day and hid by night. In 1911 his brother, already in New York City, sent him money for a ticket to America.

Dubinsky landed in New York on July 1. His relatives hoped he might go to college and become a doctor, but instead he went to work in the garment industry and joined the cutters' Local 10 of the International Ladies Garment Workers Union (ILGWU). Dubinsky became an active unionist, and by the time he was twenty-six he was on Local 10's executive board. Three years later he was its business manager.

Despite the socialism of his Polish youth, Dubinsky was in favor of American participation in World War I and against the Bolshevik Revolution in Russia. When the left-wing American Socialists split off to organize the Communist party, Dubinsky proved to be their adversary. After a steady rise in the ILGWU power structure, Dubinsky became a vice president in 1922 and in 1929 secretary-treasurer. He was elected president in 1932 and remained in the post until he retired in 1966. His stance as a leader was characterized by writer IRVING HOWE as a blend of democracy and "Bonapartism." He was skillful at negotiating with employers, many of whom were immigrants like him, and dealing with non-Jewish liberals.

By 1932 the ILGWU had lost much of its membership and was on the brink of bankruptcy, but with the New Deal there was a surge in recruitment. Dubinsky took advantage of the National Industrial Recovery Act of 1933 to push organization of the industry, and in two years there were 200,000 members and a full treasury.

By 1935 Dubinsky, by then a vice president of the American Federation of Labor (AFL; see WILLIAM GREEN and JOHN L. LEWIS), had begun to doubt the effectiveness of craft-union organization, and he joined with John L. Lewis in forming the Committee for Industrial Organization (later, the Congress of Industrial Organizations, or CIO). The next year he resigned from the AFL, but he objected to making the CIO a full-fledged federation that would compete with the AFL for members and power. The ILGWU remained on its own until 1940, when Dubinsky took it back to the AFL and again became a vice president.

Dubinsky had left the Socialist party in 1928, and he supported the Democrats in the 1932 election. In 1936 he joined with SIDNEY HILLMAN and other labor leaders to form the American Labor party (ALP), primarily to give the trade unions their own voice in politics. The party, whose strength was mainly in New York City, supported the New Deal as well as some liberal Republicans. When in 1944 the ALP was perceived as being under Communist control, Dubinsky resigned and, with REINHOLD NIEBUHR and others, organized the Liberal party, whose support was critical in bringing New York State into the Democratic column for Roosevelt's election in 1944 and John F. Kennedy's election in 1960.

Pushing the unions toward stronger social responsibility, Dubinsky fought against the racketeers that plagued many of them. His campaigns against the underworld, with the support of GEORGE MEANY, led to the adoption of antiracketeering codes by the AFL-CIO in 1957.

When Dubinsky stepped down as president in 1966, the ILGWU had a half billion dollars welfare and retirement fund, which was drawn upon for relief projects and other good works in Israel and elsewhere. Under his leadership, members had higher wages, pensions, health services, and paid vacations, as well as their own vacation resort, Unity House, in the Pocono mountains of Pennsylvania. He remained close to union activities until his death at age ninety.

## BIBLIOGRAPHY

Danish, Max, *The World of David Dubinsky,* 1957; Dewey, John, *David Dubinsky: A Pictorial Biography,* 1951; Dubinsky, David, with A. H. Raskin, *David Dubinsky: A Life with Labor,* 1977; Howe, Irving, *World of Our Fathers,* 1989; Stolberg, Benjamin, *Tailor's Progress,* 1944.

# Du Bois, William Edward Burghardt

(February 23, 1868–August 27, 1963)
Author, Civil Rights Leader, Historian, Reformer

W E. B. Du Bois, called the father of Pan-Africanism for his work on behalf of the emerging African nations, devoted his life to the struggle for equality for African Americans and all people of color. He ranks among the great American historians, and his commitment and intellectual depth made him one of the foremost reformers of our time.

Du Bois was born at Great Barrington, in western Massachusetts. His father was of French and African descent; his mother, Mary Sylvina Burghardt, belonged to a black family long in Great Barrington. Deserted by her husband, she brought up her son alone, working as a domestic. Though he was often the only black child in his classes, Du Bois experienced little, if any, discrimination in the New England town.

At fifteen, having shown a literary gift, he became a correspondent for a Negro paper, *The New York Globe.* A year later, after his mother died, local people undertook to pay for his education.

In 1885 Du Bois was introduced to racism when he went south to enter Fisk University, in Nashville, Tennessee, a black institution with, at that time, a white faculty. He also encountered the black world of the South. His often humiliating experiences led him to an understanding of the dual consciousness of the African American.

At Fisk, Du Bois wrote his senior thesis on the German statesman Otto von Bismarck, who had unified his nation. Du Bois saw unification under a trained leadership as the model for African Americans. In 1888 he entered Harvard

University and earned A.B. and M.A. degrees, studying with such professors as WILLIAM JAMES and Josiah Royce. On a grant he spent two years in Europe, studying at the University of Berlin, where he first encountered socialist ideas.

In 1894 Du Bois returned to the United States and taught at Wilberforce University, in Ohio. During two years there he completed his Harvard dissertation, *The Suppression of the African Slave-Trade to the United States of America, 1638–1870* (Ph.D., 1895), published in 1896 as the first volume of the Harvard Historical Series. Also in that year he married Nina Gomer, a fellow student of part-German ancestry.

Du Bois accepted a year's nonteaching appointment at the University of Pennsylvania, to prepare a study, commissioned by local liberals, of the black population of Philadelphia. Living in a slum, he interviewed more than 5,000 people and compiled data on every aspect of their lives and relationship to the white population. *The Philadelphia Negro* (1899), one of the first studies based on empirical sociological research, emphasized Du Bois's view that a black elite (what he labeled the "Talented Tenth"), using scientific methods, should lead the black masses. His experience in Philadelphia reinforced his sense of "twoness," not only in his but in the African American personality.

In 1897 Du Bois went to Atlanta University as professor of economics, sociology, and history and leader of its annual Conference for the Study of Negro Problems. In London in 1900 for a Pan-African conference, he prophesied in a celebrated address that "the problem of the twentieth century [would be] the problem of

Library of Congress

the color line." Du Bois's consciousness of racial inequality had been deepened by the death of his infant son, for which he blamed the poor medical facilities for blacks.

Du Bois took issue with the message of BOOKER T. WASHINGTON, when, in 1902, he reviewed Washington's autobiography. He recognized the value of Washington's work at the Tuskegee Institute, emphasizing vocational training, but he could not accept Washington's tolerance of social inequality and political subordination. Unlike Washington, Du Bois never compromised his insistence that blacks be granted full political and civil rights. The next year Du Bois published his most famous work, *The Souls of Black Folk*, essays presenting a complex picture of African Americans through a mixture of sociology, history, biography, and anecdote. His move toward radicalism was reflected in the Niagara movement, which he organized in 1905 to agitate against segregation in any form, and his biography of JOHN BROWN (1909), which extolled the abolitionist.

In 1910 Du Bois helped found the National Association for the Advancement of Colored People (NAACP; see JOEL E. SPINGARN) in New York; he served as director of publications and research. He founded and for more than twenty years edited its influential monthly journal, *Crisis.* In World War I, Du Bois gave strong support to President Woodrow Wilson and the Allies. His editorial "Close Ranks," which urged blacks to forget differences and join whites in the war effort, brought criticism from many black readers. After the war he took the lead in organizing several Pan-African congresses seeking to influence the administration of colonies, though with little effect. Du Bois detested MARCUS GARVEY and his nationalist "Back to Africa" movement.

Du Bois encouraged the literary and artistic flowering in the 1920s known as the Harlem Renaissance, though he criticized the work of some of its figures as being overly free and warned young black writers against dependence upon white patrons.

In 1926 Du Bois visited the Soviet Union and deepened his sympathy with communism. During the Great Depression his stand for black self-sufficiency and self-help programs based on economic nationalism brought him into disfavor with NAACP advocates of integrated action and free enterprise. Another problem was Du Bois's often distant and cold manner, especially with whites. When he resigned in 1934, however, the NAACP praised his having created with *Crisis* "a Negro intelligentsia, and many who have never read a word of his writings are his spiritual descendants."

Having returned to Atlanta University as chairman of the sociology department, Du Bois produced a Marxist historical work, *Black Reconstruction in America, 1860–1880* (1935); carried on a weekly column in black newspapers; wrote an autobiography, *Dusk of Dawn* (1940); and encouraged a new generation of social scientists, including RALPH BUNCHE.

When Du Bois's radical pronouncements caused the university's conservative administrators to retire him at the age of seventy-six, and he had little security, the NAACP came to his aid with a modest job as special research director. Du Bois produced works criticizing capitalism and colonialism and urging Pan-Africanism, and in 1948 the NAACP dismissed him. He became active in international peace and antinuclear movements, and in 1951 was indicted as a foreign agent. Though he was acquitted, his passport was revoked. Du Bois had remarried after the death of his first wife, and at this point he devoted several years to writing a three-volume novel. After the Department of State restored his passport in 1958, he toured western Europe and the Communist countries, receiving the Lenin Peace Prize in Moscow on May Day 1959.

In 1961 Du Bois joined the Communist party and left the United States for Ghana at the invitation of its president, Kwame Nkrumah. Subsequently he renounced American citizenship and became a Ghanaian. He died of natural causes in the capital, Accra, and was buried there.

**BIBLIOGRAPHY**

Du Bois, Shirley Graham, *His Day Is Marching On*, 1971; Du Bois, W. E. B., and H. Aptheker (ed.), *The Autobiography of W. E. B. Du Bois*, 1968; Foner, P. S., *W. E. B. Du Bois Speaks, 1890–1919*, 1970; Marable, Manning, *W. E. B. Du Bois: Black Radical Democrat*, 1986; Rampersad, Arnold, *The Art and Imagination of W. E. B. Du Bois*, 1976; Rudwick, Elliot M., *W. E. B. Du Bois: A Study in Minority Group Leadership*, 1960; Weinberg, M., *W. E. B. Du Bois: A Reader*, 1970.

# Eastman, Charles Alexander

(ca. 1858–January 8, 1939)
Author, Physician

Raised to be a Sioux warrior, Charles Eastman entered the white world and championed Indian causes from the time of Wounded Knee in 1890 till he died. His writings interpreted Indian life to white Americans at a time of much misunderstanding, and his work served the cause of American Indians in numerous ways.

Charles Eastman, originally named Ohiyesa ("Winner"), was born in the year Minnesota became a state, 1858, near the village of Redwood Falls, on the Santee reservation, bordering the Minnesota River. The Santee, his family's people, were a branch of the Sioux. His mother, who died in his infancy, was Mary Nancy Eastman, the daughter of a white artist, Seth Eastman, and a Sioux woman. At birth he was named Hakadah, "The Pitiful Last," being the youngest of five children. When the father joined the Sioux uprising in 1862 and lost touch with his family, the children were taken by his mother and brother into present-day North Dakota and Manitoba, and Ohiyesa (the name given him when he was four) spent his boyhood on the plains, isolated from contact with whites.

When Ohiyesa was fifteen, his father, who had been supposed dead but was actually in a penitentiary, turned up in Manitoba searching for his family. Having become a Christian and taken the name Jacob Eastman, he was farming in a Santee colony at Flandreau, in what is now South Dakota, and there he brought Ohiyesa and an older son, John, who later became a Presbyterian pastor and tribal leader. Jacob Eastman, who had come to see education in the white pattern as the best course for Indians, sent Ohiyesa to a Santee mission school in Nebraska, where the youth chose the name Charles Alexander Eastman.

After attending several preparatory schools, Eastman graduated from Dartmouth College in 1887 and the medical school of Boston University in 1890. His first appointment was as agency physician at the Pine Ridge Reservation, in South Dakota, and he arrived shortly before the massacre at Wounded Knee (see DENNIS BANKS). His first duty as agency physician was to attend to the wounded survivors. At Pine Ridge he met and married Elaine Goodale, a white teacher who was in charge of Indian education for the Dakotas. After a dispute with the agent on the reservation, whom he accused of corruption, Eastman resigned in 1893 and moved to St. Paul, where he practiced for a year. His wife, who was herself a poet, encouraged him to write about his Indian heritage and experiences, and with her guidance he began to contribute articles to magazines.

In 1894 the Young Men's Christian Association (YMCA) appointed Eastman a traveling secretary, and he set up more than thirty Indian YMCA groups around the country. Determined to help his people more effectively, Eastman went to Washington to lobby for the restoration of Santee treaty rights lost after the 1862 uprising. Meeting with little success and in debt, he worked for a year at the Carlisle Indian School in Pennsylvania until he was reinstated in the Indian Health Service, with an appointment at the Crow Creek Reservation in South Dakota. Continuing to write, in 1902 Eastman published his first book, *Indian Boyhood*. Again, however, he got into a controversy and was able to stay in government work only through the efforts of writer Hamlin Garland, who recommended him to President Theodore Roosevelt as head of a project to standardize Indians' surnames in order to protect their land titles. He carried on that work for six years, until restlessness impelled him to seek his roots in the Minnesota woods. Supported by the University of Pennsylvania Museum, Eastman tracked in the country around Leech Lake, collecting folklore and curios among the Ojibwa. The experience yielded his book *The Soul of the Indian* (1911). In 1910 he was a cofounder of the Boy Scouts and a year later joined in forming the Society of American Indians.

In 1915 Eastman with his wife and children started a young people's camp, "The School of the Woods," on a lake in New Hampshire. Within a few years he had to close the camp. There were financial problems, owing to wartime conditions; after his daughter Irene died of influenza there in 1918, the campsite had sad associations, and he and his wife separated in 1921.

For many years, Eastman was involved with the Santees' claim on the government to restore annuity payments negotiated in early treaties. When the U.S. Court of Claims ruled in 1922 that payment be made, Eastman was dissatisfied with the compensation he received. In 1923, however, he was rewarded with an inspectorship in the Indian service, during which he traveled to reservations, dealing with problems and conditions. He also assumed responsibilities as, in a sense, an elder statesman. When British prime minister David Lloyd George visited the United States and asked to meet American Indians, Eastman led a delegation of Sioux in tribal dress who greeted the visitor and gave him a headdress, for which Eastman earned President Calvin Coolidge's praise. He investigated the facts regarding Sacajawea, the Shoshone guide of the Lewis and Clark expedition, and believed he had verified her death in Wyoming at age 100.

In his last years, Eastman lectured, wrote, and visited England for an educational foundation. At the Century of Progress exposition at Chicago in 1933, he was awarded a medal by a national Indian fraternal organization for "the most distinguished achievement by an American Indian." He died of a heart attack at the age of eighty in Detroit.

**BIBLIOGRAPHY**

Eastman, Charles A., *Indian Boyhood*, 1902, rep., 1971, and *From the Deep Woods to Civilization*, 1916; Wilson, Raymond, *Ohiyesa: Charles Eastman, Santee Sioux*, 1983.

# Eastman, George

(July 12, 1854–March 14, 1932)
Industrialist, Philanthropist

With his new film and simple box Kodak camera, George Eastman revolutionized photography by making it available to everyone. He used the fortune made from his business to become a leading philanthropist.

Born in Waterville, New York, George Eastman took up photography as a hobby in 1877 while working as a bookkeeper for a bank in Rochester, New York. Although his salary was only $1,400 a year, he spent $94 on a camera and wet-plate equipment. Displeased with the time and difficulty involved in wet-plate processing, Eastman in 1879 invented a machine for coating rigid dry plates. The following year, he left his job at the bank to devote all his time to developing, manufacturing, and selling photographic equipment.

Eastman realized that photography would remain the province of a few amateur and professional photographers until a flexible, paper-backed film replaced the heavy, breakable, and hard-to-ship plates then in use. In 1884 he invented such a flexible film and, four years later, a simple box camera. Eastman sold his camera, along with the first roll of film and the processing of all 100 pictures on the roll, for $25. His camera was not only inexpensive for its time, but it required no skill; it had no focusing apparatus and only a single speed on the shutter, so all the photographer had to do was snap the picture. As Eastman's slogan went: "You press the button, we do the rest." He also came up with a name for his camera, Kodak, that was short, unique, and, since Eastman hoped to sell his camera worldwide, pronounceable in any language.

Backed by snappy and large-scale advertising, Eastman's Kodak film and camera soon became household words. More than 100,000 Kodak cameras were sold in the first two years alone. In the 1890s Eastman continued to improve both the film and the camera, introducing daylight-loading film, a pocket Kodak, and a cheaper model, priced as low as $5. By 1900 the reorganized and expanded Eastman Kodak Company employed over 3,000 people throughout the world. Eastman followed a policy of buying all related patents and, wherever he could, persuading competitors to sell or limit their products. In this way, he was able to dominate the photographic market abroad as well as at home.

Having built the largest and most successful manufacturing company of its kind in the world, Eastman also pioneered in industrial relations. He was one of the first employers to introduce profit-sharing as an incentive for employees. Other innovations involved the establishment of health services and retirement plans for employees.

Eastman eventually became one of the nation's five major philanthropists, giving more than $75 million to the Massachusetts Institute of Technology, the University of Rochester, Hampton Institute, and Tuskegee Institute. By 1924 he had distributed half of his fortune.

A lonely bachelor who more and more kept to himself, Eastman by 1930 played little part in the company he had founded. Two years later, he committed suicide.

**BIBLIOGRAPHY**

Ackerman, C. W., *George Eastman*, 1930; Mees, C. E. K., *From Dry Plates to Ektachrome Film, A Story of Photographic Research*, 1961; Newhall, Beaumont, *The History of Photography*, 1964.

# Eastman, Max Forrester

(January 4, 1883–March 25, 1969)
Author, Editor

Author and editor Max Eastman was an intellectual leader of radical left-wing opinion in the United States during the first quarter of the twentieth century.

Eastman was born in Canandaigua, New York. After graduating from Williams College in 1905, he continued his studies at Columbia University, where he completed the qualifications for, but declined to accept, a Ph.D.

When he left Columbia in 1911, Eastman moved to Greenwich Village in lower New York City and quickly became the unofficial leader of the group of radical intellectuals intent upon combining socialist political beliefs with artistic passion. Their goal was economic liberation for the masses and personal liberation for themselves. In 1913 Eastman published *Enjoyment of Poetry*, in which he aimed to apply psychology to poetry criticism.

In 1913 Eastman agreed to become the editor of a defunct left-wing magazine, *The Masses*. He obtained the money to resurrect the publication from wealthy donors and recruited an excellent staff. For the next three years the provocative, superbly edited journal became the most influential socialist publication in America. Because of the fierce opposition to American involvement in World War I expressed in the text and cartoons of *The Masses*, the U.S. government suppressed the magazine in 1917. Eastman and two other members of the staff were tried twice in 1918 under the Sedition Act for "conspiring to promote insubordination and mutiny in the military...and obstructing recruiting and enlistment to the injury of the service." Juries refused to convict them of the charges in both cases and the indictments were finally dropped.

In 1918 Eastman and his sister, Crystal Fuller, a woman suffrage and peace activist who strongly influenced him, founded and for five years coedited a "less rambunctious" successor to *The Masses*, called *The Liberator*, which Eastman described as more "acceptable to the postmaster general." At the same time he became infatuated with the 1917 Bolshevik Revolution in the Soviet Union. He was certain that this revolution would hasten the advent of socialism in Europe and the United States. He supported efforts to establish a Communist party in the United States, and in 1922 he went to the Soviet Union to experience a communist society firsthand. During three years there, he married the daughter of a high revolutionary official and became a member of Leon Trotsky's inner circle. The power struggle he witnessed in the Soviet Union after the death of Lenin that enabled Stalin to become dictator so disillusioned him that he fled the Soviet Union for France.

Having returned to the United States in 1927, Eastman divulged in *Since Lenin Died* (1925) that Lenin on his deathbed had warned his followers about Stalin. Though rejected and isolated by the American Communist party community, Eastman refused to compromise his perspective that communism was not the panacea many in the radical left believed it to be. He dealt with his sense of rejection and the betrayal of the promise of Marxism in the Soviet Union several times in later books: *Artists In Uniform* (1934), *The End of Socialism in Russia* (1937), *Marxism: Is It Science?* (1940), and *Reflections on the Failure of Socialism* (1955). By the 1950s, Eastman styled himself a political conservative. As his views veered to the right, he joined the staff of the *National Review* and defended the activities of Senator Joseph McCarthy.

Despite his preoccupation with politics, Eastman maintained his literary and psychological interests. In addition to *Enjoyment of Poetry*, he published numerous books of his own verse; an anti-Freudian study of the psychology of humor, *Enjoyment of Laughter* (1936); and two autobiographical books: *Enjoyment of Living* (1948) and *Love and Revolution* (1964). For twelve years he earned a living as a lecturer and then, after 1941, as a roving editor for *Reader's Digest.*

**BIBLIOGRAPHY**

Aaron, Daniel, *Writers on the Left*, 1961; Cantor, Milton, *Max Eastman*, 1970; Eastman, Max, *Enjoyment of Living*, 1948, and *Love and Revolution: My Journey Through an Epoch*, 1965; Land, Myrick E., *Fine Art of Literary Mayhem*, 1969; O'Neill, William L., *The Last Romantic: A Life of Max Eastman*, 1978.

# Eddy, Mary Morse Baker

(July 16, 1821–December 3, 1910)
Religious Leader

Mary Baker Eddy founded Christian Science and established the Church of Christ, Scientist, one of America's most important religious institutions of the late nineteenth and early twentieth century, the influence of which extends to the present.

Born on a farm near Bow, New Hampshire, Mary Baker spent much of the first forty-five years of her life in a quest for health and some measure of happiness. As a child, she was often ill and therefore absent from school, but she read and studied at home. In 1843 Mary Baker married George Washington Glover, a contractor and builder; the marriage ended with his death less than a year later. She then gave birth to her only child, a son called George. Continued ill health caused her to give the boy up to the care of a neighbor, and thereafter she had little contact with him. In 1853 she married Daniel Patterson, a traveling dentist, but the marriage proved unhappy, and she divorced him twenty years later.

Meanwhile, Mary Patterson's search for a cure to her illness took her in 1862 to Dr. Phineas Parkhurst Quimby of Portland, Maine. Quimby believed that both the cause and cure of disease lay in the mind. Using positive mental processes and the laying on of hands, he made Mary Patterson well again, and she became a devoted disciple.

In 1866 Mary Patterson fell on the ice in Lynn, Massachusetts, severely injuring her spine. Although a doctor warned that she would never walk again, she was able to heal herself after reading about one of Jesus's healing miracles in the Bible. This experience, she later claimed, marked her discovery of what she called Christian Science. She spent the next several years teaching and practicing healing, while developing her ideas about Christian Science in writing.

In 1875 her book, *Science and Health,* was published. Although she denied Quimby's influence, scholars have shown a connection between his ideas and those she set forth in this 456-page volume. Like him, she believed that "Disease is caused by mind alone," and that "Science," or God's wisdom, had been revealed to human beings by Jesus, who showed how the mind could overcome sickness and death. She further believed that God was present in everything "good" and that this good was the only reality. Since health was good, ill health was evil and the result of false belief that could be wiped out through prayer and spiritual understanding.

By the time her book came out, Mary Glover, as she now called herself, had already attracted a number of followers, and in 1875 the first public Christian Science service was held in Lynn. Two years later, Mary Glover married one of her followers, Asa Gilbert Eddy, and in 1879 she founded the Church of Christ, Scientist in Boston. In 1881 she started the Massachusetts Metaphysical College in Boston, instructing students in the doctrines and practice of Christian Science until 1889 when she retired to Concord, New Hampshire.

Despite her retirement, Mary Baker Eddy remained in complete control of the "Mother Church," reorganized and established in Boston in 1892. She revised *Science and Health* more than 380 times before she died, and was a prolific contributor to the church's various publications. These included the monthly *Christian Science Journal,* started in 1883, the weekly *Christian Science Sentinel,* dating from 1898, and the daily *Christian Science Monitor,* founded in 1908.

As a science of health, substituting readers and lay practitioners of both sexes for clergymen, the Church of Christ, Scientist appealed to women, members of the middle class, and people living in cities. All of these groups found in Christian Science a means of controlling and improving their lives amidst the dislocations of an urbanized, industrialized society.

At the time of her death in 1910, Mary Baker Eddy left a church with a membership of 100,000 and an estate valued at more than $2.5 million. The church structure and theol-ogy she developed have lasted to the present day.

**BIBLIOGRAPHY**

Peel, Robert, *Christian Science: Its Encounter with American Culture*, 1958, and *Mary Baker Eddy*, 3 vols., 1966–1977; Silberger, J., *Mary Baker Eddy: An Interpretive Biography of the Founder of Christian Science*, 1980.

# Edelman, Marian Wright

(June 6, 1939–   )
Reformer

Marian Wright Edelman, during her early civil rights activity in the South and more recently as president of the Children's Defense Fund, has directed national attention to the suffering of poor children from hunger and malnutrition.

Marian Wright was born in Bennettsville, in the sandy eastern part of South Carolina, one of six children of a Baptist minister and his wife—who also brought up fourteen foster children. Civil rights were a heartfelt concern of the Wright family, and her father spent his last days in 1954 listening to broadcast news of the *Brown* v. *Board of Education* case before the U.S. Supreme Court. He died one week before the Court declared segregation in schools unconstitutional, which occurred on May 17, 1954.

While attending Spelman College, in Atlanta, Wright spent a year abroad studying in Paris, Geneva, and the Soviet Union on a

Children's Defense Fund

Merrill Scholarship. Wright graduated as valedictorian of her class in 1960. That spring she had her first civil rights experience when Spelman students joined a sit-in at the City Hall cafeteria and were arrested. A John Hay Whitney Fellowship enabled Wright to enter the law school of Yale University, where she earned the bachelor of laws degree in 1963. She became a staff attorney for the Legal and Education Defense Fund of the National Association for the Advancement of Colored People (NAACP; see JOEL E. SPINGARN), and in 1964 went to Jackson, Mississippi, to direct the fund's office. She was the first black woman admitted to the state's bar. While in Jackson, Wright developed head-start programs in many communities for the Child Development Group of Mississippi.

During the summer of 1968, Marian Wright worked in Washington as a congressional and federal agency liaison for the Poor

People's Campaign (see RALPH D. ABERNATHY). On July 14, she was married to Peter B. Edelman, also a lawyer.

Marian Wright Edelman, from fall 1968 to spring 1973, held a Field Foundation grant under which, until 1971, she was involved in the Washington Research Project of the Southern Center for Public Policy. A principal concern of hers was planning and lobbying for the Food Stamp Act, which was enacted in 1970. When Peter Edelman became vice president of the University of Massachusetts, the family moved to Boston, and for two years Marian Edelman directed the Center for Law and Education at Harvard University.

While on the Washington Research Project Edelman was working toward the idea that became the Children's Defense Fund (CDF). She founded the CDF and became its president in 1973. The CDF is pledged to giving the needs of children—in particular, poor and minority children—priority on the social agenda. It focuses on childhood health and education in all aspects, with emphasis on infant mortality, teenage pregnancy, and child abuse. The CDF lobbies Congress through continuing research and authoritative reports. Even when the Reagan administration was reducing social expenditures, Edelman was instrumental in achieving the passage of a group of programs, "The Children's Initiative."

Among numerous awards and honors, Edelman received a MacArthur Foundation Prize Fellowship in 1984 carrying $228,000, which she turned over to the CDF. She has received more than sixty honorary degrees.

**BIBLIOGRAPHY**

Edelman, Marian Wright, *Children Out of School in America*, 1974, *Portrait of Inequality: Black and White Children in America*, 1980, *Families in Peril: An Agenda for Social Change*, 1987, and *The Measure of Our Success: A Letter to My Children and Yours*, 1992; Tomkins, Calvin, "A Sense of Urgency," *The New Yorker*, March 27, 1989.

# Edison, Thomas Alva

(February 11, 1847–October 18, 1931)
Inventor

Thomas A. Edison, despite deafness from an early age and a limited formal education, became one of the nation's most prolific pioneers in the development of electronic inventions that have transformed the lives of people everywhere.

Edison's forebears included both Canadians and Loyalists during the American Revolution. He was born in the village of Milan, near Lake Erie in central Ohio, the youngest of seven children. His great-grandfather, John Edison, had been a Loyalist soldier during the War of Independence and afterward became an exile in Nova Scotia. John's grandson, Samuel, joined an insurrection at Toronto (then York) in 1837 led by William Lyon Mackenzie against the power bloc of wealthy families. Upon the failure of the revolt Samuel Edison fled to Ohio, where he became a prosperous manufacturer of lumber products. While still in Canada he had married Nancy Elliott, a schoolteacher. When Thomas was seven his father moved the family to Port Huron, Michigan, north of Detroit, and opened a firm dealing in lumber and grain. Thomas grew up in a family that enjoyed a comfortable way of life.

Because young Edison did poorly in school, he was taught at home by his mother. Mathematics was his weakest subject, but he found chemistry to his taste. When in his teens he began working on trains selling newspapers, candy, and such, and he set up a chemical laboratory in a baggage car. Getting to know telegraph operators in the stations, he became a telegrapher himself at sixteen and roamed around the Midwest, working at telegraphy and odd jobs, dabbling in chemistry, picking up information from continual reading, and trying out inventions. During these years he began to suffer from deafness, possibly owing to an accident.

In 1868 Edison went to work as an operator for the Western Union Telegraph Company in Boston, meanwhile continuing to tinker with experiments. The next year he took out a patent for his first invention, an electric vote-recording machine, which he took to Washington and demonstrated before a Congressional committee. It was turned down because it counted votes too rapidly and would prevent members of Congress from filibustering. In New York, after showing off his technical skill, he was hired as general manager by Laws's Gold Indicator Company. Soon afterward, with two other electrical engineers, he formed a company specializing in electrical work of all kinds. In 1870, when the firm was sold, Edison received $40,000 for his share and started his own electrical business, for which he hired trained technicians able to work on inventions under his supervision, as well as scientific theorists. He had an intuitive gift for judging the abilities of prospective employees.

Edison concentrated during the early 1870s on making advances in the telegraph, often improving on the work of an earlier inventor. Typically, he took the duplex system of telegraphing, by which two messages could be sent simultaneously, and made it quadruplex, allowing for four messages. In 1876 he set up an "invention plant" at Menlo Park, New Jersey, where he and his staff pursued independent research on and development of projects that were seen to be profitable. In 1877 Edison invented the phonograph, at first a crude device which he slowly improved. Two years later, he made the incandescent electric bulb a commercial possibility, working from the discov-

eries of others going back to the 1840s. His chief (and essential) contribution was to perfect the means for cheap production of the bulbs and for bringing power to them from a central source. On Pearl Street in lower New York City he established the first plant to generate power. He devised light sockets, safety fuses, junction boxes, and other elements of the electric system now familiar to everyone.

By 1887 the facility at Menlo Park had outgrown itself, and Edison moved his headquarters to West Orange, New Jersey, where work continued on a larger scale. (Edison's home and laboratory are now part of a National Historic Site, and his Menlo Park workshop was moved to Greenfield Village, in Dearborn, Michigan.) Edison organized companies to make and sell the inventions, and these were eventually merged into what is now the General Electric Company.

In experimenting with the motion picture during the 1890s, Edison and his colleagues took an existing device, improved it, patented it as the Edison Vitascope, and encouraged the formation and systematization of what became the movie industry. He experimented with synchronizing sound and cinema, anticipating the eventual development of sound movies.

Edison's other successes, often worked out from existing inventions, include the electric dynamo, the storage battery, the dictaphone (Ediphone), the mimeograph, the microphone, the electric locomotive, railway signaling devices, and lighting systems for railway cars and mines. In World War I he chaired the Naval Consulting Board, where he contributed his experience to research on torpedoes, periscopes, flamethrowers, and devices to protect ships from the torpedoes of U-boats.

At Seminole Lodge, the winter home Edison built at Fort Myers, Florida, in the 1880s, he established the Edison Botanical Research Laboratory where he experimented unsuccessfully with making rubber from the goldenrod plant and using bamboo fiber for the filament in the incandescent bulb. His friends HENRY FORD and Harvey Firestone encouraged his efforts, and Ford bought an estate adjoining

Seminole Lodge. Edison continued to spend winters in Fort Myers until the end of his life.

Edison and his first wife, Mary Stilwell, whom he married in 1871, had three children. Two years after her death in 1884 he married Mina Miller, twenty years his junior, with whom he had three more children. Her father was Lewis Miller, one of the founders of the Chautauqua Institution, a religious retreat in western New York State, and the Edisons were often there despite Thomas Edison's skepticism.

Edison made only one discovery in pure science, the "Edison effect," which he noted and patented in 1883 and which led other workers to discover the vacuum tube, in turn important for radio. Edison registered some 1,000 patents, though many of these were the result of cooperative work in his laboratories. Even during Edison's lifetime, the phenomenal character of such inventions as electric light, the phonograph, and motion pictures gave him an almost heroic stature in the common view, and a virtual mythology grew up about the events of his life and career.

**BIBLIOGRAPHY**

Josephson, Matthew, *Edison: A Biography*, 1959; Wachhorst, Wyn, *Thomas Alva Edison, An American Myth*, 1981.

# Edwards, Jonathan

(October 5, 1703–March 22, 1758)
Religious Leader

Jonathan Edwards was a theologian, philosopher, and evangelical Congregational minister who exerted an enormous influence on the course of religious history in America and helped spark the religious revival known as the Great Awakening.

Jonathan Edwards was born in East Windsor, Connecticut, the only son of a minister and schoolmaster. Educated at home by his father, he entered Yale College before he was thirteen. There he read the works of the English philosopher John Locke and the natural philosopher and mathematician Sir Isaac Newton. Graduating first in his class in 1720, Edwards underwent a religious conversion and decided to become a minister. He spent two years studying theology at Yale, then served briefly as a Presbyterian minister to a church in New York City. In 1724 he returned to Yale as a tutor in the college, leaving after two years to assist his grandfather, Solomon Stoddard, a prominent New England clergyman, as minister of the church in Northampton, Massachusetts.

In 1729, upon his grandfather's death, Edwards succeeded him as senior minister of the church in Northampton, then the most important pulpit in Massachusetts outside of Boston. Two years later, Edwards was invited to preach before the Boston clergy. With this, his first published sermon, entitled "God Glorified in the Work of Redemption, by the Greatness of Man's Dependence on Him in the Whole of It," he won fame as a theologian. Edwards contended that the new psychology of John Locke and the new psychology of Sir Isaac Newton did not destroy the Puritan belief in an all-powerful God, but rather proved the complete dependence of human beings on God. He further maintained that his fellow Congregational ministers had gone astray by stressing good works as a means of salvation. In Edwards's view, redemption came only through the gift of God's grace, independent of any human effort.

In 1735 Edwards's sermons on justification by faith alone produced a revival in Northampton, which resulted in more than 300 conversions, including that of a four-year-old girl. Edwards wrote a history of the revival, *A Faithful Narrative of the Surprising Work of God* (1737), that was read with great interest in Europe as well as America, particularly for its descriptions of the types and stages of the conversion experience.

In 1740 a huge revival known as the Great Awakening spread throughout the colonies, accompanied by mass conversions and violent emotional reactions. Though Edwards was not the only leader of this revival, he played an important role in its early stages with hellfire and brimstone sermons like his famous *Sinners in the Hands of An Angry God* (1741), in which he declared: "The God that holds you over the pit of hell, much as one holds a spider, or some loathsome insect, over the fire, abhors you, and is dreadfully provoked." Unlike some of his revivalist colleagues, however, Edwards did not engage in pulpit histrionics. He delivered his frightening sermons in a calm, low voice.

While Edwards considered the Great Awakening a genuine work of God, he was critical of its excesses and subjected the revival to careful scrutiny in *The Distinguishing Marks of a Work of the Spirit of God* (1741), *Some Thoughts Concerning the Present Revival of Religion in New England* (1742), and *A Treatise Concerning Religious Affections* (1746). In the latter work, Edwards described with great psychological insight the different kinds of religious experience so that his readers would be able to distinguish the true from the false. His treatise anticipated the philosopher and psychologist WILLIAM JAMES's *Varieties of Religious Experience* by more than a hundred years.

Edwards parted company with revivalist preachers on the question of church membership as well as preaching style. While they welcomed into the fold all who desired salvation, he stood with the traditionalists in believing that church membership should be limited to those who could provide evidence of saving grace. Edwards's position aroused great controversy at his Northampton church, and in 1750 the church voted to remove him as minister.

For most of the next eight years Edwards served as a missionary and pastor to the American Indians and a few white settlers in Stockbridge, Massachusetts. Despite the hardships of this frontier post, he managed to write several important books, notably *Freedom of the Will* (1754). The book addressed the question that was at the heart of Edwards's theology: If everything is predetermined by God, how can people exercise free will? Edwards maintained that there is freedom, because the mind can freely act out its choice, even though the origin of the choice is determined beforehand by the motive, or that which is perceived as the greatest apparent good. If individuals perceive God to be the greatest apparent good, they can choose to serve him, but only if God reveals himself to them as the greatest good, a revelation that is not given to everyone. Having the power to choose to act, individuals bear moral responsibility for their actions and are therefore deserving of reward or punishment.

While in Stockbridge, Edwards also wrote books on original sin, the nature of true virtue, and the purpose of creation that, together with his book on free will, established his influence for the next half-century. In 1757 Edwards was appointed to succeed his son-in-law, Aaron Burr, as president of the College of New Jersey (now Princeton University). Assuming this office in January 1758, he died shortly afterward of complications following a smallpox inoculation.

**BIBLIOGRAPHY**

Guelzo, Allen C., *Edwards on the Will*, 1989; Jenson, Robert W., *America's Theologian*, 1988; Miller, Perry, *Jonathan Edwards*, 1949, rep., 1981; Storms, C. S., *Tragedy in Eden*, 1986.

# Einstein, Albert

(March 14, 1879–April 18, 1955)
Physicist, Social Philosopher

Albert Einstein was the most renowned scientist of the twentieth century and one of the greatest of all time. His remarkable insights and creative imagination enabled him to bring about great advances in theoretical physics.

Einstein was born in Ulm, Germany, the son of Hermann Einstein and Pauline Koch. When Albert was a year old the family moved to Munich, where Hermann Einstein ran a small electrochemical plant. Albert was not a notably good student, but scientific subjects and geometry interested him. His parents moved to Italy in 1894, and Albert later followed them. In 1895 his desire to enter the Federal Technical Institute (ETH) in Zurich, Switzerland, was disappointed because he failed the entrance examination in subjects outside physics and mathematics, his principal interests. He went for a year to a secondary school in Aarau, Switzerland, and in 1896 was admitted to the ETH. He passed the examinations in 1902, but not brilliantly.

In 1902 Einstein went to work at the Swiss Patent Office in Bern, the capital, where he had enough free time to write. In 1903 he married a Hungarian student he had met at the ETH, Mileva Maric; she became the mother of his two sons. His earliest papers were on statistical thermodynamics. In 1905 Einstein published a series of papers in an important journal, *Annalen der Physik,* that had a notable influence on physics. In one paper he all but proved the existence of molecules by theorizing; the essay was accepted by the University of Zurich as his

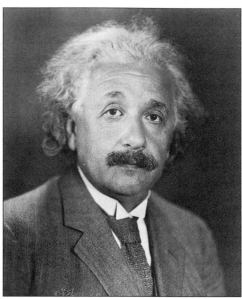

Library of Congress

Ph.D. dissertation. In another paper in the series he proved that light is a wave as well as a particle; and in still another, of major importance, "On the Electrodynamics of Moving Bodies," he developed the outline of what was eventually called the special theory of relativity. Another paper in 1905 contained his famous equation $E = mc^2$, meaning that the energy in matter (E) is equal to its mass (m) multiplied by the square of the velocity of light (c). Stars, according to this theory, can emit large quantities of light yet lose very little mass. The equation anticipated the splitting of the atom and the possibility of the atom bomb.

The major importance of Einstein's work began to be recognized. In 1909 he became a professor at the University of Zurich, and two years later he was at the German University in Prague. He returned to Zurich for a professorship at the ETH, having in the meantime taken Swiss citizenship, which he retained though also acquiring German citizenship. In 1914 he went to Berlin at the invitation of the Prussian Academy of Sciences as director of scientific research at the Kaiser Wilhelm Institute (now the Max Planck Institute), remaining there until 1933.

During World War I, Einstein maintained a quiet pacifism, being absorbed deeply in research. In 1915 he developed and published his general theory of relativity. His propositions regarding the behavior of light were tested and verified in 1919 by scientists on a British expedition that photographed a solar eclipse.

When their findings were reported, Einstein and his theory of relativity became famous.

In 1921 the Nobel Prize for Physics was awarded to Einstein for his services to theoretical physics and in particular for his discovery of the law of the photoelectric effect. A lecture engagement in Japan prevented him from attending the ceremonies in Stockholm, but he delivered his address the following year.

Einstein separated from his wife in 1914 and divorced her in 1919, later marrying his widowed cousin, Elsa Einstein. He became more conscious of his Jewish origins and spoke for Zionism during the 1920s. Though he encouraged the establishment of the Hebrew University in Jerusalem, he remained in Europe, where he supported the League of Nations in its work for peace. In the years before Hitler, Einstein had been attacked by anti-Semitic scientists, some of whom criticized his work as "Jewish physics." In 1934 the Nazi government seized Einstein's property and revoked his German citizenship. At the time he and his wife were in Princeton, New Jersey, where he had been invited to take a half-time appointment at the Institute for Advanced Study. He chose not to return to Germany and decided to become a full-time member of the institute, where he continued his work for the rest of his life. Chiefly he was seeking to create a unified field theory that would link light and electromagnetism, a goal he never fully achieved. He became an American citizen in 1940.

During the 1930s Einstein spoke out strongly against the Nazi government and in favor of world peace. After nuclear fission was achieved in Germany in 1938, a group of scientists, fearful that the Germans might develop armaments based on fission, urged Einstein to write to President Franklin D. Roosevelt warning of the danger and proposing that American scientists study the matter. The consequence was the development of the A-bomb and its explosion over Japanese cities (see J. ROBERT OPPENHEIMER). Though Einstein had abandoned pacifism and considered that Nazi German aggression could be halted only by military force, he did not involve himself in the actual development of nuclear weapons.

Einstein retired from the Institute for Advanced Study in 1945 and lived quietly in the town of Princeton, where he was regarded with affection and respect. In 1952 he was invited to become the president of Israel, but he declined. He actively promoted international government and criticized efforts in the United States to limit free speech for the sake of internal security. Not long before his death he joined the English philosopher Bertrand Russell in issuing a statement warning world leaders of the imminent peril of nuclear war.

BIBLIOGRAPHY

Bernstein, Jeremy, *Einstein*, 1973; Clark, R. W., *Einstein: The Life and Times*, 1971; Einstein, Albert, *The World as I See It*, 1949, and *Out of My Later Years*, 1950; Einstein, Albert, and R. Lawson (trans.), *Relativity: The Special and General Theory*, 1920, rep., 1961; Friedman, Alan J., *Einstein as Myth and Muse*, 1985; Hoffmann, Banesh, and Helen Dukas, *Albert Einstein, Creator and Rebel*, 1972.

# Eliot, Charles William

(March 20, 1834–August 22, 1926)
Educator

As president of Harvard University for forty years, Charles Eliot was one of the outstanding educational reformers of the late nineteenth and early twentieth centuries.

Born in Boston into a socially prominent family, Charles Eliot attended the Boston Latin School before entering Harvard at the age of fifteen. He graduated second in his class, then took a teaching position in mathematics and chemistry at Harvard. When he failed to receive tenure, Eliot studied abroad for several years, upon his return becoming professor of chemistry at the Massachusetts Institute of Technology. In 1869 Eliot published two articles on "The New Education" in the *Atlantic Monthly*. They made a great impression on officials at Harvard who were searching for a new president and in due course he became the newly elected president of the university at age thirty-five.

In the course of his long term of office, Eliot inaugurated sweeping changes at Harvard. He wanted the university to consist of a college of undergraduate studies, surrounded by autonomous graduate and professional schools. Eliot increased faculty salaries and raised the number of faculty members tenfold, from 60 to 600 in forty years. During this period, the student body grew fourfold. Eliot instituted sabbaticals to give faculty more time for research and established a liberal system of faculty retirement allowances. Moreover, he sought to ensure academic freedom and to foster an atmosphere conducive to scholarship.

On the undergraduate level, the most important change made by Eliot was the introduction of the elective system, whereby students were given a much wider range of choice in what courses they took. After 1894 the only required courses at Harvard were English and modern languages. Eliot also saw that science courses gained a secure footing in the curriculum.

On the graduate and professional level, Eliot added to the university the Graduate Schools of Arts and Sciences, Applied Science, and Business Administration. He also significantly improved the quality and methods of instruction at the law and medical schools. The law school course was lengthened to three years, and the case system became the chief method of instruction. At the medical school a four-year program including laboratory work and opportunities for clinical instruction replaced the old program (two four-months' courses of lectures), and written examinations replaced oral ones as a requirement for graduation. These changes helped make Harvard one of the leading universities in the world.

Eliot's concern with the relation between higher education and secondary education led him to exert a major influence in the latter area. As chairman (1892) of the National Education Association's Committee of Ten, Eliot helped develop a standard secondary school curriculum designed for all students, whether or not they were bound for college. He believed that secondary school subjects ought to be extended into the elementary grades as a means of reducing the age by which students were ready for college. He further believed that education ought to be adapted to individual differences not by lowering standards, but by letting students find the subjects they were best able to handle. Thanks largely to Eliot's advocacy, the Board of College Entrance Examinations, a central organization for the setting and grading of written examinations for admission to college, was established in 1901.

Eliot set forth his ideas in many books, including *The Conflict between Individualism and Collectivism in a Democracy* (1910) and

*A Late Harvest* (1924). In the last year of his presidency, he also began editing the *Harvard Classics*, a widely circulated anthology of world literature. The fifty-volume series grew out of a remark by Eliot that a person could acquire a liberal education by reading fifteen minutes a day from books that could all find room on a "five-foot shelf."

After his retirement from the presidency of Harvard in 1909, Eliot served on the Board of Overseers of the university from 1910 to 1916.

He was also a member of the General Education Board, set up by JOHN D. ROCKEFELLER, and of the Carnegie Foundation for the Advancement of Teaching. Vigorous till the end, he lived to be ninety-two.

**BIBLIOGRAPHY**

Cotton, E. H., *Life of Chas. W. Eliot*, 1926; James, Henry, *Charles W. Eliot*, 2 vols., 1930.

## Ely, Richard Theodore

(April 13, 1854–October 4, 1943)
Economist, Reformer

Sometimes called the dean of American economists, Richard T. Ely insisted that the laws of economics were "fluid and changeable." He popularized the study of economics and the ideas of Christian socialism, which provided the framework for his support of labor unions and progressive social action in general.

Richard T. Ely was born in the village of Ripley, on Lake Erie in western New York State, the eldest of three children born to parents of New England stock. His father, a civil engineer, was a rigid Presbyterian; his mother was a former schoolteacher. Richard Ely attended the Fredonia Academy and, at sixteen, taught at a country school. He entered Dartmouth College, and a year later transferred to Columbia College, in New York City, where he earned a B.A. degree in 1876. In 1879, on a Columbia scholarship, Ely went to Germany and got a Ph.D. at the University of Heidelberg. At both universities he worked under professors who, following the German historical school of economics, viewed economic activity as being influenced by cultural patterns and government policies, in contrast to the rigid concepts of classical economics.

Returning to America, Ely joined the faculty of the Johns Hopkins University as a lecturer, and by 1887 he was an associate professor of economics and a leader in the teaching of the "new economics." Woodrow Wilson was among his students. Ely was a founder of the American Economic Association and later its president. He taught that the inductive methods of modern science should be applied to economics. Economic principles were not a matter of natural law but must be based in the actual needs of people and must flow and change with society. Uncontrolled individualism, he believed, interferes with social coherence, and the state has a positive role to play in the economy. Ely's advocacies included factory regulation, labor unions, the prohibition of child labor, immigration limitation, and savings banks for the laboring classes. In 1886 he published *The Labor Movement in America*, in which he affirmed the right of working men to unionize.

Ely left the rigid Presbyterianism of his father and found his place in the Episcopal Church, where he adopted a social gospel point of view (see WALTER RAUSCHENBUSCH). In his lectures at the Chautauqua Institution, near his birthplace in New York, his message reached many clergymen and future clergymen. He urged that the churches not go along with the status quo but recognize that the mission of Christianity is "to bring to pass here a kingdom of righteousness." Ely's lectures and writings reached a large lay public as well and helped to popularize the ideas of Christian socialism.

In 1892 Ely moved to the University of Wisconsin in order to direct its new School of Economics, Political Science, and History. Inevitably he was criticized by conservatives. A state official charged that Ely had advised a strike organizer and that he taught socialism. The university regents vindicated Ely's rights, an early instance of the defense of academic freedom.

Ely did indeed advocate socialism, though of a rather mild kind. He favored socialization of such natural monopolies as public utilities, railroads, telephones, and mines, though he believed that competitive private ownership was preferable for some industrial activities. He was uncomfortable with strikes and held that public employees should rely on negotiation to settle disputes with management. In 1906 Ely accepted the presidency of the American Association for Labor Legislation.

After 1900, when Robert La Follette was elected governor of Wisconsin on a reform platform, Ely became involved in state politics and was an adviser to the governor. He broke with him, however, over American participation in World War I, which La Follette (then a senator) opposed. Ely campaigned to defeat La Follette's reelection to the Senate in 1918.

Meanwhile Ely had become interested in land economics. He invested in real estate and set up realty companies around the country. In 1920 he led in organizing the Institute for Research in Land Economics at the University of Wisconsin. His doctrines appealed to realtors and public utility officials, who helped finance the institute's work. When Wisconsin progressives attacked Ely's views, he moved his institute to Northwestern University, in Evanston, Illinois, and expanded its programs to include publications.

Ely was first married in 1884 to Anna Anderson, and they had four children. She died in 1923, and in 1931, at seventy-seven, Ely was married to Margaret Hahn, a member of his institute's staff, who was thirty-two. They had two children. Ely retired to Old Lyme, Connecticut, and died there at the age of eighty-nine.

### BIBLIOGRAPHY

Ely, Richard T., *Monopolies and Trusts*, 1912, and *Ground Under Our Feet*, 1938, rep., 1977; Ely, Richard T., with G. S. Wehrwein, *Land Economics*, 1940; Rader, Benjamin G., *The Academic Mind and Reform: The Influence of Richard T. Ely in American Life*, 1966.

# Emerson, Ralph Waldo

(May 25, 1803–April 27, 1882)
Author, Reformer

As an essayist, poet, and lecturer, Ralph Waldo Emerson was a leading exponent of the American philosophical movement known as Transcendentalism, which had far-reaching effects on literature, religion, and social reform.

Emerson was born in Boston, the son of a liberal Congregational minister, whose death when the boy was eight brought financial difficulties to the family. Nevertheless, with the help of an aunt, Emerson and his brothers were able to obtain an education. After attending the

Boston Latin School, Emerson enrolled at Harvard University in 1817. He made little impression on his fellow students but while there began keeping the journals that were to provide the material for his lectures and writings. Graduating in 1821, he was elected class poet only because six other students had declined the honor.

Emerson then taught school for several years before entering Harvard Divinity School. He was "approbated" as a Unitarian minister in 1826, and three years later was ordained as pastor of the prestigious Second Church of Boston. Though a popular preacher, Emerson soon began to question the "cold intellectualism" of his Unitarian faith. Based on the philosophy of John Locke, it maintained that the only valid knowledge was that which could be demonstrated by the senses. At the end of 1832 he resigned his pastorate on the grounds that he could no longer believe in communion as a divine sacrament. Shortly afterward he departed for Europe, where he met the English poets William Wordsworth and Samuel Taylor Coleridge, the economist and philosopher John Stuart Mill, and the historian and social critic Thomas Carlyle, with whom Emerson maintained a correspondence lasting nearly forty years. These contacts, together with Emerson's reading of German idealistic philosophers, helped shape the new set of ideas he was beginning to formulate.

Returning to Boston in the fall of 1833, Emerson began to speak on such topics as biography, literature, and the philosophy of history. Late in 1834 Emerson moved to Concord, Massachusetts, where he was to make his home for the rest of his life. His house became a gathering place for a group of writers and conversation-

Library of Congress

alists, including BRONSON ALCOTT, HENRY DAVID THOREAU, MARGARET FULLER, and ELIZABETH PEABODY, who met to discuss new philosophical ideas and were dubbed the Transcendentalists by their contemporaries.

In 1836 Emerson's first book, *Nature*, containing the essence of his Transcendental thought, was published. Emerson and the Transcendentalists believed that intuitive knowledge was superior to sensory knowledge. People have innate ideas that come, not through the five senses (by way of experience or observation) or the powers of reasoning, but directly from God. Emerson held that the physical world (society, church, customs) was not as important as the spiritual world, and that human beings can find solutions to problems by discovering the truth within themselves, emphasizing self-reliance and individualism. This optimistic philosophy with its rejection of tradition and emphasis on self-reliance proved especially attractive to the younger generation. Although the Transcendentalists believed true reform came from within the individual, many of Emerson's group joined the social reform movements of the day.

In 1837 Emerson delivered the Phi Beta Kappa address at Harvard, entitled "The American Scholar." Whereas his book *Nature* had sold poorly, the address was an instant success and in printed form sold well. In it, Emerson called on his listeners to "have done with Europe and all dead cultures" and to "explore the possibilities of our own new world." The following year, Emerson delivered his most controversial speech, the Divinity School address at Harvard, attacking formal Christianity and exhorting his listeners to rely instead on their individual intuitive experience. Emerson was denounced in the press and ostracized from Harvard.

In 1840 Emerson joined with other Transcendentalists in publishing a quarterly, the *Dial.* First under the editorship of Margaret Fuller and then under that of Emerson himself, the *Dial* served as a major organ of Transcendentalist thinking. In 1841 Emerson also published the first volume of his *Essays,* containing what was to become one of his most influential writings, "Self-Reliance," which was essentially a call for individual independence and nonconformity. A second volume of essays followed three years later; *Poems* appeared in 1847; and *Addresses and Lectures* and *Representative Men,* based on a series of lectures Emerson had given in 1845, were published in 1849 and 1850, respectively.

Emerson further cemented his reputation by lecturing. Throughout the 1840s and 1850s, he went on the lecture circuit regularly, speaking in towns and cities all over the East, and eventually the West. In 1847 he made a highly successful lecture tour of England, his lectures the following year forming the basis of *English Traits* (1856), an examination of national character.

Also during these years, Emerson sought to define himself in relation to the major reform movements of his day. Although he attended planning meetings for the utopian community of Brook Farm in 1840, he chose not to take part. Nor did he participate in Bronson Alcott's community of Fruitlands, established later. Emerson did, however, actively support abolition, giving his first antislavery address in 1844. He strongly protested the Fugitive Slave Act of 1850; and in 1855 in a major Boston address entitled "American Slavery," he advocated raising money to purchase slaves' freedom. He became an admirer of the militant abolitionist JOHN BROWN and was introduced to him by Henry David Thoreau; Emerson contributed money to Brown's efforts in Kansas, later speaking in Brown's behalf after his capture and arrest at Harpers Ferry in 1859. During the Civil War, Emerson met twice with President Abraham Lincoln to urge emancipation.

In the remaining three decades of his life, Emerson continued to write and lecture, though his influence was not as strong as before. His later writings included *The Conduct of Life* (1860), again based on a series of lectures he had given; another collection of poems, *May-Day;* and his final collection of essays, *Society and Solitude* (1870). In 1866 the rift with Harvard was finally mended when the college granted him an honorary L.L.D. degree. The following year he was invited to deliver the Phi Beta Kappa address, and in 1870 he was asked to give a course of academic lectures, "Natural History of Intellect."

By this time, however, Emerson's mind had begun to fail. He managed a trip to California in 1871, where he met the naturalist JOHN MUIR; visited Europe again; and also made a trip to the Nile Valley of Egypt. In 1879 he helped launch a short-lived Transcendentalist revival with the establishment of the Concord (summer) School of Philosophy. At the age of seventy-eight, Emerson died in Concord of pneumonia.

**BIBLIOGRAPHY**

Allen, Gay W., *Waldo Emerson: A Biography,* 1981; Bode, Carl, and Malcolm Cowley (eds.), *The Portable Emerson,* 1981; Donadio, Stephen, et al. (eds.), *Emerson and His Legacy,* 1986; Gilman, W. H., et al. (eds.), *Journals and Miscellaneous Notebooks of Ralph Waldo Emerson,* 16 vols., 1960–1982.

# Erikson, Erik Homburger

(June 15, 1902–   )
Educator, Psychoanalyst

Erik Erikson earned a reputation as one of the most influential psychoanalysts in the United States. Best known for his work on troubled youth, he introduced the term "identity crisis" and described the different stages, each with its own emotional crisis, that individuals pass through from infancy to old age.

Erikson was born in Frankfurt, Germany, to Danish parents. He completed a classical high school education at Karlsruhe, Germany, then spent several years traveling, studying art, and drawing. In 1927 he settled in Vienna, where at the invitation of his friend, the child analyst Peter Blos, he began teaching at an experimental school. He met members of the Vienna Psychoanalytic Institute, which had developed under Sigmund Freud, and studied there, mainly with Freud's daughter Anna. Also during this period he was certified as a Montessori teacher.

In 1933 Erikson graduated from the Vienna Psychoanalytic Institute. With the rise to power of Adolf Hitler in Germany, he decided to immigrate to the United States soon after taking his degree. He settled in Boston, where he set up a private practice as the city's first child analyst; he was also associated with Massachusetts General Hospital and the Harvard Psychological Clinic. While in Boston, he came into contact with such anthropologists as MARGARET MEAD and RUTH BENEDICT, and he began to develop a perspective combining psychoanalytic theory with anthropology. In 1936 Erikson joined the Institute of Human Relations at Yale, where he also taught at the medical school. Continuing to pursue his interest in anthropology, Erikson studied early childhood training methods of the Sioux Indians on a reservation in South Dakota in 1938.

From 1939, the year he became a U.S. citizen, to 1950, Erikson taught and conducted research at the San Francisco Psychoanalytic Institute and at the University of California at Berkeley. The Berkeley project was a long-term study of normal children through their first ten years of life. Also during these years, Erikson studied childhood training among the Yurok Indians of northern California, and he worked with emotionally disturbed war veterans. In 1950 Erikson was widely acclaimed for the publication of *Childhood and Society*. In this classic study, Erikson extended the work of Sigmund Freud by maintaining that the psychosexual stages set forth by Freud are paralleled by psychosocial stages covering the entire life cycle.

In the same year that *Childhood and Society* appeared, Erikson left the University of California rather than sign an oath that he was not a communist (he was not) and went to the Austin Riggs Center in Stockbridge, Massachusetts, where he worked with emotionally disturbed young people. Also during this time, Erikson worked with disturbed children at the Western Psychiatric Institute of the University of Pittsburgh School of Medicine, where he collaborated with Dr. BENJAMIN SPOCK. While doing this work, he developed the concept of identity, or the individual's sense of inner continuity in the midst of change, and the accompanying concept of an "identity crisis," which normally precedes the emergence of a firm identity at the end of adolescence and in some individuals may be prolonged. In 1958 Erikson published *Young Man Luther*, a psychohistorical study of the Protestant leader Martin Luther. The book reflected Erikson's interest in the lives of gifted individuals, how they discover themselves and how their lives can express the conflicts of their particular historical era.

In 1960 Erikson returned to Harvard as professor of human development and lecturer in psychiatry, remaining there until his retirement in 1970. He was a fellow at Harvard's

Center for Advanced Study in the Behavioral Sciences, and he also taught at the Massachusetts Institute of Technology. During these years, Erikson wrote essays on many topics, including the attitudes of young people and a wide range of political and social issues. Many of his essays were later published in two collections: *Insight and Responsibility* (1964) and *Identity: Youth and Crisis* (1968).

Beginning in 1962, Erikson spent time in India working on a study of the Indian leader Mohandas K. Gandhi that was published in 1969 as *Gandhi's Truth: On the Origins of Militant Nonviolence*. In it, Erikson traced both Gandhi's personal history of nonviolent civil disobedience and the history of India, showing how the two intersected. Erikson dedicated the book to black civil rights leader MARTIN LUTHER KING, JR., and expressed the hope that humankind would be ready to accept "Gandhi's truth" in order to prevent the destruction of the world. The book won a Pulitzer Prize and the National Book Award.

After retiring from Harvard, Erikson continued with fieldwork among such groups as the Sioux, black farmers in Mississippi, and ghetto children. He has also continued to develop and elaborate his ideas in such books as *Life History and the Historical Moment* (1975), *Identity and the Life Cycle* (1980), *The Life Cycle Completed* (1982), and *Vital Involvement in Old Age* (1986).

**BIBLIOGRAPHY**

Coles, Robert, *Erik Erikson: The Growth of His Work*, 1970; Kotre, John N., *Outliving the Self: Generativity and the Interpretation of Lives*, 1984; Stevens, Richard, *Erik Erikson, an Introduction*, 1983; Wright, Eugene, *Erik Erikson: Identity and Religion*, 1982.

# Evans, George Henry

(March 25, 1805–February 2, 1856)
Editor, Reformer

Editor of the first important labor paper in the United States, George Henry Evans was also among the early eastern advocates of the homestead movement. His ideas on land reform anticipated those of HENRY GEORGE and influenced the labor movement for many years afterward.

Born at Bromyard, Herefordshire, England, George Henry Evans immigrated to the United States in 1820 when he was fifteen, along with his father and a younger brother, Frederick William. While working as a printer's apprentice in Ithaca, New York, Evans and his brother avidly read and discussed the works of Thomas Jefferson and Thomas Paine. Frederick William later became a Shaker.

Evans started his first labor newspaper, *The Man*, in Ithaca in 1822. Moving to New York City, he then edited and published from 1829 to 1837 and again from 1844 to 1856 *The Working Man's Advocate*, the first major labor journal in the country. In 1829, the same year that Evans started publishing his paper, the Workingman's party was established in New York. Evans soon became involved in the party's activities, reporting its meetings and using his paper to advocate the party's calls for improved working conditions and free public education.

When the Workingman's party lost in the local and state elections of 1830, Evans began to look for another solution to the workers' problems. Increasingly he became convinced that the answer lay in what he termed "the new agrarianism," or the opening up of cheap or free western lands as a means of providing workers with greater opportunities. In 1840 Evans published *History of the Origin of the Working Men's Party,* in which he argued that the party had been mistaken in relying on politics to achieve its goals and called instead for an Agrarian League to push for free land.

In 1844 Evans resumed publication of the *Advocate,* which now became a vehicle for the advancement of his new agrarianism. His proposals represented an outgrowth of the thinking of Thomas Jefferson and Thomas Paine with regard to the individual's inalienable right to life. Evans held that along with other gifts of nature, every individual had a right to a homestead of 160 acres. His advocacy of this idea was so effective that the reformist editor HORACE GREELEY was among those who took up the homestead cause in the 1850s.

Evans also pushed for other reforms in the *Advocate* and in the *Daily Sentinel* and *Young America,* two papers which he later edited. He called for an end to imprisonment for debt, the abolition of all forms of slavery, and equal rights for women. He also took a stand against the United States Bank, which he regarded as a monopoly, and as a member of the Young America movement called for territorial expansion, along with a truly distinctive national literature. At age fifty Evans died at his farm in Granville, New Jersey, purchased in the 1830s when his new agrarianism was beginning to take shape.

**BIBLIOGRAPHY**

Persons, Egbert, and S. Persons (eds.), *Socialism and American Life,* 2 vols., 1952; Whitman, Alden, *Early American Labor Parties,* 1943.

## Evers, Medgar Wiley

(July 2, 1926–June 12, 1963)
Civil Rights Leader

Medgar Evers's career as a fighter for the civil rights of African Americans was cut off when he was assassinated by a segregationist in Jackson, Mississippi.

Medgar Evers was born in Decatur, in eastern Mississippi. His father was a sawmill hand, his mother did domestic work, and on their small plot the family raised their own livestock, vegetables, and even cotton. He joined the U.S. Army in his teens and saw action in Europe. The GI Bill enabled him to go to Alcorn Agricultural and Mechanical College (now a state university), in southwest Mississippi. While working as an insurance salesman, in 1954, he tried to enter the University of Mississippi law school, but the race barrier prevailed.

During his time in the army, Evers became absorbed in the writings of Jomo Kenyatta, the Kenyan nationalist leader, and had the hope of emulating his fight for the freedom of blacks. Though he named his son after Kenyatta, he put aside Kenyatta's revolutionary example in favor of nonviolence and became a volunteer worker for the National Association for the Advancement of Colored People (NAACP; see JOEL E. SPINGARN). In 1954 he was appointed state field secretary for the association.

Evers acquired a name as a civil rights activist, not only in his home state but with the central office of the NAACP. He worked to further voter registration and urged African Americans to combat segregation by nonviolent means. In 1961, when JAMES MEREDITH came to his NAACP office for advice about his intention to enroll in the University of Mississippi, the NAACP, through Evers, was of vital assistance to Meredith, and he was the first black to enter the university, in October 1962.

During the crucial days of 1963, Evers and other rights leaders focused on the situation of blacks in the city of Jackson. They strove to end discrimination in public facilities and to see blacks enlisted in the police force. Evers led boycotts of stores that practiced segregation and organized sit-ins at lunch counters. Events in Jackson were national news, and Evers's name was prominent. On June 11 President John F. Kennedy addressed the country on television, announcing that he was submitting the Civil Rights Bill to Congress. Evers saw the broadcast, and shortly after midnight on June 12, he

ABC-TV/D.C. Public Library

was shot as he was arriving home. He died soon afterward. Byron de la Beckwith was tried for the murder, but the jury was hung, and he disappeared. In 1991 he was apprehended and held for retrial.

After Medgar Evers's assassination, his elder brother James Charles Evers took his place as NAACP field secretary. In 1969 Charles Evers was elected mayor of Fayette, in southwest Mississippi, and served sixteen years; he then became clerk of the chancery court and an official of the state department of human services.

**BIBLIOGRAPHY**

Evers, Charles, *Evers,* 1971; Evers, Mrs. Medgar, *For Us, The Living,* 1967.

# Falwell, Jerry

(August 11, 1933– )
Clergyman, Political Activist

J erry Falwell has been one of the most prominent of the fundamentalist and business-oriented preachers who have come out of the South. Reaching millions by television, his Moral Majority, Inc., at its most influential was a force in national politics.

Jerry Falwell was one of twin sons born to Carey H. and Helen Falwell in Lynchburg, Virginia, in the foothills of the Blue Ridge mountains. His father, a businessman and occasional bootlegger, died of alcoholism in 1948, a few weeks after he had repented. After excelling as a student and athlete in high school, Jerry was to be the valedictorian until it came out that he had used stolen lunch tickets to get free meals in the cafeteria.

Falwell, an honor student at Lynchburg College, planned on a career in engineering until he experienced a conversion to "born again" Christianity. This occurred on January 20, 1952, during a service led by Paul Donnelson, the pastor of the Park Avenue Baptist Church in

Lynchburg. Falwell, not a churchgoer, was looking for a girl to date, and Donnelson's preaching brought him to the altar. He also met the church pianist, Macel Pate, whom he married later. His sudden conversion has also been credited to a Sunday-morning radio program, the "Old Fashioned Revival Hour," which his mother always turned on for the benefit of her late-rising family.

Having switched to the Baptist Bible College, in Springfield, Missouri, Falwell graduated in 1956. He went back to Lynchburg and started a separate Baptist church with thirty-five families who had left the Park Avenue Baptist Church. They met in a derelict building that had been a soft-drink bottling plant on Thomas Road. Immediately after the first service, on June 24, 1956, Falwell began evangelizing door-to-door. On July 1 he inaugurated a daily half-hour radio broadcast, and six months later, on television, the "Old-Time Gospel Hour," which is still on the air.

Owing to Falwell's effective preaching and business sense, the Thomas Road Baptist Church grew rapidly in membership and activities. By the late 1960s its congregation approached 10,000 families, and Falwell had established the Lynchburg Christian Academy, kindergarten through twelfth grade; a home for alcoholics; programs for children, unmarried mothers, people in jail, the deaf, and the poor; a seminary and Bible institute; a cable television network; and a missionary program training teams to go all over the world. In the 1970s Falwell founded Lynchburg Baptist College, later renamed Liberty University, with more than 10,000 students on campus and in correspondence courses. Fully accredited, the university has graduated hundreds of evangelical preachers and businesspeople.

During the observance of the 1976 American Bicentennial, Falwell sent students around the country to stage "I Love America" rallies intended also to bring people "back to God." The rallies offset the effect of a federal suit brought against Falwell's church in 1973, charging financial mismanagement. The suit was later dismissed, though the church's finances were put in the care of an advisory board. At the peak of the Falwell enterprises, income from contributions was estimated at $1 million per week.

Though Falwell had originally been against political activism in his preaching, in 1979 he founded a secular organization, Moral Majority, Inc., together with Roman Catholic and Jewish conservatives. Moral Majority has condemned abortion, homosexuality, pornography, the Equal Rights Amendment (ERA; see ALICE PAUL), divorce, "secular humanism," and civil rights leaders such as MARTIN LUTHER KING, JR. It has spoken for voluntary prayer in the public schools, free enterprise, and military power. In the 1980 elections, voters following Moral Majority's message defeated several liberal representatives and senators and helped to elect President Ronald Reagan. In 1988 Moral Majority supported President George Bush's election.

Falwell's entry into politics involved him in some complications. When he visited South Africa in 1985, in support of the government's apartheid policy, he spoke of the Anglican bishop Desmond Tutu, who had been awarded the Nobel Prize for Peace, as a "phony." Later that year he visited the Philippines to give his support to the regime of President Ferdinand Marcos.

Several "televangelists"—ministers who led television programs—organized a network called the PTL, standing for "Praise the Lord," under the directorship of Jim Bakker, an evangelist whose enterprises were on a lavish scale. When Bakker became involved in scandals, Falwell replaced him as director. In the late 1980s Falwell withdrew from the leadership of the PTL as well as Moral Majority, as his television audiences and the income therefrom showed a distinct decline.

**BIBLIOGRAPHY**

Falwell, Jerry, *Listen America!* 1980; FitzGerald, Frances, *Cities on a Hill,* 1986; Martz, Larry, *Ministry of Greed,* 1988; Young, P. D., *God's Bullies,* 1982.

# Farmer, James Leonard

(January 12, 1920–    )
Civil Rights Leader

Civil rights leader James Leonard Farmer was a founder of the Congress of Racial Equality (CORE) in 1942 and played a major role in organizing its successful nonviolent integration efforts until 1966.

Farmer was born to African American parents in Marshall, Texas. He received a B.S. degree in chemistry in 1938 from Wiley College in his hometown and a Bachelor of Divinity degree in 1941 from Howard University.

He refused to be ordained as a Methodist minister when he realized that he would have to practice in a segregated ministry. "I didn't see how I could honestly preach the Gospel of Christ in a church that practiced discrimination. . . . But I never abandoned His teaching. It is still very much part of my thinking."

Instead of becoming a minister in 1941, Farmer became the race relations secretary of the Quaker-sponsored Fellowship of Reconciliation group. The following year Farmer organized the first chapter of CORE at the University of Chicago. Influenced by the techniques of Gandhi, he directed the group toward nonviolent forms of protest—sit-ins, boycotts, and marches. In June 1943 CORE staged the first successful sit-in demonstration at a restaurant in the Chicago Loop.

Throughout the 1950s Farmer continued to organize nonviolent civil rights protests through CORE while also serving as a radio and television commentator on programs sponsored by the United Auto Workers union (UAW; see WALTER REUTHER). He also served as a program director for the National Association of Colored People (NAACP; see JOEL E. SPINGARN) and published articles in *Crisis*, an African American periodical founded by W. E. B. DU BOIS.

A wave of sit-ins by student volunteers at lunch counters throughout the South in 1960 received extensive television coverage and first brought CORE to national attention. But the organization's most dramatic success began in 1961 when it introduced "Freedom Rides" to the civil rights movement. Freedom Rides were trips by CORE volunteers, many of them white, aboard buses heading from the North into the South. The object was to test whether interstate bus terminal facilities were still segregated in violation of a 1960 Supreme Court ruling. The Freedom Riders, though subjected to physical violence and intimidation—viciously attacked in Alabama and arrested in Mississippi—carried on with determination, nonviolently. Freedom Rides attracted enough media attention to force the integration of all 120 interstate bus terminals in the South.

Farmer, as full-time national director of CORE from 1961 to 1966, was the person chiefly responsible for bringing Freedom Riders into the CORE strategy. He even served forty days in an Alabama jail for his efforts, but by the mid-1960s it had become increasingly clear to him that he could no longer lead the organization he had helped to create.

CORE had been founded on the belief that interracial cooperation was essential for the success of the organization as well as for the nation. The new, young, more militant African American recruits to CORE did not agree with this strategy and advocated implementing a policy of racial separatism. Rather than support the decision to restrict the activities of whites who had played an important role in winning significant civil rights goals during the 1950s and early 1960s, Farmer reluctantly resigned as national director.

After an unsuccessful bid to win a seat in Congress, Farmer accepted appointment by President Richard M. Nixon in 1969 as assistant secretary for administration in the U.S. Department of Health, Education, and Welfare. He was the first nationally known African American leader appointed to high office by the Nixon administration. Farmer quickly discovered, however, that the post offered him little opportunity to accomplish anything of substance. He resigned his position just a few months after accepting it and moved to Howard University in 1970 to head a "think tank" concerned with domestic policy issues.

Farmer officially resigned from CORE in 1976. The decision of CORE director ROY INNIS to encourage African American "volunteers" to participate along with Cuban troops in the Angolan civil war provoked Farmer's action. The following year he became executive director of the Coalition of American Public Employees in Washington, D.C., a post he held until 1982, when the coalition was terminated. After teaching for a year at Antioch University in Philadelphia, Farmer went to Mary Washington College of the University of Virginia, in Fredericksburg, as Virginia Commonwealth Professor; in 1985, he was made the distinguished visiting professor of history. To celebrate the thirtieth anniversary of the Freedom Riders in July 1991, Farmer chaired a commemorative conference at Tougoulou College, in Jackson, Mississippi.

**BIBLIOGRAPHY**

Farmer, James, *Lay Bare the Heart,* 1985; Meier, August, and Elliott Rudwick, *CORE: A Study in the Civil Rights Movement, 1942–1968,* 1975; Weisbrot, Robert, *Freedom Bound: A History of America's Civil Rights Movement,* 1990.

# Filene, Edward Albert

(September 3, 1860–September 26, 1937)
Merchant, Reformer

Described by one of his associates as the "philosopher of our machine economy," Edward Filene was the president of one of Boston's best-known department stores and a forward-looking leader in business and civic affairs.

Edward Filene was born in Salem, Massachusetts, into a German American family. Shortly after his birth, the family moved to Lynn, Massachusetts, where he was educated in the local public schools. Though accepted at Harvard, Filene never enrolled, in part because of recurring eczema and in part because of his father's deteriorating health, which meant that Edward and his younger brother Lincoln were needed to help run the retail store their father had started in Boston. The brothers took control of the store in 1891, having by then developed it into one of America's outstanding department stores. The store's success was due in large measure to the innovations started by Edward Filene, who was president, including installment buying and the bargain basement, where slow-moving merchandise was sold cheaply.

Filene's business philosophy included enlightened ideas for employee benefits that would eventually undermine his authority. He believed there would be greater harmony in the workplace and that business (as well as world peace) would grow if employees had greater incentives to work harder and more efficiently. These incentives, he maintained, should include medical and unemployment insurance, minimum wage standards, and other benefits. He worked for a Filene Cooperative Association that included a profit-sharing plan as well as limited voting rights for workers. As a result, some of Filene's new associates feared an employee takeover, though there was no evidence of that, and they began in 1911 a long legal battle that resulted in 1928 with the ouster of

Filene from any control of the store, though he retained his title as president. His disappointment at not being able to leave his business to his employees would last the rest of his life.

Filene's philosophy also took a social form when he began to take part in public affairs. A struggle over streetcar franchises in Boston in the 1890s made Filene aware of the divisions that existed within the city's business community. To foster cooperation, he took the lead in organizing first the Boston, and eventually the U.S., Chamber of Commerce. In 1909 he tried, with LINCOLN STEF-FENS, to organize Boston citizens in the reform of public health and education—a plan called the 1915 Movement. It made little progress owing to the failure of business leaders to back reform vigorously and to Filene's impatience and lack of political know-how.

Filene succeeded better in speaking to policy-making groups. He advised the U.S. government during World War I and helped raise money for the League for Peace. Through his

Library of Congress

contacts abroad, he was influential in getting the Dawes Plan (which restructured the German reparations payments following World War I) accepted in Europe.

In 1919 Filene founded the Cooperative League, later called the Twentieth Century Fund, for social and economic research. Continuing his interest in business cooperatives, in 1935 he started the Consumer Distribution Corporation to promote cooperatives, and in 1936, the Good Will Fund, to support education about cooperatives. He was a staunch backer of President Franklin D. Roosevelt's New Deal programs and a critic of the nation's business leaders, who he thought had failed during hard times to promote reforms. He died on a trip to France in 1937.

**BIBLIOGRAPHY**

Filene, Edward, *Speaking of Change,* 1936; Johnson, Gerald W., *Liberal's Progress,* 1948; LaDame, Mary, *The Filene Store,* 1930.

## Finney, Charles Grandison

(August 29, 1792–August 16, 1875)
Educator, Evangelist

Charles Grandison Finney was the leading Protestant evangelist of the great religious revival that swept nineteenth-century America and helped to spark the many social reform movements of the mid-century.

Born in Warren, Litchfield County, Connecticut, Finney at a young age moved to Oneida County, New York. He spent two years studying at the Hamilton Oneida Academy and then taught school. He then completed the Yale undergraduate curriculum on his own while teaching school in New Jersey. In 1818 he began reading law in Adams, New York, and was admitted to the bar in 1820.

Finney underwent a religious conversion following a period of Bible reading and spiritual turmoil. He then decided to give up the law and become an evangelist. In 1823 he became a candidate for the ministry at the St. Lawrence Presbytery and was ordained a Presbyterian minister in 1824. During the next decade Finney conducted revivals in the Midwest and the East. In his sermons, he stressed the dire consequences of disobedience to God's will. He emphasized repentance and urged converts to accept salvation. People responded strongly to his preaching. Emotional outbursts and trances were a feature of Finney-led revivals; but by combining emotional appeals with lawyerly logic, Finney was able to reach a wide audience that included all social classes.

In 1832 a group of merchants, among them ARTHUR TAPPAN and LEWIS TAPPAN, invited Finney to come to New York City as pastor of the Second Free Presbyterian Church. In New York, Finney again made many converts and was so successful that within a few years several other churches were established, including the Broadway Tabernacle, built for Finney with the help of such wealthy religious patrons as the Tappans. Increasingly dissatisfied with conservative Presbyterian theology and discipline, Finney withdrew from the Presbyterian Church and embraced Congregationalism in the Tabernacle.

Besides working to save souls, Finney took a stand against intemperance and slavery. He joined THEODORE DWIGHT WELD when Weld left the Lane Theological Seminary in Cincinnati, Ohio, because discussion of slavery was forbidden and went to the newly created Oberlin College, becoming in 1835 the chairman of Oberlin's department of theology. Two years later, he left his post at the Broadway Tabernacle and moved permanently to Oberlin.

At Oberlin, Finney served as pastor of the First Congregational Church from 1835 to 1872 and as president of the college from 1851 to 1866. Under his guidance, the school became a center of antislavery agitation and a station on the Underground Railroad (see HARRIET TUBMAN). Finney also made evangelistic tours of the United States and Great Britain and was a frequent contributor to the *Oberlin Evangelist*. He wrote many books, including two collections of his sermons, *Lectures on Revivals* (1835) and *Lectures on Systematic Theology* (two vols., 1846, 1847), and his *Memoirs* (1876). By the time of his death at the age of eighty-two, the evangelical movement that he had done so much to shape and direct was firmly established within American Protestantism.

**BIBLIOGRAPHY**

Fletcher, R. S., *History of Oberlin*, 1943; McLoughlin, William G., *Modern Revivalism: Charles Grandison Finney to Billy Graham*, 1959; Smith, T. L., *Revivalism and Reform in Nineteenth Century America*, 1957.

# Flexner, Abraham

(November 13, 1866–September 21, 1959)
Education Reformer

Abraham Flexner brought reform to American medical education. His other important legacy was the Institute for Advanced Study at Princeton, New Jersey, which remains a major center for scholarship.

Born in Louisville, Kentucky, Abraham Flexner earned his B.A. from the Johns Hopkins University in 1886 after only two years of study. While at Johns Hopkins, he was influenced by its president, DANIEL COIT GILMAN, who built the university into a first-rate institution using the German university system as a model. Back in Louisville, Flexner taught school for four years, then started his own experimental school to prepare boys from wealthy families for college. He directed the school until 1905 when he left to study psychology and philosophy at Harvard, earning a master's degree after a year. He then studied comparative education at the University of Berlin.

Convinced of the superiority of the German university system, Flexner wrote his first book, *The American College: A Criticism* (1908), in which he made the case for an environment more conducive to intellectual development. Shortly thereafter, he made a comprehensive study of medical education for the Carnegie Foundation for the Advancement of Teaching.

In preparing his famous report, *Medical Education in the United States and Canada* (1910), Flexner read everything he could on the subject and visited all of the 155 American and Canadian medical schools, including those backed by universities, providing detailed descriptions of each one. His findings were shocking. Many medical schools were run solely for profit, admitting students with less than a high school education and assuring them of graduation if they paid their tuition. Facilities were often inadequate, including unsanitary teaching hospitals and poorly equipped medical schools.

Flexner's report established his reputation as an authority on medical education. As a result of his recommendations, more than 100 inferior medical schools were shut down, while standards at the better ones were upgraded. Within a few years of his report, medical education in the United States had dramatically improved. Flexner followed the report with one on medical schools in Germany, Britain, and France, also sponsored by the Carnegie Foundation and published as *Medical Education in Europe* (1912).

Impressed with Flexner's work, John D. Rockefeller, Jr., in 1913 invited him to join the permanent staff of the General Education Board, a foundation started by JOHN D. ROCKEFELLER, to improve education in the United States. Flexner's study, "A Modern School" (1916), which made use of aspects of his Louisville school, resulted in the founding of the progressive Lincoln School of Columbia University's Teachers College. In 1917 Flexner became secretary of the General Education Board, and eight years later, he was named director of its Division of Studies and Medical Education. He strongly believed that faculties of medical schools should be restricted to teaching and research and not be allowed to practice privately. Flexner used his remarkable skills as an organizer and fund-raiser to persuade philanthropists like Rockefeller, GEORGE EASTMAN, and ANDREW CARNEGIE to contribute about $600 million toward helping medical schools improve their faculties and institute other reforms.

After retiring from the General Education Board, Flexner wrote *Universities: American, English, German* (1930), in which he attacked American universities for teaching nonacademic courses that detracted from pure learning and called for an academic center specifically devoted to higher learning.

Though criticized by some as being elitist, Flexner's ideas inspired Louis Bamberger and his sister Carrie Bamberger Frank Fuld to give $5 million for the establishment of the Institute for Advanced Study at Princeton, New Jersey. As director of the new institute, Flexner assembled a group of distinguished scholars, including the scientist ALBERT EINSTEIN. After his retirement from the institute in 1939, Flexner remained intellectually active by writing books, lecturing, and taking courses at Columbia University, though he was well into his eighties. He died at age ninety-two.

**BIBLIOGRAPHY**

Brown, E. R., *Rockefeller Medicine Men: Medicine and Capitalism in America*, 1979; Harris, Michael R., *Five Counterrevolutionists in Higher Education*, 1970.

# Flynn, Elizabeth Gurley

(August 7, 1890–September 5, 1964)
Communist and Labor Leader

Elizabeth Gurley Flynn was a crusader in the struggle for a better society and a world without war. Her participation in radical causes began in her teens. With her eloquence as a speaker she inspired millions to work for woman suffrage, civil liberties, socialism, and peace.

Flynn was born in Concord, New Hampshire, eldest daughter of Thomas Flynn, a granite quarry worker, and Annie Gurley, an Irish-born tailor. Both parents were working-class intellectuals, and their daughter grew up among Marxist tracts and radical debate. When she was ten, the family moved to the Bronx, New York, and at sixteen she joined the Industrial Workers of the World (IWW; see WILLIAM D. HAYWOOD), soon becoming prized as an organizer and speaker. She was first arrested that year, for blocking traffic while addressing a socialist street meeting on Broadway. At seventeen, on a speaking tour in Minnesota, she met and married another labor activist, Jack A. Jones, a miner. They had a son but separated before his birth, and Flynn raised him alone. In later years she had a long love affair with the Italian anarchist Carlo Tresca, who moved into the Flynn household in the Bronx.

Flynn participated in many of the great strikes of those days. She was a leader in textile strikes at Lawrence, Lowell, and New Bedford, Massachusetts, and at Paterson and Passaic, New Jersey; she was active in IWW free-speech campaigns in Montana and the state of Washington. She led efforts to save JOE HILL from execution for murder in Utah and after visiting him in prison was the inspiration of his labor song "The Rebel Girl."

During World War I, Flynn worked closely with the IWW in defending opponents of the war and, afterward, in seeking amnesty for people locked up on war-related charges. Those activities led to her joining ROGER BALDWIN and others in founding the American Civil Liberties Union (ACLU) in 1920. For seven years, from 1920 to 1927, Flynn played a leading part in action to free Bartolomeo Vanzetti and Nicola Sacco, Italian-born anarchists convicted of a murder in Massachusetts—many believed unjustly.

Though she dedicated her life to left-wing activism, Flynn did not join the Communist party until 1936, after a period of retirement from public activity owing to heart trouble. She began making speeches again; wrote a column for the *Daily Worker,* the party's newspaper; and in 1938 was elected to its national committee. Two years later, Flynn was expelled from the ACLU because of her Communist party affiliation. Thereafter she championed her leftist and liberal causes within the structure of the party. In 1951, with other party leaders, she was prosecuted under the Smith Act for conspiring to teach and advocate the overthrow of the U.S. government and was imprisoned for more than two years. Flynn was elected chair of the national committee of the American Communist party in 1961, the first woman to hold the post. She aimed to fight legislation that prevented the party from exercising its rights as a political party. While she had little success in that effort, in June 1964, in a case that Flynn had brought, the U.S. Supreme Court struck down a provision of the National Security Act that denied passports to members of the Communist party. Soon after, Flynn was invited to make her first visit to the Soviet Union, as a guest of the Soviet government. She had been there a month when she died, at seventy-four, in a Moscow hospital. Her body lay in state in the Hall of Columns of the Trade Union House.

In 1978 the board of the ACLU voted to rescind posthumously Flynn's expulsion in 1940.

### BIBLIOGRAPHY

Flynn, Elizabeth Gurley, *I Speak My Own Piece: Autobiography of "The Rebel Girl,"* 1955, and *The Alderson Story,* 1963; Lamont, Corliss, *The Trial of Elizabeth Gurley Flynn by the American Civil Liberties Union,* 1968.

## Ford, Henry

(July 30, 1863–April 7, 1947)
Industrialist, Philanthropist

Henry Ford revolutionized the automobile industry, American life, and possibly Western culture with the Model T. His assembly-line production method enabled cars to be made in quantity at a cost that brought them within reach of the average person. But his career was stained by his bigotry and antilabor bias.

Ford was born on a farm in Greenfield Township, Michigan, now in the city of Dearborn, adjoining Detroit. He was one of eight children of William Ford, of Protestant Irish ancestry, and Mary Litogot, of a Dutch or Flemish family, who died in childbirth when Henry was twelve. The boy went to country schools and early on showed a remarkable mechanical aptitude. At age fifteen he was an expert watchmaker. The next year he left school and worked days as an apprentice in a Detroit machine shop and nights repairing watches to make ends meet. He went on to other mechanical work, becoming familiar with steam engines and early power plants. Young Ford helped occasionally on his father's farm but was determined to leave farming and work with machines.

In 1896, drawing on inventions by automotive engineers in Europe and America, Ford constructed his first "horseless carriage," powered by a gasoline motor, in his own workshop. Meanwhile, a job as an engineer for the Edison Illuminating Company (see THOMAS A. EDISON) supported him as he continued experimenting. In 1899 Ford left the Edison Company and became chief engineer of the Detroit Automobile Company, backed by a group of businessmen. The company did not survive; when another, organized in 1901 as the Henry Ford

Company, met with dissension, Ford left and the firm became the Cadillac Motor Car Company. His chief interest at the time was in producing a fast racing car; he was determined, however, to make a car that could be sold at a low price.

The Ford Motor Company was founded in 1903, to produce a car that would compete with the Oldsmobile. Ford was vice president in charge of design and production. As the company prospered, Ford bought out most of the other shareholders, and by 1906 he was president and the major shareholder. Two years later, when the company was capitalized at

Ford Motor Company

$2 million, Ford introduced his Model T, which was light, durable, cheap, and efficient to run; it sold for $800 to $1,000. By 1916, when 730,000 cars were being turned out, assembly-line production had brought the price down to as low as $345. During the first years the Model T's came in a variety of colors, but after 1914 all were black. The ideal car for rough country roads, farms, and small towns, the Model T took the automobile out of the luxury class and made it an affordable necessity for the ordinary family. It also speeded up the urbanization of the United States and stimulated a transportation revolution the world over.

The assembly-line method meant tedious monotony for the worker, who typically repeated a certain movement many times as the belt went past. Labor discontent and turnover were an inevitable consequence. The year 1914 saw Ford's introduction of a remedy: a minimum wage of $5 for the eight-hour shift, contrasted with an average daily wage of around $2 at other Detroit auto factories. This seemingly revolutionary policy made Ford world famous as a humanitarian, though less atten-

tion was paid to the reality that numerous Ford workers did not qualify for the $5 rate. Ford candidly said that he wanted his employees to be able to afford the price of a Model T.

With the outbreak of World War I, Ford displayed another aspect of his humanitarianism—his conviction that the war was started by a ring of international financiers. In 1915 he sponsored a "peace ship" that carried him and pacifist delegates to Europe. The American public, increasingly pro-Allied, was hostile to Ford's expedition, and nothing came of it. When the United States entered the war in 1917, Ford's factories filled numerous government contracts for trucks, tanks, airplane motors, submarine chasers, and armaments, and he declared he would operate without profit. In fact, no profits were turned over to the government.

Though nominally a rather unpolitical Republican, Ford (after the fiasco of the peace ship) had supported President Woodrow Wilson's reelection in 1916 and his internationalist policies. Wilson persuaded him to run for the United States Senate on the Democratic ticket. He lost by a thin margin and blamed it on the international financiers and the Jews. When the *Chicago Tribune* called him an "ignorant idealist," he sued the newspaper. At the trial, cross-examination exposed his ignorance of general knowledge. The jury found the newspaper guilty of libel and awarded Ford damages of 6 cents. Embittered, Ford became more and more preoccupied with anti-Semitism and printed attacks on Jews in the newspaper *Dearborn Independent,* which he had acquired as a propaganda medium. Later he apologized publicly for his tirades against the Jewish people.

By 1920 Henry Ford (with his wife Clara and his son Edsel, who had become president) was the sole owner of one of the world's largest manufacturing enterprises, by then worth $100 million. Two years later he began making a luxury car, the Lincoln. In 1927 the outmoded Model T was discontinued (after 15 million had been made) in favor of the Model A, designed to compete with General Motors' Chevrolet and the Chrysler Corporation's Plymouth. Not a success, the Model A was replaced in 1932 by the V-8. By 1936 the Ford company had sunk to third place in the car industry.

Ford controlled his company despotically, discouraged the introduction of modern ways of management, and fiercely resisted unionization. In 1934 he refused to sign the New Deal's industry-wide code. After General Motors and Chrysler recognized the United Auto Workers of America (UAW; see WALTER REUTHER) in 1937, Ford held out and allowed his security boss to use intimidation, brutality, and terror against union organizers until 1941, when he accepted the UAW contract. Split by factions and losses, the company had seriously declined.

When World War II broke out in Europe in 1939, Ford supported the isolationist stand of the America First Committee through his friend CHARLES LINDBERGH. He had been accused of Nazi sympathies after he accepted a decoration from the Hitler government in 1938. The company, however, became heavily involved in American defense production by 1941, notably at its huge Willow Run plant, where thousands of B-24 Liberator bombers were built.

In his retirement, Ford gave his attention to the historical restorations, reproductions, and museums that he had endowed, including Greenfield Village in Dearborn, Michigan, a shrine to his close friend Edison. After his death, his grandson Henry Ford II took over the company and began to rebuild it. The preponderant share of the stock passed to a small family trust, which became the richest private foundation in the world—the Ford Foundation.

**BIBLIOGRAPHY**

Collier, Peter, and David Horowitz, *The Fords: An American Epic*, 1987; Nevins, Allan, and Frank E. Hill, *Ford*, 3 vols., 1954–1963.

# Foster, William Zebulon

(February 25, 1881–September 1, 1961)
Communist and Labor Leader

William Z. Foster, after a youth of poverty and a wide range of experience as an itinerant worker, dedicated his life to labor organization and ultimately to the American Communist party, of which he was an influential leader for the forty years of its rise and decline.

William Edward Foster was born in Taunton, Massachusetts, the son of James Foster, an Irish anarchist who had come to the United States to escape arrest for his Irish nationalist activities. The elder Foster, who worked chiefly as a stable hand, married a devout Roman Catholic woman of Scotch-Irish descent, Elizabeth McLaughlin, who bore him twenty-three children (of whom five reached adulthood). When William was six, the family moved to a Philadelphia slum neighborhood. The boy had but three years of schooling and worked at odd jobs—selling newspapers, assisting an artist, working in a type foundry and a paint works. He read voraciously, and his mother's hope that he become a priest was dashed by his exposure to secular thought. Foster identified closely with the working class, and when, at nineteen, he heard a street orator expound socialism, he made a lifetime commitment and, two years later in 1901, joined the Socialist party.

In his young manhood Foster wandered far and wide as an itinerant worker—a lumberman in Florida; a motorman on New York trolleys; a merchant seaman; a shepherd in Oregon; a circus roustabout; a railway, mill, and mine laborer; a journalist. In 1909 he was in Spokane, covering a protest by members of the Industrial Workers of the World (IWW, the "Wobblies"; see WILLIAM D. HAYWOOD) against an ordinance forbidding their meetings. He met the labor activist ELIZABETH GURLEY FLYNN and, possibly inspired by her, joined the IWW, was arrested, and spent weeks in jail. (It was at this time that Foster took as his middle name the Old Testament name Zebulon, possibly hoping to facilitate delivery of his mail.) As a Wobbly, Foster left socialism for syndicalism, which based the class struggle on militant trade union action (such as strikes) rather than on electoral politics.

Foster spent a year in Europe studying labor movements and learning French and German. He returned to the United States in 1911, and the next year he quit the IWW; got a railroad job in Chicago; joined a craft union of the American Federation of Labor (AFL; see WILLIAM GREEN and JOHN L. LEWIS), the Brotherhood of Railroad Carmen; and founded the Syndicalist League of North America. The AFL was not a revolutionary/syndicalist organization. Foster, the radical, found the AFL a useful political vehicle despite its conservative brand of unionism. Also in 1912 he married Esther Abramowitz, a Russian-born anarchist, and intensified his commitment to revolution. With the support of the Chicago Federation of Labor, he organized packing-house workers and won an eight-hour day and other benefits. As an AFL organizer, he led the nationwide steel

strike of 1919, which failed in its aim of organizing the steelworkers, though Foster's work was described as "a miracle of organization." His first book, *The Great Steel Strike* (1920), is an analytical history of the event.

Now well known as a radical, Foster found himself blacklisted and unable to work. He turned to full-time organizing, and in 1920 formed the Trade Union Education League, which stood for industrial unionism within the AFL. His work attracted interest in Moscow, and Foster was invited to visit the Soviet Union and study the Communist movement. He was impressed and, returning home, joined the American Communist party, which had been founded two years earlier. Foster devoted the rest of his life to the Communist movement, which he now believed to be the road to socialism. In 1924 the party made Foster its candidate for president and Benjamin Gitlow its candidate for vice president. On the ballot in thirteen states, the ticket received 33,316 votes; in 1928, in thirty-two states, 48,228 votes; and in 1932 (with an African American, James W. Ford, as running mate), in forty states, 102,991 votes. While in the midst of a strenuous campaign in September 1932, suffering still from the effects of a six-month prison term in 1930 for leading an unemployed demonstration, Foster had a severe heart attack and was ill for almost three years.

In 1935, when Foster returned to active life, Earl Browder had become general secretary of the American Communist party. Foster was at odds with Browder's policy of the "united front"—cooperation with the Democratic administration and liberal groups—and devoted himself to problems of the unemployed and to writing: notably, *Toward a Soviet America* (1932), *From Bryan to Stalin* (1937), and *Pages from a Worker's Life* (1939).

Foster's was the only nay vote in the Communist party leadership when Browder proposed to dissolve the party in 1944 and reorganize it as the Communist Political Association. A little more than a year later, cued by

Moscow, the party was revived under Foster's leadership. In 1948, a time of the stresses of the cold war, Foster and eleven other Communist party leaders were indicted under the Smith Act for planning the overthrow of the American government by force and violence. Foster escaped trial and imprisonment because of his health, but the others served time in prison.

In the 1950s, as a result of the cold war and of the Soviet Union's admission that Joseph Stalin had committed grave crimes against his own people, party membership and activity declined, and doubt was cast on Foster's leadership. His critics said he had become rigid and bitter. In 1957, after he was relegated to chairman emeritus, he had a serious stroke. After he had sought for two years to get the indictment against him dismissed so that he could go to the Soviet Union for medical treatment, in 1960 the government approved his passport. He was in a sanitarium near Moscow when he died. Foster was given a state funeral in Red Square and his ashes were returned home for interment in a Chicago cemetery.

**BIBLIOGRAPHY**

Draper, Theodore, *The Roots of American Communism*, 1957; Flynn, Elizabeth Gurley, *Labor's Own William Z. Foster*, 1949; Foster, William Z., *The Twilight of World Capitalism*, 1949, and *The History of the Communist Party in the United States*, 1952.

# Franklin, John Hope

(January 2, 1915–   )
Educator, Historian

John Hope Franklin is the most prominent African American historian in the United States and the first to serve as president of the Organization of American Historians.

Franklin was born in Rentiesville, Oklahoma. His father, a prominent local attorney, was one of the first African Americans to be admitted to the Oklahoma bar. Franklin graduated from Fisk University in 1935 and continued his study of history in graduate school at Harvard University, where he earned his M.A. degree in 1936 and his Ph.D. in 1941.

In addition to working to complete his doctoral thesis, from 1939 to 1943 he was professor of history at St. Augustine's College in Raleigh, North Carolina. His doctoral thesis, *The Free Negro in North Carolina, 1790–1860,* was published in 1943.

From 1947 until 1956 Franklin taught at Howard University. In 1947 he published his first book of general interest, *From Slavery to Freedom,* which examined African American progress in the United States with an optimistic viewpoint. Although it became a college textbook, Franklin's reputation as an important American historian was not firmly established until the publication of *The Militant South, 1800–1861* in 1956. This work was a more pessimistic interpretation that traced the self-destructive impulse in southern leaders that led to the Civil War and the violence that followed.

In addition to his history research and teaching duties, during this period Franklin also acted as an adviser to the National Association for the Advancement of Colored People (NAACP; see JOEL E. SPINGARN). It was in this capacity that he helped to prepare the legal brief that the NAACP submitted to the U.S. Supreme Court on segregation in public schools, which the court outlawed in its historic 1954 decision.

In 1956 Franklin left the African American college scene to become chairman of the history department at Brooklyn College, part of the City University of New York. His appointment marked the first time an African American had ever led a college department in the state of New York.

Franklin wrote two more books while at Brooklyn College: *Reconstruction After the Civil War* (1961), which, in examining the political, economic, and social aspects of the post bellum period, aimed to revise the entrenched white view of the horrors of Reconstruction; and *The Emancipation Proclamation* (1963), which analyzed the importance of the proclamation as a war measure and moral statement. He also edited a number of other books over the course of his career and in 1967 collaborated on a widely utilized collection of readings in African American history.

In 1964 he joined the history department at the University of Chicago. Three years later he broke another color barrier when he became chairman of that prestigious department. In

1974 American historians bestowed their highest honor by electing Franklin president of the Organization of American Historians.

Franklin believed that the advancement of blacks in America depended upon an increased understanding by whites about the historical legacy of slavery. Helping to provide that understanding was the role he saw himself fulfilling as a historian. Furthermore, he saw himself as a beneficiary of that understanding. "There have been Negroes as talented as I before me," he explained in an interview in *Time*, "but they could not get where I have because the white man was not advanced enough to let them."

**BIBLIOGRAPHY**

Franklin, John Hope, *Race and History: Selected Essays 1938–1988*, 1990; Thorpe, Earl E., *Negro Historians in the United States*, 1958.

# Friedan, Betty Naomi Goldstein

(February 4, 1921–    )
Author, Feminist

Few individuals played as important a role in the 1960s rise of the feminist movement as did Betty Friedan, author of *The Feminine Mystique* and cofounder of the National Organization for Women (NOW).

Betty Friedan was born Betty Naomi Goldstein in Peoria, Illinois. At Smith College she majored in psychology, edited the college newspaper, and helped found the Smith literary magazine. In 1942, after receiving her B.A. degree, she studied for a year as a psychology research fellow at the University of California in Berkeley.

After deciding not to go on to a doctorate in psychology, Friedan moved to New York and earned a living as a reporter for a news service.

In 1947 she married Carl Friedan, an advertising executive.

Friedan wanted to continue working as a reporter while raising her children, but that proved impossible. When she gave birth to her first child in 1949, she was granted a maternity leave. However, upon her request for a second maternity leave five years later, she was fired and replaced by a man. At the time she didn't mind losing her job—it meant she could concentrate her energy upon raising her children, three altogether. Later in life she attributed to the incident the awakening of her consciousness of the unfair choice that women were forced to make between a family and a career. Men could have both.

Friedan found life as a full-time suburban housewife intellectually demeaning and emotionally unsatisfying. The next eight years were "schizophrenic years of trying to be a kind of woman I wasn't, of too many lonesome, boring, wasted hours. . . ," she said in an interview.

In 1957, while conducting a questionnaire survey of her Smith class, she discovered that many of her classmates felt the same emptiness about suburban living that she did. When these preliminary results were corroborated by a more detailed and broader survey of women who graduated from other colleges, she concluded that she had discovered a social phenomenon. The widespread interest aroused by an article she published in the September 1960 issue of *Good Housekeeping,* entitled "Women Are People Too!" convinced her to delve further. The result was her writing of *The Feminine Mystique* (1963), perhaps the single most popular treatise of the modern feminist movement.

In *The Feminine Mystique,* Friedan identified a feeling of discontent among American women with a life-style that consisted fully of being a housewife, a mother, and a consumer. The depression that she claimed afflicted so many middle-aged, college-educated women arose, she decided, because they had neglected their own development in order to further the development of their husbands and children. Well-educated women had done this because they had accepted a view that women should expect development by men rather than by women. This "feminine mystique" had led women to deny their own aspirations, to conceal their abilities, and to submerge their true identities for the sake of familial harmony. It was time, she argued, for women to stop being an oppressed majority and to dismiss the feminine mystique—to embrace a new feminine life-style based on valuing a career outside of the home as of equal importance to their husbands' careers. This meant that women should no longer accept being secretaries and not executives, nurses and not doctors, church workers and not ministers.

*The Feminine Mystique* aroused a storm of controversy, among women as well as between women and men. Many women did not agree with Friedan's characterization of their lives as unsatisfying. Friedan eloquently defended her position and became a celebrity. She accepted teaching positions at New York University and the New School for Social Research, and used her access to the media to espouse feminist political activism.

In 1966, inspired by the civil rights movement, Friedan cofounded NOW and became its first president. In addition to seeking full workplace equality for women through education, legislation, and court action, NOW also worked for the establishment of child-care centers and paid maternity leave, the legalization of abortion, the guarantee of a woman's right to return to her job after childbirth, and the addition of an amendment to the Constitution prohibiting discrimination on the basis of sex (the equal rights amendment).

In 1970 Friedan declined to run for reelection as NOW president because she felt the organization had become too preoccupied with inappropriate and radical goals such as excluding men as members and securing equal rights for lesbians.

Friedan's insistence during the 1970s that the woman's movement needed to avoid alienating moderates with attacks on the sanctity of the family angered many young feminist radicals. She stuck to her guns, and in her next book, *The Second Stage* (1981), she argued that "for us [the founding mothers of NOW] equality and the personhood of women never meant destruction of the family, repudiation of marriage and motherhood, or implacable sexual war with men."

Throughout the 1970s and 1980s, Friedan remained an active advocate for women's rights in the Democratic party while pursuing her career as a writer and college teacher. After helping to found the National Abortion Rights Action League (NARAL), Friedan joined with other well-known feminists in 1971 to found the National Women's Political Caucus (NWPC). In

1976 she played a major role in persuading the Democratic party to establish the policy of reserving 50 percent of its delegate slots for women.

In 1975, 1980, and 1985 Friedan took part in International Women's Conferences sponsored by the United Nations. In 1988 she became a distinguished visiting professor at the University of Southern California's journalism school and its Institute for the Study of Women and Men. She also began an affiliation with USC's Andrus Gerontology Center that reflected her concern with the need to eliminate the demeaning aspects of growing old in America.

**BIBLIOGRAPHY**

Friedan, Betty, *The Feminine Mystique*, 1963, *It Changed My Life*, 1976, and *The Second Stage*, 1981.

# Friedman, Milton

(July 31, 1912–   )
Economist

As a major champion of the free market economy, Milton Friedman has had a profound impact on twentieth-century economic thought through his many books and years of teaching, and as the leader of the Chicago school of economics.

Milton Friedman was born in Brooklyn, New York, into an immigrant Jewish family from Austria-Hungary. Raised in Rahway, New Jersey, he attended the local high school, then enrolled at Rutgers University, graduating with a major in economics in 1932. The next year, he received his M.A. in economics from the University of Chicago, where he stayed for two years as a research assistant. In 1935 he went to Washington, D.C., to work as an economist for the National Resources Committee and the National Bureau of Economic Research, dur-

D.C. Public Library

ing which time he helped write *Consumer Expenditures in the United States*. From 1937 to 1940 Friedman taught part-time at Columbia University and from 1940 to 1941 took the position of visiting professor of economics at the University of Wisconsin. Returning to Washington in 1941, he worked for two years as principal tax economist for the U.S. Treasury Department and coauthored *Taxing to Prevent Inflation* (1943).

In 1943 Friedman resumed graduate work at Columbia; after earning his Ph.D. three years later, he taught for a year at the University of Minnesota. In 1948 he joined the faculty of the University of Chicago as a full professor, having taught there for several years, and in 1962 took the position of Paul Snowden Russell Distinguished Service Professor of Economics (at Chicago).

At Chicago Friedman soon attracted attention with his conservative economic views, which he set forth in a series of books, including *Studies in the Quantity Theory of Money* (1956), *A Theory of the Consumption Function* (1957), *A Program for Monetary Stability* (1959), and the monumental *A Monetary History of the United States, 1867–1960* (1963), coauthored by Anna J. Schwartz. Friedman campaigned for the resumption of economics based on the "quantity" theory of money, which sees the money supply, not government spending, as the chief force influencing a nation's economy. This theory had been accepted until the Great Depression of the 1930s, when the government had put into practice Keynesian principles, named for their formulator, British economist John Maynard Keynes. According to Keynesian principles, fiscal policy, which applies to taxes and federal spending, is more important than monetary policy. The Keynesian view calls for government to try to restrain business and consumer spending by raising taxes during inflationary times and to try to encourage spending by either lowering taxes or increasing the government deficit during recessionary periods. Friedman, however, attacked the U.S. government's fiscal policy as "inept" and blamed its monetary policy (under which the Federal Reserve Board tightened money during boom times and loosened money in hard times) as the main cause of economic depressions and periods of inflation. He urged that the Federal Reserve Board lose its up-and-down control over the money supply and, instead, increase that supply at a steady rate.

In *Capitalism and Freedom* (1962), written with his wife, Rose D. Friedman, Friedman further called for a return to the free market system. He argued that economic freedom was necessary to political freedom and that the role of the federal government in the economy ought to be both limited and dispersed to the state and county levels. Contending that government regulatory agencies had not only failed to stabilize the economy but were a threat to individual liberty, Friedman urged that they be abandoned. In addition, he advised the abandonment of such accepted institutions as the public school system and licensing boards for occupations and professions. Friedman's most progressive proposal called for a "negative income tax" to replace welfare. Under this plan, sometimes called the guaranteed annual income, the Internal Revenue Service would make direct payments to families when their incomes did not reach a given level. Critical of much of the social legislation passed since the New Deal of the 1930s, Friedman maintained that social problems could be better handled by the private sector.

Through his writing and teaching Friedman attracted many followers to what became known as the Chicago school of economics. His influence also spread outside of the academy. In 1964 he served as an adviser to the conservative Republican presidential candidate, Barry Goldwater, in the election of 1964, and later often advised President Richard M. Nixon. From 1967 to 1984 Friedman also wrote a regular column for *Newsweek* magazine. In 1976 he was awarded the Nobel Memorial Prize in Economic Sciences "for his achievements in the fields of consumption analysis, monetary history and theory, and for his demonstration of the complexity of stabilization policy."

In the 1980s Friedman achieved even greater prominence as the host of a ten-part television series, "Free to Choose," and as the discussion leader of a three-part series, "Tyranny of the Status Quo," both based on books written by Friedman with his wife for a popular audience. He had the further satisfaction of being an important member of President Ronald Reagan's Economic Policy Advisory Board. In 1982 he became professor emeritus at the University of Chicago and since 1977 has been a senior research fellow at the Hoover Institution of Stanford University.

Friedman has developed a large following in the nations of the former Soviet Union and in other eastern European countries where attempts are being made to dismantle the communist system of state socialism and replace it with a free market economy.

**BIBLIOGRAPHY**

Butler, Eamonn, *Milton Friedman: A Guide to His Economic Thought,* 1985; Hirsch, Abraham, and Neil de Marchi, *Milton Friedman: Economics in Theory and Practice,* 1990; Rajack, Elton, *Not So Free to Choose: The Political Economics of Milton Friedman and Ronald Reagan,* 1987.

# Fuller, Richard Buckminster, Jr.

(July 12, 1895–July 1, 1983)
Inventor, Philosopher

Buckminster Fuller, a brilliant and eccentric scientist and writer best known for his invention of the geodesic dome, maintained that technology could solve many problems of present-day life. In pursuit of his credo, he devoted his life to numerous inventions and to lecturing, teaching, and writing.

"Bucky" Fuller, as he was widely known, was born in 1895 in Milton, a suburb of Boston, Massachusetts, in a family of New England pioneers. His father's antecedents included MARGARET FULLER, the social reformer and feminist. At the age of six, using toothpicks and dried peas, he built his first tetrahedronal octet truss, a framework made of four-sided triangles arranged in eights that anticipated his invention of the geodesic dome. Following family tradition he attended Milton Academy and Harvard University, which expelled him twice—first for misbehavior and again for lack of interest. Fuller then worked two years for Armour and Company, as a meat lugger and then as a cashier. In 1917, with the start of World War I, he joined the U.S. Navy and after officer training commanded crash boats at a flying school. At that time he produced his first inventions, devices for aircraft safety. He married Anne Hewlett, daughter of an architect, James Monroe Hewlett. They had two daughters.

After his discharge in 1919, Fuller worked at a variety of jobs—for Armour again, for a trucking company, and for his father-in-law's building company. When his four-year-old daughter died in 1922, he sank into a grave depression that persisted for years, worsened by heavy drinking and unemployment. Determined to put himself right, he spent two years in virtually silent contemplation, searching for the principles that govern the universe and resolving to help advance humanity accordingly.

Out of Fuller's period of meditation came designs of revolutionary structures, such as a twelve-decked hexagonal apartment house, or "living machine," mass-produced at low expense and light enough to be transported by an aircraft, and his Dymaxion house, whose glass-walled rooms hung from a central mast, to be sold at the price of a Ford automobile. ("Dymaxion" comes from "dynamic" and "maximum.") In 1932 he founded the Dymaxion Corporation to develop his inventions. These included a three-wheeled streamlined car capable of going 40 miles on a gallon of gasoline (its production was halted after it was struck by another car and rolled over) and the Dymaxion world map, which projects a spherical world on a flat surface. The corporation survived only briefly owing to inadequate commercial support. Fuller meanwhile worked for other companies, was a technical consultant for *Fortune* magazine, and during World War II was an official of the government's Board of Economic Warfare. His Dymaxion house was revived as a portable emergency shelter for military use.

In the late 1940s Fuller worked out the science of geodesics, the theoretical basis of his invention of the geodesic dome, which is a half sphere based on a grid of thin but strong metal-alloy triangles supporting a skin of plastic or fiber glass. These have been widely used for industrial, military, institutional, and other purposes. One of the largest, designed for a tank car company in Louisiana, was 384 feet in diameter and as high as a 10-story building. A famous example was the beautiful dome housing the United States pavilion at Expo 67 in Montreal, considered the most imposing structure at the fair.

A chair as research professor created for him in 1959 at Southern Illinois University, in Carbondale, was Fuller's base for world travels; he attended conferences and lectured to propagate his philosophical and technical ideas, embracing conservation, educational reform, the humane distribution of natural resources, and do-it-yourself construction. During the 1960s and 1970s many young members of the counterculture were attracted to Fuller's principles, particularly during the Vietnam War, when he preached the need to reorient the nation from "killingry" to "livingry" (words he coined). Home-made geodesic domes turned up in hippie communes.

Fuller had a poetic way with words— exemplified in another coinage, "Spaceship Earth"—and in 1961 Harvard appointed him to its Norton Chair of Poetry for the academic year. In 1972 Fuller was made World Fellow in Residence at the University City Science Center, a consortium of thirty institutions in the Philadelphia area.

Fuller wrote some twenty-five books (including poetry), which have sold more than 1 million copies. He was active into his mid-eighties. In 1983 Fuller (already the recipient of thirty-nine honorary doctorates) was awarded the Presidential Medal of Freedom. Later that year, having moved to Pacific Palisades, California, he died in a Los Angeles hospital after a heart attack, the day before his wife's death.

**BIBLIOGRAPHY**

Fuller, Buckminster, *Ideas and Integrities*, 1963, *Operating Manual for Spaceship Earth*, 1969, and *Approaching the Benign Environment*, 1970; Hatch, Alden, *Buckminster Fuller*, 1974; Kenner, Hugh, *Bucky*, 1973; Marks, Robert W., *The Dymaxion World of Buckminster Fuller*, 1960; Meller, James (ed.), *The Buckminster Fuller Reader*, 1970; Sieden, L. S., *Buckminster Fuller's Universe*, 1989.

# Fuller, Sarah Margaret

(May 23, 1810–July 19, 1850)
Author, Critic, Feminist, Transcendentalist

Perhaps the most brilliant woman in nineteenth-century America, Margaret Fuller was a pioneer in advocating women's rights and in pursuing a career as a literary and social critic and as a professional newspaperwoman. She was also influential as a Transcendentalist.

Born in Cambridgeport, Massachusetts, Margaret Fuller was the precocious eldest child of a former schoolteacher turned lawyer and politician, who educated her like a son. After two years (1824–1825) at Miss Prescott's School for Young Ladies in Groton, she returned home, where she gained a reputation for her formidable intellect, and was accepted into the intellectual circles of Cambridge.

In the summer of 1836, Fuller became friends with RALPH WALDO EMERSON during a three-week stay in Concord. It was here she became familiar with the American philosophical movement known as Transcendentalism (see Ralph Waldo Emerson for further discussion), which had lasting effects on religion, literature, and social reform movements in the nineteenth century and later. Emerson's colleague, BRONSON ALCOTT, was so impressed with her abilities that he invited her to serve as his assistant at his Temple School in Boston, a position she held for about a year. After two years of teaching at another experimental school, the Greene School in Providence, Rhode Island, Fuller returned to the Boston area. She began attending discussions at ELIZABETH PEABODY's bookstore and also meetings of the Transcendental Club, which she helped to found.

From 1839 to 1844 Fuller supported herself by leading discussions on such topics as education, the fine arts, and Greek mythology in women's groups from the city's intellectual elite. In 1840 she joined with Emerson and others in launching the *Dial*, a quarterly journal of Transcendentalist thought. A dearth of contributors sometimes meant that Fuller had to accept second-rate material or to supply the missing copy herself. But during the two years of her vigorous editorship, the *Dial* drew international acclaim as a journal of independent thought. Also during this period, Fuller took active part in the planning of a utopian community, Brook Farm, in West Roxbury.

A trip to the Midwest in 1843 provided Fuller with the material for her first book, *Summer on the Lakes* (1844), notable for its descriptions of frontier life, particularly the problems faced by American Indians and women. The book made such an impression on HORACE GREELEY that he offered her a position as literary critic for his progressive paper, the New York *Tribune*. Before assuming her new post, Fuller took time out to complete a second book, *Woman in the Nineteenth Century* (1845), an outgrowth of an essay she had written for the *Dial*, entitled "The Great Lawsuit: Man versus Men; Woman versus Women." In this book, which soon became a feminist classic, Fuller argued that women should be allowed to develop their talents and abilities to the utmost.

Late in 1844 Fuller moved to New York and began her work for the *Tribune*, producing literary criticism that would earn her a reputation as one of the leading critics of the time, along with Edgar Allan Poe. In New York her concern for social reform also deepened through visits to prisons and various charitable institutions, about which she wrote articles for the *Tribune*.

In the summer of 1846, Fuller seized the opportunity to make a long-desired European tour as a foreign correspondent for the *Tribune*. In England and France she met a number of prominent people, including the Italian patriot and exile, Giuseppe Mazzini, and reported on the political and social unrest she observed. In Italy her role of observer began to shift toward that of active participant as a result of her friendship, then love affair, with Marchese Giovanni Angelo d'Ossoli, a young Italian nobleman with liberal principles. In September 1848, a son, Angelo Eugenio Filippo Ossoli, was born to the couple. Fuller was in Rome when a republic was proclaimed in February 1849. During the French siege of the city that followed, Fuller directed an emergency hospital while Ossoli took part in the defense of the city.

After the republic was overthrown by the French, Fuller and Ossoli fled to Rieti and then with their child to Florence, where Fuller continued work on a history of the Italian revolution she had begun earlier. Although the couple (Fuller and Ossoli had married in the summer of 1849) had many friends in Florence, difficulties with finances and with the police made them decide to journey to America. They set sail with their son in May 1850 and were within sight of New York harbor when the ship struck a sandbar in the midst of a storm and sank. The family perished.

**BIBLIOGRAPHY**

Allen, Margaret V., *The Achievement of Margaret Fuller*, 1979; Blanchard, Paula, *Margaret Fuller: From Transcendentalism to Revolution*, 1978; Huspeth, Richard N. (ed.), *The Letters of Margaret Fuller*, 4 vols., 1983.

# Galbraith, John Kenneth

(October 15, 1908–    )
Author, Economist

Perhaps the best known and most widely read of all American economists, John Kenneth Galbraith is noted for his biting critiques of the American economy in such books as *The Affluent Society* and *The New Industrial State.*

The only son of Scottish immigrant parents, Galbraith was born on a small farm near Iona Station, Ontario, Canada. He graduated from the University of Toronto in 1931, then studied at the University of California, earning his Ph.D. in economics in 1934. He taught at Harvard University from 1934 to 1939 except for one year as a research fellow at Cambridge University in England. He then took the position of assistant professor of economics at Princeton University (1939–1942).

In the 1940s Galbraith entered government service, holding posts in the National Defense Advisory Committee, the Office of Price Administration, the U.S. Strategic Bombing Survey, and the Office of Economic Security Policy. He was an editor of *Fortune* magazine for five years until he returned to Harvard in 1948 as professor of economics.

While at Harvard, Galbraith began writing books aimed at a popular audience that promoted alternative perspectives on the American economy. Like THORSTEIN VEBLEN before him, Galbraith combined economic analysis with social observation and satire. In *American Capitalism: The Concept of Countervailing Power* (1952), he sought to explain the efficiency and moderate prices of an economic system controlled largely by monopolies with the notion of a "countervailing power" that serves as a check on monopolies. According to Galbraith, blocs such as labor unions, consumer organizations, and competing companies exercise this countervailing power and help to keep the American economy stable and prosperous in normal times. In periods of inflation, however, this power is unable to offset the effects of high consumer demand. Therefore, in Galbraith's view, inflation must be curbed by such government action as tight monetary and fiscal policy or wage and price controls.

In *The Affluent Society* (1958), written at the close of a decade of prosperity, Galbraith took another hard look at the American economy and was sharply critical of its emphasis on consumer goods. According to Galbraith, the overproduction of consumer goods had several negative effects. Galbraith argued that such overproduction increased the likelihood of both inflation and recession and starved the public sector of necessary revenues, creating what he called "private opulence and public squalor." Galbraith called on Americans to reassess their national priorities and support public needs such as more and better schools, decent housing, and cleaner air rather than private luxuries like bigger automobiles. An international best-seller, in the United States the book stimulated an interest in liberal ideas and contributed to a resurgence of the Democratic party under Presidents John F. Kennedy and Lyndon Johnson.

Galbraith's third major book, *The New Industrial State,* appeared in 1967. In it, Galbraith described how economic power had moved from landowners to capitalists to what he called a "techno-structure," the managerial, technical class that planned and controlled production for 500 major companies. According to Galbraith, individual free choice no longer played a significant role in the economic system. Instead, the large corporations were able to convince the government to maintain full employment and total demand for their output. They further attempted through advertising to persuade consumers to buy their products. Galbraith was sharply critical of both the industrial system and the state, because they had no higher purpose than consumption to use up the products of industry. He believed that quality of life was more important than the quantity of goods produced, and he called upon the educational and scientific class to use their growing power to correct society's flaws.

In addition to writing and teaching, Galbraith involved himself in liberal Democratic politics. He served as a speech writer and economic adviser to Adlai E. Stevenson, the Democratic presidential candidate in 1952 and 1956, and as an adviser to Presidents Kennedy and Johnson. Galbraith also wrote major speeches for Attorney General Robert Kennedy and for Senator Edward Kennedy. From 1961 to 1963 Galbraith was American ambassador to India, an experience he described in his *Ambassador's Journal: A Personal Account of the Kennedy Years* (1969). He was chairman of the liberal organization Americans for Democratic Action from 1967 to 1969. A strong opponent of the Vietnam War, Galbraith campaigned for presidential candidate Eugene McCarthy in 1968.

In the 1970s Galbraith kept up his criticism of big business in such books as *Economics and the Public Purpose* (1973), in which he argued that the close bureaucratic relationship between corporations and government agencies frequently went against the public interest. Advocating what he termed a "new socialism," Galbraith made a case for public support of the arts and public ownership of housing, health care, and transportation.

In 1975 Galbraith retired as Paul M. Warburg, professor of economics at Harvard. Since then he has continued to provide highly readable and provocative commentary on the social, political, and economic scene in both nonfiction books and novels, including *A Tenured Professor* (1990).

**BIBLIOGRAPHY**

Gambs, John S., *John Kenneth Galbraith*, 1975; Hession, Charles H., *John Kenneth Galbraith and His Critics*, 1972; Okroi, Loren J., *Galbraith, Harrington, Heilbroner: Economics and Dissent in an Age of Optimism*, 1988; Sharpe, Myron E., *John Kenneth Galbraith and the Lower Economics*, 1974.

# Gallaudet, Thomas Hopkins

(December 10, 1787–September 10, 1851)
Educator

Thomas Hopkins Gallaudet established the first public school for deaf children in the United States.

Gallaudet was born in Philadelphia into a family with French Huguenot ancestry. When he was thirteen, he moved with his parents to Hartford, Connecticut. Two years later, Gallaudet entered the sophomore class at Yale, graduating in 1805. He then studied law briefly, tutored at Yale, and worked as a traveling salesman before enrolling at the Andover Theological Seminary in 1812. Graduating in 1814, he decided not to take a position as a minister because of ill health.

Gallaudet became interested in the education of the deaf because of a deaf young neighbor child he had befriended. Because no qualified teacher was available, the child's father raised the money to send Gallaudet, who had done some research on the subject, to Europe in 1815 to study methods of teaching the deaf. By this time, two such methods had been developed. The oral method, using speech and speechreading, was favored in England, while the manual method, involving a manual alphabet and sign language, was the preferred technique in France. (Both methods are used today.)

Gallaudet went first to England, where, as it turned out, he was financially unable to study the oral method with the Braidwood family, well-known English educators of the deaf. However, at the invitation of Abbé Roche Ambroise Sicard, he was able to go to Paris for several months of study of the manual method at the Institut Royal des Sourds-Muets, one of the earliest schools for the deaf. In 1816 Gallaudet returned to the United States, and founded the first American school for the deaf in Hartford in 1817. Although originally a private institution, the Hartford school was soon granted federal funds, and later state money, thus becoming the first free or public school for the deaf in the United States.

Gallaudet became the first principal of the Hartford school, holding this position for the next thirteen years. During this period, he helped train a number of teachers, who then went on to head schools for the deaf that were started elsewhere. The New York Institute for the Deaf was founded in 1818 and began receiving state funds a year later. In the next few years, institutions were opened in Pennsylvania and Kentucky, and by 1863 there were

Library of Congress

twenty-two schools for the deaf in the United States.

After leaving the Hartford school, Gallaudet helped establish public normal schools in Connecticut and became interested in the education of African Americans. He also supported higher education for women, emphasizing the need for qualified women teachers. While pursuing these efforts, he wrote a number of articles on the education of the deaf, as well as several children's books.

Gallaudet married Sophia Fowler, a pupil at the Hartford school. Their son, Thomas Gallaudet, became a well-known Episcopalian minister to the deaf in New York City. Another son, Edward Miner Gallaudet, founded in 1864 a school for the deaf in Washington, D.C., that later became Gallaudet College—the only liberal arts college in the world today devoted exclusively to the education of deaf students.

**BIBLIOGRAPHY**

Barnard, Henry, *Tribute to Gallaudet*, 1852; Gallaudet, E. M., *Life of Thomas Hopkins Gallaudet*, 1888; Humphrey, Herman, *The Life and Letters of the Rev. T. H. Gallaudet*, 1857.

# Gallup, George Horace

(November 18, 1901–July 26, 1984)
Public Opinion Statistician

Though George Gallup did not invent the public opinion poll, he was a pioneer in perfecting modern polling methods and in making them a serious force in American society and abroad. He once estimated that one-fifteenth of adult Americans had been interviewed in at least one of his surveys.

George H. Gallup was born in Jefferson, a small town in the central Iowa plains. His father was a land speculator specializing in "dry farming" of crops that resist drought. Gallup attended the University of Iowa, in Iowa City, and after his father had financial difficulties Gallup supported himself by running a towel service in the gymnasium. He edited the university newspaper, the *Daily Iowan*, and developed it to a point where it also served the town. After graduating with a B.A., he taught journalism while doing graduate work toward an M.A. in psychology. In 1928 he earned a Ph.D. with a thesis entitled "A New Technique for Objective Methods for Measuring Reader Interest in Newspapers," which contained the germ of the idea of his opinion polls.

For two years Gallup headed the journalism department at Drake University, in Des Moines, and for another year he taught at Northwestern University. At the same time he was conducting reader-interest surveys for midwestern newspapers and suggesting promotional projects. In 1932 he became director of research for the advertising agency Young and Rubicam, in New York, and in 1937 became a vice president. He devised a system of measuring public response to the firm's advertisements by means of surveys based on interviews. In 1935 (originally with Harold R. Anderson, who later left the firm) he founded the American Institute of Public Opinion, which conducted what came to be called the Gallup polls. Gallup first gained prominence when his poll predicted that Franklin D. Roosevelt would win the 1936 presidential election over Alfred M. Landon. In the public mind, the idea of polling continues to be associated chiefly with political campaigns. In 1958 Gallup formed the Gallup Organization Inc., which opened affiliates abroad and at home to include market research and surveys in such areas as movie audiences' preferences, religious beliefs, and attitudes toward alcohol.

The Gallup Organization has stated its aim as "impartially to measure and report public opinion on political and social issues of the day without regard to the rightness or wisdom of the views expressed." The results of the polls were syndicated and published in numerous newspapers, originally under the heading "America Speaks."

At the Gallup headquarters in Princeton, New Jersey, the organization's staff plans a survey according to the founder's complex methods. A sample of respondents, usually 3,000, is carefully chosen to represent a cross section of people, taking into account age, sex, income, place of residence, and political coloration. Interviewers, in seeking opinions, ask for an answer of "yes," "no," "no opinion," or "undecided." Some surveys require a fuller reply to such questions as "What is the most important problem facing the country?"

In polling for the 1948 presidential election, Gallup underestimated Harry S Truman's vote and overestimated Thomas E. Dewey's, thus incorrectly forecasting Dewey's victory. Gallup blamed the error on having stopped the polling too early so that "undecided" voters were overlooked. In 1952, having further refined his method, Gallup accurately predicted Dwight D. Eisenhower's winning, even though the polling underestimated the Republican vote. The Gallup Organization has occasionally undertaken a "private" poll. Before John F. Kennedy campaigned in 1960, the result of a private poll persuaded him to discuss his Roman Catholicism with the public openly and come out for civil rights.

Other public opinion survey organizations have been active in the United States and abroad, but the reputation of Gallup's has been such that in some European countries the word "galluppoll," for any opinion poll, has entered the language.

At eighty-two—still chairman of the board, though he had turned over operations to his two sons—Gallup died of a heart attack at his summer home on a Swiss lake near Bern. A year before his death he had told an interviewer, "I've always thought of us as simply a fact-finding organization. It's our job to get the facts, and what people do about them is something else."

**BIBLIOGRAPHY**

Gallup, George, *The Pulse of Democracy,* 1940, and *The Sophisticated Poll Watcher's Guide,* 1972.

# Garnet, Henry Highland

(ca. 1815–February 13, 1882)
Abolitionist

Henry Garnet was a prominent African American abolitionist who advocated black nationalism and militancy with the slogan "Let Your Motto Be Resistance."

Born a slave at New Market, Maryland, Garnet escaped with his family to New York City, where he studied at the African Free School Number 1. In 1835 he enrolled at the Noyes Academy in New Canaan, New Hampshire, but shortly afterward the school was destroyed by a mob, enraged at the presence of black students. Garnet next attended the forward-looking Oneida Institute in Whitestown, New York. After graduation in 1840, he settled in Troy, New York, where he taught in a school for African American children, served as coeditor of the black *National Watchman,* and studied for the ministry, becoming licensed to preach in 1842. He was made pastor of the town's one African American Presbyterian church and began to gain a reputation as an antislavery lecturer, often for the American Anti-Slavery Society.

At a national black convention held in Buffalo, New York, in 1843, Garnet created a sensation with "An Address to the Slaves of the United States of America," in which he urged armed rebellion. He was opposed by the up-and-coming black abolitionist leader, Frederick Douglass, and the delegates refused by one vote to endorse his speech. Yet as the decade wore on, black and white abolitionists, including Douglass himself, became more militant. Garnet, meanwhile, continued to press for African American independence. At the national black convention held in Troy, New York, the delegates voted in favor of Garnet's proposal for a national black press, over the objections of Frederick Douglass.

Interested in developments abroad as well as within the United States, Garnet was a delegate to an 1850 international abolitionist convention in Germany and later served two years in Jamaica as a Presbyterian missionary. As events moved toward a crisis in the United States, he became a contributing editor of the *Weekly Afro-American,* helped form the African Civilization Society, and continued to lecture widely on abolition. In 1859 he helped John Brown prepare for his attack on Harpers Ferry, Virginia.

Garnet worked hard for the cause of the Union, trying to dissuade the British on a trip to England from helping the South, as well as actively helping to recruit black soldiers at home. In 1864, as pastor of the Fifteenth Street Presbyterian Church in Washington, D.C., Garnet worked for the relief of destitute black troops after their discharge. The war over, he toured the South as a lecturer and editor of the *Weekly Anglo-African.*

Having advocated the colonization of blacks in Africa since the late 1840s, Garnet became in 1881 the United States minister and consul general to Liberia. He died there of a fever shortly after his arrival.

**BIBLIOGRAPHY**

Otari, Earl, *Let Your Motto Be Resistance,* 1972; Pease, Jane H., and William H. Pease, *They Who Would Be Free: Black's Search for Freedom, 1830–1861,* 1974; Quarles, Benjamin, *Black Abolitionists,* 1969.

# Garrison, William Lloyd

(December 10, 1805–May 24, 1879)
Abolitionist, Reformer

For thirty five years the abolitionist editor William Lloyd Garrison served as the moral conscience of the nation, goading Americans to acknowledge the evil of slavery and end it immediately. As a propagandist, he perhaps more than any other single abolitionist polarized the nation on the issue of slavery.

Born in Newburyport, Massachusetts, Garrison grew up pious and poor. Aged thirteen, he was apprenticed as a printer on the Newburyport *Herald*, to which he later contributed essays. In 1826 he began editing a county paper, but it failed. Moving to Boston, Garrison served as coeditor of the *National Philanthropist*, a temperance paper.

Garrison became an abolitionist as a result of an 1829 meeting with BENJAMIN LUNDY, a Quaker abolitionist who converted him to the cause and invited him to come to Baltimore to help edit the *Genius of Universal Emancipation*. While Lundy believed in gradual emancipation and the colonization of the freed slaves in Africa, Garrison during his stay in Baltimore became convinced of the need for immediate and unconditional emancipation and of the futility of colonization. The tone of his writing for the paper grew increasingly violent; an especially harsh attack on a merchant for trading in slaves resulted in Garrison being fined and imprisoned for libel. After seven weeks in prison, Garrison was released when New York philanthropist ARTHUR TAPPAN paid his fine.

Wanting a vehicle of his own, Garrison began *The Liberator*. Its first issue, January 1, 1831, made clear his position in the opening lines:

> I will be as harsh as truth and as uncompromising as justice. On this subject [slavery] I do not wish to think, or speak, or write with moderation. . . . I am in earnest—I will not equivocate—I will not excuse—I will not retreat a single inch—and I WILL BE HEARD.

Heard he was. Although *The Liberator* was supported mainly by free blacks and never had more than 3,000 subscribers, it created a stir by sternly denouncing slavery as a crime and a sin and calling for its immediate abolition without compensation. For the next thirty-five years the paper was the leading vehicle of antislavery thought. Southerners were so angered by Garrison's uncompromising stance and inflammatory language that *The Liberator* was banned throughout the South.

Also in 1831, Garrison helped found the New England Anti-Slavery Society, the first such society to be based on the principle of immediate emancipation. Garrison drafted the organization's constitution and served as its corresponding secretary. The following year, he wrote *Thoughts on African Colonization*, an attack on the idea promoted by the American Colonization Society. Visiting England in 1833, he was welcomed by British abolitionists as the leader of the American movement. Upon his return, Garrison took part in the launching of the American Anti-Slavery Society in Philadelphia late in 1833. Its *Declaration of Sentiments*, written by Garrison, also called for immediate emancipation but rejected violent means, relying instead on "moral suasion," or an appeal to the religious conscience of Americans.

During this period, resentment of abolitionists was strong in the North as well as the South, and Garrison and his followers were often subject to attack. In 1835 Garrison barely escaped lynching at the hands of an angry Boston mob.

Meanwhile, disagreements over tactics and emphasis were beginning to divide the abolitionist movement. While Garrison remained committed to moral suasion as the means of ending slavery, other leaders began to look to political action. Also, while Garrison embraced other reforms such as women's rights, pacifism, and a stop to both capital punishment and imprisonment for debts, more conservative abolitionists preferred to support a single cause.

At the World Anti-Slavery Convention in London in 1840, Garrison refused to take part because of the exclusion of women. That same year, differences within the movement came to a head at the annual meeting of the American Anti-Slavery Society, where after a bitter battle Garrison and his followers managed to retain control of the organization. The political abolitionists left to form their own organization, the American and Foreign Anti-Slavery Society, and the Liberty party.

Throughout the 1840s and after, Garrison kept up his attacks on both the government and organized religion for sanctioning slavery. He urged people to "come out" of churches that did not take a stand against slavery. With the motto "No Union With Slaveholders," he also called on the North to secede peacefully from the Union, because, in his view, the U.S. Constitution and the federal government were proslavery. On July 4, 1854, Garrison went so far as to publicly burn a copy of the Constitution. By this time, however, Garrison's moral approach had won more widespread acceptance in the North. In particular, the passage of the Fugitive Slave Act of 1850 seemed to show that slavery would never be ended by political action.

Ill health and financial troubles prevented Garrison from playing much of a role during the five years preceding the Civil War. Despite his philosophy of nonresistance, he endorsed JOHN BROWN's 1859 raid on Harpers Ferry, Virginia, and with outbreak of war accepted the fighting as necessary to the achievement of emancipation. In 1865, convinced that the battle had been won, Garrison recommended the breakup of the American Anti-Slavery Society. That same year, after the ratification of the Thirteenth Amendment, he ceased publication of *The Liberator.*

By now an elder statesman of reform, Garrison supported education for the freed slaves and crusaded for a wide range of causes, including women's rights, prohibition, and justice for American Indians and Chinese immigrants. He died in New York City at the age of seventy-three.

**BIBLIOGRAPHY**

McPherson, James M., *The Struggle for Equality,* 1964, and *The Abolitionist Legacy,* 1975; Merrill, Walter M., *Against Wind and Tide: A Biography of William Lloyd Garrison,* 1963; Stewart, James Brewer, *William Lloyd Garrison and the Challenge of Emancipation,* 1991.

# Garvey, Marcus Mosiah

(August 17, 1887–June 10, 1940)
African American Nationalist

A forceful and energetic leader, Marcus Garvey launched the first mass movement of African Americans in the United States that was based on racial pride, self-help, and separatism. The spirit of black nationalism he aroused became a potent new force in American race relations.

Garvey was born in St. Ann's Bay, Jamaica. He attended public school there until he became a printer's apprentice at age fourteen. Garvey's participation in an unsuccessful printer's strike in 1907 and other experiences he had while working in Costa Rica and Panama made him keenly aware of the discrimination suffered by blacks. In 1912 he went to London, where he met African nationalists and discovered BOOKER T WASHINGTON's autobiography *Up From Slavery*. The book's message of self-help strongly influenced Garvey.

Returning to Jamaica in 1914, Garvey founded the Universal Negro Improvement Association (UNIA), aimed at "drawing the peoples of the race together" for educational and commercial activity and the development of Africa. Unable to recruit support for a trades school in Jamaica, Garvey immigrated to the United States.

Garvey arrived in New York City in 1916 and opened a branch of the UNIA in Harlem. Despite a charismatic speaking style and a busy travel schedule, he did not manage to recruit significant numbers of followers until 1918 when he began publishing the *Negro World*, a weekly newspaper for African Americans. Its message of the need for racial pride and solidarity struck a powerful chord among African Americans and catapulted Garvey from obscurity to national prominence. The *Negro World*'s circulation quickly reached 50,000 and included subscribers in the Caribbean, Latin America, and even Africa. By 1919 the UNIA had branches in most major cities, and during the 1920s, the organization boasted a membership of nearly a million African Americans.

In 1919 Garvey founded the Black Star Line, the first steamship company owned and operated by African Americans, for the purpose of linking African American communities in the United States and the Caribbean with Africa. Garvey financed this daring and unique venture by selling stock exclusively to African

Library of Congress

Americans at the low price of $5 a share. In 1919 Garvey also established the Negro Factories Corporation to help African Americans trying to start small businesses.

Garvey reached the pinnacle of his career in 1920 when he organized an international convention of UNIA in New York. Thousands of people attended and adopted a Declaration of the Rights of the Negro Peoples of the World and called for the liberation of Africa from European colonial rule, naming Garvey provisional president of the government in exile of the Republic of Africa.

Even before the convention, Garvey had approached the government of Liberia, one of the two independent African states, about the possibility of a UNIA "back-to-Africa" colonization program. But the program languished when Garvey was forced to turn his attention to other, more pressing problems.

Garvey came under sharp attack from African American leaders like W. E. B. DU BOIS and A. PHILIP RANDOLPH, who were more intent on securing equal rights for African Americans within an integrated United States and on promoting indigenous African American cultural achievements. These critics, together with Garvey's white enemies, used the failure of the Black Star Line to secure his fall.

In 1922 faulty ships and mismanagement brought about the Black Star Line's collapse. Garvey and several associates were arrested and charged with mail fraud to sell stock in the company. During his trial, Garvey put forward his ideas of race pride and separatism. He was given the maximum five-year sentence, while his codefendants went free. Garvey exhausted his appeals in 1925 and served two years of his sentence before President Calvin Coolidge ordered him released and deported back to Jamaica.

Without an American base, Garvey was unable to maintain enthusiasm for UNIA. The organization withered and collapsed during the economic hardships of the Great Depression. After his efforts to launch a political career in Jamaica failed, Garvey moved to London in 1935; he died there five years later. Although largely forgotten at the time of his death, Garvey was hailed by later generations of African Americans as an early proponent of Black Power and African independence.

**BIBLIOGRAPHY**

Hill, R. A. (ed.), *The Papers of Marcus Garvey and the Universal Negro Improvement Association,* 1983; Stein, Judith, *The World of Marcus Garvey: Race and Class in Modern Society,* 1986; Vincent, Theodore G., *Black Power and the Garvey Movement,* 1972.

# Gellhorn, Martha

(ca. November 1908–   )
Author, Journalist

The distinguished war correspondent Martha Gellhorn has reported on every major twentieth-century conflict from the Spanish Civil War (1936–1939) through Vietnam. In novels as well as nonfiction she has written about both the horrors of war and social injustice on the domestic front.

Martha Gellhorn was born in St. Louis, the daughter of a prominent physician and of a social reformer. In her junior year of college, she left Bryn Mawr to become a reporter for the Albany, New York *Times-Union,* then the St. Louis *Post-Dispatch.* In 1934 her first novel, *What Mad Pursuit,* based on her three years at Bryn Mawr, was published. It was followed two years later by *The Trouble I've Seen,* a collection of stories chronicling her experiences as an investigator for the Federal Emergency Relief Administration during the Great Depression.

In 1937, at the height of the Spanish Civil War, Gellhorn went to Madrid. There she became acquainted with two veteran war correspondents, Ernest Hemingway and Robert Capa, and had her first article on wartime conditions in Madrid published by the popular American magazine *Collier's.* Thereafter Gellhorn traveled throughout Europe, covering the rise of fascism in Germany and in Italy and the Russo-Finnish War of 1939. Her novel, *A Stricken Field* (1940), grew out of her reporting on the situation in Czechoslovakia before and after the Munich Pact. Gellhorn and Hemingway were married in 1940 and divorced five years later.

During World War II, Gellhorn witnessed the Normandy Invasion and flew with British pilots on night bombing missions over Europe. She spent V-E Day investigating conditions at the notorious Nazi concentration camp, Dachau, in southern Germany. During these years, Gellhorn also produced the two novels considered her best. *Liana* (1944), the tragic story of an island woman in the Caribbean, was written while Gellhorn was living in Cuba with Hemingway. *The Wine of Astonishment* (1948) deals with the theme of racial prejudice through the experiences of two American soldiers, one a Jew and the other a bigot, during the Battle of the Bulge.

After the war Gellhorn covered the Nuremberg war-crimes trial and later the trial of Nazi war criminal Adolph Eichmann. Gellhorn also covered the Arab-Israeli Six-Day War in 1967 and the Vietnam War. Her war articles were collected in the much-praised volume, *The Face of War*, originally published in 1959 and revised and updated in 1967 and 1986.

In addition, Gellhorn has continued to publish novels and collections of stories. *The View from the Ground* (1988) is a collection of her peacetime reports, focusing on injustices throughout the world and expressing Gellhorn's concern with the threat of nuclear war.

**BIBLIOGRAPHY**

Rollyson, Carl, *Nothing Ever Happens to the Brave: The Story of Martha Gellhorn*, 1990.

# George, Henry

(September 2, 1839–October 29, 1897)
Author, Reformer

Henry George helped launch an entire generation of economic and social reform with his best-selling book, *Progress and Poverty* (1880). He advocated a single tax on land as a means of dealing with the wide disparity between enormous wealth and poverty in America.

George was born in Philadelphia and grew up in a devoutly religious household. Although he quit school just before his fourteenth birthday, he was an avid reader and worked to perfect his writing style. As a young man, George embarked on a life of romantic adventure, sailing in 1855 to Melbourne, Australia, and Calcutta, India, where he got his first glimpse of extreme poverty. Returning to Philadelphia a year later, he worked as a typesetter, then in 1857 sailed to San Francisco, where, after an unsuccessful attempt to join the gold rush in British Columbia, he worked as a printer, and later as a reporter and editor for several newspapers. During this period, George was often unemployed, and with a wife and two children to support, he learned what it was like to be hungry and penniless.

While on a journalistic assignment to New York City in 1869, George was struck by the "shocking contrast between monstrous wealth and debasing want." This experience, together with George's increasing dismay at monopolies, especially land monopolies, led him to make a critique of the U.S. economic system. In 1871 he published a pamphlet, *Our Land and Land Policy*. He later developed and elaborated the ideas in this pamphlet into a book, which he initially had printed at his own expense and which was later published by Appleton and Company as *Progress and Poverty* in early 1880.

In clear and often eloquent prose, George set forth the striking paradox of his times and proposed a solution. "Amid the greatest accumulations of wealth," he wrote, "men die of starvation, and puny infants suckle dry breasts." George believed that America had become divided into "the House of Have and the House of Want" because of the injustices involved in the system of private land ownership. Rising land values, he maintained, were not the result of anything landlords had done but rather a product of social evolution. For example, it was "the presence of the whole great population" that made land in New York City worth millions of dollars per acre. Therefore landowners and land speculators, who bought land at a low price and simply waited for it to rise in value, did not deserve to make a profit on what they had not really earned. Since land took on value because of the people who lived and worked on it, this unearned rent ought to revert to the public by means of a "single tax" on land values.

George argued that this single tax on land would render all other taxes unnecessary, while at the same time bringing about "the Golden Age of which poets have sung and high-raised seers have told us in metaphor!" George also attacked all forms of monopoly and called for government ownership and operation of all public utilities.

George's ideas were not new; in particular, he owed a debt to the English economist David Ricardo. Yet he expressed his views in such a sincere and moving way, invoking the tenets of Christianity as well as the political ideals upon which the nation had been founded, that *Progress and Poverty* was an immediate and spectacular success. More than 2 million copies of the book were sold in the United States, and it was translated into most of the major languages. Although George's single-tax program was never enacted, he exerted an enormous influence on reformers of the Progressive era.

George devoted the rest of his life to spreading his message throughout the United States and abroad. He moved to New York City in 1880 and a year later published *The Irish Land Question,* which led to an assignment from the radical New York *Irish World and American Industrial Liberator* to cover land troubles in Ireland. Remaining in Ireland for almost a year, George wrote and lectured in England as well as Ireland on the land question. He later made two additional lecture tours of Great Britain and published two more books, *Social Prob-*

*lems* (1883), a collection of articles, and *Protection or Free Trade* (1886), in which he advocated free trade.

In 1886 George, who had made several unsuccessful bids for public office while living in California, decided to run for mayor of New York City as the candidate of the United Labor Party (ULP) against Abram Hewitt, a conservative Democratic businessperson, and the young Republican, Theodore Roosevelt. The campaign was a fierce one with the Democrats attacking George as a dangerous radical who wanted to destroy private property and George defending himself in as many as a dozen speeches a day. Amid charges of election fraud, Hewitt came in first, with George running a strong second, trailed by Roosevelt.

After the election George and his followers fell out with the socialists in the ULP and the party went into a decline. George now sought to advance his single-tax program by starting a weekly, the *Standard,* which he published from 1887 to 1892. With his encouragement, Land and Labor clubs were organized throughout the country. In 1897 George died of a stroke after a day of strenuous campaigning once again to be mayor of New York City.

**BIBLIOGRAPHY**

Andelson, R. V., *Critics of Henry George,* 1979; Barker, Charles A., *Henry George,* 1955; Cord, S. B., *Henry George: Dreamer or Realist,* 1965; Oser, J., *Henry George,* 1974.

# Gilman, Charlotte Perkins

(July 3, 1860–August 17, 1935)
Author, Feminist, Reformer

As an advocate of economic independence for women, Charlotte Perkins Gilman made a major intellectual contribution to the American feminist movement of her day.

Charlotte Perkins was born in Hartford, Connecticut, into the illustrious Beecher family.

Her father was a grandson of the prominent minister LYMAN BEECHER, and her great-aunts and great-uncles included HENRY WARD BEECHER, CATHARINE BEECHER, and HARRIET BEECHER STOWE. Charlotte's childhood was difficult because her father abandoned the family early on, forcing them to depend on help from relatives and to move often. Moreover, her mother was overly strict and deliberately withheld her affection from her children to spare them disappointment in later life. Charlotte's schooling was erratic, but at age sixteen she managed to attend the Rhode Island School of Design briefly, and began to earn a living as a commercial artist.

In 1884, after experiencing much uncertainty about her role in life, she married Charles Stetson, an up-and-coming Providence painter. After the birth of a daughter, Katherine Beecher, about a year later, Charlotte Stetson began suffering from acute depression which kept her in bed and in tears much of the time. Seeking treatment from the famous Philadelphia neurologist, S. Weir Mitchell, she was told to devote herself to domesticity rather than to artistic ambitions. This "cure" brought on complete nervous collapse, and in the fall of 1887 she and her husband agreed to separate. In 1888 she moved with her daughter to Pasadena, California, and in 1894 was divorced. Soon afterward, her husband married one of her old friends and Stetson, under a friendly arrangement, sent her daughter East to live with Charles Stetson and his new wife and to complete her education.

Despite periods of depression which dogged her for the rest of her life, Charlotte Stetson had, meanwhile, begun writing. She published numerous poems and short stories, including "The Yellow Wall-Paper," a frightening account of her breakdown that was intended as an indictment of Dr. S. Weir Mitchell and his methods. Moving to San Francisco in 1894, she edited the journal of the Pacific Coast Woman's Press Association and made a

Library of Congress

living as a lecturer before women's groups and reform clubs.

In 1895 Charlotte Stetson left California to embark on an itinerant existence, lecturing on feminist issues throughout the country and abroad. She lived for several months at JANE ADDAMS's Hull House in Chicago and in 1896 journeyed to London as a delegate to the International Socialist and Labor Congress. While there, she met several members of the Fabian Society (a British group dedicated to a gradual shift to socialism), including Beatrice and Sidney Webb and the playwright George Bernard Shaw, whose views she endorsed.

In 1898 Charlotte Stetson published *Women and Economics*. In it, she argued persuasively for women's economic independence, maintaining that the status of women could and should be changed by rational effort. She pointed out that women had become dependent on men for their economic security and had not been able to develop their abilities to contribute to the good of society. Teach women to earn their own living, she asserted, and not just women, but society as a whole, would benefit. In a day when for the first time large numbers of women were leaving the home to enter the workplace, *Women and Economics* struck a responsive chord. The work was widely read not only in America but also abroad, and it was eventually translated into seven languages.

In 1900 Charlotte Stetson married her first cousin, George Houghton Gilman, a New York City lawyer who was also a great-grandson of Lyman Beecher and a nephew of DANIEL COIT GILMAN, the first president of the Johns Hopkins University. They lived in New York, and

Charlotte Perkins Gilman further developed her ideas on planning for work and child care in two more books, *Concerning Children* (1900) and *The Home* (1903). In *Human Work* (1904) she argued that labor ought to be regarded as "the highest joy and duty" of people. Having been a frequent contributor to leading magazines, Gilman in 1909 began publishing her own small-circulation magazine, the *Forerunner*, which carried much of her own writing. Among the works she wrote for the magazine were *Herland*, a utopian fantasy, and *Man-Made World* (1911). The latter and *His Religion and Hers* (1923) compared women's roles in society and religion to those of men. Publication of the *Forerunner* came to an end in 1916. Meanwhile, in 1915, Gilman had joined with Jane Addams and others in forming the Woman's Peace party, though she later supported the U.S. entry into World War I.

Gilman hailed the greater economic opportunities and improvements in child-rearing of the postwar period, while deploring the increasing emphasis on sex, which she blamed on the work of Austrian psychologist Sigmund Freud. One of her most frequently delivered lectures was entitled "The Falsity of Freud." Gilman also deplored the fact that women remained "slaves of fashion" and did not grasp the opportunity to join in reforming society.

George Gilman died suddenly in 1934, and a year later, knowing she had breast cancer, Charlotte committed suicide in Pasadena.

**BIBLIOGRAPHY**

Gilman, Charlotte Perkins, *The Living of Charlotte Perkins Gilman*, 1935; Hill, M., *Charlotte Perkins Gilman: The Making of a Radical Feminist, 1860–1896*, 1980.

# Gilman, Daniel Coit

(July 6, 1831–October 13, 1908)
Educator

As president of the Johns Hopkins University for twenty-five years, Daniel Coit Gilman was one of the chief shapers of the modern American university with its stress on graduate training and research in an atmosphere of academic freedom.

Born in Norwich, Connecticut, the son of prosperous and public-spirited parents, Gilman entered Yale College in 1848. While at Yale, he became close friends with Andrew D. White, who was later to become president of Cornell University and an educational leader in his own right. After graduation in 1852, Gilman studied briefly at Harvard, then went to Russia with White to serve as an attaché of the American legation at St. Petersburg.

Returning to the United States in 1855, Gilman spent the next seventeen years at Yale, where he helped to organize the Sheffield Scientific School and taught geography. Arguing that religion had nothing to fear from science, he helped win acceptance for the evolutionary theories of Charles Darwin.

In 1872 Gilman left Yale to become president of the University of California. Frustrated by the politics at Berkeley, which Gilman concluded was controlled more by the legislature than by the Board of Regents, he remained only three years.

In 1875 Gilman accepted an offer to become the first president of the Johns Hopkins University. He spent the next year visiting European universities and selecting faculty. Gilman was on the lookout for scholars engaged in original research. He always emphasized the importance of combining teaching with research and of providing German-style professional graduate training. A talented administrator, Gilman was also adept at public relations, earning the nickname "Oily Dan." Under his guidance, Johns Hopkins, which opened its doors in 1876, became a major center for graduate study and research and a model for the rest of the country.

One of Gilman's greatest accomplishments as president was to make both the hospital and medical school affiliates of the university. Backed with an endowment that came principally from Baltimore & Ohio Railroad stock, these institutions opened in 1889 and 1893 respectively. The Hopkins plan was the first in the country to admit only college graduates as medical students, a policy which had far-reaching effects on all of American medical education.

In addition to his pathbreaking role in higher education, Gilman worked to reform public schools in Connecticut, California, and Baltimore. Nevertheless, he turned down the superintendency of the New York City schools when it was offered to him in 1896.

In 1901, the year of his seventieth birthday, Gilman retired as president of Johns Hopkins. At the celebration of the university's twenty-fifth anniversary, Woodrow Wilson, then a professor at Princeton, paid this tribute to Gilman:

> If it be true that Thomas Jefferson first laid the broad foundation for American universities in his plans for the University of Virginia, it is no less true that you were the first to create and organize in America a university in which the discovery and dissemination of new truth were conceded a rank superior to mere instruction, and in which the efficiency and value of research as an educational instrument were exemplified in the training of many investigators.

After leaving Johns Hopkins, Gilman served as the first president of the newly formed Carnegie Institution of Washington, D.C., for the advancement of science and the encouragement of particular talent. He resigned at the end of three years when he discovered he did not have as free a hand as he would have liked. Gilman also served as president of the National Civil Service Reform League, from 1901 to 1907, and was a member of numerous educational boards. His writings include *University Problems in the United States* (1898) and *The Launching of a University* (1906).

**BIBLIOGRAPHY**

Franklin, Fabian, *The Life of Daniel Coit Gilman*, 1910; Gilman, Arthur, *Daniel Coit Gilman, First President of the Johns Hopkins University, 1876–1901*, 1908.

# Gladden, Solomon Washington

(February 11, 1836–July 2, 1918)
Reformer, Religious Leader

Congregational minister Washington Gladden was an early and major leader of the late-nineteenth-century movement within American Protestantism that was known as the Social Gospel movement. Supporters of this movement sought to find Christian solutions for social problems.

Washington Gladden was born in Pottsgrove, Pennsylvania. When he was six, his father died, and Gladden was raised on his uncle's farm near Owego, New York. At age sixteen he went to work for the Owego *Gazette,* and later studied at the Owego Academy. After earning his bachelor's degree from Williams College in Massachusetts in 1859 and briefly teaching, he was licensed as a Congregational minister. His first pastorate was the First Congregational Methodist Church of Brooklyn, New York, in 1860. Later he served in Morrisania, New York (1861–1866), North Adams, Massachusetts (1866–1871), and Springfield, Massachusetts (1875–1882). In the latter two places, both factory towns, he gained firsthand experience of the conflict between workers and their employers. Taking the side of the workers, Gladden advocated labor's right to organize—a view he set forth in his 1876 book, *Working People and their Employers.* His social consciousness was further developed by his work as religious editor of the New York *Independent,* an influential reformist journal. From 1871 to 1875 he wrote on church matters for the *Independent* and attempted to reconcile Christian theology with Darwinian evolutionary theories.

In 1882 Gladden became minister of the First Congregational Church of Columbus, Ohio, a position he held for the rest of his life. Here Gladden came into his own as a social reformer, seeking through his preaching, lectures, and writings to advance the Social Gospel (see WALTER RAUSCHENBUSCH), or as he described it, "a religion that laid hold upon life with both hands, and proposed, first and foremost, to realize the Kingdom of God in this world." Rejecting the Social Darwinism used by some of his contemporaries to justify the status quo, Gladden pushed for social reform, particularly of such practices as sweatshops and child labor. Though he advocated government ownership of utilities, he opposed socialism, believing instead that the present social order could be reformed by applying the basic Christian principle of loving your neighbor as yourself.

In demand as a lecturer, Gladden frequently spoke on college campuses and at theological schools. A scholar and a prolific author, he wrote nearly forty books. Among them were *Applied Christianity* (1886), *Tools and the Man: Property and Industry under the Christian Law* (1893), and *The Church and Modern Life* (1908).

An activist as well as a popularizer of the Social Gospel, Gladden helped found a settlement house, tried to mediate strikes, inspected local housing, and worked to reorganize local charities. Concerned with civic reform, he served on the city council of Columbus from 1900 to 1902. Gladden joined the new American Economic Association, an organization founded in 1885 by economists who disagreed with the prevailing school of classical economics. He also served as moderator of the National Council of Congregational Churches from 1904 to 1907. In 1905 Gladden won national attention by criticizing the American Board of Commissioners for Foreign Missions for accepting a gift of $100,000 from JOHN D. ROCKEFELLER, the president of Standard Oil. Gladden maintained that the money was "tainted" because of Rockefeller's business practices.

Gladden's views became more extreme as he aged. In labor, he abandoned his early cause of individual self-help for workers in favor of the program of the American Federation of Labor. In views on race he went from the conservatism of the African American leader BOOKER T. WASHINGTON to the more militant position of W. E. B. DU BOIS. In politics, he ignored his lifelong Republicanism to support Bull Moose candidate Theodore Roosevelt in 1912 and the Democrat Woodrow Wilson in 1916.

Gladden supported both the Spanish-American War and—once the United States entered World War I—participation in that conflict. He died before the end of the war.

**BIBLIOGRAPHY**

Dorn, Jacob H., *Washington Gladden: Prophet of the Social Gospel,* 1968; Gladden, Washington, *Recollections,* 1909; Hopkins, C. H., *The Rise of the Social Gospel in American Protestantism, 1865–1915,* 1940.

# Godkin, Edwin Lawrence

(October 2, 1831–May 21, 1902)
Journalist, Reformer

The founder and editor of *The Nation*, Edwin L. Godkin was one of the most influential critics of post–Civil War American society In his writings, Godkin sought to improve the moral tone of both business and politics.

Godkin was born in Moyne, Wicklow County, Ireland. His father, the Reverend James Godkin, was a dissenting clergyman (that is, he chose not to conform to the Church of England), and a writer and editor for Irish newspapers. Graduating from Queen's College, Belfast, Edwin Godkin studied law briefly in London, then switched to journalism. He wrote for *Cassell's Illustrated Family Paper* and in 1853, at the age of twenty-two, published his first book, *The History of Hungary and the Magyars: From the Earliest Times to the Close of the Late War*. From 1853 to 1855, Godkin covered the Crimean War for *The London Daily News* and the *New York Times*. His experiences as a war correspondent gave him an excellent knowledge of military strategy, along with a strong hatred of war.

In 1856 Godkin immigrated to the United States, settling in New York City. He studied law and was admitted to the bar in 1858. During the Civil War, Godkin served as a battlefield correspondent for *The London Daily News*, touring the South on horseback. Godkin's promise as a journalist led Henry Raymond of the *New York Times* to offer him a partnership in the paper, which Godkin declined in the hopes of starting a weekly of his own. In 1865 Godkin realized this dream with the founding of *The Nation*, which was launched with $100,000 in capital and forty stockholders. A year later, financial difficulties caused Godkin to take over the weekly himself.

Under Godkin's editorship, *The Nation* became a major molder of public opinion, providing lively and intelligent commentary on a wide range of issues. Charles Dudley Warner, editor of *The Hartford Courant*, called it "the weekly judgement day." Like Warner, many of *The Nation*'s readers were editors themselves, and these, together with the many professors who read the magazine, passed on Godkin's views in their own writings and lectures.

Although *The Nation* had been founded to serve the interests of the freed slaves, it vigorously opposed the carpetbaggers—those Northerners who went South after the Civil War, some in the interests of reform, but many for personal gain. In general, *The Nation* took a moderate stand on Reconstruction, reflecting Godkin's belief that the North should approach the South in a manner "which persuades men and not that which exasperates them."

On the other important issues of the day, Godkin emerged as a prominent spokesperson for well-to-do, educated, liberal reformers. He was sharply critical of the corruption of the Grant administration and as a Liberal Republican tried to see that Grant was not renominated in 1872. Yet when the Liberal Republicans nominated HORACE GREELEY, the controversial editor of the New York *Tribune*, as their candidate, Godkin quietly supported Grant. Later, in 1884, Godkin led the Mugwumps—eastern, liberal Republicans of an independent bent—who bolted the Republican party and its candidate, James G. Blaine, and supported instead the Democrat Grover Cleveland.

Godkin opposed Blaine because as a product of the spoils system, he embodied the kind of political corruption Godkin abhorred. One of the major crusades of Godkin's journalistic career was to replace the spoils system with a civil service based on merit instead of on political connections. Godkin attacked Tammany Hall, the Democratic party machine in New York, so frequently and so fearlessly that he was several times sued unsuccessfully for libel.

In his economic views, Godkin was a disciple of such English liberals as Adam Smith, Jeremy Bentham, and John Stuart Mill. Like them, he believed that government should pursue a *laissez-faire*, or hands-off, policy toward business. Godkin favored free trade, supporting a tariff for revenue only. He took a strong stand against imperialism and territorial expansion. He backed a sound currency based on the gold standard and opposed such inflationary schemes as the issuing of large quantities of paper money, or greenbacks, and the coinage of silver. Godkin also decried the widespread willingness to engage in speculative ventures that characterized the so-called Gilded Age.

While keenly aware of the problems of an industrialized, urbanized society, Godkin believed that many abuses could be corrected if both business and political leaders would assume a higher moral tone. In this, he showed a tendency to accept simplistic, overly optimistic solutions to complex problems.

In 1881 Godkin sold *The Nation* to Henry Villard, the owner of the New York *Evening Post,* but remained editor of the magazine, which became the *Post*'s weekly section. When the paper's editor in chief, Carl Schurz, retired two years later, Godkin served in this capacity until his own retirement in 1900.

As editor of the *Post,* Godkin was mainly concerned with the editorial page. He was the first New York editor to hold a daily editorial conference for the purpose of discussing the main stories and assigning writers to cover them. In his own writing, Godkin employed a direct, spirited style that greatly influenced an entire generation of journalists and editors.

Toward the end of his life, Godkin became disillusioned because he felt that reform had made little headway. He grew increasingly skeptical about the ability of the democratic masses to govern themselves and expressed his doubts about democracy in a number of books, including *Reflections and Comments* (1895), *Problems of Modern Democracy* (1896), and *Unforeseen Tendencies of Democracy* (1898).

Godkin was particularly troubled by the rise of imperialism and a warmongering foreign policy that culminated in the Spanish-American War of 1898. Godkin moved to England in 1900, where two years later he died, believing that because of imperialism the United States was doomed to repeat the European experience.

Godkin's long career as a journalist and editor is best summed up by his epitaph, which reads "Publicist, Economist, Moralist."

**BIBLIOGRAPHY**

Armstrong, W. M., *Godkin: A Biography,* 1978; Sprout, John G., *The Best Men: Liberal Reformers in the Gilded Age,* 1968.

# Goldman, Emma

(June 27, 1869–May 14, 1940)
Anarchist, Author, Reformer

As an anarchist writer, lecturer, and agitator, Emma Goldman was one of the most outstanding rebels in American history. "Red Emma," as she became known, boldly championed individual freedom despite prison terms and eventual deportation.

The daughter of Orthodox Jewish parents, Emma Goldman was born in Kovno, Lithuania, which was then part of the Russian Empire. Her childhood was unhappy because of her father's disappointment that she was a girl and her mother's coldness toward her. When she was eight, the family moved to the Prussian capital of Königsberg, where she received most of her formal schooling. In 1881 the family moved to the Russian city of St. Petersburg, where Goldman went to school for six more months before going to work in a glove factory. Here she met leftist students and from them learned about Russian revolutionaries.

In 1885 Goldman and a half-sister immigrated to the United States, settling in Rochester, New York. She found work in a clothing factory, and, lonely, married a fellow worker in 1887, but the two eventually divorced. During this period, Goldman was deeply shocked and angered by the trial and execution of the anarchists accused of the May 1886 bombing in Chicago's Haymarket Square (see JOHN PETER ALTGELD). Three years later she joined the anarchist cause.

Moving to New York City that year, Goldman became a disciple of Johann Most, a leading anarchist writer and speaker. While earning a living in the city's sweatshops, she began speaking at anarchist meetings and demonstrations, earning a reputation as a highly effective, charismatic speaker. She also met and fell in love with fellow anarchist Alexander Berkman. Both Goldman and Berkman believed in the use of violence to overthrow the government, which, as anarchists, they hoped to replace with a society based on voluntary cooperation and the free association of individuals and groups. So in 1892 at the time of the strike at the Carnegie steel plant in Homestead, Pennsylvania, they plotted the murder of Carnegie's manager, Henry Clay Frick. Berkman, who insisted on acting alone, failed in the attempt to assassinate Frick; he spent the next fourteen years in prison. In October 1893, Goldman was arrested for "inciting to riot"; she had told unemployed workers to steal bread to prevent starvation. She spent a year in prison on Blackwell's Island.

Having done some nursing while in prison, Goldman decided to seek professional training in Europe. In 1895 she spent a year studying nursing and midwifery in Vienna, Austria. Back in the United States, she worked as a nurse and midwife among the immigrant poor on the Lower East Side of New York. In 1899 Goldman again visited Europe, where she met the anarchist leader, Peter Kropotkin, whose ideal of a stateless communism she shared. Back in America again, Goldman dropped out of public life for a time because of efforts to implicate her in the 1901 assassination of President William McKinley by Leon Czolgosz, an unbalanced young man who had once heard Goldman speak.

By 1906 Goldman was again active in the anarchist movement on several fronts. She began editing an anarchist monthly, *Mother Earth*, which until its suppression in 1917 was one of the most important radical journals in the country. She was assisted in this work by Alexander Berkman, who had been released from prison, and who with her help wrote his notable *Prison Memoirs of an Anarchist.* Goldman also published tracts and several books of her own, including *Anarchism and Other Essays* (1910).

Also during these years, Goldman embarked on a number of lecture tours, which earned her much notoriety. A forceful, witty speaker with a gift for repartee, Goldman impressed audiences with her energy and intelligence and the strength of her convictions. Besides anarchism, she lectured on the new European theater of social protest, introducing her listeners to such playwrights as Henrik Ibsen, Anton Chekov, and August Strindberg. Goldman also lectured on feminism, calling on women to emancipate themselves from oppressive customs and traditions and demand sexual and reproductive freedom. A pioneer of the birth control movement, Goldman followed MARGARET SANGER's example in lecturing on preventive methods; as a result, she spent fifteen days in jail in 1916.

With the entry of the United States into World War I in 1917, Goldman and Berkman formed a group to help men resist the draft. These efforts led to a two-year prison sentence. After their release in October 1919, the radicals were two among hundreds of anarchists deported to the Soviet Union. According to FBI director J. Edgar Hoover, deporting Emma Goldman was one of his finest achievements.

Though initially sympathetic toward the Soviet Union, Goldman soon became disenchanted with the Bolsheviks' ruthless suppression of all political dissent. She left the Soviet Union in 1921 and two years later published *My Disillusionment in Russia*. During this period, Goldman lived and lectured in a number of countries, including England, France, and Canada. She returned to the United States for a three-month lecture tour in 1934 but was again forced into exile after being denied a permanent visa. Despondent over Berk-

man's suicide in 1936, Goldman threw herself into generating support for Spain's anarchists during the Spanish Civil War. In 1939 she went to Canada to aid the Spanish exiles there. She died the following year in Toronto.

### BIBLIOGRAPHY

Marsh, M. S., *Anarchist Women, 1870–1920*, 1981; Shulman, Alix Kates (ed.), *To the Barricades: The Anarchist Life of Emma Goldman*, 1971, and *Red Emma Speaks: Selected Writings & Speeches by Emma Goldman*, 1983; Wexler, A., *Emma Goldman*, 1984.

## Gompers, Samuel

(January 27, 1850–December 13, 1924)
Labor Leader

President of the American Federation of Labor (AFL) for nearly forty years, Samuel Gompers helped shape the American labor movement along the lines of "pure and simple" unionism, emphasizing the economic role of unions and eschewing political and revolutionary aims.

Samuel Gompers was born in a London tenement, the son of a Dutch Jewish cigarmaker. After only a few years at a Jewish free school, he was apprenticed at the age of ten to a shoemaker, but soon switched to cigarmaking. In 1863 the Gompers family immigrated to America, settling in New York City, where young Samuel went to work in a cigar factory. Although his formal education had ended at an early age, Gompers improved his intellect by hearing lectures at the

Library of Congress

Cooper Union and taking part in the debates among workers at the cigar shop.

In 1864 Gompers joined the New York City local of the Cigar Makers' International Union. When the union was badly hurt by the depression of 1873, he undertook to rebuild it, becoming president of the local in 1875. He went on to reorganize the Cigar Makers' International Union into a well-knit, financially viable organization, in which national officers had complete authority over local unions, dues were increased to build up a financial reserve, and provision was made for unemployment, sickness, and death benefits. By 1881 Gompers had made the union the strongest in the country.

That same year Gompers helped establish the Federation of Organized Trades and Labor

Unions of the United States and Canada. Five years later the Federation was reorganized as the American Federation of Labor with Gompers as president. With the exception of the 1895 term, Gompers held this position for the rest of his life. Though the AFL constitution limited the president's power, Gompers used both the prestige of his office and his own force of character to wield a wide influence.

With the decline of the Knights of Labor (see TERENCE POWDERLY) in the late 1880s, the AFL emerged as the dominant labor organization. Under Gompers's leadership, it recognized the autonomy of each trade and stressed practical demands like wages and hours, avoiding involvement with theorists and radicals. The AFL sought to improve the lot of the worker within the existing economic system. To accomplish this, it relied chiefly on collective bargaining.

Although initially against political activity of any sort, Gompers eventually decided that political action was required. Rather than endorsing one party, his policy was to support friends of labor and oppose its enemies. He remained opposed to the idea of an independent labor party, however. In the area of labor legislation, Gompers was particularly concerned with securing an amendment to the Sherman Anti-Trust Act so that it could not be used to restrict the activities of trade unions.

Unlike the Knights of Labor, which had embraced all workers—skilled and unskilled, black and white, women and men—the AFL was limited to skilled workers, which at the time of its formation constituted the bulk of the American work force. Yet despite the growth of unskilled labor, Gompers continued to oppose its inclusion in the AFL. Having at the outset advocated organizing black workers, Gompers soon gave way to those forces who were determined to exclude blacks. He also displayed a racist attitude toward Asian workers. Gompers supported woman suffrage and urged the unionization of women workers. At the same time, however, he felt that most women were

not working to support families and worried that their presence in the work force suppressed wages.

After a period of slow but steady growth in the late 1800s, the AFL's membership swelled from less than 600,000 to about 2 million between 1900 and the outbreak of World War I. With the AFL's expansion, Gompers as its president became an important public figure. He made numerous public speeches and frequently wrote articles to explain or defend labor's policies in the *American Federationist*, the AFL's official organ, which he founded and edited from 1894 until his death. Gompers also joined the National Civic Federation, an organization of large employers that worked to promote mediation of labor disputes and was particularly successful from 1900 to 1905.

While advising caution in the use of the strike, Gompers regarded it as an important tool in collective bargaining. He therefore championed the labor section of the Clayton Act (1914), forbidding the use of the injunction in labor disputes, and viewed it as one of his major achievements.

With the outbreak of war in Europe in 1914, Gompers, a pacifist, initially denounced the conflict. Yet by the end of 1915, he had reversed himself and was urging the United States to aid the Allies. The following year, President Woodrow Wilson appointed Gompers to the Council of National Defense, where he helped marshal labor support for the war and counteract the antiwar influence of the socialists. Wilson also appointed Gompers to the Commission on International Labor Legislation at the Versailles Peace Conference.

AFL membership doubled, to 4 million, in the war years, leading Gompers to hope that labor would continue to make gains in the postwar period. But the switch from a wartime to a peacetime economy, combined with a rising antiunion movement and the "Red Scare" sparked by the Bolshevik Revolution in Russia, brought hard times for workers. They fought back in a series of crippling strikes that swept the country from 1919 to 1920. Deeply dismayed by labor's new militancy, Gompers refused to support most of the strikes. He was further dismayed by several Supreme Court decisions undermining the labor provisions of the Clayton Act.

Despite these setbacks, Gompers remained committed to the labor movement he had played such an important role in shaping. Though gravely ill, he undertook the journey to Texas to lead the 1924 AFL convention. He died shortly after the convention.

### BIBLIOGRAPHY

Foner, Philip S., *History of the Labor Movement in the United States*, 5 vols., 1947–1980; Kaufman, S. B., *Samuel Gompers and the Origins of the American Federation of Labor, 1848–1896*, 1973.

# Graham, Sylvester

(July 5, 1794–September 11, 1851)
Health Reformer

Sylvester Graham preached a doctrine of diet and hygiene reform that attracted a wide following in the 1830s and 1840s. Though his adversaries called him a crackpot and a fanatic, his ideas are echoed in present-day recommendations for good health.

Sylvester Graham was a sickly, ill-educated child, afflicted with tuberculosis and handed about by various relatives. He had been born in West Suffield, a village north of Hartford, Connecticut, to a seventy-two-year-old father, John Graham, a clergyman and physician of Scottish ancestry who died when the boy was two. Little is known of his much younger mother, Ruth, a second wife. Sylvester worked as a teacher, a farmhand, and a clerk. Only when, at age twenty-nine, he was threatened by the relapse of an early tuberculosis did he decide on the ministry and enroll at Amherst Academy, in Amherst, Massachusetts. After a few months he left because of unpleasant relations with other students and teachers. During another long illness he was nursed by two women who were sisters. Upon recovering, in 1826, he married one of them, who bore him several children.

Graham was ordained a Presbyterian minister and in 1831 was sent to a church in Morris County, New Jersey. Meanwhile he had enlisted as an agent for the Pennsylvania Temperance Society and, after studies of his own, became an ardent advocate of temperance reform, vegetarianism, and other health regimens. He left the clergy and launched a career as a lecturer along the Atlantic seaboard, attracting a considerable following, including such prominent people as HORACE GREELEY and WILLIAM LLOYD GARRISON. Graham's chief message concerned bread, which he believed should be baked at home from unsifted, coarsely ground whole-grain wheat and should best be eaten when a day old. Thus he introduced Graham bread and Graham crackers. He recommended hard mattresses, open bedroom windows, cold showers, lighter clothing, regular exercise, pure drinking water, fresh vegetables and fruits, and good humor at meals. The eating of meat, he believed, caused abnormal cravings. A course of Graham's lectures recommending sexual abstinence was published as *The Young Man's Guide to Chastity* (1834) and reached a wide public in this country and abroad. He extended his program to include lectures on comparative anatomy, cholera, biblical teachings regarding wine and meat, and a dietetic system he devised for blacks.

While Graham's enthusiasm and energy brought his ideas to wide public attention and attracted followers, his frank and commonsense attitude toward personal hygiene and women's health problems shocked the prudish. He was the butt of attacks, occasionally violent, by bakers and butchers, though his *Treatise on Bread and Bread-Making* (1837) encouraged millers to profit by milling and selling Graham flour for home baking. Lampoons and jokes were circulated about him, and RALPH WALDO EMERSON wrote of him as "the poet of bran bread and pumpkins."

In 1839 Graham published *Science of Human Life,* an exhaustive two-volume textbook on physiology with a complete program for the good life. After 1840 his popular influence as a diet and hygiene reformer declined and, re-suming his religious interests, he began to deliver and publish lectures on the Bible. Of the four volumes Graham had planned, only one, *The Philosophy of Sacred History,* was completed; it was published posthumously (1855). His health failed, and he died at Northampton, Massachusetts, in 1851.

**BIBLIOGRAPHY**

Nissenbaum, S., *Sex, Diet and Debility in Jacksonian America: Sylvester Graham and Health Reform,* 1980; Whorton, J. C., *Crusaders for Fitness: The History of American Health Reformers,* 1982.

# Graham, William Franklin

(November 7, 1918–    )
Evangelist

Having devoted most of his life to spreading the Christian message throughout the United States and the rest of the world, Billy Graham is regarded as America's foremost modern-day evangelist.

Born on a farm near Charlotte, North Carolina, Graham was converted at a revival meeting when he was sixteen; he gave up his interest in baseball for preaching. He spent six months at Bob Jones University, a Christian fundamentalist institution in Cleveland, Tennessee, before he transferred in 1937 to the Florida Bible Institute near Tampa. There he became a Southern Baptist and earned a reputation for his dramatic mode of delivery. Graduating from the institute in 1940, he went on to Wheaton College in Illinois, where he continued to polish his preaching style. After earning his B.A., Graham served as minister of the First Baptist Church in Western Springs, Illinois, a Chicago suburb (1943–1946). After preaching to returning servicemen in Chicago, Graham was invited by Torrey Johnson, a radio preacher, to take over one of his programs.

In 1944 he joined Johnson's national crusade called Youth for Christ.

In 1947 Graham published his first book, *Calling Youth to Christ,* and became president of Northwestern Schools, a religious institution run by the First Baptist Church of Minneapolis. During his five years' tenure, Graham left administration of the school to others, devoting himself to evangelical work. In 1949 Graham scored his first major success as an evangelist. His Christ for Greater Los Angeles crusade reached 350,000 people and brought him national attention. Newspaper magnate WILLIAM RANDOLPH HEARST, impressed with Graham's preaching and anticommunist rhetoric, ordered his papers to cover Graham favorably.

In 1950 Graham formed the Billy Graham Evangelical Association in Minneapolis and began preaching on an ABC radio show called "The Hour of Decision." Graham further spread his message by producing religious films, writing a daily newspaper column, and publishing numerous books, including *Revival in Our Times* (1950), *World Aflame* (1965),

*Angels: God's Secret Agents* (1975), *How to Be Born Again* (1977), and *Approaching Hoofbeats: The Four Horsemen of the Apocalypse* (1983). He also continued to conduct highly successful campaigns. In 1957 Graham held a four-month campaign in Madison Square Garden in New York City, winning more than 50,000 conversions from among the nearly 2 million people present and an additional 30,000 conversions from the television viewers. Also during the 1950s, Graham held crusades in many parts of the world, including Europe, Africa, India, Australia, the Far East, and Latin America.

In the United States, meanwhile, Graham increased his fame by becoming associated with various presidents. He met with President Dwight D. Eisenhower once or twice a year during Eisenhower's two terms, was invited to the White House several times by President John F. Kennedy, and visited regularly during the administration of President Lyndon B. Johnson. A long-time friend of Richard Nixon and preacher at Sunday services at the Nixon White House, Graham suffered a temporary setback to his reputation when the Watergate scandals forced Nixon to resign the presidency. In 1983 Graham was awarded the Presidential Medal of Freedom by President Ronald Reagan.

Graham was controversial, partly for his political views. He opposed the banning of prayer in the schools and attacked the Supreme Court for being too easy on criminals. A year before the Supreme Court's desegregation decision, he began preaching to racially integrated audiences in the South. An outspoken opponent of communism, Graham backed the war in Vietnam, to the dismay of the antiwar movement. On occasion Graham has spoken in favor of nuclear disarmament.

Graham's religious views have also come under fire. Some fundamentalist leaders chided him as too liberal because he has cooperated with mainstream Protestant clergy and eschewed sectarianism. Other opponents have said that his preaching is too simplistic. Firmly in the tradition of such evangelists as CHARLES GRANDISON FINNEY, DWIGHT MOODY, and BILLY SUNDAY, Graham exhorts his listeners to repent of their sins and to accept Christ as their savior.

Despite these criticisms, Graham has enjoyed a successful career due to his highly effective preaching, to his sophisticated organization, and to his skillful use of the media. Moreover, during the 1980s, when other television evangelists became involved in scandals, Graham's reputation remained intact. As the elder statesman of the American evangelical movement, he continues to set an example of piety and moral uprightness.

**BIBLIOGRAPHY**

Bishop, M., *Billy Graham*, 1978; Frady, Marshall, *Billy Graham: A Parable of American Righteousness*, 1979; Streiker, Lowell D., and Gerald S. Strober, *Religion and the New Majority: Billy Graham, Middle America, and the Politics of the 70s*, 1972.

## Greeley, Horace

(February 3, 1811–November 29, 1872)
Journalist, Reformer

Editor of the famous New York *Tribune*, Horace Greeley was a major figure in both American journalism and in Republican party politics.

Horace Greeley was born in Amherst, New Hampshire, the son of a poor farmer and laborer. At age fourteen, he began his journalism career with an apprenticeship as a printer to the editor of *The Northern Spectator*, a Vermont paper. When the paper folded five years later, Greeley found work as a printer in Erie, Pennsylvania, where his family was then living.

In 1831 Greeley arrived in New York City with only twenty-five dollars, but he was determined to make his fortune. In 1834 Greeley founded the *New Yorker,* a weekly. His editing earned him a literary reputation but little money in the journal's seven years of publication. At the same time Greeley sold pieces to a number of New York newspapers, including the *Daily Whig.* In 1838 Thurlow Weed, William H. Seward, and other Whig leaders offered Greeley the editorship of the state party's weekly, *Jeffersonian.* (Greeley allied himself with the two politicians for years.) Two years later, Greeley served as editor of another Whig weekly, *Log Cabin,* during William Henry Harrison's successful campaign for president.

Library of Congress

Having for some time dreamed of publishing his own penny paper, Greeley in 1841 began publication of the New York *Tribune.* Possessed of a vigorous, lucid prose style, Greeley became the best-known and most often quoted public figure of his era. He brought high standards of literary excellence as well as factual reporting to his paper, partly because of the high quality of his staff, which included such luminaries as MARGARET FULLER and WILLIAM DEAN HOWELLS. The foreign correspondent was a German philosopher and socialist named Karl Marx. Greeley's *Tribune* inaugurated a number of new journalistic features, such as regular book reviews, interviews using direct quotes, and an editorial page.

During Greeley's thirty-one-year editorship of the *Tribune,* he used its pages to advance a wide variety of causes and reforms, including utopian socialist communities, women's rights, and labor unions. He also became an ardent proponent of agrarian reform, advocating free land for settlers and urging westward expansion. Although the famous remark, "Go West, young man," did not, in fact, originate with Greeley, he adopted it as an accurate reflection of his views. He acted on this view during a brief term in Congress, when he introduced in 1849 the first Homestead Bill. Finally passed as the Homestead Act of 1862, the law entitled settlers to 160 acres of free public land after five years of residence.

The cause to which Greeley gave his most consistent and long-lasting support was the antislavery movement. He attacked the Kansas-Nebraska Act of 1854 and helped in the supply of arms to antislavery elements struggling for control of Kansas. Breaking with his old allies Weed and Seward in 1854, Greeley assisted in the formation of the Republican party, which opposed the extension of slavery into the territories. When Seward—now a Republican—barred Greeley from a place in the New York delegation to the Republican convention of 1860, Greeley attended as a delegate from Oregon. By helping to defeat Seward's candidacy, he opened the way for the nomination of Abraham Lincoln.

During the Civil War, Greeley became increasingly critical of Lincoln because of Lincoln's slowness over emancipation. In "The Prayer of Twenty Millions" (August 1862), he called on Lincoln to free all those slaves who were now behind Union lines. When Lincoln did issue the Emancipation Proclamation, the *Tribune* blessed him in a banner headline. Nevertheless, Greeley's hatred of war led him in 1864 to attempt peace talks with the Confederacy on the basis of the "Union as it was"; the negotiations failed.

After the Civil War, Greeley, joining with the Radical Republicans, endorsed the

Fourteenth and Fifteenth Amendments, which would provide equal rights to the former slaves. While also supporting the impeachment of President Andrew Johnson, Greeley advocated a universal amnesty and a conciliatory policy toward the South. When he signed the bail bond releasing Jefferson Davis, the former president of the Confederacy, from prison, he aroused a storm of protest in the North, which cost him half the circulation of his *Weekly Tribune* and a big drop in the sales of his two-volume history of the war, *The American Conflict* (1864, 1867).

Both before the war and afterward, Greeley had harbored political ambitions of his own that were repeatedly thwarted. He was not re-elected to Congress in 1850 and lost subsequent bids for election to the Senate in 1863 and the House of Representatives in 1868 and 1870. Though Greeley reluctantly backed Ulysses S. Grant as the Republican candidate for president in 1868, he withdrew his support over the administration's policy toward the South and the administration's apparent corruption. In 1872 Greeley spearheaded a revolt by the reform element within the Republican party, which left it to form the Liberal Republicans. At their national convention in Cincinnati, the Liberal Republicans nominated Greeley as their presidential candidate; the platform promised civil service reform and universal amnesty. The Democrats also chose him as their standard-bearer.

In a bitter campaign, Greeley was attacked as a traitor, a crank, and a fool, and ridiculed in a series of savage cartoons by THOMAS NAST in *Harper's Weekly*. Greeley was badly beaten, carrying only six states and receiving only 2.8 million votes compared to the almost 3.6 million cast for Grant. Worn out by the rigors of the campaign and by watching at the sickbed of his wife, who died a week before the election, Greeley was shattered by the magnitude of his loss and also by the fact that the *Tribune*, the paper he had begun, had passed into the control of another editor. He soon became gravely ill and died at the end of November.

**BIBLIOGRAPHY**

Horner, H. H., *Lincoln and Greeley*, 1953; Lunde, Eric S., *Horace Greeley*, 1981; Van Deusen, G. G., *Horace Greeley, Nineteenth Century Crusader*, 1953.

## Green, William

(March 3, 1873–November 21, 1952)
Labor Leader

Wﬁﬀilliam Green entered the coal mines at sixteen and rose to be president of the United Mine Workers of America and then of the American Federation of Labor. He sought—with only marginal success—to show that the interests of capital, organized labor, and the state could work in harmony.

In 1868 Hugh Green left his coal-mining town in the west of England, with his Welsh wife Jane and his younger brother, for a new life in America. The mining industry of the British Isles seemed nearly played out. The Greens—illiterate, deeply religious, deeply trade-unionist—made their way to another mining town, Coshocton, in central Ohio. Hugh Green's eldest child, William, the first of six, was born in Hardscrabble Hill, the drab mining neighborhood of Coshocton. As soon as he learned to read, it was William's duty to read the Scriptures aloud to his devout family, in which drinking, smoking, and gambling were forbidden. William taught Sunday school at the Baptist church and felt a call to the ministry, but the family's poverty ruled that out. At fourteen, having completed the eighth grade, Green went to work as water boy for railroad workers, and two years later he joined his father in the mines.

Young Green was elected secretary of the Coshocton Progressive Miners Union at the age of eighteen. He studied economics at night and continued to work as a miner until 1908, when he became a full-time union official. Green rose through the ranks of the United Mine Workers of America (UMW) to become, in 1912, its secretary-treasurer, a post of great responsibility, and then one of its vice presidents. (He also acquired experience as a two-term member of the Ohio state assembly, where he introduced progressive legislation that was passed, and in 1919 he was a representative of the United States on the committee that led to the founding of the International Labor Organization.)

Upon the death of SAMUEL GOMPERS, in 1924, Green was elected president of the American Federation of Labor (AFL) with the strong backing of JOHN L. LEWIS, then president of the UMW. Green held that post till the end of his life. Earlier a supporter of the organization of workers according to industry, Green led the AFL in the organization of skilled workers by crafts. Eight of the largest AFL unions, including the UMW, after forming the Committee for Industrial Organization, were expelled from the AFL and, led by Lewis, became the Congress of Industrial Organizations (CIO). The ensuing struggle between the two labor giants ended with a merger in 1955.

Though Green was viewed as a conservative force in labor, in contrast to Lewis and to Lewis's successor as head of the CIO, PHILIP MURRAY, he nevertheless held views that some adversaries found progressive, if not radical. Early on he advocated universal health insurance, old-age pensions, government semiownership of railroads, and (during World War II) price control and rationing. Conversely, he called for outlawing the Communist party, and some critics claimed that in the interests of labor peace he maintained unduly cordial relations with industrial leaders.

Green lived in Washington during most of his career, but when his health failed he went for treatment at the hospital in his hometown, Coshocton, and there died at age eighty-two after a heart attack.

**BIBLIOGRAPHY**

Goldberg, Arthur, *AFL-CIO: Labor United,* 1956; Green, William, *Labor and Democracy,* 1939; Phelan, Craig, *William Green: Biography of a Labor Leader,* 1989.

# Grimké, Archibald Henry

(August 17, 1849–February 25, 1930)
Author, Civil Rights Leader, Lawyer

# Grimké, Francis James

(1850–1937)
Civil Rights Leader, Minister

# Grimké, Charlotte L. Forten

(August 17, 1837–July 23, 1914)
Abolitionist, Author, Educator

A lawyer and a minister respectively, Archibald and Francis Grimké were the African American nephews of the well-known white abolitionists and feminists, SARAH GRIMKÉ and ANGELINA GRIMKÉ. The brothers themselves figured prominently in movements in behalf of African American rights in the late nineteenth and early twentieth centuries.

Charlotte Forten Grimké, who became the wife of Francis Grimké, is best remembered for her participation in the Port Royal experiment, an effort to educate the freed slaves on the islands off the South Carolina coast during the Civil War, and for the account she left of her experiences.

Archibald and Francis Grimké were born on a plantation near Charleston, South Carolina, the sons of Henry Grimké, a white planter, and his black slave. Although their father left instructions in his will that they be freed, Francis was temporarily enslaved by his white half-brother. During the Civil War, however, the brothers became legally free. They received a secondary education at a school in Charleston that was run by a northern white abolitionist, Sarah Pillsbury. In 1866 Francis and Archibald Grimké entered Lincoln University in Pennsylvania. While they were there, their white aunts, Sarah Grimké and Angelina Grimké Weld, learned of their existence and publicly acknowledged the family connection. Their aunts also provided the young men with encouragement and financial support for their education. Both brothers received two degrees from Lincoln, the B.A. in 1870 and the M.A. in 1872.

In 1872 Archibald Grimké enrolled at Harvard Law School, again with financial support from his aunts. He received his degree two years later, the second African American to receive a law degree from Harvard. Settling in Boston, he started a law practice. In the early 1880s he also took up journalism, editing from 1883 to 1886 *The Hub*, which was devoted to the advancement of his race and was the first African American newspaper in the New England area. After the paper failed, Grimké wrote articles protesting race prejudice and discrimination for two white Boston papers, and published two biographies: *The Life of William Lloyd Garrison: the Abolitionist* (1891) and *The Life of Charles Sumner, the Scholar in Politics* (1892).

From 1894 to 1898 Archibald Grimké served as consul at Santo Domingo in the Dominican Republic. Upon his return to the United States, he again became active in African American affairs, serving as president of the American Negro Academy from 1903 to 1916 and lecturing and writing against race discrimination at the polls. In 1905 Grimké retired from his law practice and moved into the Washington, D.C., home of his brother Francis to devote the remainder of his life to civil rights. An early supporter of the Niagara movement led by W. E. B. Du Bois in opposition to the accommodationist policies of BOOKER T. WASHINGTON, Grimké became president of the Washington branch of the National Association for the Advancement of Colored People (NAACP; see JOEL E. SPINGARN). In 1919 the NAACP awarded Grimké its Spingarn Medal "for the highest achievement of an American citizen of African descent." Retiring from active work for the NAACP in 1925 because of poor health, Grimké died five years later at the age of eighty.

Francis Grimké, after graduating from Lincoln, had enrolled at the Princeton Theological Seminary in 1875, graduating three years later. In 1878 he became pastor of the Fifteenth Street Presbyterian Church in Washington, D.C., and married Charlotte L. Forten of Philadelphia. In numerous sermons circulated in pamphlet form and in such books as *God and the Race Problem* (1903) and *Jim Crow Christianity and the Negro*, Grimké protested the racial discrimination of his times, especially within the churches.

Like his brother, Francis Grimké was active in the American Negro Academy, an organization he helped to found in 1897. He also served as a trustee of Howard University. Francis Grimké also rejected the accommodationist policies of Booker T. Washington in favor of W. E. B. Du Bois's more militant approach. After a race riot in Atlanta in 1906, Grimké argued that it was the duty of African Americans to defend themselves. In 1908 he joined with other leaders in signing the call for the meeting which led to the formation of the NAACP. He continued to speak out against discriminatory practices by white churches until his retirement in 1925. Francis Grimké survived his brother by seven years, dying in Washington, D.C., at the age of eighty-seven.

Charlotte Forten was born in Philadelphia into a family that included several important black abolitionists. Her grandfather, James Forten, was a wealthy businessman who provided the main funding for WILLIAM LLOYD GARRISON and his newspaper, *The Liberator.* Her father, also an abolitionist, served in an African American regiment during the Civil War. When her mother died young, Charlotte spent her childhood in the households of her grandfather and her uncle, Robert Purvis, another well-to-do abolitionist.

Charlotte Forten was tutored at home to avoid Philadelphia's segregated schools, then sent in 1854 to Salem, Massachusetts, to continue her education. In Salem she lived at the home of Charles L. Redmond—another prominent black antislavery leader. Graduating from the Higginson Grammar School in 1855, she completed the one-year course at the State Normal School at Salem, then taught for two years at a grammar school in Salem, where she became the first black teacher of white students in the town. Overworked and ill, she resigned in 1858.

In 1862 Charlotte Forten was one of seventy volunteers who traveled to the sea islands off the coast of South Carolina as part of a federally funded project to teach the freed slaves, both children and adults, living there. (The islands had been recently occupied by Union forces.) Although fired with idealism when she arrived, the climate, the fleas, and the difficulties of teaching students who were not used to classwork all took their toll. By the time Charlotte Forten left in 1864, she was worn-out. Soon afterward, her account of these experiences appeared in *The Atlantic Monthly.*

Back in Philadelphia for seven years, Charlotte Forten wrote articles and taught. She worked for five years as a clerk in the Treasury Department in Washington, D.C., before marrying Francis Grimké, whose church she had joined, in 1878. She died in Washington, at the age of seventy-six.

**BIBLIOGRAPHY**

Cooper, Anna J., *Life and Writings of the Grimké Family,* 1951; Meier, August, *Negro Thought in America, 1880–1915,* 1963; Rose, Willie Lee, *Rehearsal for Reconstruction,* 1964; Woodson, Carter (ed.), *The Works of Francis James Grimké,* 4 vols., 1942.

# Grimké, Sarah Moore

(November 26, 1792–December 23, 1873)

# Grimké Weld, Angelina Emily

(February 20, 1805–October 26, 1879)
Abolitionists, Feminists

Sarah and Angelina Grimké occupy a special place in the abolitionist and women's rights movements. Not only were the sisters the first southern women to become antislavery activists, but they were also the first to advocate women's rights through their lectures and writings.

Sarah and Angelina Grimké were born in Charleston, South Carolina, of a wealthy slave-owner and judge. They had many siblings; Sarah was the sixth child and Angelina the fourteenth (and last). They were educated privately and at home in a manner that was considered appropriate for young ladies of their high social station. Both sisters were frustrated by the limits of their education and of the role that as women they were expected to play in Charleston society. Both were also deeply religious and distressed by their firsthand experience of slavery.

Sarah was the first to rebel. Following a trip to Philadelphia with her dying father in 1819, she met a number of prominent Quakers, who touched her with their simplicity and piety. Two years later, she took the bold step of moving to Philadelphia and becoming a Quaker. Angelina, meanwhile, began attending Quaker meetings in Charleston. Finally, after her family refused to discuss the subject of slavery with her, she left Charleston in 1829 to join her sister in her voluntary "exile."

During the first years of their exile, the sisters occupied themselves with charitable and religious work, while gradually moving closer to the antislavery movement. This time Angelina was the first to act. In 1835 she joined the Philadelphia Female Anti-Slavery Society. More important, that same year she wrote a letter to the abolitionist leader WILLIAM LLOYD GARRISON denouncing a recent mob attack on him in Boston and stating her sympathy with abolition. When Garrison published her letter in *The Liberator*, Angelina's name became publicly linked to the cause.

In 1836 Angelina Grimké wrote *An Appeal to the Christian Women of the South*. Published by the American Anti-Slavery Society and widely circulated in the North, this tract stands as the antislavery piece directed at southern women to be written by a southern woman. Postmasters in the South destroyed most of the copies that reached the region, however, and Angelina received a warning never to go back to Charleston. Having been converted to abolition by her sister, Sarah Grimké followed with *An Epistle to the Clergy of the Southern States*, also published and distributed by the American Anti-Slavery Society.

Also in 1836, Angelina Grimké accepted an appointment from the American Anti-Slavery Society to speak before small groups of women in the New York City area. Sarah soon joined her in this work, and in 1837 the sisters embarked on an extensive speaking tour of New England. The tour sparked great controversy, as the sisters spoke to audiences containing both men and women, a first for American-born women. The press and the clergy attacked them, but the sisters vigorously defended their right as women to speak in public in two pamphlets: Angelina Grimké's *Letters to Catharine Beecher, in Reply to An Essay on Slavery and Abolition, Addressed to A. E. Grimké*, and Sarah Grimké's *Letters on the Equality of the Sexes and the Condition of Woman: Addressed to Mary Parker, President of the Boston Anti-Slavery Society*, both published in 1838. The pamphlets, along with their lecturing, established the sisters as pioneers in the women's rights movement a decade ahead of the first women's rights convention in Seneca Falls, New York, in 1848. In particular, Sarah's pamphlet on the equality of the sexes has been hailed as the first serious discussion of women's rights by an American woman.

In February 1838, Angelina Grimké became the first American woman to address a legislative body when she testified before a committee of the Massachusetts legislature about the antislavery cause. In May of that same year, she married abolitionist THEODORE WELD in Philadelphia in a ceremony that emphasized sexual equality and that was attended by many prominent black and white abolitionists, including Garrison. Two days after the wedding, despite a mob so hostile that it later burned down the hall, she made an eloquent speech to a Philadelphia antislavery convention in what was to be her last important public appearance.

The couple and Sarah Grimké, who lived with them for the rest of her life, then moved to New Jersey, settling first in Fort Lee, and later on a farm near Belleville. They researched hundreds of newspapers from the South to compile Weld's *American Slavery As It Is: Testimony of a Thousand Witnesses* (1839), an indictment of slavery that HARRIET BEECHER STOWE relied on when she wrote *Uncle Tom's*

*Cabin.* After its publication, however, the sisters and Weld largely retired from active involvement in abolition. Weld was dismayed by the political direction the movement now took, and the sisters focused on running the household and raising the Welds' three children.

In the late 1840s and early 1850s, the sisters and Weld started schools at Belleville and then at a utopian community near Perth Amboy, to which they had moved. Here they taught the children of many of their former colleagues in the antislavery movement. Maintaining an interest in women's rights, the sisters also took part in women's rights conventions either directly or by correspondence.

In 1862 the trio gave up their Eagleswood school at Perth Amboy and moved to Fairmount (later Hyde Park), near Boston. All three taught at a progressive school for girls in Lexington until its destruction by fire in 1867. The following year, learning that two African American students enrolled at Lincoln University in Pennsylvania were their nephews, the sisters befriended ARCHIBALD GRIMKÉ and FRANCIS GRIMKÉ and assisted them with their education.

In 1870 the sisters joined a group of Hyde Park women in an attempt to vote in a local election. Three years later, Sarah Grimké died at the age of eighty-one. Shortly afterward, Angelina Grimké Weld had a stroke that left her paralyzed until her death at seventy-four.

**BIBLIOGRAPHY**

Lerner, Gerda, *The Grimké Sisters from South Carolina: Rebels Against Slavery,* 1967; Lumpkin, Katherine D., *The Emancipation of Angelina Grimké,* 1974; Lutz, Alma, *Crusade for Freedom: Women of the Antislavery Movement,* 1968; Perry, L., and M. Fellman, *Antislavery Reconsidered: New Perspectives on the Abolitionists,* 1979.

# Guggenheim, Meyer

(February 1, 1828–March 15, 1905)

# Guggenheim, Daniel

(July 9, 1856–September 28, 1930)

# Guggenheim, Simon

(December 30, 1867–November 2, 1941)
Industrialists, Philanthropists

Having gained wealth from a vast worldwide empire in mining and metallurgy, the Guggenheim family was notable for philanthropy, setting up several important foundations to sponsor work in education, science, medicine, aeronautics, and other areas.

Meyer Guggenheim, the head of the family, was born in Langnau, Switzerland. Immigrating to the United States at the age of nineteen, he settled in Philadelphia, where he engaged in various businesses, including peddling, until 1872. That year, he established the firm of Guggenheim and Pulaski, importers of Swiss lace and embroidery. In 1881 the firm was reorganized as M. Guggenheim's Sons with the four oldest of his seven sons as partners.

In 1887 Guggenheim acquired an interest in two copper mines in Colorado, but he soon decided that greater profits lay in the area of processing metals than in mining. Quitting the embroidery business, Guggenheim in 1888 formed the Philadelphia Smelting and Refining Company and built his first smelter at Pueblo, Colorado. He then built a second smelter in Mexico, which was the first complete silver-lead smelter in that country, and a refinery at Perth Amboy, New Jersey.

As before, Guggenheim brought his sons into the business, relying on them to manage operations in the field. The second son, Daniel, emerged as the leader by virtue of his intelligence and business acumen. Born in Philadelphia, Daniel left high school to go to Switzerland, where he spent the next eleven years learning the embroidery business. Returning to the United States in 1884, he joined his father and brothers in the rapidly growing metallurgy industry. In 1899 the major companies in the field formed the American Smelting and Refining Company (ASARCO). The Guggenheims, however, refused to join out of fear of losing control over their enterprise. Instead they entered into a fierce competition with the trust by forming alliances with the mine owners, aiding them financially when necessary, and in 1899 forming the Guggenheim Exploration Company to seek new ore deposits throughout the world. This strategy worked; in 1901 ASARCO was reorganized under the control of Daniel Guggenheim and his brothers.

As chairman of the board of directors of ASARCO and later as president (1905–1919), Daniel Guggenheim built the company into the world leader in nonferrous metal mining. In addition to establishing more smelters and refineries, he continued with explorations for new sources of ore and, once a discovery had been made, saw that it was exploited and integrated with the smelting and refining processes. Accomplishing his goals often involved solving great engineering problems. For example, in order to get to a large deposit of copper in Alaska, the company had to build a railroad over a moving glacier. It also successfully surmounted daunting obstacles to exploit an immense copper mine at Chuquicamata, Chile. In addition, the company developed nitrate fields in Chile, tin mines in Bolivia, gold mines in the Yukon region of Canada, and diamond fields in the Belgian Congo (now Zaire) and in Angola, Africa.

Daniel Guggenheim's remarkable success was due to his bold vision and insistence on using the latest and most efficient production methods and technological techniques available. As an employer, he held liberal, though paternalistic, views on labor, favoring the passage of social legislation but believing in the open shop and individual bargaining and remaining ignorant of actual conditions and wages at his plants.

Besides continuing and expanding upon his father's shrewd business practices, Daniel Guggenheim followed his example in philanthropy. During his lifetime (he died in Palm Beach, Florida, at the age of seventy-eight), Meyer Guggenheim had given generously to the hospitals and charities of Philadelphia and New York. Daniel Guggenheim subsidized free band concerts in Central Park in New York City and created two important foundations: the Daniel and Florence Guggenheim Foundation and the Daniel Guggenheim Fund for the Promotion of Aeronautics.

In 1919 Daniel Guggenheim was forced to retire as president of ASARCO because of illness. He died at his home in Port Washington, New York, at the age of seventy-four.

Daniel Guggenheim's successor as president of ASARCO was a younger brother, Simon, who was also instrumental in enlarging the family business. In addition to serving as president of ASARCO from 1919 until his death, Simon Guggenheim was a U.S. senator from Colorado from 1907 to 1913. In 1925, in honor of his dead son, he established the John Simon Guggenheim Memorial Foundation, often called the Guggenheim Foundation, to provide fellowships to scholars and artists pursuing advanced study abroad. Yet another Guggenheim son, Solomon, started the

Solomon R. Guggenheim Foundation "for the promotion of art and education in art." This foundation maintains the Guggenheim museum of modern art in New York City.

**BIBLIOGRAPHY**

O'Connor, Harvey, *The Guggenheims: The Making of An American Dynasty*, 1937.

# Guthrie, Woodrow Wilson

(July 14, 1912–October 3, 1967)
Folk Musician

Woody Guthrie's folk songs and his singing of them touched millions of Americans. His brilliance as a writer and composer, his sympathy with the exploited and luckless, and his love of freedom were cut off in mid-career, but he is remembered for bringing folk music into the American consciousness.

Woody Guthrie was born in Okemah, in central Oklahoma, soon after Woodrow Wilson was nominated for the presidency by the Democrats;

Alfred A. Knopf/D.C. Public Library

Woody's father, Charley E. Guthrie, a small-town politician, picked his son's name. Woody's mother, Nora Belle Sherman, played the piano and sang, and Woody learned her songs. The Guthrie family had more than enough hard luck. Three of their homes burned down, a sister died from burns, Charley Guthrie's business failed, and Belle Guthrie developed a disease of the nervous system called Huntington's chorea.

The Guthrie family moved to Pampa, in the Texas panhandle, where Woody as a teenager began to play guitar at dances. He married Mary Jennings in 1933; they had three children. He drifted about the country, hobo style, playing and singing the country songs he knew, occa-sionally turning up at home. Having taken the road to Los Angeles like other out-of-luck Oklahomans, Guthrie began to perform on a daily radio program, where his folksy humor and country music caught on. He became friendly with labor and groups including both socialists and communists, and sang his Dust Bowl songs at radical meetings. One of his leftist friends, Will Geer, urged Guthrie to try his luck in the East. In 1939 he left his wife (whom he later divorced) and children in Pampa and hitched his way to New York City. Geer put him on the program at a benefit concert for refugees from the Spanish Civil War and then another for John Steinbeck's committee for migrant workers, where the folk song collector Alan Lomax first heard him. Lomax got Guthrie down to the Library of Congress, in Washington, to record for the Archive of American Folksong and for Victor Records. The Victor album *Dust Bowl Ballads,* containing six two-sided records, was Guthrie's first commercial recording. Suddenly he was nationally known. In Washington he also encountered PETE SEEGER, a young volunteer at the archive deeply interested in folk music and eager to learn from Guthrie. Seeger and Guthrie became close, traveling together by car to Pampa, where Guthrie paid a brief visit to his neglected family before heading back east with a carful of Oklahoma comrades going to a Communist party convention in New York. A year later, the two singers joined up with Lee Hays and Millard Lampell as the Almanac Singers and performed for labor and antifascist audiences. Guthrie had moved close to the Communist party, but it appears that he never became a member. As he said, "I ain't a communist necessarily, but I been in the red all my life."

During World War II, Guthrie was a messman in the merchant marine and shipped out successively on three freighters that got torpedoed. In 1943 his book *Bound for Glory* was published—an autobiography, vividly written and often likened to a novel. Just at the end of the war he was drafted into the army. On a furlough to New York, he married Marjorie Greenblatt Mazia, a Martha Graham dancer. They had four children, one of whom, Arlo, grew up to be a folksinger of note.

It is estimated that between 1932 and 1952 Guthrie wrote more than a thousand songs, most to his own music, some to other tunes. The Weavers, a folksinging group led by Pete Seeger, made many of them well known during the fifties. The most famous is "This Land Is Your Land," written (in the Dust Bowl days of the 1930s) as a reply to Irving Berlin's "God Bless America." Others are "Union Maid," "Reuben James" (about a torpedoed Navy ship), "So Long, It's Been Good to Know You," "Pastures of Plenty," "Tom Joad" (inspired by Steinbeck's *The Grapes of Wrath*), and on and on.

In 1953 Guthrie divorced his wife and married Anneke Van Kirk, with whom he had a child. At about this time he began to show symptoms of Huntington's chorea, the disease his mother had died of. The remaining years were a slow decline, in various state hospitals. He could no longer perform or even write. In 1956 Pete Seeger and other old associates put on a concert in New York for the benefit of Guthrie's children, and as the audience joined in "This Land Is Your Land," Guthrie, a wisp of himself, stood in the balcony with his clenched fist raised. That event marked the beginning of a folk music revival and, in the words of his biographer, Joe Klein, of Woody Guthrie's canonization. Guthrie died eleven years later in a state hospital, in Queens, New York. His second wife, Marjorie, who had come back to help care for him, founded and devoted her life to the Committee to Combat Huntington's Disease.

Guthrie bequeathed his love of folk music to the counterculture of the 1960s through his son, Arlo, and Bob Dylan, who had visited Guthrie in his last years.

**BIBLIOGRAPHY**

Guthrie, Woody, *American Folksong,* 1947, and *Born to Win,* 1965; Guthrie, Woody, and Marjorie Guthrie (ed.), *Woody Sez,* 1975; Klein, Joe, *Woody Guthrie: A Life,* 1980; Lomax, Alan (ed.), *Hard-hitting Songs for Hard-hit People,* 1967.

# Guttmacher, Alan Frank

(May 19, 1898–March 18, 1974)
Family Planner, Physician

Dr. Alan Guttmacher, once called the father of birth control in the United States, devoted much of his career as a physician to advocating family planning and freedom of choice in bearing children. He was president of the Planned Parenthood Federation of America from 1962 until his death in 1974.

Guttmacher was one of twin sons, born in 1898 in Baltimore, Maryland. His father was a rabbi, his mother a social worker. He graduated from the Johns Hopkins University with a B.A. in 1919. After serving briefly as a private in the army, at the end of World War I he entered the Johns Hopkins School of Medicine. He earned his M.D. degree in 1923 and spent several years in residency and teaching at various hospitals. In 1925 Dr. Guttmacher married Leonore Gidding; they became parents of three daughters. He was an instructor in obstetrics at Johns Hopkins, continuing there until 1952, when he moved to New York City as director of obstetrics and gynecology at Mount Sinai Hospital. During the ten years he was at Mount Sinai, Dr. Guttmacher also taught at the College of Physicians and Surgeons at Columbia University and later at Albert Einstein Medical School in New York and at the School of Public Health of Harvard University.

In 1962 Dr. Guttmacher became president of Planned Parenthood. Since the early 1920s, he had believed that a woman had a basic right to choose whether or not she wanted a child and that the medical question of an abortion should be decided only by a physician. He strongly believed, further, that information about contraception, pregnancy, delivery, and aftercare was a basic, mandatory part of the medical profession's service to all people, whether rich or poor. Helping people to take care of their personal needs, he felt, could only contribute to the solution of society's larger problems. Responding in the 1950s to the view that it was not the responsibility of city hospitals to give out birth control information, Guttmacher charged that the failure of New York City to provide such information deprived women of good modern medical attention. By the time he had been at Planned Parenthood for two years, many of the city hospitals were dispensing birth control services, services that were extended to some of the city's poorest neighborhoods in 1965.

By 1965 there were 275 Planned Parenthood centers in the United States, and the International Planned Parenthood Federation was at work in twenty-eight countries and had thirty-eight national member organizations. As an advocate of population control, Dr. Guttmacher urged the government to sponsor birth control and fertility studies at home as well as abroad. He traveled tirelessly around the world, speaking to physicians, government leaders, and ordinary people. While his concern was always for free choice by women and for preventing discrimination in providing knowledge and good medical care, he also argued that the dangers of overpopulation had to be confronted.

In addition to technical medical books, Dr. Guttmacher wrote several books for the lay public, including *Pregnancy, Birth and Family Planning.* (His identical twin brother, Dr. Manfred Guttmacher, also a physician and a proponent of birth control, was a psychiatrist and a medical adviser to the Baltimore courts. He died in 1967.)

Before Dr. Guttmacher's death in 1974, the national family planning program had expanded to include thousands of hospitals, health departments, and community agencies as well as Planned Parenthood centers. A memorial that appeared in *Family Planning Perspectives* in March 1974 ended with these words: "We can pay Alan F. Guttmacher the homage and respect he richly deserves by completing the social changes for which he fought and by building a society in which every child is wanted, loved, healthy and brought into the world with the best care that modern medicine can offer."

**BIBLIOGRAPHY**

Guttmacher, A. F., *Birth Control and Love,* 1969, and *Understanding Sex,* 1970.

# Hall, Granville Stanley

(February 1, 1844–April 24, 1924)
Educator, Psychologist

G Stanley Hall played a major pioneering role in the development of psychology in the United States and was president of Clark University for thirty years.

Born in Ashfield, Massachusetts, Hall attended Williams College in Massachusetts and upon graduation in 1867 entered the Union Theological Seminary in New York. In 1868 he left for Germany to study philosophy at Bonn. Returning to the United States in 1871, he completed his studies at Union Theological Seminary, then taught literature and philosophy at Antioch College in Ohio. His interest in the new science of psychology was sparked by reading Wilhelm Wundt's *Foundations of Physical Psychology,* and in 1876 Hall enrolled at Harvard, earning his Ph.D. in 1878. He then went to Germany for two years of additional study.

Upon his return to America in 1880, Hall taught a very successful course in pedagogy at Harvard and in 1882 was invited by DANIEL COIT GILMAN, the president of the Johns Hopkins University, to become professor of psychology and pedagogy there. At Johns Hopkins, Hall established one of the country's first laboratories of experimental psychology and gathered around him a group of brilliant young associates, including JOHN DEWEY. Five years later Hall began the country's first professional journal in the field, the *American Journal of Psychology.*

The publication of Hall's first book, *The Contents of Children's Minds* (1883), along with various articles that followed, earned him a reputation as a leading commentator on education and led to an invitation in 1889 by philanthropist Jonas Gilman Clark to become the first president of the newly founded Clark University, in Worcester, Massachusetts. Serving as president for the next thirty years, Hall persuaded Clark, who had originally planned an undergraduate men's school, to make Clark, like Hopkins, a university devoted to

scientific research. Clark never seemed to have abandoned his original plan, however, and he kept trying to return to it.

In 1893 Hall resumed teaching and research in experimental psychology as the head of the university's psychology department. At Clark he established the first institute of child psychology in the United States. The institute conducted numerous studies, many of them using the questionnaire method favored by Hall. He also helped to found the American Psychological Association, serving as its first president in 1894. In 1904 Hall's involvement in the child study movement resulted in the publication of *Adolescence, Its Psychology and Its Relation to Physiology, Anthropology, Sociology, Sex, Crime, Religion, and Education.* A two-volume work, *Adolescence* synthesized a vast amount of literature. Its influence is evident from its sales—more than 25,000 copies—and the widespread use in colleges and teacher's colleges of a shortened version called *Youth; Its Education, Regimen and Hygiene,* published in 1906.

Seeking to give psychology a broad base, Hall helped introduce American psychologists to the ideas of Charles Darwin and the famous Austrian psychiatrist and founder of psychoanalysis, Sigmund Freud, among others. In 1909 Freud delivered a series of lectures at Clark; he received an honorary degree from the university. Continuing with his own research and writing, Hall in 1912 published *Founders of Modern Psychology* and, five years later, *Jesus, the Christ, in the Light of Psychology.*

After his retirement from the presidency of Clark in 1919, Hall occupied himself with scientific and literary projects and occasional lectures. His main published works from his later years were *Recreations of a Psychologist* (1920) and *Life and Confessions of a Psychologist* (1923). Hall died in Worcester at the age of eighty.

**BIBLIOGRAPHY**

Pruette, Lorine, *G. Stanley Hall: A Biography of a Mind*, 1926; Ross, Dorothy, *G. Stanley Hall: The Psychologist as Prophet*, 1972; Strickland, Charles E., and Charles Burgess (eds.), *Health, Growth, and Heredity: G. Stanley Hall on Natural Education*, 1965.

# Hamer, Fannie Lou Townsend

(October 6, 1917–March 14, 1977)
Civil Rights Leader

Until she was in her forties, Fannie Lou Hamer worked as a field hand on a Mississippi plantation. When she became aware of the struggle for voter registration she joined it, at risk, and became a highly effective civil rights activist and a prominent figure in the national Democratic party.

Fannie Lou Townsend was born in Rulcville, in the Delta region of northwest Mississippi, the youngest of a family of fourteen boys and six girls, and grew up in adjacent Sunflower County. Her parents, James and Lou Ella Townsend, were impoverished sharecroppers. Fannie began picking cotton at the age of six; nevertheless, she succeeded in completing six years of school. At that time, black children only attended four months of school each year because of their value to plantation owners as field hands. When she was twenty-four Fannie married Perry Hamer, a tractor driver on a nearby plantation. When it was noticed that she was literate, she was made a timekeeper. In 1962, upon hearing James Forman, of the Student Nonviolent Coordinating Committee (SNCC; see ELLA BAKER) speak at a rally, she and several other blacks tried to register to vote. They were harassed and turned away, and Fannie Hamer was fired from the plantation. To protect her husband and children, she moved out of her house and stayed with friends; the friends' house became the target of bullets.

In 1963 Hamer passed the state literacy test, registered to vote, and decided to devote her time entirely to the voter registration drive led by SNCC and the Southern Christian Leadership Conference (SCLC; see RALPH D. ABERNATHY and MARTIN LUTHER KING, JR.) and to helping black families receive welfare benefits. College students came South in 1964 for Freedom Summer, an ambitious voter registration campaign. Hamer conducted workshops, instructing the young volunteers about southern ways and cautioning them to avoid antireligious remarks in talking with blacks. She got threatening phone calls, and her husband was often fired from his jobs. Once, returning from a voter registration meeting, she was arrested and badly beaten by the police for attempting to use a bus-station restroom for whites; she suffered internal injuries and the near loss of sight in one eye.

As Mississippi's Democratic party refused black members, Hamer helped form the Mississippi Freedom Democratic Party (MFDP), whose members attempted to unseat the regular party delegation at the Democratic National Convention in 1964. The attempt failed, but Hamer's testimony to the credentials committee about the brutal treatment she and others had suffered because of their work for civil rights was broadcast on television and shocked the nation. At the 1968 Democratic convention, in Chicago, Hamer was one of twenty-two southern blacks seated as delegates, and in 1972 the MFDP delegates displaced the regular Mississippi Democrats and the state party was thenceforward integrated.

Hamer was a member of the Democratic National Committee from 1968 to 1971. In

1969 she, Dr. Martin Luther King, Sr., and Vice President Hubert Humphrey received honorary degrees from Morehead College in Atlanta. That year she founded the Freedom Farm Cooperative, a nonprofit enterprise which, having acquired 59 acres of Delta land, helped poor black and white families grow food crops on their own homesteads, provided scholarships, and set up a garment factory in Ruleville.

Hamer died of cancer at a hospital near her hometown, not long after the mayor of Ruleville had declared a Fannie Lou Hamer Day. She was fifty-nine.

**BIBLIOGRAPHY**

Jordan, June, *Fannie Lou Hamer,* 1972; Silver, J. W., *Mississippi: The Closed Society,* rev., 1966; Zinn, Howard, *SNCC: The New Abolitionists,* 1964.

# Hamilton, Alice

(February 27, 1869–September 22, 1970)
Physician, Reformer

Alice Hamilton pioneered in industrial medicine, arousing public concern about occupational diseases and the safety of workers on the job.

Born in New York City, Alice Hamilton grew up on the family estate in Fort Wayne, Indiana. After attending Miss Porter's School in Farmington, Connecticut, she chose medicine as a career. She received her M.D. from the University of Michigan in 1893, interned at the Northwestern Hospital for Women and Children in Minneapolis and the New England Hospital for Women and Children in Boston, and studied at the Universities of Leipzig and Munich in Germany. Upon her return, she did a year of postgraduate work at the Johns Hopkins Medical School, then in 1897 moved to Chicago, where she lived at JANE ADDAMS's Hull House and taught pathology at the Woman's Medical School of Northwestern University. When the

Library of Congress

Woman's Medical School closed in 1902, she became a bacteriologist at the new Memorial Institute for Infectious Diseases, winning praise for her study of an outbreak of typhoid.

Through her residency at Hull House, Hamilton became aware of the plight of immigrant workers, many of whom contracted fatal diseases in the workplace. She also read Sir Thomas Oliver's book *Dangerous Trades* (1902). Making a thorough study of the subject, Hamilton was horrified to discover that in contrast to Germany and England, the United States made practically no provision for the health and safety of workers. There were no laws about occupational safety, no system for inspecting factories, and no plans for workers' compensation for injuries. In 1908 Hamilton was appointed to the Illinois Commission on Occupational Diseases, and in 1910 she became supervisor of the state's survey of industrial poisons. Concentrating on lead, one of the most widely used industrial poisons, Hamilton inspected factories and mines, pored over medical records, and interviewed workers in their homes. Her carefully compiled survey led to a state law requiring safety measures and medical examinations of workers.

Appointed special investigator for the U.S. Bureau (later Department) of Labor in 1911, Hamilton continued her work on the national level, investigating the lead industries and later those involving rubber and munitions. Eschewing the sensationalism of the muckraking journalists, Hamilton's reports, nevertheless, provided dramatic documentation of high disease and death rates in these industries and contributed to improved industrial hygiene as well as to the passage of workers' compensation laws. Hamilton also campaigned for a federal child labor law, state health insurance, birth control, and woman suffrage.

During World War I, Hamilton expressed her pacifist sentiments by accompanying Jane Addams to the International Congress of Women at The Hague in the Netherlands and on a mission to present the women's peace proposals to the leaders of the various warring nations. In 1919 she visited Germany to investigate the famine there, becoming involved in relief work. Shortly after her return, Hamilton left Hull House to take a position as assistant professor of industrial medicine at the Harvard Medical School. The university's first woman professor, Hamilton was barred from the Harvard Club and from marching in the commencement exercises. Undaunted, she continued with her investigations, and in 1925 published the textbook *Industrial Poisons in the United*

*States*, the first of its kind in America, which established her reputation as one of the world's two leading authorities on the subject. In 1934 Hamilton published a second text, *Industrial Toxicology*, which she revised in 1949.

Also during these years, Hamilton served two terms on the Health Committee of the League of Nations (1924–1930). On a trip to the Soviet Union in 1924, where she was invited to make a survey of industrial hygiene, Hamilton was appalled by the repression of rights but admired other aspects of the Soviet system. Visiting Nazi Germany in 1933, she wrote a highly critical series of articles, and by 1940 she concluded that the United States should go to war to oppose Hitler.

Hamilton's social activism made her unpopular at Harvard, and in 1935 the university forced her to retire. She then took a position as a consultant to the Division of Labor Standards in the Department of Labor. In this capacity, she conducted her last field survey, an investigation of the viscose rayon industry. Hamilton published her autobiography, *Exploring the Dangerous Trades*, in 1943, and from 1944 to 1949 served as president of the National Consumers' League. She remained active in politics into her nineties. At age 101, Hamilton died at home in Hadlyme, Connecticut, where she had moved after leaving Harvard.

**BIBLIOGRAPHY**

Grant, Madeline P., *Alice Hamilton: Pioneer Doctor in Industrial Medicine*, 1967; Sicherman, Barbara, *Alice Hamilton: A Life in Letters*, 1984.

# Harper, Ida A. Husted

(February 18, 1851–March 14, 1931)
Author, Journalist, Suffragist

Ida Harper played a major role in the final campaign that won women the vote. She also documented the last years of the suffragist movement and the life of one of its most important leaders, SUSAN B. ANTHONY.

Born in Fairfield, Indiana, Ida Husted moved with her family to Muncie, Indiana. In Muncie's public schools, she began to display writing talent. She left Indiana University after a year to become principal of a high school in Peru, Indiana. In 1871 she married Thomas Winans Harper, a lawyer. The Harpers, who had one child, divorced nineteen years later, the chief cause being disagreement over her journalism. Ida Harper began writing for newspapers in Terre Haute, where she contributed articles using a male pseudonym to the *Terre Haute Saturday Evening Mail*. The occasional pieces turned into a regular column despite her husband's objections. In 1881 that column was called "A Woman's Opinion" and finally acknowledged Ida Harper's authorship. Harper also edited the "Woman's Department" in the union journal, the *Locomotive Firemen's Magazine*.

After her 1890 divorce, Harper became managing editor of the *Terre Haute Daily News*. Later that year, she moved to Indianapolis to be close to her daughter, who was attending school there. In that city she began to work for the *Indianapolis News*.

An advocate of woman suffrage since college, Harper befriended Susan B. Anthony when she came to speak at Terre Haute; the two friends became coworkers in the movement. Harper began attending state and national suffrage meetings, and in 1887 she was made secretary of the Indiana chapter of the National Woman Suffrage Association.

In 1896, after Harper moved to California to be with her daughter, who was attending Stanford University, Susan B. Anthony asked her to join the campaign for a state amendment for suffrage by overseeing press relations. After the unsuccessful campaign, Anthony asked Harper to write her official biography. The next year, Harper moved into Anthony's home in Rochester, New York, to begin researching and writing the book. The first two volumes of *The Life and Work of Susan B. Anthony* appeared in 1898; a third volume was published ten years later. Harper also helped Anthony edit the fourth volume of the *History of Woman Suffrage*, published in 1902. In addition she edited a women's column in the New York *Sunday Sun* and wrote for the women's pages of *Harper's Bazaar*. She accompanied Anthony on the suffrage leader's lecture tours and developed her own abilities as a public speaker.

Harper figured prominently in the successful drive for suffrage. Placed in charge of national publicity in 1916, Harper wrote hundreds of letters over the next three years to newspaper editors and scores of articles and pamphlets aimed at gaining support for a federal suffrage amendment. Late in 1918, when the amendment seemed likely to be passed by Congress, Harper began to edit the last two volumes of the monumental *History of Woman Suffrage*, which was published in 1922.

Harper lived her last years in Washington, D.C., where she died of a cerebral hemorrhage at the age of eighty.

**BIBLIOGRAPHY**

Harper, Ida, *A National Amendment for Woman Suffrage*, 1915, and *A Brief History of the Movement for Woman Suffrage in the United States*, 1917; Jones, N. B., "A Forgotten Feminist: The Early Writings of Ida Husted Harper, 1878–1894," *Indiana Magazine of History*, 1977.

# Harrington, Edward Michael

(February 24, 1928–July 31, 1989)
Author, Socialist

Michael Harrington, author of *The Other America*, a book which encouraged the federal government's War on Poverty in the 1960s, was an eloquent spokesman and political activist for socialist ideals in the United States.

Harrington was born into an Irish, Roman Catholic family in St. Louis, Missouri. After earning a B.A. from Holy Cross College in Worcester, Massachusetts, in 1947, he attended Yale Law School for one year. While at Yale, Harrington was persuaded by the logic of the arguments of fellow radical students to become a democratic socialist.

In 1949, after earning an M.A. in English literature from the University of Chicago, Harrington returned to St. Louis. He planned to become a poet, and New York seemed to him the place to be. To earn enough money for the move, Harrington accepted a position as a social worker. The experience of working among the poor of St. Louis changed the course of his life. The deplorable conditions he saw convinced him to dedicate the rest of his life to eliminating such economic hardship.

Harrington moved to New York the next year, and after a brief stint as a writer for the magazine *Life,* in 1951 he joined the staff of *The Catholic Worker,* a monthly paper cofounded and published by DOROTHY DAY. The *Worker* advocated combining aid to the poor with Christian renewal and pacifism. For the next two years, in addition to participating in the group's social work, he served as coeditor of the paper.

When the Korean War began in 1950 Harrington enlisted as a medical corpsman in the Army Reserves, but within a year he secured a discharge as a conscientious objector.

Harrington left both the Catholic church and *The Catholic Worker* in 1953. He could no longer believe that a supreme being would decree the infinite punishment of hell for any

finite human act. For the rest of his life he described himself as an atheist who was "culturally and psychologically a Catholic." But the energies he had once poured into *The Catholic Worker* he now committed to socialism. Taking the risky step of declaring his views in the politically conservative 1950s, Harrington would eventually become the most respected and admired socialist in modern America.

In the 1950s Harrington served as organization secretary of the Socialist party's Workers' Defense League, became a college campus organizer and lecturer for the Young Socialist League, and participated in civil rights demonstrations. In 1960 he joined the national executive committee of the Socialist party. From 1961 to 1962 he served as editor of *New America,* the party's official newspaper, and wrote the book that brought him national fame.

*The Other America: Poverty in the United States* (1962), reminded Americans living in an age of affluence that poverty still afflicted millions of their fellow citizens. Harrington showed how poor people in America were trapped in a harsh cycle of economic hardship that led to despair and rendered them virtually invisible to the rest of society. *The Other America* became a best-seller and helped convince President John F. Kennedy of the need to design what became known under President Lyndon B. Johnson as the War on Poverty.

Harrington turned down offers of a post in the Johnson administration, but he did briefly serve as a consultant. In 1964 he served as chairman of the board of the League for Industrial Democracy and wrote his second book, *The Accidental Century* (1965), a defense of socialism. It was followed by *Toward a Democratic Left* (1968), which called for socialist solutions to America's many domestic problems and also criticized U.S. involvement in Vietnam and Southeast Asia. At the same time, however, Harrington was a determined foe of communism, which he saw as betraying socialism's democratic promise, and a sharp critic of the Soviet Union's foreign and domestic policies.

In 1968 Harrington was elected national chairman of the Socialist party, a position he held until 1972, when he resigned to found the Democratic Socialist Organizing Committee (DSOC). DSOC merged with the New American Movement to form the Democratic Socialists of America (DSA) in 1981. The merger symbolized the reconciliation of the socialist Old Left with the New Left that had emerged on college campuses in the 1960s to protest racism and the Vietnam War. Harrington was cochairman of the DSA until his death.

In addition to his socialist political activities, Harrington continued to write books and to pursue a career as a college teacher. In 1972 he was appointed professor of political science at Queens College of the City University of New York. He was named a distinguished professor in 1988.

Besides his idealism, morality, and commitment to democracy, what characterized Harrington's socialism was his pragmatism. His intellectual conviction that fundamental structural changes in American society had to occur did not prevent him from working within the system for incremental change.

**BIBLIOGRAPHY**

Gitlin, Todd, *The Sixties: Years of Hope, Days of Rage*, 1987; Harrington, Michael, *Fragments of the Century: A Social Autobiography*, 1973, and *The Long-Distance Runner: An Autobiography*, 1988.

# Harris, LaDonna Vita Crawford

(February 15, 1931–  )
American Indian Civil Rights Leader

LaDonna Harris, a member of the Comanche tribe, spent her twenties and thirties serving civil rights and American Indian causes in her home state of Oklahoma before going to Washington, D.C., to found Americans for Indian Opportunity (AIO).

LaDonna Crawford, the daughter of an Irish-American father, Donald Crawford, and Lily Tabbytite, of pure Comanche ancestry, was born in Cotton County, in southwestern Oklahoma near the Chisholm Trail; after her parents separated, she was brought up on her Comanche grandparents' farm. Her grandfather belonged to the American Indian Church; her grandmother, a "psychic Comanche," converted to Christianity. LaDonna spoke only Comanche until she started grade school. In 1949 she finished high school in Walters, the county seat, and married a classmate, Fred Harris.

While Fred Harris went through the University of Oklahoma at Norman, his wife worked in the extension division to support the family. After obtaining his law degree in 1954, Fred Harris set up a practice in Lawton, Oklahoma, served in the state legislature, and in 1969 was elected to the U.S. Senate. During the 1970s he was chairman of the Democratic national committee and a candidate for the Democratic nomination for president.

LaDonna Harris, while living in Lawton, launched her career as an activist for civil rights generally. She was a leader in the women's movement and in bringing about the racial integration of Lawton. In 1965 she was a principal organizer of the first statewide assembly that brought together members of over sixty tribes to discuss their common problems. Out of that convocation came the organization called Oklahomans for Indian Opportunity, of which Harris was president. She was also on the board of the Southwest Center for Human Relations Studies in Norman, which addressed a broad civil rights agenda.

In 1968, when the Harrises moved to Washington, President Lyndon B. Johnson appointed LaDonna Harris chairperson of the National Women's Advisory Council of the War on Poverty and a member of the National Council on Indian Opportunity. In 1970 she went on to found AIO, devoted to encouraging dialogue between federal and tribal officials and to strengthening tribal government and leadership. As president and chief executive officer of AIO, one of Harris's first legislative victories, in 1971, was saving the sacred Blue Lake from commercial development and effecting its return to the Taos Pueblo in New Mexico. In 1973 she helped the Menominee Tribe, of Wisconsin, regain its federal recognition, which had been terminated in 1950.

Harris has devoted herself to encouraging tribes to reestablish traditional value-based ways of consensus in their systems of government. She has worked directly with the Winnebagos, the Creeks, the Apaches, the Comanches, the Pawnees, and other Indian nations. In the area of environmental protection, Harris has organized four regional forums involving federal agencies, tribal authorities, and environmental groups, designed to assist tribes in managing their resources in an ecologically sensitive way. She has represented American Indians at international meetings in ten foreign countries. In 1976 Harris was appointed United States representative to UNESCO (the United Nations Educational, Scientific, and Cultural Organization).

As a founder of the National Women's Political Caucus, Harris has been a spokesperson and model for Indian women. In 1980 she ran for vice president on the Citizens' party ticket and brought environmental issues into political debates then and subsequently. In 1991 she was in the southwest Pacific, in the republic of Vanuatu (formerly the New Hebrides), participating in the Women for Mutual Security Conference.

LaDonna Harris was divorced from her husband in 1981; he became a professor of political science at the University of New Mexico. Of their three children, two work in organizations committed to American Indian interests.

**BIBLIOGRAPHY**

Harris, LaDonna, *You Don't Have to Be Poor to Be Indian*, 1979; Harris, LaDonna, and Robert S. Peck (ed.), *Beyond Tribal Allegiance: The Indian Citizen*, 1988.

# Hayden, Thomas Emmett

(December 11, 1939–  )
Civil Rights/Antiwar Leader

Tom Hayden epitomized the radicalized middle-class college student of the 1960s. He was a cofounder of the Students for a Democratic Society (SDS) and a leader in the civil rights and antiwar movements of that turbulent decade. He continued his political activism into the 1990s.

Thomas Emmett Hayden was born in a working-class neighborhood of Royal Oak, a suburb of Detroit, Michigan. His father, a Republican, was an accountant for the Chrysler Corporation; his mother, a Democrat and a librarian, raised Tom alone after divorcing her husband. Tom attended the grammar school of the Shrine of the Little Flower Church, where the pastor was the former right-wing agitator CHARLES COUGHLIN, though young Hayden was unaware of Coughlin's previous history.

In 1957 Hayden enrolled at the University of Michigan at Ann Arbor. Radical causes first caught his attention during his junior year. In the summer of 1960 he visited the University of California at Berkeley and met students who demonstrated against the congressional committee investigating un-American activities; the Democratic party convention at Los Angeles, where he met Robert Kennedy and MARTIN LUTHER KING, JR.; and the congress of the National Student Association at the University of Minnesota, where he met black leaders of the student sit-in movement in the South.

In his senior year, as editor of the *Michigan Daily*, Hayden urged support for civil rights. After graduating, he worked with the Student Nonviolent Coordinating Committee (SNCC; see ELLA BAKER) in Georgia and Mississippi (where he was beaten up by a segregationist). Back at Ann Arbor as a graduate student, he helped form Students for a Democratic Society (SDS), which aimed to coordinate student activists nationally. In 1962, at a convention at Port Huron, north of Detroit, Hayden drafted an SDS manifesto (the "Port Huron Statement") which, in its final form, was considered "a classic document in the history of the New Left."

Hayden made radical activism his profession. In 1964, as national president of SDS, he established the Economic Research and Action Project (ERAP) in impoverished areas of northern cities and ran the project in Newark, New Jersey, where he attempted to organize the jobless poor. Hayden's 1967 book *Rebellion in Newark*, about the Newark riots that summer, describes the frustration he and his colleagues encountered, as well as the frustrations of the poor themselves. Meanwhile Hayden had joined the antiwar movement. In early 1965, with a Quaker historian, STAUGHTON LYND, and Herbert Aptheker, a Marxist, he visited North Vietnam hoping to establish contact between the American peace movement and the North Vietnamese. One result was the release

by the North Vietnamese of three American prisoners of war, whom Hayden escorted home.

In June 1968 Hayden was a pallbearer at the funeral of Robert F. Kennedy, who had been assassinated. In August, he helped plan the demonstrations of the National Mobilization Committee to End the War in Vietnam staged at the Democratic National Convention in Chicago. He and seven others, including ABBIE HOFFMAN, were indicted for inciting to riot. In the course of a lengthy trial, contempt of court was added to the charge. The convictions for riot were eventually voided on appeal, and the contempt charges cleared in a new trial. From his experiences Hayden wrote two books, *Rebellion and Repression* (1969) and *Trial* (1970).

Hayden was joined in antiwar activism by the actress Jane Fonda, whom he married in 1973. They traveled the country, speaking against the continuation of the Vietnam War. Having settled with his wife and their son Troy in Santa Monica, Hayden went into politics, styling himself a "grass-roots Democrat." After an unsuccessful run for the U.S. Senate in 1976, he continued his progressive concerns. In 1982 he was elected to the state assembly from his home district, and he has continued to serve into the 1990s, giving primary attention to environmental initiatives and higher education. His marriage to Jane Fonda ended in divorce in 1988.

**BIBLIOGRAPHY**

Gitlin, Todd, *The Sixties: Years of Hope, Days of Rage*, 1987; Hayden, Tom, *Rebellion and Repression*, 1969, and *Reunion: A Memoir*, 1988; Hayden, Tom, with Staughton Lynd, *The Other Side*, 1967; Miller, James, *"Democracy in the Streets": From Port Huron to the Siege of Chicago*, 1987.

# Haywood, William Dudley

(February 4, 1869–May 18, 1928)
Labor Leader

B ill Haywood helped found the Industrial Workers of the World (IWW) and, until its collapse during World War I, inspired its members with his simple message of the brotherhood of man and the eternal irreconcilability of boss and worker.

"Big Bill" Haywood was born in Salt Lake City, Utah. His father, also named William Dudley Haywood, who came of early New England stock, went west from his Ohio birthplace in his youth. His mother was born in South Africa of Scotch-Irish parents who immigrated to Utah during the gold rush. When Haywood was three his father died, and a few years later his mother married a hard-rock miner, who first took young Haywood to work in the mines at the age of nine. The family, with five other children, was poor; there was little schooling to be had. He worked at odd jobs until he was fifteen, when his stepfather got him work at a mine at Eagle Canyon, in northern Nevada. In that remote place he first became aware of the "labor question" when he read about the Haymarket riot in Chicago (see JOHN PETER ALTGELD). At the time, organized labor was using strikes and demonstrations to obtain improved working conditions, and many people associated the labor movement with radicals. Four years later, after a spell as a cowboy on a ranch where he met (and later married) "Nevada Jane" Minor, and after trying homesteading and other jobs, he resumed mining at Bingham Canyon, Utah. Five years later

Library of Congress

Haywood was mining at Silver City, Idaho. Two daughters were born, and then his wife's health failed; for a while Haywood turned to a dissolute life and apparently abandoned his family. At some point he lost the sight of an eye.

Haywood joined the Western Federation of Miners (WFM) in 1896 and was elected its secretary-treasurer in 1900. Thus he entered on full-time union work and never went back to the mines. Ed Boyce, president of the union and himself a radical, recognized Haywood's potential as an effectively militant labor leader. He was at the forefront of the union ranks during the industrial conflicts in Colorado during the 1900s, when the mining interests resisted unionization with violence while the miners responded in kind. Haywood (who had joined the Socialist party in 1901) became a partisan of industrial unionism (the organizing of all workers—skilled and unskilled, Yankee and immigrant, men and women) and an opponent of the craft unionism of the American Federation of Labor (AFL; see WILLIAM GREEN and JOHN L. LEWIS). In June 1905 he presided at the WFM convention in Chicago and, with other radicals, founded the Industrial Workers of the World (IWW), committed to the idea of "one big union" that would free all workers from the bonds of capitalism. He aspired to an organization for "the unskilled, the unorganized, the powerless." Haywood became nationally famous as "Big Bill"—more than 6 feet tall, powerfully built, and blind in one eye, he was a forceful, memorable speaker with a down-to-earth style.

In December 1905 a former Idaho governor, Frank R. Steunenberg, who had crushed a WFM strike in 1899, was murdered. Haywood and two other union officials were accused of instigating the crime; they were arrested in Denver and imprisoned. Indicted for murder, they were held for a year without bond. EUGENE V. DEBS called for an uprising of workers. Unions around the country raised the money to retain CLARENCE S. DARROW for the defense. While in prison, Haywood ran as the Socialist party's candidate for governor of Colorado and polled 16,000 votes. In May 1907 Haywood was acquitted. As a worker for the Socialist party he supported Debs's campaign for the presidency in 1908; as an IWW activist he was a leader of the Lawrence textile and Paterson silk workers' strikes in 1912 and 1913 and was lionized at Mabel Dodge's artistic gatherings in New York City's Greenwich Village (see LINCOLN STEFFENS).

Having become president of the IWW in 1914, Haywood improved the organization's management and directed membership drives among western miners, migratory farmworkers, and lumberjacks in the Northwest. When the United States entered World War I in 1917, the IWW denounced the war as an attack of capitalists upon the working class. Haywood and all the other IWW officials (approximately 100 total) were tried and convicted of sedition and sentenced to long prison terms. Released on bail while awaiting a new trial, Haywood toured the country speaking to raise funds for the convicted IWW leaders. When in 1921 the last legal appeal failed, Haywood jumped bail (he refused to surrender and serve his term) and escaped to the Soviet Union. Sick and exhausted, he worked on his autobiography (with Louise Bryant, JOHN REED's widow, as ghostwriter) and received visiting radicals from home. He died in a Moscow hospital in May 1928 after a paralytic stroke and was buried there.

**BIBLIOGRAPHY**

Conklin, J. R., *Big Bill Haywood and the Radical Union Movement,* 1969; Dubofsky, M., *We Shall Be All: A History of the IWW,* 1969; Haywood, William D., *Bill Haywood's Book: The Autobiography of Big Bill Haywood,* 1929; Renshaw, P., *The Wobblies: The Story of Syndicalism in the United States,* 1967.

# Hearst, William Randolph

(April 29, 1863–August 14, 1951)
Journalist

Through the sensationalism he promoted in his journalistic empire and his own lavish life-style, William Randolph Hearst became one of the best-known public figures of his day.

Hearst was born in San Francisco, California, the son of a millionaire miner and rancher. Enrolling at Harvard in 1882, he was expelled three years later because of a tasteless prank. Undaunted, Hearst persuaded his father to let him take over his father's failing newspaper, the San Francisco *Examiner,* in 1887. He modeled the paper after JOSEPH PULITZER's New York *World,* with its mixture of sensationalism and reform, and hired a talented, well-paid staff. After going into debt, Hearst finally began to make a profit.

With the purchase of the New York *Journal* in 1895, Hearst challenged Pulitzer on his own turf. He brought the best of his San Francisco staff to New York, lured other talented people away from the New York papers, and slashed the price of his paper to 1 cent. When the Cubans revolted against Spanish rule, Hearst tried to outdo Pulitzer in printing exaggerated accounts of Spanish "atrocities." The circulation war between the two papers produced "yellow journalism," or an excessively lurid style of reporting. Also, by firing public sentiment against Spain, Hearst and Pulitzer helped cause the Spanish-American War of 1898.

Harboring political as well as journalistic ambitions, Hearst made a successful bid for a seat in Congress in 1903, serving until 1907. Despite an undistinguished record, he made a determined but ultimately losing effort to win his party's presidential nomination in 1904. He then tried for the mayoralty of New York City, taking on the Democratic machine of Tammany Hall and almost winning in 1905. The following year, he struck a bargain with Tammany Hall that he hoped would win him the governorship, but he was defeated. Hearst then launched his own personal third party, the Independence party, but in the presidential election of 1908 it polled less than 100,000 votes and soon sank into oblivion.

Despite political activity, Hearst did not ignore newspapers. His journalistic empire grew through buying or starting newspapers in Chicago, Los Angeles, Boston, Baltimore, Pittsburgh, Atlanta, Seattle, and other cities. He also acquired such magazines as *Cosmopolitan, Good Housekeeping,* and *Harper's Bazaar,* and created both the King Features Syndicate and the International News Service to supply newspapers throughout the country with news and features. In 1913 he branched into motion pictures with a weekly newsreel.

Not afraid of taking unpopular stands, Hearst opposed the U.S. entry into World War I and was accused of being pro-German as a result. After the war, Hearst took a stand against America's joining the League of Nations and helped to keep the nation from participating in the World Court.

Throughout the 1920s Hearst was riding high. His handpicked candidate, John F. Hylan, was mayor of New York, enabling Hearst to influence city government for eight years. Hearst also started a motion picture company aimed at making a star of a Ziegfield Follies girl, Marion Davies, whom Hearst had met and fallen in love with in 1917 and who became his closest companion despite the fact that he was already a married man with a family. Indulging his taste for luxury, Hearst began building a mansion at San Simeon on the California coast, where he entertained prime ministers and film stars in a princely manner.

In 1932 Hearst wielded political clout by swinging the Democratic presidential nomination in Franklin D. Roosevelt's favor through his control of the California delegation. But he soon turned against Roosevelt because of the latter's attempts to regulate business, and by 1935 Hearst papers called Roosevelt's New Deal the "Raw Deal."

The Great Depression, combined with Hearst's spendthrift ways, almost cost him his empire. He not only lost control of his publishing ventures, but also suffered the humiliation of seeing many of his art treasures sold at auction at Gimbels department store in New York City. With World War II and the return of prosperity, Hearst succeeded in regaining a measure of control over a publishing conglomerate that, though diminished in size, was still the largest in the nation. After suffering a heart seizure in 1947, Hearst spent his last few years as an invalid, who, nevertheless, managed to read the various papers he owned and issue instructions to editors. Hearst died at Marion Davies's Beverly Hills, California, home at the age of eighty-eight.

**BIBLIOGRAPHY**

Coblentz, Edmund D., *William Randolph Hearst, A Portrait in His Own Words,* 1952; Swanberg, W. A., *Citizen Hearst,* 1961; Winkler, John K., *William Randolph Hearst—A New Appraisal,* 1955.

# Helper, Hinton Rowan

(December 27, 1829–March 8, 1909)
Antislavery Author

Hinton Rowan Helper wrote *The Impending Crisis of the South and How to Meet It*, a passionate argument for the abolition of slavery because of its negative effect on the nonslaveholding whites of the South. This book by one of their own kind infuriated Southerners and intensified the sectional conflict that led to the Civil War.

The son of a yeoman farmer, Helper was born in Rowan (now Davie) County, North Carolina, and grew up in relative poverty. After graduating from Mocksville Academy in 1848, he worked in a store in nearby Salisbury. In 1850 he went to New York and from there joined the gold rush to California. Upon his return three years later, he tried to recover his financial losses by writing his first book, *The Land of Gold* (1855). In it, he bitterly described California as "rich in nothing and poor in everything."

In his second book, *The Impending Crisis of the South and How to Meet It* (1857), Helper blamed the South's economic stagnation on slavery, which he claimed hindered the development of a free white labor sector. Helper did not concern himself with the immorality of slavery or its harmful effects on the slaves; his only concern was improving the lot of nonslaveholding Southern whites. He violently denounced slaveholders and threatened a slave uprising.

*The Impending Crisis* aroused so much hostility against Helper throughout the South that he was forced to flee from North Carolina to New York. In the North, an abridgment of the book became a best-seller. Republicans campaigning for Congress even distributed free copies at political rallies.

In 1861 President Abraham Lincoln appointed Helper consul in Buenos Aires, Argentina. Upon his return to the United States in 1866, Helper wrote three fiercely racist books: *Nojoque* (1867), *Negroes in Negroland, the Negroes in America, and Negroes Generally* (1868), and *Noonday Exigencies in America* (1871), which were prompted by his dismay with the course of Reconstruction. Helper was appalled at the thought of giving African Americans equal civil rights.

In 1871, by capitalizing on his government contacts and experience in Argentina, Helper managed to establish a successful business as an agent for Americans who had claims against South American governments. He might have accumulated a substantial fortune had he not become obsessed with the idea of constructing a railroad from Hudson Bay to the Strait of Magellan. His last two books, *Oddments of Andean Diplomacy* (1879) and *The Three Americas Railway* (1881) sought to popularize this dream.

His financial resources exhausted by the railway plan, Helper spent his last years in poverty. He committed suicide in Washington, D.C.

**BIBLIOGRAPHY**

Ashe, S. A., *Biographical History of North Carolina*, vol. VIII, 1917; Bailey, Hugh C., *Hinton Rowan Helper: Abolitionist-Racist*, 1965.

# Henry, Joseph

(December 17, 1797–May 13, 1878)
Scientist

Through his work in electricity, Joseph Henry became the first American scientist since Benjamin Franklin to be acclaimed internationally. As the secretary and first director of the Smithsonian Institution, he was responsible for building it into a strongly research-oriented institution that until his time had not existed in America.

Born the son of a day laborer in Albany, New York, Henry had little formal schooling but read widely. When he was sixteen, he came upon a popular book on natural science that made him decide to become a scientist. He studied at the Albany Academy. When he became an instructor at the academy in 1826, he started doing experiments in electricity.

Henry's first major success came three years later. By wrapping layers of insulated coils around an iron core, a new technique, he was able to greatly increase the possible strength of an electromagnet. The next year he discovered the principle of induction or induced current. Although Henry's responsibilities as a teacher kept him from publishing his results before the Englishman Michael Faraday, who also discovered the principle, he is generally credited with the discovery. Thus the name for the unit of induction is the henry. In 1831 Henry invented and demonstrated the first electromagnetic telegraph, later to be developed commercially by Samuel F. B. Morse. He rang a bell by transmitting an electric impulse to it over a mile of wire. Earlier Henry had also invented an electric motor using electromagnets.

As professor of natural philosophy at the College of New Jersey (now Princeton University), a post he assumed in 1832, Henry continued with his experiments. He developed the electromagnetic relay, discovered the princi-

ple of the modern transformer, and worked on long-distance discharges of electricity. This latter work helped pave the way for the development of radio.

In 1846 Henry became the first secretary and director of the Smithsonian Institution in Washington, D.C. The Smithsonian had recently been created by an act of Congress with a private endowment from the English scientist James Smithson, "for the increase and diffusion of knowledge among men." Henry believed that the institution should use its limited funds to support original scientific research and scholarly publications rather than lectures, libraries, and museums. At the time, the nation lacked such an institution dedicated to pure research. As director of the Smithsonian, Henry aided and encouraged many American scientists over the next generation. He also started a service for the free publication and distribution of scientific ideas. After Henry's death, however, the Smithsonian expanded to become the world's largest museum complex, overshadowing his original intent for the institution.

One of the Smithsonian's largest programs was in meteorology. Around 1850 Henry organized a corps of volunteer weather observers and introduced the system of transmitting weather reports by telegraph and using them to forecast weather conditions. This work was so successful that it led to the creation of the U.S. Weather Bureau. As a member of the federal lighthouse board, Henry also made improvements in fog signaling.

Henry helped organize the American Association for the Advancement of Science and was elected its first president in 1849. He assisted in founding the Philosophical Society of

Washington in 1871 and served as president. An original member of the National Academy of Sciences, Henry was president of this organization from 1868 until his death ten years later.

**BIBLIOGRAPHY**

Coulson, Thomas, *Joseph Henry: His Life and Work,* 1950; Reingold, N. (ed.), *Science in Nineteenth Century America, A Documentary History,* 1964.

# Higginson, Thomas Wentworth Storrow

(December 22, 1823–May 9, 1911)
Reformer

Thomas Wentworth Higginson played such an important role in the nineteenth-century women's rights movement that he has been hailed as the leading male feminist of his generation. The other cause to which he dedicated his life was abolition.

Born in Cambridge, Massachusetts, Higginson entered Harvard as a thirteen-year-old, graduating the second in his class in 1841. He spent two years teaching before returning to Harvard as a graduate student. In 1846 he enrolled in Harvard's divinity school. The next year he graduated from the divinity school, married, and took the position of minister at the Unitarian First Religious Society in Newburyport, Massachusetts.

At Harvard Higginson had already become active in the abolition and women's rights movements. These views caused political and professional difficulty in 1850. He ran unsuccessfully for Congress on the ticket of the Free-Soil party, which opposed the extension of slavery into the territories of the United States. That same year he lost his ministerial position. In 1852, however, he accepted a call to become pastor of a nonsectarian Free Church in Worcester, Massachusetts.

An early believer in the use of force to resist slavery, Higginson joined a Boston vigilance committee in 1851. An early attempt by the committee to rescue a fugitive slave failed. In 1854 he joined a celebrated effort to rescue another runaway. The fugitive, Anthony Burns, had been arrested in Boston. Higginson and others battered down the door of the courthouse where Burns was being held before being returned south. Higginson got a bad cut on the chin in the fight with the police. He also got an indictment—along with WENDELL PHILLIPS and several others. The abolitionists were charged with the murder of a deputy who had been killed in the fracas, but an error in the indictment led to their release.

Two years later, Higginson became involved in the struggle to make Kansas a free state. While traveling in this effort, he met the militant abolitionist JOHN BROWN; the two became friends. Higginson publicized the cause in letters to the *New York Tribune.* Later the letters were published as a tract called *A Ride Through Kansas.*

With the outbreak of the Civil War, Higginson continued his forceful abolitionism, helping raise and drill a volunteer regiment, of which he was a captain. He left that post to become colonel of the First South Carolina Volunteers, the first African American regiment in the Union army. From November 1862 until May 1864, when he retired from the army on account of a wound, he led the First South Carolina, which acquitted itself with bravery. Higginson's book *Army Life in a Black Regiment* (1870) was based on those experiences.

The war over, Higginson threw his energies into the women's rights movement. The cause was not new to him; he had espoused women's rights before the war. Now, though, it became a focus for him. He participated in state, regional, and national suffrage associations, editing the *Woman's Journal*, the organ of the Massachusetts suffrage association, from 1870 to 1884. In articles written for this weekly and for other magazines and in lectures, Higginson advocated woman suffrage and coeducation, maintaining that women were the intellectual equals of men. He championed these causes while in the Massachusetts legislature (1880–1881) as well.

The author of a number of books as well as a frequent contributor to the major periodicals of his day, Higginson served as a mentor to aspiring women writers. He helped both HELEN HUNT JACKSON and Emily Dickinson. His con-

nection with Dickinson embraced a sixteen-year correspondence that ended when the poet died in 1886. After Dickinson's death, he helped edit two volumes of her poetry. Higginson died in Cambridge at the age of eighty-seven.

**BIBLIOGRAPHY**

Leach, William, *True Love and Perfect Union: The Feminist Reform of Sex and Society*, 1980; Tuttleton, J. W., *Thomas Wentworth Higginson*, 1978; Wells, A. M., *Dear Preceptor: The Life and Times of Thomas Wentworth Higginson*, 1963.

# Hill, Joe

(October 7, 1879–November 19, 1915)
Labor Song Writer, Union Organizer

As he wandered the country in the years before World War I, Joe Hill, or Hillstrom, wrote the words of labor songs that made him an American legend. He was executed for a murder that many people believe he did not commit.

The man known today as Joe Hill was born Joel Emmanuel Hägglund in Gävle, Sweden, one of nine children in the orthodox Lutheran family of a railroad conductor. Music was a strong part of family life. Joel played the organ for family singing, and he also played the guitar and the violin. When Joel was eight, his father died after a railroad injury, and the family was reduced to bare subsistence. The children had to work, and Joel found factory jobs. At around age twenty he fell ill with tuberculosis and went to Stockholm for treatment, supporting himself with any work he could find. He learned English at a YMCA. After their mother died in 1902, the family broke up; the six surviving children divided up $1,300 realized from selling the family house and went their separate

ways. Joel and a brother took passage for New York, where he began his career as an itinerant worker.

Joel Hägglund apparently began to call himself Joe Hill in Chicago, where while working in a machine shop he tried to organize the workers, was fired, and changed his name to escape the blacklist. His restless life is hard to trace. He was in San Francisco at the time of the earthquake of 1906 and wrote an account, for his hometown paper in Sweden, of doing rescue work. In 1910 he joined the IWW (Industrial Workers of the World, nicknamed the "Wobblies"; see WILLIAM D. HAYWOOD) at San Pedro, California, and his articles, letters, and songs began to appear in IWW publications. He shipped out of San Pedro as an ordinary seaman, and he joined labor action in British Columbia and in many American cities. In 1911 he recruited IWW members to join an ill-starred rebellion in Mexico.

Everywhere Joe Hill went he wrote his songs and sang them to inspire union organizers and workers generally. As he witnessed inequities of American life, he moved far from his pious Swedish background. Though his tunes were often borrowed from Protestant hymns, the words were scornful of religion. Other tunes from popular songs of the day had the effect of parodying conventional mores. Joe Hill's *Little Red Song Book*, which went through many editions, contains barely two dozen songs, and many, such as "The Preacher and the Slave" and "Casey Jones—The Union Scab," are still familiar.

On January 13, 1914, Joe Hill was arrested in Salt Lake City, Utah, and charged with the shooting of a groceryman and his son. On June 28 he was found guilty of murder and sentenced to death. Evidence was circumstantial, and Hill (who was then using the name Joseph Hillstrom) refused to disclose facts that could have helped his case. It was evident that his IWW connection provoked feeling against him. Appeals of the verdict were made by Presi-

The Archives of Labor and Urban Affairs, Wayne State University

dent Woodrow Wilson, the Swedish government, SAMUEL GOMPERS, HELEN KELLER, and numerous others. The IWW organizer ELIZABETH GURLEY FLYNN (for whom Joe Hill wrote a song, "The Rebel Girl," during his year in prison) was a leader of the effort to save his life.

Joe Hill was executed by a firing squad on November 19, 1915. In a last letter to Haywood, he wrote, "Don't waste any time mourning—organize." At his request his ashes were scattered in all of the forty-eight states except Utah and on every continent except Antarctica. The song "I Dreamed I Saw Joe Hill Last Night," by Alfred Hayes and Earl Robinson, keeps Joe Hill's name alive.

**BIBLIOGRAPHY**

Foner, Philip S., *The Case of Joe Hill*, 1965, and (ed.), *The Letters of Joe Hill*, 1965; Smith, M. Gibbs, *Joe Hill*, 1969; Stavis, Barrie, and Frank Harmon (eds.), *Songs of Joe Hill*, 1955.

## Hillman, Sidney

(March 23, 1887–July 10, 1946)
Labor Leader

As an influential labor movement leader, Sidney Hillman had the creative will to go beyond the narrow visions of many of his fellow unionists and develop new ways for the unions to help the disadvantaged in American society.

Sidney (originally Simcha) Hillman was born in a *shtetl*, or market town, in a part of Lithuania then in the Pale, the area of Czarist Russia where Jews were legally allowed to settle. His father, Samuel Hillman, though from a line of rabbis, was a grain and flour merchant and was poor; his mother was Judith, born Paiken. Sidney, the second of seven children, the second son and the studious one, was chosen to carry on the rabbinical tradition and at age fourteen went to study at a seminary in Kovno (now Kaunas). Dissatisfied with Talmudic training, he left and found work in a chemical factory, where he joined the Bund, the outlawed Jewish socialist movement. Hillman was jailed in 1904 for taking part in a parade and again during the 1905 revolution, when he had switched to the Mensheviks, the minority branch of the social democratic party. After the collapse of the revolution, Hillman fled to the United States, as many other Russian radicals did. Settling in Chicago, he went to work as a stock clerk for Sears, Roebuck and Company, seventy hours a week at wretched wages. Then he became an apprentice cutter of men's clothing for Hart, Schaffner & Marx, a well-known garment manufacturing firm.

A bitter strike broke out in 1910, set off when five young women led a walkout against Hart, Schaffner & Marx. It soon involved the entire men's clothing industry of Chicago. Hillman, having started as a picket, was put on a committee to combat the influence of WILLIAM HAYWOOD, who wanted to bring the striking workers into the Industrial Workers of the World. Thanks to his training in the Bund, Hillman became the leader of the strike. He had a gift for holding together the diverse ethnic groups—Jewish, Italian, Slavic—among the strikers. The union's cause, furthermore, was helped by the sympathy of progressives such as CLARENCE DARROW and JANE ADDAMS, both of whom exerted a strong formative influence on young Hillman's ideas (and his mastery of English). In settling the strike, he put over a compromise requiring arbitration, got the union on a stable footing, and won the trust of management.

Hillman married one of the five young women who had started the Chicago strike, Bessie Abramowitz, herself prominent in the labor movement. They had two daughters.

In 1914 Hillman, then twenty-seven, became president of the Amalgamated Clothing Workers of America, a job he held for the rest of his life. The union gave full support to the American role in World War I, and Hillman, by

then a presence in Washington, helped create a federal board of control and labor standards for army clothing. By 1920 the Amalgamated covered 85 percent of the men's clothing industry. Hillman worked to broaden the consciousness of unionism, offering to employers active cooperation (and even loans) and helping union members to attain such social programs as cooperative housing, unemployment insurance, and their own banks. Many of Hillman's ideas would be embraced, in the 1930s, by broad sectors of the trade union movement.

In 1933, at the depth of the Great Depression, Hillman saw that only government intercession could solve the nation's economic problems. His service on the National Industrial Recovery Board further broadened his outlook. Having finally led the Amalgamated Clothing Workers into the American Federation of Labor (AFL; see WILLIAM GREEN and JOHN L. LEWIS) in 1933, he led them out when he aligned himself with John L. Lewis in forming the Congress of Industrial Organizations (CIO). As the CIO's vice president he was in the forefront of organizing the steel and auto industries and the textile field. He led union support for President Franklin D. Roosevelt's reelection in 1936. He was the pivotal figure in brokering the alliance between labor and the Democratic party that lasts to this day.

Roosevelt appointed Hillman the labor member of the National Defense Advisory Commission in 1940, to oversee armaments production, and also associate director general of the Office of Production Management, posts he filled until 1942. After leaving the government, Hillman was director of the CIO's political action committee, which mobilized organized labor to support the reelection of Roosevelt. At the Democratic National Convention of 1944, he threw his support to Harry S Truman as the vice presidential candidate. Though Roosevelt's words to the party managers, "Clear it with Sidney," became legendary, Hillman's actual influence had sharply declined. During the war, Roosevelt had drawn closer to conservative business interests and distanced himself from Hillman and like-minded reformers.

After World War II, Hillman was the CIO delegate at international labor conferences and, employing his gift for conciliation, helped found the World Federation of Trade Unions, which (for a while) united the labor movements of communist and noncommunist countries. Hillman worked himself hard, suffered several heart attacks, and died at the age of fifty-nine in 1946.

**BIBLIOGRAPHY**

Fraser, Steven, *Labor Will Rule: Sidney Hillman and the Rise of American Labor,* 1991; Josephson, Matthew, *Sidney Hillman: Statesman of American Labor,* 1952.

## Hine, Lewis Wickes

(September 26, 1874–November 3, 1940)
Photographer

Lewis Hine's eloquent photographs of immigrants, from their arrival at Ellis Island to their lives in tenements and sweatshops, and of child labor provided a stark and often shocking commentary on social conditions in early twentieth-century America and served as an impetus for reform.

Born in Oshkosh, Wisconsin, Lewis Hine left school at the age of fifteen and worked at a variety of odd jobs while continuing his education on his own. Encouraged to become a teacher by Frank A. Manny, the head of the psychology and education department of the state normal school at Oshkosh, he studied at the University of Chicago from 1900 to 1901. After Manny became principal of the Ethical Culture School in New York City, he offered Hine a position as a teacher of nature study and geography.

While at the Ethical Culture School, Hine began taking photographs at the suggestion of Manny, who wanted him to record activities at the school. Through Manny also, Hine became involved in a project of photographing immigrants at Ellis Island. This was a time of massive immigration from southern and eastern Europe; every year millions of immigrants passed through the immigration station on Ellis Island. Manny wanted the students at the Ethical Culture School to have the same regard for these new immigrants as they had for the Pilgrims who landed at Plymouth Rock. Using a cumbersome tripod-mounted 5 × 7 view camera with plates, flash pan, and powder, Hine managed to capture the looks of bewilderment—but also hope—in the immigrants' faces. His photographs paid tribute to the courage that brought these people across the ocean to start a new life in a strange land. Hine went on to record the immigrants' lives in New York City, photographing them in their crowded tenements and dingy sweatshops.

When Hine began his work, there was little precedent for this type of documentary photography. Before him, JACOB RIIS had photographed New York City slums to publicize the plight of the poor, but whether Hine had any contact with Riis is not known. Through the sociology classes Hine took at New York and Columbia universities during these years, he did, however, come to know such leading reformers as FLORENCE KELLEY, the young Frances Perkins, John Spargo, and PAUL KELLOGG, the editor of *Charities and the Commons.* In 1907 Kellogg invited Hine to take pictures for the Pittsburgh Survey, the first in-depth study of an industrial city. Although Hine only worked in Pittsburgh for three months, his photographs helped make the survey a success.

Also in 1907, Hine received his first assignment from the National Child Labor Committee (NCLC), which a year later hired him as a staff photographer. Hine's concern with child labor stemmed from his own early experiences as a young boy in Wisconsin working thirteen hours a day, six days a week, for a paltry $4 in weekly wages. To document the harsh realities of child labor at this time, Hine often risked physical harm at the hands of angry foremen and factory police. To even get into mines, mills, and factories where children were employed, he frequently had to assume a variety of disguises ranging from fire inspector to Bible salesman. When he was unable to gain entry to a factory, he visited the children's homes in the early morning and photographed them on their way to another grueling day's work. In his pocket he kept hidden a small notebook, in which he scribbled notes about the children that he used for captions for his photographs. Of his work for the NCLC Hine later wrote:

> For many years I have followed the procession of child workers winding through a thousand industrial communities from the canneries of Maine to the fields of Texas. I have heard their tragic stories, watched their cramped lives, and seen their fruitless struggles in the industrial game where the odds are all against them.

Hine's moving photographs of these exploited children created a nationwide furor that led to the eventual passage of child labor legislation.

In 1919, at the end of World War I, the American Red Cross commissioned Hine to document its relief work in war-ravaged Europe. Back in the United States in the 1920s and early 1930s, Hine returned to the subject of working-class America, this time celebrating in his photographs the dignity of human labor. His most outstanding work in this connection was a series of 1,000 photographs that recorded each day's construction of the Empire State Building in New York City. In 1932 Hine published a collection of his industrial photographs entitled *Men at Work*. Yet commercial success eluded Hine. By the time of his death eight years later, he was impoverished and virtually forgotten.

**BIBLIOGRAPHY**

Gutman, Judith Mara, *Lewis W. Hine and the American Social Conscience*, 1967; Rosenblum, Walter, Naomi Rosenblum, and Alan Trachtenberg, *America and Lewis Hine: Photographs 1904–1940*, 1976.

# Hoffa, James Riddle

(February 14, 1913–ca. 1975)
Labor Union Leader

Jimmy Hoffa went from an impoverished childhood to the leadership of the Brotherhood of Teamsters, which he helped make the largest and wealthiest labor union in the world. His involvement with the world of crime sent him to prison and probably put an end to his life.

Jimmy Hoffa was born in the town of Brazil, in central Indiana, one of four children. His father, a coal miner, died of a lung disease in 1920, and four years later Hoffa's mother, who took in washing and worked as a domestic and cook, moved her family to a working-class part of Detroit. Hoffa dropped out of school after finishing the ninth grade and got a job as stock boy in a department store. Two years later he began working as a warehouseman for the Kroger Company, a grocery and baking chain.

Low pay and wretched working conditions contributed to making Hoffa labor-conscious, and he organized an effective strike against Kroger with the help of four other workers, who remained loyal to him as union officials through his career. The union he organized was taken into the American Federation of Labor (AFL; see WILLIAM GREEN and JOHN L. LEWIS), and a year later Hoffa became a full-time organizer for the International Brotherhood of Teamsters, Chauffeurs, Warehouseman, and Helpers (IBT) and brought the Kroger union into the IBT. He was soon running the local union as its business agent, and in his first year, 1931 to 1932, he was beaten up by strikebreakers or police twenty-four times, in several instances suffering serious injuries. Hoffa's own strong-arm methods and organizing success accompanied his rise in the IBT bureaucracy. At the same time, the Teamsters were expanding nationally, as the hard times of the Great Depression made hundreds of thousands of workers receptive to the union message. Hoffa's hardboiled personality and know-how made him popular with the rank-and-file membership.

Hoffa became president of the Michigan Conference of Teamsters in 1942. In 1952, when Dave Beck was elected president of the IBT, Hoffa was elected an international vice president and acted as chief negotiator for all the truck drivers in twenty southern and midwestern states. In the late fifties, a Senate committee looking into crooked labor practices began investigating allegations of corruption in the Teamsters leadership, including the charge that Hoffa had been involved with racketeers and had taken payoffs from the trucking companies. The committee's findings led the AFL-CIO to expel the Teamsters. Hoffa was acquitted of the allegations in 1957, but a federal court found Beck guilty of stealing union

funds and income tax evasion and he went to prison.

Late in 1957 Hoffa replaced Beck as president of the IBT and encouraged centralization, so that local leaders would have to apply directly to him for authority to strike or for disbursement of funds from the union's treasury. Under Hoffa the membership grew from 800,000 to almost 2 million. In January 1964 he negotiated the first national contract, and the trucking industry came to trust him for sticking to the letter of contracts and discouraging wildcat (unauthorized) strikes. The suspicion of corruption and of involvement with organized crime, however, still hung over Hoffa. Robert F. Kennedy, as chief counsel of the aforementioned Senate committee and after 1960 as U.S. attorney general, was determined to prosecute Hoffa and other labor transgressors. In 1964 Hoffa was sentenced to a thirteen-year term in prison for jury tampering and mishandling of union funds. After unsuccessful appeals, he began serving his sentence in 1967. He continued to hold the IBT presidency, but after he resigned in 1971, President Richard M. Nixon commuted his sentence on condition that he refrain from union activity until 1980. Hoffa was released on December 23, 1971.

Though ostensibly devoting himself to prison reform and job assistance to former convicts, Hoffa was maneuvering to regain the presidency. On July 30, 1975, he disappeared after having been last seen in front of a Detroit restaurant. It was generally believed that he had been abducted. According to the *New York Times*, a gangster testifying before a Senate subcommittee in 1981 claimed that "Jimmy was killed, ground up in little pieces, shipped to Florida and dumped in a swamp." In December 1982, a Michigan court declared Hoffa to be "presumed dead," and his estate of more than $1 million was distributed to his son and daughter. The habits of corruption that Hoffa brought to the Teamsters continued to characterize the union's national leadership throughout the 1980s.

BIBLIOGRAPHY

Franco, Joseph, with Richard Hammer, *Hoffa's Man*, 1987; Hoffa, James R., *The Trials of Jimmy Hoffa*, 1970; Mollenhoff, Clark R., *Tentacles of Power: The Story of Jimmy Hoffa*, 1965; Sheridan, Walter, *The Fall and Rise of Jimmy Hoffa*, 1972; Sloane, A. A., *Hoffa*, 1991.

## Hoffman, Abbott

(November 30, 1936–April 12, 1989)
Antiwar Leader, Author

During the 1960s, Abbie Hoffman, as leader of the Youth International Party (Yippies), became a standard-bearer for the radical youths of the counterculture, often resorting to outrageous behavior to dramatize the causes to which he was committed.

Abbott Hoffman, famous as Abbie, was born in Worcester, Massachusetts, the son of a pharmacist. As he liked to say, he was a troublemaker from the start. He was expelled from high school because of an altercation with one of his teachers. He finally graduated from a private school in Worcester, then studied at Brandeis University, in Waltham, Massachusetts, where he earned a B.A. in psychology (1959). At Brandeis, Hoffman was influenced by the radical views of the political philosopher HERBERT MARCUSE. Graduate work toward an M.A. at the University of California at Berkeley, a center of political activism, pushed Hoffman further into radicalism.

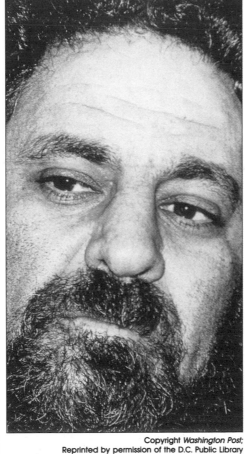

Copyright *Washington Post;*
Reprinted by permission of the D.C. Public Library

In the early 1960s Hoffman combined a conventional job as a pharmaceutical salesman with action in the growing civil rights movement. He had his first arrest in Mississippi when he arrived with the Freedom Riders (see JAMES FARMER). In 1966 he founded Liberty House, in New York City, an outlet for crafts made by poor people in Mississippi. Hoffman's next cause was opposition to the Vietnam War. As a protester he became a charismatic leader of the hippies, those radical youths of the 1960s who expressed their rebellion against mainstream American society through drug experimentation, open sexuality, rejection of prevailing dress codes, interest in esoteric religious cults, and immersion in rock and roll music.

Hoffman used satire and theatrical maneuvers to make his points. He threw dollar bills from the visitors' gallery down onto the floor of the New York Stock Exchange and ridiculed the traders rushing to grab the money. He sent 3,000 marijuana cigarettes to persons selected at random from the telephone directory, with instructions how to smoke them. He had antiwar protesters surround the Pentagon and attempt to exorcise its evil forces by spiritual energy.

With some of his followers he founded the Youth International Party, "YIP," whose members called themselves Yippies. At the 1968 Democratic National Convention in Chicago the Yippies demonstrated against the nomination of Hubert H. Humphrey as presidential candidate. Hoffman nominated a pig for president. A peaceful protest march he led was attacked by the police, in full view of the television audience tuned in to the convention. Hoffman and his fellow demonstrators, the so-called Chicago Seven, were indicted for conspiracy and inciting a riot, and the trial that followed became a raucous, often comical proceeding. Convictions on lesser charges and numerous contempt citations were later overturned, and Judge Julius Hoffman was censured for prejudicial behavior.

A few years later, threatened with a heavy sentence on cocaine charges, Hoffman went underground for seven years, having changed his appearance by plastic surgery. Under an assumed name he traveled abroad or lived quietly in a small town, sometimes taking part in environmentalist protests. His manner of coming out of hiding in 1980 was typically flamboyant: he was interviewed on national television by Barbara Walters. He acknowledged his guilt to the cocaine charges and served a year in prison.

Hoffman made a living by writing books that were a mixture of serious social and political commentary and mocking humor. Toward the end of his career he lectured on public issues, such as American interference in Central America and the excessive power of the Central Intelligence Agency (CIA). He moved to New Hope, Pennsylvania, to join in a protest against a nuclear power plant in the vicinity. He had become discouraged over the decline of his health and energy, and at the age of fifty-two he died, an apparent suicide.

**BIBLIOGRAPHY**

Hoffman, Abbie, *Soon to Be a Major Motion Picture,* 1980; Hoffman, Abbie, with Anita Hoffman, *To america with Love: Letters from the Underground,* 1976; Hoffman, Abbie, with foreword by Norman Mailer, *The Best of Abbie Hoffman,* 1989.

# Hofstadter, Richard

(August 6, 1916–October 24, 1970)
Historian

Richard Hofstadter presented a new perception of American history, bringing to bear an iconoclastic but ultimately fair and insightful view of events, individuals, and ideas, combining professional detachment and political engagement.

Hofstadter was born in Buffalo, New York, the son of Emil Hofstadter, from Poland, who worked as a furrier, and Katherine Hill, of German Lutheran ancestry. He majored in philosophy and history at the University of Buffalo, graduating with a B.A. in 1937. The left-wing student group he came to know there included Felice Swados, whom he married in 1936.

While Hofstadter was a graduate student at Columbia University, he was refused financial aid and made ends meet with part-time college teaching while his wife worked for labor unions and *Time* magazine. Both became involved in leftist politics, and in 1938 Hofstadter joined the Communist party—reluctantly, because he had misgivings about the purge trials in the Soviet Union, though as a Marxist he believed that "the party is making a very profound contribution to the radicalization of the American people." By February 1939 he had dropped out, disillusioned with the party's regimentation, and the Soviet-Nazi pact in September confirmed his turn away from communism, though he was still opposed to capitalism. The strongest influence on Hofstadter's thinking at this stage was CHARLES BEARD and his view that economic self-interest underlay political activity.

Hofstadter earned his Ph.D. from Columbia in 1942 with a dissertation, *Social Darwinism in American Thought, 1860–1915*, which upon its publication in 1944 won an important history prize. After teaching at the University of Maryland for four years, he returned to Columbia and by 1952 was a full professor. In 1959 he assumed the DeWitt Clinton professorship. Except for a year at Cambridge University, England, Hofstadter was at Columbia until his death.

In 1948 Hofstadter published *The American Political Tradition: and the Men Who Made It*. The book, which demonstrated his break with Marx and Beard, brought him attention from both scholars and the general public. His portraits depicted American political figures from the eighteenth century to the New Deal with an honest skepticism but finally showed that all held the same basic beliefs. This book came to be interpreted as a key work in the so-called "consensus" school of American historians. These historians, who rose to prominence in the 1950s, asserted that all Americans, since the Revolution or before, had shared a belief in capitalism, individualism, liberty, and other core values and that American politics as a result was not characterized by the deep and violent conflicts that haunted European politics. This school lost some credibility in the 1960s as historians began to assemble mounting evidence of conflict in American his-

tory. Hofstadter himself would admit in 1968 that his earlier work had underestimated the extent and violence of ethnic and racial divisions in America, past and present.

*The American Political Tradition* exemplified the unusual range of Hofstadter's interests in both time and detail. Throughout his career he was a productive writer, and each of his books was quite different from the others. If there was a uniting theme, it was the weight of ideas in politics and society; the uniting point of view was always a revision of conventional interpretation. While he was sometimes called a debunker, he searched for the core of truth and disclaimed being either a conservative or a radical.

In *The Development of Academic Freedom in the United States* (with W. P. Metzger, 1955), Hofstadter reacted to the repressive efforts of Senator Joseph R. McCarthy as he examined the sources of hostility to independent thinking. In the same year he published *The Age of Reform*, on the Populist, Progressive, and New Deal movements, which he was sympathetic to but still could regard critically. Both these works revealed Hofstadter's growing attraction to psychological, as opposed to economic, explanations of political movements. *Anti-Intellectualism in American Life* (1963) was, in the words of another historian, Peter Gay, "a despairing anatomy of a pervasive trait in the American character." *The Paranoid Style in American Politics* (1965), which offered a psychosocial view of history, revealed the influence of Sigmund Freud, Lionel Trilling, and Karl Mannheim on Hofstadter's work.

In spring 1968, Hofstadter gave the commencement address at Columbia, speaking with moderation and detachment about the future of the university in the light of the student uprising of the previous spring. His rhetorical question: "How can it not go on?" His publication of *American Violence* in 1970 revealed his formal break with the "consensus" school historians.

Hofstadter's first wife had died in 1945, and two years later he married Beatrice Kevitt. When he died of leukemia at the relatively young age of fifty-four, he left a son by his first marriage and a daughter by his second. A posthumous work, *America at 1750: A Social Portrait* (1971), was to have been the opening of a three-volume study of American society.

**BIBLIOGRAPHY**

Elkins, Stanley, and Eric McKitrick (eds.), *The Hofstadter Aegis: A Memorial*, 1974; Hofstadter, Richard, *The Progressive Historians: Turner, Beard, Parrington*, 1968, and *The Idea of a Party System*, 1969; Hofstadter, Richard (ed.), with Michael Wallace, *American Violence*, 1970.

# Hooks, Benjamin Lawson, Jr.

(January 31, 1925–   )
Civil Rights Leader

Benjamin L. Hooks, after his effective work as the first black on the Federal Communications Commission, led the National Association for the Advancement of Colored People (NAACP; see JOEL E. SPINGARN) during the crucial period following the height of the civil rights movement.

Born in Memphis, Tennessee, Benjamin Hooks was one of seven children of a photographer. He went through the local segregated schools and had two years of prelaw study at a Memphis college before being drafted into the U.S. Army and seeing action in Italy. On the GI Bill, Hooks went to law school at De Paul University in Chicago, since Tennessee schools of law did not admit black students. But, having earned his J.D. degree in 1948, he returned to Memphis, resolved to help end segregation.

Despite insults from white officials, Hooks practiced and argued cases in his hometown's courts. During the early sixties he joined lunchroom sit-ins encouraged by the NAACP and was on the board of the Southern Christian Leadership Conference (SCLC; see RALPH D. ABERNATHY and MARTIN LUTHER KING, JR.). Fulfilling a youthful ambition to preach, he was ordained in the Baptist ministry, serving at churches in Memphis and in Detroit.

In 1961 Hooks was made assistant public defender for the Memphis courts, and in 1965 the governor of Tennessee appointed him to a vacancy in the county criminal court, which was confirmed by election the next year. Meanwhile he joined in founding a savings and loan association, was president of a chain of restaurants, and produced television programs.

Hooks first came to national prominence in 1972 when President Richard M. Nixon, fulfilling an election promise, appointed him a commissioner on the Federal Communications Commission, which regulates television, radio, and other electronic media. Hooks, seeing his mission as the improvement of minority participation in broadcasting, was successful in bringing about fair portrayal and increased employment of blacks.

Upon the retirement of ROY WILKINS from the executive directorship of the NAACP in 1977, Hooks was elected his successor. Responding to the appeal of young black activists during the previous decade, Hooks brought the NAACP to a more aggressive posture in its social and political policies. One of his first acts, in 1979, was to organize and lead a prayer vigil in Washington against antibusing legislation, which was defeated in Congress. He strongly defended affirmative action. The NAACP, through demonstration and lobbying, influenced government policy toward African countries.

Hooks led a strong recruiting drive that brought NAACP's membership to a half million.

In order to cooperate in dealing with such problems as teenage pregnancy, substance abuse, AIDS, school dropouts, single-woman-headed households, and economic development, he led the NAACP in creating a cooperative body, the National Association of Black Organizations. The magnitude of urban problems in combination with the hostility of successive Republican administrations to civil rights and social welfare issues, however, made the 1980s a tough and demoralizing decade for these black organizations.

Hooks received the Spingarn Medal in 1985. In February 1992, he announced that he would retire from the executive directorship of the NAACP on March 30, 1993, and return to his Baptist pastorates.

**BIBLIOGRAPHY**

*New York Times*, November 7, 1976; *Washington Post*, November 8, 1976.

# Howe, Frederic Clemson

(November 21, 1867–August 3, 1940)
Author, Public Official, Urban Reformer

Urban reformer Frederic Howe implemented new methods of city management that influenced a generation of Americans. He envisioned and worked toward a "civic revival" in the United States that would combine urban renewal with an economic, moral, and cultural renaissance.

Born and raised in Meadville, Pennsylvania, Frederic Howe grew up in a conservative, predominantly Methodist environment. After graduation from Allegheny College in 1889, he earned his Ph.D. in 1892 at the Johns Hopkins University, then did postgraduate work at the University of Halle, Germany. Upon his return to the United States, he earned a law degree; settling in Cleveland in 1894, he joined the law firm of Harry and James Garfield, sons of President James A. Garfield. While serving on the city council, Howe came to know and admire reform mayor TOM JOHNSON, who converted Howe to HENRY GEORGE's single-tax and free-trade ideas and also to the idea of public ownership of the street railways. Although defeated in his bid for reelection as an independent, Howe became chairman of the Cleveland City Finance Commission and served in the Ohio senate from 1906 to 1908.

Howe, meanwhile, began to develop views on how cities could be improved, which he set forth in his 1905 book, *The City: The Hope of Democracy*. In this and in later books on British and European cities, Howe expressed his hope for a "civic revival," or moral, cultural, and economic renewal to be achieved through proper environmental planning. He had great admiration for European cities, where distinguished individuals served as mayors and where social services were provided. The city, in Howe's view, ought to be an instrument of social betterment, ever responsive to the needs of the less fortunate.

By 1910 Howe had become wealthy as a lawyer, and he decided to leave both the law and Cleveland. Moving to New York City, he became the director of the People's Institute, a reform organization. He also became active in progressive politics on the local and national level, helping to elect reformer John Purroy Mitchel as mayor of New York and becoming one of the founders of the National Progressive

Republican League, which unsuccessfully backed the nomination of Robert M. La Follette for president in 1912.

In the actual election, Howe voted for his professor from Johns Hopkins, Woodrow Wilson, and two years later Wilson appointed him Commissioner of Immigration of the Port of New York, in charge of Ellis Island. Howe tried to improve conditions for newly arrived immigrants on the island. But he soon ran afoul of congressional investigating committees, angered by his outspoken denunciation of munitions makers and other interests who in 1915 and 1916 were accused of seeking to bring the United States into World War I. When the nation did enter the war, Howe's stands on free speech and politically motivated deportation of aliens brought him under fire from some members of Congress, who called him a socialist. Howe in 1919 resigned as commissioner.

In 1919 Howe attended the Paris Peace Conference as a consultant on eastern Mediterranean affairs. Along with other progressives, he was sharply critical of President Wilson for abandoning his ideals in the face of pressure from the Allies and for creating a League of Nations, which, in Howe's view, was "a league of conquest rather than a covenant of freedom."

After the war Howe helped organize the Conference for Progressive Political Action, which launched the candidacy of Robert M. La Follette on the Progressive party ticket in 1924. Howe backed the election of Franklin D. Roosevelt in 1932 and was appointed consumers' counsel in the newly created Agricultural Adjustment Administration. In 1937 he served as an agricultural consultant in the Philippines. While engaged in a study of European banking in 1940, Howe died of a heart ailment at the age of seventy-two.

**BIBLIOGRAPHY**

Howe, Frederic, *Wisconsin: An Experiment in Democracy,* 1912, *European Cities at Work,* 1913, *The Modern City and Its Problems,* 1915, and *Confessions of a Reformer,* 1925.

# Howe, Irving

(June 11, 1920–  )
Critic, Social Historian

I rving Howe, brought up in poverty, became a distinguished literary critic, an authority on Jewish culture, and a standard-bearer of the anti-Communist left wing.

Born in New York City, Irving Howe was the only child of immigrants from the Ukraine. Both parents had crossed the ocean on the same vessel but only met and married later, on the Lower East Side. After moving to a tenement in the Bronx, Howe's parents ran a grocery store. In 1930, during the Great Depression, the store went bankrupt, Howe's father became a door-to-door peddler of linens, and the family had to share a small apartment with relatives. Later, both parents worked in a women's garment factory. Howe has written that in the midst of poverty, "Jews felt obligated to look after each other, [and] they fought desperately to avoid going on relief."

Howe's parents joined the International Ladies Garment Workers Union (see DAVID DUBINSKY) and, though not labor militants, went on the picket line during an industry-wide strike in 1933. Irving Howe's political leanings may have been started from that event. While he was a student at De Witt Clinton High School, in the northwest Bronx, he began to read Marx and joined the Young People's Socialist League

(YPSL). He looked to the socialist Norman Thomas as a leader. In 1936 Howe enrolled in the College of the City of New York (CCNY), where political radicalism was widespread. He acquired a reputation as the chief voice of the college's Trotskyist group, which stood for anti-Stalinist communism.

After graduating from CCNY in 1940, Howe briefly worked in a factory, sampled graduate study at Brooklyn College, and edited and produced a labor weekly. His political alignment was with the short-lived Workers party. In 1942 he was drafted into the army and sent to a post in Alaska, where he did clerical work and managed to read hundreds of books on a vast range of subjects.

After his discharge at the end of World War II, Howe did not return to political sectarianism but launched his career as a writer, combining his literary and political concerns. He collaborated with a labor union official, B. J. Widick, on *The UAW and Walter Reuther* (1949); wrote studies of the novelists William Faulkner and Sherwood Anderson; and later wrote two esteemed books, *Politics and the Novel* (1957) and, with Lewis Coser, *The American Communist Party: A Critical History* (1958). Howe produced book reviews for the magazine *Time* and essays for *Partisan Review* and was assistant to Dwight Macdonald on his journal *Politics.*

The year 1953 was a watershed for Howe: though without a Ph.D., he began to rise in the academic world. That spring he was invited to give a Gauss Seminar at Princeton University and that fall was appointed an associate professor of English at Brandeis University, in Waltham, Massachusetts. He had become a full professor when, in 1961, he moved on to Palo Alto, California, for a professorship at Stanford University. Two years later he gratefully returned east as professor of English at Hunter College, part of the City University of New York. From 1970 until his retirement in 1986 he held the title of distinguished professor.

Also in 1953, though secular in his point of view, Howe embarked on a concern with the literature and culture of Yiddish, which had been his first language. With Eliezer Greenberg, he translated a number of books of Yiddish prose and poetry, and he is credited with discovering the famous writer in Yiddish (and Nobel laureate) Isaac Bashevis Singer.

In 1954 Howe was a leader of the group who founded *Dissent: A Quarterly of Socialist Opinion*, which has continued publication into the 1990s. The contents of *Dissent* have been articles by a range of anti-Stalinist left-wing writers, both European and American, who, in examining socialism, have stressed its moral values and the indispensability of democracy. In 1979 Howe published a collection, *Twenty-Five Years of "Dissent": An American Tradition*, with an introduction surveying the history of radicalism in the United States and twenty-six articles representing the journal's best work.

Always preserving a reverence for Norman Thomas, in the 1960s and 1970 Howe took note of the New Left—such figures as Tom Hayden, Herbert Marcuse, Stokely Carmichael, and Noam Chomsky—but, also noting its neglect of humanistic values, did not join its ranks. He remained a scholar-intellectual, regarding Richard Hofstadter as his model. In 1976, just after his father's death, Howe published his most famous book, *World of Our Fathers*, a 700-page study of the journey of East European Jews to America and the life they found and made, which enjoyed a remarkable critical and commercial success. He was made a McArthur Fellow in 1987.

**BIBLIOGRAPHY**

Howe, Irving, *A World More Attractive: Modern Literature and Politics*, 1963, *A Treasury of Yiddish Poetry*, 1970, *A Margin of Hope: An Intellectual Autobiography*, 1982, and *Socialism and America*, 1985.

# Howe, Julia Ward

(May 27, 1819–October 17, 1910)
Author, Reformer

Julia Ward Howe is best known as the author of "The Battle Hymn of the Republic," one of the great rallying songs of the Civil War era that is still popular today. She was also a leader in the woman's club and suffrage movements.

Julia Ward was born in New York City into a wealthy and long-established family. Educated at private girls' schools and at home by tutors, she grew into a lively and intelligent young woman who enjoyed parties but also possessed a strong literary bent. In 1843 she married the distinguished Boston reformer SAMUEL G. HOWE, who was nearly twenty years her senior. The marriage was a stormy one. Despite Howe's support of numerous reform movements, he strongly objected to his wife's speaking in public and to her literary career. Indeed, he became physically ill when her first volume of poems, *Passion Flowers*, was published anonymously in 1854. Despite her husband's disapproval, Howe published another volume of poetry and wrote two plays. Otherwise she remained on the sidelines while her husband played an active role in abolitionist causes, such as providing financial backing for JOHN BROWN's raid on Harpers Ferry, Virginia, and helping with Brown's defense afterward.

In the fall of 1861, after the outbreak of war, Julia Ward Howe accompanied her husband on a trip to Washington, D.C., to inspect the sanitary conditions of the Union soldiers camped there. Inspired by the sight of the "watch-fires of a hundred circling camps," she

Library of Congress

rose in the predawn hours and began scribbling verses of the poem that was to become famous as "The Battle Hymn of the Republic." The poem was published in the *Atlantic Monthly* in February 1862 and, set to the tune of a popular abolitionist and army song, "John Brown's Body," it was soon being sung by regiments all over the North. Perhaps more than any other song, "Battle Hymn" captured the moral fervor of the Union cause with its stirring opening stanza:

Mine eyes have seen the glory of the coming of the Lord; He is trampling out the vintage where the grapes of wrath are stored; He hath loosed the fateful lightning of His terrible swift sword: His truth is marching on.

In the postwar years, Julia Ward Howe was finally able to shake off her husband's domination and emerge as a leader in her own right. In 1869 the suffrage movement bifurcated over goals. Howe joined with LUCY STONE to form the American Woman Suffrage Association and push for a suffrage amendment. She also served as president of the Massachusetts Woman Suffrage Association (1870–1878, 1891–1893) and of the New England Woman Suffrage Association (1868–1877, 1893–1910). In these roles she spoke frequently at conventions and legislative hearings. In addition, she was a founder, editor, and contributor to a weekly called *Woman's Journal*.

A leader in the woman's club movement as well, Howe helped to start the New England Women's Club in 1868 and served as its president from 1871 until her death. In 1873 she joined in the founding of the Association for the Advancement of Women (AAW), an organization of women scientists, educators, lawyers, ministers, and reformers, which met at annual conventions to discuss their work and the obstacles encountered by young women seeking an education or entry into the professions. She was elected president of the organization in 1881, and in the 1890s, after the General Federation of Women's Clubs had largely replaced the AAW, she served as director of the new organization.

By the time she reached her eighties, Julia Ward Howe had become almost a national institution, "the Dearest Old Lady in America,"

and the beloved author of the "Battle Hymn of the Republic," which was sung whenever she lectured. In 1908, two years before her death at the age of ninety-one, she was the first woman to be elected to the prestigious American Academy of Arts and Letters.

**BIBLIOGRAPHY**

Clifford, Deborah P., *Mine Eyes Have Seen the Glory*, 1978; Howe, Julia Ward, *Reminiscences*, 1899; Leach, William, *True Love and Perfect Union: The Feminist Reform of Sex and Society*, 1980.

## Howe, Samuel Gridley

(November 10, 1801–January 9, 1876)
Physician, Reformer

Samuel Gridley Howe pioneered in the education of the sight and hearing impaired at his famous Perkins Institution in Boston. He was the first to show that blind-deaf children could be successfully educated.

Born in Boston into a long-established middle-class family, Samuel Gridley Howe graduated from Brown University in 1821 and received his medical degree from Harvard in 1824. That same year, Howe's romantic spirit led him to Greece to join in the Greek struggle for independence from the Turks. During a six-year stint in Greece, Howe served as an army surgeon, a guerrilla fighter, and medical director of the Greek fleet.

Returning to Boston in 1831, Howe became the director of the New England Asylum for the Blind and went to Europe to study methods of teaching the blind and to recruit trained teachers for the school. While in Paris, he helped organize a committee to help Polish political refugees; related work in Prussia led to a six-week imprisonment by that nation.

Back in Boston in 1832, Howe began the work of building the school, now to be known as the Perkins Institution and Massachusetts School for the Blind, into one of the foremost institutions of its kind in the United States. He generally followed trial-and-error methods to develop new techniques of instruction and to improve upon old ones. Students received a common-school education with special emphasis on music and handicrafts. Howe personally developed and had printed large quantities of reading materials with raised type to help teach the students to read. He felt that his students should learn what their natural bents were, and he encouraged them to use their other senses and made it clear that they were not to be regarded with pity. Thanks to Howe's efforts, schools for the blind were started in Ohio, Virginia, and Kentucky, and other states set aside money to send their blind children to special schools.

Howe also worked with blind-deaf children and with the mentally retarded. Howe's most famous blind-deaf student was seven-year-old Laura Bridgman, whom he taught to read, write, and communicate despite the widespread belief that blind-deaf children could not be educated. Convinced that mentally retarded children could be trained to do work, Howe persuaded the state legislature to establish in 1848 an experimental school at the Perkins Institution that was the first publicly supported educational facility of its kind in the country. The Massachusetts School for Idiotic and Feeble-Minded Youth was later established on a permanent basis with Howe as its head, a position he held for more than twenty-five years.

A firm believer in public education, Howe supported HORACE MANN in his efforts to improve public schools and to establish teacher-training schools in Massachusetts. He also worked for prison reform and aid to discharged convicts and helped DOROTHEA DIX in her campaign for better treatment of the mentally ill.

As the abolitionist movement gained momentum in the 1850s, Howe became increasingly active in it. Together with his wife, JULIA WARD HOWE, he founded and edited an abolitionist journal, *The Commonwealth,* in 1850. That same year, he also helped form a Boston vigilance committee to help fugitive slaves pass safely through Boston on their way to Canada, and later provided support to the antislavery forces in Kansas. Howe knew in advance of the militant abolitionist JOHN BROWN's proposed raid into Virginia and gave him financial backing, though he later denied any connection with the raid and fled to Canada to avoid arrest.

With the outbreak of the Civil War, Howe became one of the founding members of the United States Sanitary Commission. He was later chosen as a member of the Freedman's Inquiry Commission, advocating equal civil and political rights for blacks and the establishment of a school system whereby they could receive training.

The war over, Howe returned to the Perkins Institution and also worked for various philanthropic groups as chairman of the Massachusetts State Board of Charities. He saw to the establishment of the Clark Institute for the Deaf Mute in 1867. Also in that year, he raised funds for Cretans who were in revolt against the Turks, and opened a school for Cretan refugees in Athens, Greece. After several years of ill health, Howe died in Boston at the age of seventy-four.

**BIBLIOGRAPHY**

Howe, Julia Ward, *Memoir of Dr. Samuel Gridley Howe,* 1876; Schwartz, Harold, *Samuel Gridley Howe, Social Reformer, 1801–1876,* 1956.

# Howells, William Dean

(March 1, 1837–May 11, 1920)
Author, Critic, Editor

A leading advocate of realism in literature, novelist William Dean Howells presented an unvarnished picture of industrial America in his books.

Born in Martins Ferry, Ohio, William Dean Howells had little formal schooling but was an avid reader. While working as a reporter and editorial writer for various Ohio newspapers, he had a few poems accepted by the *Atlantic Monthly.* His 1860 campaign biography of Abraham Lincoln resulted in his appointment as consul to Venice, Italy, when Lincoln won. His stay there gave him the material for two travel books, *Venetian Life* (1866) and *Italian Journeys* (1867).

Returning to the United States in 1865, Howells worked briefly for the *Nation* in New York under the editorship of EDWIN L. GODKIN, then moved to Boston to become subeditor of the *Atlantic Monthly* in 1866. Appointed editor in chief in 1871, Howells filled this position for the next ten years. He maintained the journal's reputation for literary excellence, while introducing articles on controversial issues like monopolies and labor unions. In this position he was able to publish works by two literary talents with whom he became friends—Mark Twain and Henry James. The *Atlantic* also saw Howells's own first novel, called *Their Wedding Journey*, published in serial form in 1871. Howells followed this lighthearted novel of manners and morals with other novels in a similar vein, which established his reputation as a literary figure of note.

In 1881 Howells left the *Atlantic* to devote himself to fiction. The novels he wrote during this period reflected his greater willingness to confront social problems head-on. *A Modern Instance* (1882) dealt with divorce and the unethical practices of Boston journalists. In *The Rise of Silas Lapham* (1885), Howells's hero was a self-made millionaire who tried to launch his daughters into caste-conscious Boston society.

During the 1880s, Howells was increasingly disturbed by the divisions within American society. In 1886 he took the controversial step of pleading for the commutation of the death sentences of the seven anarchists who had been convicted of inciting Chicago's Haymarket riot (see JOHN PETER ALTGELD), in which seven policemen were killed. Howells argued that there was no evidence to indicate that these men were guilty. About this time, he also came under the influence of the Russian novelist and reformer, Leo Tolstoy, and labeled himself a Christian socialist.

Beginning in the 1880s Howells began to promote literary realism. An 1885 contract with the New York publisher, Harper's, called for him to produce a novel a year and edit a column in *Harper's Monthly* magazine. Howells used this column to attack "romance" and "sentimentality" and advocate realism in literature, which he defined as "the truthful treatment of commonplace material," and to praise the work of the leading European realistic novelists, including Leo Tolstoy, Gustave Flaubert, and Honoré de Balzac.

Howells's novels of this period continued to express his criticism of competitive struggle and the extremes of social inequality. In *Annie Kilburn* (1889), he portrayed a New England town torn by industrial unrest, while in *A Hazard of New Fortunes* (1891), considered his best novel of this time, he offered up the complete panorama of New York City life from the very rich to the very poor. In *A Traveler from Altruria* (1894) Howells depicted a socialist utopia without poverty or injustice.

Moving to New York City in 1891, Howells served a brief stint as editor of *Cosmopolitan* magazine and continued producing a range of fiction, drama, criticism, and autobiography. Though he could now afford to bask in his literary celebrity, he did not avoid controversy, joining his friend Mark Twain in protesting the government's tilt to imperialism in the Spanish-American War. In his column in *Harper's* he kept up the campaign for realism. As he had helped Twain and James earlier, he supported such new writers as Stephen Crane, Hamlin Garlin, Frank Norris, and the African American poet Paul Dunbar.

Hailed as "the dean of American letters," Howells received many academic awards in his later years. In 1908 he became the first president of the newly founded American Academy of Arts and Letters. The following year he helped establish the National Association for the Advancement of Colored People (see JOEL E. SPINGARN). Howells published his last novel in 1916; four years later, he died at the age of eighty-three.

**BIBLIOGRAPHY**

Lynn, Kenneth S., *William Dean Howells: An American Life*, 1971; Vanderbilt, K., *The Achievement of William Dean Howells: A Reinterpretation*, 1968.

# Hutchins, Robert Maynard

(January 17, 1899–May 14, 1977)
Educator

Robert Hutchins greatly influenced American education with his unorthodox philosophical views, which he applied in the 1940s as University of Chicago president and as a founder of the "Great Books" program. Later he became a director of the Ford Foundation and head of the Center for the Study of Democratic Institutions.

Robert Maynard Hutchins was born in Brooklyn, New York, the son of a Presbyterian minister. When he was eight, his father was appointed a professor of theology at Oberlin College, in Ohio. Hutchins entered the college when he was sixteen. Two years later, an avowed pacifist, he volunteered in the army ambulance corps and served in Italy in World War I.

Back from the war, Hutchins switched to Yale University and began a meteoric rise to prominence as a university leader and innovator. He graduated from Yale with honors in 1921, became secretary of the university, graduated from Yale Law School in 1925, and was appointed dean of the law school in 1928. He raised the entrance requirements, started an honors program, and broadened the curriculum with social science courses—innovations that were noticed in the world of education. At the young age of thirty, Hutchins was appointed president of the University of Chicago and soon became a controversial figure.

University of Chicago

Hutchins believed that higher education was trivialized by too much emphasis on extracurricular activities such as athletics and fraternities. (He abolished the university's football team.) All students, in his view, should have a basis in the humanities as well as the sciences. He introduced the so-called Chicago Plan, which allowed qualified high school sophomores to enter the university's liberal arts program. Actually, any student who passed a placement test could enroll; class attendance was not required and the final examination could be taken whenever the student felt prepared. His innovations at Chicago stimulated an intellectual intensity among undergraduates which continues to distinguish the university to this day.

A professor of psychology, Mortimer J. Adler, whom Hutchins had met while at Yale, instilled in him a deep interest in the classics. Hutchins brought Adler to Chicago, and they inaugurated a "Great Books" course that was based on some fifty volumes comprising works by authors from Homer to Sigmund Freud. Hutchins was for a time editor in chief of *Great Books of the Western World*, published by the Encyclopaedia Britannica, Inc.

Hutchins's pacifist background was evident when he opposed American entry in World War II, though he declared that he was not an isolationist in the "America First" camp (see

CHARLES A. LINDBERGH). Rather, he said, he was for "Humanity First." He enabled research toward the atomic bomb to go on at the University of Chicago when, at the government's request, he appointed as professors several atomic scientists—including the Nobel laureates Enrico Fermi and Harold C. Urey—to work in secrecy. In December 1942, tests under the university stadium demonstrated that a controlled nuclear chain reaction was practical and could power a bomb. Hutchins believed that the reality of the bomb could scare humanity into uniting for world peace.

In 1945 Hutchins resigned as president and became chancellor of the university, devoting himself to fund raising and working for cooperation with other universities. He organized a project to rebuild interchange between American and German universities. During the late 1940s Hutchins was concerned with issues of academic and press freedom.

Hutchins left the University of Chicago in 1951 to become associate director of the Ford Foundation, which had been endowed by HENRY FORD's family and was committed to supporting peace, democratic government, education, the humanities and sciences, and social programs. Some of the foundation's activities, considered too left-wing and overly generous to some foreign countries, were attacked by conservatives, notably by Senator Joseph R. McCarthy. In 1954 Hutchins was appointed president of an independent offshoot of the foundation, the Fund for the Republic, which was concerned with the protection of civil liberties. The Fund for the Republic made grants to organizations working in such fields as in-

terracial relations and the study of federal loyalty programs and political blacklisting.

During his last twenty years Hutchins was the head of the Center for the Study of Democratic Institutions, in Santa Barbara, California—in turn a creation of the Fund for the Republic, though backed by donations from other sources, including the Xerox Corporation and ordinary citizens. The center operated like an academic community, with resident and visiting fellows who made studies of influences that affected democratic societies. It was not an "ivory tower," however. Among the center's concerns were proposals to end the Vietnam War.

Hutchins's career after 1951 is considered a disappointment, given the influence and power he wielded in the academic community in the 1930s and 1940s. He died in Santa Barbara at age seventy-eight, having led the Center for the Study of Democratic Institutions until the end of his life. In 1979 the center was taken over by the University of California at Santa Barbara and continued on a reduced scale. Subsequently the name was bought by private interests and applied to a new organization.

**BIBLIOGRAPHY**

Dzuback, Mary Ann, *Robert M. Hutchins: Portrait of an Educator*, 1991; Hutchins, Robert M., *The Higher Learning in America*, 1936, *Education for Freedom*, 1943, and *The Learning Society*, 1958; Kelly, Frank K., *Court of Reason: Robert Hutchins and the Fund for the Republic*, 1981.

# Hutchinson, Anne Marbury

(ca. July 1591–ca. August 1643)
Religious Leader

Anne Hutchinson led the first organized attack on the male-dominated Puritan religious establishment. Banished from the Massachusetts Bay Colony for her independent views, she has been hailed as one of America's earliest feminists.

She was born in Alford, Lincolnshire, England, the daughter of a dissenting Anglican clergyman, Francis Marbury, who a year before her birth lost his ministry because of his liberal views. The oldest daughter and the second of thirteen children, Anne Marbury got her religious instruction from her father and absorbed his penchant for conscientious dissent. In 1605 the family moved to London, where Anne remained until her marriage in 1612 to William Hutchinson, an Alford businessman of means. The couple would eventually have fifteen children.

Over the next twenty years, Anne Hutchinson was drawn to the preaching of John Cotton, vicar of St. Botolph's Church in Boston, Lincolnshire. Cotton was an Anglican minister with nonconformist Puritan leanings, holding that redemption could only come through the gift of God's grace, rather than from a person's behavior or works (known as the Covenant of Works, in which most Puritan theologians believed). People who did not believe in the Covenant of Works were known as antinomians and considered heretics by the church.

In 1633 Cotton was condemned by the Anglican authorities for his dissenting views and forced to flee to Boston in the Massachusetts Bay Colony. With her husband's agreement, Anne Hutchinson decided to follow him there, and in the summer of 1634 the family sailed for America. In Boston the Hutchinsons prospered and bought land and made profitable business investments. William entered public life as a judge, and Anne held a prominent position among the women of the colony as a midwife.

When Anne discovered that most Boston women believed in the Covenant of Works, she began holding weekly meetings in her home to exchange views. At first the meetings were limited to restatements of John Cotton's sermons, but gradually Anne Hutchinson began to add her own interpretations. The meetings became very popular, drawing as many as seventy or eighty people, men as well as women. Among the men were many prominent and influential citizens, including the colony's young governor, Henry Vane.

Although in interpreting sermons Anne Hutchinson was assuming the role of a minister—unheard of for a woman—her meetings did not generate open controversy until the Reverend John Wilson joined John Cotton in the pulpit. Dismayed by Wilson's views, she began criticizing his sermons at her meetings. Wilson then denounced her teachings in his sermons, accusing her of trying to upset the dominant role of men in the family. Dissension within the community grew and spread throughout the colony, as Hutchinson's followers preached in other towns. Governor Vane, John Cotton, and the majority of townspeople were on Anne Hutchinson's side, though a powerful minority, led by Wilson and John Winthrop, opposed her.

In the spring of 1637, Hutchinson's brother-in-law and supporter, John Wheelwright, was found guilty of preaching a seditious sermon. About the same time, John Winthrop was elected governor of the colony, and Hutchinson's followers lost out to the minority, orthodox faction. When Henry Vane left for England in August, Hutchinson was deprived of an important friend and supporter.

Also in August 1637, a synod of the churches was organized to deal with heresies in the colony. It condemned Hutchinson and declared her meetings disorderly. John Cotton accepted this sweeping judgment against Hutchinson. In November 1637 John Wheelwright, Hutchinson's only clerical supporter, was sentenced to banishment for sedition and contempt, as were those who defended him.

Hutchinson herself was brought to trial for "traducing the ministers and their ministry." Brilliantly holding her own against her accusers, claiming her right to discuss sermons in her home, she made the mistake of announcing that God had revealed to her that he would destroy her persecutors. The horrified court promptly banished her. In the custody of John Cotton, and under stress, she was partially convinced of her theological error; when placed on trial again in March 1638, she publicly recanted. Her inquisitors were unconvinced of her sincerity and so formally excommunicated her.

Hutchinson and her family then moved to the colony of Portsmouth in Rhode Island. After coming into conflict with the authorities there and leading an unsuccessful revolt, the Hutchinsons joined the Newport settlement, where William Hutchinson died in 1642. Worried that the Rhode Island settlements would be taken over by the Massachusetts Bay Colony, Anne Hutchinson and several children moved to New Netherlands, settling in what is now the Bronx, New York. Hutchinson and five of her children were killed by Indians in August or September 1643.

**BIBLIOGRAPHY**

Koehler, L., *A Search for Power: The "Weaker Sex" in Seventeenth Century New England*, 1980; Lang, Amy, *Prophetic Woman: Anne Hutchinson and the Problem of Dissent in the Literature of New England*, 1987; Williams, S. R., *Divine Rebel: The Life of Anne Marbury Hutchinson*, 1981.

# Ingersoll, Ralph McAllister

(December 8, 1900–March 8, 1985)
Editor, Publisher

Ralph Ingersoll was a "mover and shaker" of the American press in the mid-twentieth century. After having been a guiding spirit behind *The New Yorker, Fortune, Time,* and *Life,* he founded the short-lived newspaper *PM.*

Ralph Ingersoll was born in New Haven, Connecticut, the youngest of four children of Colin Macrae Ingersoll, of a six-generation Connecticut family, and Theresa McAllister, from Georgia. Ralph went to the Hotchkiss School, in Lakeville, Connecticut, and Yale University, where he earned a degree in mining engineering. He spent two years at mining work in the Southwest, gave that up to become a writer, and in 1923 was hired as a reporter by the New York *American.*

Two years later, shortly after the founding of *The New Yorker,* its editor, Harold Ross, hired Ingersoll on his staff. A few months later, Ingersoll became the magazine's first managing editor. He was one of the original group of gifted editors who enabled *The New Yorker* to succeed during its first five years. Ingersoll had temperamental differences with Ross, however, and he resigned in 1930 to become managing editor of another new magazine, *Fortune,* which had been started by HENRY R. LUCE, the cofounder of Time Inc. Again Ingersoll played a key part in the success of the magazine, a monthly devoted to business and industry, with emphasis on the literary quality of its writing and the elegance of its design. Subsequently, Ingersoll became publisher of the news magazine *Time* and then vice president and general manager of the entire Time Inc. organization. In 1936 he was involved in the founding of *Life,* an illustrated weekly news magazine in the Time Inc. group.

As early as 1933, Ingersoll had been pondering the idea of starting a newspaper that would be radically different. The notion did not interest Time Inc., and Ingersoll pursued it on his own. In April 1939 he resigned from *Time* and set about finding capital for the project. Through stock sales he raised $1.5 million from a group of backers that included Marshall Field III, DOROTHY THOMPSON, and Lessing Rosenwald and his sister Marion Rosenwald Stern, both children of JULIUS ROSENWALD. The first issue of *PM* appeared on June 18, 1940. It was a thirty-two-page tabloid daily, without advertising, priced at 5 cents a copy (other city papers then cost 2 or 3 cents). *PM*'s politics favored the liberal policies of President Franklin D. Roosevelt, but it also cultivated a populist air. In a prospectus Ingersoll stated, "We are against people who push other people around, . . . against fraud and deceit and greed and cruelty. . . . We are for people who are kindly and courageous and honest. . . . We are Americans and we prefer democracy to any other principle of government." Circulation, at first

encouraging, dropped. In three months, the paper faced bankruptcy. Marshall Field took over the financing of *PM,* declaring that its policies would not be affected. *PM* supported America's entry into World War II months before that occurred and continued publication during the war years.

Ingersoll was in the army during most of the war, having enlisted as a private and risen to the rank of lieutenant colonel. He wrote several books about his war observations, of which *The Battle Is the Payoff* (1943) and *Top Secret* (1946) are notable. Upon returning to *PM,* he disagreed with Marshall Field and resigned in late 1946. The paper, accepting advertisements, went on for two more years before it folded.

In semiretirement, Ingersoll operated Ingersoll Publications, a group of small newspapers in the Northeast, and published a partial autobiography and two novels. He died in a Miami Beach hospital at the age of eighty-four.

**BIBLIOGRAPHY**

Hoopes, Roy, *Ralph Ingersoll: A Biography,* 1985; Ingersoll, Ralph, *Point of Departure,* 1961.

# Innis, Roy Emile Alfredo

(June 6, 1934–   )
African American Nationalist, Civil Rights Leader

As the director of the Congress of Racial Equality (CORE) since the 1960s, Roy Innis changed its goals from nonviolent integration to African American nationalism.

Roy Innis's birthplace was St. Croix, in the Virgin Islands of the United States. His father, a police officer, died in Roy Innis's childhood, and his mother brought him to New York City when he was twelve. Growing up in Harlem, he was a good student in high school, but at six-

teen he joined the army, claiming to be eighteen. Supposing the North was integrated, he was surprised to find himself in an all-black company at a Massachusetts army base. When he was discharged, he completed high school and then went to the College of the City of New York to study chemistry. He worked as a laboratory assistant on cardiac research at a hospital in the east Bronx and was active in the local chapter of the Hospital Workers Union.

Innis was determined to play a part in the rising civil rights movement. In 1963 he joined the Congress of Racial Equality (CORE; see JAMES FARMER), which at the time, though committed to nonviolence, was one of the most radical and activist of the rights organizations. In the South, CORE sponsored Freedom Riders and sit-ins. JESSE JACKSON called CORE "the very soul of the civil rights movement."

In 1964 Innis became chairman of the education committee of CORE's Harlem chapter and led a campaign to set up independent school boards for Harlem and other predominantly black areas. In spring 1967 he resigned his hospital job and took an appointment as resident fellow (the first) of the Metropolitan Applied Research Center, which was concerned with planning for American cities and their poor. In July, Innis was elected national vice chairman of CORE. His growing interest in black nationalism and black power motivated his successful effort, with others, to remove the word "multiracial" from CORE's membership conditions. Two months later, he was made executive director of the Harlem Commonwealth Council, an antipoverty project under federal auspices that community leaders organized to foster neighborhood industries that would employ the jobless.

Innis was elected national director of CORE in 1968, and a new constitution was adopted that incorporated the principle of Black Power. He became coeditor of the *Manhattan Tribune*, a weekly paper for Harlem and the upper West Side. Innis's emphasis was on black nationalism, power, and progress. His coeditor, William Haddad, a white liberal, favored integration. Both joined to direct a journalism school for young Hispanics and African Americans.

During Innis's directorship CORE has been troubled by controversy. Many members resigned because of what was considered his autocratic style. Farmer, the founder, wanted to remove Innis because Innis encouraged black volunteers to join Cuban soldiers in the Angolan civil war. When the New York State attorney general investigated CORE's alleged misuse of donated funds, mismanagement was not proved, but Innis was required to contribute $35,000 from his own funds to the organization. CORE's membership dropped during the 1980s, though it continued to promote black-development projects in the inner-city neighborhoods. Innis remained at its head, but he became more interested in politics and made several unsuccessful tries for public office.

**BIBLIOGRAPHY**

Bell, I. P., *CORE and the Strategy of Nonviolence,* 1968.

# Itliong, Larry Dulay

(October 25, 1913–February 8, 1977)
Labor Leader

Larry Itliong organized thousands of Filipino farm workers in California in the 1960s and launched a battle against the growers that would eventually bring major economic improvements to agricultural workers throughout the state.

Larry Dulay Itliong was born in San Nicolas, Pangasinan, Philippines, and, after completing the sixth grade, came to the United States in 1929. He worked as a farm laborer in Seattle, Washington, and also in the salmon canneries of Alaska before moving to California in the late

1930s. His experiences as a farm laborer himself and later as a labor contractor in the San Joaquin Valley made him keenly aware of the poor conditions under which Filipinos worked. Most were single men who came to the United States in the late 1920s to work in the fields where vegetables and table grapes were grown. There they performed backbreaking labor for a maximum wage of about $1 an hour with no significant fringe benefits. They lived in unclean camps on the farms and spoke so little English that they had to depend on their crew leaders to communicate with their employers and the outside world.

The Archives of Labor and Urban Affairs, Wayne State University

Itliong became determined to improve conditions for Filipino farm workers. Having earlier been involved with the United Cannery, Agriculture and Packing House Workers of America, an early CIO affiliate, he formed the Filipino Farm Labor Union in 1956. Three years later, when the AFL-CIO (see WILLIAM GREEN and JOHN L. LEWIS) Council organized the Agricultural Workers Organizing Committee (AWOC), it hired Itliong to serve as an organizer of the new union. During the early 1960s Itliong organized Filipino vegetable and grape workers into a cohesive, though small, force with headquarters in Delano, California.

In the summer of 1965, Filipino farm workers, under Itliong's leadership, began demanding $1.40 an hour and 25 cents a box for the grapes they picked. The growers in Delano, however, stood firm at $1.20 an hour and 15 cents a box. Itliong was faced with a problem, because the camps at Delano had been the winter home of Filipino workers for thirty years, and they were afraid that if they walked out and set up a picket line, they would lose their homes. Finally, Itliong came up with the tactic of a sit-down strike. On September 8, 1965, his union members "sat down" in their camps, refusing to go into the fields to work. Twelve days later, the National Farm Workers Association (NFWA), under the leadership of CESAR CHAVEZ, joined their strike, shutting down grape production throughout California. The strike lasted four and a half years and attracted nationwide attention.

Midway into the strike, Itliong's AWOC merged with Chavez's NFWA to become the United Farm Workers Union with Chavez as national director and Itliong as his assistant. In this capacity, Itliong traveled throughout the country making speeches in behalf of the farm workers. He met with many prominent political leaders and the leaders of the major labor unions, spoke at grassroots community organizations, and conducted numerous press conferences with church leaders sympathetic to the farm workers' cause. Under Itliong's and Chavez's joint leadership, the United Farm Workers eventually won the strike and secured higher pay and better working conditions for their members.

When Chavez moved the union's headquarters from Delano to La Paz in 1971, Itliong kept his office in Delano. That same year, he resigned his position with the United Farm Workers because he felt that its bureaucratic organization had removed its leaders from actual contact with the workers. Itliong continued his involvement with the local farm worker community through the Filipino Service Center he had established in Delano with the goal of providing for the needs of senior citizens in the area, especially retired Filipino American farm workers.

Itliong also became involved in politics as national president of the Filipino American Political Association. In 1972 he served as a delegate to the Democratic National Convention.

In 1977, after being stricken with amyotrophic lateral sclerosis (Lou Gehrig's disease), Itliong died in Delano at the age of sixty-three.

**BIBLIOGRAPHY**

Levy, Jacques, *Cesar Chavez: Autobiography of La Causa*, 1975; Taylor, Ronald B., *Chavez and the Farm Workers*, 1975.

# Jackson, Helen Maria Fiske Hunt

(October 15, 1830–August 12, 1885)
Author, Reformer

A successful and prolific author, Helen Hunt Jackson is best remembered for *A Century of Dishonor* (1881) and *Ramona* (1884), books which helped to advance the cause of American Indian rights.

Helen Maria Fiske was born in Amherst, Massachusetts, where she was a friend of the poet Emily Dickinson. In 1852 she married Lieutenant Edward Bissell Hunt, but by 1865 both her husband and their two sons had died. Shattered by these losses, Hunt took up writing with the encouragement of author and critic THOMAS WENTWORTH HIGGINSON. She wrote poetry, magazine and newspaper articles, children's stories, and novels.

Library of Congress

Hoping to cure a bronchial condition, Hunt spent the winter of 1873 to 1874 in Colorado Springs. There she met and married William Sharpless Jackson, a railroad promoter and banker.

On a visit to Boston in 1879, Helen Hunt Jackson heard the Ponca chief Standing Bear and a young Ponca woman, Susette La Flesche Tibbles, who also went by the name of Bright Eyes, lecture on government treatment of their tribe. Two years earlier, the federal government had forcibly removed the Poncas from their homeland on the Dakota-Nebraska border to the Indian Territory, where more than a third of the tribe died of illness. When Standing Bear, along with a group of followers, tried to return to his homeland, he was pursued by the military, arrested, and ordered back to the Indian Territory.

Jackson was so outraged by what she heard that she joined with other Boston humanitarians like WENDELL PHILLIPS and the young LOUIS BRANDEIS in a crusade for American Indian rights that continued for the rest of her life. She gained national attention by writing letters to newspapers, appealing to government officials, and engaging in a public controversy with Carl Schurz, who, as secretary of the interior, was responsible for the removal of the Poncas from their homeland.

Frustrated by Schurz's lack of response, Jackson researched and wrote *A Century of Dishonor*, an attack on the U.S. government's Indian policy, published in 1881 and sent to every member of Congress. In vivid detail, Jackson described the treaties that had been made, then broken with each tribe, the forced marches they had endured, and the many times they had been massacred by whites. She begged white people to stop "cheating, robbing, breaking promises" in their relations with Indians.

In 1882 Jackson was appointed by the Interior Department to investigate the condition of the California Mission Indians. When her 1883 report brought few results, Jackson turned to fiction to try to increase public awareness of the problems facing the Indians. Her romantic novel, *Ramona*, published in 1884,

chronicled the breakup of both Indian and Spanish cultures in California. An instant success, the book remains in print perennially and has inspired several movie versions, as well as an annual pageant in southern California.

Both *Ramona* and *A Century of Dishonor* helped bring about reform of the government policy toward American Indians that resulted in the passage of the Dawes Act of 1887, allotting reservation land and citizenship rights to individual Indians. Jackson herself considered these books to be the most important of all her writings.

**BIBLIOGRAPHY**

Banning, E., *Helen Hunt Jackson*, 1973; Odell, Ruth, *Helen Hunt Jackson*, 1939.

## Jackson, Jesse Louis

(October 8, 1941–  )
Civil Rights Leader, Politician

Jesse Jackson succeeded MARTIN LUTHER KING, JR., as the foremost African American leader in the country, twice running for president, in 1984 and 1988.

Born in Greenville, South Carolina, to parents who were not married, Jesse Jackson was raised in poverty by his mother, a domestic, and by his stepfather, a janitor, whose last name he took. He later said that taunts about his illegitimacy while he was a child gave him the drive to succeed. Excelling as an athlete at the all-black Sterling High School in Greenville, Jackson upon graduation in 1959 won a football scholarship to the University of Illinois. But when he was told that blacks at the school could only be linemen and not quarterbacks, Jackson left after a year to attend the all-black North Carolina Agricultural and Technical State College in Greensboro. There he became an outstanding quarterback and an honors student.

Also while in college, Jackson joined the campus civil rights movement, organizing sit-ins and other demonstrations in Greensboro, work that brought him statewide recognition for integrating the city.

After he graduated in 1964, Jackson worked for North Carolina governor Terry Sanford briefly, then entered Chicago Theological Seminary on a scholarship, where he was ordained in 1968. While at the seminary, he also took part in the civil rights march in 1965 from Selma to Montgomery, Alabama, with Martin Luther King, Jr., and worked with King in Chicago with local civil rights organizations. In 1966 King appointed Jackson in charge of the Chicago branch of Operation Breadbasket, an organization that worked for jobs and benefits for African Americans through boycotts and picketing. Jackson quickly built Operation Breadbasket into a powerful organization that won agreements from major companies, such as A&P supermarkets, to hire more blacks in supervisory positions and to stock goods made by black manufacturers. Because of his successes in Chicago, Jackson was named national director of Operation Breadbasket in 1967.

Jackson was with King when King was assassinated in April 1964. The Reverend RALPH D. ABERNATHY was King's choice as his successor to leadership of the Southern Christian Leadership Conference (SCLC), and while Jackson remained with SCLC for several more years, many people thought he was at odds with Abernathy. In 1971 Jackson left the organization to found Operation PUSH (People United to Save Humanity) in Chicago to continue programs started by Operation Breadbasket. For ten years Jackson worked hard to build PUSH into a strong national presence, adding PUSH-Excel (PUSH for Excellence), an organization aimed at young people, with the special goal of keeping them in school.

In 1979 Jackson went to South Africa, where he made speeches stressing racial pride and urging civil disobedience to apartheid laws. Shortly afterward he made a controversial trip to the Middle East to encourage American and Israeli acceptance of the Palestine Liberation Organization, angering people on all sides. Nevertheless, by the early 1980s Jackson had emerged as a recognized world figure who was rumored to be running for the U.S presidency. He announced his candidacy in November 1983, opposing the conservative economic and social policies of President Ronald Reagan and backed by a "rainbow coalition" of the poor and dispossessed of all races. African American leaders were split over his candidacy; Jackson's campaign was ill-organized; and there was no money for a television and radio blitz around the country. Nonetheless, Jackson was a powerful and inspiring speaker, and personal appearances were well covered by the news media. He also led an extensive voter registration drive among African Americans. His success at obtaining the release of a captured U.S airman whose plane had been shot down by Syrians over Lebanon also won him considerable attention.

Jackson came under strong attacks from Jews in the United States when a journalist reported a private conversation in which Jackson had used the derogatory term "Hymies" to refer to Jews and "Hymietown" to refer to New York City. Jackson apologized, but his campaign had suffered. Yet despite this setback and considerable resistance to Jackson among white voters throughout the country, Jackson finished a strong third in the Democratic primaries, winning more than 3 million votes. His success was due to his powerful charisma and the ability of the African American churches to mobilize voters. A year after the election, a Gallup Poll showed that Jackson was the "third most admired man" in America.

In 1986 Jackson presented his Rainbow Coalition to a Democratic party conference in Chicago, and in his 1988 bid for the presidency won 6.7 million votes in the primaries. In 1989 Jackson was awarded the Spingarn Medal (see JOEL E. SPINGARN) for his achievements in civil rights and politics. The following year he was elected a nonvoting member of the U.S. Senate from the District of Columbia, a position he has used to lobby for statehood for the largely black District of Columbia. Also in 1990 Jackson won another victory on the international front when he helped bring about the release of several Americans held prisoner in Iraq. Although Jackson chose not to run for the presidency in 1992, he remained a power to be reckoned with in Democratic party politics.

**BIBLIOGRAPHY**

Celsi, Teresa, *Jesse Jackson and Political Power*, 1991; Colton, Elizabeth O., *The Jackson Phenomenon: The Man, The Power, The Message*, 1989; Gurin, Patricia, *Hope and Independence: Blacks' Response to Electoral and Party Politics*, 1989; Reed, Adolph L., *The Jackson Phenomenon*, 1987.

# James, William

(January 11, 1842–August 26, 1910)
Philosopher, Psychologist

William James not only pioneered in the study of psychology in America but also achieved international fame as a philosopher with his doctrine of pragmatism, a method for determining truth by testing the consequences of ideas.

William James was born in New York City, the son of an independently wealthy religious writer and lecturer, and the brother of the famous novelist Henry James. Since the family was often on the move, traveling throughout Europe and the United States, William was educated by tutors and in private schools in America and abroad. He studied art in Paris, and later, under the painter William Morris Hunt, at Newport, Rhode Island. Deciding not to become an artist, William James entered the Lawrence Scientific School at Harvard University in 1861, beginning a connection with Harvard that was to last for the rest of his life. In 1864 he enrolled at the Harvard Medical School, but he interrupted his studies a year later to take part in a zoological expedition to the Amazon led by LOUIS AGASSIZ, and again in 1867 to study physiological psychology in Germany. By the time he received his medical degree in 1869, he was well grounded in science as well as in German, French, and English literature.

In 1872, after a period of ill health and extreme depression, to which James was subject throughout his life, he became an instructor in physiology at Harvard. Having long been interested in the relationship between the mind and the body, he taught his first course in psychology in 1875. The following year, James started the first experimental psychology laboratory in the country. He thereby helped establish psychology as a separate laboratory science instead of a branch of philosophy. Among James's students at Harvard was the pioneer child psychologist G. STANLEY HALL. He also trained many who went on to teach psychology on the graduate level in the United States. In 1878 James signed a contract to produce a general book on psychology, which he worked on for the next twelve years. During this period, he became interested in psychic phenomena such as prophetic dreams and trances, helping to found the American Society for Psychical Research in 1884.

In 1890 *The Principles of Psychology* was finally published, in two volumes. James included in the book some of his own discoveries about the role of the will, the nature of emotional states, and the interrelation of all experience in a "stream of consciousness." But for the most part, *Principles* was a comprehensive summary of late–nineteenth-century psychology. Because of this and also because of its lively colloquial style, the book was widely read. Especially in its abridged, one-volume form published two years later, *Principles* was the leading textbook in psychology for many years. In demand as a lecturer after the publication of *Principles*, James further spread his ideas in *Talks to Teachers on Psychology; and to Students on some of Life's Ideals* (1899).

James had taught his first course in philosophy in 1879, and during the 1890s he directed his attention increasingly toward the field, though without abandoning psychology. In 1897 he published *The Will to Believe and Other Essays*, a collection of essays that dealt with the philosophy of religion and other topics. Also during these years, James involved himself with current issues and problems. He shocked colleagues by opposing a Massachusetts bill mandating Spiritualists and Christian Scientists to qualify as physicians in order to practice healing. In addition, James took a strong stand against the Spanish-American War of 1898 and against American imperialism. Later, in a famous essay called "The Moral Equivalent of War" (1910), James raised the possibility of finding a constructive outlet for the warlike spirit in human nature.

James did not belong to a church and was leery of most religious organizations. Nevertheless, he felt the need of a personal faith, and much of his philosophical writing was concerned with the quest for such a faith. Having begun to collect material on the psychology and philosophy of religion several years earlier, James in 1902 published what became his most popular book, *The Varieties of Religious Experience,* which included the histories of many people who had had mystical experiences.

In 1907 James made a major contribution to philosophy with the publication of *Pragmatism,* based on a series of lectures he had given at Columbia University and at the Lowell Institute in Boston. Rejecting fixed systems of belief, James maintained that the validity of ideas was to be determined by their consequences. Since an idea may be useful in one situation and not in another, truth is relative. Like James's earlier books, *Pragmatism* was written with grace and wit. As a philosophy of action as well as a method of thinking, his doctrine of pragmatism attracted followers, among them the philosopher and psychologist JOHN DEWEY, but also aroused much controversy. James's critics charged that pragmatism was only another name for expediency, or the idea that whatever works is good. However, by consequences James did not mean worldly success but rather psychological, moral, and artistic consequences. He answered his critics in a series of articles later collected and published as *The Meaning of Truth* (1909).

In the same year that *Pragmatism* appeared (1907), James resigned from Harvard. The following year, he delivered the Hibbert lectures at Oxford, taking the opportunity to present in a coherent form his views about the nature of the universe. In 1909 the lectures were published as *A Pluralistic Universe.* Underlying James's pragmatism was his belief in an ever-changing or "pluralistic" universe rather than a static one. In his emphasis on the importance of change, James was one of the first American thinkers to apply Darwinian evolutionary theories to philosophy and psychology. He held that ideas put to work in the world were inevitably modified during the course of their application; likewise, applying an idea to the world itself brought change. Thus by acting on ideas, human beings could contribute to the ongoing processes of the universe.

James spent the spring and summer of 1910 in Europe trying to regain his health. He died shortly after his return to the United States at his summer home in Chocorua, New Hampshire.

**BIBLIOGRAPHY**

Barzun, Jacques, *A Stroll with William James,* 1984; Bjork, Daniel W., *William James: The Center of His Vision,* 1988; Feinstein, Howard M., *Becoming William James,* 1984; Myers, Gerald E., *William James: His Life and Thought,* 1986.

## Johnson, Tom Loftin

(July 18, 1854–April 10, 1911)
Reformer

In the early years of the twentieth century, reform mayor Tom Johnson transformed Cleveland, Ohio, into one of the best-governed cities in the country, setting an important example for other progressive reformers on the local, state, and finally national level.

Born in Blue Spring, Kentucky, Tom Johnson was raised primarily in Staunton, Virginia, and Louisville, Kentucky. In 1869 he took a job in Louisville working for a street railway company. The company was owned by Alfred V. and Bidermann Du Pont, members of the wealthy industrial family; Johnson would later use his association with the Du Ponts to advantage. At Louisville, he demonstrated his ingenuity by inventing the first fare box for tolls. When he moved to Indianapolis, Indiana, in 1876, the twenty-two-year-old Johnson bought and rehabilitated the Indianapolis Street Railroad. The financial backing for the venture was supplied by the Du Ponts.

With the profits from his venture, Johnson in 1879 bought a broken-down street railway in Cleveland, Ohio, built it up, and operated it in competition with the street railway system owned by business and political leader Mark Hanna. Through this railroad and the others he acquired in Detroit, Michigan, and Brooklyn, New York, Johnson had become a wealthy man by the age of twenty-five. He also collaborated with the Du Ponts in establishing two steel mills—the Cambria Company at Johnstown, Pennsylvania, and the Lorain Steel Company at Lorain, Ohio.

Johnson's career as a public servant began in the aftermath of the Johnstown, Pennsylvania, flood of 1889. As a member of the relief commission he proved energetic and skillful in dispensing the $3 million relief fund that had been raised for victims of the disaster.

While still involved with street railway systems, Johnson read HENRY GEORGE's *Progress and Poverty* and was converted to George's single-tax and free-trade programs. Becoming one of the chief proponents of George's ideas, Johnson campaigned hard for George in the New York mayoral elections of 1886 and 1897. His own political career began in 1888 when he ran for Congress as a Democrat. He was defeated but went on to be elected in 1890 and again in 1892 on a single-tax and free-trade platform, despite his interests in the steel industry, which was protected from foreign competition by high tariffs.

After losing a bid for reelection to Congress in 1894, Johnson returned to his railway and steel ventures, which he began to dispose of in 1898. A year later, he went to Detroit to assist his friend, Michigan governor HAZEN PINGREE, in a campaign to bring the street car system under public ownership and reduce the fares.

The battle in Detroit was lost, but in Cleveland Johnson found an opportunity to make a difference.

In 1901 Johnson won the election for Cleveland's mayoralty. In this and subsequent campaigns—Johnson was mayor four times—he took his case directly to the people. He traveled around the city with a circus tent capable of holding more than 4,000 people. At these mass meetings people were invited to ask questions about the operation of city government, and even the most shy among the audiences were encouraged to take part.

Once elected in 1901, Johnson set out to make good his campaign slogan of "Home rule; three cent fare; and just taxation." Home rule was important to Johnson, because without it he had little hope of achieving his two other goals—a lower fare on the street railway and a tax system that did not favor the wealthy at the expense of the poor. Since state legislatures had legal jurisdiction over cities, political bosses on the state level were able to block municipal reform. For example, when Johnson tried to break the monopoly of the local street railway, his opponents convinced the legislature to make this more difficult for him by altering the municipal code. Nevertheless, Johnson's struggle for greater control of the street railway ended with the establishment of municipal supervision of the line in 1907. Three years later, his campaign for municipal home rule resulted in an amendment to the Ohio constitution giving cities more control over their own affairs, including the right to enact fairer tax laws.

Hailed by journalist and reformer LINCOLN STEFFENS as "the best mayor of the best governed city in the United States," Johnson served until 1909 when he lost his bid for a fifth term. He died two years later at the age of fifty-six.

**BIBLIOGRAPHY**

Avery, E. M., *A History of Cleveland and Its Environs*, 1918; Johnson, Tom, with Elizabeth J. Hauser, *My Story*, 1911; Lorenz, Carl, *Tom L. Johnson*, 1911.

# Jones, Mary Harris

(May 1, 1830–November 30, 1930)
Labor Leader

An itinerant and tireless organizer of workers all over the nation, Mary "Mother" Jones made an important contribution to the labor movement of the late nineteenth and early twentieth centuries.

Born in Cork, Ireland, Mary Harris immigrated with her family to America at age eleven. After she gained a normal school education while living in Toronto, Canada, she taught school in Michigan, worked as a dressmaker in Chicago, and returned to teaching in Memphis, Tennessee. In 1861 she married George Jones, a member of the Iron Molders' Union.

When a yellow fever epidemic struck Memphis in 1867, Jones lost her husband and four children in the same week to the disease. Remaining in the city to help nurse the ill until the epidemic subsided, Jones then moved to Chicago, where she worked as a dressmaker again. Four years later she lost everything she owned in the Great Chicago Fire.

Alone and financially ruined, Jones found comfort in the burned-out shell of a local Knights of Labor (see TERENCE POWDERLY) union hall. She began to participate in labor union meetings and by 1880 had decided to dedicate herself to the cause. For the rest of her life, without a home of her own and with only the personal belongings she could carry, Jones went from coal mines to logging camps, factories to train yards, anywhere there was labor strife, to provide help and to spread the word

Library of Congress

about unions. Though arrested, jailed, and threatened at gunpoint, Jones kept up the fight. "I am not afraid of the pen, or the scaffold, or the sword," she once said. "I shall tell the truth wherever I please."

Jones began her crusade by organizing women's auxiliaries to unions and attacking child labor practices in the South. In the 1890s she became affiliated with the United Mine Workers. In 1902 Jones attracted widespread public attention to a coal miners' strike by directing strikers' wives to attack strikebreakers with brooms and mops.

Jones's independent and uncompromising spirit made it difficult for her to remain associated with any one union for long. In 1903 she broke with the United Mine Workers when the union's president disavowed a strike by workers in Colorado she had helped to organize.

Besides her courage, compassion, and gift for eloquent, rousing speeches, Jones became well known for her ability to organize vast parades of solidarity that won public sympathy. Her most famous use of the technique occurred in 1903 when, to dramatize child labor abuse, she led striking children from the textile mills of Kensington, Pennsylvania, to the home of President Theodore Roosevelt at Oyster Bay, New York.

At times Jones's opponents underestimated her influence. As a result of her aid to a coal miners' strike in 1913, a West Virginia militia military court convicted her of conspiracy to commit murder and sentenced her to twenty years in jail. Labor leaders protested, and the U.S. Senate voted to investigate the case. Quickly freed by the newly elected governor, Jones traveled to Colorado to aid another coal miners' strike. Although arrested and deported from the area three times, she continued to return to the scene of danger. After the machine-gun "massacre" of mine families in a tent colony at Ludlow, Colorado, in 1914, Jones went all the way to Washington for help, persuading President Woodrow Wilson to urge a settlement of the strike.

Although doing what she could to help working people, Jones failed to develop a consistent philosophy. She never endorsed socialism, but she did help to found the Social Democratic party in 1898 and was one of the organizers of the Industrial Workers of the World (see WILLIAM D. HAYWOOD) union in 1905.

Jones remained active in the labor movement throughout her eighties and early nineties. In 1921, at age ninety-one, she attended the Pan American Federation of Labor meeting in Mexico City. Three years later, in 1924, she delivered her last major public address at the convention of the Farmer-Labor party. Jones lived to celebrate her 100th birthday. After her death several months later, her body was taken to the coal fields of southern Illinois, where she was buried in the Union Miners Cemetery at Mount Olive, next to the victims of the Virden, Illinois, mine riot of 1898.

**BIBLIOGRAPHY**

Cornell, Robert J., *The Anthracite Coal Strike of 1902,* 1957; Jones, Mary Harris, and Mary F. Parton (ed.), *The Autobiography of Mother Jones,* 1925; Steele, Edward M., "Mother Jones in the Fairmont Field, 1902," *Journal of American History,* September 1970.

# Kameny, Franklin

(May 21, 1925– )
Astronomer, Gay Rights Activist

Frank Kameny, forced out of a promising career in government work by the disclosure of his sexual orientation, became one of the most effective activists for homosexual civil rights in Washington, D.C., and nationally. He has encouraged aggressive action by the gay community.

Kameny, the son of an electrical engineer, grew up in the borough of Queens, New York City. By the time he was eight he knew he would become an astronomer, and at sixteen he entered Queens College. In 1943 he enlisted in the Army Special Training Program and saw action in Europe as a private first-class. He returned to college and in 1948 got a B.S. with honors in physics, specializing in optics. He entered Harvard University for graduate work and spent 1953 to 1954 doing research as an observational astronomer at the University of Arizona in Tucson. There he had his first homosexual experience and discovered the city's gay subculture. He took time off from his studies to work at an observatory in Armagh, Northern Ireland, and returned to Harvard to receive his Ph.D. in 1956.

Appointed to the faculty of Georgetown University, Kameny moved to Washington, D.C., which became his permanent home. In the summer of 1957 he was offered a civil service job in the U.S. Army Map Service that promised better opportunities. He was soon receiving ratings of "superior" for his sky surveys, made to determine more precisely the interrelations of land masses. In December, while assigned to an observatory in Hawaii, Kameny was suddenly ordered to Washington and informed by a Civil

Service Commission (CSC) investigator that he was known to be a homosexual. He was dismissed from his job, and the CSC barred him from further federal employment.

Kameny expected that his case would be favorably resolved through the administrative appeal process. That having failed, by spring 1959 Kameny was in desperate circumstances, living on handouts of food and suffering from malnutrition. Ironically, scientists of his specialty were in great demand as it was the beginning of the space age, but Kameny was a "security problem." His astronomy career was ended, but he found a job not subject to security clearance and settled in northwest Washington.

In 1960 Kameny found a lawyer to help him approach the federal courts. Appeals failed, and there was only the U.S. Supreme Court for redress. After his lawyer gave up, Kameny prepared his own brief arguing that the CSC policy on homosexuality discriminates against an entire group and "has no basis in reason." In March 1961, when the Supreme Court denied Kameny's petition for a hearing, he wrote to leaders of the Mattachine Society in New York, asking for help starting a local chapter. (The first Mattachine Society had been founded in Los Angeles in 1950 by Harry Hay and Charles Rowland to champion the civil rights of homosexuals.) A dozen men and women met that fall to form the Mattachine Society of Washington (MSW) and elected Kameny its president. Its founding statement gave as its purpose "to act by any lawful means . . . to secure for homosexuals basic rights and liberties guaranteed to all Americans." Kameny constantly urged gay activists to employ aggressive action, as the civil rights activists were doing.

MSW was indeed assertive, circulating the announcement of its founding to members of Congress, the president and his cabinet, every high official in Washington, and the press. In 1963 Kameny took a leading role in organizing a regional federation, East Coast Homophile Organizations, later expanded nationally. That year he appeared before a subcommittee of the U.S. Civil Rights Commission and presented MSW's statement on discrimination against the employment of homosexuals. He persuaded the Washington chapter of the American Civil Liberties Union (ACLU; see ROGER BALDWIN), of which he was a member, to oppose the federal ban on hiring gays, which led to the ACLU's joining in test cases. MSW published pamphlets, written mostly by Kameny, entitled "How to Handle a Federal Interrogation" and "What to Do if You Are Arrested," which were distributed in the homosexual community and offered to government employees. Kameny began serving as a paralegal counsel to gays brought up for CSC hearings as security risks.

In 1965 MSW members began to picket the White House, the Pentagon, the State Department, and the Civil Service Commission. On July 4 that year, Kameny promoted a symbolic picketing at Independence Hall in Philadelphia, and the event was staged annually until 1969.

When Congress conceded that the District of Columbia could have a nonvoting delegate elected to the House of Representatives, Kameny ran for the office in 1971, calling himself the Personal Freedom candidate. Besides gay rights, he took positions on welfare, drugs, crime prevention, and civil liberties and popularized the slogan "Gay Is Good." Kameny lost, as he expected, but he considered the effort a consciousness-raising experience for the gay community. His next cause was to challenge the American Psychiatric Association, and in 1974 the Association eliminated homosexuality from its list of mental illness.

The MSW dwindled away in the 1970s, succeeded by other organizations such as the National Gay Task Force (NGTF), which put Kameny on its board of directors. In 1975 the battle with the CSC was won: the CSC changed its antigay policy so that homosexuals may openly hold the jobs they are qualified for. Kameny still wages the battle with the military, which is far from won, though now, at least, many people thrown out of the service are given honorable rather than undesirable or dishonorable discharges.

In the 1980s, Kameny served as a member of the District of Columbia's Human Rights Commission. Besides his paralegal work counseling security clearance cases and his continuing concern with gay rights, he is involved in Democratic party activities.

**BIBLIOGRAPHY**

D'Emilio, John, *Sexual Politics, Sexual Communities*, 1983; Marcus, Eric, *Making History: The Struggle for Gay and Lesbian Equal Rights, An Oral History*, 1992.

# Keller, Helen Adams

(June 27, 1880–June 1, 1968)
Lecturer, Social Activist, Writer

Helen Keller, though blind and deaf from infancy, learned to communicate and to speak and became an American legend, not only because of what she accomplished for herself but also because of her example of strength and courage for hundreds of millions and her humanitarian crusading for many beneficent causes.

Keller was born on a farm near Tuscumbia, a small town in northern Alabama, to Kate Adams Keller and Arthur H. Keller, who had been an officer in the Confederate army. She had a younger sister and brother and two older half-brothers. When she was nineteen months old an illness, possibly scarlet fever, left her blind and deaf. With no formal education until she was seven, she was unruly and wild, able to communicate with her family only by hand signals that she had invented. Her father consulted Alexander Graham Bell, the great inventor, who was an authority on deafness. Bell advised him to write to the Perkins Institution for the Blind, in Boston, whose founder, SAMUEL GRIDLEY HOWE, had been able to teach Laura Bridgman, a child who was also deaf and blind, to read and write. Howe's successor at Perkins, Michael Anagnos, Bell's son-in-law, recommended as teacher Anne Sullivan. As a student at the institution, Sullivan had poor vision herself and had learned a manual alphabet (an alphabet for the deaf in which letters are represented by finger positions) to talk with Laura Bridgman.

Sullivan reached Keller's mind through the sense of touch, having used the manual alphabet, as Howe had done, to spell words in the girl's hand. Going further, she used practical situations, such as having the child feel water as it came from the pump and spelling it in her hand at the same time. Keller learned rapidly: in a month she knew words in the manual alphabet and could make the connection with objects. By the time she was ten and had gone to the Perkins Institution, she could read and write in Braille and could use a typewriter specially made for her.

Early on, Keller showed a literary gift, and her letters and diary came to the attention of Anagnos and Bell. What both of them wrote about her made her a celebrity. Inseparable from Sullivan, whom she called "Teacher," she traveled and met distinguished writers as well as President Grover Cleveland.

Even as a child, Keller was eager to be able to speak and worked with a specialist, Sarah Fuller, at the Horace Mann School for the Deaf in Boston. Thus she was better able to attend preparatory schools—the first one in New York City, where she developed the skill of lipreading by placing her fingers over the speaker's nose, mouth, and larynx, and another in Cambridge, Massachusetts. After working for two years with a tutor, Keller passed the entrance examinations and began at Radcliffe College. Sullivan went to class with her as an interpreter, but Keller sat for examinations alone. She earned a B.A. cum laude in 1904. Eventually, besides English, she learned French, German, Greek, Italian, and Latin.

While Keller could speak, her voice was difficult to understand for one unfamiliar with it. To communicate she usually relied on the lipreading method, or on the manual alphabet spelled into her hand by an interpreter, who in turn understood Keller's replies by the same means.

In 1903, when Keller was in her second year at Radcliffe, she produced *The Story of My Life*, made up of her own account, Sullivan's, and a number of letters. She was helped in preparing it by John Macy, an instructor at Harvard. Two years later, Sullivan and Macy were married, but "Teacher" continued until her death in 1936 to work with Keller.

As Keller grew up she began to make adult choices. She had made her religious decision when she was sixteen: she adopted the Swedenborgian faith, a Christian doctrine based on the teachings of Emanuel Swedenborg, an eighteenth-century Swedish mystic. (In 1927 she published *My Religion*, a treatise on Swedenborgianism.) Keller joined the Socialist party in 1909 and wrote much on its principles, which she wished to see applied to the handicapped as well as everyone. In 1914, feeling the Socialists moved too slowly, she resigned from the party and joined the Industrial Workers of the World (see WILLIAM D. HAYWOOD). Keller also took a prominent part in the woman suffrage movement. After the adoption of the Nineteenth Amendment to the Constitution, in 1920, Keller was less involved in political activity.

Although Keller received donations from wealthy people, she wanted to achieve financial independence. In 1908 she published *The World I Live In*, which was admired but brought little income. She and Sullivan were engaged by the Chautauqua Association to appear "on the road," demonstrating how Sullivan had taught her and how she could speak. From 1919 to 1923, they toured in vaudeville,

doing a similar demonstration after which Keller took questions from the audience. She was too radical in her ideas for the general public, however, and the vaudeville tours were given up.

Thereafter Keller and Sullivan turned their stage experience to good use on behalf of the American Foundation for the Blind, appearing before groups that would assist the foundation's work. Keller's political opinions did not enter into presentations to assist the blind. After an interlude to write *Midstream: My Later Life* (1929), Keller resumed fund raising for the foundation, the principal concern of her remaining years. She established the Helen Keller Endowment Fund with contributions from the wealthy, and through the American Foundation for Overseas Blind she sought to help people in underdeveloped countries and places devastated by war and disasters. During and after World War II, Keller worked with blinded servicemen. Throughout it all, she traveled widely in many countries and received numerous honorary degrees and decorations.

Sullivan had been responsible for Keller's financial planning, but after "Teacher"'s death in 1936, the American Foundation for the Blind administered her affairs under a trust. Sullivan's place was taken by a Scotswoman, Polly Thompson, who had joined Keller's staff in 1914 and had learned the necessary skills. In 1955 Keller published *Teacher*, a memorial to the woman who had opened the world to her and had been her closest friend.

After Thompson's death in 1960, Winifred Corbally was Keller's companion. In 1964 Keller was awarded the Medal of Freedom by President Lyndon B. Johnson. Four years later she died in her sleep at home in Westport, Connecticut.

**BIBLIOGRAPHY**

Braddy, Nella, *Anne Sullivan Macy: The Story behind Helen Keller*, 1933; Keller, Helen A., *Let Us Have Faith*, 1940, and *The Open Door*, 1957.

# Kelley, Florence

(September 12, 1859–February 17, 1932)
Reformer

Florence Kelley was a consumer movement leader and labor reformer who devoted her life to securing laws protecting children and women in the workplace.

Kelley was born in Philadelphia into a family with solid reformist credentials. Her father was a Republican congressman, an abolitionist, and an advocate of woman suffrage; her mother, the adoptive daughter of Quaker abolitionists. Often ill as a child, Kelley received much of her education at home, where she read widely from her father's library. In 1876 she entered Cornell University, one of the rare colleges of that time to admit women, and graduated in 1882. Refused admission to the law school of the University of Pennsylvania because she was a woman, Kelley started a night school for working women. During an 1883 trip to Europe she met M. Carey Thomas, future president of Bryn Mawr College, which marked a turning point in her life. Learning from Thomas that the University of Zurich allowed women to study for the doctorate, Kelley enrolled there.

At Zurich, Kelley was exposed to socialist ideas, which she adopted. She joined the Socialist party and over the years translated into English Friedrich Engels's *The Conditions of the Working Classes in England in 1844* and Karl Marx's *Address on Free Trade*.

Also in Zurich, Kelley met and married a fellow socialist, Lazare Wischnewetzky, a medical student from Russia. After coming to the United States in 1886, the couple joined the Socialist Labor party, in which Kelley was very active. The next few years produced the couple's expulsion from the party in 1887 because of ideological differences and their own separation in 1891. Kelley moved to Illinois, where she obtained a divorce under that state's more liberal divorce laws, resumed the use of her maiden name, and secured custody of the couple's three children.

Late in 1891 Kelley became a resident of JANE ADDAMS's Hull House settlement in Chicago. Building from her concern with the problem of child labor—expressed in her pamphlet called *Our Toiling Children*—Kelley persuaded the Illinois Bureau of Labor Statistics to hire her in 1892 to investigate garment industry sweatshops. Also in 1892, the federal commissioner of labor hired her to survey Chicago slums. She conducted both surveys despite the dangers posed by the smallpox epidemic of 1893.

Illinois passed its first factory law, based on Kelley's findings, in 1893. The new law prohibited factory owners from hiring children, placed controls on sweatshops, and limited the number of hours women could work. Reformist governor JOHN PETER ALTGELD appointed Kelley as chief of the new unit formed to inspect factories and bring those who violated the new law before the public, a post she held until 1897. In the course of this work, Kelley once had a warning shot fired at her. Frustrated by the difficulty of getting violators prosecuted, Kelley studied the law in evening courses at the Northwestern University Law School. She graduated in 1894 and was admitted to the bar shortly thereafter.

In 1899 Kelley was named general secretary of the newly created National Consumers' League, which sought to exert consumer pressure to improve working conditions. Moving with her family to LILLIAN D. WALD's Henry Street Settlement in New York City, she spent the following years lecturing widely on consumerism and organizing consumer leagues. By 1913, thanks largely to her efforts, nine states had laws providing a minimum wage for women and children. Kelly undertook other reform efforts as well. In the next few years, she helped organize the NAACP (National Organization for the Advancement of Colored People; see JOEL E. SPINGARN), joined the Socialist party, took a strong stand against the U.S. entry into World War I, and after the war helped found the Women's International League for Peace and Freedom.

Despite this variety of activity, Kelley's main efforts were always directed at ending the exploitation of children. In 1902 she was instrumental in creating a New York Child Labor Committee and two years later in organizing a national committee. She advocated the establishment of a federal children's commission, and, once the Children's Bureau was created in 1912, she publicized its work and supported legislation like the Keating-Owen Child Labor Act of 1916 and the Sheppard-Towner Maternity and Infancy Protection Act of 1921. Progress seemed checked in 1918 and 1922, when the conservative Supreme Court struck down various protective laws for women and children as violations of states' rights and de-

nial of children's freedom to work. Kelley then directed her work to petition for a child labor amendment to the Constitution.

Described by one associate as a "guerilla warrior" in the "wilderness of industrial wrongs," Kelley brought to the crusade for social justice an enormous energy, a keen mind, and a single-minded determination. She died in Philadelphia at the age of seventy two.

**BIBLIOGRAPHY**

Blumberg, Dorothy Rose, *Florence Kelley: The Making of a Social Pioneer*, 1966; Chambers, Clarke A., *Seedtime of Reform: American Social Service and Social Action, 1918–1933*, 1963; Ginger, Ray, *Altgeld's America*, 1958; Goldmark, Josephine, *Impatient Crusader: Florence Kelley's Life Story*, 1953.

# Kellogg, John Harvey

(February 26, 1852–December 14, 1943)
Health Reformer

John Harvey Kellogg revolutionized American eating habits with the introduction of flaked breakfast cereals. At his famous sanitarium in Battle Creek, Michigan, he also worked to increase public awareness of the importance of proper nutrition, exercise, fresh air, and rest.

Born in Tyrone Township, Michigan, Kellogg was raised a Seventh-Day Adventist in Battle Creek, Michigan, which became the world headquarters of the Adventists. At age twelve, he began to learn the printing trade in the Adventist publishing house. There he set type for articles by the church leader, in which she urged the adoption of healthful practices as part of the Adventists' religious duty. Convinced, Kellogg became a vegetarian. After leaving the publishing house, Kellogg studied

nontraditional as well as traditional medicine, earning a medical degree from the Bellevue Hospital Medical College in New York City in 1875.

In 1876 Kellogg became medical superintendent of the ten-year-old Western Health Reform Institute in Battle Creek, which aimed to treat illness naturally. Kellogg renamed the institute the Battle Creek Sanitarium, defining this last word as "a place where people learn to stay well."

Kellogg's program for "biologic living" involved total abstinence from alcoholic drinks, tea, coffee, meat, chocolate, tobacco, and condiments. He also frowned on milk, cheese, eggs, and refined sugars, maintaining that humankind's natural foods were vegetables, whole grains, nuts, and fruits. Even these foods should be eaten in moderate amounts and thoroughly chewed. Drugs were not to be taken to cure illness. The best medicine in Kellogg's view was preventive and included proper nutrition, along with sensible clothing, good posture, regular exercise and rest, and plenty of exposure to fresh air and sunshine.

Library of Congress

To develop a scientific basis for his program, Kellogg studied medicine. He became a highly skilled surgeon, setting a record in the 1890s by performing 165 successive abdominal operations without a fatality and operating on over 22,000 patients during his career. He used special techniques to prevent shock and created a program of bed exercises, both steps intended to reduce the chances that surgical patients would suffer from complications.

Under Kellogg's vigorous direction—he regularly put in sixteen-hour days—the Battle Creek Sanitarium prospered. Kellogg helped contribute to the institution's financial security by donating his surgical fees to it and to similar institutions for use in treating poor patients and to promote healthful practices. In the early part of the twentieth century the roster of people who came for treatment there read like a "Who's Who" of prominent Americans. Patients benefited from the new programs that Kellogg was constantly developing.

These included an experimental food laboratory, which in the 1890s produced the first flaked cereal, created by pressing cooked wheat through rollers. Kellogg's brother Will used this process to make cornflakes and build a lucrative and well-known breakfast food business.

As Kellogg departed more and more from the Adventist religious orientation in his work, friction developed between him and church leaders. After Kellogg's excommunication on November 10, 1907, he fought for years with the church over his control of the sanitarium.

A prolific author, Kellogg wrote more than fifty popular books, including an early sex education manual, *Plain Facts About Sexual Life* (1877). He also lectured throughout the country. Energetic until the end, Kellogg was in the midst of planning still more new programs when he was stricken with pneumonia and died at the age of ninety-one.

**BIBLIOGRAPHY**

Carson, Gerald, *Cornflake Crusade*, 1957; Deutsch, Ronald M., *The Nuts Among the Berries*, 1961; Schwarz, Richard M., *John Harvey Kellogg, M.D.*, 1970.

# Kellogg, Paul Underwood

(September 30, 1879–November 1, 1958)
Editor, Reformer

As editor of the social workers' magazine *Survey*, Paul Kellogg exerted a major influence on social reform from the presidency of Theodore Roosevelt through the New Deal of Franklin D. Roosevelt.

Born in Kalamazoo, Michigan, Paul Kellogg began his career as a journalist by working as a reporter and city editor on the *Kalamazoo Daily Telegraph*. In 1901 he moved to New York City, where he studied at Columbia University for a year, then became assistant editor of *Charities*, a magazine about the delivery of charitable services. Kellogg broadened the magazine's scope to include discussion of the important social issues of the day. In 1905 he became managing editor.

In 1907 Kellogg left the magazine briefly to head the first major in-depth social survey of an American city, in which a team of scholars and community leaders amassed information on daily life and working conditions over several years in Pittsburgh. Published first as articles and later in six large volumes titled *Pittsburgh Survey* (1910–1914), the work became a model for other such studies, while giving support to national movements for better housing and workers' compensation and fueling the fight to end the twelve-hour day in the steel industry.

Kellogg returned to the magazine *Charities*, which was renamed *Survey* in 1909, and three years after became editor in chief with his brother Arthur serving as managing editor. *Survey* backed government regulation of workers' hours and wages, unemployment insurance and pensions, public housing, minority rights, and other reform programs. Many of these programs became part of Franklin D. Roosevelt's New Deal in the 1930s, and Kellogg helped draft the Social Security Act of 1935. And with the editors of *Survey*, he worked to influence the making of more progressive social policy.

In addition to *Survey*, Kellogg was associated with a wide range of liberal political, social, and educational causes. At the end of World War I, he helped found the American Civil Liberties Union (see ROGER BALDWIN) and the Foreign Policy Association. In 1927 he took a stand against the execution of Nicola Sacco and Bartolomeo Vanzetti, anarchists accused of robbery and murder in Massachusetts. During the Spanish Civil War (1936–1939), he sought to lift the American embargo on shipping arms to the Spanish government. He served as president of the National Conference of Social Work in 1939. A man imbued with ideas of progressive reform, he devoted his life to touching upon and linking as many activities as possible, whether human-oriented or intellectually directed.

Kellogg continued to edit *Survey* until 1952 when the journal had to cease publication as a result of financial difficulties. He died six years later at the age of seventy-nine.

**BIBLIOGRAPHY**

Chambers, Clarke A., *Paul U. Kellogg and the "Survey": Voices for Social Welfare and Social Justice*, 1971; Kellogg, Paul, with Arthur Gleason, *British Labor and the War*, 1919.

# Kellor, Frances Alice

(October 20, 1873–January 4, 1952)
Reformer, Sociologist

Frances Kellor's studies of the problems faced by different social groups, especially immigrants, and her calls for government action on their behalf made her a leading reformer of the Progressive era.

Born in Columbus, Ohio, Kellor moved with her mother to Coldwater, Michigan, after her father reputedly abandoned the family. Too poor to finish high school, Kellor became a typesetter and then a journalist for the *Coldwater Republican*. She lived with Mary A. and Frances E. Eddy, who made it possible for her to enroll at Cornell Law School. After earning an L.L.B. in 1897, Kellor moved to Chicago, where with the help of a scholarship from the Chicago Women's Club she studied sociology at the University of Chicago. As part of her work there, Kellor studied women criminals, black migrants, and unemployed women to confirm her belief that crime was related to environmental factors. Using the data she had gathered, Kellor made this argument in her first book, *Experimental Sociology* (1902), in which she also called for the establishment of rehabilitation programs within prisons.

In 1903 Kellor moved to New York City on a fellowship to study unemployment at the New York Summer School of Philanthropy. In her research, Kellor investigated the ways in which employment agencies often exploited southern black women who had migrated to the North, later expanding the study to include the plight of new immigrants. The study was published in book form as *Out of Work: A Study of Employment Agencies* (1904) and pointed out the need for federal action. Also in 1904, Kellor helped found the Inter-Municipal Committee on Household Research, whose legislative committee proposed laws regarding child labor, tenement houses, and employment bureaus. In 1906, largely due to the work of this committee and the impact of Kellor's book, a

stronger law governing employment agencies was passed. That same year, Kellor helped found the National League for the Protection of Colored Women.

In 1908 Governor Charles Evans Hughes appointed Kellor and LILLIAN D. WALD to the newly created New York Commission on Immigration. In its investigations of living and working conditions among immigrants, the committee found much evidence of exploitation and recommended the creation of a Bureau of Industries and Immigration in the Department of Labor. This was done in 1910 with Kellor serving as director and chief investigator.

After resigning from the Bureau of Industries in 1912, Kellor continued to work in behalf of immigrants through the Progressive party's national service committee. The following year, she became director of the legislative committee of the New York branch of the North American Civil League for Immigrants, which she had earlier organized. In this capacity, Kellor explored the possibilities of government action regarding immigrants' employment, education, and standard of living. In 1914 the New York branch became known as the Committee for Immigrants in America, with Kellor serving as vice chair.

With the outbreak of World War I, Kellor's and the committee's emphasis shifted to naturalization, citizenship, and Americanization efforts to encourage national unity. In the 1920s she founded the Inter-Racial Council and the Association of Foreign Language Newspapers. Kellor's concern with the peaceful settlement of differences among groups both within the United States and abroad brought her into the field of arbitration. In 1926 she became a founding member and an officer of the American Arbitration Association. She prepared a code of ethics for arbitration that was used for many years and wrote several books on the use of arbitration in industrial relations. Kellor also believed in the use of arbitration to solve international disputes and advance world peace. She was actively involved in this cause until her death in New York City at the age of seventy-eight.

**BIBLIOGRAPHY**

Bennett, Helen Christine, *American Women in Civic Work*, 1915; Hartmann, Edward George, *The Movement to Americanize the Immigrant*, 1948; Higham, John, *Strangers in the Land*, 1955.

## Keyserling, Leon H.

(January 22, 1908–August 9, 1987)
Economist, Government Adviser, Lawyer

Leon Keyserling was instrumental in drafting major New Deal legislation and throughout his government career urged the use of Keynesian policies—federal spending on social programs—to maintain full employment during slack economic periods.

Keyserling was born in Charleston, South Carolina, the son of William Keyserling and Jennie Hyman. He grew up and went through high school in Beaufort, South Carolina, and earned his B.A. at Columbia University, where he was elected to Phi Beta Kappa. He graduated from Harvard Law School and, in 1931, was admitted to the bar in New York. The next year he became an assistant in the economics department at Columbia.

In 1933, drawn to government service in the first administration of President Franklin D. Roosevelt, Keyserling briefly served on the legal staff of the Agricultural Adjustment Administration. Later that year he became secretary and legislative assistant to Senator Robert F. Wagner, of New York. Keyserling assisted Wagner in drafting such important New Deal legislation as the National Industrial Recovery Act (1933), the Social Security Act (1935), and the National Labor Relations Act (1935), known as the Wagner Act, which created the National Labor Relations Board to stop employers from engaging in unfair labor practices. Keyserling also helped write Wagner's bill providing for federal assistance in the building of low-rent housing for the poor. In 1937 he left Wagner's staff to become general counsel of the United States Housing Administration (USHA), serving as its acting administrator in 1941. He also served briefly as commissioner of the body that succeeded the USHA, the National Housing Agency.

In 1940 Keyserling married another government economist, Mary Dublin, who later was chief of the Women's Bureau in the Department of Labor during the administration of President Lyndon B. Johnson.

As World War II ended and the transition to a peacetime economy was in view, Keyserling submitted an essay in a contest (sponsored by the Pabst Brewing Company) for a solution to problems of postwar employment. One of 36,000 entrants, Keyserling won second prize, $10,000. In his essay he made proposals that led to the Employment Act of 1946, stipulating that full employment must be the nation's economic goal, and to the establishment of the Council of Economic Advisers. Carrying through his earlier concern for federal housing, Keyserling was instrumental in gathering conservative as well as liberal backing for the Wagner-Ellender-Taft Housing Bill of 1945, which created the General Housing Act, providing for slum clearance, low-cost housing, urban redevelopment, and loans for private construction, all under a single federal agency.

In 1946 President Harry S Truman appointed Keyserling vice chairman of the Council of Economic Advisers, which had the duty of administering the provisions of the Employment Act. In 1949 Keyserling became chairman and used his position, along with other liberals, to advance Keynesian economic policies. By arguing that the government could spur economic growth through deficit spending, Keyserling was able to justify massive federal expenditures on both military preparedness and liberal social programs. The economic prosperity of the 1950s and 1960s appeared to support his economic views.

Keyserling held the council chairmanship until 1953, when he left federal office and worked as a consultant and lawyer for public employees' unions and foreign governments. He founded the Conference on Economic Progress, a nonprofit body concerned with public-interest projects. During the administration of President Jimmy Carter, Keyserling worked with other economists to draft the Full Employment and Balanced Growth Act of 1978.

Throughout his public service, Keyserling wrote extensively on legal questions and economics. In the 1930s he edited with Rexford G. Tugwell, another economist and an adviser to Roosevelt, two volumes entitled *Redirecting Education*. His chapter, "Social Objectives in the American College," emphasized the importance of the social sciences for politics.

**BIBLIOGRAPHY**

Keyserling, Leon H., *"Liberal" and "Conservative" Economic Policies and Their Consequences, 1919–1979*, 1979.

# King, Coretta Scott

(April 27, 1927–  )
Civil Rights Leader

Coretta Scott King worked at the side of her husband, MARTIN LUTHER KING, JR., during his years in the civil rights crusade, and after his death she continued to devote herself to his message of nonviolence and peace.

Coretta Scott was born in Heiberger, in central Alabama. Her father ran a country store; her mother drove a school bus. Coretta, however, was not entitled to ride in one and walked 5 miles to a one-room schoolhouse. She was able to attend a private school in Marion, the county seat, maintained by northerners, and then went to Antioch College, in Ohio, an institution known for its progressive politics and approach to schooling. Her interests were music and education, though she was not allowed to be a practice teacher in the local public schools. Scott's voice was admired, and upon graduating in 1951, she decided to make her career in music. She entered the New England Conservatory of Music in Boston, with a fellowship she eked out by doing domestic work for her lodging. Later she received financial support from her home state, which had an aid program for students who were not admitted to Alabama's white colleges.

Coretta Scott met Martin Luther King, Jr., a promising theological student at Boston University. Both young people shared a dedication to good works, in particular to helping American black people. On June 18, 1953, they were married by the Reverend Martin Luther King, Sr., at the Scott home in Alabama, then returned to Boston—Coretta Scott King to complete her Mus.B. degree in voice, her husband to complete his Ph.D.

The Kings settled first in Montgomery, where in 1955 and 1956 the bus boycott brought Martin Luther King to public notice as a civil rights crusader—and where the King residence was hit by a bomb that endangered his family.

In 1960 the Kings moved to Atlanta. During these years, though Coretta King was concerned with their children—four by 1964—she participated in her husband's work, at his side in marches and demonstrations, sometimes speaking in his place. She taught in the music department of an Atlanta college and toured with her "freedom concerts," in which she lectured, sang, and recited poetry on the civil rights movement. The proceeds went to the Southern Christian Leadership Conference (SCLC; see RALPH D. ABERNATHY and MARTIN LUTHER KING, JR.), of which her husband was president. Coretta King accompanied him when he lectured abroad and was in Oslo when he received the Nobel Prize for Peace. In 1962, on her own, she represented the Women's Strike for Peace at an international disarmament conference in Geneva, Switzerland.

After Martin Luther King was assassinated on April 4, 1968, Coretta King displayed courage and presence. The day before his funeral she led the march of striking garbage men in Memphis which her husband was to have led, and soon afterward she spoke from notes of his at a peace rally in New York City. In June she addressed a mass meeting at the Lincoln Memorial in Washington, exhorting women to unite and fight racism, war, and poverty.

Coretta Scott King's later life has been dedicated to the Martin Luther King, Jr. Center for Nonviolent Social Change, in Atlanta, which she founded. The center, a historic site under the National Park Service, comprises King's tomb and birthplace, a chapel, a conference and cultural center, and other features. Coretta King directs programs that promote her husband's nonviolent philosophy through an interracial coalition of labor, religious, civil rights, and other organizations. In August 1983 she led the Twentieth Anniversary March on Washington, in which a half million people participated. She led another Washington demonstration, "Housing Now!" in 1989 and protested Reserve Officers' Training Corps (ROTC) programs at schools named in memory of her husband.

**BIBLIOGRAPHY**

King, Coretta Scott, *My Life with Martin Luther King, Jr.,* 1969, and (ed.), *The Words of Martin Luther King, Jr.,* 1983.

# King, Martin Luther, Jr.

(January 15, 1929–April 4, 1968)
Civil Rights Leader

Martin Luther King, Jr., led the African American struggle to achieve full rights of American citizenship and showed how mass peaceful action could solve intractable social and political questions. He eloquently voiced the hopes and grievances of American blacks, persuading the majority of them to take him as their leader.

King was born in Atlanta, Georgia, the son of the assistant pastor of the Ebenezer Baptist Church and the grandson of the Reverend Adam Daniel Williams, who had been the pastor of Ebenezer Baptist for more than thirty years. Martin's parents, the Reverend King, Sr., and Alberta Williams, had an older child, Christine, and a younger, Alfred Daniel ("A.D."), who also became a minister. When Reverend Williams died in 1931, the Reverend King, Sr., succeeded him and was pastor for more than fifty years, until his death in 1984.

The young King went to segregated public schools and then to Booker T. Washington High

School, which he left after two years when he qualified to enter Morehouse College, now part of Atlanta University. As he pursued a major in sociology, his concern with social betterment was aroused. King got his A.B. in 1948, but the year before he had been ordained a Baptist minister and had become assistant pastor to his father.

In 1948 King went north to Chester, Pennsylvania, where he entered Crozer Theological Seminary as one of six black students among some ninety whites. At Crozer he first became acquainted with the Social Gospel movement of WALTER RAUSCHENBUSCH and the works of Mohandas K. Gandhi, who had been assassinated in early 1948. He graduated with a bachelor in divinity degree in 1951, having been president of the senior class, the top student, and winner of a graduate fellowship.

The Crozer fellowship enabled King to enter Boston University, which he had chosen over an offer from Yale because of his desire to study with its philosophy department. By 1953 he had completed the course requirements for the Ph.D., and he had met Coretta Scott (see CORETTA SCOTT KING), who was studying voice at the New England Conservatory. That summer they married and returned to Boston, Coretta King to finish her work at the conservatory, her husband to write his Ph.D. dissertation on the concept of God in the thought of Paul Tillich and H. N. Wieman, while taking courses at Harvard in Plato and in existential philosophy and preaching in local churches. In 1955 Boston University awarded him the Ph.D.

The previous year, however, King had been called to his first ministry, at the Dexter Avenue Baptist Church, in Montgomery, Alabama, a strictly segregated city like any other in the South. King was beginning to be known for his preaching when, on December 1, 1955, ROSA

Library of Congress

PARKS, a seamstress, was arrested for not giving up her bus seat to a white passenger. Her action, coming after the Supreme Court declared the segregation of schools unconstitutional (*Brown* v. *Board of Education*, 1954) indicated the electrifying effects that decision had on blacks, who henceforth would not tolerate situations they had long endured. The consequence was an almost total boycott of Montgomery's segregated bus system by the black community. The Montgomery Improvement Association (MIA), formed by the ministers of the black churches, chose King as its president to lead the protest. As the nonviolent boycott and the violence of the white community went on during 1956, national and international attention focused on Montgomery, and King became prominent for his eloquence and his personal courage in the face of attacks on his home and himself. In November the U.S. Supreme Court declared Alabama's laws segregating buses unconstitutional.

Some sixty southern black leaders met in January 1957 at the Ebenezer Baptist Church in Atlanta to form a larger organization, the Southern Christian Leadership Conference (SCLC; see also RALPH ABERNATHY), to lead the struggle against segregation. King, elected its president, emphasized Gandhi's teaching of nonviolence and made the winning of black voting rights the first goal. His career was transformed as his fame and dedication grew. In March he was invited to attend the ceremonies for the independence of Ghana, in West Africa. In May he led a prayer pilgrimage of 25,000 people in Washington, D.C., demanding federal action on civil rights. In June 1958 he met with President Dwight D. Eisenhower to urge stronger federal protection of civil rights, and in September his book *Stride Toward*

*Freedom* was published, giving his account of the Montgomery protest. In February 1959 he and his wife went to India at the invitation of the Gandhian National Memorial Fund. In January 1960 he left his Montgomery pastorate for Atlanta, where the SCLC headquarters had been established, and he became cominister of his father's church.

The Gandhian techniques of civil disobedience that King and the SCLC supported included not only the boycott but the sit-in, the protest march, and the Freedom Rides (see JAMES FARMER). The action of the Freedom Riders, traveling across state lines, was an effort to force the federal government to protect the rights of southern citizens. In that and other aspects of his work King gradually gained the support of President John F. Kennedy and his brother Robert Kennedy, the U.S. attorney general.

The struggle to integrate Birmingham, Alabama, during spring 1963 involved King's most strenuous and courageous action. The city's police, under the commissioner Eugene "Bull" Connor, used brutal means—dogs, cattle prods, fire hoses—against the demonstrators. The American public witnessed horrifying scenes on television and in newspapers, bringing home the reality of the violence. King was arrested and thrown into a solitary cell, where he wrote a stirring "Letter from Birmingham Jail," defending nonviolent protest in answer to a statement by a group of local clergymen objecting to his tactics. Though sporadic violence continued, the Birmingham campaign was finally successful and black and white leaders agreed on a gradual procedure of desegregation. King gave his account of the Birmingham struggle in *Why We Can't Wait* (1964).

The March on Washington in August 1963, organized by King and the SCLC, was attended by a quarter of a million people, at least a fourth of whom were white. From the steps of the Lincoln Memorial, King gave his most famous speech, with its repeated words "I Have a Dream." In fall 1964 King was awarded the Nobel Prize for Peace, and in his laureate address in Oslo, Norway, he saw the award as an affirmation of nonviolent protest. "The Movement," he declared, "seeks to liberate American society and to share in the self-liberation of all the people." His movement's efforts compelled Congress to pass the Civil Rights Act of 1964, which committed the federal government to eliminating racial discrimination from American life.

In spring 1965 King organized two marches of many thousands from Selma to Birmingham, to emphasize the need for a federal voting rights law. President Lyndon B. Johnson signed the Voting Rights Act on August 6, in King's presence. His support of Johnson began to waver, however, and in 1967 he declared his opposition to the Vietnam War, as he became cochairman of an organization concerned about the war. He further broadened his concerns from racism to include unemployment and poverty. An attempt to improve slum conditions in Chicago was a failure. Some of his younger, more radical followers fell away as they found King unacceptably moderate. Riots in the ghettos of Newark, Harlem, Detroit, and Los Angeles challenged his nonviolent teaching.

To highlight the problems of the poor, both black and white, King planned a Poor People's Campaign in the form of a march and campground in Washington during April 1968 (see RALPH D. ABERNATHY). In March he led protesters in Memphis in support of a strike of sanitation workers. "I've been to the mountaintop . . . and I've seen the Promised Land," he told his followers, shortly before, on April 4, he was shot by a sniper as he stood on the balcony of his motel room talking with JESSE JACKSON and other followers.

King's work is carried on at the Center for Nonviolent Social Change in Atlanta. In 1986 King's birthday, January 15, became a federal holiday.

**BIBLIOGRAPHY**

Branch, Taylor, *Parting the Waters: America in the King Years,* 1988; Carson, Clayborne (ed.), *The*

*Papers of Martin Luther King, Jr.*, vol. 1, *Called to Serve, 1929–1951*, 1992; D'Emilio, John, *The Civil Rights Struggle: Leaders in Profile*, 1979; Garrow, David J., *Bearing the Cross: Martin Luther King, Jr., and the Southern Christian Leadership Conference*, 1986; King, Coretta Scott, *My Life with Martin Luther King, Jr.*, 1969.

# Kinsey, Alfred Charles

(June 23, 1894–August 25, 1956)
Scientist

D r. Alfred Kinsey, a biologist trained to study wasps, was the first scientist to apply the empirical techniques of scientific and statistical research to human sexual behavior. His findings in the famous "Kinsey Reports" liberalized popular attitudes about sexuality.

Kinsey was the son of a teacher at the Stevens Institute of Technology, in Hoboken, New Jersey, where he was born. Later the family moved to South Orange, a dozen miles westward, where Alfred finished high school. Despite a strong interest in wildlife, he followed his father's wishes and entered Stevens Institute as a mechanical engineering major. But after two years, determined to work in life sciences, he transferred to Bowdoin College, in Maine, where he earned his B.S. in biology (1916). He chose entomology for graduate work at Harvard University, narrowing his specialization to a single genus of insect, the Cynips, or gall wasp, which lays its eggs on plants, causing a growth called a gall. For his field study Kinsey traveled thousands of miles in the West and South, collecting some 300,000 specimens. His notable collection is housed today in the American Museum of Natural History in New York City.

With his Sc.D. from Harvard, Kinsey was appointed an assistant professor of zoology at Indiana University, in Bloomington, where he spent his entire career, achieving a full professorship in 1929. He continued entomological research, traveling in Central America and Mexico and publishing learned works on the Cynips as well as general textbooks in biology. He won international renown for his precise scholarship on the taxonomy of the gall wasp and on genetic theories.

In the late 1930s, after students requested faculty to teach a course in marriage, Kinsey became interested in studying human sexual behavior by the use of scientific norms. To obtain accurate information, he began to interview students, colleagues, and others, eventually using a standardized format, a comprehensive series of topics, a special code for replies, and a policy of full confidentiality. He depended upon the empirical techniques that he had applied in his work on gall wasps.

Despite criticism from more conservative quarters, Kinsey moved on with what had become his primary project, and he obtained the support of the university administration. In 1941, having received funding from the Rockefeller Foundation through the National Research Council, he enlisted research assistants and extended the scope of the project. In 1947 he established a nonprofit corporation, the Institute for Sex Research, which maintains the records of interviews, tabulations of data, and collections of letters and other documentation. Kinsey's statistical method resembled that of sociological poll-takers such as GEORGE GALLUP.

The first publication of the institute was *Sexual Behavior in the Human Male* (1948), by Kinsey and two of his research assistants, Clyde E. Martin and Wardell B. Pomeroy. Based on a statistical sample of 5,300 case histories of men and boys, it was brought out by a publisher of medical books, and the first printing was 5,000 copies. Within a few weeks the Kinsey Report, as it was popularly called, was a best-seller, the subject of extensive public interest and discussion. *Sexual Behavior in the Human Female,* which followed in 1953, was based on interviews with 5,940 women and girls.

The Kinsey reports were the first reliable surveys of human sexual behavior, exploring its distribution, range, frequency, and variety. They documented the fact of wide variations in sexual behavior. Among Kinsey's findings: sexual behavior varies notably between different economic and social classes; homosexual experience is more common than has been supposed; the average man achieves a peak of virility in his teens, steadily declining thereafter, though continuing well beyond the sixties; women have a greater range of sexual capacity than commonly thought; premarital intercourse is more usual, among both sexes, than formerly believed.

Kinsey drove himself hard, and his health suffered. Though the royalties from the publications went entirely to the Institute for Sex Research, he was anxious over the decline of funding from other sources. Increasing scientific and moral criticism made foundations reluctant to support his research. He died of a heart ailment complicated by pneumonia. The institute, renamed in 1982 the Kinsey Institute for Research in Sex, Gender, and Reproduction, continues its studies and publications.

**BIBLIOGRAPHY**

Christenson, Cornelia V., *Kinsey: A Biography,* 1971; Institute for Sex Research, *Pregnancy, Birth and Abortion,* 1958, *Sex Offenders: An Analysis of Types,* 1976, *The Kinsey Institute New Report on Sex,* 1990, and others; Pomeroy, W. B., *Dr. Kinsey and the Institute for Sex Research,* 1972.

## Koop, Charles Everett

(October 14, 1916–    )
Government Official, Surgeon

As surgeon general of the United States during the 1980s, C. Everett Koop attracted widespread attention with his outspokenness on such controversial issues as AIDS and abortion.

A descendant of Dutch colonists, Charles Everett Koop was born in Brooklyn, New York. He earned his B.A. at Dartmouth College in 1937 and his M.D. at Cornell Medical College in 1941. After several internships and residencies, Koop joined the faculty of the University of Pennsylvania School of Medicine and was appointed surgeon-in-chief at Children's Hospital in Philadelphia in 1948. Koop became one of the few surgeons in the country to devote his practice exclusively to pediatrics.

An expert clinician, Koop successfully reconstructed the chest of a baby with a heart born outside its body and separated three pairs of Siamese twins. Koop also established the first neonatal intensive surgical care unit in the country, helped make anesthesia safe for children, and drew national attention to the problem of children with cancer.

Koop generated controversy with his stand on abortion, which he opposed on moral and religious grounds. In 1979 and 1980 he toured the country with a multimedia antiabortion presentation. Largely because of his antiabortion position, Koop was nominated by President Ronald Reagan in 1981 to be surgeon general of the United States. Despite strong opposition by feminist groups and by the American Public Health Association, Koop was confirmed by the Senate and sworn in on January 21, 1982.

In 1982 Koop issued the strongest attack on cigarette smoking yet made by the Public Health Service, stressing the link between smoking and cancer. He pushed for legislation to strengthen the health warning labels on cigarette packages. Koop also emerged as a strong, if controversial, champion of the rights of handicapped children.

Koop's stands on AIDS and abortion sparked the most heated debate and set him at odds with the Reagan administration. After finally getting clearance to prepare a report on AIDS in 1986, Koop described the AIDs virus and how it was transmitted and urged more sex education for children, as well as the use of condoms to prevent the spread of the disease. The report infuriated conservatives who had hitherto supported Koop, while it pleased liberals.

Koop again became the target of conservatives when he refused to write a report for President Reagan on the negative mental and physical effects of abortion on women. In researching the subject, Koop learned that there were no credible scientific studies showing that abortions were either harmful or not harmful to women's health, and he thought that such evidence, in any case, would dilute his moral position that abortions killed human lives.

Since leaving government service in 1989, Koop has presented a series of television programs on health care reform, served as chairman of the "Safe Kids" campaign at the Children's National Medical Center in Washington, D.C., and lectured throughout the country.

**BIBLIOGRAPHY**

Brownstein, Ronald, and Nina Easton, *Reagan's Ruling Class*, 1982; Koop, C. Everett, *Koop, The Memoirs of America's Family Doctor*, 1991.

## Kuznets, Simon Smith

(April 30, 1901–July 10, 1985)
Economist

Simon Kuznets, of Ukrainian origin, became a master of twentieth-century economics. He helped transform economics into a more exact science by his system, which was the basis for the "gross national product" concept.

Kuznets was born in Kharkov to Abraham Kuznets, a fur dealer, and Pauline Friedman. In 1907 his father immigrated to the United States, meaning to have his family join him when he was established, but World War I and the Russian Revolution intervened. Meanwhile Simon Kuznets, the second of three sons, went to a gymnasium (high school) and became interested in economics. Only in 1922 could Kuznets, with a younger brother, join his father in New York. The brothers taught themselves English in their first months there, and that fall Kuznets entered Columbia University. A year later he was awarded a B.A. in economics; he received his M.A. in 1924. He went on into graduate work and earned his Ph.D. in 1926. His dissertation, entitled "Cyclical Fluctuations: Retail and Wholesale Trade, United States, 1919–1925," expressed his determination to understand economic behavior by means of statistical data that demonstrated the regularities in economic development.

After eighteen months as a research fellow of the Social Science Research Council (SSRC), Kuznets was invited by his Columbia mentor, Wesley C. Mitchell, to join the staff of the National Bureau of Economic Research (NBER), where during an affiliation of some thirty years he did pioneer work on business cycles. During those years he held professorships at the University of Pennsylvania (1930–1954), the Johns Hopkins University (1954–1960), and Harvard University (1960–1971).

Economists had long sought to quantify a country's prosperity by analyzing all its sources of income, but the available statistics were too uneven to be useful. In 1941 Kuznets published a seminal two-volume work, *National Income and Its Composition, 1919–1938*, which revised earlier statistics and provided a conceptual framework as the basis for such research. He computed income as the sum of wages, profits, interest, and rents. Measurements of this kind are the foundation of macroeconomics, which is concerned with the totality of forces working in an economy and the interrelationships of various divisions of the economy.

Kuznets's system of measurement enabled the Commerce Department to make frequent estimates of the gross national product and revisions of its growth. Indeed, the concept of "gross national product" as a measure of economic output is usually credited to Kuznets. International agencies, such as the World Bank and the World Monetary Fund, have used Kuznets's system to calculate the economic progress or retrogression of industrial and developing nations. Economists in the private sector likewise rely on the system for industrial and fiscal calculation.

During World War II, Kuznets was associate director of the Bureau of Planning and Statistics of the powerful War Production Board, which had been set up in 1942 to direct production and also the procurement of materials. The board expanded and converted the economy to a maximum, assigning priorities for scarce materials and halting nonessential industry. Kuznets continued his researches meanwhile and in 1946 published *National Product Since 1869*, which gave historical estimates of U.S. income growth over a seventy-year period. In 1949 he became chairman of SSRC's Committee on Economic Growth, which, working with students at Johns Hopkins, produced a major comparative study of national income growth for various countries over periods of time.

Kuznets's last important work, published in 1979, was *Growth and Structural Shifts*. The book dealt with the development of Taiwan beginning in 1895, when the island was occupied by Japan and subsequently industrialized, up to its present independent status. Taiwan furnished an example of "Kuznets's law" for the economies of developing countries: during the early phase of development, inequalities of income distribution will rise sharply, followed by a turn toward equalization.

In 1971, the year he became emeritus at Harvard, Kuznets was awarded the Nobel Memorial Prize in Economic Sciences for his work on national income accounting.

**BIBLIOGRAPHY**

Kuznets, Simon, *Population, Capital, and Growth*, 1973, and *Essays in Growth, Population, and Income Distribution*, 1979.

# Lathrop, Julia Clifford

(June 29, 1858–April 15, 1932)
Reformer

Social worker and reformer Julia Lathrop was a pioneer in child welfare legislation.

Julia Lathrop was born in Rockford, Illinois, into a wealthy, reform-minded family. Her father was a supporter of women's rights, an abolitionist, and a founder of the Republican party; her mother was an early advocate of woman suffrage. After graduation from high school, Lathrop studied for a year at the Rockford Seminary, then transferred to Vassar College, graduating in 1880. She spent the next ten years working as a secretary in her father's law office.

Library of Congress

In 1890 Lathrop joined in the work at Hull House, the Chicago settlement founded by JANE ADDAMS and Ellen Gates Starr, remaining as a full-time resident for the next twenty years. Her first experience in public welfare occurred during the depression of 1893 when she volunteered to investigate relief applications in the Hull House district. Her stark account of conditions in the county charities appeared in *Hull-House Maps and Papers* in 1895. Also in 1893 Lathrop began serving as the first woman on the Illinois Board of Charities, a position to which she was appointed by reform governor JOHN PETER ALTGELD. In the course of her work, she visited county farms and almshouses, interviewing directors, staff, and inmates—and even at one point, testing the safety of a fire-escape chute. In articles and speeches Lathrop strongly objected to the lumping together of young and old, the sick and the mentally ill in the same institutions, urging separate institutions for young people and hospitals to care for the mentally ill. Her concern with delinquent children led her to join with Jane Addams and other women in securing a law establishing the first juvenile court in the United States in 1899. Recognizing the need for properly trained attendants at state institutions, she helped launch in 1903 and 1904 a series of social work courses at what became known as the Chicago School of Civics and Philanthropy.

In 1912 President William Howard Taft appointed Lathrop head of the new Children's Bureau of the Department of Labor. Under her guidance the bureau made studies of infant and maternal mortality, nutrition, juvenile crime, and the rights of children. The bureau also enforced the first child labor law, passed in 1916. After the United States entered World War I, the bureau organized a study of child welfare under war conditions and a Children's Year for 1919.

Lathrop resigned from the Children's Bureau in 1921 for health reasons but continued to support its work. She was also active in immigration affairs and in the League of Women Voters. Death followed goiter surgery in 1932.

**BIBLIOGRAPHY**

Addams, Jane, *My Friend, Julia Lathrop*, 1935; Chambers, Clarke A., *Seedtime of Reform: American Social Service and Social Action, 1918–1933*, 1963.

# Lease, Mary Elizabeth Clyens

(September 11, 1853–October 29, 1933)
Populist Orator

Mary Elizabeth Lease won fame and notoriety with her fiery speeches for the People's (Populist) party in the 1890s. She was born Mary Clyens in Ridgway, Pennsylvania, the daughter of Irish immigrants. Mary grew up on the family farm, attended parochial schools, and taught school for two years before moving to Kansas in 1870 to teach at a Catholic girls school in Osage Mission. In 1873 she married Charles L. Lease, a pharmacist. After various moves, the Leases settled in Wichita, Kansas, where she organized a woman's club, served briefly as president of the Wichita Equal Suffrage Association, spoke on behalf of woman suffrage, and studied law at home, gaining admittance to the bar in 1889.

Before long, Lease was caught up in the revolt among Kansas farmers. Drought and hard times had arrived in 1887. Farmers who had heavily mortgaged their farms to pay for improvements now faced huge debts. Adding to their discontent were the high freight rates they had to pay to ship their produce east and a deflated currency that had caused a drop in agricultural prices. Lease stumped the state for the farmer-supported Union Labor party in the campaign of 1888 and afterward edited its organ, the *Union Labor Press*. She also joined the Knights of Labor (see TERENCE POWDERLY) and the Kansas Farmers' Alliance.

In 1889 when angry Kansas farmers organized the state People's party, later known as the Populists, and ran candidates in the state elections of 1890, Lease again took to the platform. She made over 160 speeches throughout Kansas and won fame throughout the state as a speaker. Whether or not Lease actually called on farmers "to raise less corn and more hell," the phrase became a powerful slogan of the farmers' crusade.

Lease emerged as a national leader of the Populist movement. She spoke in western and southern states and helped launch the national People's party in 1892 in St. Louis. She seconded the nomination of James B. Weaver for president at the party's nominating convention later that year and campaigned with him around the country. Although Weaver did poorly in the national election, the Populists were swept into office in Kansas, and Lease was appointed president of the Kansas State Board of Charities. However, she lost this post after quarreling with the governor and became alienated from the party leadership. At the presidential nominating convention of 1896, Lease tried unsuccessfully to keep the Populists from joining forces with the Democrats. But after the Populists chose the Democratic nominee, William Jennings Bryan, as their candidate, she gave him her support.

After the election of 1896 and the collapse of the Populist movement, Lease moved to New York City. She continued to give occasional lectures, but for the most part she lived out the remaining thirty-some years of her life in quiet obscurity.

**BIBLIOGRAPHY**

Goodwyn, L., *Democratic Promise: The Populist Movement in America*, 1976; Stiller, R., *The Queen of the Populists: The Story of Mary Elizabeth Lease*, 1970; White, William Allen, *Autobiography*, 1946.

# Leontief, Wassily

(August 6, 1906–   )
Economist

Wassily Leontief, who was born and raised in Russia, became an innovative American economist whose methods have had an international impact. He has constantly tried to instill reality into economic research.

Leontief was born in St. Petersburg, Russia, son of an economics professor (of the same name) and Eugenia Bekker. He grew up in a time of social and political turmoil and remembers seeing Lenin, the leader of the Russian Revolution, address a mass rally in what by then was called Leningrad. At the University of Leningrad, which he entered at the age of fifteen, Leontief studied sociology, philosophy, and economics. In 1925, with the rest of his family, Leontief chose to leave the Soviet Union and entered the University of Berlin for a Ph.D., awarded in 1928. During the preceding year he was a research associate in economics at the University of Kiel, Germany.

In 1929 and 1930 Leontief was in Nanking, China, as an economic adviser to the Ministry of Railroads, and from there he immigrated to the United States and joined the National Bureau of Economic Research. He joined the faculty of Harvard University soon afterward as an economics instructor, and in 1948, having become a full professor, he founded a center for research in "input-output analysis" called the Harvard Economic Research Project, which he directed. In 1953 Leontief was appointed to the Henry Lee Chair of Political Economics, which he held until 1975. Two years earlier, he had closed the Economic Research Project, and coincidentally in that year he was awarded the Nobel Memorial Prize in Economic Sciences for the development of the input-output method, employing mathematical formulas and transactions tables, which divide the economy into numerous sectors.

Leontief's first book, *The Structure of the American Economy, 1919–1929: An Em-*
*pirical Application of Equilibrium Analysis* (1941), was devoted to his method of analyzing economic input and output. With that he made his reputation as an innovator in his field. By using Leontief's method, economists are able to predict how changes in one part of the economy will affect the behavior of other parts: this is called general equilibrium analysis. The first significant applications of Leontief's model occurred at the beginning and the end of World War II, when the U.S. Bureau of Labor statistics used it to predict how employment would change as the economy went from peace to war and back again. At the latter stage, the factor of disarmament become a major concern of Leontief's. The invention of the computer has made the application of this type of analysis feasible, and it has been used advantageously for economic forecasting by some fifty industrialized nations, noncommunist and communist. The collection of international economic data in recent years has improved largely because of Leontief's system, which requires methodical assembly of a huge amount of such material.

When more advanced computers became available in the 1950s and 1960s, Leontief refined his system, increasing the number of economic sectors. The construction of the required tables became usual procedure with the U.S. Department of Commerce. The United Nations, the World Bank, and many governments have adopted input-output analysis as an essential feature of economic planning and budgeting.

Leontief was one of the first economists to take into account the impact of economic activity on environmental quality. In his Nobel lecture, he described a simple input-model of the world economy in which pollution was treated as a separate sector. He pointed out that in less developed countries, strict antipollution standards would foster expanded employment though requiring some sacrifices in the consumption of goods. In 1977 Leontief and collaborators prepared *The Future of the World Economy,* a summary of research on the effect of economic strategies on the environment and on international economic development.

In 1975 Leontief moved to New York University as director of the Institute for Economic Analysis, virtually a one-man organization that works closely with the United Nations on world economic problems and interindustrial relations. Going beyond economics, Leontief has been interested in using his method to study the interrelation between fields of knowledge.

**BIBLIOGRAPHY**

Agarwal, J. P., et al., *The Future of the World Economy: An Appraisal of Leontief's Study,* 1978; Leontief, Wassily, *The Future Impact of Automation on Workers,* 1986; Leontief, Wassily, with Faye Duchin, *Military Spending,* 1983; Leontief, Wassily, with E. Leontief, *A Memoir,* 1983.

# Lewis, John Llewellyn

(February 12, 1880–June 11, 1969)
Labor Leader

John L. Lewis rose from impoverished origins to become one of the most powerful labor leaders in the nation's history. As the founder of the Congress of Industrial Organizations (CIO) he brought millions of workers into the labor movement and enabled them to have security and benefits previously undreamed of.

Lewis was born in Lucas County, in southern Iowa, the eldest of eight children of Welsh parents: Thomas, a coal miner and farm hand, and Ann Louisa Watkins. As the family moved about central Iowa, John attended a variety of public schools and finished the junior year of high school. When the family went back to Lucas County, John worked in the coal mines and, by 1901, had become secretary of a United Mine Workers of America (UMW) local. Little is known of his next five years, when apparently

National Archives

he knocked about the West as a miner and a construction worker. In 1906 he returned to Lucas, the county seat, and tried to make good with a feed and grain business. He became a Mason, and married Myrta Bell, a physician's daughter.

His attempts at business having failed, Lewis decided to try a newly opened coal-mining area in central Illinois and in 1908 moved his family (including his parents, a sister, and five brothers) to a village called Panama. All the men in his family worked in the mines, and John Lewis pursued his career in the labor movement. He became an Illinois legislative agent for the UMW and used his position to get workers' compensation and mine safety laws enacted. By 1910 he was a salaried organizer for the American Federation of Labor (AFL; see WILLIAM GREEN) and spent the next six years organizing locals and getting acquainted with union leaders. On behalf of the AFL he worked for Woodrow Wilson in the 1912 campaign. In 1917 he was appointed the official statistician for the UMW and editor of its journal and began taking part in negotiations with coal mine proprietors.

In 1919 Lewis became acting president of the UMW—by then, with more than 400,000 members, the country's largest trade union—and led a national strike of coal miners. The strike ended when he steered events to a compromise, and the next year he was elected president of the UMW. He held that post for forty years.

The 1920s were years of general prosperity, but not for the coal industry. A surplus of coal meant unemployment for miners, and the UMW membership began to fall. Lewis negotiated an agreement with coal operators in 1924 that was designed to stabilize the industry and called for three no-strike years. The industry, however, took advantage of nonunion mining in the South, to the detriment of union membership in the North. Lewis found his power base receding.

With the New Deal in the 1930s, Lewis saw an opportunity to restore power, rebuild the UMW, and organize the industrial workers. President Franklin D. Roosevelt's economic advisers proposed national economic planning similar to what Lewis wanted for the coal industry. The National Industrial Recovery Act of 1933 protected the right of workers to organize, and Lewis proceeded to build up the UMW to more than 300,000 members and make numerous new contracts with coal mine operators, even in the South. In 1935 Lewis became a vice president of the AFL. His aim was to organize millions of workers in the big mass-production industries, but when other AFL leaders would not join, he formed the Committee for Industrial Organization (CIO) and took its members out of the federation. The CIO, renamed Congress of Industrial Organizations, succeeded in signing collective-bargaining contracts with General Motors and U.S. Steel, two powerful corporations that had been strongly

antiunion. Two years after its creation, the CIO had a far greater membership than the AFL.

Lewis had swung the UMW behind Roosevelt for his reelection in 1936, and his own position had profited from the alliance with the New Deal administration. Relations began to cool, however. An economic decline in 1937 and 1938 brought a rise in unemployment. CIO membership declined, and Lewis's call for greater concern for labor failed to move the government. A further blow was the CIO's defeat in the Little Steel strike of summer 1937 (see PHILIP MURRAY). With the threat of war in Europe, Roosevelt's interest turned from domestic problems to foreign affairs. Lewis opposed Roosevelt's interventionism and sided with the isolationists. In the 1940 election Lewis supported Wendell Willkie, on the Republican ticket, and promised to resign from the CIO presidency if Roosevelt won. In November 1940 Lewis stepped down. In 1942 he ordered the UMW to leave the CIO.

During World War II, Lewis led the UMW in several nationwide strikes against wartime wage restrictions that alienated the public but did gain advantages for the workers. After the war, further strikes brought condemnation from President Harry S Truman because they threatened the country's security. The government seized the mines, and Lewis was convicted of contempt. The strikes, again, won benefits for UMW members. Lewis took the UMW back into the AFL in 1946, then out again because the AFL members would not join in resisting the Taft-Hartley Act (see PHILIP MURRAY).

After 1950 Lewis emphasized harmonious relations with the mine operators and in so doing created a peaceful phase for a coal industry that was on the decline. He spoke for "cooperative capitalism," an approach reminiscent of the time of President Herbert Hoover—and Hoover, in his eighties, complimented him. Lewis quietly retired from the UMW presidency in 1960 and lived on to the age of eighty-nine. The legacy he left behind was mixed. On the one hand, he had been the indispensable leader during the greatest surge of union organizing in this country's history. On the other hand, he ran the UMW in an autocratic fashion, choosing to maintain his power at all costs. He so weakened democratic procedures within his union that he made it possible for crooked and ruthless leaders to take over the UMW after his death. This union is only now recovering some of the qualities that, in the early years of this century, made it one of the brightest stars in labor's firmament.

**BIBLIOGRAPHY**

Alinsky, Saul, *John L. Lewis,* 1949; Dubofsky, Melvin, and Warren Van Tine, *John L. Lewis: A Biography,* 1986, and *Labor Leaders in America,* 1987.

## Lewis, John Robert

(February 21, 1940–　)
Civil Rights Activist

In his early twenties, John Lewis became one of the most courageous leaders of the civil rights movement. As a believer in non-violent protest, he suffered many severe beatings and arrests during his activist years. He later moved on to a career in civic organizations and politics.

John R. Lewis, the third of ten children of Eddie and Willie Mae Lewis, was born near Troy, in southern Alabama. On the family-owned farm the crops were mainly cotton and peanuts, which yielded poor return, so Eddie Lewis also drove a school bus and his wife took in laundry. The children were bused eighteen miles to a one-room school. As a youngster, John wanted to be a minister, and when the children played church, he was always the preacher. In his teens he began preaching in rural churches, learning from the radio gospel broadcasts conducted by the Reverend MARTIN LUTHER KING, JR., in Montgomery.

Lewis alone in his family aspired to a college education and joined the civil rights movement. At age seventeen he went to the American Baptist Theological Seminary, a black institution in Nashville, Tennessee, earning his way as a janitor and kitchen worker. After a year, he asked King and the Reverend RALPH D. ABERNATHY to help him transfer to Troy State College, an all-white school, so that he could live at home while a student. Both ministers agreed to help and proposed bringing suit, but Lewis's parents, afraid of repercussions, would not sign the papers, and nothing came of the plan. Lewis went back to Nashville and attended Fisk University. (After dropping out for several years to take part in the civil rights movement, he earned a B.A. in philosophy from Fisk in 1967. He also earned a degree from the American Baptist Theological Seminary.)

John Lewis launched his civil rights career in 1959 while at Fisk, when his attempt to start a chapter of the National Association for the Advancement of Colored People (NAACP; see JOEL E. SPINGARN) was halted by the university authorities. He attended workshops on nonviolence conducted by the Reverend James M. Lawson, Jr., for the Fellowship of Reconciliation (see A. J. MUSTE), joined sit-ins at Nashville lunch counters, and was arrested several times. In 1960 he was one of the founders of the Student Nonviolent Coordinating Committee (SNCC; see ELLA BAKER), and the next year he was in the first party of Freedom Riders, organized by JAMES FARMER of the Congress of Racial Equality. Thirteen white and black volunteers left Washington on May 4 by Greyhound bus for points south, determined to integrate southern bus terminals. They were repeatedly met with violence. On a later Freedom Ride, Lewis was knocked unconscious by a white segregationist in Montgomery.

Notwithstanding, Lewis continued to make Freedom Rides that year and the next, consistently adhering to his creed of nonviolence.

In June 1963, Lewis was elected chairman of SNCC and, in order to give it his full time, dropped out of college. That August he was a leader of the famous March on Washington and planned a speech that would attack President John F. Kennedy's civil rights bill as inadequate and dated. Other leaders, including ROY WILKINS, the executive secretary of the NAACP, were alarmed at Lewis's aggressive tone and persuaded him to subdue his speech, but it was nevertheless the most radical given that day. The following year, Lewis organized antisegregation events in several southern towns and the "Mississippi Freedom Summer," a broad campaign to register black voters. In March 1965, Lewis was coleader of a march from Montgomery to Selma to protest the refusal of voting rights to most African Americans in the South. On the approach to Selma the marchers were set upon by troopers, and Lewis suffered a fractured skull.

While Lewis was moving away from strict nonviolence, he was still seen as moderate by the majority of SNCC members, and in April 1966 STOKELY CARMICHAEL defeated him for the chairmanship of SNCC. After leaving SNCC, Lewis continued his civil rights activity. He spent a year in New York as associate director of the Field Foundation, responsible for its programs supporting civil rights and child welfare, and after a year completing his degree at Fisk he joined the Southern Regional Council, sponsored by the Ford Foundation. Over the six years he was director of the council's Voter Education Project (VEP), nearly 4 million minority voters were added to the rolls.

In 1977 Lewis left VEP to run for the U.S. House of Representatives from Georgia's fifth district, which includes Atlanta, but lost to a liberal white candidate. That summer, President Jimmy Carter appointed him an officer of the federal volunteer agency, ACTION, which oversees antipoverty programs. He resigned in 1980 and returned to Atlanta as community affairs director of a consumer cooperative bank. For five years he served on the Atlanta City Council. In 1986 Lewis successfully ran for the fifth congressional district seat. He defeated JULIAN BOND in the primary, with the support of 80 percent of the white electorate—who, in the opinion of some observers, considered Lewis the less militant candidate. He has been reelected for two successive terms.

**BIBLIOGRAPHY**

Viorst, Milton, *Fire in the Streets: America in the 1960s*, 1979.

# Lewis, Oscar

(December 25, 1914–December 16, 1970)
Anthropologist

Oscar Lewis, in his highly readable books on family life in the slums of Mexico, Puerto Rico, New York City, and Cuba, threw a harsh light on the realities of poverty. He sought to establish his thesis that the culture of poverty is the same among people everywhere.

Lewis was born in New York City and grew up on a small farm in upstate New York. His father, Herman Lewis, was a Polish-born rabbi and cantor, who married Bertha Biblow. Lewis attended the City College of New York (CCNY), majoring in history but also studying philosophy with a great teacher, Morris Raphael Cohen. Like many young people at urban colleges in the 1930s, he was influenced by Marxist ideas. He graduated from CCNY in 1936 and entered Columbia University meaning to major in history, but he found the work not to his liking. He had married Ruth Maslow, whose brother, the psychologist Abraham H. Maslow, introduced him to RUTH BENEDICT, a Columbia professor of anthropology, and she persuaded Lewis to switch to her field of study.

Lewis and his wife went to the Canadian province of Alberta to do fieldwork at a reservation of the Blackfoot Indians, an Algonquian tribe. His dissertation, published as *The Effects of White Contact upon Blackfoot Culture,* earned Lewis his doctorate in 1940. After teaching at Brooklyn College and Washington University, in St. Louis, in 1948, he founded the department of anthropology at the University of Illinois, in Urbana, which he headed until the end of his life.

During the 1940s Lewis went to Mexico as a field representative for the United States National Indian Institute. Visiting the village of Tepoztlán, in central Mexico, he undertook research on its people starting from earlier anthropological studies. The result was *Life in a Mexican Village: Tepoztlán Restudied* (1951), considered a landmark in anthropological research on communities, which opened a new direction in independent revisionist studies. Lewis evolved a controversial theory of the subculture of poverty within the larger culture: the poor in different societies, he concluded, have more in common with one another than with other classes in their own society, and the rural poor are closer to the urban poor than either class is to its more affluent neighbors. Ways of life, he aimed to show, are passed down in poor families from generation to generation. In the 1960s his work profoundly influenced Democratic policymakers, who launched the War on Poverty as part of President Lyndon Johnson's Great Society reforms.

Lewis's method was to conduct extensive tape-recorded interviews in which his subjects spoke for themselves. These were transcribed, translated, and edited for the most part as first-person pseudonymous accounts with realistic dialogue, as readable as fiction. His books, which achieved notable popularity and sales, brought home the reality of poverty to countless readers, though some critics questioned whether they were representative of the cultures they depicted. As the Black Power movement gained force in the late 1960s, his theories fell into liberal disfavor.

From 1952 to 1954, while in India on a Ford Foundation appointment, Lewis produced a study of village life in northern India, but the focus of the greater part of his work was Latin America. *Five Families* (1959) presents five days in the lives of five families in a Mexico City slum. He centered on one of the families in *The Children of Sánchez* (1961), about a widower and his four children, and on another in *Pedro Martínez: A Mexican Peasant and His Family* (1964). In 1966 Lewis published his best-known work, *La Vida: A Puerto Rican Family in the Culture of Poverty—San Juan and New York,* which received the National Book Award.

Lewis was working on a study of life in Cuba after the Castro revolution when he died of a heart attack while visiting New York. His research, which convinced him that the Cuban poor were better off after the revolution, challenged his thesis that the culture of poverty was universal. His data were used by his widow, Ruth Maslow Lewis, and Susan Rigdon in *Living the Revolution: An Oral History of Contemporary Cuba* (1977), presenting the lives of eight Cubans.

**BIBLIOGRAPHY**

Lewis, Oscar, *Anthropological Essays,* 1970; Rigdon, Susan, *The Culture Façade: Art, Science, and Politics in the Work of Oscar Lewis,* 1988.

# Lindbergh, Charles Augustus, Jr.

(February 4, 1902–August 26, 1974)
Aviator, Conservationist, Isolationist

Culver Pictures

Charles Lindbergh's solo nonstop flight from New York to Paris in 1927 made him an American hero. In later years, his isolationist stand regarding American entry into World War II and his belief in "Nordic supremacy" set him apart from many of his fellow citizens.

Charles A. Lindbergh, Jr., was born in Detroit, Michigan, an only son. His Swedish-born father, who grew up in Minnesota, was a lawyer and, from 1907 to 1917, a congressman of Progressive Republican politics who attacked the big industrial trusts, sponsored various reforms, and denounced propaganda and profiteering during World War I. Charles, Jr., was brought up in Little Falls, Minnesota, mainly by his mother, Evangeline Land, a schoolteacher. His parents were often separated.

After finishing high school in 1918, Lindbergh spent two years working on a farm, then studied civil engineering at the University of Wisconsin. During his sophomore year he left to take a flying course at a school in Lincoln, Nebraska, and made his first solo flight in 1923 in a war-surplus training plane. He enrolled as a cadet in the Air Service Reserve (renamed the Air Corps Reserve in 1926) at an airfield in San Antonio, Texas, and upon graduating first in his class in 1925, was commissioned a second lieutenant. For a time Lindbergh flew mail between Chicago and St. Louis.

In 1927 Lindbergh resolved he would win the $25,000 Orteig Prize for the first nonstop New York–Paris flight. A group of St. Louis businessmen financed Lindbergh's work designing a single-engine monoplane, which he christened *The Spirit of St. Louis*. In early May 1927, he flew from California to New York in twenty-one hours and twenty minutes, setting a coast-to-coast speed record. On the morning of May 20 Lindbergh took off from Roosevelt Field, near New York City, and crossed the Atlantic to Paris, some 3,600 miles, in thirty-three and a half hours. The French gave Lindbergh a wildly enthusiastic welcome, and President Calvin Coolidge sent a U.S. Navy cruiser to bring him home. He received the Distinguished Flying Cross and was made a colonel in the air reserve. After touring the country to promote interest in aviation, he made several long test flights. In Mexico, he met Anne Morrow, the daughter of the U.S. ambassador, Dwight W. Morrow, and married her in 1929.

Anne Lindbergh became a pilot and radio operator and shared her husband's career in aviation. The Lindberghs set a new transcontinental air record in 1930 and made an official goodwill tour of the Orient. As technical adviser to several commercial airlines, Charles Lindbergh laid out many of the air routes across the Pacific and to South America.

In March 1932, the Lindberghs' infant son was kidnapped and murdered. The incessant publicity surrounding the tragedy and the trial of Bruno Hauptmann for the crime caused Charles and Anne Lindbergh to leave the United States in 1935 and move to England. (In

1932 Congress had enacted the so-called Lindbergh Act, making interstate kidnapping a federal crime.)

During the years abroad, Lindbergh worked with the surgeon Dr. Alexis Carrel on the development of a "mechanical heart," and also worked with the rocket expert Robert Goddard. During visits to Nazi Germany to observe and report on German air power for the American military, Lindbergh formed the opinion that the German air force was invincible and accepted a decoration from the Nazi government. Returning to the United States in 1939, he became associated with the America First Committee, which opposed entering World War II, and claimed in his speeches that the prowar advocates were influenced by the Jewish "race." He called his position "the wave of the future," a phrase used as the title of a book by his wife advocating isolationism, a policy of avoiding alliances or commitments to other nations. After President Franklin D. Roosevelt criticized him for his statements, Lindbergh resigned his commission in the Air Corps Reserve.

When the United States entered the war, Lindbergh worked as a technical adviser to HENRY FORD and other builders of military aircraft, and as a civilian he tested P-38 fighter planes, extending their range by 500 miles, and flew some fifty combat missions. As a journalist remarked, "Lindbergh's genius lay in aviation, not politics." In 1954 President Dwight D. Eisenhower appointed him brigadier general in the Air Force Reserve. In his last years he was an effective promoter of nature conservation. He made his home on the Hawaiian island of Maui, and in 1974 he died of cancer and was buried there. He was survived by his wife, three sons, and two daughters.

**BIBLIOGRAPHY**

Lindbergh, Charles A., *We*, 1927, and *The Spirit of St. Louis*, 1953; Ross, Walter S., *The Last Hero: Charles A. Lindbergh*, 1964.

# Lindsey, Benjamin Barr

(November 25, 1869–March 26, 1943)
Judge, Reformer

Judge Benjamin Lindsey played a major role in establishing the juvenile court system in the United States.

Born in Jackson, Tennessee, Ben B. Lindsey moved with his family to Denver, Colorado, when he was eleven. He attended preparatory schools in Indiana and Tennessee, returning to Denver when he was sixteen. Ill and in debt, his father committed suicide, leaving Ben and a younger brother in charge of the family. Unable to finish school, Ben did odd jobs. Finally he began to read law, and in 1894 was admitted to the bar. Appointed public guardian and administrator of orphaned children in 1899, Lindsey heard a case that influenced the rest of his life.

A boy had been caught stealing coal. Lindsey at first sentenced the boy to reform school, but upon learning that the boy's father was dying and that the family had no money, he arranged for the boy to be put on informal probation, even though there was no legal basis for such action. At this time in Colorado, there was no separate system of juvenile justice; by the age of fourteen, juvenile offenders were tried in adult courts and treated the same as adult criminals.

Lindsey's concern with juvenile justice led him to draft and secure legislation creating a juvenile court in Denver. (The first juvenile court in the country had been established in

Illinois in 1899.) In 1900 Lindsey was appointed a justice on the new juvenile court and served in this capacity for the next twenty-seven years. Lindsey's work on the court soon attracted wide attention. He held informal Saturday morning meetings with boys on probation, in which he spoke to them in their own language, reinforcing positive behavior and helping build the boys' self-esteem. He also allowed boys sentenced to reform school to report there without an escort, and in all the years this honor system was in operation, Lindsey lost only five boys.

Believing that many juveniles committed crimes because they were influenced by the actions of adults, Lindsey drafted and successfully lobbied for the passage of the Colorado Adult Delinquency Act of 1903, which made it a crime to contribute to the delinquency of a minor. By 1920 forty states and the District of Columbia had passed similar laws, often because of personal appeals by Lindsey to legislative committees.

Lindsey won national prominence as a progressive reformer through a series of articles published in *Everybody's Magazine* in 1909 as *The Beast and the Jungle* and later in book form as *The Beast.* According to Lindsey, the beast was the capitalist system which enabled the few to enrich themselves at the expense of the many, whose poverty was one of the main causes of juvenile delinquency. The articles led to many invitations to lecture and to friendships with such leading progressives as UPTON SINCLAIR, LINCOLN STEFFENS, and Theodore Roosevelt.

In the 1920s Lindsey gained notoriety as a proponent of the sexual revolution with the publication of two books: *The Revolt of Modern Youth* (1925) and *The Companionate Marriage* (1927). In the first he made the case for sexual education, including information about birth control; in the second, for a form of marriage that could be more easily dissolved, provided there were no children involved.

Coming under attack by the Ku Klux Klan in Denver, Lindsey lost his position on the court in 1927 and was even disbarred on a trumped-up charge. He was reinstated in 1935, but by that time he had already moved to California, where he helped set up a Children's Court of Conciliation, which sought to save failed marriages and thereby keep families together. Lindsey presided over the Los Angeles division of this court until his death at the age of seventy-three.

**BIBLIOGRAPHY**

Goldman, Eric, *Rendezvous with Destiny,* 1953; Larsen, Charles E., *The Good Fight: The Life and Times of Ben B. Lindsey,* 1972; Levine, M., and A. Levine, *A Social History of the Helping Services,* 1970.

# Lippmann, Walter

(September 23, 1889–December 14, 1974)
Journalist, Political Analyst

Walter Lippmann was a profound political thinker and an astute commentator on national and international events, who influenced presidents for nearly sixty years. In his championing of liberal democracy—an open society governed by law—he set a standard and established a tradition in American journalism.

Lippmann's father was a well-to-do New York clothing manufacturer, Jacob Lippmann, whose father, Louis, had emigrated from Germany at the time of the 1848 revolution. His mother, Daisy Baum, came from a similar background. An only child, Walter Lippmann grew up in quiet comfort; he read widely and was taken to Europe almost every summer. In 1906 he entered Harvard University, where he got his B.A. cum laude in three years.

Lippmann stayed on in Cambridge for another year, working as assistant to the philosopher George Santayana. Having become interested in socialism, he wrote on social reform for student publications, served as president of the Harvard Socialist Club, reported for the left-wing weekly *Boston Common,* and became a "leg man" for the muckraker LINCOLN STEFFENS. When Steffens assigned him to prepare an article for *Everybody's Magazine,* Lippmann took as his subject the professor who had most influenced him, WILLIAM JAMES. Steffens gave the byline to young Lippmann, bringing him national attention and a place on the staff. For a few months he worked as an assistant to the socialist mayor of Schenectady.

In 1913 Lippmann published his first book, *A Preface to Politics,* which while partial to socialism was the beginning of a move away from it. The book caught the attention of HERBERT CROLY, who enlisted Lippmann to join him in founding the *New Republic,* a liberal weekly, which supported President Woodrow Wilson's policies. Getting to know the Washington, D.C., scene, Lippmann took leave of the journal in 1917 to serve as an assistant to Newton D. Baker, secretary of war, and moved shortly to a post under Wilson's adviser, Edward M. House, on a committee charged with drafting data for the president's use at the eventual peace conference. In 1918 he was commissioned an army captain and sent to France to work in military intelligence. With the armistice, he rejoined House in Paris and helped

Library of Congress

formulate Wilson's Fourteen Points for the Versailles peace conference.

Lippmann returned to the *New Republic* in 1919 but left soon after to write *Public Opinion* (1922), in which he dealt with the difficulties of informing the public about the complexities of contemporary society. That book helped to establish Lippmann's position as a leading American political thinker of his time. In 1921 he joined the staff of the New York *World,* the most liberal of the city's papers, and in 1923 became editor. During his years on the *World,* Lippmann wrote some 2,000 of his clear-sighted editorials. Though a religious skeptic, in his book *A Preface to Morals* (1929) he observed that the absence of religious faith made for a serious emptiness in society.

In 1931, after the *World* closed down, Lippmann went to the conservative New York *Herald Tribune* to write—with full freedom—his column "Today and Tomorrow," which appeared several times a week and was eventually syndicated in more than 200 papers with nearly 40 million readers. (Lippmann's impact was less on the general reader than on presidents and other statesmen, scholars, and intellectuals.) After President Franklin D. Roosevelt took office in 1933, Lippmann was favorable toward the New Deal, but he became hostile to what he considered collectivism, and in 1936 he supported the Republican candidate, Alfred M. Landon. After observing Roosevelt's conduct of foreign policy during the early years of World War II, Lippmann decided he was one of the greatest presidents. In 1943 he published another influential book, *U.S. Foreign Policy: Shield of the Republic,* in which he urged an internationalist policy after the war. As relations with the Soviet Union became troubled, Lippmann spoke for diplomacy and political settlement. His "Today and Tomorrow" columns stating his position were published in book form as *The Cold War* (1947).

Lippmann left the moribund *Herald Tribune* in 1962 to write "Today and Tomorrow" for the *Washington Post*, in addition to occasional articles for *Newsweek*, which the *Post* owned. He continued to focus on foreign policy and, in the main, supported President John F. Kennedy's policies. The Vietnam War he regarded as a catastrophe that could have been avoided. During the sixties Lippmann continued to press for a Soviet-American understanding and realistic dealings with Communist China. He gave up newspaper work in 1967, though he contributed now and then to *Newsweek* until 1971.

A few years before his death Lippmann told an interviewer, "The supreme question before mankind—to which I shall not live to know the answer—is how men will be able to make themselves willing and able to save themselves."

**BIBLIOGRAPHY**

Blum, John Morton (ed.), *Selected Letters of Public Philosopher Walter Lippmann*, 1985; Harrison, Gilbert (ed.), *Early Writings*, 1970, and *Public Persons*, 1976; Rossiter, Clinton, and James Lare (eds.), *The Essential Lippmann*, 1963; Steel, Ronald, *Walter Lippmann and the American Century*, 1980.

## Livermore, Mary Ashton Rice

(December 19, 1820–May 23, 1905)
Reformer, Suffragist

Mary Livermore made an important contribution as an organizer of medical relief services for the Union army during the Civil War. A popular lecturer, she also gave her support to the woman suffrage and temperance movements.

Born in Boston, Mary Ashton Rice was educated at a local female seminary; she then taught for several years before marrying Daniel Parker Livermore, a Universalist minister, in 1845. The Livermores settled in Chicago, where he became pastor of the Second Universalist Church. In addition to raising their family, Mary Livermore helped her husband edit *The New Covenant*, a Universalist monthly; engaged in charity work; and took part in the antislavery movement. On his part, her husband would accommodate his life to her work.

With the outbreak of the Civil War, Mary Livermore volunteered her services to the Chicago (later Northwestern) Sanitary Commission, an organization formed to help the army medical department in getting medical supplies to battlefield hospitals. Livermore, along with Jane C. Hoge, assumed full charge of the Chicago office, speaking and raising money all over the Midwest and later visiting Union hospitals.

Her wartime experiences convinced Livermore that women needed political power if they were to bring about reform. She became a supporter of woman suffrage, helping to found and serving as the first president of the Illinois Woman Suffrage Association in 1868. A year later, Livermore established her own suffrage paper, *The Agitator*, and helped found a national organization, the American Woman Suffrage Association, of which she was later president.

Late in 1869 Livermore accepted an offer from LUCY STONE and other suffrage leaders to edit the *Woman's Journal*. She and her family moved to the Boston suburb of Melrose for this purpose. In 1870 Livermore helped to found the Massachusetts Woman Suffrage Association and went on to be active in many feminist and suffrage organizations.

Having gained valuable experience as a public speaker during the war, Livermore decided to embark on a career as a professional lecturer, under the management of James Redpath, a lecture promoter whose speakers included many celebrities. She made her first speaking tour in 1870, and two years later resigned from the editorship of the *Woman's Journal* to lecture full-time across the country. For many years Livermore spoke on a great range of topics, including improved education for women.

Livermore also became interested in temperance work, speaking often for the national Woman's Christian Temperance Union (WCTU) and founding the Massachusetts WCTU.

Livermore remained on the lecture circuit until 1895 when she was in her mid-seventies. During the last decade of her life, she continued to make occasional speeches for both suffrage and temperance and worked for local philanthropies.

**BIBLIOGRAPHY**

Hersh, B. G., *The Slavery of Sex: Feminist-Abolitionists in America*, 1978; Livermore, Mary, *My Story of the War*, 1888, and *The Story of My Life*, 1897.

# Lloyd, Henry Demarest

(May 1, 1847–September 28, 1903)
Journalist, Reformer

One of the early muckrakers, crusading journalist and author Henry Demarest Lloyd exerted a major influence on reform in the late nineteenth and early twentieth centuries with his attacks on monopolies and his call for a democratic and capitalistic system aimed at promoting social justice and the general welfare.

Born in New York City, Henry Demarest Lloyd earned his B.A. from Columbia College in 1867 and a law degree from Columbia Law School in 1869. He was admitted to the New York bar, but instead of going into practice, he took part in reform activities. He helped defeat the New York Democratic machine, Tammany Hall, in the elections of 1871. He also worked, unsuccessfully, to prevent the nomination of the protectionist editor of the New York *Tribune*, HORACE GREELEY, at the Liberal Republican convention of 1872.

Disillusioned with politics, Lloyd became an editor on the *Chicago Tribune*, where he began to attack monopolies and cover social issues. In 1881 WILLIAM DEAN HOWELLS published in *The Atlantic Monthly* Lloyd's article called "The Story of a Great Monopoly." The article was an indictment of the methods by which the Standard Oil Company got the railroads to charge it lower freight rates as a means of forcing competitors out of business. "The Story of a Great Monopoly" attracted wide attention.

In 1885 Lloyd left the *Tribune*. After the Haymarket riot of 1886 (see JOHN PETER ALTGELD) in which seven Chicago policemen were killed by a bomb, Lloyd joined with labor lawyer CLARENCE DARROW and a few others in taking up the cause of the anarchist labor leaders convicted of instigating the crime. He and his associates were able to get two of the death sentences commuted. In 1890 Lloyd's investigation of the Spring Valley, Illinois, coal miners' strike led to his first major book, *A Strike of Millionaires Against Miners*, a powerful appeal for social justice. In 1893 Lloyd served as an unofficial organizer for the Milwaukee streetcar workers. A year later, he again joined forces with Clarence Darrow to defend union organizer EUGENE V. DEBS for his role in the Pullman strike of 1894.

Also in 1894, Lloyd published *Wealth Against Commonwealth,* a thoroughly researched attack on Standard Oil and other monopolies. He advocated government regulation of industry and public ownership of all monopolies. Yet though his book reached a broad audience, it did not bring about the reforms Lloyd had hoped for.

Turning to political action, Lloyd ran for Congress as a Populist in 1894 and was defeated. When the Populists fused with the Democrats in the election of 1896, Lloyd's political orientation shifted leftward. Although he did not join the Socialist party until several years later, he supported the party as the only one with a program aimed at ending monopolies and freeing the working class from its oppression.

From 1897 to 1901 Lloyd traveled abroad, studying labor and social movements in various countries. As a result, he wrote *Labour Co-partnership* (1898), about producers cooperatives in England, and *A Country Without Strikes* (1900), about compulsory arbitration of industrial disputes in New Zealand. But Lloyd was unable to get the pragmatic American Federation of Labor (see WILLIAM GREEN and JOHN L. LEWIS) to adopt such idealistic practices.

In 1902 Lloyd supported the Pennsylvania miners during the long anthracite coal strike. When the mine owners finally agreed to arbitrate, Lloyd teamed up with Clarence Darrow and John Mitchell, president of the United Mine Workers, in presenting the miners' case. Barely finished with these intense negotiations, Lloyd began working for city ownership of Chicago's street railways. In the midst of this campaign he died in Chicago at the age of fifty-six.

Two of Lloyd's books were published posthumously. *A Sovereign People* (1907) was his examination of democracy in Switzerland, while *Man, the Social Creator* (1906) advanced the social welfare philosophy that was to influence the progressive policies of President Theodore Roosevelt and later the New Deal of Franklin Roosevelt.

**BIBLIOGRAPHY**

Destler, Chester M., *Henry Demarest Lloyd and the Empire of Reform,* 1963; Lloyd, C., *Henry Demarest Lloyd, 1847–1903,* 2 vols., 1912.

## Lovejoy, Elijah Parish

(November 9, 1802–November 7, 1837)
Abolitionist, Journalist

Killed while defending his press against an angry mob, antislavery editor Elijah Lovejoy became famous as the first martyr of the abolition movement.

Elijah Lovejoy was born in Albion, Maine, into a long-established and deeply religious family. He was educated at Waterville (now Colby College) in Maine, and taught school and edited a Whig political paper before attending the Princeton Theological Seminary. Licensed to preach in 1833, Lovejoy moved to St. Louis, where he preached and served as the editor of a Presbyterian weekly journal, *The St. Louis Observer.*

In the paper's pages, Lovejoy attacked both the Catholic church and slavery. Lovejoy advocated gradual emancipation, but even this position antagonized the citizens of St. Louis, in the slave state of Missouri. Faced with mounting threats and refusing to moderate his views, Lovejoy in 1836 decided to move his press to Alton, Illinois.

No sooner had Lovejoy moved to Alton than his press was thrown into the river. When a public meeting pledged money for a new press, a grateful Lovejoy promised not to write about slavery in his paper—a promise he soon broke in order to set forth his increasingly radical views. He now began to call for immediate emancipation, and on July 4, 1837, when he called for an American Anti-Slavery Society state auxiliary, the citizens of Alton decided he had gone too far. Angry mobs twice threw his presses into the river, only to have them replaced by the Ohio Anti-Slavery Society.

In an atmosphere of growing tension, Lovejoy and his opponents awaited the arrival of his fourth press. Though begged to leave by prominent local citizens, Lovejoy held his ground, declaring that he was ready for martyrdom. When the press arrived on November 7, 1837, it was placed in a guarded warehouse. Nevertheless, an armed mob stormed the warehouse, and Lovejoy was shot and killed in the melee.

Lovejoy's death sparked antislavery sentiment throughout the North and brought new converts to the abolitionist movement, most notably WENDELL PHILLIPS. Hailed as the "abolitionist martyr," Lovejoy has also been viewed as a martyr to the cause of free speech, because he died defending his right to publish his views, however unpopular.

**BIBLIOGRAPHY**

Dillon, Merton L., *Elijah P. Lovejoy, Abolitionist Editor*, 1961; Simon, P., *Lovejoy, Martyr to Freedom*, 1964.

## Lowell, Josephine Shaw

(December 16, 1843–October 12, 1905)
Reformer

Josephine Shaw Lowell exerted a major influence on the charitable movement of late-nineteenth-century America by emphasizing the need to formulate principles and to manage public philanthropy in an efficient and professional manner.

Josephine Shaw was born in West Roxbury, Massachusetts, into an affluent, public-spirited family. She received her formal education abroad and in schools in Boston and New York City, where the family moved. She also benefited from contact with such important literary and political figures as James Russell Lowell, LYDIA MARIA CHILD, and MARGARET FULLER, who visited the family home. Her first involvement with charitable work occurred during the Civil War when she joined the Woman's Central Association of Relief, an auxiliary of the U.S. Sanitary Commission. After losing both her brother, Robert Gould Shaw, who commanded the first black regiment, and her husband of a year, Colonel Charles Russell Lowell, to the war, she raised money for the National Freedmen's Relief Association, and in 1866 inspected schools for African Americans in Virginia.

In the 1870s Lowell joined the New York Charities Aid Association, which had been founded by other women veterans of wartime relief work for the purpose of inspecting state charitable institutions, including hospitals, orphanages, and jails. In her reports, Lowell expressed her outrage at the miserable conditions under which inmates lived and the lack of any effort at rehabilitation. In 1876 Governor Samuel J. Tilden appointed her to be the first woman member of the New York State Board of Charities, a position she held for thirteen years.

Lowell's reports also exposed political corruption and led directly to several important reforms. These included the establishment of the Women's House of Refuge (later the State Training School for Girls) in Hudson, New York, and an asylum for mentally ill women in Newark, New York. She also helped bring about passage of a law placing matrons in police stations in 1888.

Combining theory with practical work, Lowell set forth her ideas in *Public Relief and Private Charity* (1884) and other articles. She believed in turning recipients of charity into productive members of society and limiting community support to those whom it could completely rehabilitate and reform.

These theories were, nevertheless, tempered by Lowell's contention that poor wages, more than unemployment, were responsible for poverty and its accompanying problems for families. When a Tammany-backed governor was elected in New York in 1889, hindering the possibility for further reforms, Lowell turned her attention to the problems of workers. In 1890 she founded the Consumers' League of New York, an organization which sought to improve conditions in the workplace by putting consumer pressure on employers. Lowell served as president of the Consumers' League until 1896. She also supported the efforts of labor unions, emphasizing their positive aspects in her 1893 compilation, *Industrial Arbitration and Conciliation.*

Lowell's growing conviction that reform could only be achieved by political action led her in 1894 to found the Woman's Municipal League, one of the many organizations formed during the Progressive era in the last decade of the nineteenth century and the first two decades of the twentieth century. In 1895 Lowell also founded the women's auxiliary of the Civil Service Reform Association of New York State, serving for many years as its executive committee chair. A leader of the anti-imperialist movement during the Spanish-American War, Lowell helped bring many prominent speakers to rallies in New York.

For thirty years Lowell's home in New York City was a gathering place for philanthropists, reformers, and social workers. She helped attract many talented people to the field of social work, while making the general public more aware of both the problems and potential benefits of charitable efforts.

**BIBLIOGRAPHY**

Stewart, William Rhinelander, *The Philanthropic Work of Josephine Shaw Lowell,* 1911; Taylor, Lloyd C., "Josephine Shaw Lowell and American Philanthropy," *New York History,* October 1963.

# Luce, Henry Robinson

(April 3, 1898–February 28, 1967)
Editor, Publisher

Henry R. Luce was probably the nation's most influential magazine publisher during the first half of the twentieth century. He introduced and perfected the first weekly newsmagazine, *Time,* and the first magazine devoted to photojournalism, *Life.*

Luce, eldest of four children of a Presbyterian missionary, Henry Winters Luce, and a YWCA (Young Women's Christian Association) worker, Elizabeth Middleton Root, was born in Dengzhou (now Penglai), on the coast of the Shandong promontory in northeast China. Aside from fifteen months in America when the Reverend Luce had a furlough in 1906 and 1907, the boy grew up in China. As a student at a British school, however, he had little familiarity with the Chinese people. In 1912 young Luce traveled alone to England for a year at an English school, where he was treated for his stammer. He then entered the Hotchkiss School, in Lakeville, Connecticut, helped by a wealthy family friend, Mrs. Cyrus H. McCormick, of Chicago. At Hotchkiss he felt an outsider among boys from families of means, but he found a friend in Briton Hadden, and they both entered Yale University in 1916 and worked on the *Yale Daily News*. After a summer in an army training camp, Luce finished his A.B. at Yale in 1920 and, thanks to Mrs. McCormick, spent a year at Oxford.

Library of Congress

Luce and Hadden, while reporters on the *Baltimore News*, began to plan a new kind of weekly magazine, to be called *Time*, which would give the most important news in a concise and interesting style, covering both sides analytically while telling the reader which side *Time* considered had the better case. The venture's stock was bought by a number of wealthy friends, though Luce and Hadden retained financial control. The first issue, with Hadden as editor and Luce as business manager, was dated March 3, 1923.

By 1930 *Time* had a circulation of 300,000. It favored a progressive sort of Republicanism, and early on it had adopted the style that came to be called Timese, using distinctive language, sometimes reversing sentence order, and introducing novel words and unusual items of information. Objective reporting was not required of *Time*'s writers, who originally were anonymous.

The publishers, incorporated as Time Inc., bought the *Saturday Review of Literature* and started an advertising trade journal, *Tide*, both of which were later sold. After Hadden died of septicemia in February 1929, Luce assumed control of the editorial and business sides of the firm. He brought in as managing editor Hadden's cousin John S. Martin, who carried on Hadden's policies and stylistic color. Luce founded still another magazine in 1930, *Fortune*, a monthly focusing on business, notable for its staff of well-known writers, its comprehensive articles, and its high price.

During the 1930s Luce entered the newsreel and radio world with *The March of Time*, presenting the salient events of the week in *Time* style. That events were sometimes dramatized by actors drew criticism from some journalistic purists. In any event, neither the radio program nor the newsreel survived beyond the late 1940s.

In November 1935, having divorced his first wife, Luce married Clare Boothe, an editor and later a well-known playwright. While she had no appointive position, she undoubtedly influenced her husband's publications and is said to have inspired his creation of *Life* magazine a year later.

Certainly it was Luce's interest in the image and his awareness of the technical advances in photography and printing that led him to plan another pioneer periodical, whose title he bought from a long-lived humor magazine. In November 1936 the first issue of *Life* appeared. Its editorial method, using pictures as *Time* used words, was an instantaneous success. In a month circulation passed a half million and a year later approached 2 million. *Life* became the principal vehicle for Luce's editorial statements as he began to concern himself with public issues.

Though Luce had been impressed by "strong men" like Benito Mussolini and Francisco

Franco—though not Franklin D. Roosevelt, whose hostility to big business made him uneasy—he saw Adolf Hitler as a serious danger to the United States and Europe and supported aid to Great Britain and intervention in World War II. In China, which he and his wife visited in 1941, he saw General Chiang Kai-shek as a paragon of leaders, despite the military gains of the Chinese communist forces. After the success of the revolution, he opposed recognition of the government of Mao Tse-tung and, through his editorial pronouncements and connections, may have influenced American policy for decades.

In the 1940 presidential election, Luce favored Wendell Willkie's candidacy as the most reliably interventionist possibility among Republican hopefuls. He and Clare Boothe Luce had a hand in Willkie's campaign speeches, and the Time Inc. publications were at the service of the campaign. Willkie's defeat, it is said, ended Luce's hope of becoming secretary of state. Once the United States entered World War II, Luce fell in with Roosevelt's leadership. In early 1941, Luce published an editorial essay in *Life* entitled "The American Century," claiming that the United States would now take Great Britain's place as the leader among nations. It provoked much controversy. Soviet leader Norman Thomas attacked Luce's "nakedness of imperial ambition," though DOROTHY THOMPSON found merit in it.

Even during the war Luce began to see the Soviet Union as an eventual impediment to America's leadership. He was pleased with President Harry S. Truman's postwar challenges to Moscow, though his hope of encouraging military aid to Chiang Kai-shek came to nothing. *Life* and *Time* supported Dwight D. Eisenhower's campaign with enthusiastic coverage, though Luce found his foreign policy as president too moderate.

Luce was obsessed with competition to best the Soviet Union in space exploration. When Eisenhower appointed Clare Boothe Luce ambassador to Italy, Henry Luce spent most of the years 1953 to 1957 with her in Rome, commuting as necessary to New York. He pressed President John F. Kennedy to take a more forceful stand toward Communist Cuba, and he urged aggressive involvement in Vietnam. While the international views Luce voiced in his publications encountered ongoing criticism from liberals, they were probably approved by most of his upper-middle-class readers.

After he became Editorial Chairman of Time Inc., in 1964, Luce and his wife lived mostly at a winter home in Phoenix, Arizona. During the remaining three years of his life they continued to travel, and Luce took up the study of religion and supported a movement to achieve world peace through law.

**BIBLIOGRAPHY**

Baughman, James L., *Minister of Information*, 1987; Elson, Robert T., *Time Inc., 1923–1941*, 1968, and *The World of Time Inc., 1941–1960*, 1973; Kobler, John, *Luce: His Time, Life, and Fortune*, 1968; Prendergast, C. D., *The World of Time Inc., 1960–1980*, 1986; Swanberg, W. A., *Luce and His Empire*, 1972.

# Lundy, Benjamin

(January 4, 1789–August 22, 1839)
Abolitionist

A pioneer in the establishment of anti-slavery newspapers and societies, Benjamin Lundy served as an inspiration to later abolitionists, notably WILLIAM LLOYD GARRISON.

Born in Hardwick, New Jersey, Benjamin Lundy was raised on a farm by Quaker parents. Having received little formal education, he was apprenticed to a saddlemaker in Wheeling, Virginia (now West Virginia), where he was introduced to the slave system and became convinced of its evil. After moving to St. Clairsville, Ohio, Lundy in 1816 started an antislavery society, the Union Humane Society, as the first step in what he hoped would become a national organization. He also began to contribute to an antislavery newspaper, *The Philanthropist.*

After living two years in St. Louis, Missouri, during which he organized antislavery societies and lectured and wrote articles on the subject, Lundy moved to Mount Pleasant, Ohio, where *The Philanthropist* was published. In 1821 he began publishing his own antislavery paper, *The Genius of Universal Emancipation,* which would concentrate on the abolitionist cause and exclude other reforms. The following year, he moved the paper to Greenville, Tennessee. His aim was to foster antislavery sentiment in the South and thus destroy the institution from within. Circulating in more than twenty-one states and territories, Lundy's paper helped keep the abolitionist movement going throughout the 1820s. In 1824, after a trip to the East to attend an antislavery convention in Philadelphia, Lundy again moved his paper—this time to Baltimore, Maryland, in order to be closer to centers of political power and financial support. He founded the Maryland Anti-Slavery Society, which, in an effort to end slavery by political means, unsuccessfully ran candidates for the state legislature in 1825 and 1826. Lundy, meanwhile, continued his print attacks on slavery and the slave trade and worked to form new antislavery groups in the United States and Canada.

Getting no support for the idea of settling freed slaves on land in the Deep South, Lundy became interested in the colonization of freed slaves abroad. In an attempt to find an appropriate site for such colonies, he made trips to Haiti (1825, 1829), to the Wilberforce colonization project in Canada (1832), and to Texas (1830–1831, 1833–1834, and 1834–1835), before Texas became a part of the United States.

On a lecture tour of the Northeast in 1828, Lundy met William Lloyd Garrison, a young journalist who had been converted to the cause of abolition by reading Lundy's paper. Lundy convinced Garrison to move to Baltimore the following year as an associate editor of the *Genius.* However, the two men soon differed on the issue of when slavery should be ended. While Lundy favored gradual emancipation, Garrison called for immediate and total freedom. Garrison's outspokenness on the subject involved the paper in a number of libel suits, and in 1830 the partnership came to an end. Facing growing hostility in Baltimore, Lundy moved the paper to Washington, D.C., and then to Philadelphia. Over the next several years, publication became increasingly irregular because of Lundy's travels and poor financial condition. By the end of 1835 Lundy closed the paper.

In 1836 Lundy's concern over the situation in Texas led him to start another paper, *The National Enquirer and Constitutional Advocate of Universal Liberty,* in which he attacked the proposed annexation of Texas as a plot on the part of slaveowners to gain more power. That same year, Lundy published his pamphlet called *The War in Texas,* setting forth vigorous arguments against annexation. He gave former president and congressman

John Quincy Adams material for his antislavery speeches, which had the effect of consolidating public opinion in the North against the division of Texas into several slaveowning states, as some southern leaders had hoped.

In 1838 failing health made it necessary for Lundy to sell the *National Enquirer;* the buyer was poet and abolitionist John Greenleaf Whittier. Lundy moved to Illinois and published *The Genius* until his death from a fever at the age of fifty.

**BIBLIOGRAPHY**

Dillon, Merton L., *Benjamin Lundy and the Struggle for Negro Freedom*, 1966; Dummond, D. L., *Antislavery: The Crusade for Freedom in America*, 1961; Landon, F. (ed.), *The Diary of Benjamin Lundy*, 1921.

## Lynd, Helen Merrell

(March 17, 1896–January 30, 1982)
Educator, Sociologist

## Lynd, Robert Staughton

(September 26, 1892–November 1, 1970)
Educator, Sociologist

## Lynd, Staughton Craig

(November 22, 1929–   )
Civil Rights Activist, Historian, Lawyer

Robert and Helen Lynd, in their groundbreaking work *Middletown*, produced a classic sociological study of Middle America. Their son Staughton has been a leader on the civil rights and antiwar fronts and a defender of the legal rights of workers.

Robert S. Lynd, born in New Albany, Indiana, grew up across the Ohio River in Louisville, Kentucky. His father, Staughton Lynd, was a banker; his mother was Cornelia Day. He graduated from Princeton University in 1914, having been the first in his family to have a college education. After working in New York publishing for four years, he served in World War I, sustaining wounds. While convalescing in an army hospital his social conscience was awakened by a book by the English economist John A. Hobson, maintaining that economic theory is tied up with social welfare and should influence social reform.

Lynd returned to New York and worked for Charles Scribner's Sons (publishers) and for a magazine, *The Freeman*. In September 1922, having married Helen Merrell, he left publishing and entered Union Theological Seminary, which granted him a D.D. in 1923.

Helen Merrell was born in La Grange, a suburb of Chicago, and grew up in Framingham, Massachusetts. She graduated from Wellesley College as a Phi Beta Kappa in 1919 and then taught at a girls' school in New York City, where she met Robert Lynd.

The Lynds went to a village in the oil country of eastern Montana, Wolf Basin, where Robert Lynd was a missionary preacher. The poverty and exploitation of the oil workers made a deep impression, and Lynd's interest in his congregation became more sociological than religious. Returning east, he became involved with the Institute for Social and Religious Research, a

Rockefeller-sponsored organization, and directed "Small City" studies. Articles he published about his ministry in Wolf Basin, though critical of the plight of the oil workers and of the Rockefeller interests, stimulated the institute to commission the Lynds to undertake a study of religion in the social context of a typical American town. Their choice was Muncie, in central eastern Indiana, which, being neither southern nor eastern nor western, was, Lynd wrote, "as representative as possible of contemporary American life."

The Lynds, subsidized by the institute, spent several years researching in Muncie. They soon discovered that the religious emphasis, in isolation, was too limiting, and they enlarged the study to include all aspects of the city's society. This approach was not acceptable to the institute, which declined to publish the study but allowed the Lynds to bring it out on their own. *Middletown: A Study in Contemporary American Culture,* the first major sociological profile of an American city, was published in 1929 by a New York firm and was an immediate commercial success. The book documented the day-to-day life of all classes of Muncie people—their economy, recreations, how they interrelated, and how they brought up their children. Contrasting the town in the 1890s and the 1920s, the Lynds—without moralizing or satire—portrayed a community that moved from altruistic civic values to a life dominated by consumerism.

A sequel, *Middletown in Transition* (1937), researched during the Great Depression, was more concerned with social change. The city had become more industrialized, and there was deeper class feeling as well as greater tolerance. The Lynds were more concerned with the power structure and how it governed the flow of information.

After publishing *Middletown,* Robert Lynd went to Columbia University for graduate work and received his Ph.D. in 1931, the same year he was named a full professor of sociology. He continued to be concerned with social inequalities and injustices, as his stance moved further left; while he was a social activist and on some

questions in agreement with communists, he was never a communist. He became disillusioned with the possibility of using social science to effect social change, a view he expressed in his last book, *Knowledge for What?* (1939). He retired from Columbia in 1960.

The year before the publication of *Middletown,* Helen Lynd became a founding member of the faculty of Sarah Lawrence College, in Bronxville, New York. She taught literature, history, and social philosophy and helped devise the college's interdisciplinary curriculum, designed for each student, and its flexible system of grading. Rather than grades, students were given detailed written evaluations. Helen Lynd did graduate study at Columbia and earned a Ph.D. in history and philosophy in 1945. A book based on her dissertation, *England in the Eighteen-Eighties,* was published that year. In 1958 she published *On Shame and the Search for Identity,* which brought psychoanalytical insights to a discussion of the differences between guilt and shame. Helen Lynd retired from Sarah Lawrence in 1964. In 1981 her son Staughton Lynd edited *Possibilities,* her account of how *Middletown* came to be written.

Staughton Lynd was born in Philadelphia and educated at the Ethical Culture School and the Fieldston School, in New York City. At Harvard University in the class of 1951 he joined the John Reed Club (see JOHN REED) and other left-wing organizations. After graduate work in urban planning at Harvard and at the University of Chicago, he went into the U.S. Army, but in 1954, after a year, he was given an undesirable discharge as the result of an investigation of his "leftist past." In 1958 the U.S. Supreme Court ruled that such discharges, made on political grounds, should be changed to honorable ones.

Lynd and his wife, Alice Niles, worked with cooperative and social organizations until 1959, when he began graduate work at Columbia. His Ph.D. in 1962 was for a dissertation on revolutionary war history. He taught at Spelman College, a black institution in Atlanta, and, having become involved in the civil rights movement, was head of the Freedom Schools project in Mississippi during the summer of 1964. That fall he was appointed an associate professor of history at Yale University.

In spring 1965, during an anti–Vietnam War demonstration in Washington, Lynd was arrested as he and others tried to storm the House of Representatives to urge a Declaration for Peace. In January 1966, he joined TOM HAYDEN and Herbert Aptheker, a communist historian, on a trip to North Vietnam in hopes of furthering negotiations to end the war. The State Department revoked his passport, which he was able to retrieve only two years later thanks to a U.S. Court of Appeals ruling. While Lynd took on other teaching jobs in Chicago, his post at Yale was in suspension until he formally resigned in 1968. He taught in various colleges, worked in the antiwar movement, and with Hayden wrote an account of their trip to Hanoi, *The Other Side* (1967). The next year he published *Intellectual Origins of American Radicalism,* treating currents of the eighteenth and nineteenth centuries; it was received as a major work in the history of American thought. He continued the history in *The Resistance* (1971), written with Michael Ferber.

After working for several years as an organizer for the United Steel Workers Union, mainly in Gary, Indiana, Lynd decided he could help workers more effectively as a labor lawyer. After receiving his degree from the University of Chicago Law School in 1976, Lynd moved to Niles, Ohio, near Youngstown, one of the largest steel centers though suffering industrial decline, where he established a law practice in partnership with his wife. The Lynds specialize in legal services law, mainly serving parties short of finances. In 1992 Staughton Lynd published *Solidarity Unionism: Rebuilding the Labor Movement from Below.*

**BIBLIOGRAPHY**

Fox, Richard, "Epitaph for Middletown: Robert S. Lynd and the Analysis of Consumer Culture," in Richard Fox and Jackson Lear (eds.), *The Culture of Consumption,* 1983; Lynd, Helen M., *Towards Discovery,* 1965; Lynd, Robert S., *Knowledge for What?* 1939; Lynd, Staughton, *Class Conflict, Slavery, and the U.S. Constitution,* 1968.

## Lyon, Mary

(February 28, 1797–March 5, 1849)
Educator

Mary Lyon pioneered in education for women with the founding of Mount Holyoke Female Seminary (later Mount Holyoke College), one of the first permanently endowed institutions of higher learning for women to offer an education equivalent to that offered by the men's colleges.

Lyon was born in Buckland, Massachusetts, and grew up on the family farm there. She joined the Buckland Congregational church and attended the local district schools of Buckland and Ashfield. In 1814, at age seventeen, she

began teaching in summer schools for small children and, three years later, continued her own education by enrolling in the Sanderson Academy in Ashfield, one of the few schools to offer an academic program to women as well as men.

In the ensuing years, Mary Lyon studied at Amherst Academy, at Sanderson again, and at the Byfield (Massachusetts) Female Seminary. Byfield's head, the Reverend Joseph Emerson, believed that women's education should stress academic subjects rather than accomplishments like painting and dancing, and that schools for women ought to be established. At Byfield Mary Lyon became good friends with Emerson's assistant, Zilpah Grant. Later the two women each started her own school along the lines of Byfield. In 1828 Zilpah Grant founded the Ipswich (Massachusetts) Female Seminary and, with Mary Lyon's help, made it into an outstanding institution, emphasizing academic subjects along with a strong religious component. Ipswich, however, had no endowment, and Mary Lyon's growing conviction of the need for this eventually led her to found Mount Holyoke.

Early in 1834 Lyon began circulating a plan for a residential seminary for students of limited means. Costs would be kept down by having students perform domestic work and by paying teachers minimal salaries. The seminary's financial affairs would be handled by a board of trustees who would serve without profit. Lyon raised the first thousand dollars and resigned from Ipswich Seminary to continue with fund raising. In 1837 Mount Holyoke

Library of Congress

Female Seminary, one of the country's first institutions to offer women a college education, became a reality, with Mary Lyon at its head. Its first class numbered eighty students. Lyon included, among others, classes in natural sciences, mathematics, modern history, and Latin in the program. College-level textbooks were used, and in time the three-year course expanded to four years. Many Mount Holyoke graduates became schoolteachers and missionaries.

By 1849, the year of Mary Lyon's death at the age of fifty-two, Mount Holyoke had trained more women teachers than any other institution in the country. It paved the way for the numerous women's colleges that would be founded later in the century.

**BIBLIOGRAPHY**

Cole, Arthur C., *A Hundred Years of Mount Holyoke College*, 1959; Green, Elizabeth A., *Mary Lyon and Mount Holyoke: Opening the Gates*, 1979.

# McClure, Samuel Sidney

(February 17, 1857–March 21, 1949)
Editor, Publisher

As the editor and publisher of *McClure's Magazine*, Samuel McClure helped launch the muckraking crusade against the abuses of large corporations and government corruption.

Born in County Antrim, Ireland, McClure immigrated to America with his widowed mother when he was nine. He grew up in poverty in Indiana. After obtaining his B.A. by working his way through Knox College in Galesburg, Illinois, McClure moved to Boston and obtained a position as an editor for *The Wheelman*, a bicycle magazine.

After less than a year in Boston, McClure moved on to New York City. He worked briefly as an editor, then decided to invest his meager savings in a literary syndicate that would resell purchased stories to newspapers. McClure had a knack for recognizing talented young writers. Through his syndicate he introduced to the American public such English writers as Rudyard Kipling, A. Conan Doyle, and Robert Louis Stevenson. He also purchased and resold stories by writers like Mark Twain, O. Henry, Jack London, and Stephen Crane. The McClure Syndicate was the first successful literary syndicate in America.

In 1893 McClure founded his own literary journal, *McClure's Magazine.* The journal's low price and the high quality of its stories and articles soon made it a huge success. With a circulation of 400,000 by 1900, the magazine exerted a powerful cultural and social influence in the period prior to World War I.

Always on the lookout for new ideas, McClure crisscrossed the country, talking with everyone from newspaper editors to people on the street and jotting down notes. He then had his staff writers, including the previously unknown Willa Cather, develop his ideas into lively, well-documented articles. This practice resulted in the magazine's chief claim to fame: its series of muckraking articles, beginning in 1903. The series included IDA TARBELL's "The History of the Standard Oil Company," LINCOLN STEFFENS's "The Shame of Minneapolis," and RAY STANNARD BAKER's "The Right to Work."

Muckraking pieces in *McClure's* exposed corruption in government and chronicled abuses of fair competitive practices by large "monopolistic" corporations. The articles generated support for the enactment of reform legislation.

A brilliant editor but dismal businessperson, McClure lost control of both his magazine and literary syndicate in 1912. Ten years later he regained control of *McClure's* briefly, but in 1929 the magazine ceased publication.

McClure himself was more interested in profits than in social reform for its own sake. When the United States entered World War I, he helped in the production of prowar propaganda for the government and spoke out in favor of Prohibition. In his eighties, after a trip to Italy, he sanctioned Mussolini's dictatorship. He died at age ninety-two.

**BIBLIOGRAPHY**

Harrison, J. M., and H. H. Stein (eds.), *Muckraking: Past, Present, and Future,* 1974; Lyon, Peter, *Success Story: Life and Times of S. S. McClure,* 1967; McClure, Samuel Sidney, *My Autobiography,* 1914.

# Macdonald, Dwight

(March 24, 1906–December 19, 1982)
Author, Journalist, Political Commentator

Dwight Macdonald was a man of letters and a man of politics, who moved through a spectrum of radical views. Styling himself a "conservative anarchist," he had a gift for seeing the underlying significance of events in politics and culture and in detecting what was phony in either.

Dwight Macdonald was born in New York City to (in his own words) "one of the few happily married couples I've known." His father, after whom he was named, was a lawyer of modest background; his mother, Alice Hedges, belonged to a wealthy Brooklyn family. The boy was sent to "good" schools in New York and New England. At Phillips Exeter Academy in New Hampshire and at Yale University, he made a name as a prize-winning writer and an editor of publications. After graduating from Yale with a degree in history, Macdonald had a brief try at executive training for Macy's department store. In 1929 he joined the staff of *Fortune* magazine, newly founded by HENRY R. LUCE. He was an associate editor until 1936, when he resigned in protest because of editorial tampering with an article he had written on the United States Steel Corporation. Having acquired a distaste for capitalism, Macdonald began reading the Communist "founding fathers," Lenin, Marx, and Trotsky, and evolved, in his words, "from a liberal into a radical and from a tepid Communist sympathizer into an ardent anti-Stalinist." (Josef Stalin, the leader of the Soviet Union from 1924 to 1953, was a terrifying dictator whose ruthless pursuit of power and communist vision prompted him to kill millions of Soviet citizens, including many of those, like Trotsky, who had been heroes of the 1917 Russian Revolution. Anti-Stalinists were radicals who, in the 1930s and 1940s, exposed the true horror of Stalin's rule, but who still believed that a decent leftist politics could be built on Marxist or Leninist principles.)

Thereafter, Macdonald's career continued mainly in magazines. In 1937 he joined the staff of the *Partisan Review*, which professed political independence and socialism of an anti-Stalinist cast. Macdonald joined the Trotskyist Socialist Workers Party for a time and contributed to its monthly journal, *New International*. Having taken a pacifist position toward World War II, in 1943 he broke with the prowar stance of the *Partisan Review* and started *Politics*, a "little" magazine that he owned, published, and edited. *Politics*, though declared Marxist, welcomed all varieties of radical opinion. Submissions were judged on quality of writing and thought, and noted European and American writers contributed articles on literary as well as political subjects. Two years later, as Macdonald's views evolved, his magazine moved toward anarchism and pacifism. It ceased publication in 1949 for lack of funds. In 1951 Macdonald became a staff writer for *The New Yorker*, whose editor allowed him wide latitude of expression as well as of space.

Macdonald's expressly political books, derived from his articles, were *Henry Wallace, the Man and the Myth* (1948), *The Root Is Man: Two Essays in Politics* (1953), and *Memoirs of a Revolutionist* (1957), which is full of political criticism. Throughout the 1950s, he was a fierce critic both of Soviet-style communism and America-style capitalism. In 1963 his favorable *New Yorker* review of the socialist Michael Harrington's *Poverty in America* brought the issue of poverty to President John F. Kennedy's attention and helped to launch the "War on Poverty." In 1967 and 1968, Macdonald protested involvement in the Vietnam War, refused to pay taxes for the war, and counseled young men to defy the draft. Civil disobedience for him meant "the deliberate, public and nonviolent breaking of a law because to obey it would be to betray a higher morality."

Cultural, social, and literary criticism was the focus of Macdonald's later career. For *The New Yorker* he wrote profiles of DOROTHY DAY and ROGER NASH BALDWIN, and acerbic critiques of the Revised Standard Version of the Bible (versus the King James Version) and the Great Books of the Western World. He deplored mass and middlebrow culture and the relaxed standards of the *Webster's Third New International Dictionary*.

Macdonald and his first wife, Nancy Rodman Macdonald, founded Spanish Refugee Aid, which raised funds for exiled Republican veterans of the Spanish Civil War. They had two sons. In 1950 he divorced his first wife and married Gloria Kaufman. At age seventy-six he died of heart failure in a New York hospital.

**BIBLIOGRAPHY**

Macdonald, D., *The Ford Foundation: The Men and the Millions*, 1956, *Against the American Grain*, 1963, *Essays and Afterthoughts*, 1974, and (ed.) *Parodies*, 1960; Whitfield, Stephen J., *A Critical American*, 1984.

# McDowell, Mary Eliza

(November 30, 1854–October 14, 1936)
Reformer

As a reformer and the director of a Chicago settlement house, Mary McDowell sought to promote social justice during a career spanning forty years.

Mary McDowell was born in Cincinnati, Ohio. She was educated in the public and private schools of Ohio and Chicago, Illinois, where her family moved. At the age of sixteen she had her first social work experience during the Great Chicago Fire of 1871 when she assisted in relief efforts. She led a Sunday school class in the 1880s in Evanston, Illinois, and met temperance leader FRANCES WILLARD.

Library of Congress

McDowell became involved in the Woman's Christian Temperance Union (WCTU) and, through her work for the WCTU, the kindergarten movement.

McDowell went to live in JANE ADDAMS's Hull House in Chicago in 1890, and started a kindergarten. Four years later, McDowell was asked to head a new settlement house project that was being started by University of Chicago faculty members; she led the project for twenty-five years. It was located in an immigrant neighborhood near the stockyards. McDowell set up a day nursery for working mothers and arranged clubs and outings for children. She also campaigned successfully for a public library.

McDowell's concern with the open garbage pits surrounding the neighborhood and with "Bubbly Creek," a branch of the Chicago River that was little more than an open sewer, led her

into public health reform. She launched a campaign to educate the public about the health hazards of the open pits and kept after city officials and meat packers from the stockyards until the pits were closed, Bubbly Creek was filled, and a City Waste Commission was established.

McDowell also became involved in the labor movement. Together with Michael Donnelly, president of the meat packers' union, she established the Illinois Women's Trade Union League in 1903, serving as its president from 1904 to 1907. She was also a chief organizer of the National Women's Trade Union League in 1903. In the Chicago stockyard strike of 1904, McDowell mediated between the packers and union officials. Although the strike was lost, she managed to secure recognition of the union. McDowell then wrote a letter to President Theodore Roosevelt about conditions in the meat-packing plants. UPTON SINCLAIR's novel *The Jungle* appeared about the same time, and a federal investigation of the stockyards ensued.

In 1907 McDowell was also able to persuade Roosevelt to conduct a federal investigation of women and children in industry. She pushed for laws to limit working hours and was one of the leaders of the campaign to establish a Women's Bureau within the Department of Labor in 1920.

After the Chicago race riots of 1919, McDowell organized an Interracial Cooperative Committee to oversee legislation and civic activities involving blacks and whites. She was also active in the National Association for the Advancement of Colored People (NAACP; see JOEL E. SPINGARN), the Urban League of Chicago, and the Immigrant's Protection League. In 1923 reform mayor William Dever appointed McDowell commissioner of public welfare. In 1929 McDowell retired as director of the University of Chicago Settlement House. She died seven years later at the age of eighty-one.

**BIBLIOGRAPHY**

Tyler, Helen E., *Where Prayer and Purpose Meet,* 1949; Wilson, Howard E., *Mary McDowell, Neighbor,* 1928.

## McNickle, William D'Arcy

(January 18, 1904–October 15, 1977)
American Indian Rights Advocate, Author, Ethnologist

D'Arcy McNickle was a man of diverse talents—a novelist, a historian, a public official, and a tireless worker for the cause of American Indians. He has been called the grandfather of modern American Indian literature and ethnohistory.

McNickle was born at St. Ignatius, on the Flathead Indian Reservation in northwestern Montana. His mother, Philomene Parenteau, was of a Canadian *métis* (mixed blood) family that moved south, and she had been adopted into the Flathead (or Salish) tribe. She married an Irish rancher, William McNickle. Though living on the reservation, young McNickle's parents wanted him to identify with white society and not with the poverty and hopelessness of the reservation. The boy felt a strong attachment to the Indian people, however, and became a member of the Confederated Salish and Kootenai tribes, qualifying under the Dawes Allotment Act of 1887 (see HENRY ROE CLOUD) for a parcel of reservation land.

Around 1915, after his parents divorced, McNickle was sent for three years to the Chemawa Indian School, run by the Bureau of Indian Affairs (BIA) in Salem, Oregon, a school where students were punished if they spoke their native language. He had some public schooling and, in 1921, entered the University of Montana, where he began to write poetry and fiction. During his senior year, when he won a statewide poetry contest, a professor urged him to leave and study at Oxford University, in England. To finance that, McNickle sold his allotment on the reservation.

After his year at Oxford and a period in Paris, McNickle settled in New York City, working as an automobile salesman and a free-lance writer. From 1928 to 1934, he was on the editorial staff of the *National Cyclopaedia of American Biography,* took courses at Columbia University and the New School for Social Research, and was involved in the intellectual and artistic life of New York. In 1931 he went to France for a semester at the University of Grenoble.

In 1935 McNickle took a job in Washington with the Federal Writers Project. The next year was important. His first novel, *The Surrounded,* which he had begun writing in 1927, was published, to critical praise. The novel grew out of McNickle's youthful experiences. It is the story of a young man, half Salish, half Spanish, torn by his conflicts. Long out of print, *The Surrounded* was republished in 1978.

Also in 1936, McNickle joined the staff of the BIA under its new commissioner, John Collier, who had instituted the policy of hiring qualified Indians. He spent sixteen years with the BIA, first as Collier's personal assistant, then as a field representative, and finally as director of tribal relations. His work included setting up reservations for dispossessed Indians, helping to establish tribal councils and courts, and protecting water rights. McNickle was a representative to the first Pan-American conference on Indian life at Patzcuaro, Mexico, in 1940. In 1946 he was a founder of the National Congress of American Indians, the first national organization of Indian tribes working independently to protect their rights. During these busy years McNickle produced his most important book, *They Came Here First: The Epic of the American Indian* (1949; revised, 1975), which is an ethnological and historical study that gives a full picture of Indian/white relations.

McNickle resigned from the BIA in 1954, at a time of declining official interest in Indians, when the spirit of the Collier years had waned. Moving to Boulder, Colorado, he founded American Indian Development, Inc. (AID), which raised private funds to support health and education projects and other social programs. Under McNickle's direction, AID sponsored summer leadership training workshops at western colleges for young Indians, many of whom became outstanding activists. During this time he was on the John Hay Whitney Foundation's committee that awarded Opportunity Fellowships to many young Indian scholars.

In 1966 the University of Saskatchewan, at Regina, Canada, appointed McNickle to a professorship as founding chairman of its department of anthropology. With more time for scholarship, he completed *Indian Man: A Life of Oliver La Farge* (1971) and edited the volume on contemporary affairs in the Smithsonian Institution's *Handbook of North American Indians.*

After five years at Regina, McNickle retired to Albuquerque, New Mexico, where writing projects awaited completion. In 1972, however, he was invited to be founding director of the Center for the History of the American Indian at the Newberry Library, in Chicago. Commuting from Albuquerque, he served until 1976, when he became chairman of the Center's Advisory Council.

McNickle died suddenly of a heart attack a few months after he had visited the Flathead Reservation for the first time in fifty years. He left two daughters by two earlier marriages. The Newberry Library center has been renamed the McNickle Center.

**BIBLIOGRAPHY**

McNickle, D'Arcy, *Runner in the Sun,* 1954, rev., 1987, *The Indian Tribes of the United States,* 1962, rev. as *Native American Tribalism,* 1973, and *Wind from an Enemy Sky,* 1978; McNickle, D'Arcy, with H. E. Fey, *Indians and Other Americans,* 1959, rev., 1970; Parker, Dorothy, *Singing an Indian Song: A Biography of D'Arcy McNickle,* 1992; Purdy, J. L., *Word Ways: The Novels of D'Arcy McNickle,* 1990; Ruppert, James, *D'Arcy McNickle,* 1988.

# Malcolm X

(May 19, 1925–February 21, 1965)
African American Activist, Civil Rights Leader

Malcolm X was important in shaping a Black Muslim and Black Power movement that challenged the nonviolent and integrationist struggle for black equality favored by MARTIN LUTHER KING, JR.'s civil rights movement.

Born Malcolm Little in Omaha, Nebraska, Malcolm was one of eight children of Earl Little, a Baptist minister and follower of MARCUS GARVEY, the black nationalist, and Louise Little. For many years, Malcolm knew only poverty and violence. In 1929 the family moved to

East Lansing, Michigan, where white racists tried to burn down their house. Two years later, Earl Little was run down by a trolley car, probably an act of murder. By that time the country was mired in the Great Depression, and Louise Little found it impossible to feed and care for her children. The children were placed in separate foster homes and institutions, and Louise was declared incompetent and placed in a mental hospital, where she spent the next quarter century.

At thirteen, Malcolm was sent to a juvenile detention home for a minor act of mischief. Three years later, he went to live with a sister in Boston. No longer

*U.S. News & World Report* Collection, Library of Congress

attending school, he took on odd jobs and learned about street life in the black ghetto. Eventually he got a job as sandwich man on trains between Boston and New York and was quickly introduced to drugs and crime in Harlem. Sporting a zoot suit (a fad in the 1940s, it was a suit with long, draped pants, tight at the ankle, and a jacket with wide shoulders), Malcolm became a recognized underworld figure. He talked his way into a draft exemption from the armed forces during World War II. Back in Boston, he was arrested in 1946 for burglary and sentenced to ten years in prison. He was twenty years old.

Prison was to be Malcolm's salvation. He began to read history, philosophy, and religion. Through his brother, he learned about the Nation of Islam, also known as the Black Muslims, led by ELIJAH MUHAMMAD. Based in Chicago, Elijah Muhammad preached against white racism and advocated a Muslim way of life, which forbade drinking, smoking, and drugs; he insisted that members have jobs. The move-

ment's separatist ideology was extreme. Not only did it dismiss the civil rights movement's goal of full black integration into white society as illusory, it also depicted all whites as descended from the devil, born to harm blacks.

By the time Malcolm was released from prison in 1952, he was committed to the Nation of Islam and took the name Malcolm X, dropping what the Muslims considered a slave name. He progressed through the ranks rapidly, recruiting first in Detroit, then Boston and Philadelphia, and finally in New York. Malcolm had become an eloquent speaker; and, owing largely to his efforts, which included starting a national Muslim newspaper, the movement attracted thousands of members. In 1959 the nation watched a television documentary on the Muslims called "The Hate That Hate Produced" on the Mike Wallace Show, and by the end of the year the Muslims could claim 100,000 followers. One source of new recruits for the Muslims was the country's jails. An estimated 600 convicts joined the movement each year, most of them staying out of jail when released and dramatically altering their values and behavior.

On one hand, the Muslims were effective in organizing schools and businesses and in providing encouragement and moral support for their members. On the other hand, the movement frightened whites and the growing civil rights movement. Since the Muslims were anti-integration, they considered nonviolence absurd and would not cooperate in demonstrating with such groups as the National Association for the Advancement of Colored People (NAACP; see JOEL E. SPINGARN) or the Congress of Racial Equality (CORE; see JAMES FARMER).

Malcolm X was especially extreme in his statements of hate for whites.

By the early sixties, Malcolm's position of leadership had brought him into conflict with Elijah Muhammad as well as with some of the other leaders, who criticized him for forgetting the original religious intentions of the Muslims and being swayed by the glory of politics. When in 1963 Malcolm spoke of President John F. Kennedy's assassination as a case of "the chickens coming home to roost," suggesting that the hate directed at blacks had been responsible for the killing of the president, Muhammad suspended him from the movement.

On his part, Malcolm had become suspicious of Muhammad's life-style and morals and the general Muslim policy of "nonengagement" from active confrontation with racism. In 1964 he broke with Muhammad and formed his own group, called the Muslim Mosque, Inc., determined to make the group international and to initiate a back-to-Africa movement. The same year, he made a pilgrimage to Mecca and visited several African countries, meeting and having discussions with prominent Muslim leaders and scholars. He discovered that the views of many Muslims differed from his racist views, and he seriously reconsidered his position. When he returned to the United States, he announced that his visit in the Islamic world had helped to alter his view that all whites were evil and racist. He now believed that the plight of American blacks was caused by Western civilization and hoped that Islamic leaders abroad would help him bring before the United Nations the issue of American racism and its capitalistic ramifications in Africa. He formed the Organization of Afro-American Unity to unify black groups he had previously feuded with. This willingness to work with integrationists offended more militant Muslim followers at the same time that his anticapitalism brought support from Marxists, though he was not actually committed to Marxism.

In early 1965, Malcolm's house was firebombed, and a week later he was assassinated while speaking at a rally at the Audubon Ballroom in Harlem. He was thirty-nine years old. He had long believed he would be killed by the Black Muslims, but although two of the three men convicted of shooting him were members of the Nation of Islam, no conspiracy was ever proved.

Malcolm, who had renamed himself el-Hajj Malik el-Shabazz after his pilgrimage to Mecca, was survived by his wife Betty Shabazz, whom he had married in 1958, and four children. His funeral was attended by many black leaders, including BAYARD RUSTIN, who had differed with him, and a huge crowd of followers. His words and actions have continued to fuel separatist tendencies in black communities, especially during moments, such as the late 1960s and late 1980s, when progress toward the integration of black and white America has been halted or reversed.

That people responded so strongly in different ways to a man who began his life by hating whites and ended it by having questioned his own deepest convictions is evidence of Malcolm X's influence and at the same time characteristic of an era of great struggle in the American conscience.

### BIBLIOGRAPHY

Breitman, George (ed.), *Malcolm X Speaks: Selected Speeches*, 1965, and *The Last Year of Malcolm X*, 1967; Epps, Archie (ed.), *The Speeches of Malcolm X at Harvard*, 1968; Lomax, L. E., *To Kill a Black Man*, 1968; Malcolm X, with Alex Haley, *The Autobiography of Malcolm X*, 1964.

# Mann, Horace

(May 4, 1796–August 2, 1859)
Educator, Reformer

Declaring that "In a republic, ignorance is a crime," Horace Mann set out to reform the system of public education in Massachusetts until it became a model for the rest of the country.

The son of a poor farmer in Franklin, Massachusetts, Mann himself never attended school for more than eight or ten weeks at a time until he was sixteen years old. After six months of preparation under a private tutor, he was admitted to Brown University, graduating with high honors in 1819. Mann tutored Brown students in Latin and Greek for two years, then studied law at the Litchfield Law School in Connecticut from 1821 to 1823. He was admitted to the bar in 1823 and practiced in Dedham, Massachusetts, for the next decade and then in Boston from 1833 to 1837.

Mann entered the Massachusetts House of Representatives in 1827, serving there until he moved on to the state senate in 1833. He was elected senate president in 1835. As a legislator, Mann supported a number of reforms, including the establishment of state hospitals for the insane, the restriction of slavery, and educational improvements. In 1837 Mann helped secure the passage of an education bill providing for a state board of education. That same year, Mann gave up a successful law practice and a promising political career to become the first secretary of the new state board of education.

Although Massachusetts, along with the other New England states, offered better public education than other parts of the country, its school system had begun to show the ill effects of decentralization and inadequate funding. Local school districts seldom kept public schools open for more than a few months a year; teachers were often poorly prepared and underpaid; and a viable high school program, authorized by 1827 legislation, had yet to be created.

Mann threw himself into his work as secretary with passionate conviction. The progress he made in remedying the shortcomings of the educational system during his twelve years in office earned him the title of "the father of American public education."

To arouse public interest in education, Mann organized annual educational conventions in every county for the benefit of teachers, school officials, and the public. He addressed these meetings himself and enlisted the aid of prominent professional people and educators.

In 1838 Mann also began to publish a semimonthly magazine, the *Common School Journal*, to explore public school problems. More importantly, Mann used the annual reports he was required by law to prepare to discuss problems and possible solutions in clear, concise language. These widely distributed reports provided a coherent progressive educational vision.

Convinced of the need for improvement in the teaching profession, Mann advocated the establishment of teachers' institutes and normal schools. He was able to obtain funds from wealthy donors to support the creation of normal schools and convince the legislature to match these philanthropic donations with tax revenues. Thanks to these efforts, the first state normal school in the United States opened in Lexington, Massachusetts, in 1839.

Mann also won higher salaries for teachers, and during his time in office, appropriations for public education more than doubled. Some of these funds were used to establish fifty new high schools, while other monies went to reshaping the curriculum and methods of instruction. Mann also succeeded in getting the minimum school year attendance requirement extended to six months.

To those who protested that school taxes violated the rights of private property, Mann replied that private property was, in effect, held in trust for the general welfare. In his annual report of 1846, he wrote, "The property of this commonwealth is pledged for the education of all its youth up to such point as will save them from poverty and vice, and prepare them for the adequate performance of their social and civil duties."

Mann viewed the public school as the "great balance wheel" of society. He felt that it could prevent class conflict by providing equal opportunities for economic and social advancement while at the same time inculcating all children with a common set of beliefs.

Mann also believed that children could be easily molded by teachers and school officials. He favored instruction in moral values over the use of corporeal punishment, a position that angered schoolteachers who saw the rod as their most effective disciplinary tool.

Even more controversial was Mann's stance on the teaching of religion in the schools. He argued that the Bible should be read in school but not discussed there. Religious leaders accused Mann of trying to create a godless school system.

In 1843 Mann traveled to Europe to study the schools there. He returned with high praise for the German educational system. This led to conflict with Boston teachers, who read into Mann's report criticism of their own practices.

Despite the controversy he aroused, Mann's tenure as secretary of the state board of education was remarkably productive. In 1848 he resigned to take a seat in the U.S. House of Representatives as an antislavery Whig to succeed John Quincy Adams. Four years later in 1852, Mann made an unsuccessful bid for election as the governor of Massachusetts on the Free-Soil ticket (see GERRIT SMITH).

The following year Mann became the first president of Antioch College in Yellow Springs, Ohio. Mann was excited by the prospect of presiding over a school open to students regardless of their race, sex, or religion. But the tension of coping with the school's precarious financial condition over the next few years exhausted him and undermined his health, and he died in 1859.

**BIBLIOGRAPHY**

Downs, R. B., *Horace Mann: Champion of Public Schools*, 1974; Messerli, Jonathan, *Horace Mann*, 1972; Tharp, Louis H., *Until Victory: Horace Mann and Mary Peabody*, 1953.

# Marcuse, Herbert

(July 19, 1898–July 29, 1979)
Philosopher, Social Critic

Late in his relatively quiet academic life, Marcuse's ideas of radical socialism, drawn from both Marxist and Freudian sources, suddenly came to the fore among university students in this country and abroad to provide a libertarian rationale for civil rights and pacifist activism.

Herbert Marcuse was born in Berlin, son of an upper-class family prominent in Prussian society since the eighteenth century. While a student at the University of Berlin, Marcuse joined the Social Democratic party, but he became disillusioned in 1919. What triggered his break was the brutal murder that year, allegedly on orders of the Social Democratic government, of the communist leaders Rosa Luxemburg and Karl Liebknecht. Marcuse earned a doctoral degree in 1922 at the University of Freiburg and then embarked on postdoctoral studies at the Frankfurt Institute of Social Research, which he helped to found. This institute, which included such individuals as Theodore Adorno, Erich Fromm, and Max Horkheimer, would become famous both in Europe and the

United States. During the twenties Marcuse's thinking was strongly influenced from three directions: the failure of democracy in the newly formed German (Weimar) republic, opening the way to Nazism; the new sociology voiced in the ideas of the Frankfurt Institute; and the work of Wilhelm Reich, a maverick Viennese psychoanalyst who drew on Marxist interpretations. Marcuse's first book, a study of the theory of history held by the German philosopher G. W. F. Hegel, was published in 1932.

When Adolf Hitler took power in 1933, the Nazis forced the Frankfurt Institute to close, and Marcuse, who was Jewish, fled to Switzerland. In 1934 he came to the United States and was appointed a lecturer at Columbia University. He became an American citizen in 1940. His first book in English was *Reason and Revolution* (1941), defending Hegel from the charge that his ideas aided Nazism. After the United States entered World War II, Marcuse was recruited by the Office of Strategic Services (OSS) to work in Washington as a European intelligence analyst. At the end of the war the OSS became the Office of Intelligence Research (OIR), and Marcuse stayed on for four years, focusing on research involving communism and the Soviet Union for the Central Intelligence Agency (CIA) and the Department of State. His work led to the book *Soviet Marxism* (1958), an analysis of the psychology of Soviet leaders and Soviet myths. Thereafter he taught at Columbia, Harvard University, and Brandeis University. In 1965 Marcuse retired from Brandeis and moved to the University of California at San Diego.

Marcuse belonged to a group of German-Jewish refugee intellectuals, known as the Frankfurt School, that began to receive attention in the United States after World War II. Especially important were their studies of why totalitarianism of the left (Stalinism) and right (Nazism) had vanquished democracy throughout Europe. Marcuse, in the 1950s, was a lesser-known member of this group, but he contributed significantly to the exploration of this problem. In 1955 he published *Eros and Civilization*, in which he drew on Marxist and psychoanalytic thought to argue for the erotic nature of all social and political repression. In 1964 he extended this argument to contemporary American life in his *One-Dimensional Man*. His popularity with students had begun at Brandeis, where many students began to regard his work as a basis for the politics of the radical New Left—notably, for their view that America's ostensibly free and democratic society was, in reality, deeply repressive and intolerant. At San Diego, Marcuse's lectures were received with growing enthusiasm by students. During the campus revolts of 1968 at many universities in the United States and abroad, students and others who supported the civil rights and anti–Vietnam War movements were won over to his libertarian hope of a society where people, freed from restraints, could reach their full potential. Marcuse was attacked from both left and right: *Pravda*, the newspaper of the Communist party in the Soviet Union, called him "a werewolf," and he was reviled by Ronald Reagan, governor of California at the time, and Spiro T. Agnew, then the vice president of the United States.

As the radical tumult of the 1960s died down, Marcuse's fame as "the father of the New Left" (a label he disliked) dwindled. Upon retiring in 1970, Marcuse stayed on in San Diego. In May 1979, he was invited by the Max Planck Society (a research foundation, named in honor of a distinguished physicist) to lecture at one of its branches, in Starnberg, near Munich. After suffering a stroke, Marcuse died in Starnberg on July 29.

**Bibliography**

Lind, Peter, *The Genesis and Development of a Theory of Human Liberation*, 1985; MacIntyre, Alasdair, *Herbert Marcuse: An Exposition and a Polemic*, 1970; Marcuse, H., *Negations*, 1968, *An Essay on Liberation*, 1969, and *Counterrevolution and Revolt*, 1972; Mattick, Paul, *Critique of Marcuse*, 1972.

## Masters, William Howell

(December 27, 1915– )

## Johnson, Virginia Eshelman

(February 11, 1925– )
Researchers in Sexual Behavior

The research team of William Masters and Virginia Johnson is known for pathbreaking laboratory studies of human sexual behavior, which have changed the attitudes of many American women and men.

Born in Cleveland, Ohio, William Masters studied science at Hamilton College in New York, graduating in 1938. After earning his M.D. from the University of Rochester Medical School in 1943, he interned in obstetrics and gynecology and then taught at Barnes Hospital, in the medical school of Washington University, St. Louis.

In 1954, after publishing numerous articles in medical journals, Masters decided to undertake research into sexual behavior. Like ALFRED KINSEY before him, he was concerned about the lack of adequate knowledge in this area. But unlike Kinsey, who had to rely on secondhand data, Masters was determined to make use of modern scientific equipment in the laboratory to study the human body's response to sexual stimulation. To assist with his research and serve as a female interviewer, he hired Virginia Johnson. Born in Springfield, Missouri, Johnson had studied psychology and sociology at the University of Missouri (1944–1947), though without earning a degree.

Masters and Johnson conducted their research at the Washington University School of Medicine on a grant from the U.S. Institutes of Health from 1955 until 1964, when the agency withdrew its funding and Masters established

Copyright *Washington Post;*
Reprinted by permission of the D.C. Public Library

the nonprofit Reproductive Biology Research Foundation (now called the Masters and Johnson Institute). Johnson became a research associate and later codirector of the institute. Over a period of eleven years, several hundred male and female paid volunteers took part in research, whereby the physiological changes occurring during sexual activity were measured by electrocardiographs and other scientific equipment.

In 1966 Masters and Johnson published the results of their work in *Human Sexual Response.* Though intended for a medical and scientific audience, the book soon became a best-seller with sales of more than 250,000. One important consequence of the work was to help free women from a limiting definition of sexuality. Whereas both popular and medical opinion had held that men were aggressive and active sexually, while women were passive, Masters and Johnson demonstrated that women's sexual responses were at least as intense as men's, if not more so. They also showed that aging did not significantly impede either male or female sexuality; and in other ways, too, their findings expanded the definition of normal sexual behavior.

Having begun in 1959 to treat husbands and wives with sexual problems, Masters and Johnson published *Human Sexual Inadequacy* in 1970. In their discussion of sexual dysfunction and unhealthy sexual attitudes, they stressed the importance of sex education for young people and adults alike. They also conducted clinical programs to treat sexual inadequacy and trained other therapists in their techniques. In 1971 Masters and Johnson were married. Their other books include: *The Pleasure Bond—A New Look at Sexuality and Commitment* (1975), *Ethical Issues in Sex Therapy and Research* (two vols., 1977, 1980), *Homosexuality in Perspective* (1979), *Human Sexuality* (1982), and *Crisis: Het-* *erosexual Behavior in the Age of AIDS* (1988).

**BIBLIOGRAPHY**

Lehrman, Nat, *Masters and Johnson Explained*, 1971; Robbins, Jhan, *An Analysis of Human Sexual Inadequacy*, 1970; Robinson, Paul A., *The Modernization of Sex: Havelock Ellis, Alfred Kinsey, William Masters and Virginia Johnson*, 1976.

# Mather, Increase

(June 21, 1639–August 23, 1723)

# Mather, Cotton

(February 12, 1663–February 13, 1728)
Religious Leaders

Father and son, Increase and Cotton Mather were prominent Puritan leaders and ministers. Of the two, Cotton was the more famous—indeed, perhaps the most famous of all the Puritans. He played a leading role in the transition from extreme religious orthodoxy to a more secular outlook in New England.

Increase Mather was born in Dorchester, Massachusetts, the son of Richard Mather, first pastor of the Dorchester Church. Raised a strict Puritan, he graduated from Harvard College in 1656 and received his M.A. from Trinity College, Dublin, Ireland, in 1658. After preaching in England and on the island of Guernsey, he returned to Boston in 1661. In 1664 he became minister of the Second Church of Boston, a position he held for the rest of his life.

Chosen a fellow of Harvard in 1674, Mather served as president with the title of rector from 1685 to 1701. He encouraged the study of science at Harvard but stood firm against efforts to undermine the college's strict Congregationalism. From 1688 to 1692, Mather served as an able ambassador for the Massachusetts Bay Colony at the courts of James II and William III while the colony's original charter was being renegotiated.

A prolific writer, Increase Mather produced more than 100 books and pamphlets, including *A Brief History of the War with the Indians* (1676) and *Remarkable Providences* (1684). Unlike his son, Cotton, he was cautious during the Salem witchcraft trials of 1692 and 1693. In *Cases of Conscience Concerning Evil Spirits* (1693), he argued against the use of "spectral evidence," maintaining that it was better for ten guilty witches to escape than for one innocent person to die. The tract made an impression on Governor William Phips and helped end the trials. In 1721 Increase Mather joined his son Cotton in advocating inoculation for smallpox, against the opposition of laypersons and many doctors. He died in Boston two years later at the age of eighty-four.

Increase Mather's oldest son, Cotton, was born in Boston. By his own account, he "began to pray, even when [he] began to speak."

Entering Harvard at the age of twelve, the youngest student the college had ever admitted, Cotton Mather graduated in 1678. Fearful that his habit of stammering would interfere with his preaching, he studied medicine for a time before earning his M.A. from Harvard in 1681. By 1680 he had overcome his stammer enough to begin preaching. In 1685 he was ordained and joined his father in the pulpit of the Second Church of Boston, holding this position until his death.

As minister of this church, one of the largest in Boston, Cotton Mather earned a reputation for his pastoral care. Mather was the first American minister to organize clubs for young people, and he started the practice of making regular calls upon elderly and ill church members and upon prisoners. He also helped set up a school for the education of slaves and organized efforts to promote peace, build churches in poor communities, provide relief for needy ministers, and establish missions among the American Indians.

Mather's role in the Salem witchcraft trials of 1692 has been much debated. An intensely religious and introspective man given to swooning and moments of sudden illumination, he had a strong sense of evil and of the power of the devil, which he believed could result in diabolical possession. He published *Memorable Providences, Relating to Witchcrafts and Possessions* in 1689, which, along with two other works on the subject, probably helped foster an awareness of witchcraft that may have contributed to the Salem hysteria. Yet at the time of the actual trials, Mather wrote a statement to the judges, warning them about the overuse of "spectral evidence" and advising milder punishments than execution. When the trials were done, he defended the verdicts, both in writing and by speech when he attended one of the resulting executions. He also defended the justice of several of the witchcraft trials in *Wonders of the Invisible World* (1693). Yet later still, in his most famous work, *Magnalia Christi Americana* (1702), a monumental ecclesiastical history of New England, Mather presented the Salem witchcraft trials as having unjustly condemned to death many innocent people.

After 1692 Mather's influence diminished somewhat because of the trend away from Puritan dominance, and also because of his own hot temper and arrogance. Although he had hoped to follow in his father's footsteps as president of Harvard, Mather was denied this honor. In 1703, when the lower house of the Massachusetts legislature, consisting largely of religious conservatives, appointed Mather president, their action was overruled by the more liberal upper house. Thereafter, Mather looked to a new institution to be the stronghold of Congregational orthodoxy, persuading Elihu Yale to contribute generously to it and convincing the governor of Connecticut to name the college after Yale.

Although at the outset of his career Mather bitterly attacked those with differing religious beliefs, he grew more tolerant with age. He even boasted that his church had welcomed into the fold not only Anglicans but also Baptists, Presbyterians, and Lutherans. Also, toward the end of his life, Mather began to expound doctrines that placed him at a distance from the strict Calvinism of his youth and closer to the deism of the eighteenth century with its emphasis upon a rationally ordered universe and a benevolent God.

An even more prolific author than his father, Mather wrote more than 450 books, cementing his reputation not only as a religious leader but also as a man of letters and a scientist. His interest in science was evident in *The Christian Philosopher* (1721) and other works. Mather had a wide-ranging curiosity about the natural world and saw no conflict between his religious beliefs and science, because, in his view, an understanding of nature was the best cure for atheism. He conducted many experiments of his own and published the results, including one of the earliest known descriptions of plant hybridization. Mather's concern with the useful in everyday life produced such observations as: "The very wheelbarrow is to be with respect looked upon." In this, he anticipated Benjamin Franklin, who claimed that

Mather's essays had provided the inspiration for many of his own practical devices. Mather corresponded with some of Europe's leading scientists and was a great admirer of Sir Isaac Newton. In 1712 he became one of the few American colonists to be elected to the Royal Society of London. In 1721, when smallpox broke out in Boston, Mather advocated inoculation against the protests of most physicians, the general populace, and some clergy, who regarded it as both a dangerous and godless practice. Mather's role in the inoculation campaign, together with his many other activities, reflected the tireless zeal with which he worked for what he considered to be the best interests of his fellows. He died in Boston at the age of sixty-five.

**BIBLIOGRAPHY**

Hall, Michael G., *The Last American Puritan: The Life of Increase Mather, 1639–1723*, 1988; Middlekauf, Robert, *The Mathers: Three Generations of Puritan Intellectuals, 1596–1728*, 1971; Silverman, Kenneth, *The Life and Times of Cotton Mather*, 1984.

# Mauldin, William Henry

(October 29, 1921–  )
Cartoonist

Bill Mauldin won fame during World War II with his series of cartoons depicting two battle-weary soldiers, Willie and Joe. He has since become a leading satirist of the social and political scene.

Mauldin was born in Mountain Park, New Mexico, and grew up there and in Phoenix, Arizona. While still in high school he sold his first drawings and with his earnings took a correspondence course in cartooning; in 1939 he studied at the Chicago Academy of Fine Arts. Back in Phoenix, he tried with little success to sell cartoons to national magazines. In 1940, when he was eighteen, Mauldin began training with the 45th Infantry Division of the U.S. Army. He did cartoons for the 45th Division *News* and in 1943 went with his division overseas to Sicily, where he joined the staff of the army's newspaper, *Stars and Stripes.* Mauldin covered the fighting in Sicily (he was wounded at Salerno and received the Purple Heart), and later elsewhere in Italy, France, and Germany.

Mauldin's cartoons initially featured a fresh-faced, clean-shaven young recruit much like himself, who over time developed into the bearded, dirty, and disgruntled pair of seasoned soldiers, Willie and Joe. His cartoons appealed to servicemen and to the general public alike but at the same time irritated some of the top army officers, notably General George Patton. Patton worried that the cartoon characters of Willie and Joe would have a negative effect on army morale and wanted them spruced up. After a meeting between the general and Mauldin arranged by General Dwight D. Eisenhower, who himself enjoyed the cartoons, Mauldin continued to draw the same bedraggled pair, and Patton remained miffed. Mauldin's cartoons for the 45th Division *News* and for *Stars and Stripes* were brought together in several collections, including *Star-Spangled Banter* (1941 and 1944), *Mud, Mules and Mountains* (1944), and *Up Front* (1945). In 1945 Mauldin won the Pulitzer Prize for a cartoon captioned "Fresh American troops, flushed with victory," which showed grimy soldiers trudging through the mud and rain.

After his discharge from the army in June 1945, Mauldin focused on the problems of returning veterans in his Willie and Joe cartoons. He also developed a new series which he used to ridicule racists, overzealous patriots, and stereotyped liberals. His cartoons of the early postwar years were collected in *Back Home* (1947). In 1950 and 1951 Mauldin worked in Hollywood as a technical consultant and actor in the war film *Teresa,* and he costarred with Audie Murphy in the film version of Stephen Crane's Civil War novel, *The Red Badge of Courage,* both of which were released in 1951. Also that year, *Up Front,* a film version of Mauldin's Willie and Joe cartoons, was released. Early the following year, Mauldin visited the war front in Korea, reporting on his experiences in the illustrated volume *Bill Mauldin in Korea* (1952). In 1956 Mauldin ran unsuccessfully as a Democrat for a seat in the House of Representatives from New York.

Joining the staff of the St. Louis *Post-Dispatch* as an editorial cartoonist in 1958,

Mauldin that same year won his second Pulitzer Prize. Mauldin's *Post-Dispatch* cartoons were eventually syndicated to 140 newspapers. As a satirist of the social and political scene, Mauldin was compared to the *Washington Post*'s editorial cartoonist, HERBERT BLOCK.

In 1962 Mauldin moved to the Chicago *Sun-Times,* where he has remained as an editorial cartoonist ever since.

**BIBLIOGRAPHY**

Mauldin, Bill, *Back Home,* 1947, *Sort of a Saga,* 1949, *What's Got Your Back Up?* 1961, *I've Decided I Want My Seat Back,* 1965, *The Brass Ring,* 1972, *Mud and Guts,* 1978, and *Let's Declare Ourselves Winners and Get the Hell Out,* 1985.

# Mead, Margaret

(December 16, 1901–November 15, 1978)
Anthropologist

Through her innovative work among the people of the South Pacific, Margaret Mead drew the world's attention to the social science of anthropology. In the course of enhancing the popular image of her profession, she helped to develop ideas about sex, culture, education, and child rearing that influenced several generations.

Mead was born in Philadelphia and studied at DePauw University in Indiana for one year before attending Barnard College in New York, where she graduated in 1923. While at Barnard she met the noted anthropologist FRANZ BOAS and decided to pursue graduate work in anthropology under his guidance at Columbia University. She earned her M.A. from Columbia in 1924 and immediately began her doctoral studies.

Mead was eager in 1925 to find a "people" of her own to study and become identified with, as her mentors Franz Boas and RUTH

BENEDICT had done. She settled on the people of the South Pacific and was determined to study the primitive cultures still alive there before they perished under the impact of economic development.

For her first and only solo mission as a field investigator, Mead chose to spend a year on an island in American Samoa. Her determination to live among the Samoans and not to let her Western cultural norms bias her observations was exceptional for an anthropologist at that time.

The goal of her research was to find out whether "the disturbances which vex our adolescents are due to the nature of adolescence itself or the civilization (cultural environment)." Having established that the tensions which existed in America did not exist for adolescents in Samoa, Mead concluded that civilization was the culprit. The relaxed attitude toward sex in Samoa minimized conflict and the incidence of neuroses due to guilt feelings. Cultural environment, not innate programming by nature, was the source of the problem. She remained a cultural relativist for the rest of her life.

Mead published the results of her work in Samoa in 1928 and was awarded her doctorate the following year. *Coming of Age in Samoa* described adolescent sexuality and guilt-free love in vivid, descriptive language. Mead applied her findings to contemporary American society and suggested that relaxing prohibitions on premarital sex might be desirable. The book shocked readers, became a best-seller, and made Mead famous, associating her name forever with sex and freedom.

Critics attacked *Coming of Age in Samoa* for being based more on Mead's personal agenda than on the life-style of the people of Samoa. Fellow anthropologists charged that it lacked the statistical data necessary for them to do an independent verification of her conclusions. (This critique has recently resurfaced in the book *Margaret Mead and Samoa: The Making and Unmaking of an Anthropological Myth,* by Derek Freeman.) Nevertheless, the detailed descriptions of daily Samoan life she provided in combination with her innovative blending of psychological and sociological insights concerning sexual temperament continued to make her work popular with readers around the world.

Mead returned to the South Pacific many times over the course of the next four decades to study the Manus people of the Admiralty Islands; the Arapesh, Mundugumor, and Tchambuli of New Guinea; and the Balinese. Repeated visits to the Manus over forty-seven

Copyright *Washington Post;*
Reprinted by permission of the D.C. Public Library

years enabled her to chronicle how their culture changed under the pressure of modernization. The results of her investigations are available in *Growing Up in New Guinea* (1930); *Sex and Temperament in Three Primitive Societies* (1935), with Gregory Bateson, then her husband; *Balinese Character* (1942); and *New Lives for Old: Cultural Transformation* (about the Manus; 1956).

Mead dealt specifically with how American male and female relations compared to those relations in the seven other cultures she had studied in *And Keep Your Powder Dry: An Anthropologist Looks at America* (1942) and *Male and Female: A Study of the Sexes in a Changing World* (1949). Among her suggestions were that men should assume more of the early child-rearing tasks so that the contrasts between the sexes could be reduced; and women should pursue careers so that they did not become dependent upon their husbands. (Mead was married and divorced three times.)

Mead's lifelong association with the American Museum of Natural History—she became assistant curator of ethnology in 1926, associate curator in 1942, curator in 1964, and curator emeritus in 1969—provided her with a professional home-base during her long career. She also taught anthropology courses at Columbia and Fordham universities.

Like her teachers Franz Boas and Ruth Benedict, Mead consistently championed anthropology as a human science, one both reflective and relevant. During World War II, she and Benedict, in work for the government and private organizations, played an important role in discrediting Nazi ideas of racial inferiority and in stimulating support for fighting against racial and cultural prejudice both at home and abroad. She felt a special need to improve people's understanding of themselves, especially in the case of women. She endeavored to meet this need through her many books and articles. She never hesitated to speak out in support of equal rights for women, civil rights legislation, better care for the elderly, nuclear disarmament, protection of the environment, and improved public education.

**BIBLIOGRAPHY**

Cassidy, Robert, *Margaret Mead: A Voice for the Century,* 1982; Grosskurth, Phyllis, *Margaret Mead,* 1988; Mead, Margaret, *Blackberry Winter: My Earlier Years,* 1972, and *Letters From the Field,* 1925, 1975, 1977.

# Meany, George

(August 16, 1894–January 10, 1980)
Labor Leader

George Meany was for almost sixty years a highly effective labor leader, having risen to be president of the largest and most powerful labor movement, the AFL-CIO, whose merger he engineered. He was an adamant foe of communist influence in the unions.

Meany was born in the Harlem area of New York City, second of eight children of Michael Joseph Meany, a plumber and staunch Democratic party worker, and Anne Cullen, both Americans born of Catholic Irish families. When he was five, the family moved across the Harlem River to the Port Morris section of the south Bronx. After leaving school at sixteen, he worked as a plumber's helper while going to night school to study for the journeyman's examination. In 1915 he qualified and joined the local of the plumber's union, over which his father presided. Joseph Meany died of a heart attack in late 1916, and the next year an older son, John, enlisted in the U.S. Army. George Meany had to support his mother and six younger siblings. He worked irregularly at construction jobs and pitched on a semiprofessional baseball team, while maintaining his union activity.

In 1919 Meany married Eugenia McMahon, who belonged to the International Ladies Garment Workers Union. Three years later George Meany was elected business agent of the Bronx local, which was affiliated with the American Federation of Labor (AFL; see WILLIAM GREEN and JOHN L. LEWIS). It was a full-time job. He never worked again as a plumber; his life career was as a union official.

Having taken on the secretaryship of the New York City Building Trades Council in 1923, Meany became well acquainted with local and national labor leaders and politicians. In 1934 he became president of the New York State Federation of Labor and became a highly visible figure in Albany, the state capital. As a capable lobbyist before the legislature, he furthered the passage of many prolabor bills. In his father's footsteps he was active in Democratic politics, working for Franklin D. Roosevelt's reelection in 1936 and also for that of Fiorello La Guardia, reform mayor of New York City, a Republican but an ally of Roosevelt. And he had strong labor support as a tenacious bargainer in disputes over wage rates for government workers.

At the beginning of 1940 Meany moved onto the national scene when he became secretary-treasurer of the AFL. In March 1941, Roosevelt named Meany one of four union officials on the new National Defense Mediation Board. Strongly anticommunist, Meany joined with DAVID DUBINSKY in opposing communist influence in the unions. At the end of World War II, in 1945, Meany led a boycott by the AFL of the inaugural meeting of the United Nations–sponsored World Federation of Trade Unions (WFTU), whose membership included unions from the Soviet Union. He was against any collaboration with Soviet labor organizations. At home, he fought vainly against passage of the antilabor Taft-Hartley Act, which Congress passed in June 1947 over President Harry S Truman's veto.

After William Green's death in 1952, Meany was elected president of the AFL. He worked thereafter for the merger of the AFL and the CIO (Congress of Industrial Organizations; see JOHN L. LEWIS), and when it came to pass he was elected president of the new federation. He directed a campaign against corruption in the unions, which brought about the expulsion of the International Brotherhood of Teamsters (see JAMES R. HOFFA) and two other big unions in 1957.

Meany had a cordial relationship with President John F. Kennedy and was in despair when Kennedy was assassinated. He was even friendlier with President Lyndon B. Johnson, and he backed the Vietnam War (a position he later retracted when he learned of the bombing of civilians). In the 1972 election, affronted by George McGovern's antiwar platform, he ordered the normally Democratic AFL-CIO to take a neutral position, possibly contributing to Richard M. Nixon's victory. Meany later broke with Nixon over the Watergate scandal and led the AFL-CIO in calling for Nixon's impeachment.

During the civil rights struggle Meany gave nominal support and encouraged AFL-CIO unions to stop discriminatory practices, but he had no patience with black activism during the 1960s and would not permit AFL-CIO members to take part in the great march on Washington led by MARTIN LUTHER KING, JR., in which the UAW president, WALTER REUTHER, joined. Toward the end of his career he was increasingly criticized for keeping the AFL-CIO separate from the social justice crusades of the day (such as civil rights), for failing to undertake vigorous organizing campaigns that would expand labor's ranks, and for tolerating the slippage of power away from rank-and-file members and toward labor chieftains like himself. Meany set the American labor movement on a course of declination from which it has never recovered.

After the death of his wife and a siege of serious illness, Meany resigned the presidency of the AFL-CIO in November 1979. He died two months later.

**BIBLIOGRAPHY**

Robinson, Archie, *George Meany and His Times: A Biography,* 1981; *Labor's Heritage,* 1988.

# Mencken, Henry Louis

(September 12, 1880–January 29, 1956)
Critic, Journalist, Philologist

HL. Mencken, as editor, newspaperman, iconoclastic critic, and literary stylist, was a liberalizing influence on American literature and social thought through the years before and after World War I. After 1930 his conservative political views tended to take over. In his late years he produced a much admired autobiography.

Harry Mencken, as he was called in his boyhood, was born into a German American family in Baltimore, Maryland, where he lived all his life. He was the eldest of four children of

August Mencken and Anna Abhau and the descendant of a line of lawyers and professors in Germany. His father and an uncle owned a successful cigar factory. (The adult Mencken was seldom seen without a cigar.) Young Mencken went to a private school, Knapp's Institute, favored by German Americans, and to a high school called the Baltimore Polytechnic, but much of his education came from the Enoch Pratt Free Library, which he frequented. He played the piano well and loved music. Harry Mencken graduated from the Polytechnic as class valedictorian in 1896 and, obedient to his father, took a job in the cigar factory. After his father's death in 1899, Mencken followed his ambition and became a reporter on the *Baltimore Morning Herald.*

By 1906 Mencken had advanced through police reporter, city editor, and managing editor on the *Evening Herald* (successor to the *Morning Herald*) and had become editor in chief when the paper failed. He joined the *Baltimore Sun* as Sunday editor and in 1910 moved to the *Evening Sun,* writing on local issues in a daily column that was usually controversial. With the outbreak of World War I, Mencken went to Germany as a correspondent for the *Sun.* When, upon returning to Baltimore in early 1917, he advocated that the United States enter the war on the German side, the paper declined to publish his articles. Mencken considered the rise of anti-German feeling to be hysterical, a product of Anglo-Saxon puritanism and government propaganda.

During the interlude when he was not writing for the *Sun,* Mencken began work on a remarkable philological study, *The American Language* (1919), which emphasized the difference between British and American usage. Throughout his career he continued his linguistic research, through four editions of the book, each revised and expanded, with supplements in 1945 and 1948. *The American Language* did much to create a consciousness of the distinct character of American speech, and Mencken's lively scholarship did not discourage an enthusiastic popular response, though professional linguists never accepted

him as a peer. In 1920 Mencken returned to the *Sun,* staying until 1948 and writing on every subject from the national political scene to local cuisine.

Mencken conducted a separate literary career beginning in 1905, when he published a critique of George Bernard Shaw's plays. In 1908 he brought out *The Philosophy of Friedrich Nietzsche,* and that year he began to review books for the monthly *Smart Set,* which he coedited with George Jean Nathan from 1914 to 1923. As a superb editor, he discovered and encouraged many new young writers. In 1917 he published *A Book of Prefaces,* and during the postwar years he brought out six volumes of *Prejudices,* essays of iconoclastic criticism and social satire. In 1923 Mencken and Nathan founded the *American Mercury* with the goal of enlightening the "civilized minority." The influential monthly featured diverse opinions on a wide range of issues affecting American culture. During the Great Depression, however, the *American Mercury*'s readership declined, and Mencken retired as editor in 1933.

Mencken's writings were required reading for up-to-date college students and those in American literary circles during the 1920s. His prose style was admired not only for its humor and liveliness but also for its clarity, grace, and truthfulness. The targets, or victims, of Mencken's typewriter were certain members of the American middle class—the conventional, genteel, fundamentalist, commercial-minded, philistine sort, for whom he introduced the term "booboisie." Always favoring realism, skepticism, and satire, Mencken helped to win a public for the work of Sinclair Lewis, Theodore Dreiser, Sherwood Anderson, Frank Norris, Willa Cather, Joseph Hergesheimer, and Stephen Crane.

While Mencken seemed the prototype of an independent bachelor, enjoying an evening of music and beer with his cronies, in 1930 he married Sara Powell Haardt, a novelist and short-story writer, and moved out of the family house into a more stylish part of Baltimore. His wife's health was delicate, and after she died in

1935, Mencken returned to Hollins Street and his bachelor life for good.

Mencken was called a liberal during the conservative 1920s and a conservative during the liberal 1930s, when his reputation went into decline. He was an adversary of the New Deal and President Franklin D. Roosevelt but was in no way the Nazi sympathizer and anti Semite that some of his detractors called him. On the contrary, he championed civil rights and freedoms.

In the 1940s Mencken's reputation revived when he began publishing his memoirs in installments in *The New Yorker*. They appeared in three volumes, *Happy Days, 1880–1892, Newspaper Days, 1899–1906,* and *Heathen Days, 1890–1936,* and were collected in one volume in 1947. Mencken continued to contribute to the *Sun,* his last assignment being to cover the presidential conventions of the Democratic, Republican, and Progressive parties in 1948. Soon afterward he suffered a stroke and, while not immobilized, spoke with difficulty and was unable to read or write. He died at home some seven years later.

**BIBLIOGRAPHY**

Cooke, Alistair (ed.), *The Vintage Mencken,* 1955; Fecher, Charles A. (ed.), *The Diary of H. L. Mencken,* 1989; Fitzpatrick, Vincent, *H. L. Mencken,* 1989; Forgue, Guy J. (ed.), *Letters of H. L. Mencken,* 1981.

# Meredith, James Howard

(June 25, 1933– )
Civil Rights Activist

James Meredith's application to the University of Mississippi in 1961 sparked a violent crisis that opened the way to the desegregation of the university and eventually of the state at large.

J. H. Meredith (as he was christened) was born and raised near Kosciusko, in central Mississippi, one of ten children of Moses and Roxie Meredith, who owned a large farm. After attending local segregated schools he went to St. Petersburg, Florida, where an uncle lived, and finished high school, again at a segregated institution. Looking toward a good education, in 1951 Meredith enlisted in the U.S. Air Force (at which time he expanded J. H. to James Howard).

Meredith spent nine years in the air force and was discharged a staff sergeant in summer 1960. During his service he had earned credits for college-level courses by correspondence. While he had his sights on the University of Mississippi, he had a wife and child, and realistically he decided to begin by entering Jackson State, a black college.

Meredith discussed his intentions with MEDGAR EVERS, the state field secretary for the National Association for the Advancement of Colored People (NAACP; see JOEL E. SPINGARN). Evers agreed that the association's legal defense and education fund could help Meredith with his effort to transfer to the University of Mississippi. His application was submitted on January 31, 1961. Nearly two years passed before Meredith's registration on October 1, 1962. Both the university and the state of Mississippi interposed resistance—political, legal, and finally, on Governor Ross R. Barnett's part, physical. A federal court order and the presence of federal troops brought the crisis to an end, but not before the campus was the scene of violence, rioting, and two deaths. Calm returned to the university, though troops remained, and Meredith graduated in August 1963. The attention this controversy attracted in the media made Meredith's name well known and raised national consciousness of the civil rights struggle.

During 1964 and 1965, Meredith was at the University of Ibadan, Nigeria, taking graduate courses in economics. He returned to the United States the following year to enroll in the college of law at Columbia University but interrupted his studies in 1966 to take part with STOKELY CARMICHAEL and others in a "March Against Fear" from Memphis to Jackson, the aim of which was to encourage voter registration. Segregationists shot at the marchers and wounded both leaders. Meredith, despite the lingering effects of his injuries, continued at Columbia and earned his law degree in 1968.

In later years Meredith lectured at American and African colleges and undertook various business ventures, including stockbroking and property investments in New York. After returning to Mississippi, in 1972 he ran unsuccessfully on the Republican ticket for the U.S. Senate against James Eastland. Despite his prominent role in the civil rights movement, Meredith was a political conservative at heart, and, in 1989, he joined the staff of Senator Jesse Helms, of North Carolina. For two years he devoted his time to an intensive study of American social policies from the eighteenth century to the present. Meredith then returned to Jackson to write a book and engage in local politics.

**BIBLIOGRAPHY**

Lord, Walter, *The Past That Would Not Die*, 1965; Meredith, James H., *Three Years in Mississippi*, 1965.

# Milk, Harvey Bernard

(May 22, 1930–November 27, 1978)
City Official, Gay Rights Activist

Harvey Milk was the first acknowledged homosexual official in San Francisco and possibly in the nation. He not only worked to protect gay rights but as a liberal Democrat championed many social causes.

Milk was born in Woodmere, on the south shore of Long Island near the edge of New York City. His grandfather, Morris Milch, had emigrated from Lithuania and worked up from peddling dry goods to owning a prestigious department store. Harvey's parents, William Milk and Minerva Karns, had both served in the U.S. Navy during World War I. There was an elder son, Robert, born four years before Harvey.

As a teenager, Harvey Milk was in love with opera and went in alone to the Metropolitan Opera House in Manhattan to buy standing room. It was at this time that he began to have secret homosexual experiences.

At high school in Bay Shore, a larger Long Island town where the family had moved, Milk was known as a jokester and a fairly good athlete—a tall basketball player and a football linebacker. After graduating in 1947, Milk went to the New York State Teachers College at Albany to major in liberal arts. He wrote up sports for the college newspaper and in his senior year was sports editor. Three months after graduating from college he enlisted in the navy, was sent to Officers Candidate School in Newport, Rhode Island, and by 1953 was a lieutenant junior grade on an aircraft carrier based at San Diego.

Having been honorably discharged in 1955, Milk went back east and taught history and mathematics at a Woodmere high school while coaching basketball for two years. After spending a year with a companion in Dallas, Texas, he came back to New York and began working as a statistician for an insurance company. In 1963, having switched to a job as a researcher for a Wall Street investment firm, Bache & Co., he discovered an intuitive gift for anticipating business trends that influenced investment futures. Within a year he was supervising the information center, and he continued to ascend the corporate ladder. In that milieu, his politics were strictly conservative. In 1967 Milk restlessly transferred to Bache's Dallas office. After a year, he resigned. His companion then was a stage director for the "tribal love-rock musical" *Hair,* and Milk began moving toward a countercultural viewpoint.

San Francisco Public Library

When his friend moved to San Francisco to direct another company of *Hair,* Milk followed and got a job as a financial analyst for a downtown firm. In spite of his success in that world, Milk found his political views steadily more liberal-to-left. In April 1970 he was so infuriated over the American invasion of Cambodia that he burned his BankAmericard before a crowd of protesters. His firm fired him, and he returned to New York and went into theater work. A *New York Times* reporter described him at the time as an aging hippie. The year 1972 found him back in San Francisco with a new consort, living on unemployment and tax refunds until he opened a camera shop in the gay neighborhood, where he became known as the Mayor of Castro Street.

Angered at politicians because of the televised Watergate hearings, Milk decided to run for the board of supervisors, the chief governing body of the city, in 1973. His local popularity encouraged him; he made his homosexuality known from the start. He campaigned for gay rights but also for expanded child-care facilities, low-rent housing, a civilian police-review board, and free municipal transportation. He was unsuccessful, but then did a little better in the 1975 election. In 1976 he was appointed by Mayor George Moscone to the Board of Permit Appeals but was removed after five weeks, whereupon he ran an exuberant campaign for the state assembly ("Harvey Milk vs. the Machine") and lost by a thin margin. In 1977, having attracted a solid liberal constituency in addition to his strong gay following, Milk was elected a supervisor. His wit and showmanship were never a political handicap.

In early 1978, Milk and Moscone put through a municipal ordinance protecting homosexual rights, the strongest such law in the nation. It passed the board of eleven supervisors with one negative vote, that of Dan White. Later in the year, after an antihomosexual state proposition was voted down, White resigned as supervisor. During his time in office, Milk's performance was regarded with strong approval by the majority of the electorate.

On November 27, 1978, Dan White, who had wanted to be reappointed and had learned that the mayor had decided against it, came to City Hall and shot Moscone and Harvey Milk dead in their offices.

**BIBLIOGRAPHY**

Shilts, Randy, *The Mayor of Castro Street: The Life and Times of Harvey Milk,* 1982; Weiss, Mike, *Double Play: The San Francisco City Hall Killings,* 1984.

# Miller, William

(February 15, 1782–December 20, 1849)
Religious Leader

William Miller was a Protestant leader who attracted a large and enthusiastic following by prophesying the Second Coming of Christ between 1843 and 1844. Miller's followers founded the Adventist Church, which later split into such groups as the Seventh-Day Adventists and the Advent Christian Church.

Born in Pittsfield, Massachusetts, Miller became a farmer first in Poultney, Vermont, and then in Hampton, New York. He also served as justice of the peace and deputy sheriff, and fought in the War of 1812. A self-educated man, Miller initially adopted the Deist belief in a rational, orderly universe in which God had only a limited role. But in 1816 he experienced a religious conversion and became a Baptist. After fifteen years of careful study of the Bible, especially the Book of Daniel, Miller became convinced that Christ would return to earth about 1843, and that the present world would give way to the millennium—a period of great holiness.

Such Adventist views were already being circulated as part of the religious revival known as the Second Great Awakening that swept the country in the early nineteenth century. But Miller was able to express these views in a clear and convincing manner. He began preaching in 1831, was ordained a Baptist minister in 1833, and published a book of his sermons in 1836. Wherever he preached, people converted. The Millerite movement also grew as a result of the efforts of the promoter, Joshua Vaughan Himes, who saw that Adventist papers like *Signs of the Times* of Boston and *The Midnight Cry* of New York were published in major cities and that reams of literature about the movement were distributed.

By 1843 Miller estimated his following at from 50,000 to 100,000. The Millerites, or Adventists, disposed of their worldly goods in preparation for the Second Coming of Christ. When the year passed without this occurring, some of Miller's associates recalculated the date, setting it at October 22, 1844. As the day approached, excitement reached a fever pitch.

When the day passed uneventfully, many of Miller's followers left the movement. But enough remained to form with Miller the Adventist Church in 1845, affirming their belief in the millennium, though without setting a specific date. After Miller's death in 1849, the Adventist movement continued, despite disputes over doctrine, which caused it to split into the Seventh-Day Adventists and the Advent Christian Church.

**BIBLIOGRAPHY**

Bliss, Sylvester, *Memoirs of William Miller*, 1853; Nichol, F. D., *The Midnight Cry*, 1944; Sears, C. E., *Days of Delusion*, 1924.

# Montezuma, Carlos

(ca. 1865–January 31, 1923)
American Indian Rights Leader, Physician

Carlos Montezuma (born Wassaja, which means "Signaling"), one of the most distinguished American Indians of the early twentieth century, was a physician who ministered both to his people and to urban American whites. Critical of the Bureau of Indian Affairs, he spoke out for American Indian rights and sought to publicize conditions on the reservations.

Soon after the Territory of Arizona was organized out of New Mexico Territory, Wassaja was born, in the Superstition Mountains east of Mesa. His parents were of the Yavapai tribe, though later in life he was thought to be an Apache, because the Yavapai were also called the Mohave-Apache. In 1871 he was captured by a warring band of Pima Indians; his parents later died. The Pimas sold the boy for $30 to an itinerant photographer, Carlos Gentile, who had him baptized Carlos Montezuma, perhaps after the Montezuma Castle ruins in Arizona. During their wandering life, the boy, a quick learner, went to schools in Illinois and New York City. After Gentile had business reverses and committed suicide, Montezuma had various guardians until he ended up with W. H. Steadman, a Baptist minister in Urbana, Illinois, who brought him into his fold.

Steadman helped Montezuma enter the University of Illinois, where he earned a B.S. degree in chemistry in 1884. He found work with a druggist who, learning that he wanted to study medicine, arranged for him to enroll at the Chicago Medical College. He received his M.D. degree in 1889 and soon afterward joined the Indian Service. Montezuma served as physician at several reservations in the West until, discouraged by the conditions he saw, he came east to practice at the Carlisle Indian School in Pennsylvania. There he found kindred spirits in the school's founder, Richard H. Pratt, and a teacher, GERTRUDE BONNIN, later an activist for Indian rights, to whom he was briefly engaged. The three opposed the reservation system of the Bureau of Indian Affairs and the inferior place it gave to American Indians. Montezuma called the reservation "a demoralized prison; a barrier against enlightenment, a promoter of idleness, beggary, gambling, pauperism, ruin and death."

In 1896 Montezuma moved on to Chicago and set up a successful practice in gastroenterology while teaching at the College of Physicians and Surgeons. In the early 1900s he revisited his home country and saw an abandoned army base, Fort McDowell, become a Yavapai reservation, where some of his relatives lived. Though Montezuma continued to argue for the abolition of the Bureau of Indian Affairs, in 1906 President Theodore Roosevelt proposed that he become its head, an offer he declined. Despite his interest in forming a Pan-Indian organization, when other activists organized the Society of American Indians, Montezuma refused to join, claiming that the bureau had contaminated it. In 1913, however, he agreed to serve on the society's executive committee and addressed its meetings, calling for an end to the bureau. At his own expense, in 1916 he launched a journal called by his Yavapai name, *Wassaja*, devoted chiefly to his campaign against the Bureau of Indian Affairs, and the next year when he protested against the draft of Indians into the armed forces he was imprisoned. President Woodrow Wilson obtained his release—and again a president offered him the post of Commissioner of Indian Affairs, and again Montezuma refused. He resumed his criticism of the Society of American Indians for working with the bureau, though when the society voted to recommend abolishing the bureau, in 1918, he praised its new officers, which included CHARLES EASTMAN, HENRY ROE CLOUD, and GERTRUDE BONNIN, and urged Indians to join.

In 1913 Montezuma had married Marie Keller, a non-Indian of Romanian ancestry, who was half his age. The Reverend W. H. Steadman performed the ceremony. In the early 1920s a threat from land speculators to move the Yavapai off the Fort McDowell reservation preoccupied Montezuma, who brought his prestige and wisdom to bear and saved the reservation. In December 1922, ill with tuberculosis, he went back to Fort McDowell to be among his people. Insisting on living in a brush shelter, he declined during winter weather and, with his wife beside him, died in January.

**BIBLIOGRAPHY**

Iverson, Peter, *Carlos Montezuma and the Changing World of American Indians,* 1982; Montezuma, Carlos, *Let My People Go,* 1914.

# Moody, Dwight Lyman

(February 5, 1837–December 22, 1899)
Religious Leader

Dwight Moody was a very popular and effective late–nineteenth-century evangelist. The creator of modern mass evangelism, he preached to audiences of thousands in the United States, Canada, and Great Britain.

Born in Northfield, Massachusetts, Moody left school at age thirteen to help support his widowed mother and his siblings. Moving to Boston when he was seventeen, he worked in a shoe store and underwent a religious conversion that led him to join the Congregational church. In 1856 he moved again, this time to Chicago, where he worked as a shoe salesman and became involved in religious work. In 1858, after volunteering to teach poor children in a mission Sunday school, Moody organized the North Market Sabbath School. The school became a center of evangelical activity and social services.

Library of Congress

Moody decided to give up his successful business career in 1860 and devote himself to religion as an independent city missionary. During the Civil War he helped erect prayer tents and nursed wounded and ill soldiers under the auspices of the Chicago Young Men's Christian Association (YMCA) and the United States Christian Commission. In 1864 he started the Illinois Street Church, a nondenominational "mission" church to minister to the urban poor. From 1865 to 1869 he served as president of the Chicago YMCA.

Moody's remarkable career as a popular revivalist began in 1873 when he teamed up with singer and organist Ira B. Sankey for the first of several evangelical tours of Great Britain. While Sankey sang such hymns as "Saved by Grace" and "Safe in the Arms of Jesus," Moody preached a message of friendship, kindness, and forgiveness to large, enthusiastic audiences. Upon his return to the United States in 1875, Moody settled in Northfield, using it as a base from which to conduct evangelical campaigns in every large city in the country, and also in Canada. Combining "old time" religion with business competence, Moody attracted a huge following, including many businessmen. A fundamentalist, he rejected the theory of evolution. He viewed the salvation of souls as the answer to many pressing social problems but steered clear of the Social Gospel movement with its emphasis on social reform. He did not choose to be ordained and remained a lay preacher all his life.

In 1879 Moody founded the Northfield Seminary for Girls with funds from the sale of the Sankey and Moody hymnal. Two years later, he founded the Mt. Hermon School for Boys. In the mid-1880s, Moody began conducting annual Bible conferences at Northfield to encourage young people to follow a religious life. In 1889 he founded the Moody Bible Institute in Chicago for lay foreign missionaries.

During the last twenty years of his life, Moody traveled to Great Britain and to many U.S. cities with his evangelical message. He conducted numerous student conferences, which in turn stimulated Christian voluntary organizations and the recruitment of missionaries. In 1899, in the midst of one of his many evangelical tours, he became ill; he died at the age of sixty-one, after his return to Northfield.

### BIBLIOGRAPHY

Abbott, Lyman, *Silhouettes of My Contemporaries*, 1921; Bradford, Gamaliel, *D. L. Moody, A Worker in Souls*, 1927; Farwell, J. V., *Early Recollections of Dwight L. Moody*, 1907; Findlay, James F., *Dwight L. Moody: American Evangelist, 1837–1899*, 1969; Moody, W. R., *The Life of Dwight L. Moody*, 1930.

# Morgan, Lewis Henry

(November 21, 1818–December 17, 1881)
Social Scientist

Lewis Henry Morgan was a pioneering nineteenth-century American anthropologist. He made the first scientific study of an American Indian nation and did important early work on kinship systems and successive stages in human society.

Born on a farm near Aurora, New York, Morgan attended Union College in Schenectady, New York, graduating in 1840. He then read law in Aurora, was admitted to the bar, and in 1844 moved to Rochester, New York, where he began a law practice. As an attorney and later director of a railroad company, Morgan acquired wealth, and he served in the New York Assembly and then the state senate during the years 1861 to 1869.

Morgan had first become interested in American Indian culture when he joined a secret society that called itself The Grand Order of the Iroquois. The club's aim was to study American Indian lore and to educate Indians into "civilized" ways. In the 1840s the club helped the Seneca, an Iroquois nation, defeat a fraudulent treaty by which the nation stood to lose its lands. Morgan went to Washington, D.C., in behalf of the Seneca, and in 1847 was adopted into the nation. Meanwhile, he had begun to collect material and write about American Indian life. In 1851 Morgan published his pathbreaking scientific study, *The League of the Ho-de-no-sau-nee, or Iroquois*.

Becoming interested in the Iroquois system of kinship, Morgan published a pamphlet on the subject in 1858, then went on to study the kinship systems of more than seventy American Indian nations in Michigan, Kansas, Nebraska, and the Dakotas. He reached the conclusion that the kinship system of the Iroquois was remarkably similar to those of nations throughout North America. Expanding the scope of his inquiries to include primitive kinship throughout the world, Morgan in 1860 had the Smithsonian Institution circulate a questionnaire on primitive kinship systems to all its foreign correspondents. The publication of his *Systems of Consanguinity and Affinity of the Human Family* (1871) established kinship as the chief organizing principle of anthropological studies of rural societies.

Morgan's work on kinship systems led him to theorize about how different forms of social life developed over the course of human history. In 1877, after much reading, correspondence, and conversations with Charles Darwin and others, Morgan published his most important book, *Ancient Society, or Researches in the Lines of Human Progress*. In it Morgan maintained that all human races had a common origin and underwent the same passage through stages of savagery, barbarism, and civilization. He linked advances in food pro-

duction to each of these stages. Morgan also postulated that the family grew out of a state of promiscuity. His ideas influenced other theorists, including Karl Marx and Frederick Engels. Although contemporary anthropologists have rejected specifics of Morgan's analysis, they have retained his general sequence of stages, now described as "hunting and gathering," followed by "horticulture," and then "urban" society.

During the 1870s, Morgan continued with his studies of American Indian culture, focusing on architecture, history, and migrations, and in keeping with his interest in Indian welfare introduced laws to help the Iroquois. His last book, published shortly before his death, was *Houses and House—life of the American Aborigines* (1881).

Morgan was elected to the National Academy of Sciences in 1875, becoming president of the American Association for the Advancement of Science in 1879. He died in Rochester at the age of sixty-three in 1881.

**BIBLIOGRAPHY**

Resek, Carl, *Lewis Henry Morgan, American Scholar*, 1960; Stern, B. J., *Lewis Henry Morgan, Social Evolutionist*, 1931.

# Moses, Robert

(December 18, 1888–July 29, 1981)
Public Official, Urban Planner

Known as the Master Builder and the Power Broker, Robert Moses transformed New York City's system of parks and parkways. His influence on city planning extended beyond New York to the entire nation and several foreign countries.

Robert Moses was born in New Haven, Connecticut, the son of a well-to-do department-store owner, Emanuel Moses, whose wife, Bella

Silverman, persuaded him to move to New York City in 1897. The Moses' only son, Robert, grew up in a luxurious town house on East 46th Street. He entered Yale University at the age of seventeen, younger than most of his class, and distinguished himself as a poet, a swimmer, and a scholar (Phi Beta Kappa). After graduating in 1909, he spent four years at Oxford University, where he was the first American student to become president of the Oxford Union. After earning an M.A. in 1913, he returned to New York for graduate work in the School of Political Science at Columbia University, which granted him a Ph.D. in 1914 for a thesis on the civil service of Great Britain.

Young Moses, noted as an idealist at Yale and Oxford, went to work for the Municipal Research Bureau, an advisory branch of the government reform movement in New York. The reform-minded mayor John Purroy Mitchel asked the Municipal Research Bureau to devise a plan for restructuring the city's civil service system, which, dominated by Tammany Hall (the name for the Democratic party machine), was riddled with influence-peddling and graft. The bureau appointed Moses for the job. His reform plan, resembling plans he had put forward in his Ph.D. thesis, was shoved aside when Mitchel was defeated for reelection in 1917. The next year Belle Moskowitz, Governor Alfred E. Smith's principal adviser, hired Moses as chief of staff of a commission that was to plan complete reorganization of the state government. Moskowitz tutored the young idealist in the realities of practical politics, and Moses too became a principal adviser to the governor. In 1924 Smith appointed him president of the New York State Council of Parks, which was based on plans Moses had presented in 1920 for statewide improvement of parks and highways. Three years later, he appointed Moses the New York secretary of state, the beginning of a long career as a power broker.

Among the city and state appointments Moses held, often simultaneously, the most prominent were those of New York City Parks Commissioner, head of the State Parks Council, head of the State Power Commission, and chairman of the Triborough Bridge and Tunnel Authority. Undoubtedly his most popular accomplishment was Jones Beach State Park, on the south shore of Long Island. Moses worked to build more than a dozen bridges and tunnels, including the Brooklyn-Battery Tunnel, Triborough Bridge, and the Verrazano Narrows Bridge; more than thirty expressways and parkways, including the Long Island Expressway and the Palisades Parkway; and hundreds of parks and playgrounds. Among other public works built under Moses's supervision were the New York World's Fair of 1964 and 1965, Lincoln Center, and the St. Lawrence Seaway. He played a crucial part in negotiations to bring United Nations headquarters to New York.

Some social thinkers, such as LEWIS MUMFORD, saw Moses's vision of the city, and New York City in particular, as disastrous. His eye was fixed on an automobile civilization, and he had an active hostility to mass transit. The funds Moses spent on highways far exceeded what he allowed to be spent on mass transit. The consequence was the chaos and congestion of untrammeled automobile traffic. His biographer, Robert Caro, wrote that "For decades . . . [Moses] systematically defeated every attempt to create the master plan that might have enabled the city to develop on a rational, logical, unified pattern."

In later years Moses's influence dwindled. He died at the age of ninety-two at a hospital near his home on the south shore of Long Island.

**BIBLIOGRAPHY**

Caro, Robert, *The Power Broker*, 1974; Moses, Robert, *Working for People*, 1956.

# Mott, Lucretia Coffin

(January 3, 1793–November 11, 1880)
Reformer, Religious Leader

As a Quaker minister, abolitionist, and women's rights advocate, Lucretia Mott played an early and major role in the American reform movement.

Lucretia Coffin was born into a long-established Nantucket, Massachusetts, family. Growing up in the island's close-knit Quaker community, in which women were considered the spiritual equals of men, she early on developed a strong sense of women's rights. She received her education at the island Quaker school, in schools in Boston after the family's move there, and at Nine Partners, a coeducational Quaker boarding school near Poughkeepsie, New York. Asked to stay on as a teacher, she met and in 1811 married James Mott, a New York Quaker who was also a teacher there. The couple settled in Philadelphia, where the Coffin family had moved and where James Mott went into business with her father. The marriage was an extremely happy one.

After the death of their baby, Lucretia Mott turned to religion and in 1821 became a Quaker minister. When the Society of Friends split into Orthodox and Hicksite branches, she and her husband joined the more liberal branch headed by Elias Hicks. Lucretia Mott's Quakerism informed her early antislavery position, as Elias Hicks opposed slavery and urged Friends not to use such products of slave labor as sugar and cotton. Her abolitionism was further fueled by a meeting with WILLIAM LLOYD GARRISON in 1830. Three years later, she attended the founding convention of the American Anti-Slavery So-

Sophia Smith Collection, Smith College

ciety in Philadelphia. Since the society did not allow women members, she helped form a women's auxiliary, the Philadelphia Female Antislavery Society. In 1837 she helped organize the Anti-Slavery Convention of American Women.

In 1840 Mott went as a delegate to the World Anti-Slavery Convention in London but could not take part because of her sex. Here she met ELIZABETH CADY STANTON. The two women organized a women's rights movement eight years later at a convention at Seneca Falls, New York. For the historic 1848 convention Mott helped draft a Declaration of Sentiments modeled after the Declaration of Independence and claiming equal rights, including the right to vote. Thereafter she regularly attended the women's rights conventions held in the following years and in 1852 was elected president of the convention at Syracuse, New York.

After the Civil War and the passage of the Thirteenth Amendment abolishing slavery, Mott worked for equal rights for African Americans and was active in the Friends Association of Philadelphia for the Aid and Elevation of the Freedmen. She also helped to raise money for Swarthmore College, which opened in 1864, and was vice president of the Pennsylvania Peace Society. Increasingly liberal in her religious views, Mott joined with other like-minded people in forming the Free Religious Association in Boston in 1867. She also remained active in the women's rights movement and was in 1866 elected president of the American Equal

Rights Association, an organization which backed civil rights for both women and blacks.

Lucretia Mott possessed great oratorical skills, along with enormous energy and an ability to make lasting friendships. Commanding the respect of fellow reformers and opponents alike, she lent credibility to even the most seemingly radical of causes. Throughout her life, Mott's overriding concern was to secure emancipation for the oppressed, whether women, African Americans, or people bound by narrow religious doctrines. Active till the end, she died peacefully at her home at the age of eighty-seven.

**BIBLIOGRAPHY**

Bacon, Margaret, *Valiant Friend: The Life of Lucretia Coffin Mott,* 1980; Greene, D. (ed.), *Lucretia Mott. Her Complete Speeches and Sermons,* 1981; Sterling, Dorothy, *Lucretia Mott: Gentle Warrior,* 1964.

# Muhammad, Elijah

(October 7, 1897–February 25, 1975)
Black Muslim Leader

Elijah Muhammad, as spiritual leader of the Nation of Islam, established a religious organization that gave poor urban black people a sense of racial pride and of economic and political self-sufficiency.

Born Elijah Poole, one of thirteen children of former slaves, he grew up on a cotton plantation in Sandersville, in central Georgia. His father, Wali Poole, sharecropped and was a Baptist preacher. The boy Elijah left school when he was nine and worked at a sawmill and in the cotton fields. Later, after a job in a Southern Railway gang, he went on the road, taking what work he could find. In his mid-twenties, with a wife and two children (eventually eight), he settled in Detroit and worked on the General Motors assembly line.

AP/Wide World Photos

In 1930, while jobless, Poole met a door-to-door silk peddler, Wali Farrad (or W. D. Fard), who called himself Allah and preached the message of the Lost-Found Nation of Islam, which he had founded. He converted Poole, who became a devoted disciple. Two years later he sent him to Chicago to establish the Nation of Islam's second temple. Farrad's doctrines included not only Muslim beliefs but the view that white treachery caused black misery. In 1934 Farrad disappeared: some thought he had gone to Mecca, others that he had met with foul play, of which Poole was suspected. Assuming the surname Muhammad to replace his "slave name," Elijah took over Farrad's library of some hundred sacred books and his movement, the headquarters of which he moved to Chicago. Elijah Muhammad declared that "Allah" had named him his Messenger. His followers were known as the Black Muslims.

Muhammad preached that white people had Christianized black people in order to control and exploit them. He advocated that blacks cherish their racial dignity and form a separate, self-sufficient nation with its own schools and economic structure. Under his authoritarian guidance, the Nation of Islam won many thousands of members, chiefly among the ghetto poor, and established a network of successful businesses, quite independent from the white community. Black Muslims were expected to abstain from drugs, alcohol, tobacco, pork, and sinful sexual behavior and were not to marry outside their race. They followed the law but did not vote. They worked hard and sought education that would bring advancement. Most Muslims gave up their "slave name" and took "X" as a surname.

Muhammad's activities attracted little notice from white Americans until the outbreak of World War II, when he supported Japan on the ground that it was not a white country. Because he advised young black men not to serve in the armed forces, he was tried for sedition. Though acquitted of that crime, he was convicted of refusing to register for selective service and spent four years (1942–1946) in a Michigan penitentiary. His behavior during imprisonment earned him respect from many black people outside his congregation. Muhammad, furthermore, converted numerous black prisoners. Even after his release from prison, his teachings were to influence such leaders as MALCOLM X and ELDRIDGE CLEAVER.

In the 1950s Malcolm X became Muhammad's leading student and, in short order, his lieutenant. But a rivalry developed, as Malcolm leaned toward an integrationist position, and in 1965 he was assassinated—some believed the gunmen were rival Black Muslims, which Muhammad denied.

In his later years Muhammad somewhat moderated his antiwhite doctrine and began to reach out to the black middle class. He divided his time between his Chicago headquarters and an estate in Scottsdale, Arizona, where he spent winters because of asthma. When he died of congestive heart failure in Chicago, the membership of the Nation of Islam was estimated at 160,000. The leadership passed to a son, Warith Deen Muhammad, who welcomed white Muslims. An offshoot headed by Louis Abdul Farrakhan restricts its adherents to African Americans.

The *New York Times,* in an editorial on Muhammad after his death, remarked that "the positive aspect of the Black Muslim movement, the success it has had in rehabilitating and inspiring thousands of once defeated and despairing men and women, suggests a need for deeper popular understanding."

**BIBLIOGRAPHY**

Lincoln, C. E., *The Black Muslims in America,* 1973; Muhammad, Elijah, *Message to the Black Man,* 1964; Weisbrot, Robert, *Freedom Bound: A History of America's Civil Rights Movement,* 1990.

# Muir, John

(April 21, 1838–December 24, 1914)
Author, Explorer, Naturalist

As a naturalist, explorer, and author, John Muir was a major figure in the forest conservation movement in the United States. Largely through his efforts, Yosemite and Sequoia national parks were established.

John Muir was born in Dunbar, Scotland, and received his early education there. In 1849 he immigrated with his family to the Wisconsin frontier, where his father started a farm near Portage. Muir later described these years on the farm in his autobiographical work, *The Story of My Boyhood and Youth* (1913). His stern, Calvinist father made him work long hours at strenuous labor. But in his spare time Muir read every book he could lay his hands on, even waking up early in the morning to be able to read. This self-education enabled him to enroll at the University of Wisconsin in 1860.

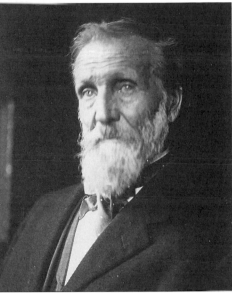
Library of Congress

Muir left the university in 1863 without taking a degree, because he preferred to select his own courses rather than follow a set curriculum. By this time, he had become deeply interested in botany, and he went on many walking trips through the midwest and into Canada. In 1867 an accidental injury to one of his eyes while he was working at a carriage factory made Muir decide to give up mechanical inventions and devote himself instead to, in his words, "the study of the inventions of God." He traveled by foot from Indiana to the Gulf of Mexico, keeping a journal in which he recorded his observations of the plants, animals, and people he met along the way. His journal was later published as *A Thousand-Mile Walk to the Gulf* (1916).

Arriving in California in 1868, Muir went immediately to Yosemite Valley, where he remained for the next six years. He made many excursions into the mountains, and also into Nevada, Utah, the Northwest, and eventually Alaska. As before, he recorded his observations and made pencil sketches of what he saw. Muir was particularly interested in forests and glaciers. Whereas earlier scientists had decided that Yosemite Valley, with its broad valley floor, steep cliffs mounted with huge rounded domes, and dramatic waterfalls must have been formed by a cataclysm in the earth's surface, Muir was the first to argue that the valley had actually been formed by glacial erosion. In 1871 he found glaciers still active in the Sierra Nevada Mountains. Continuing his explorations into Alaska, Muir in 1879 discovered Glacier Bay and a glacier was named for him.

Also during these years, Muir began a career as a nature writer. He wrote articles based on his journal entries that appeared in such publications as *Scribner's Monthly*, the *Overland Monthly*, and the *Century Magazine*, describing in vivid prose the beauties of western forests and scenery. These articles helped educate Americans about the need to preserve natural beauty.

In 1880 Muir married and moved to Alhambra, California, where for the next decade he supported himself and his family as a fruit grower. His writing diminished during this period, but by the end of it he had made enough money to devote himself to nature study, writing, and conservation.

In 1889 Muir took Robert Underwood Johnson, the editor of *Century Magazine,* on a camping trip in Yosemite Valley. Although at the time the area was a state reservation, sheep, which Muir referred to as "hoofed locusts," were allowed to graze in the valley meadows and alpine gardens, causing great destruction with their tramping and feeding. Thefts of timber were also common. Muir and Johnson were so appalled by the devastation of the valley that they launched a campaign for the establishment of Yosemite National Park. Muir wrote a series of articles for *Century* detailing how Yosemite Valley was being ruined. As a result of his efforts, Congress passed the Yosemite National Park Bill in October 1890, creating Yosemite, Sequoia, and General Grant national parks.

In 1892 Muir took part in a lobbying campaign against a congressional bill that proposed to reduce the boundaries of Yosemite National Park by one-half. That same year, he helped form the Sierra Club to coordinate the work of conservationists. As the club's first president (a post he held for the rest of his life), Muir built the Sierra Club into one of the most important and longest-lasting conservation organizations in the country. In 1894 Muir published his first book, *The Mountains of California,* which further cemented his reputation as an advocate for preserving natural beauty.

As early as 1876 Muir had urged the appointment of a national commission to look into the destruction of forests, make a survey of publicly owned forest lands, and recommend measures for their conservation. When a forestry commission was finally appointed in 1896, Muir was invited to accompany it on its investigations. Based on the commission's recommendations, President Grover Cleveland created thirteen forest reservations of more than 21 million acres. However, commercial and political interests fought successfully to restore to the public domain all the forest reserves except those of California until March 1, 1898.

In the ensuing battle—between what Muir called "landscape righteousness and the devil"—Muir again wielded his pen in behalf of conservation. Two articles, "Forest Reservations and National Parks" and "American Forests," for *Harper's Weekly* and the *Atlantic Monthly,* respectively, were so successful in winning public support that in 1898 when the opponents of the reservation policy again tried to have the forests reserves annulled, they failed.

In the spring of 1903 Muir went on a brief camping trip in Yosemite and the surrounding area with President Theodore Roosevelt. He seized the opportunity to convince the already conservation-minded Roosevelt of the need to set aside more land. As a result, Roosevelt subsequently established 148 million additional acres of forest reserves, doubled the number of national parks, and created sixteen national monuments. One of the latter, a magnificent redwood grove near San Francisco, was named the Muir Woods National Monument in Muir's honor.

Muir spent the last years of his life fighting to prevent the lovely Hetch-Hetchy Valley in Yosemite National Park from being turned into a reservoir to supply water for San Francisco. Although a board of army engineers reported that other sources of water were available to the city, Muir and his supporters ultimately lost the battle. Nevertheless, the vigorous campaign they waged did much to raise the national consciousness about the importance of wilderness preservation.

John Muir died in Los Angeles in 1914. His other books include *Our National Parks* (1901) and *The Yosemite* (1912).

**BIBLIOGRAPHY**

Cohen, Michael P., *The Pathless Way: John Muir and the American Wilderness,* 1984; Fox, Stephen, *John Muir and His Legacy: The American Conservation Movement,* 1981; Turner, Frederick, *Rediscovering America: John Muir in His Time and Ours,* 1985.

# Mumford, Lewis Charles

(October 19, 1895–January 26, 1990)
Cultural Historian, Social Philosopher

Lewis Mumford was a philosopher; a literary scholar; a historian; an essayist concerned with culture, society, politics, and morality; and a critic of city planning and of architecture in general. His influence on American thought and policy has been profound.

Mumford was born in Flushing, now part of Queens, New York. Only late in his life did he reveal that he was the illegitimate son of a businessman, Lewis Charles Mack. His mother, Elvina Conradina Baron, of German descent, had been married briefly to John Mumford, and after the marriage was annulled she kept his name. While working as housekeeper in the home of a bachelor, Jacob Mack, she had a love affair with his young nephew, Lewis. Elvina Mumford brought up her son alone, in a boardinghouse she ran on the West Side of New York. The boy Mumford went to public schools and briefly considered becoming an electrical engineer. While working as a copyboy for the *Telegram*, he attended evening classes at the City College of New York. He later took courses at Columbia University and the New School for Social Research but was not interested in a degree. In 1918 he enlisted in the navy and served less than a year ashore as a radio technician.

Early on, strongly influenced by the writings of Sir Patrick Geddes, a Scottish biologist, sociologist, and town planner, Mumford had set his sights on being a writer of similarly broad interests. In 1919 Mumford began reviewing books for *The Dial*, then a journal of opinion, mainly radical. Though its life was brief, *The Dial* attracted some of the best young radical writers and pundits in America at the time, including RANDOLPH BOURNE. After submitting only two reviews, Mumford was hired as an associate editor. At *The Dial* he met Sophia Wittenberg, an assistant editor, whom he married two years later. They had a

son and a daughter. After a year in London (arranged by Geddes) as acting editor of the *Sociological Review,* Mumford embarked on his lifetime career as a freelance writer, interspersed with many academic appointments. His work encompassed a notable range of disciplines.

Mumford published his first book, *The Story of Utopias,* in 1922; in 1924 he published his first book on architecture, *Sticks and Stones.* In 1923 he was a cofounder of the Regional Planning Association of America and helped plan Sunnyside Gardens, in Queens, where he and his family lived for ten years before moving to the village of Leedsville, in upstate New York, near his close friend JOEL E. SPINGARN. He devoted three books to nineteenth-century American culture: *The Golden Day* (1926), *Herman Melville* (1929), and *The Brown Decades* (1931). In 1932 he began contributing a column on architecture, "The Sky Line," to *The New Yorker,* where it appeared for some thirty years. In 1934 he published *Technics and Civilization,* the first volume in what he called the Renewal of Life series, which continued with *The Culture of Cities* (1938), *The Condition of Man* (1944), and *The Conduct of Life* (1951). In 1947 he published *Green Memories,* a biography of his son, Geddes, who was killed in World War II.

As a critic of architecture and city planning, Mumford clashed with ROBERT MOSES, whose large-scale public works and expressways he believed were planning at its worst. He led a campaign against Moses's plan to build a road through Washington Square in New York City. Mumford saw the domination of the machine—or the megamachine, as he called it—as the growing threat for Western civilization, in its negation of human feelings and humanistic values. A major late work, *The Myth of the Machine* (in two volumes, 1967 and 1971), was his extended statement of his ultimate philosophy. During World War II, Mumford actively supported aid to the Allies; twenty-five years later, he protested American involvement in Vietnam. The power of the military-industrial complex and the threat of nuclear disaster preoccupied him. Among his many honors were the presidency of the American Academy of Arts and Letters, the National Medal for Literature (1972), an honorary knighthood bestowed by Queen Elizabeth II, and the National Medal of Arts, awarded by President Ronald Reagan in 1986, when Mumford was ninety. Mumford died in his old house at Leedsville at the age of ninety-four.

**BIBLIOGRAPHY**

Blake, Casey Nelson, *Beloved Community: The Cultural Criticism of Randolph Bourne, Van Wyck Brooks, Waldo Frank, and Lewis Mumford,* 1990; Hughes, Thomas P., and Agatha C. Hughes, *Lewis Mumford: Public Intellectual,* 1990; Miller, Donald L., *Lewis Mumford: A Life,* 1989; Mumford, Lewis, *The City in History,* 1961, and *Sketches from Life,* 1982.

# Murray, Philip

(May 25, 1886–November 9, 1952)
Labor Leader

Philip Murray, a coal miner from childhood, became a stabilizing influence in the American labor movement and particularly in the leadership of the CIO after he succeeded JOHN L. LEWIS. He supported the New Deal and accepted the government's role in establishing labor policies.

Though born in the village of Blantyre, near Glasgow, Scotland, Murray was the son of Roman Catholics from Ireland. His mother, Rose Ann Layden, died when he was two. His father, William, remarried, and in time there were eleven children in the family. Philip, the eldest son, from the age of ten worked in the mines with his father, who was secretary of his local union. When he was sixteen, Philip and his father went to the United States and settled in the coal country east of Pittsburgh, where their international coal-union transfer cards enabled them to go to work. In a year's time they were able to bring over the rest of the family.

When young Murray got into an altercation with his weigh boss, who was cheating him, and was fired, the union called a strike. The strike came to nothing, and Murray left town to spare his family. At this point he decided to make his career in the union movement. When he was eighteen, he was elected president of a United Mine Workers (UMW) local. To make up for his meager education (which had stopped when he was ten), he studied science and mathematics by correspondence at night and proved to be a quick learner. In 1910 he married Elizabeth Lavery, a coal miner's daughter, and the next year he became a U.S. citizen.

In 1912 Murray was elected to the UMW international executive board. His rise as a union officer was rapid. Eight years later he was named vice president by John L. Lewis, whom he had backed for the presidency, and he was Lewis's right-hand man for more than twenty years. Murray handled negotiations with dissatisfied members and appeared before congressional committees.

During World War I, President Woodrow Wilson named Murray to the War Labor Board. In 1921 President Warren G. Harding asked Murray to use his position to end violence in West Virginia where thousands of coal miners were in a violent struggle against state police and mine guards. Murray was effective in settling the dispute.

Under the National Industrial Recovery Act in the New Deal years, Murray was involved in the drive to reorganize the UMW and expand its membership. The craft unions of the American Federation of Labor (AFL; see WILLIAM GREEN and JOHN L. LEWIS) were alarmed at the prospect of industrial unionization (organizing all workers in an industry into one union), which Murray argued for at the 1935 AFL convention. When his case was rejected, Murray joined Lewis in leading the UMW and seven other industrial unions out of the AFL to form the Committee for Industrial Organization, later called the Congress of Industrial Organizations (CIO; see JOHN L. LEWIS). Becoming vice president of the CIO (Lewis was president), Murray headed its Steel Workers' Organizing Committee, which set to unionizing the workers of United States Steel. Aided by the Wagner Act and the National Labor Relations Board (NLRB), the Big Steel campaign succeeded; likewise, the unionization of workers in the automobile, textile, and rubber industries was accomplished. Less success met the campaign to organize Little Steel (the smaller companies), and Murray called for a strike. On Memorial Day, 1937, violence erupted when ten Republic Steel workers were shot by police. The courts later held Republic and other companies in violation of the Wagner Act and forced them to sign union contracts.

In the 1940 election, John L. Lewis opposed President Franklin D. Roosevelt's candidacy for a third term and supported the Republican candidate Wendell Willkie. When Roosevelt was reelected, Lewis resigned as CIO president and supported Murray as his successor. In 1942, however, he forced Murray out as UMW vice president, charging that he neglected his responsibilities, and soon afterward Lewis took the UMW out of the CIO. The long friendship between Murray and Lewis was broken. Besides being president of the CIO, Murray became president of the United Steelworkers of America.

During World War II, Murray was a member of the National Defense Mediation Board. He reluctantly pledged a no-strike policy for his steelworkers, but when the war was over he led them in several winning strikes for higher wages. Murray belonged to the National Association for the Advancement of Colored People (NAACP; see JOEL E. SPINGARN) and condemned racial discrimination in the CIO unions. He supported Roosevelt's reelection in 1944 and Harry S Truman's election in 1948, having joined with President Truman in a vain attempt to defeat the Taft-Hartley Bill, which imposed strictures on unions. Though opposed to communist influence in labor, he accepted the reality of working with the Soviet Union to defeat Nazism. In 1949, however, he took the initiative in expelling communist-led unions from the CIO.

Murray campaigned for a Democratic victory in 1952 and was dejected when Adlai Stevenson lost to Dwight D. Eisenhower. In California to preside over the fourteenth convention of the CIO, he died of a heart attack four days after the presidential election.

**BIBLIOGRAPHY**

Brophy, John, *A Miner's Life*, 1964; Dubofsky, Melvyn, and Warren Van Tine (eds.), *Labor Leaders in America*, 1987.

# Murrow, Edward Roscoe

(April 25, 1908–April 27, 1965)
News Commentator

Edward R. Murrow was an independent-minded newsman who emphasized plain speaking and straightforward reporting on a high level of integrity. In the words of the *New York Times*, "No other figure in broadcast news left such a strong stamp on both radio and television."

Murrow was born at Pole Cat Creek, near Greensboro, North Carolina, son of a farmer, Roscoe C. Murrow, and Ethel Lamb. He was named Egbert Roscoe Murrow, but as he grew up he became Ed, then Edward. When he was six, the family moved to a small town, Blanchard, in northern Washington. His father became a locomotive engineer for a lumber company, and young Murrow spent summers working on a survey gang in the camps. He got a taste of frontier life and labor excitement brought on by the Industrial Workers of the World (see WILLIAM D. HAYWOOD). At his high school he was student body president and a champion debater. In 1930 Murrow graduated from Washington State College (now University), in Pullman, with a B.A. in the speech program, which included the first college course in radio broadcasting given in the United States.

At college Murrow had become president of the National Student Federation (NSF), and after graduating he went to New York City to lead the federation's work, giving talks at colleges, arranging student exchanges, and finding speakers for the University of the Air, a Columbia Broadcasting System (CBS) feature. (At an NSF conference he met Janet Brewster, whom he later married. She also became a broadcaster.) Murrow moved on to the Institute of International Education as assistant director in 1932, and the following year, as Hitler and the Nazi party took power in Germany, he became involved in bringing anti-Nazi scholars to the United States. CBS put Murrow in charge of arranging talks for its network in 1935, and

two years later it sent him to Europe as director of its programs beamed to America. As political events moved rapidly forward, Murrow's voice became well known. He broadcast eyewitness reports of historic happenings—such as Hitler's entrance into Vienna in March 1938 after German troops occupied Austria, which became part of the German Reich. Murrow and his staff originated the news roundup, in which, during a broadcast, reporters' accounts were picked up from several different cities. He recruited a remarkable team of foreign correspondents, all experienced journalists. Murrow made London his base during World War II. He brought home the realities of the war to the American people through his reports as they happened, describing the German blitz (bombing raids) on British cities as well as British and American raids on German cities. He reported from air-raid shelters, hospitals, camps, and—at the end of the war—from the Nazi concentration camp at Buchenwald, Germany, where he witnessed the camp's liberation by Allied troops. He was as much a presence to the British people as to Americans and was later honored by Queen Elizabeth II with an honorary knighthood.

Returning to the United States, Murrow was on the air for CBS every night giving the news with his commentary—a program that became the authoritative account of what had happened at home and abroad. Murrow saw radio and television as the means for informing and educating the public, and his objection to commercialization often brought him into conflict with the networks.

From 1951 to 1958, Murrow and Fred W. Friendly produced a weekly television program called "See It Now," devoted to national and international events and problems and considered the most objective, informative, and penetrating on the air. One of the most interesting episodes of "See It Now" was an attack on Senator Joseph McCarthy that aired in 1954. By weaving footage of McCarthy's anticommunist speeches and his outbursts against witnesses before the House Un-American Affairs Committee, Murrow created a harsh but accurate portrait of the senator. In the 1950s he launched "Person to Person," in which he visited with celebrities in their homes, and another, "Small World," involving conversations by telephone with distinguished personages abroad, with relevant films and photographs.

After CBS ended "See It Now" in favor of entertainment that attracted larger audiences, Murrow's disagreement with broadcasting policy became acute. In October 1958 he delivered a famous speech to a meeting of the Radio and

Television News Directors Association harshly criticizing the networks for their encouragement of "decadence, escapism, and insulation from the realities of the world in which we live." His resignation from CBS followed.

In early 1961 Murrow joined the administration of President John F. Kennedy as director of the U.S. Information Agency and served for three years, until illness forced him to retire. Well known as a three-pack-a-day smoker, he died of lung cancer a year later.

**BIBLIOGRAPHY**

Barnouw, Erik, *The Golden Web,* 1968; Kendrick, Alexander, *Prime Time,* 1969.

## Muste, Abraham John

(January 8, 1885–February 11, 1967)
Pacifist

For over half a century, the Reverend Abraham John Muste was an internationally renowned advocate of pacifism.

Muste was born in Zierikzee, the Netherlands, and immigrated to Grand Rapids, Michigan, with his family in 1891. He received his B.A. from Hope College in Holland, Michigan, in 1905, and his M.A. from Hope College in 1909 after studying at the New Brunswick Theological Seminary in New Jersey. He was also awarded a Bachelor of Divinity degree from Union Theological Seminary in 1913.

Muste first attracted public attention the winter of 1917 when he resigned as pastor of the Central Congregational Church in Newton, Massachusetts, in protest of American participation in World War I. He explained to his stunned congregation one Sunday morning that since wars could be avoided and were not in the spirit of Christ, he could not pretend to be able to provide the kind of prowar religious support the church membership expected.

For the next year and a half the unemployed Muste and his wife and daughter lived in housing provided by Quakers in Providence, Rhode

Island. He joined the Fellowship of Reconciliation (FOR), an interfaith pacifist organization which the Quakers had sponsored. Encountering socialists who were equally vocal in their opposition to war, Muste became attracted to the socialist critique of American society and especially of capitalist exploitation of labor. In February 1919, he volunteered his services to help the cause of organized labor during a strike in Lawrence, Massachusetts. He was beaten by the police and arrested for his efforts, but he persevered. When the strike was settled in labor's favor, Muste was credited with playing a major role in securing the victory. He did volunteer work also for the American Civil Liberties Union (ACLU; see ROGER BALDWIN), of which he was one of the founders.

During the 1920s and early 1930s, Muste deepened his commitment to labor, while continuing his work in FOR. He served as the Education Director of Brookwood Labor College, in Katonah, New York, a small residential school dedicated to training the children of labor families to become the future leaders of organized labor. Muste's labor union activities led to his arrest again as one of the leaders of a strike in Paterson, New Jersey, in 1931. The mass suffering caused by the Great Depression moved Muste for a time to abandon his commitment to nonviolence and to advocate the need for revolutionary and, if necessary, violent change. In 1934 he founded the American Workers' party and drew close to the Trotskyist wing of the Socialist party to forward that aim. His experience with leftist politics left him disillusioned, however, and prompted his return, by 1940, to his earlier commitment to pacifism and nonviolence.

His conviction that "war does not bring peace, it merely breeds more war" led him in 1940 to become executive secretary of FOR. When World War II broke out, he refused to support American involvement. Instead, he stood up at a Quaker meeting and said, "If I can't love Hitler, I can't love at all."

In 1948 Muste announced that he would refuse to pay federal income taxes because the revenues were used to build weapons. Ten years later, as national chairman of the Walk for Peace to Washington, he appealed for the unconditional halt of all nuclear weapons tests. His refusal to support the United States in the cold war did not mean, however, that he supported the Soviet Union. In Moscow in 1961 he protested in Red Square against nuclear testing, and he played a leading part in protests at the White House and at United Nations headquarters. With DOROTHY DAY, he joined in protests against civil-defense drills in New York City.

In 1966, during a visit to South and North Vietnam, Muste was expelled from South Vietnam for leading an antiwar protest in Saigon. After an interview with the leader of North Vietnam, Ho Chi Minh, in Hanoi, Muste proclaimed that the United States would not be able to prevent communist North Vietnam from conquering South Vietnam. At the time the United States had over 500,000 troops in Vietnam fighting to preserve the government of South Vietnam. Muste's actions in South and North Vietnam put him into the forefront of a massive antiwar movement and brought him from a marginal role to a position of political significance.

Muste explained his willingness to take unpopular stands on issues throughout his life with the comment: "Peaceableness does not mean trying to disturb nothing or glossing over realities. Nonviolence is not apathy or cowardice or passivity."

Although rigidly and militantly opposed to war, Muste's attitude toward theological doctrine was flexible enough to enable him to participate in meetings of the Friends (Quakers) and to serve with the Dutch Reformed Congregational Church and with Presbyterian groups.

**BIBLIOGRAPHY**

Allen, Devere, *Adventurous Americans*, 1932; *New York Times*, February 12, 1967.

# Nader, Ralph

(February 27, 1934– )
Consumer Advocate, Lawyer

Lawyer and activist Ralph Nader founded and has led the consumer rights movement in the United States for nearly three decades. "Naderism" has become synonymous with the use of citizen action to combat business and government practices deemed detrimental to the public interest.

Ralph Nader was born in Winsted, Connecticut, the son of Lebanese immigrants, who instilled in him strong moral and democratic values. After attending Winsted's Gilbert School, Nader enrolled at the Woodrow Wilson School of Public and International Affairs at Princeton University, graduating magna cum laude with a major in government and economics in 1955. He then entered Harvard Law School, where he became editor of the *Harvard Law Record*. As a student without a car who relied on hitchhiking for transportation, Nader had become concerned about the problem of automobile safety, and while in law school, he published his first article on the subject, "American Cars: Designed for Death," in the *Harvard Law Record*. Earning his law degree with distinction in 1958, he spent six months in the army before starting a small law practice in Hartford, Connecticut, in which he handled a number of auto accident cases.

UPI

Becoming convinced that he could accomplish little on the local level, Nader moved to Washington, D.C., in 1964. As a staff consultant on highway safety to Daniel Patrick Moynihan, then Assistant Secretary of Labor for policy planning, Nader compiled a massive report on the subject, which became the best-selling muckraking book *Unsafe at Any Speed: The Designed-in Dangers of the American Automobile* (1965). In it, Nader charged that the automobile companies sacrificed safety for speed and appearance, citing the Chevrolet Corvair as especially unsafe. General Motors (GM) hired a detective to uncover damaging material on Nader's private life. The effort not only failed to compromise Nader but also embarrassed GM president James M. Roche, who had to apologize before a Senate committee. Nader's book led Congress to pass the Traffic and Motor Vehicle Safety Act of 1966, which called on the federal government to set safety standards that must be met by all cars sold in the country.

Directing his attention to other areas involving health and safety, Nader became involved in efforts that helped bring about the Wholesome Meat Act of 1967 and legislation providing for better safety standards in the construction of natural gas pipelines and underground mining. In 1969 Nader helped establish in Washington, D.C., the Center for Study of Responsive Law, which conducted investigations of federal commissions, such as the Federal Trade Commission, suspected of being unduly influenced by the very industries they were supposed to be regulating. In 1970 he started the Public Interest Research Group (PIRG) to work for consumer and political reform on the community and college campus level; and in 1971, he launched Public Citizen, Inc., a consumer lobbying group to counteract the influence of powerful corporate lobbies.

Inspired by Nader's idealism, many young people, who became known as Nader's Raiders, joined his crusades through these and other organizations like the Center for Auto Safety, the National Insurance Consumer Organization, and the Health Research Group. Relying on individual contributions, on foundation grants, and on Nader's earnings as a writer and speaker for funds, these organizations conducted investigations of a wide range of consumer issues including the environment, nuclear power, health care, freedom of information in government, and tax reform. They also pushed for legislative and judicial remedies for the abuses they uncovered, using class-action suits and other legal tools to achieve their goals.

Nader and his various groups influenced the creation of several new government "watchdog" agencies, including the Occupational Safety and Health Administration, the Environmental Protection Agency, and the Consumer Product Safety Commission. They were also largely responsible for at least eight federal consumer protection laws, among them laws regulating radiation dangers, the use of cyclamates in diet foods, and the use of DDT in the control of insect pests. On the local level, Nader and his associates sparked the establishment of consumer affairs commissions in most major cities and aroused public concern about product safety and value.

Despite their accomplishments, Nader and his associates drew fire for being fanatics and for conducting superficial and slanted research. Moreover, in the conservative climate of the 1980s, Nader's brand of activism seemed doomed to extinction. Nevertheless, he and his associates kept up their crusades on a variety of fronts.

In 1980 Nader resigned as president of Public Citizen, Inc., so that he could devote more time to organizing citizens on the community level. With Ronald Reagan's election to the presidency in 1981, Nader attacked the administration for offering a government that favored business and ignored consumer interests. The following year, a Nader group published a study of the Reagan Administration entitled *Reagan's Ruling Class: Portraits of the President's Top One Hundred Officials.*

Continuing his critique of corporate influence, Nader in 1986 coauthored *The Big Boys: Power and Position in American Business,* a study of nine powerful chief executive officers of corporations. Two years later he helped bring about the passage of Proposition 103 in California, a law that lowered some auto insurance costs. The following year, GM announced that air bags would become standard equipment on many 1990 models, something that Nader had fought for during the past decade. Also around this time, Nader used national radio talk shows to forestall a congressional pay hike.

A firm believer in the power of the ordinary citizen to effect change, Nader in the early 1990s set out to make his Connecticut hometown a model democracy. As the leader of the consumer movement for a quarter century, he remains a living symbol of the importance of individual commitment to reform.

**BIBLIOGRAPHY**

Bollier, David, *Citizen Action and Other Big Ideas: A History of Ralph Nader and the Modern Consumer Movement,* 1989; Buckhorn, Robert F., *Nader: The People's Lawyer,* 1972; Burt, Dan, *Abuse of Power: A Report on Ralph Nader's Network,* 1982; Whiteside, Thomas, *The Investigation of Ralph Nader: General Motors Vs. One Determined Man,* 1972.

# Nast, Thomas

(September 27, 1840–December 7, 1902)
Cartoonist

Thomas Nast was the most important political cartoonist in nineteenth-century America, known for exposing government corruption. His legacy lives on—it was he who made the donkey and the elephant the symbols of the Democratic and Republican parties and who created the roly-poly image of Santa Claus, modeled on himself.

Born in Landau, Germany, Thomas Nast came to New York City with his family in 1846. Educated in the local public schools, he demonstrated a talent for drawing and in 1853, at the age of thirteen, entered the Academy of Design. Two years later, he was hired as an illustrator by Frank Leslie, publisher of the popular *Frank Leslie's Illustrated Newspa-*

*per.* He gained valuable experience at the newspaper, while studying on his own the work of such notable illustrators as the Englishman John Tenniel.

On March 19, 1859, Nast's first important drawing—a page of biting satire involving a current police scandal—appeared in *Harper's Weekly*, beginning an association that was to last for nearly thirty years. Meanwhile, in 1860 Nast traveled to England to make drawings of a heavyweight boxing match for the New York *Illustrated News.* Then, learning of the rebellion led by Giuseppe Garibaldi in Italy, he decided to take part in the campaign as a war correspondent, sending illustrations to periodicals in London and New York.

Returning to New York in February 1861 with only a dollar and fifty cents, Nast got the opportunity he needed with the outbreak of the Civil War. Nast sent sketches of war activities to various publications including *Harper's*, which made him a staff artist in 1862. He built a solid reputation with drawings that depicted battle scenes, attacked those who opposed a vigorous prosecution of the war, and hailed the emancipation of the slaves. Abraham Lincoln called Nast "our best recruiting sergeant."

After the war, Nast continued his often savage political commentary, portraying President Andrew Johnson as a dictator and lambasting northerners who urged a conciliatory policy toward the South. His greatest triumph occurred in 1869 when he launched a campaign to expose the corruption of the Tweed Ring, which under the leadership of Tammany Hall boss William Marcy Tweed had robbed New York City of a whopping $100 million. Through such famous cartoons as "The Tammany Tiger Let Loose" and "Who Stole the People's Money?" Nast not only aroused enough public indignation to cause Tweed's downfall but also made Tweed's face familiar throughout the world. In this way, Nast contributed to Tweed's eventual arrest after the latter had escaped to Spain.

Over the years *Harper's* published about 3,000 Nast illustrations. His political cartoons generally expressed his continued support for the Republican party, which he left only to back the Democratic winner Grover Cleveland over the Republican, James G. Blaine, in 1884. In the mid-1880s, his contributions to *Harper's* began to dwindle, ending altogether in 1886. He continued to contribute to other journals and in 1892 and 1893 tried unsuccessfully to establish his own *Nast's Weekly.* Losing both his audience and his inventiveness, Nast turned his pen against Populists and blacks late in his career. He fell heavily into debt because of unwise investments, and in an attempt to pay his debts he accepted an appointment by President Theodore Roosevelt as U.S. consul in Guayaquil, Ecuador. Nast died there of yellow fever at the age of sixty-two.

**BIBLIOGRAPHY**

Keller, M., *The Art and Politics of Thomas Nast,* 1968; St. Hill, Thomas Nast, *Thomas Nast's Christmas Drawings for the Human Race,* 1971, and *Thomas Nast: Cartoons and Illustrations,* 1974.

# Nation, Carry

(November 25, 1846–June 9, 1911)
Reformer

Notorious for her hatchet-smashing attacks on saloons, Carry Nation did more than anyone else to publicize the cause of prohibition that led to the passage of the Eighteenth Amendment in 1919.

She was born on a farm in Garrard County, Kentucky, the oldest daughter of George Moore, a successful cattle trader, and his wife, Mary, who was mentally unbalanced and eventually had to be institutionalized. Often ill as a child, Carry Moore had little education. In 1867 she married Charles Gloyd, a Civil War veteran and physician, whom she discovered to her horror was an alcoholic. Even though she was pregnant and still loved Gloyd, she left him and went back to her family. After Gloyd's death six months later, she returned to Holden, Missouri, where the couple had been living, with her daughter, Charlien. There she taught school for several years before marrying, in 1877, David Nation, a newspaper editor, lawyer, and minister who was nineteen years her senior.

Library of Congress

After various moves, the Nations settled in Medicine Lodge, Kansas, where Carry launched her crusade against the sale of liquor. Although Kansas had been legally "dry" since 1880, alcohol was still sold at pharmacies and other so-called joints. In 1892 Carry Nation helped found the county chapter of the Woman's Christian Temperance Union. Seven years later, she and a few other women entered a Medicine Lodge saloon and through prayer and emotional appeals managed to close the place down. After using these tactics to dry up the entire town, Nation moved on to the neighboring town of Kiowa, where for the first time she resorted to physical force, destroying bottles and saloon furniture with bricks.

She began closing saloons throughout the state, attracting national publicity when she wrecked the barroom of the Hotel Carey in Wichita and landed in jail for two weeks. Nation's violent methods (which by this time included the use of a hatchet), colorful personality, and imposing appearance—she was almost six feet tall and strongly built—made good copy for newspapers throughout the country. This publicity helped stir up public sentiment in favor of stricter enforcement of state and local prohibition laws.

Nation's frequent arrests forced her to begin lecturing in order to raise money to pay her fines. She also sold copies of her autobiography, *The Use and Need of the Life of Carry A. Nation* (1904), and miniature hatchets engraved "Carry Nation, Joint Smasher." She received numerous small donations from temperance supporters. Part of her income went to finance several short-lived prohibition magazines; some also supported a home for the wives of drunkards. Her own husband had earlier divorced her on grounds of desertion.

Continuing with her crusade, Carry Nation harangued state legislators and even caused the U.S. Senate to suspend business once as she shouted her opinions of the body from the galleries. She abandoned the hatchet in 1910 after being badly beaten by the woman owner of a Montana saloon. The next year, she collapsed on a stage in Arkansas, and died six months later.

**BIBLIOGRAPHY**

Beals, Carleton, *Cyclone Carry*, 1962; Taylor, R. L., *Vessel of Wrath*, 1966.

# Newton, Huey Percy

(February 17, 1942–August 22, 1989)
Civil Rights Leader

Huey Newton, cofounder of the Black Panthers party, was a hero for millions of African Americans for his message: know and protect your rights by any means. He ended a troubled life in violence.

Huey P. Newton, named for the Louisiana populist leader Huey Pierce Long, was born in Monroe, Louisiana (seven years after Long was assassinated), youngest of seven children of a sharecropper. When Huey was one year old, his father decided to move the family to Oakland, across the bay from San Francisco. He worked as a laborer, barely making ends meet. At school Huey was unruly and often absent. He refused to learn to read but counted on a talent for memorizing what others read to him. He barely graduated from high school, whereupon he taught himself to read and went through Plato's *Republic* five times. "This was a trigger point in my life because [then I] . . . gobbled up everything I could get," he told an interviewer. Newton took a two-year course at Merritt College and a year of prelaw at a San Francisco school, where he met Bobby Seale.

Meanwhile, Newton was piling up a police record for minor offenses. In 1964 he was sentenced to three years' imprisonment for assault with a deadly weapon—having pulled out a kitchen knife during a political argument at a party. He was released on probation after serving six months, and he and Seale got jobs doing youth work with a poverty program.

In October 1966, Newton, Seale, and Bobby Hutton (aged fifteen) organized the Black Panthers Party for Self-Defense, which soon recruited numerous members from ghetto youth in Oakland and other cities. The party's immediate aim, stated in its manifesto (written by Newton), was to combat police brutality in the black neighborhoods. The Panthers became familiar with police methods; they followed police cars to encounters with black people and stood witness, armed and carrying law books. Seale was chairman, Newton minister of defense; STOKELY CARMICHAEL and ELDRIDGE CLEAVER, who joined in 1967, were respectively prime minister and minister of information. The Panthers insisted that members observe discipline, abstain from drugs, and read the books of revolutionary leaders such as MALCOLM X, Mao Tse-tung, and W. E. B. DU BOIS. They modeled themselves on the armed bands of Marxist guerrilla fighters who were then employing success in South America and Vietnam, and who had already triumphed in China and Cuba. And like these guerrillas they intended to combine their military prowess with concern for their people's welfare. They set up social programs—health clinics, children's lunch programs, psychological counseling—and a newspaper, *Black Panther.*

Early on October 28, 1967, Newton was in a brush with police in which a patrolman was shot to death and Newton was wounded. What actually occurred was never clear. At his trial, in July 1968, Newton was convicted of voluntary manslaughter and sentenced to two to fifteen years. The conviction was reversed in May 1970 because of judicial errors, and in 1972 the charges were dismissed. Newton had begun to steer the Panthers in a nonviolent direction and preached "inter-communalism—the relatedness of all people." He directed a nonviolent boycott of liquor stores that resulted in the owners' contributing to a fund for social services for the poor.

After three years in Cuba to escape a charge for another felony, Newton returned for trial in 1977; the charge was dropped. He did graduate work at the University of California for a Ph.D. degree in 1980 for a thesis on repression in America and, in 1982, officially disbanded the Black Panther party. But he had further run-ins with the law and with drugs and alcohol. On August 22, 1989, he was shot dead on the street by a drug dealer, and Seale delivered his funeral eulogy.

**BIBLIOGRAPHY**

Newton, Huey P., *To Die for the People*, 1972; Newton, Huey P., with J. H. Blake, *Revolutionary Suicide*, 1973; Seale, Bobby, *Seize the Time*, 1970.

## Niebuhr, Reinhold

(June 21, 1892–June 1, 1971)
Political Activist, Theologian

Reinhold Niebuhr was prominent among American Protestant leaders during the decades before, during, and after World War II. Teaching a realistic and neoorthodox theology, he fortified his biblical insights with the wisdom of thinkers far outside Protestant Christianity, while playing an active role in practical politics nationally, internationally, and locally.

Niebuhr was born in Wright City, a small town near St. Louis, Missouri, the son of Gustave Niebuhr, a clergyman of the Evangelical Synod sect of Lutheranism, and Lydia Hosto, daughter of a pastor of that sect. The Reverend Niebuhr had emigrated from Germany in 1876, when he was seventeen, and was pastor of the church in Wright City when Reinhold was born, one of four children. The father died when the children were young, and Lydia Niebuhr brought them up alone. A younger son, Helmut Richard, and a daughter, Hulda, also became theologians.

Reinhold Niebuhr attended Elmhurst College, in a suburb of Chicago, for both high school and college. In 1910 he transferred to Eden Theological Seminary, near St. Louis, and three years later to Yale Divinity School. He earned a Bachelor of Divinity degree in 1914 and an M.A. in 1915, when he was ordained a minister and took the pastorate of the Bethel Evangelical Church, in Detroit. During thirteen years there, he helped lead his Evangelical Synod denomination in a merger with the Reformed church as the Evangelical and Reformed church, finally joining with the Congregational church to form the United Church of Christ.

In Detroit, Niebuhr became deeply concerned with social problems. After violent race riots in 1925, he served as chairman of the mayor's committee on race relations. His church was in a neighborhood where many auto workers lived, and he worked on their behalf, lecturing and writing as a critic of the labor policies of the Ford Motor Company (see HENRY FORD) and other Detroit industries.

In 1928 Niebuhr went to the Union Theological Seminary in New York City as an associate professor of the philosophy of religion, and two years later he was made professor of applied Christianity. While he became a major influence in the world of theology, he was best known as a political and social thinker and activist. He was vice chairman of the Socialist party and a founder of the Fellowship of Socialist Christians. Niebuhr's commitment to socialism and to his Christian philosophy is given voice in a famous book, *Moral Man and Immoral Society* (1932). As a pacifist, he joined the Fellowship of Reconciliation (see A. J. MUSTE).

In 1940, however, Niebuhr resigned from the Socialist party and supported Franklin D. Roosevelt's reelection. Rejecting pacifism, he had come to believe that "the halting of totalitarian aggression is a prerequisite to world peace and order." During the early years of World War II, he headed American Friends of German Freedom, an anti-Hitler group, and the ex-pacifist Union for Democratic Action. In February 1941 he founded the journal *Christianity and Crisis*, often a vehicle for his opinions, which he edited until 1966. He carried on his left-wing but noncommunist political activity as vice chairman of the Liberal party (see DAVID DUBINSKY).

Niebuhr was a founding member of the Americans for Democratic Action, a new liberal group founded in 1947 to fashion a disciplined and realistic liberalism capable of resisting tyrannies of the left (communism) and right (fascism). After the war he joined in its declaration asking the government to take economic steps to unseat Francisco Franco, the dictator of Spain, and to give quick approval to the Marshall Plan for European recovery. He became and remained a vigilant anticommunist, and called on the United States to assume leadership in world affairs.

Niebuhr urged the clergy to accept the doctrine of Christian Realism—which teaches that human beings are sinners and that self-interest controls society—and to help establish a socially constructive Christianity through involving themselves in social and political activism.

Niebuhr was a notably prolific and lucid writer. His most important theological contribution was a two-volume work, *The Nature and Destiny of Man* (1941, 1943). Hubert H. Humphrey, while vice president of the United States, said of Niebuhr, "No preacher or teacher, at least in my time, has had a greater impact on the secular world." After suffering a stroke in 1952, Niebuhr's activism flagged, though he still produced such works as *The Irony of American History* (1952) and *Faith and Politics* (1968). Marking the centennial of Niebuhr's birth, ARTHUR M. SCHLESINGER, JR., recalled one of his characteristic observations: "Man's capacity for justice makes democracy possible; but man's inclination to injustice makes democracy necessary."

### BIBLIOGRAPHY

Bingham, June, *Courage to Change: An Introduction to the Life and Thought of Reinhold Niebuhr*, 1961; Fox, Richard Wightman, *Reinhold Niebuhr: A Biography*, 1985; Kegley, Charles (ed.), *Reinhold Niebuhr: His Religious, Social, and Political Thought*, 1984; Stone, Ronald H., *Reinhold Niebuhr: Prophet to Politicians*, 1972.

# Niles, Hezekiah

(October 10, 1777–April 2, 1839)
Editor

Editor and publisher for twenty-five years of the *Niles' Weekly Register*, one of the first newspapers to achieve a national readership, Hezekiah Niles was an important figure in early American journalism.

Hezekiah Niles was born in Jefferis' Ford, Chester County, Pennsylvania, and raised in Wilmington, Delaware. At the age of seventeen, he was apprenticed to a printer in Philadelphia. He returned to Wilmington in 1797 and helped publish an almanac and worked as a printer. In 1805 he started his own magazine, *The Apollo*, which soon failed. Next, Niles moved to Baltimore, Maryland, where he became editor of *The Evening Post.*

In 1811 Niles began publishing the *Weekly Register* (later known as *Niles' Weekly Register*). In its wide appeal, the *Weekly Register* anticipated HORACE GREELEY's New York *Weekly Tribune*, the first nationally significant paper in the United States. Though the *Weekly Register* never became as influential as the

*Tribune,* it was, nevertheless, a voice to be reckoned with, and is today regarded as an important source for the history of the period.

Many of the *Weekly Register*'s readers were editors and politicians, since politics was its chief focus. Niles was a personal friend of the Whig statesman Henry Clay. He used his paper to advocate the latter's program of economic nationalism. Known as the American System, the program included a protective tariff to help build up American industry, internal improvements, and a centralized banking system. Besides calling for a protective tariff in the *Weekly Register,* Niles served as the guiding spirit behind protectionist conventions held at Harrisburg, Pennsylvania, in 1827 and at New York City in 1831. Though initially opposed to the rechartering of the first Bank of the United States in 1811, he came out in favor of the rechartering of the second Bank of the United States during the administration of President Andrew Jackson.

In his editorials Niles also took a stand against slavery. He believed that it ought to be abolished but that the change should be made gradually. While living in Delaware, he was an officer of the state abolition society.

A vigorous, incisive writer, Niles also distinguished himself for his factual reporting. While many of his contemporaries relied on sheer eloquence, Niles backed up his arguments with statistical evidence. In addition to his work on the *Weekly Register,* he wrote pamphlets and books on American government. The best known of these was *Principles and Acts of the Revolution in America* (1822).

After retiring as editor and publisher of the *Weekly Register,* Niles returned to Wilmington. He died there in 1839.

**BIBLIOGRAPHY**

Stone, R. G., *Hezekiah Niles as an Economist,* 1933.

## Noyes, John Humphrey

(September 3, 1811–April 13, 1886)
Reformer

John Humphrey Noyes was the founder and for thirty years the head of the Oneida Community, the most successful of the utopian socialist communities established in nineteenth-century America.

Born in Brattleboro, Vermont, Noyes entered Dartmouth College at the age of fifteen, graduating in 1830. He then studied law for a year, but happening to attend a revival meeting held by the evangelist CHARLES GRANDISON FINNEY, he gave up the idea of a career in the law in favor of the ministry. Noyes enrolled at the Theological Seminary at Andover, Massachusetts, but decided the atmosphere was too secular and so entered the theological department at Yale College.

At Yale, Noyes became associated with a group of revivalists and with them organized an ecumenical church. He also pursued Bible studies on his own and from these studies developed the doctrine of perfectionism. Noyes maintained that since the second coming of Christ had already occurred, it was possible for individuals to achieve a state of sinlessness in this life. Others before Noyes had advanced this doctrine, but he was the first to assert that any person who accepted that the kingdom of heaven had been established by Christ on earth could live without sin. In February 1834, after Noyes announced that he personally had attained perfection, he lost his license to preach and was expelled from Yale.

For the next few years, Noyes traveled in New York and New England trying to interest others in his views. Eventually settling in Putney, Vermont, he organized a small community and in 1836 founded the Bible School, which developed into a society of Bible Communists, most of whom were well-to-do people. These people shared their resources and worked to spread Noyes's ideas through publications like the *Perfectionist* and the *Spiritual Magazine.* In his "Battle-axe Letter" of 1837, Noyes first set forth the idea of complex marriage, maintaining that monogamy did not square with perfectionism because in heaven there were no "simple" marriages. He first acted on this idea in 1846 when he and his wife exchanged partners with another couple in the group. Arrested on charges of adultery and released on bail, Noyes escaped to central New York. There he and eighty-seven followers established the Oneida Community.

Unlike many utopian communities, which failed after a few years, Oneida prospered. By the 1870s it comprised over 200 members, who were the joint owners of 664 acres of prime land. The community included a farm, a sawmill, and factories for canning and for the manufacture of such goods as chains, suitcases, silverware, woolens, and silk thread. The community was governed democratically, with all decisions made by consensus. Noyes gave informal Bible instruction, and the society adhered to a vegetarian diet and banned the use of both alcohol and tobacco. Members dressed simply, with women wearing pants. The community attracted the most attention for its sexual practices. Community members could take multiple partners, although they had to receive permission to do so. Men were responsible for birth control, which was achieved through continence, and only the most spiritually advanced couples were supposed to have children.

Oneida flourished until 1875. That year Noyes tried unsuccessfully to appoint his son Theodore as the new leader. Four years later, Noyes left for Canada, escaping the possibility of an arrest for statutory rape. Without his leadership, the community yielded to outside pressures, giving up the practice of complex marriage as well as economic communism. The community reorganized as a privately owned joint stock company, of which the present-day Oneida Corporation is the offshoot.

Noyes died in Ontario, Canada, at the age of seventy-four. In addition to a thriving economic enterprise, Noyes left behind an advanced body of social thought aimed at freeing people from both capitalism and sexism. His ideas on religion and society are contained in such works as *Bible Communism* (1848), *Male Continence* (1848), *History of American Socialisms* (1870), and *Scientific Propagation* (ca. 1873).

**BIBLIOGRAPHY**

Carden, M. L., *Oneida: Utopian Community to Modern Corporation,* 1969; Robertson, C. N., *Oneida Community: An Autobiography, 1851–1876,* 1970, and *Oneida Community: The Breakup, 1876–1881,* 1972; Whitworth, J. M., *God's Blueprints,* 1975.

# O'Leary, Jean

(March 3, 1948–    )
Gay Activist

After four and a half years in a Roman Catholic order of nuns, Jean O'Leary left to become an outspoken and effective leader for lesbian and gay rights and a voice in national politics.

O'Leary grew up in Cleveland, Ohio, the eldest of four children in a devout Roman Catholic family, and was educated in parochial schools. Her father, Jim O'Leary, was an advertising sales manager; her mother, Betty

Higgins, though she had polio when Jean was a child, raised the family. At Magnificat High School, a girls' institution taught by nuns, Jean was conscious that she was attracted to women, but she concealed it. She played drums, the only girl in a boys' rock band, and later she played in an all-girl band; loving to organize, she ran high school election campaigns. In 1966 O'Leary became a novice in the convent of the Sisters of the Holy Humility of Mary, in Youngstown, a teaching and nursing order. It was "one of the best experiences of my life, on every level," she has said. She took her temporary vows and, looking toward a career in clinical psychology, attended classes at Youngstown University. Having switched to the Lourdes Convent of her order, in Cleveland, she continued her studies at Cleveland State University and graduated with a B.S. magna cum laude in 1971. That she was a lesbian had become evident in the convent, however, when she got involved in "particular friendships." After four and a half years she left the order.

O'Leary learned that a Ph.D. program in organizational development was offered at Yeshiva University, and she became a doctoral candidate. That coincided with her interest in Greenwich Village, which, she had read in *Cosmopolitan* magazine, was a haven for lesbians. Arriving in summer 1971, she shared an apartment in Brooklyn Heights with a man from Cleveland also interested in organizational development—who, she discovered, was also gay and had moved to New York in the same spirit of exploration as hers. They together attended meetings of the Gay Activists Alliance (GAA) in Manhattan, at the time a large, well-run organization with a building in Soho called the Firehouse, used for gay cultural events.

O'Leary discovered that there was sexism in the GAA: male members discriminated against female and excluded them from leadership. To offset that she joined in forming the Lesbian Liberation Committee (LLC) and served as its chairwoman. She would go up to Albany to lobby legislators on issues of sexual

privacy and sexual orientation. In 1973 O'Leary led the LLC out of the GAA to join up in the Lesbian Feminists Liberation, Inc., which she chaired. From 1976 to 1981 she was coexecutive director of the National Gay Task Force. During that time she compiled studies of lesbianism and homosexuality at the request of the nomenclature committee of the American Psychiatric Association. Her studies helped form the basis for the association's eventual declassification of homosexuality as a psychiatric disorder (see FRANK KAMENY). In the late 1970s O'Leary organized meetings of gay leaders with presidential aides in the White House and subsequently with key federal agencies, including the State Department, the Department of Justice, and the Civil Rights Commission, elevating issues of gay equality to national attention.

As her interest moved toward national politics, O'Leary was appointed by President Jimmy Carter to the National Commission on the Observance of International Woman's Year, which sponsored the National Women's Conference in Houston in fall 1977. At that event BETTY FRIEDAN reversed an earlier stand and agreed that it was appropriate for the women's movement to make lesbian issues an official concern. The conference led to the creation of the National Advisory Committee for Women, to which the president also appointed O'Leary.

Beginning in 1976, O'Leary was a delegate to each Democratic convention, and in 1988 Michael Dukakis appointed her to the Democratic National Committee. She was a whip for Dukakis, and again for Bill Clinton. In 1978 Mayor Ed Koch of New York City named her to his Commission on the Status of Women, and she also served on the advisory committee for the Human Rights Commission for the State of New York.

Having moved to Los Angeles in 1981, O'Leary assumed the executive directorship of National Gay Rights Advocates (NGRA), which she held until 1989. With 30,000 members it was the country's largest civil rights organization working for gay rights; NGRA organized the first Coming Out Day, on October 11, 1988. O'Leary heads a firm marketing computer supplies and runs a fund-raising office for political causes in California and nationally.

**BIBLIOGRAPHY**

Marcus, Eric, *Making History: The Struggle for Gay and Lesbian Equal Rights*, 1992; Marotta, Toby, *The Politics of Homosexuality*, 1981.

# Oppenheimer, Julius Robert

(April 22, 1904–February 18, 1967)
Theoretical Physicist

J Robert Oppenheimer, "the father of the atomic bomb," was a pioneer researcher in quantum physics, a great teacher, and a sensitive leader. During the McCarthy era he was labeled a security risk because he had opposed the nuclear arms race.

Oppenheimer, born in New York City, was the son of a well-to-do importer of textiles, Julius Oppenheimer, and an artist, Ella Friedman. He was an excellent student at the Ethical Culture School, in New York, and graduated in

Library of Congress

and in one year was granted the Ph.D. for a thesis on an aspect of the quantum theory. From 1927 to 1928, he held a National Research Council fellowship at both Harvard and the California Institute of Technology, in Pasadena, then went abroad again for a year at the University of Leiden (Netherlands) and the Federal Technical Institute (ETH) in Zurich. In 1929 Oppenheimer took up a unique joint appointment at the University of California at Berkeley and CalTech, dividing his time between

1921. That summer he fell ill with dysentery while visiting relatives in Germany, and his plans to study at Harvard were put aside while he recovered. He spent the next summer exploring the mountains of New Mexico, and that fall he entered Harvard. He was elected to Phi Beta Kappa in his second year and received the B.A. summa cum laude, in chemistry, after his third year. His interest veered to physics when he went to Cambridge University, England, in 1925 for a year at the Cavendish Laboratory.

At the invitation of the physicist Max Born, Oppenheimer moved on to the University of Göttingen, where he collaborated with Born

them. He performed important research and was a stimulating teacher, under whom Berkeley became the ranking institution in the United States for work on quantum physics. He trained a number of leading scientists in the field.

Oppenheimer's interests involved not only physics but the arts, literature, and the outdoors. In the 1930s, with the rise of fascism in Europe and the Great Depression at home, Oppenheimer gave his support to progressive organizations. He did not join the Communist party, but many of the causes he embraced—the Loyalists in the Spanish Civil War, desegregation, improved conditions for migratory workers—were also supported by the party.

The discovery of nuclear fission in 1939, coincidental with the beginning of World War II as Germany invaded Poland, drew Oppenheimer into research for the atomic bomb, a concern of the government because of suspicions that the Germans were developing such a weapon. In 1942 he was appointed director of the project at Los Alamos, New Mexico, working on the design and construction of the A-bomb, as well as looking toward nonmilitary uses of nuclear energy. He was notably successful as an administrator, sympathetic to the needs of his staff. On July 16, 1945, the first A-bomb was exploded at Alamogordo, New Mexico, and three weeks later Hiroshima and then Nagasaki were devastated.

Later that year Oppenheimer resigned from the project and resumed his professorship at Berkeley and Caltech, while serving as a consultant to the government on atomic energy, which he believed should be under civilian supervision. He recommended plans for the control of nuclear arms and energy by an international agency under the United Nations, which was defeated by the Soviet Union's rejection.

In late 1947 Oppenheimer became director of the Institute for Advanced Study at Princeton, New Jersey, which under him became an international center for research in theoretical physics as well as for humanistic studies. Brilliant young postdoctoral students were invited as fellows, joining a nonteaching faculty that included ALBERT EINSTEIN.

In the same year Oppenheimer became chairman of the general advisory committee of the U.S. Atomic Energy Commission, which in 1949 voted against the government's program for a crash program to build the hydrogen bomb, more powerful than the A-bomb and, as the cold war developed, seen as a deterrent to the Soviet Union. His opposition to the H-bomb and his radical associations in the 1930s made him vulnerable to attacks by Senator Joseph McCarthy and the military. In 1954 Oppenheimer's enemies secured the revocation of his security clearance, a decision widely protested by scientists and intellectuals.

Oppenheimer continued as director of the Institute for Advanced Study, while lecturing and writing on science and education. In 1963 the Atomic Energy Commission awarded him its highest honor, the Enrico Fermi Award, for his contributions to the development of atomic energy.

**BIBLIOGRAPHY**

Goodchild, Peter, *J. Robert Oppenheimer: Shatterer of Worlds*, 1980; Oppenheimer, J. R., *Science and the Common Understanding*, 1954, and *Some Reflections on Science and Culture*, 1960; Stern, Philip M., and Harold P. Green, *The Oppenheimer Case: Security on Trial*, 1969.

# Ortiz, Alfonso Alex

(April 30, 1939–   )
American Indian Activist, Anthropologist

Alfonso Ortiz has become the most respected scholar of American Indian culture and religion, in particular that of the Southwest, and has worked resolutely through his government and academic associations for American Indian rights.

Ortiz was born a Tewa at the San Juan Pueblo, the largest and most isolated of the six Tewa pueblos on the Rio Grande north of Santa Fe, New Mexico. His mother, Lupe Naranjo, was Spanish American; his father, Sam Ortiz, was a full-blood Tewa. He was raised by his Tewa grandparents in the pueblo and learned English when he went to school. When Ortiz graduated from Española High School, he was awarded a scholarship for outstanding citizenship which, together with National Merit Scholarships, enabled him to attend the University of New Mexico, at Albuquerque. He earned an A.B. in sociology in 1961 and, on an archaeological dig that summer, met and married Margaret Davisson, of Boston. Considering a career as a schoolteacher, he studied for a year at Arizona State University.

Ortiz decided instead on anthropology, and he entered the University of Chicago in 1962 on a John Hay Whitney Opportunity Fellowship. There he encountered the scholar who had the strongest influence on his career, Fred Eggan, the leading authority on the Pueblo Indians. Eggan suggested that Ortiz make his own people the subject of his doctoral dissertation. Ortiz began fieldwork in summer 1963 and in 1965 continued on a research grant from Project Head Start, under the U.S. Office of Economic Opportunity. He completed the work and earned his doctorate in 1967. His book *The Tewa World: Space, Time, Being, and Becoming in a Pueblo Society*, based on the dissertation, was published in 1969, with a foreword by Eggan.

Ortiz's activism on behalf of Indians began when he was an undergraduate at Albuquerque, where he was a leader of the Kiva Club, an organization for Indian students that was named after the communal ritual house. In his senior year he was president of the Southwestern Indian Regional Youth Council.

After teaching a year at Pitzer College, in Claremont, California, Ortiz became assistant professor of anthropology at Princeton University in 1967. In 1970 he became a tenured associate professor. During March of that year he was chairman of the first convocation of American Indian scholars, held at Princeton University, and editor of its proceedings, *Indian Voices* (1970). In 1971 he was elected vice president of the Association on American Indian Affairs and in 1973 succeeded to the presidency, which he held until 1988. For many years he has also been chairman of the National Advisory Council for the D'Arcy McNickle Center for the History of the American Indian (see D'ARCY MCNICKLE).

Ortiz returned to his alma mater, the University of New Mexico, as professor of anthropology in 1974; he continues to teach at the university. In his career he has combined social activism for Indian rights with scholarship in Indian religion and culture, focusing on ritual drama, movements toward revitalization, oral traditions, myth, and the history of Indian and white relations. He is the editor of volumes 9 and 10 of the Smithsonian Institution's *Handbook of North American Indians*, which deal with the Indians of the Southwest.

Ortiz and his former wife, Margaret D. Ortiz, edited *To Carry Forth the Vine: An Anthology of Traditional Native North American Poetry* (1977). Of their three children, two are working in the Pueblo community.

**BIBLIOGRAPHY**

Ortiz, Alfonso, with Richard Erdoes, *Myths and Legends of North American Indians*, 1984.

# Owen, Robert Dale

(November 9, 1801–June 24, 1877)
Author, Public Official, Reformer

Robert Dale Owen was a reformer who helped his father, Robert Owen, found the utopian community of New Harmony in Indiana and was later prominent in other reform efforts, including abolition, women's rights, and public education.

Robert Dale Owen was born in Glasgow, Scotland, the son of British industrialist and reformer Robert Owen. A few years before his son's birth, Robert Owen had acquired from his father-in-law, David Dale, the New Lanark Mills in Scotland, where Owen proceeded to put into practice his ideas about social reform. He provided his workers with better housing, schools for their children, and company stores where they could buy goods at reasonable prices. Robert Dale Owen attended the New Lanark school and was also educated by private tutors and at a progressive school in Switzerland.

In 1825 Robert Dale Owen accompanied his father to the United States, where he was to spend most of the rest of his life. The following year, father and son traveled to New Harmony, Indiana, where they established a utopian community based on socialist principles. His father then returned to England, but Robert Dale Owen remained to teach school and edit the *New Harmony Gazette*. While there, he met the reformer FRANCES WRIGHT. After New Harmony failed in 1827, Owen accompanied her to her own utopian community at Nashoba, Tennessee, and from there to Europe, where he met such leaders and intellectuals as the Marquis de Lafayette, William Godwin, Jeremy Bentham, and Mary Wollstonecraft Shelley.

Owen returned to the United States in 1828 even more determined to realize his father's reformist vision. After a year at New Harmony, he moved to New York City, where together with Wright he founded the *Free Enquirer* as a successor to the *New Harmony Gazette*. The journal was opposed to organized religion, and it supported reform of divorce laws, a program of industrial education, and a more equitable distribution of wealth. Along with a group of like-minded reformers, Owen was able to persuade the New York Workingmen's party to replace its original goal of a more equal distribution of property with a program of public education.

In 1832 Owen rejoined his father in England, helping him for six months to edit a weekly penny paper in support of cooperative societies, which was called *The Crisis*. Upon his return to the United States and New Harmony, Owen entered into an even more productive phase of his career. He served three terms in the Indiana legislature (1836–1838) and during his tenure was successful in getting money for public schools from surplus state funds. In 1842 Owen was elected to Congress as a Democrat, serving two terms (1843–1847). One of his main achievements as a congressman was the drafting of the bill (in 1845) setting up the Smithsonian Institution (see JOSEPH HENRY), which thanks to Owen became a teaching as well as a research center.

Back in Indiana after 1847, Owen lobbied successfully for property rights for married women and for more liberal divorce laws. He also engaged in a debate with the well-known editor HORACE GREELEY on the subject of divorce in Greeley's paper, the New York *Tribune*. Widely circulated in pamphlet form, the debate aroused much comment. In 1853 Owen was appointed charge d'affaires at Naples, and in 1855, minister to Italy. While abroad, he came under the influence of spiritualism and later wrote two books on the subject: *Footfalls on the Boundary of Another World* (1860) and *The Debatable Land between this World and the Next* (1870).

Returning to the United States in 1858, Owen took up the cause of emancipation. In 1863 the War Department appointed Owen to investigate the condition of the freedmen, and the investigations of his committee led to Owen's book *The Wrong of Slavery* (1864).

Though he had been an ardent emancipationist, Owen was against giving the freedmen the vote immediately; instead he believed that the franchise ought to be withheld for ten years. After the war, Owen spent much of his time writing articles on social and political questions, as well as a series of autobiograph-ical articles that were published in book form as *Threading My Way* (1874). Three years after the book appeared, Owen died at his summer home on Lake George, New York.

**BIBLIOGRAPHY**

Leopold, Richard W., *Robert Dale Owen,* 1969.

# Park, Robert Ezra

(February 14, 1864–February 7, 1944)
Sociologist

Robert Park exerted a major influence on the development of American sociology. A professor at the University of Chicago in the 1920s, he became a leader of the "Chicago school" of sociology and pioneered in the study of race and ethnic relations.

Robert Park was born in Harveyville, Luzerne County, Pennsylvania, and grew up in Red Wing, Minnesota, where he attended the local high school. He spent a year at the University of Minnesota, then transferred to the University of Michigan, where he became interested in the study of human behavior through contact with the young philosopher JOHN DEWEY. Graduating in 1887, Park spent the next decade working as a reporter for newspapers in Minneapolis, Detroit, Denver, and New York City.

In 1891 and 1892, Park, along with John Dewey and Franklin Ford, a New York journalist, attempted to create a new type of newspaper. Called *"Thought News,"* the paper was to offer in-depth coverage of current events in the context of social analysis. Park's interest in the connection between social change and news made him decide to leave journalism and pursue graduate study. He studied for a year at Harvard under the philosopher WILLIAM JAMES, who deeply influenced him. After earning his M.A. in 1899, Park went to Europe, where he studied under the philosopher and sociologist Georg Simmel and under Wilhelm Windelband at the University of Heidelberg in Germany. He wrote his dissertation on public opinion and, with a Ph.D. from the University of Heidelberg, returned to Harvard as an assistant in philosophy in 1904.

Park embarked on a career applying his studies, accepting an invitation to become secretary of the Congo Reform Association and going to Africa. Park exposed the exploitation of African workers by Belgian authorities in the Congo (now Zaire) in a series of articles published in *Everybody's Magazine* in 1906 and 1907. Through this work Park met BOOKER T. WASHINGTON, who persuaded him to study African Americans in the South under the auspices of Tuskegee Institute. During the next seven winters Park studied black folkways and race relations in the South, winning a reputation as a world authority on race relations. In 1912 at a conference on race relations he had organized at Tuskegee, Park met the University of Chicago sociologist William I. Thomas, who became his mentor.

In 1913 Park was invited to join the staff of the sociology department at the University of Chicago, teaching there until his retirement in

1929. An outstanding teacher, Park helped inspire many advanced students. In 1921 he published an influential textbook, *Introduction to the Science of Sociology*, written with E. W. Burgess, in which they stressed the study of social processes, especially interaction, rather than institutions like the family, and stressed the importance of empirical research. Park's other writings during this period included *The Immigrant Press and Its Control* (1922) and *The City, Suggestions for the Study of the Urban Environment* (1929). Encouraged by Park, a generation of sociologists focused on urban problems and race relations and used empirical research to produce such trailblazing studies as *The Hobo* (1923), *The Gang* (1927), and *The Ghetto* (1928).

Park also introduced a number of important concepts into sociology. These included "human ecology," which deals with the spatial and temporal interrelationships between people and their economic, social, and political organizations; "collective behavior," the processes by which an existing consensus is broken and then a new consensus formed; and the "marginal man," a person who has a confused identity because he belongs to more than one distinct culture.

Park was president of the American Sociological Society from 1925 to 1926 and received an honorary degree from the University of Michigan in 1937. After his retirement from the University of Chicago in 1929, he spent several years traveling, lecturing, and studying multiethnic societies in China, India, Africa, and South America. In 1935 he accepted an appointment as a visiting professor at Fisk University in Nashville, Tennessee, where he taught and did research until his death a week before his eightieth birthday. Park's collected papers were published posthumously in three volumes: *Race and Culture* (1950), *Human Communities* (1952), and *Society* (1955).

**BIBLIOGRAPHY**

Faris, Robert E. L., *Chicago Sociology, 1920–1932*, 1967; Persons, Stow, *Ethnic Studies at Chicago*, 1987; Ross, Dorothy, *The Origins of American Social Science*, 1990.

# Parkhurst, Charles Henry

(April 17, 1842–September 8, 1933)
Reformer, Religious Leader

Presbyterian minister Charles Parkhurst preached a form of the social gospel, emphasizing the need for social reform as well as the saving of souls. The antivice crusade he launched in New York City in the 1890s anticipated later efforts at municipal reform.

Parkhurst was born on his parents' farm in Framingham, Massachusetts, and educated at home until he was eleven. After five years of public schooling his father found him work as a clerk in a grocery store. Preferring scholarly pursuits, he prepared for college at an academy, enrolling at Amherst College in 1862. After graduation four years later, he became principal of Amherst High School, serving in this capacity for the next three years. Parkhurst then spent two periods of study in Germany, in between which he taught Greek and Latin at Williston Seminary in Easthampton, Massachusetts. In 1874 Parkhurst was ordained by the South Berkshire Association of Congregational Ministers, and that same year became pastor of the First Congregational Church in Lenox, Massachusetts.

In 1880 Parkhurst became minister of the Madison Square Presbyterian Church in New

York City, where he soon became concerned with the problem of corruption, particularly the police graft that was encouraging vice. He began to speak out against this in his sermons. Parkhurst also joined the Society for the Prevention of Crime, an association of clergy, lawyers, and merchants, and was elected president of the organization in 1891.

A year later, Parkhurst delivered his most blistering attack yet on the corrupt Democratic politicians of Tammany Hall, whom he described as "polluted harpies that, under the pretense of governing this city, are feeding day and night on its quivering vitals. . . ." When a reporter who happened to be present that Sunday publicized the sermon, Parkhurst was called before a grand jury to prove the charges. Lacking such proof, he hired a free-lance detective, Charles W. Gardner, to guide him through the vice district. Parkhurst and the detective spent four nights making the rounds of various brothels, saloons, gambling houses, and an opium den in the city's Chinatown.

Parkhurst and Gardner then made sworn affidavits about their findings, and on March 13, 1892, Parkhurst preached a second sermon, producing the affidavits as proof. He was criticized by many members of his congregation and by some of his fellow clergymen for his "sensationalism." But his disclosures aroused public opinion; a second grand jury was called and a number of individuals named in Parkhurst's affidavits were indicted. Parkhurst, however, was more interested in prosecuting the police officers who accepted bribes to protect the owners of brothels and other vice establishments than in closing down these places. As a result of his charges, the superintendent of the police force resigned, and all precinct

Library of Congress

captains except one were transferred—a decision Parkhurst protested on the grounds that simply moving officers from one area to another was unlikely to end corruption.

An even more important result of Parkhurst's crusade was the appointment of State Senator Clarence E. Lexow to investigate corruption in the city. The Lexow committee investigation of 1894 led to the downfall of the Democratic party machine at Tammany Hall, sending its chief packing to Europe and forcing the city police department to reorganize. Thanks to the wave of favorable publicity produced by the investigation, a reform-minded Republican candidate, William L. Strong, was swept into office as mayor of New York. One of his first acts of the new administration was to name a new four-man police board that included future president Theodore Roosevelt. In the company of the crusading journalist JACOB RIIS, Roosevelt patrolled the city streets at night on the lookout for police officers who were neglecting their duty.

Parkhurst, meanwhile, launched a second crusade in 1904 directed against poolrooms and the back rooms of saloons, but it made little impression. He continued at his church until retiring in 1918. During the 1920s Parkhurst opposed Prohibition, believing that drinking ought to be controlled by education rather than by law. In 1933 he died after a fall caused by sleepwalking.

**BIBLIOGRAPHY**

Gardner, C. W., *The Doctor and the Devil; or Midnight Adventures of Dr. Parkhurst*, 1931; Parkhurst, Charles, *My Forty Years in New York*, 1923; Werner, M. R., *It Happened in New York*, 1957.

# Parks, Rosa Louise McCauley

(February 4, 1913–    )
Civil Rights Activist

Rosa Parks has been called the mother of the civil rights movement for her courage when she would not give up her bus seat to a white man, which set off a boycott of the Montgomery, Alabama, bus system which in turn activated the movement against segregation.

Born in Tuskegee, Alabama, daughter of a carpenter and a teacher, Rosa McCauley grew up on a farm, then attended an industrial school for girls and the high school of Alabama State Teachers College in Montgomery, the state capital. At nineteen, she married Raymond Parks, a barber. Rosa Parks joined the Voters League and the youth council of the National Association for the Advancement of Colored People (NAACP; see JOEL E. SPINGARN), while her husband took part in voter registration. In those years involvement in such causes was risky.

On the evening of December 1, 1955, Parks boarded a bus to go home from the downtown department store where she worked as a seamstress. While cities outside the South, and even some southern cities, no longer enforced segregated seating on public transport, Montgomery still had discriminatory ordinances. Seats in the front rows were for whites, those at the back for blacks, and if a white passenger found all the seats taken a black passenger had to surrender his or her seat. Such was the case when the driver ordered Parks to give up her seat to a white man. She refused politely, and the driver called the police. Parks was arrested, charged, fined, and held in a cell.

Three friends arrived to post bail for Parks: two white civil rights activists, Clifford and Virginia Durr, who knew Parks through their work in the NAACP, and E. D. Dixon, former president of the state NAACP. Dixon asked Parks if she were willing to be a test case, and she agreed. More significant than the judicial aspect of the case, however, was the boycott of Montgomery's buses by the black community, which provided 70 percent of riders. A one-day boycott had been planned by civil rights activists, and now Rosa Parks—a respected, unassuming, religious person of strong character—was an ideal subject on whose behalf to stage it.

When the boycott took place on Monday, December 5, scarcely any black passengers were on the buses. At a mass rally that night, called by the ministerial alliance at one of the black churches, the clergymen and the people agreed to continue the boycott, under the leadership of a young Baptist pastor, MARTIN LUTHER KING, JR. Another clergyman, RALPH D. ABERNATHY, read the modest demands—courteous treatment, fair though segregated seating, black drivers on the mainly black routes—which were refused by the city government. The boycott, exceeding all expectations, continued for months. On February 1, the boycotters demanded complete integration, meaning that black riders were to be allowed to sit anywhere on the buses. As the boycott went on, the black community endured brutal violence from the police and other white persons. Rosa and Raymond Parks and many others lost their jobs. King's house was bombed. The boycotters maintained their resolve, and their protest drew national attention. On November 13, the U.S. Supreme Court declared bus segregation unconstitutional, and on December 21, after U.S. marshals served the court order, Montgomery complied. The first battle in the civil rights movement had been fought, and the integrationists had triumphed.

Though she and her husband were harassed and threatened, Rosa Parks worked as a volunteer coordinating the boycott. In 1957, unable to find employment in Montgomery, they moved to Detroit. Working as a seamstress, Rosa Parks devoted free time to fund raising for the NAACP.

In 1965 Parks was hired as office manager by a U.S. congressman from Michigan, John Conyers, Jr. She also traveled around the country making speeches on the history of civil rights, addressed to young people. In 1987, having retired, she founded the Rosa and Raymond Parks Institute for Self-Development, which seeks to guide black youths in their career plans.

**BIBLIOGRAPHY**

Branch, Taylor, *America in the King Years 1954–63,* 1988; Parks, Rosa, with Jim Haskins, *Rosa Parks: My Story,* 1992; Raines, Howell, *My Soul Is Rested: Movement Days in the Deep South Remembered,* 1983; Robinson, Jo Ann, *The Montgomery Bus Boycott and the Women Who Started It,* 1987.

# Paul, Alice

(January 11, 1885–July 9, 1977)
Reformer

As a feminist and suffragist favoring the use of militant tactics, Alice Paul devoted her life to fighting for women's rights, not just in America but worldwide. The suffrage battle won, she wrote the Equal Rights Amendment and worked hard, though unsuccessfully, to secure its passage.

Alice Paul was born in Moorestown, New Jersey, into a well-to-do Quaker family, whose ancestors included colonial leader WILLIAM PENN and a founder of Swarthmore College. Educated privately, she attended Swarthmore, graduating in 1905. She then spent a year doing graduate work at the New York School of Social Work, while living at the New York College Settlement.

In 1906 Paul went to England to do social work and continue her graduate education. Through the influence of Emmeline and Christobel Pankhurst, she joined the militant wing of the British suffrage movement. Her activities led to three periods of imprisonment. When, in protest, she went on hunger strikes, she was subjected to painful forced feedings. During this period in England, she managed to pursue graduate work at the universities of Birmingham and London, which led to an M.A. degree (1907) and a Ph.D. (1912) from the University of Pennsylvania.

Back in the United States in 1912, Paul led the congressional committee of the National American Woman Suffrage Association (NAWSA). However, her preference for militant tactics made her break with that organization the following year, forming the Congressional Union for Woman Suffrage, which she chaired. That same year, the Congressional Union organized a march of 5,000 women in Washington, D.C., at the time of Woodrow Wilson's first inauguration. Disagreeing with NAWSA's state-by-state approach, the new organization pushed for a woman suffrage amendment to the Constitution and singled out the party in power—in this case, the Democrats—as the culprit for failing to endorse such an amendment. Paul's organization worked to defeat Democratic congressional candidates in the off-year elections of 1914. As a result, both houses of Congress decided to consider woman-suffrage bills in 1914. With the Senate bill's defeat—by just one vote—both houses formed committees on woman suffrage. At the same time, NAWSA, under the leadership of CARRIE CHAPMAN CATT, shifted its strategy to focus on a constitutional amendment.

With the entry of the United States into World War I in 1917, NAWSA supported the war effort, but members of the Congressional

Union continued to picket the White House, get arrested, and go on hunger strikes. Paul herself was sentenced to prison several times during this period. In the end, Paul's tactics, combined with persuasion from Carrie Chapman Catt, convinced President Wilson to give priority to a federal suffrage amendment as a war measure. The Congressional Union joined the Woman's party to form the National Woman's party in 1917, with Paul heading the national executive committee for four years and the committee on international relations subsequently.

Following ratification of the Nineteenth Amendment in 1920, the National Woman's party worked to secure an Equal Rights Amendment (ERA) to the Constitution, which Paul drafted and was able to get introduced in Congress in 1923. The ERA sparked a great deal of controversy among women's groups. Many opposed it, afraid that it would end labor legislation that protected women and children, which had been won only after a long battle.

Paul, meanwhile, decided to attend law school in order to be better able to deal with women's rights issues. She earned three degrees: an L.L.B. from Washington College of Law in 1922 and an L.L.M. and D.C.L. from the American University in 1927 and 1928. In 1927 she became chair of the Woman's Research Foundation.

In the 1930s Paul's work assumed an international scope. From 1930 to 1933 she served as head of the nationality committee of the Inter-American Commission of Women, an organization which sought to obtain equal rights for women in Latin America. In addition, Paul served on the Women's Consultative Committee on Nationality of the League of Nations and on the executive committee of the Equal Rights International, which was also called the World Women's party. In the late 1930s, Paul began pushing for an Equal Rights Treaty guaranteeing equality to women in all nations that signed. While the United Nations (UN) was being organized after World War II, Paul was able to get a statement recognizing equal rights incorporated into the charter. She considered the UN Assembly's adoption of a woman suffrage resolution in 1946 an important victory.

Back in the United States, Paul's work for the ERA continued. By 1942 the Senate Judiciary Committee reported out the bill, and in 1944 both the Democratic and Republican parties included support for the ERA in their platforms. But when the Senate first voted on it in 1946, the ERA won only a simple majority, short of the two-thirds vote necessary to send it to the states for ratification. In 1950 it finally passed the Senate, with a rider stating that no protective legislation was to be affected. It passed again with this same clause in 1953 but became a dead cause until picked up by the women's movement of the 1960s.

When that renewed support for ERA began, Paul joined in the effort, even though she was in her eighties. She worked from the headquarters of the National Woman's party in Washington, D.C., from 1970 to 1972, when failing health made her relocate to Connecticut. Even then she managed to keep up the fight for the ERA until she suffered a stroke. She died in Moorestown, New Jersey, at the age of ninety-two.

**BIBLIOGRAPHY**

Irwin, Inez Haynes, *Up Hill with Banners Flying*, 1964; Lunardini, Christine A., *From Equal Suffrage to Equal Rights: Alice Paul and the National Woman's Party, 1910–1928*, 1986.

# Pauling, Linus Carl

(February 28, 1901– )
Humanitarian, Scientist

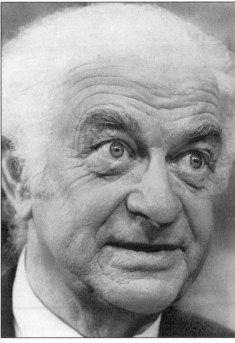

NBC/D.C. Public Library

One of the world's most distinguished scientists and a dedicated humanitarian, Linus Pauling has made significant contributions to such varied fields as chemistry, molecular biology, immunology, genetic diseases, and peace.

Pauling was born in Portland, Oregon, the son of a pharmacist. At age sixteen he enrolled at Oregon State College, graduating in 1922 with a major in chemistry and physics and having served as an assistant in quantitative analysis. He received his Ph.D. from the California Institute of Technology (Caltech) in 1925, then spent a year abroad studying the new concept of quantum mechanics on a Guggenheim fellowship in Munich, Zurich, and Copenhagen. In 1927 he returned to Caltech as an assistant professor, becoming a full professor four years later. In 1937 Pauling became chair of the division of chemistry and chemical engineering and director of the Gates and Crellin Laboratories of Caltech.

Pauling's early work exploring the structure of crystals led him to consider the nature of the chemical bond and the structure of molecules. Applying quantum mechanics to the structure of molecules, he developed his theory of resonance in chemical bonding. This explained how many substances were formed and eventually led to the development of many new drugs, plastics, and synthetic fibers. Pauling's book called *The Nature of the Chemical Bond*

*and the Structure of Molecules and Crystals* (1939) became a classic in the field.

During World War II, Pauling worked with the medical research committee of the Office of Scientific Research and Development. The latter committee used his recent research on proteins to help produce the first synthetic antibodies from blood globulins, thereby advancing the field of immunology. In 1948 Pauling received a Presidential Medal for Merit for his war work.

Having spent fourteen years studying more complex chemical structures, particularly the amino acids and peptide chains that make up proteins, Pauling in 1951 discovered what he called the "alpha helix" structure of several protein molecules. This important discovery led to new developments in disease control, plastics, and synthetic fibers. Pauling then worked on the connection between molecular abnormalities and such hereditary diseases as sickle-cell anemia. He also investigated the link between mental retardation and body chemistry and advanced a new theory of anesthesia. In 1954 Pauling was awarded the Nobel Prize for Chemistry for his work on chemical bonds and molecular structure.

As a scientist aware of the diseases and hereditary defects that can result from excessive radiation exposure and also of the destructive capacity of nuclear weapons, Pauling became convinced of the need to take a stand against the testing of nuclear weapons and in favor of multilateral disarmament. As a result of his antinuclear activities, Pauling came under suspicion by the State Department of being pro-Soviet and was denied a passport in 1952 and 1954. He was also accused of being a communist by Senator Joseph R. McCarthy. Nevertheless, Pauling courageously kept up his peace activities, publishing a book on disarmament entitled *No More War!* in 1958. Also that year, he presented to the United Nations a petition signed by more than 11,000 scientists calling for a halt in nuclear testing and participated in a televised debate with Edward Teller, the architect of the hydrogen bomb. On October 10, 1963, the day that a partial nuclear test ban went into effect, Pauling was awarded the Nobel Prize for Peace for 1962, his second Nobel Prize.

In 1963 Pauling left Caltech to work on peace and disarmament projects at the Center for the Study of Democratic Institutions in Santa Barbara, California. Two years later, he circulated a letter signed by eight Nobel Prize winners calling for the withdrawal of U.S. troops from Vietnam. In 1967 Pauling, along with political philosopher HERBERT MARCUSE, educator and linguist NOAM CHOMSKY, pediatrician BENJAMIN SPOCK, and others called U.S. involvement in Vietnam unconstitutional and urged resistance to the draft.

Also in 1967 Pauling became research professor of chemistry at the University of California at San Diego and subsequently professor of chemistry at Stanford University (1969–1972). In 1970 Pauling created a stir by endorsing the theory that large doses of vitamin C could prevent or cure the common cold. He wrote a popular book on the subject and on vitamin C as a cure for the flu and for cancer. In 1973 Pauling founded the Linus Pauling Institute of Science and Medicine in Palo Alto, California, to pursue work in orthomolecular medicine. Throughout the 1980s and early 1990s, he has remained active as an author and lecturer on social and political issues.

**BIBLIOGRAPHY**

Serafini, Anthony, *Linus Pauling: A Man and His Science,* 1989; White, Florence, *Linus Pauling, Scientist and Crusader,* 1980.

# Peabody, Elizabeth Palmer

(May 16, 1804–January 3, 1894)
Educator, Transcendentalist

Elizabeth Peabody founded the first kindergarten in America. As a bookstore owner, author, and publisher, she also did much to publicize the philosophy of Transcendentalism.

Born at Billerica, Massachusetts, Peabody attended the private school her mother conducted in nearby Salem on the principle that all children should be educated as if they were geniuses. While still in her teens, Peabody became a teacher, first at her mother's school, then in Maine, before returning to Massachusetts in 1825 to open a school of her own in the Boston suburb of Brookline.

While conducting this school, Peabody became acquainted with the Unitarian minister and Transcendentalist, WILLIAM ELLERY CHANNING, and served as his copyist and secretary for nine years. Through Channing, Peabody met other Transcendentalists, like Emerson, and later became a charter member of the Transcendental Club. Transcendentalism (see RALPH WALDO EMERSON for further discussion) was an American philosophical movement that had lasting effects on religion, literature, and social reform movements in the nineteenth century and later.

In 1834 Peabody gave up both her school and her work as Channing's secretary to assist BRONSON ALCOTT at his experimental Temple School in Boston. The publication of her *Record of a School* in 1835 helped establish Alcott as an eminent, if highly controversial, educational reformer. A year later, Peabody left the school and went back to Salem to live with her family.

Moving her family to Boston in 1840, Peabody opened her famous bookstore in the parlor of her West Street House. Featuring books by foreign authors as well as ones by native-born radical thinkers, Peabody's bookstore soon became a favorite gathering place for the Transcendentalists. MARGARET FULLER held her celebrated "conversations" there, and Emerson, George Ripley, and others met to discuss plans for the *Dial* and for Brook Farm, an experimental utopian community (see MARGARET FULLER and RALPH WALDO EMERSON). Besides running the bookstore, Peabody became the first woman publisher in Boston. She published early works by her friend and brother-in-law, Nathaniel Hawthorne; several of Margaret Fuller's translations from the German; and for two years, issues of the *Dial*. She also published one issue of her own transcendental journal, *Aesthetic Papers*, containing HENRY DAVID THOREAU's influential essay, "Civil Disobedience."

In 1850 Peabody closed her bookstore and devoted herself to writing and lecturing on education, as well as teaching. Learning of the kindergarten movement started in Germany by Friedrich Froebel, she opened in Boston in 1860 the first kindergarten in the United States. Although both the school and Peabody's book, *Moral Culture of Infancy, and Kindergarten Guide* (1863), written with her sister, Mary Peabody Mann, were well received, Peabody decided that the school was not in accord with Froebel's theories. In 1867 she closed it and went to Europe to study kindergartens there. Upon her return, she worked to promote the kindergarten movement, publishing a magazine, *The Kindergarten Messenger*, in 1873 and in 1877 organizing the American Froebel Union, serving as its first president. Peabody helped establish the kindergarten and teacher-training school at New York City's Normal College (now Hunter College of the City University of New York) and contributed money for the establishment of a kindergarten for the Paiute Indians in the West.

In the 1880s, when she was in her eighties, Peabody taught at Bronson Alcott's Concord School of Philosophy and wrote two more books, *Reminiscences of William Ellery Channing* (1880) and *Last Evenings with Allston* (1886), a book of reminiscences that included some of the essays she had written for the *Dial*. Active until the end, Peabody died at her home in Jamaica Plain, Boston, at the age of eighty-nine.

**BIBLIOGRAPHY**

Baylor, Ruth M., *Elizabeth Palmer Peabody: Kindergarten Pioneer*, 1965; Brooks, G., *Three Wise Virgins*, 1957; Sayder, A., *Dauntless Women in Higher Education, 1856–1931*, 1972; Tharp, L. H., *The Peabody Sisters of Salem*, 1950.

# Peabody, George

(February 18, 1795–November 4, 1869)
Business Leader, Philanthropist

The first American to take up philanthropy on a large scale, George Peabody anticipated such later philanthropists as ANDREW CARNEGIE and JOHN D. ROCKEFELLER with his generous gifts to a variety of educational and cultural institutions.

Born into a poor family in South Danvers (now Peabody), Massachusetts, George Peabody was apprenticed to a grocer in Danvers at the age of eleven. He later worked in Newburyport, Massachusetts, and in the District of Columbia, where in 1814 he became a partner in a dry-goods firm. He moved with the firm to Baltimore a year later, and in 1829 became the sole owner. He made a number of business trips to England, and in 1835, while in London, negotiated an $8 million loan that saved the state of Maryland from bankruptcy. Settling permanently in London the following year, Peabody started the investment banking house of George Peabody & Co.

Peabody prospered, and he became increasingly involved in philanthropy. Peabody believed that rich people had an obligation to make wise gifts of their money. He chose as the objects of his benefactions educational and cultural institutions such as libraries, schools, museums, and colleges.

Among Peabody's major gifts were $1.5 million to found the Peabody Institute in Baltimore, Maryland, including a free library, an academy of music, and an art gallery. He also established the Peabody Institute in Peabody, Massachusetts, which provides a library and an endowment for lectures; and museums at Yale and Harvard universities. In 1862 Peabody also donated $2.5 million to the city of London for the construction of low-cost housing for the poor. Peabody's last significant benefaction was $3.5 million for the Peabody Education Fund to advance education in the American South to be distributed without regard to the race of the beneficiary. The Peabody Education Fund was important as a precursor of today's philanthropic foundation.

Peabody's generosity made him much admired in both England and the United States. Though offered a baronetcy and the Grand Cross of the Bath by Queen Victoria, he declined both. Upon his death, he was given a funeral in Westminster Abbey, then his body was returned to the United States for burial in his native city of South Danvers, renamed Peabody in his honor.

**BIBLIOGRAPHY**

Corey, Lewis, *The House of Morgan*, 1930.

# Penn, William

(October 14, 1644–July 30, 1718)
Colonial Leader

William Penn was an English Quaker who advocated religious and civil liberty and founded Pennsylvania as a "Holy Experiment," where these liberties could exist.

Penn was born in London, the son of Admiral Sir William Penn, a wealthy naval officer, landowner, and good friend of King Charles II. Although his father was an Anglican, Penn was drawn to the Puritans. In 1662, after two years' study at Christ Church College, Oxford, he was expelled because of his refusal to accept the university rule that all students must attend the Church of England. Hoping to change his son's nonconformist religious beliefs, Penn's father sent him to Italy and France. Upon his return, Penn studied law in London, then went to Ireland to manage his father's estates there.

In Ireland, Penn met the Quaker preacher Thomas Loe and became convinced of the truth of the Quaker faith. To his father's great chagrin, Penn gave up a promising future to associate himself with a plain-living and plain-thinking sect whose members were scorned, ridiculed, and often imprisoned.

Penn himself was imprisoned several times for preaching and writing about the Society of Friends (Quakers). While locked up in the Tower of London, he wrote his celebrated *No Cross, No Crown* (1669), setting forth the Quaker doctrines of humility and nonviolence. Although his father secured his release after eight months, Penn was again arrested in 1670 for preaching on a London street. He defended himself so eloquently that the jury found him not guilty. When it refused to change its ver-

Library of Congress

dict, the jury was imprisoned by an angry judge but then later released.

In 1670 Penn's father died after having become reconciled with his son. The admiral's legacy to Penn included his extensive estates in England and Ireland as well as his personal friendship with King Charles II and his brother, James, Duke of York. Penn spent the next decade writing pamphlets in defense of Quakerism and going on preaching missions throughout England, the Netherlands, and northern Germany.

Also during these years, Penn developed an interest in America. In 1677 he helped settle the affairs of a Quaker colony in New Jersey, for which he took part in the drafting of a liberal charter. Then in 1680 Penn asked King Charles II to repay a debt of £16,000 owed to his father with a grant of wilderness land in America. In 1681 Penn's dream of a "Holy Experiment" came true when he was granted a charter giving him proprietary rights over the territory west of the Delaware River between New York and Maryland.

In 1682 Penn drew up a "Frame of Government," providing for an elected assembly. Penn's "Frame" may have had an influence on the Constitution of the United States. Other laws guaranteed free elections and trial by jury and established a humane penal code.

Attracted by promises of cheap land and religious freedom, settlers from the Netherlands and Germany as well as England poured into Pennsylvania, or Penn's Woods, as the new colony was called. Penn went there himself in 1682. He helped get the government set up and held friendly councils with the American Indians to negotiate for the transfer of their lands and ensure peaceful relations. A pioneer in city planning, Penn laid out Philadelphia in an orderly checkerboard pattern and had a fine manor house built for himself in Pennsbury on the Delaware River. But after less than two years, a border dispute with neighboring Maryland forced Penn to return to England.

Back in England, Penn's friendship with the new king, James II, a devout Catholic, was at first a boon, then a liability. Penn was able to use his influence with the king to free from prison hundreds of Quakers and political prisoners. But when the Glorious Revolution of 1688 replaced James II with the Protestant rulers William and Mary, Penn found himself under suspicion and was arrested several times. In 1692 Pennsylvania was taken away from him and put under royal control. It was restored to him in 1694.

By the time Penn returned to his colony in 1699, it was beset by problems over government and other matters. Penn tried to resolve these problems by issuing a new constitution, the Charter of Privileges, creating a one-house elected legislature with greater powers while at the same time reducing the powers of the proprietor and his governor. He also allowed the lower counties (now Delaware) to set up an independent government, united with Pennsylvania only through the governor. Penn held more meetings with the American Indians to make new agreements and foster friendly relations. In addition, he tried to lessen the evils of slavery in Pennsylvania and made a will providing for the freeing of his own slaves at a later date.

Although Penn had hoped to remain in Pennsylvania, within two years' time he was again obliged to return to England. He never set foot in America again.

Penn's last years were darkened by tragedy. In 1708 he had to spend nine months in debtors' prison due to his steward's mismanagement of his funds. In 1712 Penn was about to sell his proprietorship of Pennsylvania to the crown when he suffered a stroke that left him incapacitated. His wife managed his proprietary affairs until Penn's death in 1718.

**BIBLIOGRAPHY**

Bronner, Edwin B., *William Penn's "Holy Experiment": The Founding of Pennsylvania, 1680–1684,* 1978; Trussell, John B., Jr., *William Penn: Architect of a Nation,* 1980; Wildes, Harry Emerson, *William Penn,* 1974.

# Phillips, Wendell

(November 29, 1811–February 2, 1884)
Reformer

A brilliant orator, Wendell Phillips was famous as the "golden trumpet" of the abolitionist movement. He remained concerned with the plight of the freedmen after Emancipation and was also an early supporter of the labor movement.

Phillips was born in Boston into a wealthy, long-established mercantile family. At the Boston Latin School and later at Harvard, from which he graduated in 1831, Phillips demonstrated a flair for oratory. In 1834 he received his law degree from Harvard and seemed destined for a successful practice until he was converted to the abolitionist cause by Ann Terry Greene, whom he married in 1837. That same year, Phillips made his debut as an abolitionist orator with a speech at Faneuil Hall in Boston, denouncing the murder of antislavery editor ELIJAH LOVEJOY. The speech established Phillips as one of the leaders of the movement. In 1840 Phillips and his wife attended the World Anti-Slavery Convention in London, where Phillips joined with WILLIAM LLOYD GARRISON in protesting the barring of women delegates from the floor.

Library of Congress

Throughout the 1840s Phillips worked with Garrison, serving on the executive committee and as recording secretary of the American Anti-Slavery Society, and was a frequent contributor to *The Liberator*. Like Garrison, Phillips criticized the Constitution of the United States because of its compromises on slavery and did not believe that the abolitionist cause could be advanced through political action. Nevertheless, Phillips differed with Garrison's doctrine of nonresistance, arguing that laws like the Fugitive Slave Act of 1850 ought to be forcibly resisted.

In the turbulent decade of the 1850s, Phillips became increasingly militant. By this time he had won a national reputation as a lecturer, and he used the platform to fire public sentiment against slavery. He also helped organize a vigilance committee in Boston to ensure the safe passage of fugitive slaves to Canada, and in 1854 he took part in an unsuccessful attempt to free captured fugitive Anthony Burns. Although impressed with the radical abolitionist JOHN BROWN, whom he met in 1857, Phillips stopped short of aiding Brown in his raid on Harpers Ferry, Virginia. He did, however, organize the legal defense of those who had helped Brown and provided legal counsel for Brown in Virginia—Phillips later delivered the eulogy at Brown's funeral.

With the outbreak of the Civil War, Phillips insisted that it was more important to free the slaves than to save the union, and he criticized President Abraham Lincoln for failing to make emancipation his war aim. Phillips welcomed both the Emancipation Proclamation and the passage of the Thirteenth Amendment, freeing the slaves, in 1865. But when William Lloyd Garrison called for the disbanding of the American Anti-Slavery Society, Phillips strongly objected. Arguing that with emancipation the society's real work had just begun, Phillips replaced Garrison as president of the American Anti Slavery Society. He now pushed for the passage of the Fourteenth Amendment, giving African Americans equal rights, and of the Fifteenth Amendment, giving them the vote. With the passage of the latter in 1870, Phillips urged that a system of free public education be established in the South, so that all children, black and white, rich and poor, would receive an equal education. And when most Americans, including some of Phillips's former colleagues in the abolitionist movement, lost interest in the plight of the free slaves, Phillips kept up the cry for social justice.

A supporter of other reform efforts, including woman suffrage, prison reform, and the rights of American Indians, Phillips in the years after the war took up the cause of labor. Arguing that wage earners were as much the victims of corporate capital as slaves had been of slavery, he urged workers to use the ballot to defend their interests. Phillips advocated the eight-hour day and an end to child labor. In 1870 he made an unsuccessful bid for the governorship of Massachusetts on the Labor Reform ticket.

Having made reform his profession early on, Phillips remained an agitator, "with no bread to earn, no candidate to elect, no party to save, no object but truth" until the end of his life. He died in Boston at the age of seventy-two.

BIBLIOGRAPHY

Bartlett, Irving H., *Wendell Phillips: Brahmin Radical,* 1961; McPherson, James, *Struggle for Equality: Abolitionists and the Negro in Civil War and Reconstruction,* 1964.

## Phillips, William

(ca. 1906–   )
Editor, Writer

William Phillips was one of the founders and for fifty years has been an editor of the *Partisan Review,* one of the nation's most important literary-political journals.

The son of Russian immigrants, Phillips was born in Manhattan and grew up in the Bronx. He enrolled at City College, graduating in 1926. While there, he discovered modernism (an artistic and literary movement characterized by a searching for new forms of expression); later, as a graduate student at New York University, from which he earned an M.A. in 1930, he began reading such major modernist authors as James Joyce, Ezra Pound, and Thomas Mann and also viewing modern art. By 1933 he was attending meetings of the John Reed Club (see JOHN REED), a group of writers and painters affiliated with the Communist party, through which he met PHILIP RAHV. Phillips and Rahv decided to begin a journal that would promote political radicalism and literary modernism.

From its first issue in February 1934 until 1937, *Partisan Review* was the official organ of the John Reed Club. Eventually, however, Phillips and Rahv broke with the party and the club. Publication of the *Partisan Review* was suspended for a few months in 1937, and when it resumed in December of that year, it was with a new staff and editorial policy. In the arts the magazine increased its commitment to experimentalism. In politics, *Partisan Review* consistently exposed Stalin's crimes while attempting to develop a non-Stalinist brand of leftist politics. Among the important new literary figures whose writings appeared in the pages of *Partisan Review* were Delmore Schwartz, Mary McCarthy, Lionel Trilling, and Edmund Wilson. The magazine also published such leading European and English writers as George Orwell, Franz Kafka, and Jean-Paul Sartre.

In the postwar years, *Partisan Review* supported the policy of containment of communism, but fought the anticommunism hysteria created by Senator Joseph McCarthy. In 1963 *Partisan Review* began an affiliation with Rutgers University, moving to the New Jersey campus, where Phillips became professor of English. Since the late 1950s, he had assumed more and more of the editorial responsibilities of the magazine, as Rahv devoted less and less time to it. In 1969 Rahv left to found his own magazine.

During the 1960s *Partisan Review* continued to publish important new writers, but as the decade wore on and politics became increasingly polarized, Phillips and *Partisan Review* came under fire from the left and right. Refusing to become a new (or neo-) conservative like many of his former colleagues, Phillips tried to steer a middle course between the two extremes. In the process, *Partisan Review* lost much of its influence. In 1978 Phillips moved *Partisan Review*'s offices to Boston University and became a professor of English there.

Phillips edited many volumes of short fiction and coedited three anthologies of pieces from *Partisan Review* with Rahv. He also published *A Sense of the Present* (1967), which is a volume of essays, and the memoir, *A Partisan* *View: Five Decades of the Literary Life* (1984).

**BIBLIOGRAPHY**

Barrett, William, *The Truants*, 1982; Gilbert, James Burkhart, *Writers and Partisans: A History of Literary Radicalism in America*, 1968; Hellman, Lillian, *Scoundrel Time*, 1976; Phillips, William, *A Partisan View: Five Decades of the Literary Life*, 1983; Podhoretz, Norman, *Breaking Ranks*, 1979.

# Pingree, Hazen

(August 30, 1840–June 18, 1901)
Reformer

H azen Pingree was an early progressive, who before the "official" beginning of the Progressive movement (with the presidency of Theodore Roosevelt) instituted important urban reforms as mayor of Detroit.

Born in Denmark, Maine, Hazen Pingree went to work at various jobs at the age of fourteen. During the Civil War he enlisted as a private in Company F, 14th Massachusetts Infantry (later the First Massachusetts Heavy Artillery), and was captured, then paroled, in 1864. After the war, Pingree settled in Detroit, which was then on the verge of a huge economic boom, and got a job in a shoe factory. Late in 1866 Pingree became a partner in a shoe-manufacturing concern, which under his skilled management grew into a highly successful business.

During the next twenty years, Pingree married, had three children, and established himself as a model citizen and businessman. Among other groups, he joined the Michigan Club, which was made up of Republican businesspeople, who offered him the nomination for mayor of Detroit in 1889 on a mild reform platform. He accepted and immediately created what would be a longstanding rapport with working people and the large immigrant population of the city, going far beyond the ideas of the Michigan Club to offer his support for an eight-hour work day. As a result, he won the election handily.

Pingree was elected mayor for two terms, during which he fought municipal scandal and entrenched private company strangleholds on such areas as streetlighting, railways, tollroads, gas, electric, and telephones. Having expanded his ideas about social reform, he came to believe that the public should own and control such public utilities. Though not well known outside of Michigan, he got some national attention for his plan for city gardens to help the unemployed survive in the panic of 1893.

In 1896 Pingree was elected governor and served two terms. He fought the tax evasion of railroad and mining companies and set up commissions to establish fair tax rates, but he found the larger state office more difficult to manage than the municipal one. Though his urban reform programs would later be recognized as direct forerunners to those of later Progressives (like Robert M. La Follette) and his popularity remained undiminished with the people during his terms of office, he left the governorship unhappy and under a cloud of scandal over supplies procured for the Michigan militia in the Spanish-American War.

Pingree spent his final years traveling abroad and working on a history of the Boer War. He died in England in 1901.

**BIBLIOGRAPHY**

Holli, M. G., *Reform in Detroit: Hazen S. Pingree and Urban Politics,* 1969.

# Podhoretz, Norman

(January 16, 1930– )
Author, Editor

Norman Podhoretz, who began a brilliant career as a literary critic and left-wing dissenter, moved to an extreme conservatism as the editor of *Commentary*.

Norman Podhoretz, born in Brownsville, a neighborhood of Brooklyn, New York, was the son of a milkman, who with his wife had emigrated from eastern Europe. Young Podhoretz had a dual education, in public and in Hebrew schools. He was valedictorian of his class at a Hebrew high school; at a public high school he was a superior student and graduated when he was sixteen. At Columbia University he studied with the literary critics Lionel Trilling, F. W. Dupee, and Mark Van Doren (who gave him the only B he got in English). Simultaneously he attended the Jewish Theological Seminary, near Columbia. Podhoretz graduated from both institutions with honors in 1950.

With a Fulbright Scholarship (under the student foreign exchange program sponsored by Senator J. W. Fulbright), Podhoretz studied for two years at Cambridge University, in England, where he was influenced by another literary critic, F. R. Leavis. After earning a B.A. degree in 1952, Podhoretz spent a year working toward a Ph.D., then decided not to prepare for an academic career but simply to become a "great" literary critic. He first, however, served two years in the U.S. Army, in Germany, as an information officer.

While abroad, Podhoretz published book reviews in *Commentary,* a monthly journal sponsored by the American Jewish Committee. Under the editorship of Elliot Cohen, the magazine published contributions on current issues and Jewish affairs, following in the main a left-wing line, though anticommunist and non-Zionist. (In the words of IRVING HOWE, *Commentary* at the time was "inclined ... to minimize the McCarthyite threat," preferring to "attack the delusions of those liberals, many of them Jewish, who saw no parallel threat from Stalinism.") Podhoretz was first noticed when *Commentary* published his review of Saul Bellow's novel *The Adventures of Augie March,* which, unlike most other reviews of the book, was provocatively negative.

Upon his discharge, Podhoretz joined *Commentary* as an assistant editor, while writing book reviews, often polemical, for many other journals. He left *Commentary* for two years to work in book publishing, and after Cohen's death he returned in 1960 as editor in chief. Podhoretz made extreme changes in policy and format, at first guiding *Commentary* further leftward. He aimed to make the journal a vehicle of "the long-dormant tradition of American social criticism." He caused a stir by publishing Paul Goodman's entire book, *Growing Up Absurd,* a harsh critique of American society that became a testament of the New Left.

With his autobiographical essay *Making It* (1966), however, Podhoretz began to appear in a new light. With what some considered a disarming candor, he revealed an obsession with success and an overvaluation of fame, riches, and power. He was drifting away from his radical credo and, in the next years, he turned *Commentary* into a voice of the "new conservatism." Another installment of autobiography, *Breaking Ranks: A Political Memoir* (1979), continued to show Podhoretz's defection from his earlier left-wing stance. The message of his 1980 book, *The Present Danger,* is spelled out by its subtitle, "Do We Have the Will to Reverse the Decline of American Power?"; and *Why We*

*Were in Vietnam* (1982) finds the war, as President Ronald Reagan called it, "a noble cause."

Podhoretz's views are complemented by those of his wife, Midge Decter, also a writer and editor.

**BIBLIOGRAPHY**

Podhoretz, Norman, *Doings and Undoings: The Fifties and After in American Writing,* 1964, *The Bloody Crossroads: Where Literature and Politics Meet,* 1986, and (ed.), *The Commentary Reader: Two Decades of Articles and Stories,* 1966.

# Polk, Leonidas Lafayette

(April 24, 1837–June 11, 1892)
Editor, Reformer

As an editor and an agrarian reformer, L. L. Polk was one of the Populist movement's most powerful and persuasive spokespersons until his untimely death.

Born in Anson County, North Carolina, Polk was orphaned at the age of fourteen and took up farming. Elected to the state legislature in 1860 on the eve of the Civil War, Polk opposed secession as late as April 1861, after fighting had begun at Fort Sumter. But after his state seceded, he joined the Confederate army, in which he was a lieutenant. Polk was reelected to the legislature in 1864 despite the fact that as a former Southern Unionist he was regarded with suspicion in some circles.

The war over, Polk took up the cause of agrarian reform, advocating the establishment of a state department of agriculture. After this was accomplished in 1877, he served as its first commissioner, a post he held until 1880. In 1886 Polk began publishing a journal called the *Progressive Farmer,* which sought to teach southern farmers better agricultural methods; at the same time, it reflected its editor's growing interest in politics. In his journal Polk urged farmers to form clubs through which they could exert pressure on the legislature to meet their demands. With the support of the farmers' clubs that were started, Polk saw that a state college of agriculture was founded.

While Polk was involved in this effort, the Farmers' Alliance spread through the South and the West. Soon caught up in the new movement, Polk turned his journal into an organ of the Farmers' Alliance; in 1887 he was elected vice president of the National Alliance, and two years later, president. As the head of such an organization, which by this time had over a million members, Polk became an important force in national politics. He sought to further spur the growth of the organization by embarking on nationwide speaking tours in 1890 and 1891. In his speeches Polk stressed the need for unity among southern and western farmers.

When the Democrats and Republicans failed to endorse the National Alliance's radical platform, Polk turned to the newly emerging

People's or Populist party that was based on a coalition of farmers and workers. An eloquent, impassioned orator, Polk proved especially adept at spreading the Populist message of reform. In February 1892 he presided at the convention in St. Louis, which marked the official founding of the party. Polk's reputation was such that he was assured the nomination as the Populist presidential candidate in 1892. However, three weeks before the convention, Polk died suddenly after a brief illness. His death was a major loss to the movement, especially in the South.

**BIBLIOGRAPHY**

Goodwyn, L. C., *Democratic Promise: The Populist Moment in American History*, 1976; McMath, R. C., *Populist Vanguard: A History of the Southern Farmer's Alliance*, 1975; Noblin, S., *Leonidas Lafayette Polk, Agrarian Crusader*, 1949.

# Post, Louis Freeland

(November 15, 1849–January 10, 1928)
Journalist, Reformer

As a journalist and a lecturer, Louis Freeland Post was a leading proponent of HENRY GEORGE's single-tax program. Through his work, he sought to advance the civil and economic rights of his fellow citizens.

Born on a farm in northwestern New Jersey, Post left school at the age of fourteen to become a clerk in a pawnshop in New York City. He then worked as a newspaper printer before entering a New York City law office. He was admitted to the bar in 1870.

Post was appointed clerk to Major David T. Corbin, who was U.S. attorney at Charleston, South Carolina, and a senator in the state's Reconstruction

Library of Congress

government. Post gained an inside view of conditions in the South during Reconstruction through his work on legislative committees and during Ku Klux Klan trials.

Back in New York, Post served from 1874 to 1875 as assistant U.S. attorney, then fled from the political corruption he encountered. He was a partner in the law firm of Lockwood & Post until 1880 when he became an editorial writer for the newspaper, *Truth*. Post's pro-labor editorials helped occasion the first official Labor Day in 1882.

During the 1880s Post became good friends with the reformer Henry George and a prominent advocate of George's single-tax plan.

Post edited the *Standard,* the weekly of the single-tax movement, and also lectured extensively from 1892 to 1897 on the single tax; in 1894 he published an account of George's work called *Post's Outlines.*

After working as an editorial writer for the Cleveland *Recorder,* Post and his wife established and edited a liberal journal, called the *Chicago Public,* which had among its backers the reform mayor of Cleveland, TOM JOHNSON. Appointed to the Chicago school board, Post fought for academic freedom and the formation of teachers' unions. He traveled to Great Britain in 1908 to attend a free-trade conference and in 1913 was appointed assistant secretary of labor by President Woodrow Wilson, serving until 1921.

During the so-called Red Scare of the 1920s, when aliens suspected of being communists were rounded up and thrown into jail without due process of law, Post protested these violations of civil liberties in his book, *The De-portation Delirium of Nineteen Twenty* (1923).

After retirement, Post remained in Washington, D.C., where he continued to write. His final work on Henry George, *The Prophet of San Francisco: Personal Memories and Interpretations of Henry George,* appeared in 1930, two years after Post's death at the age of seventy-eight. Post's other writings include *The Ethics of Democracy* (1903), *Ethical Principles of Marriage and Divorce* (1906), *What Is the Single Tax?* (1926), and *The Basic Facts of Economics* (1927).

**BIBLIOGRAPHY**

La Follette, Belle C., "Louis F. Post," *La Follette's Magazine,* February 1928; Reedy, W. H., "A Cabinet Photograph," St. Louis *Mirror,* January 24, 1913; Vallandigham, E. N., "Louis F. Post . . . A Personal Tribute," *New-Church Review,* January 1929.

# Powderly, Terence Vincent

(January 22, 1849–June 24, 1924)
Labor Leader, Reformer

As head of the Knights of Labor, Terence Powderly was the most popular and powerful labor leader in the United States during the 1880s. A gifted speaker with a vision of a better world, he made his most lasting contribution to the labor movement as a publicist and educator.

Born in Carbondale, Pennsylvania, to Irish immigrant parents, Powderly attended school until he was thirteen, when he left to work for the railroad. At age seventeen he became a machinist and in 1871 joined the local of the Machinists' and Blacksmiths' International Union, becoming its secretary and president the following year. In 1874 Powderly was initiated into the Knights of Labor. Founded in 1869 by URIAH STEPHENS and other Philadelphia garment cutters, the Knights was a secret organization with elaborate rituals, which functioned more as a fraternal order than a labor movement. In 1878, in response to calls from Powderly and a few others, the Knights held its first general assembly and adopted a constitution, which Powderly helped to draft, calling for the solidarity of all workers. Although Stephens was elected head of the Knights, Powderly was one of the acknowledged leaders of the national organization, and in 1879 he replaced Stephens as chief executive, or Grand Master Workman.

Under Powderly's leadership, the Knights grew from about 9,000 members in 1879 to over 700,000 in 1886. Powderly made possible this expansion by reducing the secrecy that made becoming a member a slow and restricted process, lowering the age of admission, using commissioned organizers, and opening admission to women, blacks, and new immigrants. Indeed, the Knights was the first industrial union to admit all gainfully employed persons, including unskilled workers, regardless of sex, race, or color. In the West farmers accounted for the bulk of the membership; in the East, trade unionists. The Knights established hundreds of black and many integrated locals in the South. It also played a role in the passage of the Contract Labor Act of 1885.

As head of the Knights, Powderly was more interested in a broad program of social reform than in bread-and-butter issues like higher wages and shorter hours. He viewed the Knights as an educational institution that would achieve reform by enlisting workers to demand that government own public utilities, regulate trusts, reform the currency and land system, and abolish child labor. He hoped to replace the wage system by a system in which factories cooperatively owned by workers would produce goods that would be sold by cooperatives owned by consumers. Yet while 135 such cooperatives were set up, including the ownership and operation of a coal mine, the system failed to take hold.

Although Powderly was himself elected mayor of Scranton, Pennsylvania, for three successive terms (1878–1884) on the Greenback-Labor Ticket, he shrank from involving the Knights in direct political action. Not until 1892 did the national organization take a partisan stance, and by then it was too weak to do much.

As labor tactics, Powderly preferred arbitration and education to strikes, which he considered outmoded and dangerous. Nevertheless, the hard times of 1884 and 1885 involved the rank and file of the Knights in a series of strikes and boycotts, through which they managed to successfully challenge the powerful monopolies of the day. The Knights' most notable victories in this regard were strikes by railway shopmen of the Union Pacific and the Southwest System (1884) and against the Wabash Railroad (1885), in which

they forced railroad magnate Jay Gould to negotiate with the Knights and agree to end discriminatory practices.

After reaching the peak of their influence in 1886, the Knights soon fell into a decline, in part because of several disastrous strikes, including a second one against Jay Gould's railway system in the South and the West and one by the Chicago meat packers. The Knights' decline also stemmed from the refusal of Powderly and other leaders to focus on concrete issues like higher wages and shorter hours, which were important to the trade unionists among its membership. In 1886 a group of disaffected trade unionists, led by SAMUEL GOMPERS, broke off from the Knights to form a rival organization, the American Federation of Labor (see WILLIAM GREEN and JOHN L. LEWIS).

A third reason for the decline of the Knights lay in Powderly's character. Viewing the Knights as his personal domain, he had little patience with disagreement, which to him meant disloyalty. As a result, numerous subordinates who differed with him were expelled from the Knights. And while Powderly was a gifted orator, he was not an able administrator because of his unwillingness to delegate authority. Close coordination of effort was also made difficult by the fact that Powderly stayed in Scranton 100 miles away, while the Knights' executive board was based in Philadelphia. Moreover, Powderly spent a great deal of time writing letters, in which he often complained of the burdens of his office. Then, too, in moments of crisis he was frequently incapable of acting decisively. Increasingly isolated from the rank and file of the Knights, Powderly was finally forced out of office in 1893 by a coalition led by farmers, who by this time accounted for a large majority of the membership. The Knights continued as a fraternal organization until 1917 when it disbanded.

Powderly, meanwhile, became a lawyer and civil servant. He was admitted to the Pennsylvania bar in 1894, and three years later, as a reward for campaigning for the Republican candidate, William McKinley, in the election of 1896, was appointed U.S. commissioner general of immigration. Dismissed by President Theodore Roosevelt in 1902 over a minor political matter, he was later appointed chief of the Division of Information of the Bureau of Immigration by Roosevelt, holding this post until 1921. From 1921 to 1924 Powderly served as a commissioner of conciliation in the Labor Department. He died in Washington, D.C., at the age of seventy five.

**BIBLIOGRAPHY**

Fink, Leon, *Workingmen's Democracy: The Knights of Labor and American Politics*, 1983; Foner, Philip S., *History of the Labor Movement in the United States*, vol. 2, 1964; Grob, Gerald, *Workers and Utopia*, 1961; McLaurin, M. A., *The Knights of Labor in the South*, 1978.

# Powell, John Wesley

(March 24, 1834–September 23, 1902)
Explorer, Scientist

A national hero thanks to his epic exploration of the Colorado and Green rivers, John Wesley Powell pioneered scientific land and water management in the West as head of the U.S. Geological Survey.

Born in Mt. Morris, New York, to Methodist immigrant parents, John Wesley Powell spent his boyhood in various frontier settlements in Ohio, Wisconsin, and Illinois, to which his parents moved in the hopes of spreading the gospel. Powell studied at three colleges, Wheaton (in Illinois), Illinois College, and Oberlin in Ohio, but he did not receive a degree. Also during these early years, he undertook long, solitary plant-collecting trips down the Mississippi and Ohio rivers. In 1858 he was elected secretary of the Illinois Society of Natural History.

With the outbreak of the Civil War, Powell enlisted in the Union army, rising to the rank of major of artillery. At the Battle of Shiloh in

Library of Congress

1862 he lost his arm at the elbow. After the war he taught geology at Illinois Wesleyan University (1865) and at Illinois State Normal University (1867), where he also served as curator of the museum. Powell also led groups of students and amateur naturalists on expeditions to the mountains of Colorado in 1867 and 1868. On one of these trips, Powell first envisioned a bold plan to undertake a boat exploration of the gorges of the Colorado and Green rivers.

Powell secured funding by the Smithsonian Institution and Congress and in May 1869 embarked with eleven men and four boats on a 900-mile voyage—the last major exploration within the continental United States. Starting out on the Green River in Wyoming, Powell and his men spent three difficult, dangerous months on the water before passing through the Grand Canyon to safety in August. Powell made three additional western expeditions during 1871 to 1875, publishing his findings in a book that came to be regarded as a literary classic, *Explorations of the Colorado River of the West and Its Tributaries* (1875). In it, Powell observed that many of the West's canyons were formed by water erosion acting on rocks that were gradually rising.

In 1875 Powell was appointed director of the second division of the U.S. Geological and Geographical Survey of the Territories (renamed the Survey of the Rocky Mountain Region in 1877). Making use of the staff and findings of his survey, Powell in 1878 published his pathbreaking *Report on the Lands of the Arid Region of the United States.* In Powell's view, the most important fact of life in the West was its aridity. Convinced that the lands beyond the 100th meridian (approximately central Kansas) had insufficient rainfall for large-scale agriculture, he wanted to change the 160-acre allotments established in the Homestead Act to promote smaller, irrigated farms and much larger grazing farms. He also wanted to replace the old system of conducting surveys of rectangular blocks of land with surveys based on the location of water. Unfortunately, most of the reforms Powell proposed were ignored because of pressure from western land promoters. It was not until the Dust Bowl of the 1930s that Powell's early recommendations were heeded in a desperate attempt to repair the damage caused by decades of dry-land farming.

Meanwhile, with the consolidation of all the western surveys as the United States Geological Survey, Powell in 1879 was put in charge of the Bureau of Ethnology at the Smithsonian, a post he held for the rest of his life. In 1877 Powell had published his pioneering *Introduction to the Study of the Indian Languages.* Now, under his direction, the Bureau of Eth-nology published a number of reports and monographs that marked the first systematic study of the various American Indian nations.

From 1880 to 1894, Powell also served as director of the U.S. Geological Survey, which under his guidance became a large and well-managed organization and a model for later bureaus covering other areas of science. To make the survey's work available to the public, Powell instituted a series of regular bulletins, monographs on special subjects, and magnificent folio atlases complete with geologic and topographic maps.

In 1888, following the ten-year drought of the 1880s, Powell began a program of western irrigation surveys. He believed that the arid regions could be made productive if the government undertook large-scale irrigation and damming projects. This concept of "reclamation" would be picked up and successfully advanced later on by a number of Powell's younger colleagues at the Geological Survey. But in the 1890s, Powell's opponents again defeated his program. After both the irrigation survey budget and the budget of the Geological Survey had been slashed, Powell resigned as head of the survey. He devoted his remaining years to working for the Bureau of Ethnology and to the writing of philosophical treatises. Powell died at his summer home in Maine at the age of sixty-eight.

**BIBLIOGRAPHY**

Darrah, William Culp, *Powell of the Colorado,* 1951; Stegner, Wallace, *Beyond the Hundredth Meridian: John Wesley Powell and the Second Opening of the West,* 1954; Terrell, John Upton, *The Man Who Discovered America: A Biography of John Wesley Powell,* 1969.

# Pulitzer, Joseph

(April 10, 1847–October 29, 1911)
Journalist

As the owner of the St. Louis *Post-Dispatch* and later of the New York *World,* Joseph Pulitzer contributed more than any other person to making the American newspaper what it is today.

Joseph Pulitzer was born in Makó, Hungary, and grew up in Budapest. Failing to make a military career in Europe because of poor health and eyesight, Pulitzer immigrated to the United States in 1864 and enlisted in the Union army. He served for nearly a year under General Philip Sheridan. With the end of the war, Pulitzer went to St. Louis, Missouri, where he became a reporter for a newspaper owned by German-born journalist and statesman Carl Schurz.

In spite of at first being ridiculed because of his scrawny figure and poor English, Pulitzer soon became a highly successful reporter. His reputation was such that he was elected to the state legislature as a Republican and served during the 1870 session. An ardent supporter of the Liberal Republican movement, of which Schurz was one of the leaders, Pulitzer was named secretary of the Cincinnati convention that nominated controversial editor HORACE GREELEY for the presidency in 1872. Disillusioned by the failure of the movement, Pulitzer joined the Democratic party, campaigning vigorously for Samuel J. Tilden in 1876.

In 1878 Pulitzer bought the failing St. Louis *Dispatch* at public auction for $2,500 and soon added to it the St. Louis *Post.* Using both sensationalism and campaigns against political and municipal corruption in St. Louis, he managed to double the circulation of the combined papers within a year. By the end of 1881, the St. Louis *Post-Dispatch* was bringing in annual profits of $45,000.

In 1883 Pulitzer bought the New York *World* from financier and railroad speculator Jay Gould, for $346,000, and quickly transformed it into the country's leading Democratic daily newspaper. With the *World,* Pulitzer fine-tuned the techniques of mass-circulation journalism he had started in the St. Louis *Post-Dispatch.*

Like the St. Louis *Post-Dispatch,* the *World* combined sensational crime stories with effective exposés of civic corruption. Moreover, it provided readers with entertainment as well as information through such features as sports, colored comics, illustrations, and women's fashions. The *World* further made full use of inventions that were revolutionizing publishing during this time. Among these inventions were cheaper newsprint made from wood pulp, the Linotype machine, typewriters, telephones, and the telegraph. These improvements, along with the paper's excellent news coverage, distinguished editorials, sensational stories, promotional stunts, and reform-minded crusades, brought a dramatic rise in circulation. Two months after Pulitzer assumed control of the paper, its original readership of 20,000 had doubled. By the fall of 1884, the *World* boasted a circulation of 100,000; by 1886, 250,000. In 1887 Pulitzer added the *Evening World,* and by 1896 the combined circulation of the two papers had climbed to nearly 750,000.

Newspapers in New York and other large cities soon adopted Pulitzer's successful methods. In particular, a fierce rivalry developed between the *World* and the New York *Journal* under the ownership of WILLIAM RANDOLPH HEARST. Hearst was determined to outdo the *World* in sensationalism, giving rise to "yellow journalism," a term used because of a comic strip titled the "Yellow Kid" but which came to stand for the most lurid of journalistic practices. Yellow journalism on the part of both papers helped inflame public opinion in favor of war against Spain in 1898.

Pulitzer had retired from direct control of his papers in 1889 because of failing health, but he returned after the Spanish-American War and raised the level of the *World* to what it had been. Under his renewed guidance, the paper continued to serve as an instrument of middle-class reform. In editorials and stories, the *World* supported labor, campaigned against trusts and political bosses, and helped to expose the plight of the urban poor—crusades which anticipated in daily journalism the muckraking magazines of the early twentieth century.

An extremely wealthy man by the time of his death in 1911, Pulitzer left $2 million for the establishment of the first school of journalism in the country at Columbia University in New York City. He also left $250,000 to be used for the annual Pulitzer prizes in journalism, literature, and education.

**BIBLIOGRAPHY**

Barrett, J. W., *The World, the Flesh and Messrs. Pulitzer*, 1931; Swanberg, W. A., *Pulitzer*, 1967.

# Rahv, Philip

(March 10, 1908–December 23, 1973)
Editor, Literary Critic

As coeditor of the literary magazine *Partisan Review* for thirty-five years, Philip Rahv championed radical politics and literary and artistic modernism.

Born Ivan Greenberg in Kupin, Ukraine, Russia, Rahv immigrated to the United States in 1922 when he was fourteen. After high school in Providence, Rhode Island, he moved to New York City during the Great Depression and began his literary career with the Federal Writers' Project and by contributing pieces to such leftist publications as the *New Republic, New Leader,* and *New Masses.* In 1933 he joined the John Reed Club (see JOHN REED), affiliated with the Community party, and changed his name. Along with WILLIAM PHILLIPS, Rahv launched *Partisan Review* as the club's literary journal in 1934. In 1936, however, Rahv and Phillips broke with the party over the brutality of Stalin as revealed by the Moscow purge trials and suspended publication of the journal.

The journal resumed publication in 1937 with a new editorial staff and policy. Its first new issue published many who would become major figures of the postwar literary world, including James Agee, Edmund Wilson, Mary McCarthy, Lionel Trilling, and Rahv. By publishing American and European modernist authors, *Partisan Review* influenced American culture in the 1940s and 1950s.

During this period, Rahv, though a coeditor with Phillips, was the dominant figure at *Partisan Review.* A gifted editor, he fostered and promoted the talents of other writers; and as a brilliant literary critic, he became known for his studies of American literature and for his critical work on Franz Kafka and Fyodor Dostoyevsky. Collections of his essays include *Image and Idea* (1949), *The Myth and the Powerhouse* (1965), *Literature and the Sixth Sense* (1969), and *Essays on Literature and Politics* (1974). He also anthologized the novels of Henry James and Leo Tolstoy and, with William Phillips, edited collections of writing from the *Partisan Review.*

Despite his disassociation from the Communist party, Rahv continued to be active politically. During World War II he urged support of the war against Hitler, and in the postwar period he denounced Senator Joseph McCarthy's anticommunist witch-hunt, while many associates straddled the fence or actually supported the senator. In 1958 Rahv, Saul Bellow,

Alfred Kazin, and other writers published an open letter to the *New York Times*, protesting that Jewish culture was being destroyed in the Soviet Union and urging that Jews be allowed to emigrate.

In 1957 Rahv became professor of English at Brandeis University, a post he held until his death. Earlier he had been a senior fellow of the School of Letters of Indiana University. Objecting to the changes of the sixties as much as he had to the conservatism of the forties and fifties, Rahv defended modernism and denounced literary fads. By 1965 Rahv had returned to the radicalism of his youth, and he attacked many of his associates, including Phillips, for not being radical enough. Five years later, he left his position as coeditor of the *Partisan Review* and started a journal of his own, *Modern Occasions*. In 1972 Rahv was elected to the prestigious Academy of Arts and Sciences. A year later, he died at the age of sixty-seven.

### BIBLIOGRAPHY

Barrett, William, *The Truants*, 1982; Gilbert, James Burkhart, *Writers and Partisans: A History of Literary Radicalism in America*, 1968; Phillips, William, *A Partisan View: Five Decades of the Literary Life*, 1983.

# Randolph, Asa Philip

(April 15, 1889–May 16, 1979)
Civil Rights Activist, Labor Leader

In a long life committed to racial justice, A. Philip Randolph won respect for his quiet dignity and his firmness. A union organizer and socialist early in life, he became the country's best-known black trade unionist and a nationally prominent leader in the struggle for civil rights.

Born in the small town of Crescent City, in central Florida, A. Philip Randolph was the second son of a self-educated minister of the African Methodist Episcopal Church, James William Randolph. His mother, Elizabeth Robinson, a strongly religious woman, had married at thirteen. Both parents were the children of slaves. Two years after Asa Randolph's birth, the family moved to Jacksonville. He attended Methodist-supported schools, including the Cookman Institute from which he graduated in 1907. He worked at odd jobs, acted in amateur dramatics, and gave public readings in the precise diction his father had taught him. The family atmosphere was relatively intellectual.

Young Randolph became acquainted not only with Shakespeare and Dickens, but with the writings of FREDERICK DOUGLASS, BOOKER T. WASHINGTON, and W. E. B. DU BOIS.

In 1911 Randolph headed for New York City, washing dishes on a passenger ship to pay his way. He worked at various menial jobs while attending night classes at the City College of New York, where he began reading Marx and became interested in union organizing. In 1914 he married Lucille Campbell Green, a graduate of Howard University, who owned a beauty parlor and shared Randolph's political views. Randolph and his friend Chandler Owen joined the Socialist party in 1916 and the next year, with Lucille Randolph's backing, founded a Socialist journal, *The Messenger,* which supported the Industrial Workers of the World (see WILLIAM D. HAYWOOD) and opposed the United States' entering World War I. Randolph became celebrated for his eloquent speechmaking at street-corner rallies, in which he urged blacks not to fight in the war. He was arrested by federal agents on charges of treason, which were dropped.

In the 1920s, Pullman porters—all black Americans, employed on the railway sleeping cars—had to work 400 hours a month for a salary of $67.50 and had no assured rest periods between runs. In 1925, impressed by Randolph's speaking and activism, a group of porters asked him to organize an independent labor union. The Pullman Company had forced them to join a company-controlled union. As he was not a Pullman employee he could not be fired or harassed by the company. With help from a liberal foundation, the Garland Fund, Randolph organized the Brotherhood of Sleeping Car Porters, which attracted more than 50 percent of the porters as members. In 1928 the Brotherhood joined the American Federation of Labor (AFL; see WILLIAM GREEN and JOHN L. LEWIS). Yet the union had been unable to win recognition from the Pullman Company or the Federal Railway Mediation Board. With the aid of William Green, president of the AFL, Randolph got the Railroad Transportation Act amended to cover the Pullman porters. On August 15, 1937 (the union's twelfth anniversary), the Brotherhood and the Pullman Company signed the first contract between an American corporation and a black union. The contract cut the work month by almost half and provided for a significant increase in wages.

Randolph was now an important figure in the emerging civil rights movement. He was named the first president of the National Negro Congress (NNC), which he led until 1940 when he resigned because of supposed communist influence in the organization. In the same year Randolph—with executive secretary of the National Association for the Advancement of Colored People (NAACP; see JOEL E. SPINGARN), WALTER F. WHITE, and other leaders—met with President Franklin D. Roosevelt to press for integration of the armed forces and the employment of black workers in the defense plants. The president promised that blacks would be eligible for combat duty; segregation,

however, would continue. To force an executive order to end discriminatory hiring practices in defense plants, Randolph called for a show of strength: a massive march on Washington in July 1941. The president vainly attempted to dissuade Randolph and the other black leaders. On July 1, six days before the march was to occur, Roosevelt signed an executive order barring discrimination in defense plants and in government service and creating a temporary Fair Employment Practices Committee. Though integration of the armed forces was not achieved, Randolph called off the march. Some activists accused Randolph of backing down on integration, but thousands of jobs in defense industries were opened up for blacks.

After the war ended, Randolph led in organizing the League for Nonviolent Civil Disobedience Against Military Segregation and again called for a march on Washington. Furthermore, he advised young African Americans to resist the draft. President Harry S Truman, who was also concerned about losing the black vote in the next election, issued an executive order in July 1948 banning racial discrimination in the armed forces. Again Randolph called off his campaign, having won his major battle.

Though Randolph's influence waned in the 1950s as younger black leaders came to the fore, he continued his fight against racial discrimination in the labor unions and, in 1957, was elected a vice president of the AFL-CIO. His last confrontation with an American president occurred in 1963, when John F. Kennedy attempted to dissuade black leaders from staging a demonstration for civil rights legislation. Randolph was honorary director of the March on Washington for Jobs and Freedom, on August 28, 1963, when 200,000 people congregated at the Lincoln Memorial, to be addressed by Randolph, MARTIN LUTHER KING, JR., and other leaders.

The Civil Rights Act of 1964 was passed with the active encouragement of President Lyndon B. Johnson, who that year awarded Randolph the highest civilian honor, the Medal of Freedom. Also in 1964 Randolph established the A. Philip Randolph Institute, under the direction of BAYARD RUSTIN, which pledged among other goals to foster cooperation between organized labor and the black community.

In his last years, Randolph counseled young African Americans to follow his principles of nonviolence and pacifism, not always with suc-cess. He died in his apartment in the Chelsea district of New York at the age of ninety.

**BIBLIOGRAPHY**

Anderson, Jervis, *A. Philip Randolph: A Biographical Portrait*, 1972; Harris, W., *Keeping the Faith: A. Philip Randolph*, 1977.

# Rauschenbusch, Walter

(October 4, 1861–July 25, 1918)
Reformer, Religious Leader

A leader of the Social Gospel movement, Walter Rauschenbusch helped link religion with ideas of social reform as part of the general movement known as Progressivism at the end of the nineteenth century.

Rauschenbusch was born in Rochester, New York, to German immigrants who came to the United States, like so many others, following the failed revolution of 1848 in Germany. Originally a Lutheran, his father became a Baptist in America and taught at the Rochester Theological Seminary.

Rauschenbusch studied in Germany at the Gymnasium of Gütersloh, Westphalia, and graduated at the head of his class in 1883. He earned an A.B. from the University of Rochester in 1884 and a doctorate in divinity in 1886 from the Rochester Theological Seminary. Ordained a Baptist minister, he became pastor of the Second German Baptist Church in New York City, then located in Hell's Kitchen, a poor section of the city inhabited by immigrants.

Rauschenbusch remained in his post for a decade. He became deeply involved in the lives of the immigrants around him and was awakened to ideas of social reform through his reading of Karl Marx, EDWARD BELLAMY, John Ruskin, Leo Tolstoy, and HENRY GEORGE. To George he remained philosophically indebted for the rest of his life. He determined during these years to help improve the living conditions of the poor as part of his religious commitment.

In 1888 Rauschenbusch became ill with influenza and, as a result of exposure in the great blizzard of that year, his condition worsened and he became deaf. (His handicap was somewhat lessened when, in 1893, he married Pauline Rother, another German immigrant, who had been a schoolteacher in Milwaukee. She became involved in her husband's work and helped him through the difficulties of daily life. Their household eventually included five children.)

During 1889 Rauschenbusch published a periodical of Christian socialism, *For the Right*, and in 1891 and 1892 he studied economics and theology in Berlin and the conditions of working people in England. While in England he met Sidney and Beatrice Webb, whose socialist Fabian Society influenced him, as did the work of the Salvation Army. After returning to the United States in 1892, Rauschenbusch championed the cause of the striking steelworkers in Homestead, Pennsylvania, who were defeated by a combination of corporate power and government; however, their struggle aroused much popular sympathy for labor reforms.

In 1897 Rauschenbusch became a professor at the Rochester Theological Seminary, a position he held until his death, and in 1907 he studied once again in Germany, at the universities of Kiel and Marburg.

Rauschenbusch's first book, *Christianity and the Social Crisis,* was published in 1907 and brought him immediate acclaim. In it he criticized capitalism as corrupting and immoral and decried the neglect of the social ideals of Christianity. He became a popular speaker at universities and other institutions and was soon known as the leader of the Social Gospel movement, which aimed to work for social reform based on a broader view of Christian ethics. His commitment to the poor and his firsthand knowledge of their exploitation and the appalling conditions in which many lived was as prominent in his writings as was his expertise in theology, church history, and social thought. He went on to write six more books, including, finally, *A Theology for the Social Gospel* (1917), in which he advocated both economic and moral revolution. He turned Christianity into a social movement based directly on the pressing needs of the poor in the new urban and industrial societies.

Gifted with a warm, dynamic personality, Rauschenbusch always sought justice and a higher moral consciousness for all. After the outbreak of World War I, he became disillusioned by American militarism and nationalism, which as he witnessed, led to many social ills, including discrimination against people with German surnames. Deploring the hate that had been aroused by the war, Rauschenbusch spoke out against American intervention. He died at the age of fifty-six from cancer, full of despair, before the end of the war.

**BIBLIOGRAPHY**

Rauschenbusch, Walter, *Prayers of the Social Awakening,* 1910, *Christianizing the Social Order,* 1912, *"Unto Me,"* 1912, *Dare We Be Christians,* 1914, and *The Social Principles of Jesus,* 1916; Sharpe, D. R., *Walter Rauschenbusch,* 1942.

# Reed, John Silas

(October 20, 1887–October 17, 1920)
Communist, Journalist

John Reed's spirited accounts of labor strife and of revolution and war in Mexico and Europe brought the reality of those events to the American people. He was a founder of the communist movement in the United States before the end of his brief life.

John Reed was born in Portland, Oregon. His father was a successful businessman from the East; his mother came from a wealthy pioneer family. At Harvard in the class of 1910 he was involved with the literary set, dramatics, sports, and student pranks. When Reed met the Californian muckraker LINCOLN STEFFENS, a family friend, the older man encouraged a first interest in social problems. After graduation and several months of wandering in England and France, he returned home to find his father's business in straits and himself on his own.

Having fixed his sights on being a writer, Reed headed for New York and, with Steffens's help, got a post on a popular magazine, the *American.* He soon became a well-known figure in the radical scene of Greenwich Village. He moved leftward in his political views, and in 1913 he readily accepted an invitation from MAX EASTMAN to work on the left-wing *Masses.* Reed covered the strike of 25,000 silk workers in Paterson, New Jersey, and experienced his first of many arrests, for an altercation with a policeman. The next year he went to Mexico for the *Metropolitan* magazine to cover the campaigns of the rebel leader Pancho Villa. His articles, which brought him a national reputation, were published as *Insurgent Mexico* (1914).

In spring 1914 Reed went to Colorado to report the massacre of striking coal miners at Ludlow, and he wrote articles that indicted the Rockefeller interests that owned the company. With the outbreak of World War I, the *Metropolitan* sent him to cover action in eastern Europe, and his reports were published as *The War in Eastern Europe* (1916). When the United States entered the war, Reed told the Congressional Committee on Military Affairs, "I do not believe in this war [and] I would not serve in it." (He would not have qualified for the draft, in any case, because he had lost a kidney to disease.)

Reed and Louise Bryant, whom he had married in November 1916, were determined to observe events in Russia and arrived in time to witness the October 1917 revolution. Reed became a close friend of V. I. Lenin and helped to write Bolshevik propaganda leaflets predicting an enduring proletarian government. His dispatches to the *Masses* had much to do with the American government's suspension of the magazine for sedition, and upon returning to New York Reed himself was arrested for seditious actions and his papers were seized, though the indictment was dropped. During

(John Reed Papers) By permission of the Manuscript Department, The Houghton Library, Harvard University

1918 he published his famous eyewitness account of the Russian revolution, *Ten Days That Shook the World,* for which Lenin wrote an introduction. Reed threw himself into the formation of the American Communist party and, though again indicted for sedition, left the country on a forged passport and worked passage to Russia, where he sought Bolshevik help for the American party. Seeking to return home for trial, he was arrested and detained in a Finnish prison. After he was released to Russia he became active in the Soviet government. At a congress of the Communist International, he urged American communists to work for unity of "the Negro and the white laborer in common labor unions . . . to destroy race prejudice and develop class solidarity."

Reed, in weakened health, fell ill of typhus and, with Louise Bryant beside him, died in Moscow on October 17, 1920. The Soviet government buried him in the wall of the Kremlin.

**BIBLIOGRAPHY**

Cheuse, Alan, *The Bohemians: John Reed and His Friends Who Shook the World,* 1982; Hicks, Granville, *John Reed: The Making of a Revolutionary,* 1936; Rosenstone, R. A., *Romantic Revolutionary: A Biography of John Reed,* 1975.

# Reuther, Walter Philip

(September 1, 1907–May 9, 1970)
Labor Leader, Reformer

Walter Reuther was a union organizer and social progressive who rose to head one of the country's largest unions, the United Automobile Workers of America (UAW). He was a gifted negotiator, at the forefront of labor during a time of momentous changes for industrial workers.

Reuther, born in Wheeling, West Virginia, was the son of a brewery worker, Valentine Reuther, and Anna Stocker, who both had come from Germany in childhood. The family was rooted in trade unionism and social idealism: the father brought up Walter and his three brothers to be dedicated union members and socialists of the EUGENE V. DEBS variety. Walter Reuther learned tool- and diemaking in high school and at sixteen went to work at the Wheeling Steel Company as an apprentice diemaker. Fired in 1926 because he led a protest about working conditions, he headed for Detroit and soon became a supervising diemaker for the Ford Motor Company (see HENRY FORD), which was retooling to make the Model A car. Reuther worked the night shift and went to high school during the day, got his diploma, and entered Detroit City College in 1930.

At college (later Wayne State University) Reuther was involved in campus politics and in the 1932 presidential campaign, when he supported Norman Thomas, on the Socialist ticket. After the Ford company fired him because of union activity, Walter Reuther and his brother Victor made a trip they had long planned—to go to the Soviet Union and work at an automobile plant in Gorki, east of Moscow. On the way they observed the effects of the Great Depression in England and western Europe. They were in Germany in 1933 when the Nazis came to power and, having made union contacts, acted briefly as couriers in the resistance. In November the Reuthers arrived at Gorki, where Walter taught Russian workers how to use equipment that had been acquired from the Ford company. The Reuthers had a sympathetic interest in Soviet planning but were troubled by the government's repressive ways. After two years they came home via the Trans-Siberian railway and Japan.

In 1935 Walter Reuther went to work at a General Motors plant and became involved in organizing for the UAW, which then belonged to the American Federation of Labor (AFL; see WILLIAM GREEN and JOHN L. LEWIS). In 1936 he married May Wolf, an activist in a teachers' union. Later that year he and two of his brothers played a leading part in a sit-down strike at a plant in Flint, Michigan, which led to the recognition of the union by General Motors. Walter Reuther was by then president of a local that represented some 30,000 workers. The following May, when Reuther and other UAW men were attempting to organize workers at the Ford company's River Rouge plant, company goons beat them savagely in the presence of a *Time* magazine photographer. Reuther became nationally known.

In 1939 Reuther was appointed director of the UAW's General Motors department. There had been ideological conflict in the UAW, in which the procommunist faction turned against Reuther, and he in turn adopted a strong anticommunist stance. By 1942, after the country had entered World War II, he was vice president of UAW, which by then had joined the Congress of Industrial Organizations (CIO; see JOHN L. LEWIS). He devised a plan, using his technical training, for converting automobile plants to aircraft manufacture. Such proposals made his reputation as one of the most effective younger union leaders. He used his prestige to keep the autoworkers faithful to the no-strike pledge for the war's duration.

Reuther was elected to the UAW presidency in 1946, after leading a lengthy strike against General Motors that got the workers sizable increases in pay. Politically, he had moved toward a liberal position, having resigned from the Socialist party. Recognizing the Democratic party as the best vehicle for labor politics, he helped found the Americans for Democratic Action (see REINHOLD NIEBUHR) in 1947 and supported Harry S Truman for the presidency in 1948. That year, he almost lost his life when an unknown assailant attacked him with a shotgun, crippling his right arm.

Having been elected president of the CIO in 1952 after the death of PHILIP MURRAY, Reuther succeeded three years later in engineering the merger of the AFL and the CIO and became vice president of the new entity (AFL-CIO) and director of its industrial union department. By that time he was a powerful force in the Democratic party and worked for John F. Kennedy's election in 1960 and later for President Lyndon B. Johnson's "Great Society" programs. He often disagreed with the conservative and craft-union policies of AFL-CIO president GEORGE MEANY, who merely expressed sympathy with the civil rights struggle while Reuther took part in demonstrations. In 1968 Reuther took the UAW out of the AFL-CIO and briefly joined the Teamsters' Brotherhood (see JAMES R. HOFFA) in the Alliance for Labor Action.

Reuther employed his bargaining skills to extract from the companies wide-ranging benefits for union members, including pensions, medical insurance, unemployment benefits, cost of living allowances, and profit sharing, in return for labor peace and good order in the shops. Within the union structure he fostered programs for the good of the membership—such as an education and recreation center for members' families on Black Lake, in northern Michigan. In spring 1970 he boarded his chartered jet plane to fly up and inspect the construction, accompanied by his wife and several union officials. The plane crashed and all were killed.

**BIBLIOGRAPHY**

Barnard, John, *Walter Reuther and the Rise of the Auto Workers,* 1983; Dubofsky, Melvyn, and Warren Van Tine (eds.), *Labor Leaders in America,* 1987; Howe, Irving, and B. J. Widick, *The UAW and Walter Reuther,* 1949; Reuther, Victor G., *The Brothers Reuther and the Story of the UAW,* 1976.

# Riis, Jacob August

(May 3, 1849–May 26, 1914)
Author, Photojournalist, Reformer

Jacob Riis's startling exposés, both in print and in photographs, of conditions in New York City's slums influenced a generation of investigative reporters, known as muckrakers, and set the standard for future photojournalists.

Born the son of a teacher in Ribe, Denmark, Riis was educated by his father and a private tutor, later becoming a carpenter's apprentice. Unable to find work, he immigrated to America in 1870 with $40 in his pocket. Riis spent the next seven years barely eking out a living from a variety of odd jobs, which prompted his later sympathy for the poor.

In 1877 Riis got a job as a police reporter for the New York *Tribune* at a salary of $25 a week. His beat was the Mulberry Bend, a notorious slum on New York's teeming Lower East Side. In these squalid surroundings, Riis found his lifework. As his colleague, LINCOLN STEFFENS, observed, Riis was a reporter who "not only got the news, but cared about it." He was more concerned with "the stories of people and the conditions in which they lived" than with the particular fire or murder that he was reporting.

Armed with a pencil, a notebook, and a camera, Riis documented the overcrowding, lack of proper sanitation, and grinding poverty of the slums. He took pictures with a flash so that "the darkest corner might be photographed," twice setting fire to a building and once to himself with the primitive apparatus. His haunting photographs of dingy tenements; ragged, half-starved children; and dim, garbage-strewn alleys were among the first to appear in newspapers.

In 1888 Riis left the *Tribune* to become a police reporter for the New York *Evening Sun.* In 1890 *How The Other Half Lives*, Riis's first and most famous book, was published. In it, Riis drew upon his experiences as a police reporter to tell "what the tenements are and how they grew to be what they are." Packed with harrowing details and illustrated with drawings based on Riis's photographs, *How The Other Half Lives* was a powerful indictment of slum conditions. As Riis described one tenement:

> The hall is dark and you might stumble over the children pitching pennies back there. . . . A flight of stairs. You can feel your way, if you cannot see it. Close? Yes! What would you have? All the fresh air that ever enters these stairs comes from the front door that is forever slamming, and from the windows of dark bedrooms that in turn receive from the stairs their sole supply of the elements God meant to be free, but man deals out with such a niggardly hand. . . . What sort of an answer, think you, would come from these tenements to the question "Is life worth living?"

Also during this period, Riis became involved in various reform efforts. He joined the local chapter of JOSEPHINE SHAW LOWELL's Charity Organization Society, helping to publicize its child care and work training programs. He penned editorials decrying government corruption. He worked to improve the lives of those living in tenements. He convinced members of a New Jersey women's club to volunteer to work in New York City's tenements, which later led to the founding of a settlement house on the Lower East Side that came to be called the Jacob A. Riis Settlement. He also campaigned for the destruction of the Mulberry Bend tenements.

In 1895, during the term of reform mayor William L. Strong, Riis formed an important friendship with Theodore Roosevelt. The two men toured the slums at night to learn about conditions there. Later, when Roosevelt became governor of New York in 1899, Riis advised him on urban policy. Their efforts included the creation of a state tenement house commission, whose report led to a 1901 law setting strict building codes for tenements. Riis continued to advise Roosevelt during the latter's presidency and promoted the cause of his friend, publicizing administration policies and publishing a highly favorable biography, *Theodore Roosevelt the Citizen* (1904).

Besides campaigning for tenement reform, Riis tried to help the poor in other ways. He was especially concerned with the plight of children and worked to secure parks, playgrounds, and more and better schools. He also fought for the passage of child labor laws. In addition, Riis exposed and had corrected the contamination of the city's water supply. To provide children with positive outlets, he helped establish boys' clubs and participated in forming the Boy Scouts of America.

A prolific writer, Riis wrote a number of other books, including *The Children of the Poor* (1892), *The Battle with the Slum* (1902), *Children of the Tenements* (1903), and his autobiography, *The Making of an American* (1901).

A month after suffering a heart attack, Riis died at his country home in Barre, Massachusetts, at the age of sixty-five.

**BIBLIOGRAPHY**

Cordasco, F. (ed.), *Jacob Riis Revisited*, 1968; Felt, J., *Hostages of Fortune: Child Labor Reform in New York State*, 1965; Lane, James B., *Jacob A. Riis and the American City*, 1974; Lubove, Roy, *The Progressives and the Slums: Tenement House Reform in New York City*, 1962.

# Robeson, Paul Leroy Bustill

(April 9, 1898–January 23, 1976)
Civil Rights Activist, Entertainer

Paul Robeson, son of a former slave, became an American icon as athlete, singer, and actor—a beloved figure until the McCarthy era, when he was attacked and ostracized for his outspoken criticism of racial injustice and his close ties with radicalism and the Soviet Union.

Robeson was born in Princeton, New Jersey, the youngest of eight children born to the Reverend William Drew Robeson, former pastor of the Witherspoon Street Presbyterian Church, and Anna Louisa Bustill. The Reverend Robeson had been born a slave on a North Carolina plantation in 1845, escaped at fifteen, and eventually studied for the ministry. He had been forced to resign from the Princeton church in 1901 because of some irregularity in the church's business records and had to work as a coachman. His wife, a teacher, who belonged to a free Philadelphia family of considerable distinction, died of burns in a household accident when Paul was six.

Robeson's father, with Paul and another son, Ben, after several difficult years moved to Somerville and took over a Methodist church. Paul went to the town's integrated high school, where his baritone voice began to be noticed. An athlete and top student, he won a four-year scholarship to Rutgers University (the state institution), the first of his family to attend a white college. At Rutgers he was the only black student. He was popular, an admired orator, Phi Beta Kappa in his junior year, and the leading athlete—he earned twelve varsity letters in four sports and was an All-American football end in 1917 and 1918. In 1919 he got his B.A. with honors and the next year entered Columbia University Law School.

In 1920 Robeson was persuaded by another student, Eslanda Cardozo Goode, to take the lead in a play, *Simon the Cyrenian*, at the Harlem YMCA (Young Men's Christian Association) and later at a downtown theater. (Simon was an African who helped carry Jesus's cross.) His performance was a hit; he and Eslanda Goode were married in 1921 and went to England, where he performed in another play at a provincial house and had the experience of traveling without worry of Jim Crow laws (laws in effect in the American South that banned blacks from using hotels, restaurants, train cars, and bathrooms reserved for whites). Robeson took his law degree at Columbia in 1923 and joined a New York law firm, where he encountered some bias. When the Provincetown Players approached him, he was glad to take leading parts in two plays by Eugene O'Neill at their playhouse in Greenwich Village: *The Emperor Jones* and *All God's Chillun Got Wings*. His performances were widely praised, and in 1925 he repeated the role of Brutus Jones, a black dictator, in London, where his debut was described as triumphal.

In the 1925 to 1926 season Robeson embarked on his first concert tour in America and abroad, singing spirituals and folk songs. His baritone voice became world famous in concerts and hundreds of recordings. He was able to perform songs in twenty languages. In 1934 he concertized in the Soviet Union on his first visit there. Robeson alternated recitals with roles on stage; one of the most famous was as Joe in the musical *Show Boat*, singing "Ol' Man River." His renditions of "Ballad for Americans" and "Joe Hill" were equally famous. Robeson won the greatest honors for his performance in Shakespeare's *Othello*, which he first played in London in 1930, then on the stage in New York during the winter of 1943 and 1944, and then on tour. He played in a number of films and was said to be the first African American actor not to play cinema parts that were racist stereotypes. Robeson said that he did not succeed to his satisfaction in that respect because of the movie industry's attitude toward blacks, and he gave up working in films.

During the 1930s the Robesons lived mainly in London, where he met many refugees from the fascist countries (willingly giving benefit performances for them) and got to know British radicals. He also met young pro-independence activists from the British colonies in Africa—Jomo Kenyatta, from Kenya, and Kwame Nkrumah, from the Gold Coast, now Ghana. On his 1934 visit to the Soviet Union, Robeson had been deeply impressed by the social experimentation that was proceeding; he learned Russian and often went back. He sent his son, Paul Jr., to school in Moscow in order to escape racial discrimination in the United States. Robeson gave several concerts to raise money for Spanish Republicans (those fighting against the dictator Franco to bring democratic rule to Spain), and in January 1938 he and his wife visited embattled Barcelona and Madrid, where he sang for the soldiers, including men in the Abraham Lincoln Brigade from the United States.

Robeson became more and more, as he said, a spokesman "against anti-Semitism and against injustices to all minority groups." In the late 1940s, as the cold war gathered force, he became identified with radicalism and was called a communist or a communist sympathizer, though in fact he was never a Communist party member. A large segment of the public as well as the government turned against him, but he only stated his opinion of the Soviet Union more forcefully. When in 1949 he was to sing at a left-wing music festival in Peekskill, New York, right-wing extremists stopped it by storming the gathering and injuring many people, while the police looked on. (The concert took place a week later, though with renewed violence.) The next year the State Department revoked Robeson's passport and refused to return it unless he signed an oath that he was not a communist. In 1952 the Soviet government's award to him of the Stalin Peace Prize appeared only to confirm what his adversaries claimed. A legal battle over the passport issue went on for eight years, until the Supreme Court found the government's action in such cases unconstitutional.

In 1958 Robeson gave a farewell concert at Carnegie Hall, made a brief concert tour, recorded one more album, and left the country. While he and his wife moved about in the Soviet Union, eastern Europe, and London, his health went into decline and he was often in hospitals. In 1963, after the Robesons returned to the United States, he announced his retirement from the stage and refused press interviews concerning a rumor that he had turned against Marxism. Eslanda Robeson died in 1965, and her husband moved to Philadelphia to live with a sister.

On April 15, 1973, shortly after Robeson's seventy-fifth birthday, entertainment stars and civil rights leaders organized a birthday salute at Carnegie Hall. Those on the platform included former U.S. attorney general Ramsey Clark; PETE SEEGER, singing Spanish Civil War songs; and CORETTA SCOTT KING, who said that before MARTIN LUTHER KING, JR., Robeson had "tapped the same wells of latent militancy" among African Americans. The tide of feeling against Robeson was turning. Rutgers University held a symposium on his life, and in 1975 the FBI declared that "no further investigation is warranted." When Robeson died in a Philadelphia hospital after a stroke, the white press praised him as "a great American," but Coretta King deplored "America's inexcusable treatment" of a man who had had "the courage to point out her injustices."

**BIBLIOGRAPHY**

Duberman, Martin Bauml, *Paul Robeson,* 1988; Robeson, Paul, *Here I Stand,* 1958.

# Rockefeller, John Davison

(July 8, 1839–May 23, 1937)
Industrialist, Philanthropist

As the moving force behind the Standard Oil Company, which became a great bogeyman to reformers, John D. Rockefeller helped create the American petroleum industry. He also pioneered in large-scale, systematic philanthropy, giving away millions of dollars for the advancement of education, medicine, and science.

Born in Richford, Tioga County, New York, Rockefeller grew up under the influence of his strict Baptist mother and his shrewd small businessman father. In 1853 the family moved to Cleveland, Ohio, where Rockefeller completed high school, and after three months at a commercial school, he entered business as a clerk with a commission firm. In 1858 Rockefeller started his own commission firm with Maurice B. Clark. A year later, the first successful drilling for oil took place at Titusville in western Pennsylvania. Realizing that Cleveland was well situated to dominate the oil-refining business, Rockefeller formed another partnership with Clark, two of Clark's brothers, and Samuel Andrews, an inventor of a cheaper process for refining oil. In 1863 he and his partners built and ran a refinery in Cleveland.

Two years later, Rockefeller bought out the Clarks' interest in the refinery and with Andrews expanded his operations until his refinery was the largest in the Cleveland area. He also brought his brother William into the business and sent him to New York to establish banking and shipping connections. With the addition in 1867 of Henry Flagler, a brilliant young local businessman, the firm became

Courtesy of the New-York Historical Society, New York City

known as Rockefeller, Andrews, & Flagler. Despite chaotic conditions in the oil industry, which was subject to sharp price fluctuations and unrestrained competition, Rockefeller and his associates prospered. In 1870 the partners organized the million-dollar Standard Oil Company of Ohio.

Throughout the 1870s the Standard Oil Company continued to grow and expand. It did so by keeping production costs down, obtaining favorable rates from the railroads in the form of then-legal rebates, engaging in occasional price slashing, and buying out competitors. By the mid-1870s, the company had either absorbed or forced out of business the majority of its rivals. Under Rockefeller's skilled leadership, the company also pioneered in vertical integration within the oil industry, acquiring or building its own pipelines, controlling local distributors, and using its own tank cars. Thus, by 1880 Standard Oil had managed to secure a virtual monopoly over oil refining and transportation.

From the 1870s onward, Rockefeller and Standard Oil came increasingly under attack by reformers, who were concerned with the company's vast size and influence, as well as such specific practices as price cutting and manipulating the railroads to get rebates. In 1879 the Hepburn Committee of the New York State legislature investigated railroad rebates, focusing public attention on Standard Oil's use of this practice. Public indignation was further aroused by HENRY DEMAREST LLOYD's muckraking article, "The Story of a Great Monopoly," which appeared in the *Atlantic Monthly* in 1881.

Newspaper editorials and articles attacking Standard Oil were also published in the New York *World.*

Since Standard Oil was by this time a nationwide company, it became necessary to devise a new form of organization. In 1882 the company's legal counsel came up with the idea of centralizing separate Standard Oil units in various states in a board of trustees with a central office in New York. Thus was born the first and largest of the so-called trusts. During the 1880s criticism of the trusts mounted, culminating with the passage of the Sherman Anti-Trust Act of 1890. Two years later, the Ohio Supreme Court declared the Standard Oil Trust illegal, prompting the formation of separate Standard Oil companies of Ohio, New York, Indiana, and New Jersey, and later a holding company, Standard Oil Company of New Jersey, which functioned until dissolved by the U.S. Supreme Court in 1911. Meanwhile, the attacks on Standard Oil continued, reaching a climax with Henry Demarest Lloyd's *Wealth Against Commonwealth* (1894) and IDA M. TARBELL's *History of the Standard Oil Company* (1904).

Though often bitterly assailed in books and magazine articles, Rockefeller never operated outside the law. Nor did he seek a complete monopoly over the oil industry. Rather, through consolidation he tried to prevent a return to the chaos of the early years. Moreover, by the 1890s Rockefeller had virtually retired from the oil business with a fortune estimated at $1 billion, a large part of which he devoted to philanthropy. Like ANDREW CARNEGIE, Rockefeller felt it was his moral duty to use his money for the benefit of humanity. As a lifelong Baptist, he had early in his career begun the practice of giving 10 percent of his income to the church, and in his benefactions he was often guided by Baptist ministers.

In 1889 Rockefeller made his first major gift of $600,000 to establish the University of Chicago (his family later gave more than $80 million to this institution). In the last decades of his life, he gave away an estimated $550 million to a variety of worthwhile causes. In addition to individual gifts, Rockefeller created four new philanthropic organizations: the Rockefeller Institute for Medical Research (1901), the General Education Board (1902), the Rockefeller Foundation (1913), and the Laura Spelman Rockefeller Foundation (1918). As a result of his benefactions, the hookworm was eliminated and agriculture improved in the South, numerous institutions of higher learning were strengthened, and medical research and standards were greatly improved. Rockefeller also saw to the preservation of such areas of natural beauty as Acadia National Park in Maine, Jackson's Hole in Wyoming, and the Palisades Interstate Park in New York and New Jersey. A frugal man with simple tastes, Rockefeller died at his home in Ormond, Florida, a few weeks short of his ninety-eighth birthday.

**BIBLIOGRAPHY**

Collier, Peter, and David Horowitz, *The Rockefellers: An American Dynasty,* 1977; Hawke, David F., *John D.: The Founding Father of the Rockefellers,* 1980; Nevins, Allan, *John D. Rockefeller: The Heroic Age of American Enterprise,* 2 vols., 1940, and *Study in Power: John D. Rockefeller, Industrialist and Philanthropist,* 2 vols., 1953.

# Rosenwald, Julius

(August 12, 1862–January 6, 1932)
Merchant, Philanthropist

Though Julius Rosenwald applied his mercantile and administrative gifts to building up Sears, Roebuck & Company into a preeminent mail-order firm, his greatest contribution to American life was as a philanthropist of broad, unprejudiced interests.

Born in Springfield, Illinois, almost across the street from the house where Abraham Lincoln had lived before he became president, Julius Rosenwald grew up under the influence of the Lincoln tradition. He was the son of Samuel Rosenwald and Augusta Hammerslough. After a foreshortened public school education he went to New York at the age of seventeen and worked for a wholesale clothing firm, Hammerslough Brothers, apparently a connection of his mother. When he was twenty-three Rosenwald became the president of another clothing firm, Rosenwald & Weil, in Chicago, and held that position until 1906. In 1895, however, he assumed a second office with the mail-order house of Sears, Roebuck & Company, as its vice president and treasurer, and this association became his lifetime career. From 1910 until 1925 he was president and then, until his death, chairman of the board of directors. Under Rosenwald's leadership, with the advice of shrewdly chosen experts, Sears, Roebuck became a great establishment, the country's leading mail-order company.

It was as a humanitarian and philanthropist that Rosenwald is best remembered. He once said that his social principles were inspired by his religious experience as a member of the Jewish Chicago Sinai Congregation. As early as 1910 he was making generous gifts to educational and social service institutions in the South, especially those serving African Americans. In 1917 he created the Julius Rosenwald Fund to further the "well-being of mankind." The fund contributed means to stave off starvation in postwar Germany and helped establish colleges in Turkey. Its outstanding benefactions carried forward Rosenwald's interest in the South and in helping African Americans. He did not believe in endowments and stipulated that his fund should end within twenty-five years after his death, which occurred in 1932. When the fund was actually liquidated, in 1948, it had donated $63,000,000 to improve rural education, racial relations, and health education among African Americans. It had partially subsidized a number of Young Men's and Young Women's Christian Association buildings for blacks in big cities. The fund had also made grants to individuals, such as Clementine Hunter, of Louisiana. Hunter began painting at the age of sixty and with the fund's support became a famous primitive artist; her work depicted southern life.

Julius Rosenwald's benefactions were not sectarian. In his own city he was a socially minded civic leader—a founder of the Municipal Voters League and an active member of the Public Efficiency Bureau and the Chicago Planning Commission. In 1916 President Woodrow Wilson appointed Rosenwald to the Council of National Defense; in 1918 he went on a special mission to France at the request of the secretary of war, Newton D. Baker; in 1919 he took part in the Second National Industrial Conference. He was instrumental in forming the Federation of Jewish Charities in Chicago in 1923. He gave the city of Chicago a museum of science and industry.

To the University of Chicago, Rosenwald donated nearly $5 million and served for twenty years on its board of trustees. He was a supporter of the Hebrew Union College, in Cincinnati; the Jewish Theological Seminary of America, in New York City; and (though he was not a Zionist) the Hebrew University of Jerusalem.

A little more than a year before his death, Rosenwald wrote in the *Atlantic Monthly*, "I believe that large gifts should not be restricted to narrowly specified objects, and that under no circumstances should funds be held in perpetuity.... I have confidence in future generations and in their ability to meet their own needs wisely and generously."

**BIBLIOGRAPHY**

Werner, M. R., *Julius Rosenwald*, 1939.

# Ruffin, Edmund

(January 5, 1794–June 18, 1865)
Agriculturist, Author

Hailed as the father of soil chemistry in America, nineteenth-century agricultural reformer Edmund Ruffin had an important impact on the South, helping to turn around the economic decline into which Atlantic tidewater plantations had fallen. Ruffin was also an early and major advocate of secession prior to the Civil War.

Born in Prince George County, Virginia, Edmund Ruffin was educated at home, except for a brief period at the College of William and Mary in Williamsburg, Virginia. During the War of 1812 he served as a private, returning after his father's death to take charge of the family lands at Coggin's Point on the James River. Here Ruffin, with little practical or theoretical knowledge, began his experiments in scientific agriculture. His aim was to restore the fertility of soil worn-out by years of using poor methods for single-crop farming. He discovered that the soil could be greatly improved by treating it with calcareous earth and marl (substances that are rich in lime) and then rotating crops and employing proper drainage and good methods of planting. In this way, Ruffin was able to increase wheat and corn yields by 40 percent.

In 1818 Ruffin presented his findings before the Prince George County Agricultural Society, expanding and publishing them three years later in the *American Farmer*. In 1832 he published the results of his experiments in a volume entitled *An Essay on Calcareous Manures* that was revised and went through many editions. He further advanced the cause of agricultural reform by publishing an influential journal, the *Farmer's Register*, for the next decade. Ruffin was appointed a member of the first Virginia State Board of Agriculture in 1841, and a year later he became agricultural surveyor of South Carolina. His *Report of the Commencement and Progress of the Agricultural Survey of South Carolina* (1843) marked the beginning of a new era in agriculture in that state. Active in the organization of agricultural societies, Ruffin in 1845 was elected president of the newly formed Virginia Agricultural Society. During this period, he wrote and spoke frequently on scientific agriculture for newspapers, farm journals, and agriculture societies.

Interested in politics as well as agriculture, Ruffin served in the state senate from 1823 to 1826 and during the next thirty years earned a reputation as a champion of slavery and states' rights, becoming Virginia's leading advocate of secession. He set forth his proslavery views in numerous pamphlets, including *The Political Economy of Slavery* (1857). In 1860 he published *Anticipations of the Future*, a book which made the case for secession by depicting the advantages of an independent South. As an honorary member of the South Carolina Palmetto Guard, Ruffin won Southern acclaim by firing the first shot at Fort Sumter in April 1861. Four years later, financially ruined and in despair over the collapse of the Confederacy, he took his own life.

---

**BIBLIOGRAPHY**

Craven, Avery O., *Edmund Ruffin, Southerner*, 1932.

# Rush, Benjamin

(January 4, 1745–April 19, 1813)
Physician, Reformer

One of the foremost physicians of the revolutionary era, Benjamin Rush made valuable contributions to medicine and pioneered in the treatment of the mentally ill. He also supported a wide range of reforms, including temperance, abolition, public education, and prison reform.

Born in Byberry, Pennsylvania, Rush earned his A.B. at the College of New Jersey (now Princeton University) in 1760, served as an apprentice to a prominent Philadelphia physician for six years, and then obtained his M.D. from the University of Edinburgh (Scotland) in 1768. Upon his return to Philadelphia a year later, he practiced medicine and served as professor of chemistry at the College of Philadelphia, the first such teaching position in America. In 1770 Rush wrote the first American chemistry text. Two years later, Rush published *Sermons to Gentlemen upon Temperance and Exercise,* the first American work on personal hygiene.

With the outbreak of the revolutionary war, Rush became a member of the Second Continental Congress, arriving in Philadelphia in time to sign the Declaration of Independence. In 1777 he was appointed surgeon general of the armies of the Middle Department, but he resigned when General Washington failed to follow his advice about improving the medical care of the soldiers.

After the war, Rush continued with his medical practice and with teaching, while devoting considerable time and energy to reform work. In 1784 he published a temperance tract that was the first to warn of the physiological consequences of alcohol consumption, while at the same time attacking it on moral grounds. Often quoted by temperance advocates, the tract led to Rush's later reputation as founder of the movement. Rush also opposed the use of tobacco because of its unhealthy effects.

Convinced that a sound educational system was crucial to the success of the new nation, Rush in 1786 penned the first American essay calling for government-supported schools on all levels, including a federal or national university. The latter dream was never realized, but in 1783, Rush was instrumental in the founding of Dickinson College, the first college in Pennsylvania outside of Philadelphia. Unlike most of his contemporaries, Rush was also a believer in education for women. Although he felt they should be educated differently from men, he included such subjects as geography, chemistry, and history in his proposed curriculum, along with instruction in domestic matters.

Already in 1773, Rush had written an antislavery tract in which he not only attacked slavery but also asserted that African Americans were in every way equal to white people. He had also helped to found the Pennsylvania Society for the Abolition of Slavery. In 1803 he became president of the society.

Rush was also one of the founding members of a penal reform society. An early opponent of capital punishment, Rush believed that punishment should be aimed at reforming the criminal and that prison terms should be fixed by law and adjusted to the crime.

Rush vigorously supported the new federal Constitution and, as a member of the Pennsylvania ratifying convention, helped to lead the successful fight for its adoption. He also helped secure a more liberal state constitution.

From 1783 until his death Rush served on the staff of the Pennsylvania Hospital. In 1786 he established the first free dispensary for poor people in the country. In 1789 he was appointed to the chair of the theory and practice of medicine at the College of Philadelphia, and after 1792 he taught at the newly formed University of Pennsylvania. Rush came to believe that all disease could be cured by bloodletting and purging.

This treatment was put to the test in the Philadelphia yellow fever epidemic of 1793, in which several thousand people, including members of Rush's household, died, despite his use of extensive bloodletting. Criticized for this, Rush wrote an account of the epidemic—maintaining it was the result of poor sanitation rather than of contagion—that is still regarded as a classic in medical literature.

In 1789 when Rush took charge of the mentally ill at the Pennsylvania Hospital, they were housed in small, dirty basement cells. Rush had them moved to better facilities and tried to find a cure, using "shock therapy" of hot and cold baths. His *Medical Inquiries and Observations upon the Diseases of the Mind*, published in 1812, the year before his death, was the first American work on the subject and anticipated improvements in the treatment of the mentally ill.

**BIBLIOGRAPHY**

Binger, Carol, *Revolutionary Doctor: Benjamin Rush, 1746–1813,* 1966; Goodman, Nathan Gerson, *Benjamin Rush: Physician and Citizen, 1746–1813,* 1934; Hawke, David Freeman, *Benjamin Rush: Revolutionary Gadfly,* 1971.

# Rustin, Bayard

(March 17, 1910–August 24, 1987)
Civil Rights Activist

Bayard Rustin was one of the most skillful organizers among the leaders of the civil rights movement. He was also influential in a range of other causes: pacifism, refugees, nuclear disarmament, Japanese American rights, and gay rights.

Bayard Rustin was born and grew up in West Chester, Pennsylvania, the illegitimate son of a West Indian father and a young mother, and was raised a Quaker by his grandparents. In the local high school he was an honor student, active in debating, singing, and athletics. Even in Pennsylvania, however, he sometimes encountered discrimination. After graduation he did college work at Wilberforce University in Ohio on a music scholarship and later at Cheyney State College in Pennsylvania.

In 1936 Rustin joined the Young Communist League (YCL). While studying at the City College of New York, he became a YCL organizer and peace activist, assigned to campaign against discrimination in the armed services. He once said that the communists "seemed the only people who had civil rights at heart." He supported himself by singing at Café Society and other stylish night clubs. Rustin left the YCL in 1941, however, disillusioned because the communists dropped antidiscrimination and peace campaigning in favor of military support of the USSR. He became active in the Fellowship of Reconciliation (FOR; see A. J. MUSTE), and that summer he volunteered to organize young people for A. PHILIP RANDOLPH's march on Washington to demand job opportunities for blacks. After the march was canceled (over Rustin's objection), he joined JAMES FARMER in the Congress of Racial Equality (CORE) as its first national field secretary.

Rustin went to the West Coast in 1942 with Socialist party leader Norman

Walter Naegle/Courtesy of the Bayard Rustin Fund

Thomas to help Japanese American families forcibly interned by the government. When he was called for the draft, his conscientious objector status as a Quaker would have meant noncombatant service, but he refused any kind of military service in a segregated army and got a prison sentence. He served over two years in a federal penitentiary. Upon his release in 1945, he became leader of the Free India Committee, an FOR project, and was arrested for demonstrating at the British Embassy in Washington. Later he spent a year studying with disciples of Mohandas Gandhi in India and brought knowledge of Gandhian nonviolent philosophy to the civil rights movement. In 1947, working with CORE, he organized the first Freedom Rides (see JAMES FARMER) into the South (an attempt to integrate southern bus terminals), was arrested in North Carolina, and served three weeks on a chain gang. (His published account of the experience resulted in that state's abolishing chain gangs.) As director of the Committee Against Discrimination in the Armed Forces, Rustin played a part in bringing about President Harry S Truman's executive order, in 1948, banning such discrimination. Rustin was a cofounder of the

American Committee on Africa and went to Ghana and Nigeria to advise black leaders of the emerging independent countries.

Pacifism was ingrained in Rustin's beliefs, and in 1953 he became executive director of the War Resisters League (WRL). He took his organizing skills to England to help plan the first marches for nuclear disarmament; to the Sahara Desert to protest the first French nuclear-test explosion; and to Europe to organize the San Francisco–to–Moscow Peace Walk.

In 1955 Rustin went to Montgomery, Alabama, representing the WRL and became one of the principal advisers to MARTIN LUTHER KING, JR., and the Southern Christian Leadership Conference (SCLC; see RALPH D. ABERNATHY and MARTIN LUTHER KING, JR.). He continued to be a valued strategist for the civil rights movement, one of his major successes being the planning of the 1963 march on Washington. In 1964, when the A. Philip Randolph Institute was founded, Rustin became its director and served to the end of his life. Coalition and compromise, cooperation with labor unions, and nonviolence continued to be his concerns. During the Harlem riots of 1964 and again in the black uprising in 1965 at Watts, in Los Angeles, he courageously sought to calm the violence, though the enraged demonstrators threatened him.

Rustin openly declared that he was gay and urged black leaders to join the campaign against AIDS, pointing to its disproportionate prevalence among minorities. (His open homosexuality and early YCL episode had long disquieted some of his civil rights colleagues.) In 1987, during his last months, Rustin went to Thailand for the International Rescue Committee to report on the situation of Cambodian refugees; to Chile and Paraguay to seek out organizations working for democracy; and to Haiti to consider the prospects of a proposed election.

After Rustin's death from cardiac arrest following surgery for appendicitis, the *New York Times* stated in an editorial that "other civil rights leaders wielded power; Bayard Rustin wielded influence. America is better for his having done so."

**BIBLIOGRAPHY**

Viorst, Milton, *Fire in the Streets: America in the 1960s*, 1979; Weisbrot, Robert, *Freedom Bound: A History of America's Civil Rights Movement*, 1990.

# Ryan, John Augustine

(May 25, 1869–September 16, 1945)
Reformer, Religious Leader

The career of Father John A. Ryan blended traditional Roman Catholic principles and the American progressive tradition. His achievement in the struggle for social justice was recognized both by the Catholic church and by the nation.

Michael John Ryan, as he was christened, was the eldest of ten children born to William Ryan and Maria Elizabeth Luby Ryan on a farm in Vermillion, near St. Paul, Minnesota. Both parents had emigrated separately from Ireland in the 1840s. Of six sons, three became priests; of four daughters, two became nuns. John Ryan (he dropped "Michael" and later added "Augustine") grew up on the farm and in his teens went to a school in St. Paul run by the Christian Brothers, where he recognized that he had a vocation for the priesthood. He entered St. Thomas Seminary (later St. Paul Seminary) and graduated in 1892 as valedictorian, then went on to a six-year clerical course. In June 1898 he was ordained a priest, and in the fall he began graduate work at The Catholic University of America (CUA) in Washington, D.C.

At CUA, Ryan studied under the Reverend Thomas J. Bouquillon, a theologian well known for progressive social ideas. In 1906 Ryan received a doctorate in sacred theology (S.T.D.), having written a thesis entitled "A Living Wage: Its Ethical and Economic Aspects," which drew on traditional theological sources and particularly on the encyclical *Rerum novarum* (1891) of Pope Leo XIII, the first socially progressive pontiff. Ryan voiced in "A Living Wage" the moral and economic ideas that were to dominate his lifelong social philosophy. He maintained that each person has a right, endowed by God, to share in the earth's bounty and to earn a wage that allows a life of dignity. Further, he argued, the state must if necessary compel employers to pay a living wage.

Ryan had returned to St. Paul Seminary to teach in 1902, while still preparing his thesis, and he remained there for thirteen years, meanwhile lecturing around the country, urging Catholics to become actively involved in social issues. He constructed a program of reform, published in the *Catholic World* in 1909: a legal minimum wage; an eight-hour work day; laws protecting women and children and the right to picket and boycott; employment bureaus; unemployment, accident, health, and old age insurance; public housing; public ownership of public utilities, mines, and forests; control of monopolies; progressive inheritance and income taxes; laws against speculation in stocks and commodities; and taxation on the future rise in land values, an idea Ryan got from the teachings of HENRY GEORGE.

Though sometimes called a socialist, Ryan insisted that he was applying orthodox Catholic theology to the problems of industrial society. He worked with Catholic organizations and had the support of respected clerics such as John Ireland, the liberal archbishop of St. Paul. In 1915 Ryan was appointed associate professor of political science at CUA, and the following year he published his last major scholarly book, *Distributive Justice: The Right and Wrong of Our Present Distribution of Wealth*, in which he studied the relative claims of employees and employers to the products of industry. In 1919 he became professor of theology and dean of the School of Social Sciences at CUA. In the same year he wrote the "Bishops' Program of Social Reconstruction" for the National Catholic War Council—the most progressive statement of social reform yet issued by the Catholic church. He joined the National Catholic Welfare Council in 1920 as director of its Social Action Department. At CUA, Ryan was a mentor to priests and nuns who wished to commit themselves to social reform.

Ryan's lecturing and writing brought him a broad lay audience as well. He worked with ROGER BALDWIN on the board of the American Civil Liberties Union (ACLU) and with other national leaders on a federal child-labor amendment, a minimum-wage law, and efforts for international peace. He considered the Eighteenth Amendment, which established the prohibition of liquor, to be unenforceable.

In 1933 Ryan was raised to the rank of monsignor by Pope Pius XI. In that year, as Franklin D. Roosevelt became president, Ryan welcomed the New Deal as a means of realizing social reform. He saw the National Industrial Recovery Act (NIRA) as fulfilling Pius XI's plan for industrial reorganization outlined in a 1931 encyclical. He served on the National Recovery Administration's Industrial Appeals board, and he was a consultant to other government agencies. He strongly endorsed worker efforts in the 1930s to organize unions and to bargain collectively with employers, and he established close relations with leading trade unionists of the day. A staunch supporter of Roosevelt, Ryan defended the president against the attacks of the profascist radio priest, CHARLES COUGHLIN, in 1936, and the following year Roosevelt showed his appreciation by asking Ryan to give the benediction at his second inauguration.

Ryan was obliged by administrative rules to retire from his posts at CUA when he became seventy, in 1939, but he continued to work with the National Catholic Welfare Council. He also wrote his autobiography, which, published in 1941 as *Social Doctrine in Action*, was also a history of the liberal wing of the Catholic church. He was an active supporter of American aid to the Allies in World War II. At Roosevelt's fourth inauguration, in January 1945, Ryan again gave the benediction. That summer, in failing health, he went home to Minnesota. After asking to be driven out to see the old farmhouse in Vermillion, Father Ryan died at St. Joseph's Hospital in St. Paul.

**BIBLIOGRAPHY**

Broderick, F. L., *Right Reverend New Dealer, John A. Ryan*, 1963; Richard, J. P., *John A. Ryan, Prophet of Social Justice*, 1946; Ryan, J. A., *The Church and Socialism*, 1919, *Questions of the Day*, 1931, *Seven Troubled Years, 1920–1936*, 1937, and *Can Unemployment Be Ended?* 1940.

# Samuelson, Paul

(May 15, 1915–  )
Economist

Known for his broad contributions to both abstract economic theory and practical matters of national economic policy, Paul Samuelson has won the Nobel Memorial Prize in Economic Sciences and written the most widely used elementary college economics textbook.

Born in Gary, Indiana, to Frank and Ella Lipton Samuelson, both emigrants from Poland, Samuelson received his B.A. in economics from the University of Chicago in 1935 and his Ph.D. in 1941 from Harvard University. He became an assistant professor in economics at the Massachusetts Institute of Technology (MIT) in 1940. Appointed a full professor in 1947, Samuelson since 1966 has held the rank of institute professor, helping to create a leading center of economics research. He spent some of the World War II years in Washington as a consultant to government agencies, including the National Resource Planning Board and the War Production Board. In 1944 he warned that cuts in production at the war's end would bring widespread unemployment.

Samuelson's book *Foundations of Economic Analysis,* based on his doctoral dissertation, was published in 1947 and reissued in an enlarged edition in 1983. It has become one of the most widely regarded economics books of our time. Using advanced mathematics as the basis of analyzing and solving problems, Samuelson presented a unified theory of consumer and producer activity, international trade, public finance, and welfare economics. Samuelson was a follower of the great English economist John Maynard Keynes, who argued for the use of government fiscal (spending) powers to stabilize capitalist economies.

In 1948 Samuelson published *Economics: An Introductory Analysis,* now in its thirteenth revised edition and in translations in many languages. It has become a standard college textbook, celebrated for its clear explanation of the mathematics and the principles of applied economics.

Besides carrying on his advisory role to government and private organizations, Samuelson has published papers over a wide range of economics topics, including analytic techniques, demographic and monetary economics, economic growth, and international trade. President John F. Kennedy appointed him chairman of a committee of economists to advise him on policy.

In 1970 Samuelson received the Nobel Memorial Prize in Economic Sciences "for the scientific work through which he has developed static and dynamic economic theory and actively contributed to raising the level of analysis in economic science." Subsequently his publications have included analyses of Marxist economic theory that have been attacked by Marxist economists.

Samuelson married Marion E. Crawford in 1938, with whom he had two daughters and four sons. After her death he married Risha Eckaus in 1981. At present institute professor emeritus, Samuelson is still active in research at MIT.

**BIBLIOGRAPHY**

Brown, E. C., and R. M. Solow (eds.), *Paul Samuelson and Modern Economic Theory,* 1983; Keating, Maryann O. (ed.), *Economics from the Heart: A Samuelson Sampler,* 1983; Samuelson, Paul, *Problems of the American Economy,* 1962.

# Sanger, Margaret Louise Higgins

(September 14, 1883–September 6, 1966)
Reformer

Margaret Sanger dedicated her life to the birth-control movement in the United States, of which she was the founder and controversial leader.

Margaret Higgins was born in Corning, New York, the daughter of Irish American parents. Her father was an atheist and a socialist who spent more time arguing social questions than making a living. While admiring her father for his liberal views, Margaret was upset by the family's poverty and also by the fact that her mother, worn out from raising

Library of Congress

eleven children, died at a relatively young age of tuberculosis. Margaret's two older sisters financed her education at Claverack College in Hudson, New York, a private coeducational secondary school. After graduation and a short spell teaching in Little Falls, New Jersey, she came back home to help her dying mother. Although her father expected her to remain on as a housekeeper after her mother's death, Margaret left to study nursing at the White Plains (New York) Hospital. In 1902 she married William Sanger, an architect and socialist. Ill with tuberculosis during her first pregnancy, Margaret Sanger recovered through sheer determination to lead a normal life. Two more children were born to the couple.

In 1912 the Sangers moved to New York City, where they threw themselves into radical activity. As a member of the Socialist party and a woman's labor organizer, Margaret Sanger met such leaders as EUGENE V. DEBS, EMMA GOLDMAN, and WILLIAM D. HAYWOOD of the Industrial

Workers of the World (IWW). She played a valuable role during an IWW strike at the Lawrence, Massachusetts, textile mills. By evacuating the strikers' children from the area, she and ELIZABETH GURLEY FLYNN spurred sympathy for the strikers, helping them meet success.

Influenced by Emma Goldman and other radical women, Sanger became convinced that women would never become fully free and equal without being able to control childbearing. In 1912 she authored a series of articles about female sexuality for a socialist weekly, *The Call.* The issue that published her article on syphilis was banned by the U.S. Post Office under the Comstock Act of 1873, which prohibited using the mails to disseminate information on birth control and other sex-related topics (see ANTHONY COMSTOCK). That same year, Sanger began working as a visiting nurse among poor immigrant women in New York City. This experience left her appalled by the toll exacted by venereal disease among these women and also by the numbers of deaths from botched abortions. According to Sanger, the turning point in her life came when one of her patients, who had been refused contraceptive information by her doctor, died as a result of a self-induced abortion. She vowed to educate women about birth control.

Finding that little contraceptive information was available in the United States, Sanger in 1913 traveled to Europe, where she met with members of the radical French labor movement to learn about their program for distributing information on contraception. Upon her return, she separated from her husband and began publishing *Woman Rebel*, a militant monthly that supported women's liberation, radical politics, and birth control—a term Sanger herself coined. Indicted by the Justice Department under the Comstock Act, Sanger fled to England, leaving behind thousands of copies of a contraceptive advice pamphlet, *Family Limitation*, to be distributed. While in England she became an intimate friend of the physician and sex reformer Havelock Ellis, who advised her to adopt a moderate approach to her campaign—one more likely to win wider acceptance. Sanger also spent two months visiting clinics in the Netherlands, where she learned family planning techniques.

After Sanger's return to the United States in 1915, the government dropped its charges against her, but she defied the law again, first by founding a new journal, *The Birth Control Review*, and second by opening a birth-control clinic in Brooklyn. It was the first such clinic in the United States. Police quickly closed it and arrested Sanger, who was sentenced to thirty days in jail. Sanger's imprisonment won her national sympathy. More important, perhaps, by appealing her case she obtained a modification of the New York law against the distribution of contraceptive information. The change allowed physicians to provide this information, though only to married women and solely for the purpose of treating or preventing venereal disease.

Sanger now focused on lobbying for bills allowing doctors to distribute birth-control information and to staff clinics. Distancing herself from her former radical associates, she also concentrated on winning the support of wealthy philanthropists, sometimes using eugenic arguments that birth control would reduce the birthrate of the unfit and inferior. In 1920 Sanger founded the American Birth Control League, serving as president until 1928; the organization later became the Planned Parenthood Federation of America (1942; see ALAN GUTTMACHER). In 1921 Sanger organized the first national birth-control conference in New York City. Having divorced her husband in 1920, Sanger in 1922 married J. Noah H. Slee, a wealthy industrialist, who allowed his wife the autonomy she desired while contributing generously to the birth-control cause. With money from her husband, Sanger in 1923 opened the Birth Control Clinical Research Center in New York City. The first birth-control clinic in the United States to include doctors on the staff, it provided a model for the nationwide network of over 300 birth-control clinics established by Sanger and her supporters by 1938.

Sanger worked hard raising money to keep her clinics open. To supply them with contraceptive devices, she smuggled European-made diaphragms into the United States. Also, through the National Committee on Federal Legislation on Birth Control, which she had started in Washington, D.C., Sanger fought to change the Comstock Act so that contraceptive material intended for physicians could be mailed. In 1936 in the case of *United States* v. *One Package*, she won this important victory.

Following the *One Package* case, Sanger became less active in the birth-control movement but continued to speak in its behalf in the United States and abroad. In 1952 she helped found the International Planned Parenthood Federation, serving as president for the next six years. Also in the 1950s, she convinced the wealthy philanthropist Katharine Dexter McCormick to provide the financial support needed for the research to create an oral contraceptive. This research led to a birth-control pill that came on the market in 1960. After suffering repeated heart attacks, Sanger died in a Tucson, Arizona, nursing home at the age of eighty-six.

**BIBLIOGRAPHY**

Gordon, Linda, *Woman's Body, Woman's Right: A Social History of Birth Control in America*, 1976; Gray, M., *Margaret Sanger: A Biography of the Champion of Birth Control*, 1979; Reed, J., *From Private Vice to Public Virtue: The Birth Control Movement and American Society Since 1830*, 1978.

# Schlafly, Phyllis Stewart

(August 15, 1924–   )
Author, Lecturer, Politician

Phyllis Schlafly is a leading spokesperson for the conservative viewpoint on issues ranging from women's rights to national defense. She played a major role in defeating the Equal Rights Amendment to the Constitution.

Phyllis Stewart was born in St. Louis, Missouri, into a family with strong conservative values. She attended the Academy of the Sacred Heart in St. Louis, graduating as class valedictorian in 1941. She attended Maryville College of the Sacred Heart and Washington University, from which she graduated Phi Beta Kappa in 1944. While in college, she worked the night shift at a federal munitions factory. She earned a master's degree in political science at Radcliffe College, served briefly as a researcher for several Washington congressmen, then helped run the successful campaign of Republican congressman Claude I. Bakewell of St. Louis. In 1946 she became a researcher and librarian for a local bank.

In 1949 Phyllis Stewart married Fred Schlafly, a successful lawyer from Alton, Illinois, who shared her conservative views. Although she left her job at this time to become a homemaker and eventually the mother of six children, Phyllis Schlafly found time to do community volunteer work and, in 1952, to run unsuccessfully for Congress. (Since the 1950s she has served as a delegate to the Republican National Convention.) Schlafly also did research for Senator Joseph McCarthy in the early 1950s, and founded with her husband the Cardinal Mindszenty Foundation in 1958 to publicize the threat of communism.

Schlafly's support of conservative presidential candidate Barry Goldwater in 1964 led to her first book, *A Choice Not an Echo.* Published by a company she and her husband started, the book sold over 3 million copies and helped Goldwater win his party's nomination. Following the book's success, Schlafly joined forces with Admiral Chester Ward to write a series of books on national defense policy and nuclear strategy. She argued that various presidential advisers were seriously undermining the nation's defenses.

Meanwhile, in 1964 Schlafly was elected first vice president of the National Federation of Republican Women and only narrowly lost the election as president of the organization in 1967. She started the Eagles Trust Fund to support conservative political candidates and founded a conservative monthly newsletter, *The Phyllis Schlafly Report.* In 1970 Schlafly made another unsuccessful bid for Congress.

In the February 1972 issue of *The Phyllis Schlafly Report,* Schlafly launched her first attack against the Equal Rights Amendment (ERA; see ALICE PAUL), which had been brought before Congress since 1923. Schlafly contended that the ERA, which demanded equality of rights for women under the law, represented a serious threat to women and the family, because it would thrust mothers into military combat and make wives responsible for providing 50 percent of the financial support of their families. In 1972 she founded a Stop ERA organization with chapters around the country and in 1975, as an answer to "women's lib," founded the Eagle Forum, another organization aimed at promoting the traditional roles of women as mothers and homemakers. Later the Eagle Forum also became involved in defense and foreign policy issues. Schlafly spoke against the ERA amendment in thirty state legislatures.

Making use of the media to spread her views, Schlafly from 1973 to 1978 was a commentator on the CBS radio network program "Spectrum" and on the Chicago radio station WBBM program "Matters of Opinion" (1973–1975), later serving as a commentator on the Cable News Network. In 1977 Schlafly published *The Power of the Positive Woman* to further her attack on the women's liberation movement. The following year, she earned a law degree from Washington University. Thanks largely to Schlafly's efforts and those of other conservative, antifeminist groups, the ERA was defeated in 1982.

Phyllis Schlafly has received a number of awards for her work, including the Woman of Achievement in Public Affairs award of the St. Louis *Globe-Democrat* (1963), ten George Washington Honor Medals from the Freedoms Foundation at Valley Forge, Pennsylvania, and a citation from *Good Housekeeping* magazine as one of the ten most admired women in the world (1977).

**BIBLIOGRAPHY**

Felsenthal, Carol, *The Sweetheart of the Silent Majority: The Biography of Phyllis Schlafly*, 1981.

# Schlesinger, Arthur Meier, Jr.

(October 15, 1917–   )
Author, Historian

As a historian and prize-winning author, adviser to two presidents, and one of the founders of Americans for Democratic Action, Arthur Schlesinger, Jr., is a leading spokesperson for twentieth-century liberalism.

Schlesinger was born in Columbus, Ohio, the older son of American historian Arthur Schlesinger. Growing up in Cambridge, Massachusetts, where his father was a professor at Harvard University, he was surrounded by American history from childhood on. Schlesinger attended local public schools, completing his secondary education with two years at Phillips Exeter Academy in New Hampshire. After graduation he accompanied his parents on a trip around the world, then enrolled at Harvard, graduating summa cum laude in 1938. Schlesinger spent the next year studying at the University of Cambridge in England on a fellowship. In 1939 the honors thesis he had written at Harvard about a nineteenth-century journalist and theologian was published as *Orestes A. Brownson: A Pilgrim's Progress.*

Also in 1939, Schlesinger returned to Harvard as a junior fellow, a position that enabled him to pursue scholarship without teaching responsibilities. After two years of research, he delivered an important series of lectures on Andrew Jackson at the Lowell Institute in Boston. Realizing that he had enough material for a book, Schlesinger wrote *The Age of Jackson* (1945). The book offered a new and penetrating analysis of Jacksonian democracy as a political and intellectual movement aimed at curbing the power of business. Although Schlesinger denied the book was an attempt to explain the New Deal of Franklin D. Roosevelt, the book had the effect of establishing Roosevelt's place firmly within the American reform tradition. *The Age of Jackson* became a best-seller and won the 1946 Pulitzer Prize for history.

Meanwhile, during World War II, Schlesinger worked for the Office of War Information and served in the Office of Strategic Services in Europe. Late in 1946 he returned to Harvard as an associate professor, and the following year he helped found Americans for Democratic Action, a liberal organization concerned with further carrying out the goals of the New Deal. The Americans for Democratic Action also called on liberals to be as vigilant in their fight against communism as they had been in their struggle against Nazism. Schlesinger captured the spirit of this new and toughened liberalism in his influential 1949 book, *The Vital Center.*

While at Harvard during the 1950s (he became a full professor in 1954), Schlesinger wrote a series of three major books on the age of Roosevelt: *The Crisis of the Old Order* (1957), *The Coming of the New Deal* (1958), and *The Politics of Upheaval* (1960). Also during this period, Schlesinger served as national chairman of Americans for Democratic Action (1953–1954) and as a speechwriter and adviser to the Democratic presidential candidate, Adlai E. Stevenson, in the elections of 1952 and 1956.

Schlesinger performed the same function for Democratic presidential candidate John F. Kennedy in 1960 and, with Kennedy's election, took a two-year leave of absence from Harvard to serve as a special assistant to the president. In this position, he helped develop Kennedy's "New Frontier" program of reform and later the "Great Society" of President Lyndon B. Johnson. Schlesinger wrote of his experiences during the Kennedy administration in *A Thousand Days: John F. Kennedy in the White House* (1965), a personal memoir that won him a second Pulitzer Prize and a National Book Award for history and biography.

After his resignation from the White House staff in 1964, Schlesinger became Albert Schweitzer professor of humanities at the City University of New York in 1967. In the late 1960s, Schlesinger, along with many other intellectuals, became more and more concerned about the growing U.S. involvement in Vietnam and about mounting violence at home. Deeply shocked and angered by the 1968 assassination of Robert F. Kennedy, whose presidential candidacy he had supported, Schlesinger dealt with violence as a peculiarly American trait in *The Crisis of Confidence: Ideas, Power and Violence in America* (1969).

Yet another area of concern for Schlesinger was the abuse of presidential power, especially to make war, by Presidents Lyndon B. Johnson and Richard Nixon. In Schlesinger's view, presidential power had increased to the point where it threatened the system of checks and balances established by the Constitution. He discussed the problem at length in *The Imperial Presidency* (1973). Schlesinger then devoted himself to writing a monumental biography of Robert F. Kennedy. Published as *Robert Kennedy and His Times* in 1978, the book became an instant best-seller and won its author another National Book Award. Because of his close association with liberal presidents and other members of the liberal establishment, however, Schlesinger found himself under attack by the New Left and by a younger generation of American historians who did not share Schlesinger's admiration for the American liberal tradition.

In 1980 Schlesinger worked for the presidential candidacy of Senator Edward Kennedy, and throughout the decade he continued to comment on current affairs from a liberal, Democratic perspective in articles and reviews. *Cycles of American History,* a collection of Schlesinger's essays, was published in 1986. In his *Disuniting of America* (1991), Schlesinger argued strenuously against multiculturalism and for the assimilation of ethnic and racial minorities into a common American culture. In so doing, he continued his lifelong project of defining an American liberalism strong enough to withstand attacks from both conservative and radical critics.

**BIBLIOGRAPHY**

Anderson, Patrick, *The Presidents' Men,* 1968; Cunliffe, Marcus, and Robin W. Winks (eds.), *Pastmasters: Some Essays on American Historians,* 1969; Ross, Mitchell, *The Literary Politicians,* 1978.

# Schneiderman, Rose

(April 6, 1884–August 11, 1972)
Labor Leader, Public Official

Despite a ghetto upbringing and only a grammar school education, Rose Schneiderman became a well-known trade unionist in the United States. She organized thousands of women in unions and held important positions in the federal government during the New Deal and later in the labor department of New York State.

Rose Schneiderman was born in a town (whose name she did not know) in what is now Poland and was then part of Russia. Her father, Adolph Samuel Schneiderman, a tailor, brought the family to the United States in 1890, when Rose was six, and settled the family of five in two rooms in the Lower East Side of New York City. Three years later he died of brain fever, and Rose had to leave school to care for the younger children while her mother worked in a sweatshop. Later she went back to school and had completed the sixth grade when she had to find work herself. Her wages as a store clerk were less than $3 a week. When she left for a better job, stitching cap linings, her wages were $5 a week (and the cap stitchers had to pay for their sewing machines, thread, and electric power). After three years, Schneiderman led a group of fellow workers to demand membership in the all-male United Cloth Hat and Cap Makers Union. She was elected secretary and organizer of the local chapter the women founded. In 1904 she led a successful strike against the cap factories, and soon afterward she joined the New York chapter of the Women's Trade Union League (WTUL), an alliance of woman unionists and social workers that JANE ADDAMS had helped found. In 1908 Schneiderman became an organizer for the WTUL.

Rose Schneiderman's ambition was to go to college and become a teacher, but her involvement in union activity ruled that out. Instead she educated herself through broad reading. In the winter of 1909 to 1910, Schneiderman led the WTUL in supporting a strike of some 25,000 mostly female workers in the New York City shirtwaist industry. She persuaded women prominent in New York society to help out, contributing funds and walking the picket line, and she canvassed New England, speaking at meetings to raise money. The strike was one of the most important of the Progressive era. The strike won concessions from employers in widely hailed settlements known as *Protocols for Peace*. This settlement, in turn, established the International Ladies' Garment Workers Union (ILGWU) as an important union. Schneiderman joined the ILGWU as an organizer and traveled the country to promote unionization. By then she was well known in the labor movement. She was a diminutive, red-haired, serious young woman whom the social critic IRVING HOWE described as "a tiny firebrand, vivid and articulate."

Active in the woman suffrage movement as of 1910, Schneiderman toured New York State for the Woman's Suffrage party, speaking at street rallies. She had become vice president of the national WTUL when she was appointed by President Woodrow Wilson to represent American woman workers at the Paris Peace Conference in 1920. In 1923 she was a delegate to the International Federation of Trade Unions in Vienna. During the twenties, as a leader of the national WTUL, she marched on picket lines and organized trade union locals. Under the National Recovery Act of President Franklin D. Roosevelt's New Deal, she was the only woman on the Labor Advisory Board; and she was a member of the president's "brain trust." In 1937 Governor Herbert Lehman appointed her secretary of the New York State Department of Labor, a post she held for seven years. Schneiderman resigned at age sixty but continued to serve her causes—typically, as a director of Bryn Mawr College's summer school for working women, to which she insisted that African American women be admitted.

Rose Schneiderman spent her last years in the Jewish Home and Hospital in New York City, where she died at the age of eighty-eight. She had been reelected annually as president of the National Women's Trade Union League to the end of her life.

**BIBLIOGRAPHY**

Boone, G., *The Women's Trade Union Leagues in Great Britain and the United States*, 1942; Dubofsky, Melvyn, and Warren Van Tine (eds.), *Labor Leaders in America*, 1987; Howe, Irving, *World of Our Fathers*, 1976.

# Schumpeter, Joseph Alois

(February 8, 1883–January 8, 1950)
Economist

Joseph Schumpeter was one of the most diversely talented economists during the years between World War I and World War II and one of the most influential of the Harvard economists. Little was known of his earlier life in Europe until research after his death brought new information to light.

Schumpeter (the name is pronounced "shum-pater") was born in Triesch, Moravia, then in the Austro-Hungarian Empire, and after World War I part of Czechoslovakia, where the town is now called Trest. His father, with the same name, was a German-speaking manufacturer of cloth; his mother, Joanna Grüner, a physician's daughter. His father died in 1887, and six years later his mother married a retired army officer some thirty years older, Lieutenant-Field Marshal Sigismund von Kéler. The family lived thereafter in Vienna.

Schumpeter attended the Theresianum, a school for boys of aristocratic families, where he showed a gift for languages. At the University of Vienna, though his primary interest was economics, he took a law degree in 1906. He spent a year in England, living a stylish life while doing research at the London School of Economics and the British Museum and getting to know eminent professors of economics. In 1907 he married an Englishwoman, Gladys Seaver, who was twelve years older than he was. She preferred to live in England, and eventually they were divorced.

Schumpeter spent a year in Cairo, practicing law at the International Mixed Court of Egypt and writing his first book, the title of which can be translated as "The Nature and Essence of Theoretical Economics." Upon its publication in 1908, the book made his name known in the field. At the age of twenty-six, appointed to a post at the University of Czernowitz (now Chernovtsy, Ukraine), Schumpeter was the youngest professor of economics in the empire.

In 1912 Schumpeter became a full professor at the University of Graz, somewhat closer to Vienna. He had published in 1911 what is considered his most important work, *The Theory of Economic Development* (translated in 1934), in which he held that the entrepreneur, or business manager, was the chief factor in stimulating the business cycle. In 1913 to 1914, while he was an exchange professor at Columbia University, in New York, he lectured at other institutions and met several American economists. During World War I, Schumpeter continued to teach at Graz while strengthening friendships with political figures in Vienna.

In 1919, after the war, the empire was broken up and Austria emerged as a small republic. Schumpeter became secretary of finance in the new socialist government. Unsuccessful at the job and unpopular, he was dismissed and became chairman of a private bank. By 1924, when the bank foundered, he lost his post and went into bankruptcy.

Through the help of friends, in 1925 Schumpeter was appointed professor of public finance at the University of Bonn, in Germany. In that year he married Annie Reisinger, a working-class woman of twenty-one with whom he was deeply in love. Within a year she had died in childbirth; the child died as well. A month before, Schumpeter's mother, whom he adored, had died. For some years in a mood of despair, he buried himself in writing, teaching, and lecturing and cultivated an interest in sociology. During those years, furthermore, though heavily debt-ridden, he worked at repaying the losses of people who had suffered in the bank failure.

Schumpeter had temporary appointments at Harvard University in 1927 to 1928 and in 1930; during the latter year he led in founding the Econometric Society, which is concerned with economic analysis using statistics and mathematics. In 1932, Schumpeter accepted the professorship in economics that Harvard had been urging on him, and there he remained until the end of his life, having become an American citizen in 1939. In 1937 he married Elizabeth Boody, an economic historian, who is credited with sustaining him during his periods of depression and what has been called "his punishingly hard research program."

His tireless studies at Harvard yielded first a two-volume work, *Business Cycles* (1939), which he described as a theoretical, historical, and statistical analysis of the capitalist process. It is no longer valued by most economists, who consider it an anachronistic oddity, though it comprises a useful history of modern capitalism. In 1942 he published a highly regarded work, *Capitalism, Socialism, and Democracy*, which, with a wealth of political, sociological, and historical wisdom, depicts capitalism as doomed to eventual decay, inevitably to be succeeded by socialism.

When Schumpeter died he left an unfinished major work, *History of Economic Analysis*, which his widow edited for publication. It appeared in 1954, a year after her own death. He also left, in his private papers, hundreds of aphorisms, many of them acute, which have been published by Richard Swedberg.

**BIBLIOGRAPHY**

Allen, Robert Loring, *Opening Doors: The Life and Work of Joseph Schumpeter*, 2 vols., 1991; Schumpeter, J. A., and Redvers Opie (trans.), *Theory of Economic Development*, 1934; Swedberg, Richard, *Schumpeter: A Biography*, 1991.

# Seeger, Peter

(May 3, 1919–  )
Folksinger, Reformer

Pete Seeger was a prime mover in the rediscovery of our folk songs, as a scholar, collector, organizer, and performer. His commitment to peace, justice, and environmental issues has been linked constantly to his singing and banjo playing all over the country.

Pete Seeger was born in Patterson, New York, north of New York City, to parents whose ancestry went back to colonial New England and Valley Forge. His father was a musicologist of liberal leanings, his mother a violinist and music teacher. Growing up in Nyack, New York, he heard a great deal of music but resisted studying. When, in 1935, his father, himself a scholar of folk music, took him to a folk festival in North Carolina, Pete's enthusiasm was kindled, especially for the five-string banjo, the instrument of choice for folksinging in the South. Seeger spent two years at Harvard, but he dropped out to take to the road. For several years he traveled the forty-eight United States, hitchhiking and riding freight trains, picking up songs and banjo tricks from the people he encountered. He acquired a huge repertory of folk music and got to know folk artists like WOODY GUTHRIE and the guitar player Huddie Ledbetter (Leadbelly). Seeger spent months at the Library of Congress in Washington as an assistant to the curator of the Archive of American Folk Song, John A. Lomax. Seeger listened to hundreds of recordings and traveled with Lomax and his son Alan on field trips collecting songs.

During the 1930s, partly as a reaction to the Great Depression, many artists and intellectuals as well as working people fell under the spell of the Communist party. Seeger was one of these. Though he was far from being an active member, his radical political beliefs were influenced by the experience.

In 1940 Seeger formed a group, the Almanac Singers, with Guthrie, Lee Hays, and others, that performed before enthusiastic labor audiences and recorded albums of folk and union songs. Seeger had a talent for getting audiences to sing along with him. The Office of War Information (OWI) commissioned him and Guthrie to write and perform antifascist songs. Seeger enlisted in the army in 1942 and was assigned to Special Services, entertaining troops in the Pacific theater and the States. Discharged in December 1945, he helped found People's Songs, Inc., a union of songwriters and a clearinghouse for folk music, and became its director. He was convinced that a folk music revival was on the horizon and that the unions would boost it. People's Songs, with some 3,000 members and support from the radical public, promoted widespread interest in folk and labor songs, often through concerts

called "hootenannies." The Communist party, still near the peak of its membership, took an interest in the folk song movement, and Seeger remained in its orbit through the 1940s. In the 1948 presidential campaign, People's Songs, including Seeger, joined the communists in supporting Henry A. Wallace's candidacy on the Progressive ticket.

An outgrowth of the folk song wave was an immensely popular singing group, the Weavers—Lee Hays, Ronnie Gilbert, Fred Hellerman, and Seeger (on banjo). As Seeger said in later years, "We hoped to sing for peace and civil rights. We never intended that we would be a commercial success." The group, after its debut at the Village Vanguard in New York City, sang in theaters and clubs around the country and on national television and radio. The Weavers' recordings—including hits like *Goodnight, Irene, Kisses Sweeter than Wine,* and *On Top of Old Smoky*—had sold more 4 million copies by 1952. But engagements dwindled as the anticommunist spirit gained ground, and the Weavers disbanded. Seeger struck out on his own, having broken with the Communist party in 1951.

During the fifties Seeger went on singing—touring at home and abroad, giving concerts to large crowds. In 1955 he was summoned to appear before a subcommittee of the House Committee on Un-American Activities (HUAC), which was investigating supposed subversive influences in the world of entertainment. Seeger refused to answer questions about his political beliefs. Rather than taking the Fifth Amendment to the Constitution he cited the First, which guaranteed freedom of speech and association. That did not help his case. He was indicted for contempt of Congress and went on trial in March 1961 in the U.S. District Court in New York; found guilty, he was sentenced to a year in prison. In May 1962, the U.S. Court of Appeals dismissed the indictment on a technicality.

Despite the judicial reversal, Seeger was blacklisted by some television networks and his concerts were often picketed by right-wingers. He continued to play around the country and with his family toured the world. In Moscow, he got 10,000 people to sing four-part harmony to *Michael, Row the Boat Ashore*. He recorded forty albums for Folkways Records and published songbooks and instruction manuals. He was at Selma, Alabama, in 1965, marching and singing for civil rights. He was in the forefront of the anti–Vietnam War movement and composed some of its theme songs: *Where Have All the Flowers Gone* and *Waist Deep in the Big Muddy*. Seeger was one of the few artists to be as popular with the New Left (in the 1960s and 1970s) as he had been with the Old Left (in the 1930s and 1940s).

In 1943 Seeger had married Toshi-Aline Ohta, of Virginian and Japanese parentage, who worked with him for their causes. With their three children they eventually settled down in a log cabin they had built, overlooking the Hudson River, near Beacon, New York. Seeger's driving interest in the sixties, stimulated by RACHEL CARSON's book *Silent Spring*, be-

came the environment, and he led a movement to clean up the polluted Hudson. With volunteer helpers he built an old-style sloop, the *Clearwater*, which became the symbol as well as transport of a crew of folksinging activists as they cruised the rivers and coasts, raising funds. The *Clearwater* movement has stimulated new pure-water laws that have begun to take effect. Seeger has continued to be prominent in antinuclear demonstrations and Earth Day events.

**BIBLIOGRAPHY**

Dunaway, D. K., *How Can I Keep From Singing: Pete Seeger*, 1981; Seeger, Pete, and Bob Reiser, *Carry It On! A History in Song and Picture of the Working Men and Women of America*, 1985, and *Everybody Says Freedom: A History of the Civil Rights Movement in Songs and Pictures*, 1989.

# Seton, Elizabeth Ann Bayley

(August 28, 1774–January 4, 1821)
Educator, Religious Leader

Elizabeth Seton was the first native-born American to be recognized as a saint by the Roman Catholic church. She also founded the first American sisterhood, the Daughters (or Sisters) of Charity of St. Vincent de Paul, and made important contributions to Catholic education in the United States.

The daughter of a prominent New York physician, Elizabeth Ann Bayley grew up a devout Episcopalian. She married William Seton, a well-to-do merchant, in 1794 and had five children, but she still found time for charitable work, helping to start a society to aid destitute widows.

In 1800 Seton suffered the first of several misfortunes when her husband's business

went bankrupt. The next year, she lost her father to yellow fever, then her husband died in 1803 while the couple was on a trip to Italy. There Seton was befriended by two of his business associates, the brothers Antonio and Filippo Filicchi, who introduced her to the Roman Catholic faith.

Upon her return to New York, Seton anguished over whether or not to convert to Catholicism. She finally joined the Catholic church in March 1805. Disinherited by her godmother and shunned by many of her former friends, Seton spent the next three years struggling to support herself and her five children.

In 1808, at the invitation of Father William V. Dubourg, superior of the Sulpicians, Seton went to Baltimore to found a Catholic school for girls. During the year she spent teaching in Baltimore, Seton also began to realize her dream of founding a religious community. A site was found, the first recruits to the new order began to arrive, and early in 1809 Seton took her first vows as a nun.

In June 1809 Seton and a small group of women traveled to Emmitsburg, Maryland, where they occupied a small, fairly primitive stone farmhouse. By 1810 the community had moved into a larger structure and had begun to grow rapidly with new recruits from Maryland and New York. In that year, too, Mother Seton, as she was now known, and her new order were regularized under the somewhat modified rules of the French order of the Sisters of Charity of St. Vincent de Paul.

The Sisters cared for the sick and the poor and especially devoted themselves to teaching. They also started St. Joseph's School (later a college) for girls, one of the first parochial schools in the United States.

Library of Congress

Over the next several years, the sisterhood started by Mother Seton spread to Philadelphia, New York, and eventually, Baltimore. In 1814 Mother Seton established the Orphan Asylum of Philadelphia, the first Catholic child-care institution in the United States.

Active and cheerful until the end, Mother Seton died at Emmitsburg of tuberculosis at the age of forty-six. During her lifetime, Mother Seton's contemporaries attested to her extraordinary goodness, and in 1975 she was canonized.

**BIBLIOGRAPHY**

de Barberey, Helene Bailly, and Joseph B. Code, *Elizabeth Seton*, 1929; Dirvin, Joseph I., *Mrs. Seton, Foundress of the Am. Sisters of Charity*, 1962; Melville, Annabelle M., *Elizabeth Seton*, 1951; Seton, Robert, *Memoir, Letters and Journal of Elizabeth Seton*, 1869; White, Charles I., *Life of Mrs. Eliza A. Seton*, 1853.

# Shays, Daniel

(ca. 1747–September 29, 1825)
Rebel Leader, Soldier

Daniel Shays was one of the leaders of an uprising of debtor farmers in western Massachusetts during the post-revolutionary period. Shays's Rebellion, as it was called, added momentum to the drive for a stronger central government that led to the adoption of the United States Constitution.

Born into a poor family, Shays worked as a hired man in Brookfield, Massachusetts, until the outbreak of the Revolution. He fought at Lexington and, promoted to the rank of ensign, served with distinction at Bunker Hill, Ticonderoga, Saratoga, and Stony Point. In 1777 he was commissioned captain in the 5th

Massachusetts Regiment. The French Marquis de Lafayette, who served as general in George Washington's army, presented him with a handsome sword, but Shays's poverty forced him to sell it. Criticized for doing so, Shays resigned from the army in 1780. He settled in Pelham, Massachusetts, where he held a number of town offices.

After the war, the nation entered into a period of severe economic depression. High taxes combined with low farm prices and a lack of readily available currency threw many farmers and small property owners heavily into debt. Those who could not pay their debts faced imprisonment and the loss of their farms. These conditions produced a growing discontent that flared into armed rebellion in western Massachusetts in 1786.

In the fall of that year, Shays led a mob of several hundred men that gathered in front of the courthouse at Springfield, Massachusetts, to prevent the court from meeting to foreclose on farms and imprison debtors. Later, Shays and his men forced the supreme court at Springfield to adjourn after the state legislature failed to respond to the farmers' grievances.

In January 1787, Shays and another leader, Luke Day, planned an attack on the Springfield arsenal. A communication from Day to Shays was intercepted by the commander of the county militia, however, and Shays and 1,200 men were repelled by forces under the command of General Benjamin Lincoln. Shays then offered to lay down his arms if a general pardon were granted. Shays's terms were refused, and in February 1787 Lincoln defeated the rebels at Petersham.

With a reward on his head, Shays escaped to Vermont. He was one of fourteen men excluded from the general pardon granted in June 1787 and was sentenced to death in absentia. The following year, Shays successfully petitioned for pardon and returned to Massachusetts.

Though his military uprising was a failure, Shays's original demands for tax relief and postponement of debt payments received some redress, and the rebellion underscored importantly the need for a new constitution for the country.

**BIBLIOGRAPHY**

Adams, J. T., *New England in the Republic*, 1925; Parmenter, C. O., *History of Pelham, Mass.*, 1898; Szatmary, David P., *Shays' Rebellion: The Making of an Agrarian Insurrection*, 1980; Taylor, Robert L., *Western Massachusetts in the Revolution*, 1952.

# Sinclair, Upton Beall, Jr.

(September 20, 1878–November 25, 1968)
Activist, Social Critic

During Upton Sinclair's long career he was a prolific author of novels and nonfiction works attacking the country's economic and social ills in the name of social justice. Abroad, he was one of the best-known American authors. His socialist politics repeatedly drew him into running for office, never with success.

Upton Sinclair was born in Baltimore, Maryland, an only child. His father, who came from a line of Virginia aristocrats whose luck ran out with the fall of the Confederacy, was at times a merchant and died of alcoholism. His mother's background was one of gentility and piety. Sinclair grew up in New York City and entered the City College of New York at age fourteen.

After graduating in 1897, he spent three years as a special student at Columbia University taking humanities courses and supporting himself by freelance writing. Under pseudonyms he wrote numerous adventure stories for pulp magazines.

As a youth he was deeply religious and idealistic; his idols were Jesus, Shakespeare's Hamlet, and the poet Percy Bysshe Shelley. At age twenty-three he wrote and published on his own a sentimental novel, *Springtime and Harvest*, about a woman's redemption. Not long after that, he made a marriage that proved to be unhappy and ended in divorce in 1913. In the first year of the marriage he wrote three more works of fiction notable for their painful subject-matter: loneliness, poverty, suicide. Sinclair's second marriage endured nearly fifty years, and he married a third time in his eighties.

In 1902 Sinclair was persuaded to join the Socialist party by friends, particularly George D. Herron, a preacher in the Social Gospel movement (see WALTER RAUSCHENBUSCH). When Sinclair planned to write a novel about the Civil War, Herron advanced funds for a year's support. He moved with his family to rented land near Princeton, New Jersey, where they lived in tents and later a shack while Sinclair did research at the university library. In 1904 he published *Manassas*, a well-documented work that brought him public attention as well as royalties that enabled him to buy the land and its farmhouse for his family.

Sinclair decided to base his next novel on the conditions of work and of sanitation in the meat-processing industry. With a $500 advance from a socialist weekly, *Appeal to Reason*, Sinclair spent two months researching in the Chicago stockyards and wrote his most celebrated work, *The Jungle* (1906). While

Library of Congress

Sinclair hoped his exposure of corruption and dreadful living conditions would create public sympathy for the stockyard workers and win them to socialism, his graphic account of filthy handling, spoiled meat, and generally unsanitary conditions attracted more attention and brought a public outcry and government reform of food inspection laws.

With his earnings from *The Jungle*, Sinclair started a cooperative living venture, Helicon Hall, in Englewood, New Jersey, which attracted the interest of WILLIAM JAMES and JOHN DEWEY. When it burned down the next year, Sinclair lost his life savings. With *The Jungle*, however, he had become a muckraker (see RAY STANNARD BAKER, LINCOLN STEFFENS, and IDA TARBELL), and he went on to publish other works of that kind, including *The Fasting Cure* (1911), about dietary fads; *King Coal* (1917), on working and living conditions of Colorado miners; *The Brass Check* (1919), on dishonest journalism; *Oil!* (1927), considered Sinclair's best work as literature, inspired by scandal arising from corrupt handling of the government's Teapot Dome oil reserves; *Boston* (1928), a two-volume novel about the trial and execution of the anarchists Nicola Sacco and Bartolemeo Vanzetti, an episode that provoked extensive controversy; and *The Flivver King* (1937), a hard-boiled critique of Henry Ford.

Having moved to Pasadena, California, in 1915, Sinclair had run unsuccessfully on the Socialist party ticket for the House of Representatives in 1920, the Senate in 1922, and the governorship in 1926 and 1930. In 1934 he had switched to the Democratic party and run for governor as the leader of the "End Poverty in California" (EPIC) movement. Coming at the height of the Great Depression, the EPIC platform, which included planks calling for such socialist remedies as government ownership of industry, attracted an immense following. Sinclair's victory had appeared certain, but he was attacked bitterly by the big industrial interests, including the film companies and the influential newspapers, and he lost to the Republican candidate, 879,000 to 1,138,000. The strength of Sinclair's Democratic support encouraged President Franklin D. Roosevelt to swing leftward with his New Deal policies.

The last quarter century of Sinclair's career was devoted to a celebrated literary accomplishment: the Lanny Budd series, comprising eleven historical novels that presented a panorama of the great events in world history from the beginning of World War I to the end of World War II. The hero, Lanny Budd, is an American journalist of socialist leanings who ends up working directly for President Franklin D. Roosevelt. The third volume in the series, *Dragon's Teeth* (1942), won a Pulitzer Prize.

While Sinclair maintained a steadfast faith in socialism, he had a lifelong interest in psychic phenomena and religion, and in the 1950s he carried on a lengthy correspondence with the Swiss psychologist C. G. Jung, mainly about religious and social questions. Sinclair was opposed to communism and alcohol, favored a vegetarian diet, and was considered a puritan in matters of morality. He published his autobiography in 1962, bringing to some ninety the total of his books, which, translated into over fifty languages, have had even more readers abroad than at home.

When Sinclair died at the age of ninety in a New Jersey nursing home, the *New York Times* observed that his works "will be around as literary and political history long after many of today's popular authors are forgotten."

**BIBLIOGRAPHY**

Gottesman, Ronald, *Upton Sinclair: An Annotated Checklist*, 1973; Harris, Leon, *Upton Sinclair: American Rebel*, 1975; Yoder, John A., *Upton Sinclair*, 1975.

# Skinner, Burrhus Frederic

(March 20, 1904–August 18, 1990)
Behaviorist Psychologist

B F. Skinner studied human and animal behavior in ingenious experiments that profoundly affected educational methods and theories. He mistrusted "the mysterious world of the mind" and rejected data that could not be directly observed.

Skinner was born in a small railroad town, Susquehanna, in the northeast corner of Pennsylvania, to William Arthur Skinner, a lawyer, and Grace Madge Burrhus. He had a younger brother who died in his youth. As a youngster he loved to experiment with kites, model airplanes, and perpetual-motion machines. After graduating from high school, he went to Hamilton College, in eastern New York State, majoring in English and minoring in languages. He wrote poetry and stories and one summer went to the Bread Loaf School of English, at Middlebury, Vermont, where he met Robert Frost and heard encouraging words from him. He earned his A.B. in 1926.

Skinner spent a year at his parents' home in Scranton, Pennsylvania, writing stories without commercial success. He decided he lacked a genuine literary gift and that what really interested him was human behavior. Having discovered the psychologist John B. Watson's work on behaviorism, Skinner began graduate work in psychology at Harvard. He was awarded his Ph.D. in 1931. He stayed on for five years at Harvard as a research fellow in experimental psychology and then in 1936 went to the University of Minnesota to teach psychology. Becoming an associate professor, he remained at Minnesota until 1945, when he was appointed chairman of the psychology department at Indiana University, in Bloomington. He returned to Harvard in 1947 as the William James Lecturer and the next year became a full professor. Skinner retired in 1974, but as a professor emeritus continued his laboratory work, lecturing, and prolific writing.

Behaviorism accounts for the behavior of animals and human beings by observing physical responses to stimuli from outside the organism. Skinner rejected what he could not literally observe, such as feelings, moods, thought, and the unconscious, and based his work on the patterns of responses. He believed that people could achieve self-understanding only through systematically modifying their behavior by following his principles. An important one of these was operant behavior, by which he meant that any behavior—such as a pigeon's pressing a lever to get food or a composer's creation of a symphony—is selected and strengthened by the expectation of positive results such as food or praise. New behavior that occurs accidentally through the individual's distinctive experience and genetic background can become a fixed behavior pattern through what Skinner called positive reinforcement, that is, reward of some kind. He identified both positive and negative reinforcements, the latter being what adversely affected desirable behavior. While punishment was a negative reinforcer, Skinner considered that it only induced avoidance or attempted escape and was ineffective in teaching children or dealing with public offenders. He used successive approximation in his work with learning-disabled persons: the desired behavior is broken down into its components and each learning step is reinforced until the task is mastered.

Skinner demonstrated successive approximation in 1937 when, after noting an experiment in which a chimpanzee "earned" poker chips which could be traded for food, he believed that similar behavior was possible for a less advanced animal—in this case, a rat. The laboratory rat (whom he named Pliny), in a so-called Skinner box, learned to pull a chain that released a glass marble from a rack. Pliny then carried the marble across the Skinner box and dropped it into a tube in order to be fed. Skinner constructed this pattern step by step, through successive approximation. He applied his techniques to human education by showing that illiterate and even retarded persons could learn to read with programmed instruction on teaching machines that reinforced the correct responses by praise.

As experimental subjects Skinner preferred pigeons to rats, because they lived much longer. During World War II, he designed a homing device for the guided missile by putting pigeons in the nose cone and conditioning them to peck at an image of the target and thus, through electrical impulses, steer the missile as it descended. The government's Office of Scientific Research and Development awarded a contract for promoting Skinner's idea, and it was tested but never put into practice.

While at Indiana, Skinner returned to writing fiction with a controversial novel, *Walden Two* (1948), about a utopian community founded on behaviorist principles, in which jealousy, unhappiness, and class struggle were replaced by rewarding work and ample opportunity for creative activity. Over many years the novel sold a million copies and was widely translated, and a few "Walden Two" communes were attempted.

Later Skinner devised an "air crib" for the younger of his two daughters. This was an air-conditioned soundproof box with suspended objects for "tactile and visual stimulation" and a sliding safety-glass window. A growing infant could play or sleep in it without clothing or blankets. Plans to put this baby-tender on the market did not materialize.

Skinner proposed using operant conditioning as a utopian social instrument, since, he said, all people are controllable and the kind of behavior that is socially beneficial for everyone could be reinforced. He hoped that the broad application of the principles of behaviorism could end social conflict and war. Authoritarian political systems can apply behavior modification, Skinner observed to the dismay of some critics, "and the challenge to democratic society is to develop it first."

**BIBLIOGRAPHY**

Nye, Robert D., *Three Psychologies: Freud, Skinner, and Rogers*, 1986; Skinner, B. F., *Beyond Freedom and Dignity*, 1971, *About Behaviorism*, 1974, and *Consensus and Controversy*, 1987.

# Smith, Gerald Lyman Kenneth

(February 27, 1898–April 15, 1976)
Activist, Fundamentalist Clergyman

Gerald L. K. Smith began his career as a liberal-minded minister of the Christian Church but turned into an advocate for several varieties of bigotry from the days of the Great Depression to the 1950s.

Smith was born in Pardeeville, a village north of Madison, Wisconsin. His father, Lyman Z. Smith, a traveling salesman of patent medicines, preached in the local Christian Church. When Gerald was two, his father was incapacitated by a disease, possibly pernicious anemia. The family moved to a farm in southwest Wisconsin, where Gerald helped with the chores and went to a one-room schoolhouse. The home atmosphere was strictly pious, and the boy, who was often with his invalid father, resolved to become a minister. After high school, he worked his way through Valparaiso University, in northern Indiana, and in 1917 earned a bachelor of oratory degree.

Smith served as minister to churches in several Wisconsin towns until called to a large church in Indianapolis in 1922, where his revivals drew many members and he became prominent in Indiana religious work. He tended toward liberal positions—he exposed bad working conditions in industrial plants, supported union organizing by the American Federation of Labor (see WILLIAM GREEN and JOHN L. LEWIS), and spoke against the Ku Klux Klan, a force in Indiana.

In 1928 Smith moved to Shreveport, Louisiana, to take the pulpit at a prestigious church whose congregation included many affluent people. In spite of them, he continued his liberal activities—preaching for social justice and once exchanging pulpits with a local rabbi. When he learned that Shreveport bankers might foreclose on numerous mortgages, he asked the governor of Louisiana, Huey P. Long, for help, and Long halted the move. Smith became a staunch partisan of Long, who made himself virtually the dictator of the state. In 1934 Smith gave up his pastorate and put his oratorical talent at work for Long, embracing his fierce hatred of President Franklin D. Roosevelt. He spoke around Louisiana to spread Long's message of "Every Man a King" and recruit for his "Share Our Wealth" clubs, which claimed some 5 million members.

Long was assassinated on September 8, 1935, and Smith preached at an open-air funeral in Baton Rouge attended by 150,000 people. His hope of becoming Long's successor was defeated by other Long loyalists, who made peace with the Roosevelt administration. Smith then took up the Old Age Revolving Pension Plan (OARP) organization, led by FRANCIS E. TOWNSEND. In 1936, with Townsend and CHARLES COUGHLIN, he campaigned for William F. Lemke as presidential candidate of the Union party, on a vehemently anti–New Deal platform.

When the *March of Time* (see HENRY R. LUCE) produced a newsreel about him entitled "The 'Lunatic Fringe,'" depicting his anti-

Semitic diatribes and his saluting audiences, Smith began to be seen as a fascist who attacked Jews, blacks, Catholics, millionaires, New Dealers, and communists. In 1937 he founded the Committee of One Million, a nationalist organization supported by big businessmen. His radio broadcasts from his new base in Detroit, Michigan, fulminating against the unions and winning the admiration of HENRY FORD, were a feature of the late 1930s. By 1941 isolationism was Smith's principal concern. But after December, when the United States entered World War II, he fixed on patriotism and victory rallies. He started a monthly magazine, *The Cross and the Flag*, to promote a white, Christian America, and he claimed the title America First for his own party, which ran him for president in 1944.

Smith's last enterprise was the Christian Nationalist Crusade, founded in 1947 in Los Angeles. It called for deporting Zionists, shipping African Americans to Africa, dissolving the United Nations, and restoring the right of Christian prayer in public buildings. In 1952 Smith stated that the Republican candidate for the presidency, Dwight D. Eisenhower, was a Swedish Jew and unqualified for the office. At the time of his death, Smith still claimed hundreds of thousands of followers.

**BIBLIOGRAPHY**

Jeansonne, Glen, *Gerald L. K. Smith: Minister of Hate*, 1988; Ribuffo, Leo P., *The Old Christian Right: The Protestant Far Right from the Great Depression to the Cold War*, 1983.

# Smith, Gerrit

(March 6, 1797–December 28, 1874)
Philanthropist, Reformer

Philanthropist and reformer Gerrit Smith was involved in a remarkable variety of nineteenth-century reform movements, including temperance, dress reform, woman suffrage, and vegetarianism, but he made his greatest contribution as an abolitionist.

Born in Utica, New York, Gerrit Smith in 1806 moved with his family to Peterboro, New York, an area which became a center of reform activity. Graduating from Hamilton College in 1818, Smith helped his father manage a $400,000 family fortune, which the younger Smith eventually controlled. After increasing the family wealth through shrewd investments, Smith devoted much of his time and money to good works.

Smith's involvement in philanthropy and reform began in the 1820s when he supported the Sunday School movement and the United Domestic Missionary Society. He helped to build churches and donated generous sums to both theological schools and colleges. He advocated temperance and a vegetarian diet, and along with meat gave up spices, tea, and tobacco. Among the other causes which attracted him during these years and the decade that followed was dress reform. Smith's daughter, Elizabeth Smith Miller, was the originator of the Bloomer costume popularized by AMELIA BLOOMER. Smith supported woman suffrage and, for a time, the colonization of African Americans. He was also concerned with prison reform and sought to have capital punishment abolished. Taking up the cause of oppressed peoples abroad as well as within the United States, Smith protested the harsh treatment of Irish, Italian, and Greek nationalists in their respective countries.

Although initially supporting the colonization of blacks, Smith took an abolitionist position in the 1830s and soon became a leading figure in the movement. He helped convert his cousin, the women's rights leader ELIZABETH CADY STANTON, to this cause and also to temperance. Smith served as vice president of the American Anti-Slavery Society and in 1836 assumed the presidency of the New York Anti-Slavery Society.

In the 1840s Smith tried to advance abolition through political action. He made an unsuccessful bid for the governorship of New York on the Liberty party ticket in 1840. In 1848 the Liberty party nominated Smith for the presidency, but he declined to run. Meanwhile, Smith had joined the growing free-soil movement, which was supported by discontented Democrats and Whigs who feared that new U.S. territories might become slave states. In 1848 this antislavery coalition formed the Free-Soil party. Smith was instrumental in founding the party, which adopted his slogan "Free Men, Free Soil, and Free Trade."

Becoming increasingly militant in the 1850s, Smith joined in promoting resistance to the Fugitive Slave Act. He helped runaway slaves escape to Canada and took part in the much-publicized rescue of a slave named Jerry in Syracuse in 1851. A year later, Smith was elected to Congress on an independent ticket, where he served a term until resigning and, having been recently admitted to the bar, opened a law practice in Peterboro.

When the Kansas-Nebraska Act of 1854 brought a rush of both proslavery and antislavery settlers into these territories, Smith backed the antislavery faction. He gave Eli Thayer's New England Emigrant Aid Company more than $14,000 to help eastern abolitionists settle in the West. He also urged the use of force against proslavery settlers and forcible resistance to the federal authorities in Kansas, because he felt they supported the proslavery element. From 1856 to 1858, Smith aided the radical abolitionist JOHN BROWN, perhaps giving Brown money for his 1859 raid on Harpers Ferry, Virginia. When documents implicating Smith and five other northern abolitionists in the raid were later discovered in a Maryland farmhouse, Smith suffered a breakdown and spent several weeks in an insane asylum in Utica, New York.

In 1858 Smith made another unsuccessful bid for the governorship of New York. His platform included abolition, temperance, and land reform. During the Civil War Smith became a Republican, writing and speaking on behalf of the Union cause and campaigning for Lincoln's reelection in 1864. After the war, Smith's growing conservatism led him to favor a policy of moderation toward the South, while advocating black suffrage. Smith died in New York City at the age of seventy-seven.

**BIBLIOGRAPHY**

Frothingham, O. B., *Gerrit Smith*, 1878, rep., 1969; Hammond, C. A., *Gerrit Smith*, 1900; Harlow, R. V., *Gerrit Smith, Philanthropist and Reformer*, 1939; Porter, K. W., *John Jacob Astor*, 2 vols., 1931.

# Smith, John

(ca. 1579 or 1580–June 21, 1631)
Colonial Leader

The English soldier and adventurer Captain John Smith not only helped to found the Virginia colony but also, through his bold and vigorous leadership, played a crucial role in its survival.

Born the son of a farmer in Willoughby, England, Smith left home at an early age to seek adventure as a soldier on the Continent. While serving with the Eastern European forces which were fighting the Turks, he was captured and sold into slavery. After a dramatic escape and further adventures abroad, Smith returned to England. There, by his own account, he helped organize the Virginia Company of London for the purpose of starting a colony in Virginia. In December 1606, Smith was one of the 144 colonists who sailed for America in three ships.

Landing in Virginia in May 1607, the colonists founded a settlement at Jamestown, 40 miles up the James River. From the start, Jamestown was wracked by disease and internal dissension. Unlike Smith, who at the age of twenty-seven was already a tough and experienced captain, most of the settlers were ill-prepared for the serious business of establishing a colony. They had come expecting to make their fortunes through the discovery of gold and silver and were unwilling to work to feed and defend themselves. As a later settler observed, the colonists "would rather starve in idleness . . . than feast in labor."

Smith quickly emerged as a natural leader by virtue of his energy and resourcefulness. He traded with the Algonkian Indians for corn to feed the starving settlers and went on several voyages to explore the Potomac and Rappahannock rivers and the Chesapeake Bay. On one expedition, undertaken in December 1607, Smith and seven companions were ambushed by Algonkians, and Smith was taken prisoner and brought before their chief, Powhatan. According to Smith, he was saved from death through the intervention of Powhatan's eleven-year-old daughter, Pocahontas.

In this and subsequent dealings with the American Indians, Smith showed himself a shrewd strategist. He drove a hard bargain and generally got what he wanted through bluff and a show of force, but very little bloodshed.

Upon his return to Jamestown in January 1608, Smith found that rival leaders had assumed control. Held responsible for the deaths of two of his men, he was arrested, tried, and sentenced to hang. Only the timely arrival of a supply-laden English ship, with a high official on board (who restored Smith as a leader of the colony), saved Smith from the gallows.

The following fall, Smith managed to defeat his rivals and get himself elected president of Jamestown's governing council. He soon put the colony under what amounted to martial law. Declaring that the settlers "must be more industrious or starve," Smith made them farm and work at other constructive tasks, including strengthening the settlement's defenses against Indian attack.

Smith's term as president lasted just a year. In September 1609, Smith returned to England. That winter, the colony was nearly wiped out by starvation and Indian attacks.

In 1614 Smith again sailed for America, this time to explore the area around Cape Cod, which he named "New England." He returned with a valuable cargo of fish and furs, along with accurate maps of the region. Smith's second and last voyage to America ended when he was captured by pirates. Escaping and making his way back to England, he devoted himself to writing accounts of his travels. His most important book was *The Generall Historie of Virginia, New-England, and the Summer Isles* (1624). In it, Smith emphasized the importance of products like fish, furs, and timber; criticized the fruitless quest for gold and silver; and urged that future colonists be willing to work hard. His information and maps were most helpful to later colonists.

A colorful, near-legendary figure, Smith has inevitably been the subject of much controversy. Although in the past, historians discounted Smith's overblown accounts of his exploits, modern research has largely substantiated his claims to fame.

**BIBLIOGRAPHY**

Fox, Joseph L., *Captain John Smith*, 1985; Gerson, Noel B., *Glorious Scoundrel: A Biography of Captain John Smith*, 1978; Hartzog, Henry S., *John Smith and Pocahontas*, 1979.

# Smith, Joseph

(December 23, 1805–June 27, 1844)
Religious Leader

Joseph Smith founded the Church of Jesus Christ of Latter-Day Saints (the Mormon church), an indigenous American church which today is one of the fastest-growing denominations, with a world membership of 7 million.

Born in Sharon, Vermont, Joseph Smith moved with his family to Palmyra, in western New York, in 1816. At the time this part of the state was known as "the burnt-over district" because it had undergone successive waves of religious enthusiasm and was filled with many competing religious sects. A sensitive boy with little formal schooling, Smith was deeply troubled by the existence of so many sects, each claiming to be the true faith. In 1820 and again in 1823 Smith experienced "visions," in which an angelic figure appeared to him and told him not to join any of the sects, because none of them represented God's will. According to Smith, the angel said that the true church had been withdrawn from the world and that it was Smith's mission to bring it back. The angel also instructed him where to find a book written on gold plates that contained the history of this true church.

In 1827 Smith uncovered the plates from a stone box under a large rock at a hill called Cumorah near Manchester, New York. He then set to work translating them from the language (known as reformed Egyptian) in which they were written, with the help of two magic stones called Urim and Thummim. Smith published this work as *The Book of Mormon* in 1830. The book, together with two of Smith's later revelations contained in *Doctrine and*

Library of Congress

*Covenants* (1835) and the *Pearl of Great Price* (1851), formed the basis of the Mormon faith.

*The Book of Mormon* tells how the Hebrews came from Israel to the Americas in ancient times. Although their communities were destroyed by warfare long ago and few survived, their descendants lived on as the American Indians. A latter-day prophet, Smith was to restore the ancient, primitive Christianity of the Hebrews in America. On April 6, 1830, at Fayette, New York, Smith formally founded the Church of Jesus Christ of Latter-Day Saints. Initially the church membership consisted mostly of Smith's relatives and friends, but after the arrival in November of that year of Sidney Rigdon, a brilliant leader, it grew quickly and developed into a cooperative society ruled by Smith with a firm hand. A handsome, vigorous man with a forceful personality, Smith convinced his followers that his God-given powers were great. He maintained that God had chosen him to save a doomed world. Smith alone would decide who should be admitted to heaven, pictured by him as a place of earthly delights.

In 1831 Smith moved his community to Kirtland, Ohio, and then, after his involvement in a bank fraud made him a fugitive from the law, to Jackson County, Missouri, in 1838. Friction between the Mormons and their neighbors forced another move a year later, this time into Illinois to a community which Smith renamed Nauvoo. The Mormons thrived and their numbers grew, increased by many converts from Europe as well as the United States who were drawn by Mormonism's offer of certainty in troubled times. Allowed a free rein by the Illinois government, Smith served as mayor of Nauvoo and exercised virtual one-man rule. He emerged as a prominent, though controversial, figure, who enjoyed his power and the trappings that went with it. He especially liked to dress in fancy uniforms and describe himself as commander of the Mormon militia, called the Nauvoo Legion, which, in Smith's eyes, made him the highest-ranking military officer in the United States. In February 1844 Smith's dreams of glory reached a climax when he announced he was running for president of the United States; this candidacy was cut short by his death that summer.

The Mormons had continued to be unpopular with their neighbors, and a rift had developed among church members themselves when Smith added polygamy to the tenets of Mormonism. Although the only wife Smith acknowledged publicly was his first one, Emma Hale, whom he had married in 1827, he is said to have taken at least twenty-seven, and possibly many more, wives. On June 7, 1844, the troubles came to a boil. Smith's critics published a strong attack on him in the *Nauvoo Expositor*. Smith struck back by having the press destroyed and its editor expelled. Civil authorities then threw Smith and his brother Hyrum into jail in Carthage, Illinois. On June 27 a mob of non-Mormons broke into the jail and shot both Smith and his brother.

Most of Smith's followers moved with BRIGHAM YOUNG to Utah a few years later. Those who remained formed the Reorganized Church of Jesus Christ of Latter-Day Saints, which did not practice polygamy.

**BIBLIOGRAPHY**

Brodie, Fawn, *No Man Knows My Name: The Life of Joseph Smith, the Mormon Prophet*, 1971; Bushman, Richard L., *Joseph Smith and the Beginnings of Mormonism*, 1984; Gottlieb, Robert, and Peter Wiley, *America's Saints: The Rise of Mormon Power*, 1986; Muldar, William, and A. R. Mortensen, *The Mormons in American History*, 1981.

# Spingarn, Joel Elias

(May 17, 1875–July 26, 1939)
Civil Rights Leader, Editor, Scholar

J E. Spingarn played a central part in the formation of the National Association for the Advancement of Colored People (NAACP) and established the Spingarn Medal, awarded annually to the person of African descent who has made the highest achievement in any honorable field during the previous year.

Spingarn was born in New York City, the eldest of four sons born to Elias Spingarn, a successful tobacco merchant of Austrian origin, and Sarah Barnett, from England. J. E. Spingarn was educated in New York public schools and at Columbia College, where he earned an A.B. in 1895 and a Ph.D. in 1899. His dissertation, published as *The History of Literary Criticism in the Renaissance*, made his scholarly reputation. Spingarn's mentor at Columbia, George E. Woodberry, who introduced him to the humanism that marked his life, appointed him to the department of comparative literature. In 1910 Spingarn succeeded Woodberry as department head, but in the following year he disagreed with NICHOLAS MURRAY BUTLER, president of Columbia, about departmental structure and authority and was dismissed from the faculty by Butler.

Spingarn, who had a private income, was little troubled by the loss of his academic post. He continued his career as an independent scholar, publishing poetry and works of criticism, and occasionally teaching at the New School for Social Research (see CHARLES BEARD). His interests were notably broad: he has inevitably been called a "Renaissance man." As a Republican he ran for Congress in a traditionally Democratic district and, though unsuccessful, made a strong showing. He was a partisan of Theodore Roosevelt and was active in the Progressive party. He took up the cause of woman suffrage, though he failed to interest Roosevelt in the movement. Having bought a country estate called Troutbeck, near Amenia, in upstate New York, he acquired the Amenia *Times* and published it for a dozen years as a reformist paper. In 1919 he was one of the founders of the publishing firm of Harcourt, Brace and Company, and he was an active editor for several years. In addition, his work at Troutbeck as a horticulturist brought him world fame.

Spingarn's background did not foreshadow his dedication to African American rights, though it is likely that Woodberry's humanistic influence at Columbia was a telling factor. The rise of anti-Negro sentiment in the 1900s surely evoked Spingarn's sympathy for its victims. The NAACP was formed in 1909 by a group of seven white Americans and one black, W. E. B. Du Bois. Its defense of an African American threatened with extradition to Arkansas for a murder committed in self-defense impelled Spingarn to contribute funds, and OSWALD GARRISON VILLARD invited him to become a member of the association. Before he left Columbia, Spingarn had become deeply involved in its work. His younger brother Arthur, a lawyer, soon joined him. In 1913 J. E. Spingarn became chairman of the NAACP board and established the Spingarn Medal. During World War I, in which he was commissioned a major in the U.S. Army, Spingarn worked to establish a training camp where some thousand African American officers were commissioned. He became treasurer of the NAACP in 1919, and from 1930 until his death he served as its president. His brother Arthur succeeded him.

Spingarn died of a cerebral thrombosis at his New York City home. A few weeks earlier, he had seen the Spingarn Medal awarded to the singer Marian Anderson in a presentation at Richmond, Virginia, by Eleanor Roosevelt.

**BIBLIOGRAPHY**

Ross, B. Joyce, *J. E. Spingarn and the Rise of the NAACP, 1911–1939*, 1972; Van Deusen, M., *J. E. Spingarn*, 1971.

# Spock, Benjamin McLane

(May 2, 1903–    )
Author, Pediatrician, Political Activist

Pediatrician Benjamin Spock became a household name and influenced two generations of parents who reared the children of the baby boom with his best-selling manual, *Baby and Child Care*. In the 1960s Spock also became prominent in the peace movement.

Spock was born in New Haven, Connecticut, and attended the Phillips Academy in Andover, Massachusetts. Graduating from Yale in 1925, he studied at the Yale Medical School and at the Columbia College of Physicians and Surgeons. After receiving his M.D. in 1929 he interned at Presbyterian Hospital in New York and completed residencies in pediatrics at the New York Nursery and Child's Hospital (1931–1932) and in psychiatry, the principles of which he was eager to apply to pediatrics, at the New York Hospital (1932–1933). Spock also trained for six years at the New York Psychoanalytic Institute. From 1933 to 1943 he had a private practice in pediatrics in New York City.

Also during these years, he taught pediatrics at the Cornell University Medical College, was on the pediatric staff of New York Hospital, and served as a pediatric consultant to the New York City department of Health and the Institute on Personality Development.

Spock completed *Baby and Child Care* during the two years he served as a psychiatrist in the navy (1944–1946). The book (originally published as *The Common Sense Book of Baby and Child Care*) appeared in 1946 at the beginning of the postwar baby boom. In contrast to the traditional manuals with their rigid rules, Spock sought to reassure new parents with the words: "You know more than you think you do." He emphasized flexibility in dealing with differences between individual infants and children and told parents not to worry constantly about spoiling their children. This was welcome advice to the millions of middle-class women who had left college and jobs to devote themselves full-time to marriage and motherhood. (By 1990, *Baby and Child Care* had sold over 28 million copies.)

In 1947 Spock moved to Minnesota, where he taught psychiatry at the University of Minnesota and was a psychiatric consultant to the Mayo Clinic. In 1951 he became professor of child development at the University of Pittsburgh, holding the same position at Western Reserve University from 1955 until his retirement in 1967. Also during these years, Spock contributed a regular column on child rearing to the *Ladies' Home Journal.* His articles

were later collected and published as *Dr. Spock Talks with Mothers* (1961) and *Problems of Parents* (1962).

Spock's career as a political activist began in 1962. Dismayed by President John F. Kennedy's announcement of the resumption of nuclear testing in the atmosphere, he took out a full page ad in the *New York Times* in support of the National Committee for a Sane Nuclear Policy (SANE). From 1963 to 1967 Spock served as cochairman of SANE. During this period, Spock grew increasingly concerned with the escalation of the war in Vietnam. From an embarrassed and self-conscious demonstrator he developed into a militant peace activist. As Spock later explained: "What is the use of physicians like myself trying to help parents to bring up children, healthy and happy, to have been killed in such numbers for a cause that is ignoble?" Resigning from his position at SANE, he became in 1967 cochairman of the National Conference for a New Politics, a loose coalition of New Left groups. Spock also took part in the draft-resistance movement, and his activities in this connection led to his indictment in 1968, along with four others, for conspiracy to violate selective service laws. Found guilty, he was fined $5,000 and sentenced to two years in prison. A year later, however, the U.S. Court of Appeals reversed his conviction. The experience led Spock to write *Decent and Indecent* (1970), a book expressing his concern about the direction in which the country seemed headed.

A hero to the young and the radical, Spock was nominated as the presidential candidate of the People's party in 1972. Many conservatives, on the other hand, blamed Spock for the youth revolt of the sixties, which they felt was the result of the permissive attitude in child rearing that Spock encouraged. Spock also came under fire from feminists for making women feel obligated to be full-time mothers. They charged that the child-centeredness promoted by Spock's books was unhealthy because it produced mothers consumed by guilt and spoiled children.

Responding to feminist criticisms, Spock revised his book in the 1970s to include the role of fathers, sitters, and day care centers. Nevertheless, he continued to stress that child rearing is "exciting and creative work." Since his retirement from medical practice, he has also continued to write about and speak out on political issues.

**BIBLIOGRAPHY**

Bloom, Lynn Z., *Dr. Spock: Biography of a Conservative Radical*, 1972; Michalek, Irene, *When Mercy Seasons Justice: The Spock Trial*, 1972; Mitford, Jessica, *The Trial of Dr. Spock*, 1969; Spock, Benjamin, *Spock on Spock: A Memoir of Growing Up with the Century*, 1989.

# Stanford, Leland

(March 9, 1824–June 21, 1893)
Industrialist, Philanthropist

Leland Stanford used his business abilities and his political influence to create an industrial empire in railroading. With his associates, he was instrumental in the completion of the first transcontinental railroad. He used a large part of the millions made through his railroad ventures to found and endow Stanford University.

Stanford was born in Watervliet, New York, and attended the Clinton Liberal Institute and the Cazenovia Seminary in New York. At age twenty-one, he entered the law office of Wheaton, Doolittle, and Hadley in Albany, New York, and was admitted to the bar three years later. In 1848 Stanford established a law practice in Port Washington, Wisconsin, but after a fire destroyed his office and law library in 1852, he moved to California. There he joined his younger brothers in the highly profitable business of selling supplies to miners in El Dorado County and later Sacramento. Becoming involved in state politics as a Republican, Stanford made an unsuccessful bid for governor in 1859. He ran again in 1861 and was elected due to a split in the Democratic party. As governor until 1863, he kept California in the Union during the Civil War.

Having meanwhile become interested in the construction of a transcontinental railroad, Stanford joined with three other Sacramento merchants, Mark Hopkins, Charles Crocker, and Collis P. Huntington, in organizing the Central Pacific Railroad in 1861. During his term of office as governor, he approved several public grants for the construction of the Central Pacific over the Sierra Nevada at Truckee, California; once out of office, he devoted all of his energies to the railroad. He served as president of the Central Pacific from the beginning until his death and handled the railroad's financial and political interests. As the western half of the transcontinental railroad (the Union Pacific was the eastern half), the Central Pacific received generous subsidies from the federal government, so that only a small outlay of capital was required of Stanford and his associates. They relied on borrowed money as well.

In 1863 the Central Pacific began building tracks eastward from Sacramento, California, while the Union Pacific pushed westward from Omaha, Nebraska. The Central Pacific used Chinese immigrant workers to keep costs down, and it drove its crews relentlessly through two hard winters of work in the high Sierra in order to reach the flat land beyond before the Union Pacific. Finally, on May 10, 1869, the two lines met at Promontory Point, Utah. Stanford and his associates profited enormously from the construction.

After its completion, Stanford and his associates became involved in other rail and water interests in California. Incorporated in 1870, their Southern Pacific Railroad acquired and built lines north and south from San Francisco and eventually completed a second transcontinental railroad from California to New Orleans. The "Big Four," as Stanford and his associates became known, established a virtual monopoly over transportation within the state. Their holdings were reorganized under a new Southern Pacific charter granted by the state of Kentucky, with Stanford continuing to serve as president until 1890. Although the Southern Pacific came under frequent attack as a monopolistic "octopus," Stanford remained personally popular in California.

From 1870 on, Stanford began devoting less time to railroad building and more to his extensive vineyards in the Sacramento Valley and his ranch at Palo Alto, California, where he bred and ran trotting horses and made studies of animal locomotion. He was also much concerned with the education of his son, Leland Stanford, Jr. The boy's death at the age of fifteen led Stanford in 1885 to found and finance as a memorial to his son the Leland Stanford Junior University, which opened in 1891 and grew into one of the leading universities in the country.

Also in 1885, Stanford was elected to the U.S. Senate, which caused a break between him and his railroad associate, Collis P. Huntington. In 1890 Huntington managed to replace him as president of the Southern Pacific. As senator, Stanford opposed the Interstate Commerce Act of 1887, because of its attempt to regulate business, and supported the exclusion of Chinese laborers in 1888. He served in the Senate until his death in Palo Alto at the age of sixty-nine.

**BIBLIOGRAPHY**

Bancroft, Hubert Howe, *History of the Life of Leland Stanford: A Character Study,* 1952; Tutorow, Norman E., *Leland Stanford: Man of Many Careers,* 1971.

# Stanton, Elizabeth Cady

(November 12, 1815–October 26, 1902)
Reformer, Suffragist

As one of the more radical of the nineteenth-century suffragists and women's rights leaders, Elizabeth Cady Stanton sought above all else to free women from the legal obstacles that prevented them from achieving equality with men.

Elizabeth Cady was born in Johnstown, New York, the daughter of a successful lawyer and judge. Her father's grief over the loss of his only son early on made her resolve to prove that she was as good as a boy by studying the classics and learning how to ride horseback. She excelled in both and longed to attend Union College in Schenectady, where her brother had studied. She was sent instead to EMMA WILLARD's all-female seminary in Troy, New York, where she was a student for three years (1830–1832), though she disapproved of single-sex education.

As a young adult, Elizabeth Cady was exposed to the world of reform through visits to the home of her cousin, abolitionist GERRIT SMITH, at Peterboro, New York. Here she met and was strongly attracted to Henry B. Stanton, an abolitionist orator ten years her senior. Over her father's objections, they were married in May 1840 in a ceremony from which the promise to obey was omitted. On their honeymoon the couple attended the World Anti-Slavery Convention in London. At the convention Elizabeth Cady Stanton met the Quaker abolitionist and woman's rights advocate LUCRETIA MOTT, sharing her anger that women delegates were not allowed to speak and vote at the convention. The two women decided to hold a women's rights convention as soon as they returned home and to form a women's rights organization.

Library of Congress

Eight years passed before Stanton and Mott were able to act on their plan. In the meantime, Stanton gave birth to three children (four more were to follow) and with her husband moved to Seneca Falls, New York, where on July 19 and 20, 1848, the first women's rights convention was finally held. Stanton drafted a Declaration of Sentiments, modeled after the Declaration of Independence and declaring that women were created equal to men. Against the advice of Mott as well as her husband, she also proposed a resolution asking for the vote. The resolution—the first in the long struggle for woman suffrage—was adopted.

Soon after the Seneca Falls convention, Stanton began writing articles on women's rights for AMELIA BLOOMER's temperance paper, the *Lily*, and also donned the costume of a short skirt over trousers publicized by Bloomer. Through Bloomer, Stanton met SUSAN B. ANTHONY in 1851. The two women would work together for nearly fifty years in the cause for women's rights. They complemented each other well. While Stanton excelled as a speaker and writer, Anthony was a good organizer and was more free to be an active campaigner. Nevertheless, in 1860 Stanton found the time from her busy family life to become the first woman to address a joint session of the New York State legislature in behalf of a stronger married women's property bill, which then passed. That

same year, she rocked the national women's rights convention with her proposals for liberalized divorce laws.

The Civil War turned Stanton's attention to the cause for the abolition of slavery. In 1863 she and Anthony organized the Women's Loyal National League to launch a massive petition campaign for abolition by constitutional amendment. After the war, however, Stanton's feminism led her to oppose both the Fourteenth and Fifteenth amendments, because they extended civil rights and the franchise to black males but excluded women. In 1866 Stanton unsuccessfully ran for Congress from New York State and the following year ran an equally unsuccessful campaign to win woman suffrage in Kansas.

In 1868 Stanton and Anthony started in New York City a women's rights weekly, the *Revolution*, to which Stanton contributed vigorous editorials in support of the vote, greater opportunity for working, and the right to serve on juries. In 1869 she and Anthony founded the National Woman Suffrage Association to work for the passage of a federal woman suffrage amendment. For the next twenty years Stanton served as president of this organization. (A rival organization, the American Woman Suffrage Association, was formed later that year by more conservative suffragists led by LUCY STONE.)

In 1869 Stanton began lecturing on women across the country, becoming a popular and beloved speaker. During these years, she also campaigned for woman suffrage in California with Anthony (1871), regularly addressed Congressional committees on behalf of a federal suffrage amendment, and in 1888 attempted—unsuccessfully—to vote in Tenafly, New Jersey, where she and her family were then living.

On the occasion of her eightieth birthday in 1895, Stanton was honored by the declaration of "Stanton Day" in New York City and by a gathering of 6,000 at the city's Metropolitan Opera House. Yet that same year, Stanton, ever the iconoclast, provoked a storm of controversy with the publication of *The Woman's Bible,* in which she tried to correct what she considered a degrading view of women in the Scriptures. The book was bitterly attacked by clergy, the press, and many of Stanton's suffragist colleagues.

Undaunted, Stanton continued to set forth her views on religion, divorce, and woman suffrage in newspaper and magazine articles, complaining about the state of the women's rights movement and attempting to get President Theodore Roosevelt's support. She gradually lost her eyesight but stayed up to date on woman suffrage and other issues. She died in her sleep at the age of eighty-six. At her funeral Anthony said simply, "Well, it is an awful hush."

**BIBLIOGRAPHY**

Banner, Lois W., *Elizabeth Cady Stanton: A Radical for Women's Rights,* 1980; Flexner, Eleanor, *Century of Struggle: The Woman's Rights Movement in America,* 1959, rev., 1975; Griffith, Elizabeth, *In Her Own Right: The Life of Elizabeth Cady Stanton,* 1984.

## Steffens, Joseph Lincoln, Jr.

(April 6, 1866–August 9, 1936)
Journalist, Reformer

Lincoln Steffens was one of the original muckrakers, whose investigative reporting in the 1900s revealed the corruption that often underlay American urban politics and big business. He was an influential advocate of civic reform and later embraced a hard-edged socialism that strongly colored opinion, especially among youth in the 1930s.

Lincoln Steffens was the eldest child and only son of a pioneer California family. His father, Canadian-born and Illinois-bred, came overland as a wagon-train scout in 1862 and settled first in San Francisco (birthplace of his son), where he started out as bookkeeper for a paint and glass firm. His mother, Elizabeth Louise Symes, born in England, grew up in Hoboken, New Jersey, and also came to California in the 1860s. In 1870 the family moved to Sacramento, where Joseph Steffens rose to be a partner in the paint firm and then a banker. Lincoln, with three younger sisters, grew up in a mansion. A mediocre student, he was sent to a military academy for the discipline, then with some difficulty got through the University of California at Berkeley, where the study of philosophy took hold of him.

In 1889 Steffens went to Germany and studied in a series of universities. At Leipzig, two notable experiences befell him: he found Wilhelm Wundt's lectures in experimental psychology worth his time, and he fell in love with a fellow student from Troy, New York, Josephine Bontecou (ten years older than he). They married secretly in London in November 1891 and studied at the Sorbonne, in Paris, living on the young husband's allowance.

When the couple arrived in New York City in fall 1892, Steffens found a letter from his father containing $100 and advising him to "stay in New York and hustle." A job did not materialize, and they had to rely on Josephine's mother for support. Finally, through his father's connections, Steffens became a reporter for the New York *Evening Post.* Thus began his career as an investigative reporter—a "muckraker" as his friend Theodore Roosevelt called the writers of that time who aimed at exposing corruption in politics and business. Steffens and Roosevelt became acquainted in 1895, when Steffens covered an exposé of vice that climaxed in Roosevelt's appointment as head of the New York City police board. (In 1894, Steffens had come into a bequest from a student friend in Germany which, thanks to wise investing, gave him an independent income.)

Steffens's success as an investigative journalist arose from his intelligence, sympathetic manner, knack for colorful detail without sensationalism, and, above all, his careful research of facts and statistics. In the 1900s a revolution in magazine publishing was influencing American reading habits: the appearance of low-priced, lively, mass-circulation journals whose editors could recruit writers skillful in probing the realities of industry, business, politics, and the working class. In 1901 Steffens joined the staff of McClure's (see SAMUEL S. McCLURE), along with such writers as IDA TARBELL, RAY STANNARD BAKER, Theodore Dreiser, and William Sydney Porter ("O. Henry"). He published an article on corruption in the city government of St. Louis, then dealt with Minneapolis and other cities, finding variations in corruption and occasional evidences of reform. The articles formed his first book, The Shame of the Cities (1904), which contributed in critical ways to the emergence of the major reform movement known as Progressivism. In 1906 Steffens, Tarbell, and Baker left McClure's and, with WILLIAM ALLEN WHITE and others, bought the American Magazine, which became a leading organ of reform. Three years later Steffens turned to free-lance writing, chiefly for Everybody's Magazine, and published Upbuilders, in which, applying the Golden Rule, he dealt optimistically with such reform-minded figures as Judge BEN B. LINDSEY, of Denver.

By the year 1911, as public interest in muckraking waned, Steffens's reputation suffered from charges of radicalism. That year his wife died and, soon afterward, his parents. He moved to Greenwich Village and made new friends, particularly young ones. WALTER LIPPMANN, whom he had hired on Everybody's, was his secretary, and JOHN REED was a protégé. He turned up at evening gatherings at the apartment of wealthy Mabel Dodge, attended not only by artists and intellectuals but also by radicals such as MAX EASTMAN, WILLIAM D. HAYWOOD, and EMMA GOLDMAN. In 1914 Steffens was in Mexico observing its revolution; in March 1917, he was in Russia studying the effects of the European war and the first phase of the Russian revolution, just as Czar Nicholas II was forced to abdicate. Returning home, Steffens lectured in favor of a just peace. After covering the Paris Peace Conference, he was appointed to an unsuccessful mission in 1919 to explore diplomatic recognition of the Soviet Union. He interviewed V. I. Lenin, the Communist party leader, and declared, "I have seen the future; and it works." While leading an expatriate life in London he fell in love with Ella Winter, an intellectual Englishwoman some thirty years younger than he. They married in 1924 and had a son, Pete Stanley Steffens.

In 1927 Steffens returned to the United States and settled his family in Carmel, California. His principal concern was writing his memoirs, published in 1931 as The Autobiography of Lincoln Steffens, in some 800 colorful, occasionally humorous pages, which became a best-seller. Hopeful about his country's future when he first returned home in 1927, Steffens was discouraged by the effect of the Great Depression and became more and more an admirer of the Soviet Union, which to him offered the only sensible solution to the problems of power and capitalism. Steffens was bedridden after a heart attack in 1933 and died three years later.

**BIBLIOGRAPHY**

Kaplan, Justin, Lincoln Steffens: A Biography, 1974; Palermo, P. F., Lincoln Steffens, 1978; Stinson, Robert, Lincoln Steffens, 1979; Winter, Ella, And Not to Yield, An Autobiography, 1963.

# Steinem, Gloria

(March 25, 1934–   )
Editor, Feminist Activist, Writer

As a feminist activist and founding editor of *Ms.* magazine, Gloria Steinem has been a symbol of the women's liberation movement for more than twenty years.

Gloria Steinem was born in Toledo, Ohio, the granddaughter of an early feminist, Pauline Steinem, who was president of the state suffrage association and a delegate to the 1908 International Council of Women. Gloria spent her early childhood traveling

Copyright *Washington Post;* Reprinted by permission of the D.C. Public Library

around the country in a house trailer while her father tried to make a living and, after her parents' divorce, caring for her ailing mother in a poor neighborhood in Toledo. Escaping to Smith College in 1952, she was elected to Phi Beta Kappa and graduated magna cum laude with a major in government four years later. Steinem then spent two years studying at the Universities of Delhi and Calcutta in India on a Chester Bowles Asian fellowship. After her return to the United States, she worked for a year as director of the Independent Research Service in Cambridge, Massachusetts.

In 1960 Steinem moved to New York City to begin a career in journalism. Among her early articles were a piece on the sexual revolution for *Esquire* magazine and an article about her experiences posing as a Bunny at the New York Playboy Club. Steinem also wrote feature articles for such magazines as *Vogue, Glamour,* and *Cosmopolitan;* helped put together a coffee table book, *The Beach Book,* about basking in the sun; and worked as a scriptwriter for "That Was the Week That Was," a TV show of topical satire, from 1964 to 1965. Also during these years, she attained minor

celebrity as someone who supported the "right" causes and appeared in public with the "right" men. In 1968 Steinem began writing a weekly column, "The City Politic," for the recently started *New York* magazine. A political activist as well as a journalist, she accompanied CESAR CHAVEZ on his Poor People's March in California; served as treasurer for the Committee for the Legal Defense of Angela Davis, the African American radical; and supported the Democratic presidential candidacy first of Eugene McCarthy, and later of Robert F. Kennedy.

Late in 1968, Steinem became actively involved with the feminist movement after attending a meeting of a radical women's group, the Redstockings, called to protest a hearing on New York State's abortion laws. She began writing feminist articles and served as a popular spokesperson for the movement on the lecture circuit and on television talk shows. On the organizational level, Steinem joined with BETTY FRIEDAN and black Congresswoman Shirley Chisholm to found in 1971 the National Women's Political Caucus to encourage women to run for office. She also helped start the Women's Action Alliance to mobilize nonwhite and non-middle-class women and men to fight social and economic discrimination.

Additionally in 1971, Steinem began to explore the possibility of starting a new kind of women's magazine that would be informed by feminist concerns and would be owned, operated, and edited by women. The first complete issue of *Ms.* magazine appeared in 1972 and sold out its first 300,000 copies in eight days.

The issue included a full-page petition for safe and legal abortions signed by over fifty prominent women, among them Gloria Steinem. For fifteen years under Steinem's editorship, *Ms.* served as the leading popular magazine of American feminism. In 1987, however, the demands of advertisers for control over copy proved too great, and the magazine was sold. In 1990 a new *Ms.* was started without advertising and with Steinem as consulting editor.

While editing *Ms.*, Steinem, along with other feminist leaders, lobbied state legislators around the country in behalf of the Equal Rights Amendment (ERA), which passed Congress and was sent to the states for ratification in 1972. (It was finally defeated in 1982.) In 1977 she served as one of the commissioners appointed by President Jimmy Carter to the National Committee of the Observance of International Women's Year.

From the mid-1970s on, Steinem took part in the founding of such progressive political groups as Coalition of Labor Union Women, Voters for Choice, and Women Against Pornography.

In the 1980s, Steinem served as a role model for many younger feminists. In 1983 she published *Outrageous Acts and Everyday Rebellions,* a collection of her essays and articles written over the two previous decades. She followed it with *Marilyn* (1986), a biography of the late film star, Marilyn Monroe, whom Steinem viewed as a victim of many of the kinds of exploitation of women that the women's movement was seeking to end. Steinem's most recent book is *Revolution from Within: A Book of Self-Esteem* (1992).

**BIBLIOGRAPHY**

Daffron, Carolyn, *Gloria Steinem,* 1987; Henry, Sondra, *One Woman's Power: A Biography of Gloria Steinem,* 1987; Hoff, Mark, *Gloria Steinem: The Women's Movement,* 1991.

## Stephens, Uriah Smith

(August 3, 1821–February 13, 1882)
Labor Leader

An early unionist, Uriah Stephens founded the Knights of Labor in 1869, which in its day was the most powerful workers' organization in the country.

Born near Cape May, New Jersey, Uriah Stephens apprenticed as a tailor in Philadelphia from 1845 to 1853, while educating himself, especially addressing social, political, and economic issues. In 1853 he embarked on an extended trip to the West Indies, Central America, and California. After his return to Philadelphia in 1858 he urged workers to move west for better earnings and better lives. He also became active in the Republican party, because of his interest in abolition as well as westward expansion. Stephens was a strong supporter of Lincoln in 1860, though convinced that war would add to the misfortunes of working people. In 1861 he took part in a national convention of workers opposed to the war.

In 1862 Stephens began his labor-organizing activities by forming a trade association of garment cutters in Philadelphia. Travel to Europe put Stephens in touch with the International Workingmen's Association.

Although his garment cutters' group had virtually collapsed by 1869, Stephens in that year helped found the Noble and Holy Order of the Knights of Labor. Convinced that an open labor organization could not long survive, Stephens insisted upon secrecy and developed complex symbols and rituals that drew on his experiences as a member of such fraternal orders as the Masons and the Odd Fellows. He hoped to unite all workers—unskilled as well as skilled, women as well as men, blacks as well as whites—into a huge national organization that would eventually replace capitalism with a new socialist order. Under Stephens's leadership, the Knights of Labor espoused a broad program of social reform along with the traditional unionist effort for higher wages. Stephens further stressed education as one of the keys to the spread of the movement.

The Knights of Labor grew rapidly throughout the 1870s; within five years its membership had quadrupled and by 1878 it was the biggest labor organization in the country. That year, at the Knights' first national convention, Stephens was elected General Master Workman. He served only a year, however, as ill health forced him to resign. He was succeeded as Grand Master Workman by TERENCE POWDERLY, who moved the Knights away from rituals and secrecy.

Stephens died in Philadelphia in 1882. At the time of his death and for long afterward, he was hailed as a visionary leader of the labor movement.

**BIBLIOGRAPHY**

Foner, Philip, *History of the Labor Movement in the United States*, vol. 1, 1947; Ware, Norman J., *The Labor Movement in the United States, 1860–1895*, 1929.

## Still, William

(October 7, 1821–July 14, 1902)
African American Abolitionist

William Still was an African American abolitionist who aided slaves escaping to freedom on the Underground Railroad, a network of abolitionists that sheltered fugitive slaves and helped them reach freedom. Still's book *The Underground Railroad* is an invaluable contribution to the history of slavery in the United States.

William Still was born in Shamong, New Jersey, the youngest of eighteen children. Both his parents were former slaves. Still worked on his father's farm and had little formal schooling. At age twenty he left home, finally settling in Philadelphia, where he taught himself to read and write.

In 1847 Still joined the Pennsylvania Society for the Abolition of Slavery. Because of his parents' experiences, he took a special interest in the plight of runaway slaves and became involved in helping them to escape to freedom in Canada. From 1852 to 1861 Still served as the head of the Underground Railroad in Philadelphia (see HARRIET TUBMAN), raising money, meeting new arrivals in the city, and finding temporary housing for them. During the decade, more than 800 African Americans made their way safely through Philadelphia to Canada.

Following a trip to Canada in 1855, Still reported on the successful lives of former slaves in their new country. In the late 1850s, he became a friend and supporter of the abolitionist JOHN BROWN, although he did not become actively involved in Brown's plot at Harper's Ferry, Virginia.

During the Civil War, Still, who had already made money in real estate, opened his own business in coal. He had earlier become involved in a campaign to end discrimination against African Americans on Philadelphia's streetcars, and after an eight-year struggle, the state legislature passed a law ending segregation on streetcars. In 1867 Still published a *Brief Narrative of the Struggle for the Rights of the Colored People of Philadelphia in the City Railroad Cars.*

Still's best-known book, *The Underground Railroad,* was published in 1872. Based on the careful, secret records Still had kept during the decade he was involved with the railroad, the book included names, places, and escape routes and emphasized the ingenuity and bravery of the slaves. Still's book is considered the most complete account of the Underground Railroad.

After the war, Still became a member of the Freedmen's Aid Commission and the Philadelphia Board of Trade. An active member of the Presbyterian church, he organized the first YMCA (Young Men's Christian Association) for African Americans in the country and served on the boards of several charitable institutions for African Americans. He died at the age of eighty in Philadelphia.

**BIBLIOGRAPHY**

Khan, L., *One Day, Levin . . . He Be Free, William Still and the Underground Railroad,* 1972; Quarles, Benjamin, *Black Abolitionists,* 1969.

## Stone, Isidor Feinstein

(December 24, 1907–June 18, 1989)
Journalist

I F. Stone, sometimes called a latter-day Thomas Paine, made his reputation as a radical journalist of firm integrity, scholarship, and wit. His four-page *Weekly* and his articles and books helped to influence liberal-to-left American opinion for nearly fifty years.

"Izzy" Stone, as his friends called him, was born Isidor Feinstein in Philadelphia, the son of immigrants from Russia, and grew up across the Delaware River in Haddonfield, New Jersey, where his parents ran a dry-goods store. As a youngster he read widely and favored the writings of Walt Whitman (of nearby Camden), Jack London, and the anarchist Prince Peter Kropotkin. He launched his journalistic career at age fourteen with a monthly newspaper, the *Progressive,* carrying poetry, advertisements, and editorials of a progressive slant, and then was hired as a reporter for the local daily.

Having failed to be admitted to Harvard, Stone attended the University of Pennsylvania, majoring in philosophy, while working ten hours a day as a rewrite man for the Philadelphia *Inquirer.* He dropped out of college in his junior year because "the smell of a newspaper shop was more enticing." (The university gave him an A.B. degree in 1975, making him a member of the class of 1928.) While working for the *Inquirer,* Stone was a publicist for Norman Thomas's first presidential campaign, in 1928, and joined the Socialist party, which Thomas led. He later dropped out of the party, preferring to be an independent journalist.

Stone got a thorough grounding in newspaper work during five years as a reporter on the Camden *Courier-Post,* published by J. David Stern. When Stern bought the New York *Post,* Stone joined its staff as an editorial writer (and began using the name I. F. Stone). In 1937 he published his first book, *The Court Disposes,* about the U.S. Supreme Court, and the next year he took a second job as associate editor of a liberal weekly, *The Nation.* In 1939, when he found Stern's politics too conservative, he moved to Washington as *The Nation*'s Washington editor, combining that post after 1942 with a job on *PM,* the liberal daily founded by RALPH INGERSOLL.

Stone went to Palestine in 1945 to cover the struggle of Jewish underground groups toward establishing a homeland. The next year, reporting for *PM,* he followed the secret route taken by survivors of the Nazi concentration camps from eastern Europe to Palestine. His account became a book, *Underground to Palestine* (1946), which, translated into Hebrew, was used by the Israeli army for training. In 1948 Stone was in the new Jewish state of Israel to cover the Arab-Israeli War and published his account as *This Is Israel* (1948). That year, he worked for Henry A. Wallace's campaign for the presidency on the Progressive party ticket. He opposed President Truman's cold-war policy and hoped for peaceful coexistence with the USSR.

After *PM* ceased publication in 1948, Stone wrote a column for two liberal New York papers of brief duration, first the *Star* and then the *Daily Compass,* which folded in 1952. He decided to become independent and started *I. F. Stone's Weekly,* a four-page paper devoted to unearthing hidden facts (about American politics, foreign and domestic) and presenting his own left-liberal opinions. The entire staff consisted of Stone and his wife as business manager. He started with some 5,000 subscribers at $5 per year. Its subscribers included Eleanor Roosevelt, ALBERT EINSTEIN, the United Nations secretary-general U Thant, and Marilyn Monroe, who bought subscriptions for every member of Congress. By the early sixties the *Weekly* had some 30,000 subscribers; by the late sixties, more than 70,000, still at $5 a year. Many of the subscribers were writers and college professors, who spread the paper's influence even more broadly, particularly during the years of the Vietnam War and the civil rights movement.

Stone could break with strictly leftist views, to the dismay of some of his readers. He had been partial to the Soviet Union, but after a visit in 1956 he wrote that "the worker is more exploited than in Western welfare states. . . . This is not a good society, and it is not led by honest men." He visited Israel frequently and had supported that nation's fight for independence, but after the 1967 Arab-Israeli War he urged compensation for Arab refugees and the creation of an Arab Palestine federated with Israel. He defended the Warren Commission report, rejecting the conspiracy explanation of President John F. Kennedy's assassination.

In 1971 Stone ended the *Weekly* (which had become the *Bi-Weekly*) and took up the study of classical Greek, so that he could read the literature on Socrates in the original. His book *The Trial of Socrates* (1988), which was a best-seller, took issue with Plato's interpretations of the trial. He continued to write provocative articles on political subjects for *The Nation* and the *New York Review of Books*—typically, one that was critical of Mikhail Gorbachev for being a hypocrite on human rights. "Izzy" Stone died of a heart attack at eighty-one. As another journalist wrote, Stone had become "a symbol of what the First Amendment is all about."

**BIBLIOGRAPHY**

Patner, Andrew, *I. F. Stone: A Portrait,* 1988; Stone, I. F., *The Hidden History of the Korean War,* 1952, *The Truman Era,* 1953, *The Haunted Fifties,* 1963, and *The Killings at Kent State,* 1971.

# Stone, Lucy

(August 13, 1818–October 18, 1893)
Abolitionist, Feminist, Suffragist

The foremost orator of the antebellum women's rights movement, Lucy Stone also played a major role as an organizer and propagandist for woman suffrage in the latter part of the nineteenth century.

Lucy Stone's dedication to the cause of women's rights went back to her early life on the farm where she was born in West Brookfield, Massachusetts, where her mother was subject to hard work and the absolute rule of her husband and where her brothers received preferential treatment. She began to question whether the Bible could possibly be right in stating that men should rule women and suspected inaccurate translations from the Greek and Hebrew as the source of the injustice. She decided at a young age that she must go to college to read these languages and worked hard to obtain her education.

At sixteen she was teaching school for much less than the going rate for male teachers; she applied her earnings to study at Quabog Seminary in Warren, Massachusetts, Wesleyan Academy in Wilbraham, and Mount Holyoke Female Seminary in South Hadley. In 1843, at the age of twenty-five, she was finally able to enter Oberlin College in Ohio (see CHARLES GRANDISON FINNEY), the first coeducational college and a center of antislavery thought. Through her linguistic studies, she was able to confirm her suspicions regarding the role of women in the Bible. She hoped to develop her ideas on reforming injustices for women through public speaking but found that women could not pursue public oratory at Oberlin. Graduating in 1847, she was the first Massachusetts woman to gain a bachelor's degree.

After graduation, Stone, who had long objected to the injustice done to slaves, embarked on a career as a lecturer for the Massachusetts Anti-Slavery Society. The abolitionists complained, however, when she included women's rights in her lectures, and she had to agree to speak on women's issues separately. Stone was a highly effective speaker—sincere, fervent, and fearless before hostile audiences.

In 1850 she helped organize a major national women's rights convention at Worcester, Massachusetts. The speech she made there is thought to have inspired SUSAN B. ANTHONY to join the movement. During the next decade Stone not only attended but also served as secretary of every annual women's rights convention except for one.

In 1855 Stone married Henry Brown Blackwell, a businessman, abolitionist, and brother of the pioneer women physicians ELIZABETH BLACKWELL and EMILY BLACKWELL. At their wedding the couple registered a protest against the unjust marriage laws of the time which made wives subordinate to their husbands. Stone also decided to keep her maiden name, becoming known as Mrs. Stone and giving rise to the term "Lucy Stoner" to describe a woman who kept her maiden name after marriage.

In the first years of her wedded life, Stone kept to her busy schedule of lecturing and attending women's rights conventions, but with the birth of a child, ALICE STONE BLACKWELL, in 1857, she largely retired from the public arena in order to care for her daughter. Nevertheless, in 1858, Stone made news when she refused to pay taxes while women were denied the vote. In 1863 she helped organize the Women's Loyal National League to lobby for the ratification of the Thirteenth Amendment, freeing the slaves.

After the Civil War, Stone worked to get the vote extended to women as well as to freed African American males and was disappointed when Congress passed the Fifteenth Amendment without woman suffrage. Disagreeing with fellow feminists over the best way to win suffrage, Stone and others had formed the American Woman Suffrage Association

(AWSA) in 1869 with the intent of supporting the Fifteenth Amendment. The AWSA hoped to secure the vote for women later through campaigns in the various states, while its rival, the National Woman Suffrage Association (NWSA), headed by Susan B. Anthony and ELIZABETH CADY STANTON, had refused to endorse the Fifteenth Amendment without the inclusion of the vote for women.

Besides chairing the executive committee of the AWSA, Stone in 1870 founded the *Woman's Journal*, with MARY LIVERMORE as editor, which was published without interruption for the next forty-seven years and, more than any other periodical, served as the organ of the women's movement. Stone took over the editorship of the *Woman's Journal* after 1872, along with her husband and later her daughter, Alice Stone Blackwell.

In 1890 when the AWSA and the NWSA were finally united into a single organization—

the National American Woman Suffrage Association (NAWSA)—Stone became chair of the executive committee. Three years later, she made her last public address before the World's Congress of Representative Women at the Columbian Exposition in Chicago. A few months afterward, Stone died of a stomach tumor at the age of seventy-five. At her funeral in October 1893, thousands of mourners came to pay tribute.

**BIBLIOGRAPHY**

Blackwell, Alice Stone, *Lucy Stone, Pioneer of Woman's Rights*, 1930; Hayes, Elinor Rice, *Morning Star: A Biography of Lucy Stone*, 1961; Wheeler, Leslie A. (ed.), *Loving Warriors: Selected Letters of Lucy Stone and Henry B. Blackwell, 1855–1893*, 1981.

# Stowe, Harriet Elizabeth Beecher

(June 14, 1811–July 1, 1896)
Author, Reformer

Harriet Beecher Stowe is famous as the author of the best-selling antislavery novel *Uncle Tom's Cabin*, which so aroused northern feeling against slavery that it has been named as one of the causes of the Civil War.

Harriet Beecher, a daughter of the well-known Congregational minister LYMAN BEECHER and his first wife, Roxana Foote, was born in Litchfield, Connecticut. Her mother died when she was four years old, and Harriet was raised by her older sister, CATHARINE BEECHER, who became a well-known author and educator. Harriet was also the playmate and close companion of her younger brother, HENRY WARD BEECHER, destined to become one of the most popular preachers of his day. Harriet was educated at Miss Pierce's school in Litchfield,

then at the Hartford Female Seminary started by her sister Catharine. There, at age sixteen, Harriet began teaching. Along with her brothers and sisters, Harriet was greatly influenced by her father, a leader in the evangelical movement who inspired in his family a strong sense of public duty. All of his sons except one became ministers, and Harriet and Catharine were able to exert a moral influence through writing and teaching.

In 1832 the family moved to Cincinnati, Ohio, where Lyman Beecher became president of Lane Theological Seminary and pastor of the Second Presbyterian Church and where Catharine started a school, the Western Female Institute, at which Harriet became a teacher. Also at this time, Harriet wrote a geography book for children and a number of sketches that were published in the *Western Monthly Magazine*.

In 1836 Harriet married Calvin Stowe, a professor of Biblical literature at Lane. Harriet's early married years were difficult. Her husband was moody and distant, the couple had little money, and Harriet gave birth to five children in rapid succession. She continued to write an occasional tale or sketch, and a collection of her stories entitled *The Mayflower* was published in 1843.

Also during these years, Harriet Beecher Stowe began storing up impressions that she would later use in her antislavery masterpiece. Living in a border city, she was very much aware of and disturbed by the existence of slavery across the Ohio River in Kentucky, and in 1849 she visited a Kentucky plantation, where she saw the slaves in their cabins. That same year, Stowe lost her infant son (her sixth child) to a cholera epidemic and felt that she finally understood the anguish of slave mothers who were separated from their children.

In 1850 Stowe and her husband returned to New England, where he joined the faculty of Bowdoin College in Brunswick, Maine. Caught up in the heated discussion of the Fugitive Slave Act of that year, Stowe declared the law an abomination and vowed to do something about it. She began work on a long tale about slavery, entitled *Uncle Tom's Cabin, or Life Among the Lowly.* The novel was published serially in the *National Era*, an antislavery paper in Washington, D.C., in 1851 and 1852, and in book form in 1852. Though no one expected the book to be popular or successful, more than 300,000 copies were sold within the first year. The book was several times adapted for the

Library of Congress

stage and was ultimately translated into fifty-five languages.

*Uncle Tom's Cabin* was the first book by an American author to have as its hero an African American. Uncle Tom is the saintly slave of a good-hearted family in the Upper South. Debts force the family to sell him downriver, where for two years he lives with another kindly master. But after this man's accidental death, Tom passes into the hands of the novel's villain, Simon Legree, who beats him to death. In the novel, Stowe attacks the institution of slavery rather than white southerners, who for the most part are presented as well-meaning; the evil Simon Legree is a transplanted northerner.

By turns sentimental and realistic, *Uncle Tom's Cabin* appealed strongly to nineteenth-century readers. And because the book presented the horrors of slavery in vivid human terms, it had a powerful impact. President Abraham Lincoln only slightly exaggerated when, upon meeting Stowe in 1863, he said, "So you're the little woman who wrote the book that made the big war." While fueling antislavery sentiment in the North, the book infuriated southerners, who charged that Stowe knew nothing about plantation life and grossly misrepresented it. In response to her critics, Stowe published *A Key to Uncle Tom* (1853), a nonfiction work containing documentary evidence that supported her indictment of slavery in the novel. Also in 1853, Stowe and her husband visited England, where she was warmly received.

Stowe's second (and last) antislavery novel was inspired by the growing conflict over the spread of slavery into Kansas and Nebraska. The hero of *Dred: A Tale of the Dismal*

*Swamp* (1856) is an escaped slave and outlaw living in the North Carolina swamps, who preaches to a band of fugitives and has a vision of a holy war. The novel reflected Stowe's new militancy, shared by her brother Henry, who was at this time sending rifles to aid the antislavery settlers in Kansas.

After *Uncle Tom* and *Dred,* Stowe continued to write novels, producing on average almost a book a year for the next thirty years. In the settings, characters, and themes of her later novels, however, she returned to the New England of her childhood. Her New England novels include *The Minister's Wooing* (1859), *The Pearl of Orr's Island* (1862), and *Oldtown Folks* (1869). Stowe also contributed many short sketches to the New York *Independent,* the *Christian Union,* and the *Atlantic Monthly.* One of her pieces for the latter created an international uproar. In "The True Story of Lady Byron's Life" (1869), later published in book form as *Lady Byron Vindicated,* Stowe charged that Lord Byron had a love affair with his sister and that a child was born of the affair.

After her husband's retirement from teaching in 1864, the Stowes moved to Hartford, where they lived on the income from Harriet's writing. Beginning in 1867, the family spent winters in Florida. Stowe's book *Palmetto Leaves* (1873), a series of sketches about the delights of Florida, helped spark a Florida land boom. Calvin Stowe died in 1886. In 1889 Stowe compiled her autobiography, *The Life and Letters of Harriet Beecher Stowe,* with the help of one of her sons. She died in 1896 in Hartford at the age of eighty-four.

**BIBLIOGRAPHY**

Gossett, Thomas F., *Uncle Tom's Cabin and American Culture,* 1985; Reynolds, Moira D., *Uncle Tom's Cabin and Mid-Nineteenth Century United States: Pen and Conscience,* 1985; Wilson, Forrest, *Crusader in Crinoline: The Life of Harriet Beecher Stowe,* 1941.

# Sumner, William Graham

(October 30, 1840–April 12, 1910)
Social Scientist

Social scientist William Graham Sumner was one of the leading exponents of Social Darwinism in America. Viewing life as a grim struggle in which only the fittest could survive, Sumner glorified the millionaires of his day as products of natural selection and attacked reformers for trying to preserve the unfit.

Born in Paterson, New Jersey, William Graham Sumner graduated from Yale in 1863, then studied abroad. When he returned to the United States in 1866, he became a tutor at Yale for three years during which time he decided upon a career as a minister. In 1869 he became assistant rector at the Calvary Church in New York City, and the following year became rector of the Church of the Redeemer in Morristown, New Jersey. Increasingly interested in social and economic issues, Sumner in 1872 left the ministry to accept the newly created professorship in political and social science at Yale, a position he held for the rest of his life.

Sumner proved a highly effective teacher, winning his students' admiration with his blunt, vigorous classroom manner. Sumner worked to broaden the curriculum to include more science, and was a strong champion of academic freedom.

Sumner's economic views were based on a firm belief in sound money, free trade, individual liberty, and fierce opposition to any form of government intervention. He felt that any such intervention would disrupt the proper operation of natural laws, which governed economic life as well as biological life. Sumner even opposed high tariffs, regarding them as a form of government handouts, and he was an especially outspoken critic of socialism.

Outside of the classroom, Sumner expounded his views in speeches and essays with provocative titles like "That It Is Not Wicked to Be Rich; Nay, Even, That It Is Not Wicked to Be Richer than One's Neighbor." Sumner's thinking about society was greatly influenced by the work of the British philosopher Herbert Spencer, whose textbook, *The Study of Sociology,* Sumner used in his classes. Like Spencer, Sumner applied Darwinian evolutionary theories to society, arguing that economic competition was good because it promoted the survival of the fittest. Far from accepting the idea that all humans are created equal, Sumner believed in the existence of innate inequalities. According to him, poverty was the natural result of these inequalities. He therefore rejected government welfare programs as a sentimental and absurd attempt by reformers to make the world over and believed such programs placed a financial burden on the middle class, whom he called "the forgotten man." He regarded the middle-class virtues of hard work, thrift, and sobriety as necessary to uphold family life and the public morality.

Sumner's most important book, *Folkways* (1907), did not appear until late in his career, when he had turned to an interest in sociology. In it, he maintained that people developed folkways and mores, which governed their behavior in society and were essential to their survival. He further asserted that members of a particular group took an ethnocentric view of their folkways and mores, believing them to be superior to those of any other group. Sumner's theories in *Folkways* were in keeping with his Social Darwinism, because they were based on constant conflict and the struggle to survive among different groups.

While spreading the ideas of Social Darwinism, Sumner did much to help establish sociology as an academic discipline. In recognition of his contributions, he was elected president of the American Sociological Society in 1909. Late that same year he went to New York to deliver an address before the society and collapsed, dying several months later. His notes were published posthumously as *The Science of Society* (1927) in four volumes.

**BIBLIOGRAPHY**

Keller, Albert G., *Reminiscences (Mainly Personal) of William Graham Sumner,* 1933; Starr, Harris E., *William Graham Sumner,* 1925.

# Sunday, William Ashley

(November 18, 1862–November 6, 1935)
Evangelist

Billy Sunday was the most popular evangelist of his day, especially in the years before World War I. His influence on the Americans who flocked to his tent meetings was intense, though perhaps not long-enduring. He helped shape public opinion that led to Prohibition.

The preacher universally known as Billy Sunday was born in Ames, in the heart of Iowa, youngest of three sons of William Sunday, from a Pennsylvania German family, and Mary Jane Cory. The father died during the Civil War a month or so after the boy's birth. William and his next older brother were brought up in soldiers' orphans' homes. At age fourteen William was on his own, working at odd jobs. In an Iowa village called Nevada he managed to attend high school while working as the janitor. In Marshalltown, working in a furniture store, Sunday played on the local baseball team and caught the eye of the captain of the Chicago White Sox, who recruited him in 1883. He spent eight years as a professional ballplayer. In 1887 he experienced a Christian conversion; the next year he married Helen Thompson, of Chicago. They had four children.

Sunday gave up baseball in 1891 and worked for the YMCA (Young Men's Christian Association) in Chicago. He became an assistant to J. Wilbur Chapman, an evangelist, serving as advance man and occasionally preaching. In January 1896 he began his own evangelistic career but was not ordained (as a Presbyterian) until 1903. As Billy Sunday he became famous, traveling from town to town with his musicians and big choirs, holding revivals in auditoriums or more often in tents with sawdust-covered floors. Those who chose conversion came forward to shake Sunday's hand; this was "hitting the sawdust trail." A collection was taken up at the last meeting of a revival, and such proceeds, sometimes amounting to $50,000 or more, gave Sunday his income. He was reputed to have become rich. It has been said that he preached to more than 100 million people and converted more than a million.

Billy Sunday was a master showman. He drew on his baseball background, used current slang, and performed acrobatics on the platform. His sermons were in the tradition of the hard sell revivalist religion of the nineteenth century. As the spokesman of divine wrath, he fiercely denounced not merely sinners but liberals, scientists, higher education, card-playing, dancing, and liquor. His crusade against liquor bore fruit when the states ratified in 1919 the Eighteenth Amendment to the Constitution, prohibiting the manufacture, sale, or transportation of intoxicating liquors. Sunday was earnest and sincere, and he was responsible for reforming many wayward and even criminal people and for cleaning up vice in many towns, at least temporarily. His writings included *Burning Truths from Billy's Bat* (1914) and *Great Love Stories of the Bible and Their Lessons for Today* (1917).

Billy Sunday died of a heart attack at his retirement home in Winona Lake, Indiana, shortly before his seventy-third birthday and almost two years after witnessing the repeal of the Eighteenth Amendment.

**BIBLIOGRAPHY**

McLoughlin, W. G., *Billy Sunday Was His Real Name*, 1955; Sunday, W. A., *Seventy-four Complete Sermons*, 1915; Wright, Melton, *Giant for God: A Biography of William Ashley ("Billy") Sunday*, 1951.

# Tappan, Arthur

(May 22, 1786–July 23, 1865)

# Tappan, Lewis

(May 23, 1788–June 21, 1873)
Abolitionists, Philanthropists

Brothers and successful merchants, Arthur and Lewis Tappan used their wealth to support mid-nineteenth-century religious and reform causes, notably abolition, forming an activist partnership that lasted throughout their adult lives.

Born in Northampton, Massachusetts, the Tappan brothers had strict religious training but little formal schooling. They both worked as clerks in dry goods stores in Boston as teenagers. Arthur went on to New York and started a business in the silk trade in 1826, and Lewis joined him as partner in 1828. They became very successful, and in 1841, Lewis used his experience as credit manager to start the first business credit rating agency in the United States.

The brothers were both driven by conscience to become active in religious and political causes. They backed various church schools, missionary societies, and antivice and temperance groups and supported the Broadway Tabernacle for CHARLES GRANDISON FINNEY, as well as the Oneida Community of JOHN HUMPHREY NOYES; Kenyon College; and the Lane Seminary in Cincinnati, Ohio. After many Lane students withdrew because they were not allowed to discuss slavery, the brothers helped found Oberlin College in Oberlin, Ohio, and sent Finney there as professor of theology in 1835.

Like many other religious activists of the time, they turned their attention to antislavery efforts. Arthur had once belonged to the movement to colonize freed slaves in Africa but had soon left that and with his brother joined the abolitionists. They were on friendly terms with WILLIAM LLOYD GARRISON, whose antislavery newspaper, *The Liberator*, they helped finance. In 1833 they also helped found both the New York City Anti-Slavery Society and the American Anti-Slavery Society, activities for which the next year they suffered mob action from hostile antiabolitionists.

In 1840 the Tappans broke with Garrison when he brought together many issues, such as women's rights, under the umbrella of reform. They founded the new American and Foreign Anti-Slavery Society and started an abolitionist weekly, *The National Era*. Becoming convinced that political action was necessary, they backed the Liberty party of James G. Birney in 1840 and 1844. When some of their own religious organizations failed to support abolition, they started the American Missionary Association dedicated expressly for the cause.

During the 1850s, the brothers grew more extreme in their views. They opposed the Fugitive Slave Act of 1850 and contributed their efforts to help slaves escape the South by way of the Underground Railroad (see HARRIET TUBMAN). Abandoning earlier organizations, they formed the Abolition Society in 1855. Wary of Abraham Lincoln in 1860, Lewis voted instead for the outspoken abolitionist GERRIT SMITH.

The brothers' remarkable partnership in reform ended in 1865 with Arthur's death. In 1879 Lewis published *The Life of Arthur Tappan*, but he suffered a stroke before seeing it in print. He died three years later at the age of eighty-five.

**BIBLIOGRAPHY**

Barnes, G. H., *The Anti-Slavery Impulse*, 1933; Filler, Louis, *The Crusade Against Slavery*, 1960; Wyatt-Brown, Bertram, *Lewis Tappan and the Evangelical War Against Slavery*, 1969.

# Tarbell, Ida Minerva

(November 5, 1857–January 6, 1944)
Journalist

Ida Tarbell's condemnation of the Standard Oil monopoly at the beginning of the twentieth century placed her among the leading American muckrakers and brought her international fame as a journalist.

Tarbell was born on a farm near Hatch Hollow, in northwestern Pennsylvania. Both parents came from New England stock. Tarbell's father, spurred by the discovery of oil in Erie County, gave up the idea of moving to Iowa and instead set up shop making wooden oil tanks. The family moved to Titusville, Pennsylvania, in 1870, and Ida began her first formal education in high school there. She graduated from Allegheny College, nearby, in 1880 with a bachelor's degree in biology and soon discovered that, as a woman, she could not hope to pursue a career in science. For two years she taught at Poland Union Seminary in Ohio. She then joined the editorial staff of the *Chautauquan*, a magazine of the Chautauqua movement dedicated to self-improvement through home study, later becoming its managing editor. In 1891 she left the magazine and went to Paris to study history and do research on the role of women in the French Revolution. To maintain herself abroad, she earned money writing articles for periodicals in the United States.

It was at this time that Tarbell met SAMUEL S. MCCLURE, who would revolutionize the magazine world with his *McClure's*, a mass-circulation journal with high literary content. For *McClure's* she wrote, first, feature articles on Louis Pasteur and other well-known French

Library of Congress

figures, then later, after returning home, an eight-part series on Napoleon that was hugely successful both for herself and for the magazine. In 1895 the articles were published in book form as *A Short Life of Napoleon Bonaparte,* which sold 100,000 copies. Her next assignment from McClure was a series on Abraham Lincoln, which appeared from 1895 to 1898 in twenty-two parts and then in 1900 in two volumes as *The Life of Abraham Lincoln.*

With his magazine an established success, McClure sought new content in contemporary social issues. Fired by the publisher's enthusiasm to expose corporate trusts, Tarbell began a lengthy inquiry into the history and breadth of JOHN D. ROCKEFELLER's oil interests that resulted in a strong condemnation of the business. Her work, eventually entitled "The History of the Standard Oil Company," ran to nineteen articles in *McClure's,* appearing simultaneously with LINCOLN STEFFENS's "The Shame of Minneapolis" and RAY STANNARD BAKER's "The Right to Work." These articles together gave journalism the movement known as muckraking (a term coined by Theodore Roosevelt and taken from John Bunyan's *Pilgrim's Progress*). The muckrakers exposed corruption and abuses in many areas of public life and contributed specifically to the reform movement known as Progressivism.

Tarbell was not an entirely objective investigator of the oil industry: years before her father had lost money when the Standard Oil Company had combined secretly with the railroads to regulate freight prices and drive independent oil interests out of business. Despite her prejudice against monopolies and unjust private gain, Tarbell proved an accurate researcher, and her work has withstood the test of time. When they appeared in 1901, the articles had an immediate negative effect on the public's opinion of big business as a whole and helped pave the way for the antitrust prosecution of the Standard Oil Company and its breakup in 1911.

In 1906 Tarbell, along with Baker, Steffens, and other writers, resigned from *McClure's* in a dispute over Samuel McClure's policies and took control of *The American Magazine.* Her first series was on the history of the American protective tariff, published in 1911 as *The Tariff in Our Time,* an attack on protection as a benefit for the trusts and not for workers. In recognition of her contribution, President Woodrow Wilson in 1916 offered Tarbell a place on the Federal Tariff Commission, but she refused it.

Another Tarbell series in *The American Magazine* on the history of the women's movement in the United States ran in 1909 and 1910. Tarbell was not a true feminist. While she endorsed some feminist aims, she did not support the suffrage cause, believing that women needed to strengthen their place in the home and family. These views appeared in *The Business of Being a Woman.*

From 1912 to 1915 Tarbell visited a number of American factories to examine employee conditions. She reported a developing social conscience on the part of corporations, especially in the mass-production techniques and employee welfare policies of HENRY FORD, a view that some of her admirers found surprising.

*The American Magazine* was sold in 1915, and Tarbell turned to lecturing and free-lance writing. She had become interested in peace issues before World War I and attended the Paris Peace Conference in 1919 as a correspondent, as well as the Naval Disarmament Conference in Washington in 1921. She was a supporter of President Franklin D. Roosevelt's New Deal programs, especially social security. Later in life she taught classes in biographical writing. Tarbell died of pneumonia at the age of eighty-six.

**BIBLIOGRAPHY**

Brady, Kathleen, *Ida Tarbell: Portrait of a Muckraker,* 1954; Tarbell, Ida, *Peacemakers—Blessed and Otherwise,* 1924, *The Nationalizing of Business,* 1936, and *All in the Day's Work,* 1939; Tompkins, M. E., *Ida M. Tarbell,* 1974.

# Thomas, Lowell Jackson

(April 6, 1892–August 29, 1981)
Author, News Commentator

Lowell Thomas was the first celebrated radio and television news broadcaster, whose voice brought world events to American families in evening broadcasts for nearly forty-six years, beginning in 1930.

Lowell Jackson Thomas was born in the village of Woodington, Ohio. Both parents were teachers, though his father, Harry George Thomas, of Welsh ancestry, became a physician. When Lowell was eight the family moved to Cripple Creek, Colorado, which at that time was enjoying a gold-mining boom. The boy peddled newspapers and helped in the mines. His home life, however, was cultured. His father had a good library and insisted on correct speech. Thomas worked his way through the University of Northern Indiana, at Valparaiso, and got a B.S. degree in two years. Then he attended the University of Denver, the Kent College of Law in Chicago, and Princeton University, where he studied constitutional law (1916) while teaching public speaking.

During his summer vacation in 1915, Thomas went to Alaska and hiked with camera and notebook. His friend DALE CARNEGIE helped him organize his material as a lecture with slides—an early type of travelogue. When he presented his show in Washington, it was brought to the attention of President Woodrow Wilson. Thomas consequently was assigned to head a mission to record events of World War I. With a camera crew, he made movies on the European western front and in the Near East, where in 1917 he met Colonel T. E. Lawrence, who led the Arab revolt against the Turks and became famous as Lawrence of Arabia. Thomas returned to New York with films depicting the liberation of Damascus and Jerusalem after centuries of Turkish rule and the Allied forces entering Germany. In 1919 he showed his movies to immense audiences in Madison Square Garden and, at the invitation of King George V, in Covent Garden in London.

Thomas next went on a world tour, including visits to Afghanistan and Burma and a visit to India with the Prince of Wales. The films he made were widely exhibited in America and Europe. During the 1920s he wrote such best-sellers as *With Lawrence in Arabia* (1924) and *Beyond Khyber Pass* (1925), about Afghanistan.

In 1930 Thomas began his long career as a radio news broadcaster, mainly for the Columbia Broadcasting System. For a time he also was the voice of Fox Movietone newsreels shown in movie theaters. He continued to travel and sometimes broadcast from unexpected places—a helicopter, a plane, a ship, Chungking, the Philippines, Iwo Jima. Thomas, claiming that his voice had been heard by more people than any other voice in history, estimated his total radio and television audience at 70 billion.

Thomas became wealthy and owned a large estate near Pawling, New York. After ending his news broadcasting in 1976 he continued to travel, to do radio talks based on his recollections, and to produce films made by the three-dimensional Cinerama process. In 1977, after the death of his first wife, Frances Ryan, Thomas married Marianna Munn. He interrupted his honeymoon in Hawaii to fly to Washington to receive the Medal of Freedom award from President Gerald Ford, then continued a world tour. He died of a heart attack at his Pawling home at the age of eighty-nine, four days after recording fifteen 5-minute radio talks.

**BIBLIOGRAPHY**

Edwards, Douglas, *New York Times*, September 20, 1981; Thomas, Lowell, *Good Evening, Everybody*, 1977, and *So Long Until Tomorrow*, 1978.

## Thompson, Dorothy

(July 9, 1894–January 30, 1961)
Journalist

Dorothy Thompson was one of the leading political commentators of the pre–World War II period and an effective propagandist against the rise of fascism.

Thompson was born in Lancaster, a town near Buffalo, New York, eldest child of an impoverished Methodist minister, Peter Thompson. Her mother died when she was eight, and her father married the church organist, who proved to be a severe stepmother. Dorothy Thompson graduated in 1914 from Syracuse University, where, while working her way through, she became well known as an orator and a woman suffrage activist. After college,

Thompson joined the staff of the New York State Suffrage Association, which worked successfully for a state suffrage amendment.

During World War I, Thompson hoped to go overseas but instead had to settle for a social work job in New York City. Intending to be a journalist, she made it to Europe in 1920. On shipboard she met a group of Zionists going to a conference in London, covered the event, and persuaded International News Service to hire her as a free lance. Soon she was in Vienna as a stringer for American newspapers while studying at the University of Vienna. She married a Hungarian writer, Josef Bard, in 1922 (and divorced him five years later).

Thompson was a notably good reporter. Typical of her style, she disguised herself as a Red Cross worker and got past the guards to obtain an exclusive interview with Zita, the deposed Empress of Austria. John Gunther remarked that Thompson blazed through Europe like "a blue-eyed tornado." She also had a gift for giving parties to which political and intellectual celebrities flocked. In 1925 the New York *Evening Post* and the Philadelphia *Public Ledger* made her head of their Berlin office, the first woman to head an overseas news bureau. In Berlin, Thompson met the American novelist Sinclair Lewis, with whom she embarked on a stormy marriage in 1928. Their son Michael was born in 1930, after they returned to live in New England. From her home base Thompson carried on a career lecturing, writing, and traveling. She went back to Berlin in 1931 to interview Adolf Hitler for *Cosmopolitan* and concluded that he could never take power, an erratic prediction she made again in her book *I Saw Hitler!* (1932). When she returned to Germany in 1934, her attack on the anti-Jewish campaign and belittling of the führer caused her to be the first correspondent to be expelled, and at the order of Hitler himself.

Thompson's work as a news columnist and commentator was the peak of a career during which she was on friendly terms with many of the world's leaders. In 1936 she began to write "On the Record," a column for the *New York Herald Tribune*, which eventually was syndicated in 170 newspapers. As the international crisis became graver, she warned increasingly of the danger of Nazism, and in 1939, at a pro-Nazi rally in Madison Square Garden, created a sensation (and put herself at risk) by loudly heckling the speakers. After the outbreak of war in Europe, she denounced CHARLES LINDBERGH for his isolationist views and his contacts with the Hitler government. Thompson avoided conflict with her paper's conservative political stance. She supported Wendell Willkie for the Republican presidential nomination until late in the 1940 campaign, when she endorsed Franklin D. Roosevelt as the more effective leader against fascism. The *Herald Tribune* forced her resignation and she switched to the Bell Syndicate.

In 1941 Thompson helped to found Freedom House, a liberal internationalist organization. In 1942 she divorced Lewis and soon afterward married an Austrian-Czech painter, Maxim Kopf. In the postwar years, her career began to decline. After visiting Palestine in 1945, she took up the cause of the Palestinian Arabs. Though she had consistently supported Jewish causes, she was accused of anti-Semitism, and the New York *Post* dropped her column. She became involved in the American Friends of the Middle East in 1951—an anti-Zionist body backed by oil interests and (perhaps unknown to her) by the Central Intelligence Agency. Her publishers insisted that she leave the American Friends organization in 1957. The next year, after her husband's death, she stopped writing her column. Thompson seemed to have lost her spirit, though in 1960 she published an article paying tribute to Sinclair Lewis that many considered her finest work. Dorothy Thompson died in early 1961 while visiting her grandsons and daughter-in-law in Lisbon.

**BIBLIOGRAPHY**

Kurth, Peter, *American Cassandra: The Life of Dorothy Thompson*, 1990; Sanders, Marion K., *Dorothy Thompson: A Legend in Her Time*, 1973; Sheean, Vincent, *Dorothy and Red*, 1963; Thompson, Dorothy, *Let the Record Speak*, 1939.

# Thompson, Hunter Stockton

(July 18, 1939–   )
Writer

In such books as *Fear and Loathing in Las Vegas: A Savage Journey to the Heart of the American Dream,* Hunter S. Thompson established a reputation as one of the leading practitioners of the New Journalism, a type of nonfiction writing employing fictional techniques that developed in the 1960s (see TOM WOLFE).

Hunter Thompson was born in Louisville, Kentucky, and attended public schools there before joining the U.S. Air Force. After his discharge in the late 1950s, he held a number of journalistic positions, including Caribbean correspondent for the New York *Herald Tribune* (1959–1960) and South American correspondent for the *National Observer* (1961–1963). Settling in California, he contributed articles to several magazines, including the *Nation, Harper's,* and the *Reporter.*

In 1966 Thompson published *Hell's Angels: A Strange and Terrible Saga,* an account of the year he spent riding with the motorcycle gang. In it, he sought to correct many popular misconceptions about the Hell's Angels, while at the same time locating their real menace in the social conditions that produced them.

As the decade of the sixties turned violent, Thompson increased his experiments with hallucinogenic drugs and became radicalized politically. His writing subsequently took on an increasingly antagonistic, antiestablishment tone that became identified with "Gonzo journalism." (The name Gonzo came from a fan letter in which a fellow writer pronounced a piece Thompson had written "real Gonzo.")

In 1970 Thompson became national affairs editor for *Rolling Stone* magazine. Among the articles he wrote for *Rolling Stone* was the two-part "Fear and Loathing in Las Vegas," which became the book of the same name, published in 1971. The book recounted in the first-person the nightmarish, drug-ridden misadventures of Raoul Duke, a stand-in for Thompson, and a 300-pound Samoan attorney named Dr. Gonzo. *Fear and Loathing in Las Vegas* was hailed as a brilliant piece of writing about the drug subculture and as both a barbed and hilarious portrait of Las Vegas.

Having won a reputation as an outlaw journalist, Thompson went on to cover the 1972 presidential campaign for *Rolling Stone* in his own frenetic, highly idiosyncratic style. Underneath the cultivated lunacy, however, he demonstrated a shrewd investigative and analytical ability that led one reviewer to call *Fear and Loathing on the Campaign Trail '72,* the book containing Thompson's *Rolling Stone* articles, the best political reporting in some time.

Thompson's later books include *The Great Shark Hunt* (1979), a collection of pieces written for *Rolling Stone* and other publications; *The Curse of Lono* (1983), an account of his madcap adventures while on a visit to Hawaii; and two other collections of articles, *Generation of Swine* (1988) and *Songs of the Doomed: More Notes on the Death of the American Dream* (1990).

**BIBLIOGRAPHY**

Dickstein, Morris, *Gates of Eden: American Culture in the Sixties,* 1977; Hellmann, John, *Fables of Fact: The New Journalism as New Fiction,* 1981; Klinkowitz, Jerome, *The Life of Fiction,* 1977; McKeen, William, *Hunter S. Thompson,* 1991.

## Thoreau, Henry David

(July 12, 1817–May 6, 1862)
Author, Transcendentalist

Henry David Thoreau was one of the chief representatives of Transcendentalism. He was also an important naturalist, whose eloquent writing influenced the conservation and ecology movements of the twentieth century. His famous essay, *Civil Disobedience,* inspired nonviolent protest movements in the United States and abroad.

Thoreau was born in Concord, Massachusetts, of French ancestry. After studying at Concord Academy, he entered Harvard College in 1833. While there he heard RALPH WALDO EMERSON deliver his "American Scholar" address, and he read Emerson's book, *Nature,* which set forth the main ideas of Transcendentalism (see RALPH WALDO EMERSON for further discussion). This American philosophical movement had lasting effects on religion, literature, and social reform movements in the nineteenth century and later.

Young Thoreau took to heart Emerson's advice to "Know thyself" and "Study Nature." After graduating in 1837, he returned to Concord, where Emerson lived. He began keeping a journal, which he maintained until his death, and with Emerson's encouragement wrote poems and essays and gave his first lecture at the Concord Lyceum, speaking annually there for the next twenty years. Thoreau taught briefly in the Concord public school system, and from 1838 to 1841 ran a school of his own with his brother John.

For two years beginning in 1841, Thoreau lived at Emerson's home, exchanging work as

Library of Congress

a handyman for the freedom to pursue his own writing. He attended meetings of the Transcendental Club, becoming acquainted with such other figures in the movement as MARGARET FULLER, ELIZABETH PEABODY, and BRONSON ALCOTT; and helped Emerson edit the Transcendental journal, the *Dial,* contributing a number of poems and essays to it. Emerson then arranged for Thoreau to serve as a tutor to Emerson's brother's children on Staten Island, in the hopes that Thoreau would have better success in selling his work to periodicals in New York. He did not, and after a year he returned home to Concord to assist his father in the family business of pencil making.

On Independence Day, 1845, Thoreau moved to land owned by Emerson on Walden Pond to begin his famous experiment in self-sufficient living. He built himself a one-room cabin, where he lived and wrote for the next two years and two months, his solitude broken by frequent trips to Emerson's home in Concord. While at Walden, Thoreau worked on the manuscript of what was to be his first book, *A Week on the Concord and Merrimack Rivers;* recorded his observations of nature in his journal; and wrote a lecture about his life at Walden.

In July 1846, during his stay at Walden, Thoreau was arrested for his refusal to pay his poll taxes for four years. He had withheld the tax to protest the Mexican War, which he regarded as part of a southern conspiracy to achieve the extension of slavery. He spent only one night in jail, however, for someone—probably an aunt—paid the taxes, a move that annoyed Thoreau. He told the story of this experience in his famous essay, first published in 1849 as "Resistance to Civil Government" and later, in 1866, as *Civil Disobedience.* In it, he argued that individuals have a right to disobey the laws of their government when that government acts unjustly, a view that achieved fame and influence in the twentieth century.

Leaving Walden Pond in September 1847, Thoreau spent another year at Emerson's home, managing the household while Emerson was away in Europe. From then on he lived at his family's house in Concord, working in his father's pencil factory and as a town surveyor and in his spare time going for long rambles and continuing with his writing, which he had little success in getting published. *A Week on the Concord and Merrimack Rivers* was finally published in 1849 at Thoreau's own expense. The book, which is considered the most transcendental of Thoreau's writings, was based on a boat trip he had taken with his brother ten years earlier. Thoreau used this literal journey as a vehicle to present his ideas about literature, life, and religion.

Thoreau's second and most important book, *Walden,* appeared in 1854. In it, Thoreau made clear how his Transcendentalism differed from Emerson's. Unlike his mentor, Thoreau did not believe that material things were necessary to everyday comfort and a successful life. "I went into the woods," Thoreau wrote, "because I wished to live deliberately, to front only the essential facts of life, and see if I could not learn what it had to teach, and not, when I came to die, discover that I had not lived." According to Thoreau, most people in industrial America were preoccupied with making money and as a result lived "lives of quiet desperation." His advice to them was to "simplify, simplify" and to seek spiritual development through communion with the natural world, as he had done at Walden.

Although *Walden* has become a classic, it sold poorly during Thoreau's lifetime, and most of his other writings were not published until after his death. They include *Excursions* (1863), *The Maine Woods* (1864), *Cape Cod* (1865), and *A Yankee in Canada* (1866).

While Thoreau never became a member of an antislavery society, he increasingly spoke out against slavery during the 1850s. In 1857 he met the militant abolitionist JOHN BROWN at Emerson's home in Concord, whom he regarded highly. After Brown's execution for the raid on the arsenal at Harpers Ferry, Virginia, in 1859, Thoreau was among the first to make speeches publicly defending Brown. His "A Plea for Captain Brown" hailed Brown as a martyr. At the end of 1860 Thoreau became seriously ill with tuberculosis. Despite a health-seeking trip to Minnesota in 1861, he continued to decline, and at age forty-four he died at his family home in Concord.

Fame came to Thoreau posthumously. In the early twentieth century, the Indian leader Mohandas Gandhi launched a passive resistance movement for Indian independence based on his reading of Thoreau's *Civil Disobedience.* Then in the 1950s and 1960s, MARTIN LUTHER KING, JR., and other black leaders used Thoreau's principles in their nonviolent civil rights movement in the United States. Thoreau's nature writing, particularly his *Journal* and *Walden,* have proved similarly significant to the conservation and ecology movements, influencing, among others, the forest preservationist JOHN MUIR.

**BIBLIOGRAPHY**

Anderson, Charles R., *The Magic Circle of Walden,* 1968; Richardson, Robert D., *Henry Thoreau: A Life of the Mind,* 1986; Wagenknecht, Edward, *Henry David Thoreau: What Manner of Man?* 1984.

# Thorndike, Edward Lee

(August 31, 1874–August 9, 1949)
Educator, Psychologist

Edward L. Thorndike developed psychological testing in education—the application of statistical measurement to mental traits—and was one of the most influential educational theorists of the first half of the twentieth century. He produced many widely used achievement and aptitude tests, enabling educators to study and appraise educational methods.

Thorndike was born in Williamsburg, Massachusetts, one of four children of Edward Roberts Thorndike, a Methodist minister, and Abby Brewster Ladd, both from Maine. All four of the Thorndike children became scholars of repute. Edward attended schools in New England towns where his father served as pastor and earned an A.B. at Wesleyan University in 1895. He went on to Harvard University for another A.B. and an M.A. (1897). He had first heard the term "psychology" while at Wesleyan, but his interest was not engaged until, at Harvard, he read WILLIAM JAMES's *The Principles of Psychology* and took a course with James, thereupon making psychology his chosen field. He began research (on intelligence in chickens) while still in Cambridge.

With a fellowship, Thorndike began graduate study at Columbia University in 1897, where his teachers included the psychologist James M. Cattell and the anthropologist FRANZ BOAS. He received his Ph.D. in one year, writing his dissertation on animal intelligence, which launched scientific research on animal learning. Thorndike at this stage of his career had sketched the outlines of a psychology stressing stimulus-response connections as the basis for learning.

In 1899 Thorndike was appointed instructor in genetic psychology at Teachers College, Columbia University, at the stage when the college was being transformed from a small normal school into an important training cen-

ter for educators. Thorndike became a full professor in 1904 and remained at Teachers College for the rest of his career.

Beginning with his earliest research, Thorndike stressed the employment of scientific method, especially statistical techniques, in psychological testing designed to measure the intelligence of children and their capacity for learning. During World War I, his testing methods were used in the U.S. Army and set a pattern thereafter in personnel work and placement as well as for educational guidance. Thorndike's theory of innate differences in the aptitudes of schoolchildren influenced reformers who sought to make education more flexible and individualized.

Thorndike was notably prolific. Among nearly eighty books that he wrote or edited were arithmetic texts for the early grades; *The Teacher's Word Book* (1921), a compilation of 10,000 words of greatest frequency in general use that was a basis for planning school readers; several dictionaries used in schools; and many on psychological theory. Thorndike's findings led to a reconsideration of curriculum and course material. His research proving that adults' ability to learn declines only slightly over the years stimulated adult education.

Thorndike became professor emeritus in 1941. When he died eight years later, he left four children who, like his own generation of relatives, were distinguished in the scholarly world.

**BIBLIOGRAPHY**

Joncich, Geraldine, *The Sane Positivist*, 1968;
    Thorndike, E. L., *The Measurement of Intelligence*, 1927, and *Selected Writings from a Connectionist's Psychology*, 1949.

# Tourgée, Albion Winegar

(May 2, 1838–May 21, 1905)
Author, Civil Rights Leader, Jurist

As one of the leading carpetbaggers during Reconstruction, Albion Tourgée worked to secure civil and political rights for African Americans and to end racial discrimination in North Carolina.

Tourgée was born in Williamsfield in the Western Reserve of Ohio, then a center of abolitionist activity. He attended the University of Rochester in New York but left to enlist in the Union army. Wounded in battle, he resumed his studies at Rochester, then reenlisted only to be wounded again and taken prisoner by the Confederacy. Released, he returned briefly to Ohio before serving with the army in Tennessee. Resigning from the army, he studied law and was admitted to the Ohio bar.

In 1865 Tourgée joined the flood of northerners, the so-called carpetbaggers, that poured into the South after the war, some genuinely concerned with reform, others seeking only personal gain. Settling in Greensboro, North Carolina, Tourgée practiced law, made unsuccessful investments in a nursery and a plantation, and was soon caught up in Reconstruction politics.

Tourgée helped to found the North Carolina Republican party and in 1868 was elected to the state's constitutional convention. Tourgée's platform called for reform in prisons, schools, and state and local government, as well as rights for African Americans. He helped frame the new state constitution and revise the state legal code. In 1868 Tourgée was also elected to the state superior court, serving on the bench for six years.

As a judge and political leader, Tourgée quickly gained a reputation for radicalism. Tourgée tried to see that wealthy plantation owners were taxed more heavily than those who were less well-off. But in contrast to many native-born radicals, he advocated allowing former Confederates to vote without restriction.

Working closely with African American political leaders, Tourgée sought to end racial discrimination by law in the state. Threatened by the Ku Klux Klan, he lashed out against the group's terrorist activities from the bench, and tried unsuccessfully to use the courts to stop Klan violence. Tourgée was accused of taking a bribe from some railroad promoters; further examination by historians has suggested there was nothing improper about the transaction.

When Reconstruction came to an end in North Carolina, so did Tourgée's political career. In 1879 he went to New York, where he began a new career as a novelist. In six novels written between 1879 and 1883, Tourgée dealt with such issues as the causes and results of the Civil War, the differences between northern and southern cultures, and the reasons why Reconstruction failed. Of his books, the most successful were *A Fool's Errand* (1879), a semiautobiographical account of the experiences of a former Union officer in the South, and *Bricks Without Straw* (1880), a novel about the problems facing African Americans after emancipation.

From the North, Tourgée continued to crusade for the rights of African Americans. In 1884 he published *An Appeal to Caesar*, calling for a race policy based on equality. Four years later, he began writing a weekly editorial for *The Chicago Inter-Ocean*, in which he expressed his views on such issues as labor reform and racial justice. In 1891 Tourgée founded the National Citizens Rights Association.

Tourgée played a dominant role in fighting the *Plessy* v. *Ferguson* case up to the Supreme Court and wrote a brief attacking segregation by law. The Supreme Court, however, in 1896 upheld the right of a state to provide "separate but equal" accommodations on public carriers in the *Plessy* case.

Tourgée spent his last years in Bordeaux, France, where President William McKinley had appointed him U.S. consul. Although Tourgée's pleas for racial equality went largely unheard during his lifetime, they were picked up by later generations of white as well as black Americans.

**BIBLIOGRAPHY**

Gross, T., *Albion Tourgée*, 1963; Olsen, O., *A Carpetbagger's Crusade*, 1965.

## Townsend, Francis Everett

(January 13, 1867–September 1, 1960)
Physician, Reformer

Francis E. Townsend formulated a pension plan for the elderly that he claimed would bring an end to the Great Depression. Financially unsound and poorly administered, the Old Age Revolving Pension Plan (OARP) nonetheless became a popular movement that was championed by Townsend until his death.

Townsend was born in Fairbury, in central Illinois, one of seven children of poor farmers. The family moved to the prairie town of Franklin, Nebraska, seeking better farmland, and Francis studied for two years at Franklin Academy. He and a brother went to California during a land boom in 1887, but their hopes did not prosper, and he returned to Franklin in 1890 to finish school. He tried farming on his own homestead but was unsuccessful and turned to odd jobs. Having saved enough money, Townsend entered Omaha Medical College in 1899 and worked his way through. He graduated in 1903 and took up a practice in the Black Hills of South Dakota, doctoring for miners and ranch hands. In 1906 he married a widow, Wilhelmina Mollie Brogue, with seven children, and their family increased by four more children.

Townsend enlisted in the Army Medical Corps during World War I and returned to move his family to Long Beach, California. His health was poor, and competition from younger doctors was stiff. For many years life was a struggle, and the Great Depression brought near disaster. Fortunately he found work at the Long Beach Health Office, and his family was able to live without the severe hardship others were facing in those times. By then Townsend had seen at close hand how difficult it was for many elderly people to survive hardships not of their making. In his sixties himself, Townsend conceived of his OARP, which called for the government to provide $200 monthly for retired Americans over the age of sixty, funded by a 2 percent tax on all business transactions. He announced his plan in a Long Beach newspaper in September 1933, and before long, enormous numbers of people were hailing the "Townsend Plan."

Townsend hired Robert Earl Clements, a real-estate developer, to promote the plan, which was based on a national organization of local clubs with dues-paying members. An estimated 2.25 million people joined for 25 cents a year, and a newspaper and other ventures brought in money to the national headquarters. Townsend began to exert political pressure to have OARP made into law. Economists, however, made fun of OARP, and the government showed no interest in it. When Townsend attacked the Franklin D. Roosevelt administration, especially the Social Security Act of 1935, it supported a congressional investigation of the OARP organization that resulted in uncovering financial irregularities. Townsend then joined with GERALD L. K. SMITH and CHARLES COUGHLIN in the campaign of 1936, supporting William Lemke and the Union party. Townsend's support was only halfhearted, however, and was based mainly on his dislike of Roosevelt, whom he continued to attack.

In 1937 Townsend was convicted of contempt of Congress for his refusal to cooperate with the Senate committee investigating the Townsend Plan; he was sentenced to prison, but Roosevelt commuted his sentence.

Townsend tried to improve his plan somewhat and continued to travel and lecture to elderly audiences until shortly before his death in 1960 at the age of ninety-three. Time and prosperity had dulled the impact of the Depression, however, and the enormous interest in the plan had died away.

**DIBLIOGRAPHY**

Holtzman, Abraham, *The Townsend Movement*, 1963; Townsend, F. E., *New Horizons*, 1943.

# Truth, Sojourner

(ca. 1797–November 26, 1883)
Abolitionist, Reformer

Former slave Sojourner Truth was one of the most powerful presences on the abolitionist lecture circuit in the 1840s and 1850s. She also used her considerable talents as a speaker to advance the cause of women's rights.

Born a slave on the farm of Charles Hardenbergh, in Ulster County, New York, she was given the name Isabella and spoke Dutch as her first language. After her owner's death, she belonged to a number of masters, arriving in 1810 on the farm of John J. Dumont in New Paltz, New York. Here she met a slave named Thomas and bore five children. Two of her daughters were sold away,

Courtesy of the New-York Historical Society, New York City

and her son was sold illegally out of state in Alabama. In 1827 Isabella fled Dumont's farm and took refuge with Isaac and Maria Van Wagener, after Dumont broke his promise to free her a year before the date when all slaves in New York State were to be freed. Adopting the last name of Van Wagener, she successfully sued to have her son returned—a remarkable triumph of justice for a black woman at the time.

In 1829 Isabella Van Wagener moved with her two youngest children to New York City, where she worked as a house servant. She became involved with a religious cult, which established a commune at Sing Sing (now Ossining),

New York, returning to Manhattan after the breakup of the commune. Isabella began to have visions. She took the name of Sojourner Truth in 1843 and set out alone on foot as an itinerant preacher in response to a call from her spirit voices, traveling through Long Island and Connecticut spreading the message of God's love for humanity through words and songs.

In the winter of 1843 Sojourner Truth joined a communal farm in Northampton, Massachusetts, and met such abolitionist leaders as WILLIAM LLOYD GARRISON and FREDERICK DOUGLASS. She began speaking against slavery throughout New England, and later the Midwest, making a profound impression wherever she went. She supported herself during her travels by selling copies of her biography, *Narrative of Sojourner Truth: A Northern Slave* (1850), which she had dictated to a white friend, Olive Gilbert.

Sojourner Truth spoke at her first women's rights convention in Worcester, Massachusetts, in 1850, and thereafter played a leading role in the movement. Her tall and imposing figure and her commanding delivery always made her a popular speaker. Her famous words, from an 1851 convention where male speakers had labeled women inferior to men, are proof of her extraordinary spirit:

> Look at me! Look at my arm! I have plowed, and planted, and gathered into barns, and no man could head me—and ain't I a woman? I could work as much and eat as much as a man (when I could get it), and bear the lash as well—and ain't I a woman? I have borne five children and seen them most all sold off into slavery, and when I cried out with a mother's grief, none but Jesus heard—and ain't I a woman.

During the Civil War Sojourner Truth raised contributions for Union soldiers and nursed the wounded, while striving for better conditions in army camps. In 1864 President Abraham Lincoln received her at the White House in Washington, D.C., and she remained for two years in the capital helping freedmen living in refugee camps and working for the National Freedmen's Relief Association as a counselor in Arlington Heights, Virginia. In 1870 she petitioned President Ulysses S. Grant to establish a state for Negroes on western lands, an idea which bore no fruit but helped encourage many blacks to move west to Kansas and Missouri at the time.

Sojourner Truth continued to lecture and sell copies of her book until 1875, when poor health forced her to return to Battle Creek, Michigan, where she had made her home near her children since the mid-1850s. She died there at the age of eighty-six.

**BIBLIOGRAPHY**

Loewenberg, B. J., and R. Bogin (eds.), *Black Women in Nineteenth-Century American Life: Their Words, Their Thoughts, Their Feelings*, 1976; May, J., *Sojourner Truth: Freedom Fighter*, 1973; Ortiz, V., *Sojourner Truth: A Self Made Woman*, 1974.

# Tubman, Harriet

(ca. 1820–March 10, 1913)
Reformer

Hailed as "the Moses of her people" because of her courageous rescues of hundreds of slaves on the Underground Railroad, Harriet Tubman was a living symbol of the resistance of African Americans to slavery.

Born to slave parents on a plantation in Dorchester County, Maryland, Harriet began working as a field hand when she was seven years old. Although she received no schooling, she grew up strong-willed and independent. When she was thirteen, the plantation overseer struck her on the head causing her afterward often to fall suddenly to sleep and experience visions. In 1844 she married John Tubman. Five years later, when the plantation where she lived was sold, Harriet Tubman decided to escape to the North in order to avoid being sold out of state. Her husband decided not to flee with her, so Tubman traveled by herself on the Underground Railroad, a network of secret stations run by abolitionists to help fugitive slaves.

Not long after her safe arrival in Philadelphia, Tubman found work and began making trips to the South to help other slaves escape on the Underground Railroad. In December 1850 she brought out her sister and two children from Maryland, and later she helped her brother and two other slaves. Tubman's most daring exploit occurred in 1857 when she hired a wagon and brought from Maryland her elderly parents. She had hoped to rescue her husband also, but he had remarried and was not interested in escaping.

In the decade before the Civil War, Tubman guided to freedom about 300 slaves without ever losing a slave through capture. Deeply religious, Tubman thought all her actions were guided by God. Maryland slaveowners offered a reward of $40,000 for her apprehension. Fellow abolitionists extolled her virtues, and in the late 1850s she began speaking at abolitionist meetings.

In 1858 Tubman met the radical abolitionist JOHN BROWN in St. Catherines, Ontario, where she and her parents were then residing. She became a coconspirator in planning his raid on Harpers Ferry, Virginia, in 1859, an opportunity for action she missed on account of illness and which resulted in his capture and death.

Tubman had a vision that the Civil War would start. She continued her rescue work during the first year of the war, then early in 1862 joined the Union forces at Beaufort, South Carolina, serving as a scout and spy, often behind enemy lines. She also worked as a nurse and helped the freedmen who sought refuge with the Union army.

After the war, Tubman returned home to Auburn, New York, where she had resettled her parents on a farm in the late 1850s. In 1869 she married Nelson Davis, a disabled veteran, who died in 1888. She also cared for a number of African American orphans and elderly former slaves. Part of the money that enabled her to do this came from royalties turned over to her from Sarah Bradford, who wrote two biographies: *Scenes in the Life of Harriet Tubman* (1869) and *Harriet, the Moses of Her People* (1886). Although Tubman repeatedly applied to the federal government for compensation for her wartime services, the only money she received was a small pension as the widow of Nelson Davis.

In the last years of her life, Tubman, who was herself illiterate, raised money for freedmen's schools and helped spur the growth of the African Methodist Episcopal Church in upstate New York. In 1903 she donated 25 acres of land to the church for the establishment of a shelter for poor and homeless African Americans. Tubman died of pneumonia in 1913.

**BIBLIOGRAPHY**

Daniel, S. I., *Women Builders*, 1969; Grant, M., *Harriet Tubman*, 1974; Heidish, M., *A Woman Called Moses*, 1976; Quarles, Benjamin, *Black Abolitionists*, 1969.

# Turner, Frederick Jackson

(November 14, 1861–March 14, 1932)
Historian

Historian Frederick Jackson Turner was the author of a provocative essay, "The Significance of the Frontier in American History," which opened up a new period in the interpretation of American history.

Born in Portage, Wisconsin, Frederick Jackson Turner grew up in a family that stressed learning and culture. Educated at local schools, he earned both his B.A. (1884) and his M.A. (1888) at the University of Wisconsin. He received his Ph.D. from the Johns Hopkins University, where he studied under Herbert Baxter Adams. Adams was one of a group of American historians who applied Darwinian evolutionary ideas to the study of history. According to Adams and others of this school, American democracy had originated among the primitive tribes of Germany. Turner retained the evolutionary thrust of Adams's thinking, while significantly modifying this theory.

In 1893, as a young professor at the University of Wisconsin, Turner presented his famous paper, "The Significance of the Frontier in American History," at a meeting of the American Historical Association. In Turner's view, American democracy had begun in American rather than German forests. American history, he maintained, was to a great extent the history of the conquest of the West. The availability of free land had drawn settlers farther and farther westward, and as each successive wave of immigrants struggled with the "primitive condi-

Library of Congress

tions" of the frontier, they were transformed by the experience. According to Turner:

> The advance of the frontier has meant a steady movement away from the influence of Europe, a steady growth of independence along American lines. And to study this advance, the men who grew up under these conditions, and the political, economic, and social results of it, is to study the really American part of our history.

Turner believed that the frontier had shaped the American character; from it stemmed the American's toughness, resourcefulness, and individualism, as well as American democracy. He also believed that the frontier had served as a kind of safety valve for Americans, allowing mobility and the promise of new opportunities. "So long as free land exists," he wrote, "the opportunity for a competency exists, and economic power secures political power."

Yet as of 1893, Turner observed, citing a recent bulletin from the superintendent of the census, the western frontier was officially gone. He worried what the future held in store for Americans without a western frontier, but he hoped that because of their frontier heritage, Americans would avoid many of the social ills that beset Europeans.

Turner's essay catapulted him to celebrity. By focusing on an area that until then had been neglected, he brought about a major shift in the interpretation of American history. While previous American historians had concentrated on the nation's European origins, Turner was the first to look for what was unique about the American experience. He was also among the first to apply interdisciplinary techniques to the study of history in the seminars he taught at the University of Wisconsin.

Turner remained at the University of Wisconsin until 1910 when he became a professor at Harvard. From 1909 to 1910 he served as president of the American Historical Association, and from 1910 to 1915 he was on the board of the *American Historical Review*. Upon his retirement from Harvard in 1924, he worked as a research associate at the Huntington Library in Pasadena, California. Here he devoted himself to an analysis of such problems as the depletion of natural resources, population explosions, and the prospect of another world war more terrible than the last. Turner died at the age of seventy-one, before such a war occurred.

Turner's dedication to teaching combined with the painstaking process by which he gathered and verified facts meant that his output was relatively slight. In 1906 he published *The Rise of the New West*, covering the period from 1819 to 1829 as part of *The American Nation*

series. One other book, a collection of essays entitled *The Significance of the Frontier in American History* (1920), appeared during Turner's lifetime. Two additional books were published posthumously: *The Significance of Sections in American History* (1932), which was awarded a Pulitzer Prize, and *The United States 1830–1850* (1935).

Turner is best known for his frontier theory, which started a controversy that has continued into the present, with some historians arguing that he overemphasized the role of the frontier in shaping the American past. But he also deserves to be remembered as a historian who brought to historical research a scientific and interdisciplinary approach. He preferred to think of himself not as a historian of the West, but as one seeking to explain the United States of his day through its history, defined by Turner as the interrelations of its economics, politics, sociology, culture, and geography.

**BIBLIOGRAPHY**

Jacobs, Wilbur R., *The Historical World of Frederick Jackson Turner*, 1968; Odum, H. W., *American Masters of Social Science*, 1927.

# Veblen, Thorstein Bunde

(July 30, 1857–August 3, 1929)
Economist, Social Critic

As an economist and social critic, Thorstein Veblen was one of the leading figures in the revolt against nineteenth-century social thought. Using Darwinian evolutionary theory, Veblen attacked the conservative economic doctrines of his times. He is best known for his first book, *The Theory of the Leisure Class* (1899).

Thorstein Veblen was born on a farm in Cato Township, Manitowoc County, Wisconsin, to Norwegian immigrant parents. He grew up in

rural Minnesota in a Norwegian community. He entered Carleton College at the age of seventeen in the preparatory course, completing the college course in 1880.

Veblen then taught briefly at a private school in Wisconsin, and in 1881 he entered the graduate school of the Johns Hopkins University. Before the end of his first term, he transferred to Yale University. Unable to obtain a teaching position after he earned his Ph.D. in philosophy in 1884, Veblen spent the next seven years on his family's Minnesota farm and in Iowa, where he had moved with his wife, Ellen May Rolfe Veblen. He then entered Cornell University in 1891 and studied economics under J. Laurence Laughlin, whom, two years later, he followed to the new University of Chicago. He became an economics instructor, then an assistant professor, and helped to found the *Journal of Political Economy*, serving as managing editor from 1896 to 1905. In his writing and thinking, Veblen began to apply insights from anthropology and psychology to economic theory.

In 1899 Veblen published *The Theory of the Leisure Class*, his first and most important book. Veblen rejected the "economic" man of classical economic theory, who always behaved in a rational, productive manner. Instead Veblen argued that human beings were driven by instincts that were the result of social evolution. Unlike the Social Darwinists, however, he did not believe that the millionaires of his day represented the "survival of the fittest." Rather he viewed them as latter-day barbarians. Veblen theorized that society had begun in a savage state that was peaceful, sedentary, and communal. When society accumulated a surplus of goods, it passed into barbarism, which was characterized by warfare, private property, and the emergence of the leisure class. This class did not engage in useful production that was essential to survival but rather in wastefulness and "conspicuous consumption" undertaken to demonstrate how much wealth the leisure class possessed. Moreover, according to Veblen, the lower and middle classes were driven to emulate the pecuniary mores and rituals of the leisure class. Veblen's devastating and satirical portrait of the millionaire business tycoons and his compelling questioning of the virtue of wealth outraged many, while delighting reformers and radicals.

In his next book, *The Theory of Business Enterprise* (1904), Veblen distinguished between industry, which is directed toward productivity, and business, which is directed toward profit. He believed that there was a fundamental conflict between these two types of activity, because businesspeople will restrict production in order to keep prices and profits high.

As unconventional in his personal life as he was in his writing, Veblen was forced to leave the University of Chicago because of an extramarital affair. In 1906 he joined the faculty of Stanford University as an associate professor, but three years later was again fired for the same reason. Veblen spent the next seven years (1911–1918) as an instructor at the University of Missouri. He published several more books, including *The Instinct of Workmanship* (1914), which was based on his famous course, "Economic Factors in Civilization." Veblen saw the "instinct of workmanship," or the drive toward increased productivity, as a counter to the influence of the business culture.

In 1918 Veblen moved to New York City to become the editor of the freethinking *Dial* magazine, joining the faculty of the newly created New School for Social Research in 1919. During this period he wrote a series of articles for the *Dial* that were later published as *The Engineers and the Price System* (1921). Restating his belief in the destructive effect of business on production, he called upon engineers to organize a revolution, take over the economy, and run it through a "soviet of technicians." These ideas appealed to the leaders of what became known as the Technocracy movement, a diverse group of social scientists and politicians. But hopes for a revolution proved illusory, and Veblen himself remained skeptical of organized reform. In 1926 he returned to his cabin in Palo Alto, California, where he had lived while teaching at Stanford and where he would spend the last three years of his life.

Because he focused on habitual group behavior rather than the individual acting rationally and in isolation, Veblen was one of the founders of the institutional school of economics. During the years immediately following his death, his influence among economists was at its greatest. The Great Depression of the 1930s seemed to verify Veblen's criticism of capitalism, and his vision of an industrial order dominated by a "soviet of technicians" influenced the architects of Franklin D. Roosevelt's New Deal. Although the institutional school of economics became less important after World War II, Veblen's writings continue to be read and appreciated for their trenchant insights into human behavior.

**BIBLIOGRAPHY**

Diggins, John P., *The Bard of Savagery: Thorstein Veblen and Modern Social Theory*, 1978; Riesman, David, *Thorstein Veblen: A Critical Appraisal*, 1953, rep., 1975; Seckler, David, *Thorstein Veblen and the Institutionalists: A Study in the Social Philosophy of Economics*, 1975.

# Villard, Fanny Garrison

(December 16, 1844–July 5, 1928)
Philanthropist, Reformer

As a philanthropist, suffragist, and pacifist, Fanny Garrison Villard gave generously of both her time and money.

The only daughter of seven children born to the militant abolitionist WILLIAM LLOYD GARRISON, Fanny Garrison was born in Boston and grew up in the thick of her father's reform agitation. Though named Helen Frances, she was known as Fanny from her childhood. After attending the Winthrop School in Boston, she taught piano. In 1866 she married Henry Villard, a German immigrant and newspaper reporter. Villard later became a successful financier and political activist, taking over two leading reform journals, the New York *Evening Post* and *The Nation.*

Wealthy from successful business ventures, Fanny and Henry Villard pursued philanthropy and public service. In 1878 she became involved with her first charity, the Diet Kitchen Association, which supplied food to the ill and to children living in poverty, later serving as president of the association (1898–1922). The other charitable organizations for which she was a financial supporter and dedicated worker included the New York Infirmary for Women, the Consumers' League, the Working Woman's Protective Association, and the NAACP (National Association for the Advancement of Colored People; see JOEL E. SPINGARN). Villard also helped plan and raise money for Barnard College, the women's college associated with Columbia University, and the Harvard Annex for women (later Radcliffe College). In addition, she provided financial support for schools and colleges for blacks in New York and the South, including Virginia's Hampton Institute.

Villard came to think that charity alone was not enough—the country needed social reform, which she believed could only be accomplished through women's political participation. After her husband's death, when she was in her fifties, she joined the suffrage movement with the encouragement of her son, OSWALD GARRISON VILLARD, who had taken over the New York *Evening Post.* Fanny Villard served on the executive board of the New York State Woman Suffrage Association and was also auditor and chair of its legislative committee. In New York City she was a member of three different suffrage societies, serving as president of one, the William Lloyd Garrison Equal Suffrage Club. Villard campaigned vigorously for the New York State suffrage referendum that became law in 1917, and she continued to make speeches before various groups, including street crowds, until the Nineteenth Amendment went into effect in 1920.

Influenced by the teachings of her father, Villard was a sometime participant in peace meetings and demonstrations before 1914, when she threw herself into the effort of trying to keep the United States out of World War I. In August 1914, she organized and led a peace parade of 1,500 women down Fifth Avenue in New York City. The following year, she organized the national Woman's Peace party with settlement house founder JANE ADDAMS, serving on the board and chairing its New York branch. In 1916 Villard left the party after it decided that a belligerent act by any of the warring nations against the United States was sufficient cause to enter the war. When the nation did finally go to war, Villard devoted herself to pro- grams helping refugees and conscientious objectors. In 1919 she founded her own Woman's Peace Society, serving as its president until her death at the age of eighty-three.

**BIBLIOGRAPHY**

Addams, Jane, *Peace and Bread in Time of War*, 1922; Catt, Carrie Chapman, and Nettie Rogers Shuler, *Woman Suffrage and Politics*, 1923.

## Villard, Oswald Garrison

(March 13, 1872–October 1, 1949)
Editor, Reformer

Editor of the New York *Evening Post* and *The Nation*, Oswald Garrison Villard was a well-known pacifist who vigorously opposed the U.S. entry into both world wars. Villard helped found the National Association for the Advancement of Colored People (NAACP; see JOEL E. SPINGARN) and supported many other liberal causes.

Villard was born in Wiesbaden, Germany, where his parents, entrepreneur Henry Villard and his wife FANNY GARRISON VILLARD (daughter of the abolitionist leader WILLIAM LLOYD GARRISON), were visiting. He received his B.A. from Harvard in 1893 and his M.A. three years later. After teaching American history at Harvard, Villard turned to journalism, working as a reporter on the *Philadelphia Press* and then as an editorial writer on the New York *Evening Post*, which his father owned. The paper, with EDWIN L. GODKIN as editor in chief, took a strong stand against the Spanish-American War. In 1900, following his father's death, Villard took over both the *Evening Post* and its weekly literary supplement, *The Nation*.

A firm believer in racial equality, Villard in 1909 organized an interracial conference on the 100th anniversary of Abraham Lincoln's birth. Out of this meeting of black and white social critics and reformers came the NAACP, organized by Villard, black leader W. E. B. DU BOIS, and others. Villard wanted the NAACP to safeguard the rights of African Americans without yielding to pressures from whites, as he felt earlier leaders like BOOKER T. WASHINGTON had done.

No doubt influenced by the reform efforts of his mother and grandfather before him, Villard's concern with equal rights started early and extended to a wide range of causes, including women. While still at Harvard, he had publicly supported woman suffrage, and in 1911 he marched in a women's rights parade down Fifth Avenue in New York in front of a hostile crowd.

With the election of Woodrow Wilson to the presidency in 1912, Villard hoped to be able to promote the interests of African Americans on the national level. As chairman of the NAACP, he sought presidential support for a National Race Commission, headed by JANE ADDAMS, that would study all aspects of African American life. Though initially receptive to the idea, Wilson later rejected it out of the fear of offending southern senators. Villard then embarked on a speaking tour of major Eastern cities, arguing in favor of the plan and bitterly attacking Wilson's brand of democracy as being discriminatory.

With the outbreak of war in Europe in 1914, Villard worked to keep the United States from becoming involved. Concerned that Wilson was leading the nation into war, Villard supported the Republican candidate, Charles Evans Hughes, in the election of 1916.

When the United States did enter the war in 1917, Villard maintained that African Americans, who were denied their civil rights, should not have to give their lives for a system that was unjust. He wrote articles and editorials protesting the imprisonment of the labor leader Eugene V. Debs and of conscientious objectors and was himself attacked as being pro-German. Villard denounced the Treaty of Versailles and warned of another war to follow.

Villard's views cost him his paper. In 1918 he had to sell the New York *Evening Post* after it lost circulation. He was, however, able to keep *The Nation*, which increased its circulation from 7,000 to nearly 40,000 in the next two decades and became an influential liberal journal. In its pages, Villard attacked the Palmer Raids (so-called after U.S. attorney general A. Mitchell Palmer), in which people with radical political beliefs were arrested in 1919 and 1920. He urged his readers to sympathize with the Russian Revolution, though he was later sharply critical of the totalitarian Soviet government that emerged. These and other positions were so unpopular that Villard required police protection from angry crowds when he spoke in Cincinnati in 1921.

Throughout the 1920s, Villard campaigned against the corruption exposed in Tammany Hall (the leading arm of the Democratic party in New York) and the Teapot Dome Scandal (in which government officials leased government oil deposits for private gain), and he supported a broad program of reform including regulation of the stock market, prison reform, birth control, and the extension of labor unions. Blacklisted by the Daughters of the American Revolution as a dangerous liberal, he held a "blacklist party" in 1929. A thousand people showed up.

In 1932 Villard retired as editor of *The Nation*, but continued to serve as contributing editor. He generally welcomed the New Deal legislation of President Franklin D. Roosevelt, though he worried about the effects of big government on individual freedom. He denounced the rise of fascism in Italy and Nazism in Germany, while at the same time writing sympathetically about the German people.

In 1940 Villard severed all connection with *The Nation* because he strongly disagreed with its editorial board's support of Roosevelt's defense policy. Villard's antiwar stance led him to join in the activities of the America First Committee (see Charles Lindbergh), even though its membership included right-wing elements who opposed his reformist views. He continued to advocate nonintervention until the Japanese bombing of U.S. ships at Pearl Harbor in 1941 brought the nation into the war.

After suffering a heart attack in 1944, Villard had to cut down on his activities. He died of a stroke five years later.

**BIBLIOGRAPHY**

Humes, D. Joy, *Oswald Garrison Villard: Liberal of the 1920s*, 1960; Nevins, Allan, *The Evening Post: A Century of Journalism*, 1922; Villard, Oswald Garrison, *Fighting Years: Memoirs of a Liberal Editor*, 1939.

# Vincent, Henry

(January 1, 1862–October 29, 1935)
Editor, Reformer

Though not as well-known as other more colorful Populist leaders such as IGNATIUS DONNELLY, Henry Vincent did more than any single individual to spur the growth of the People's party in the Great Plains region.

Henry Vincent was born in Tabor, Iowa, the son of an economic freethinker and abolitionist who worked at various times for both HORACE GREELEY and WILLIAM LLOYD GARRISON. In 1879 Vincent left high school to begin publishing a weekly called *The American Nonconformist.* In 1886 he and two older brothers moved to Winfield, Kansas, to start a paper—eventually also called *The American Nonconformist—* which promised always "to take the side of the oppressed as against the oppressor."

In politics, Vincent supported the Greenback movement, a campaign to help working people by increasing the supply of paper money or "greenbacks." During the 1880s he helped organize a number of political parties around this reform of the monetary system. He also organized an alliance of Kansas editors belonging to third parties and communicated with editors outside the state in order to keep abreast of political developments throughout the country. He watched with interest the rise of the Knights of Labor (see TERENCE POWDERLY), helping the union organize in the West.

Learning that a group of farmers in Texas had formed an organization called the Farmer's Alliance with a Greenback platform and a widespread program of purchasing and marketing cooperatives, Vincent visited the group's Dallas headquarters in 1888. He came away impressed with the role of the cooperative movement in educating farmers about the ways in which they were exploited and then encouraging them to organize politically to do something about it. Vincent formed an Alliance cooperative in Winfield, Kansas. He also publicized the movement, both in his newspaper and among his fellow members of the Greenback movement.

Vincent's efforts were remarkably successful; within eighteen months about 140,000 Kansas farmers joined the movement. However, the Kansas cooperatives, along with those in other states, began to go into a decline in 1891 and 1892 when they were refused access to bank credit. It then became clear that the movement could not survive without a basic overhaul of the nation's banking and monetary system. And since the two major political parties could not be depended upon to accomplish this, Vincent and other Alliance leaders looked to create a new farm-labor party to push for their demands.

Vincent was at the forefront of the efforts that launched the movement known as the People's or Populist party in 1892. He helped found the National Reform Press Association, which during populism's brief heyday, enlisted the support of more than 1,000 country newspaper editors. To be more effective in the crusade, Vincent moved the *Nonconformist* twice, first to Indiana and later to Chicago. While editing his paper, he also managed to write *The Story of the Commonweal* (1894), a book about the army of the unemployed that marched on Washington, D.C., in 1893, under the leadership of JACOB S. COXEY.

Support for the People's party declined following the 1896 presidential election, when the party joined the Democrats to support William Jennings Bryan. After the dissolution of the People's party, Vincent remained an independent with views ahead of his time, supporting industrial unionism, equality for women and blacks, and the First Amendment rights of freedom of speech and of the press. He was skeptical of the ability of the reforms of the Progressive era to effect lasting change and tried to find another mass democratic movement that could succeed where the Populists had failed. Vincent died in Ypsilanti, Michigan, at the age of seventy-three, unconvinced that the New Deal would be the answer.

**BIBLIOGRAPHY**

Goodwyn, Lawrence C., *Democratic Promise: The Populist Moment in America*, 1976.

# Vorse, Mary Marvin Heaton

(October 9, 1874–June 14, 1966)
Labor Activist, Writer

Mary Heaton Vorse was best known as a reporter of the struggles of the American labor movement between the two world wars. Throughout her long career she communicated to the general public the realities of life for human beings who were victims of forces beyond their control.

Mary Heaton was born in New York City, the daughter of New England parents from families of comfortable means. She grew up in Amherst, Massachusetts, was sent to private schools, traveled abroad, and studied art in Paris and New York. In 1898 she married Albert White Vorse, a newspaperman with literary ambitions. With their two children they moved to Europe in 1903, hoping A. W. Vorse's career as a writer would benefit where the cost of living was cheaper. It was his wife's literary gift, instead, that came to the fore. Mary Vorse's humorous stories of family life were welcomed by American magazines. Her success was sealed when she was invited to write a chapter for a composite novel, *The Whole Family* (1908), made up of the work of twelve writers, including Henry James and WILLIAM DEAN HOWELLS. She went on to publish a number of novels as well as more famous works of nonfiction.

After returning to the United States, the Vorses settled in Provincetown, Massachusetts, in a sea captain's old house that became Mary Heaton Vorse's home base for the rest of her life. She separated from her husband in 1909. On June 14, 1910, while Mary was on a transatlantic ship, she got news of his death and the next day the death of her mother. In 1912 she married Joseph O'Brien, also a newspaperman, but she retained the name Mary Heaton Vorse. O'Brien died suddenly in 1915, leaving her with a son.

Mary Vorse's first contact with labor strife was in 1904, when she was in Venice with her first husband. Upon encountering a demonstration of young women strikers, she was impelled to join them. Her first assignment as a labor reporter was the Lawrence, Massachusetts, textile strike in 1912. She went to Europe to cover international conferences on woman suffrage and world peace in 1915, the year her husband died. Determined by then to devote her writing to liberal causes, she once described herself as "a woman who in early life got angry because many children lived miserably and died needlessly."

After World War I, Vorse reported on postwar conditions in Europe for the American Relief Association, the Red Cross, and the American press; she returned home to cover the great steel strike of 1919, which covered ten states. It was the subject of her most important labor book, *Men and Steel* (1920). Vorse next covered the Russian famine in 1921 and 1922 for the Hearst syndicate.

The year 1926 found Vorse in Passaic, New Jersey, alongside her close friend, another radical activist, ELIZABETH GURLEY FLYNN, speaking to the workers during a textile strike in which the police set upon the demonstrators and reporters with clubs. Three years later she was in

Gastonia, North Carolina, speaking at a rally of the National Textile Workers Union, when the crowd was fired upon by police. That event yielded the book *Strike—A Novel of Gastonia* (1930). In 1937 Vorse herself was wounded by shots from vigilantes as she covered a strike at the Republic Steel Corporation plant in Youngstown, Ohio. Another important book, *Labor's New Millions* (1938), chronicled the 1935 formation of the CIO (Congress of Industrial Organizations; see JOHN L. LEWIS), a labor federation dedicated to unionizing the masses of unskilled and semiskilled factory workers. She was soon in Europe again, for the North American Newspaper Alliance, covering the Nazi annexation of the Sudetenland (part of Czechoslovakia) and events in Poland and France on the eve of the outbreak of World War II. After the war, Vorse served in Italy with the United Nations Relief and Rehabilitation Administration. In 1962, when she was eighty-eight (and broke), the United Auto Workers (see WALTER REUTHER) gave her its Social Justice Award, with a cash honorarium.

Mary Heaton Vorse was an admired figure in Provincetown, where she lived when she was not traveling. Her house was a gathering place for the radical and literary intelligentsia, including the writers Eugene O'Neill, Edna St. Vincent Millay, Susan Glaspell, JOHN REED, and, in later years, John Dos Passos and Edmund Wilson. She and O'Brien helped found the Provincetown Players and provided a shed on their wharf where the Players first performed before moving on to New York. Vorse wrote about herself in *A Footnote to Folly* (1935), reminiscences of experiences in Europe and the United States, and *Time and the Town* (1942), about her life in Provincetown and of the town itself. She died in June 1966 in her home at the age of ninety-two.

**BIBLIOGRAPHY**

Garrison, Dee, *Rebel Pen: The Writings of Mary Heaton Vorse*, 1985, and *Mary Heaton Vorse: The Life of an American Insurgent*, 1989; Vorse, Mary Heaton, *The Autobiography of an Elderly Woman*, 1911.

## Wald, Lillian D.

(March 10, 1867–September 1, 1940)
Public Health Nurse, Reformer, Settlement Founder

One of the most outstanding social workers of the Progressive era, Lillian Wald made her greatest contribution in public health nursing, which she developed into a profession. She also distinguished herself as the founder of the Henry Street Settlement in New York City and as a dedicated worker for child welfare.

Born in Cincinnati, Ohio, into a prosperous family, Lillian Wald grew up in Rochester, New York, where she attended Miss Cruttenden's English-French Boarding and Day School. At age sixteen she applied to Vassar College but was rejected because she was considered to be too young. After several years spent enjoying an active social life, Wald decided she wanted serious work and entered the New York Hospital training school for nurses in August 1889. Graduating in 1891, she worked for a year as a nurse at the New York Juvenile Asylum. This experience proving unsatisfactory, Wald enrolled in the Woman's Medical College in New York to obtain additional training and at the same time began teaching home-nursing classes for immigrant families.

The turning point in Wald's life occurred in March 1893 when she was called from the classroom to help a sick woman in a run-down tenement building. Horrified by the wretched living conditions, Wald decided to devote herself to public health nursing. Together with Mary Brewster, Wald set up an office first at the College Settlement on the Lower East Side and then on the top floor of a tenement on Jefferson Street.

Library of Congress

With the financial help of Mrs. Solomon Loeb and her banker/philanthropist son-in-law, Jacob H. Schiff, Wald and Brewster were able to move to a permanent home on Henry Street, where in 1895 they established the Nurses' Settlement.

The Nurses' Settlement was the only social settlement to emphasize nursing, which in Wald's view extended beyond caring for the sick to include education aimed at preventing disease. By 1896 the settlement had eleven residents, nine of whom were trained nurses, and was known as the Henry Street Visiting Nurses Service. By 1913 there were nine such houses in Manhattan and the Bronx, with a total residential staff of ninety-two nurses, who made over 200,000 visits a year. The idea of public health nursing had been born and spread rapidly.

Wald also established the country's first public-school nursing program in New York City. She was instrumental in setting up a department of nursing at Columbia University in 1910, and two years later she helped the Red Cross establish the Town and Country Nursing Service. Having played a prominent role in the creation of the National Organization for Public Health Nursing, Wald was elected president of the organization in 1912.

The Nurses' Settlement, meanwhile, soon outgrew its nursing focus and became known as the Henry Street Settlement, providing a full complement of community programs. A system of scholarships was started for children from poor families, and career guidance and vocational training were offered. In addition, the Henry Street Settlement was involved in efforts to provide better education for retarded children, to improve housing, to establish more parks and playgrounds, and to eradicate tuberculosis. Henry Street was always dependent on donations, and Wald proved to be a good fund-raiser.

Wald also became active in the child welfare movement. She pushed for legislation prohibiting child labor, and in 1904 she and FLORENCE KELLEY, who was also a Henry Street resident, founded the National Child Labor Committee. Wald's suggestion to President Theodore Roosevelt of the need for a government agency to protect the rights of children led in 1912 to the establishment of the Federal Children's Bureau, headed by JULIA LATHROP.

The outbreak of World War I in 1914 was a blow to Wald's pacifist convictions. Together with Florence Kelley and JANE ADDAMS, she helped found the American Union Against Militarism, which had as its goal ending the war by mediation. When the United States did enter the war, Wald served as head of the Council of National Defense's committee on home nursing. She also chaired the Nurses' Emergency Council, recruiting volunteer nurses and coordinating nursing agencies during the influenza epidemic of 1918.

The war over, Wald helped found the League of Free Nations Association, a forerunner of the Foreign Policy Association. She had expanded the Henry Street Settlement to include a neighborhood playhouse in 1915, and in the 1920s she added an experimental theater and a playground. Her health deteriorating, Wald stepped down as head of the settlement in 1933. She retired to Westport, Connecticut, where after a long illness she died at the age of seventy-three.

**BIBLIOGRAPHY**

Eisemann, A., *Rebels and Reformers*, 1976; Epstein, B. W., *Lillian Wald: Angel of Henry Street*, 1948; Wald, Lillian, *The House on Henry Street*, 1915, and *Windows on Henry Street*, 1934.

# Walling, William English

(March 14, 1877–September 12, 1936)
Labor Reformer, Socialist

William English Walling dedicated his life to working for the less fortunate as a socialist, labor reformer, and founder of the National Association for the Advancement of Colored People (NAACP; see JOEL E. SPINGARN).

Born in Louisville, Kentucky, Walling was educated in private schools there and abroad. He received his B.S. from the University of Chicago, attended Harvard Law School briefly, then returned to Chicago to study sociology and economics. Independently wealthy, Walling was able to pursue his concern with social reform without having to worry about making a living. In 1900 and 1901 he served as an Illinois factory inspector. He then moved to New York City, where for four years he was a resident of the University Settlement on the Lower East Side, a predominantly immigrant neighborhood. In this same period he became active in the labor movement and befriended SAMUEL GOMPERS, president of the American Federation of Labor (AFL; see WILLIAM GREEN and JOHN L. LEWIS). At the AFL's 1903 convention Walling joined with JANE ADDAMS and others in founding the National Women's Trade Union League.

After witnessing a race riot in Springfield, Illinois, in 1908, Walling wrote two articles about race relations in the North. Published in the *Independent*, they attracted the attention of social worker Mary White Ovington, who suggested forming an organization to work for African American rights. Meetings were held in Walling's apartment, and the NAACP was born, with Walling serving as the first chairman of the board of directors. It was also Walling who hit upon the name for the organization's magazine, *The Crisis*, and who brought in W. E. B. DU BOIS to become the journal's editor.

Walling's politics were socialist, as he had declared as early as his days as an inspector in Illinois. A 1905 to 1907 trip to Russia allowed him to study the revolutionary movement there, interviewing such leaders as Maxim Gorky and Vladimir Lenin. But despite this interest—and activity on behalf of the Socialist party for years—he did not join the party until 1910. Within three years, he had published two books: *Socialism As It Is* (1912) and *The Larger Aspects of Socialism* (1913), in which he argued that reform was not enough. While desirable, reform was most useful because it paved the way for socialism.

By the early 1920s, however, Walling had distanced himself from both the party and the movement. Walling broke with the Socialist party over the entry of the United States into World War I, which the party opposed and Walling did not. He also became dismayed by the antidemocratic trends of the Russian Bolsheviks, criticizing them in *Out of Their Own Mouths* (1921), which he cowrote with Gompers.

After the war, Walling worked for the AFL on a full-time basis. He wrote for the organization's publication, the *American Federationist*, and every month spent a week in Washington, D.C., on AFL business. In 1924 he ran for Congress from Connecticut on the Democratic and Progressive tickets, but lost.

During the 1930s, Walling was alarmed by the rise of fascism in Europe. He organized committees across the Continent to aid workers living in fascist countries. In 1936 he traveled to Holland, despite a severe heart attack, to meet with a group of anti-Nazi Germans. He died on the trip, in Amsterdam.

**BIBLIOGRAPHY**

Ovington, Mary White, *How the NAACP Began*, 1967; Walling, William English, *American Labor and American Democracy*, 1926.

# Washington, Booker Taliaferro

(April 5, 1856–November 14, 1915)
Educator, Reformer

As the head of Tuskegee Institute, a leading center of black education, Booker T. Washington was a major spokesperson for his race in the late nineteenth and early twentieth century. He believed that African Americans should advance through education and effort instead of seeking social and political equality with whites.

Booker T. Washington was born a slave on a plantation near Hale's Ford, Franklin County, Virginia. His father was an unknown white man; his mother, a cook on the plantation. After Emancipation in 1865, Washington's family moved to Malden, West Virginia, where he went to work in the salt furnaces and later in a coal mine. Imbued with a strong desire to get an education, Washington managed to take classes at night.

Library of Congress

In 1872 at the age of sixteen, Washington entered Hampton Normal and Agricultural Institute in Virginia. Here he came under the influence of the school's founder and principal, SAMUEL CHAPMAN ARMSTRONG. Armstrong emphasized a program of arts and sciences as well as industrial arts that would train African Americans for jobs—and instill values. He believed that African Americans would be granted political and civil rights once they had proven themselves worthy of these rights.

Graduating from Hampton with honors in 1875, Washington returned to Malden to teach school. In 1878 he studied briefly at Wayland Seminary in Washington, D.C., before returning to Hampton as a teacher in a program for American Indian students. In 1881 Washington became principal of a new state school for African Americans at Tuskegee, Alabama.

From the time of his arrival at Tuskegee, Washington assumed a leadership role. Finding that no land or buildings had been acquired for the school, he went to work winning the support of local whites and recruiting African American students. Thanks to his efforts, Tuskegee opened with forty students in a dilapidated shanty loaned by the black Methodist church. From these modest beginnings Washington had by 1888 built Tuskegee into an institution with 540 acres of land and an enrollment of more than 400.

Like Hampton, Tuskegee offered training in a variety of skilled trades. Boys also studied farming and dairying; girls learned cooking, sewing, and other homemaking skills. In the academic departments, the emphasis was on the practical applications of learning rather than learning for its own sake. Washington was also concerned that students be taught the beauty and dignity of labor. In addition, personal hygiene, manners, and moral education were stressed. Unlike Hampton, where the principal and most of the teachers were white, Tuskegee always had an all-black staff, including the famous agricultural chemist GEORGE WASHINGTON CARVER. The school became known throughout the country and abroad. Graduates taught in all the southern states, and institutions modeled on Tuskegee were started elsewhere.

Washington personally devoted a great deal of time and energy to raising money for Tuskegee and publicizing the school and its philosophy. He was remarkably successful in securing financial aid from white northern philanthropists, including ANDREW CARNEGIE, who became the largest single donor, and philanthropic foundations such as the Peabody Education Fund, started by GEORGE PEABODY.

Beginning in 1884, when Washington addressed the National Education Association at Madison, Wisconsin, he was in demand as a public speaker on education and race relations. Washington delivered his most famous speech at the Cotton States and International Exposition in Atlanta in 1895. The essence of his racial philosophy was contained in this statement: "In all things that are purely social we can be as separate as the fingers, yet one as the hand in all things essential to mutual progress." Washington also advised blacks to remain in the South instead of seeking advancement in the North.

After Washington's Atlanta speech, he was hailed as the spokesperson for his entire race and the successor to FREDERICK DOUGLASS, who had died that year. In 1896 he was awarded an honorary degree by Harvard University. Two years later, Washington received President William McKinley at Tuskegee, and in 1901 he dined at the White House with President Theodore Roosevelt, who consulted him on appointments and on southern and racial policies. During Roosevelt's administration and that of William H. Taft, Washington had more influence than any other African American and more than some white southerners.

In keeping with Washington's philosophy of economic self-help, he organized and became the head of the National Negro Business League (1900), established to help develop and support black-owned businesses. In 1901 Washington published his autobiography, *Up From Slavery.* A best-seller in the United States and translated into more than a dozen languages, the book established Washington as a prototype of the self-made black man.

Yet many African American intellectuals, notably Harvard-educated W. E. B. DU BOIS, sharply criticized Washington's philosophy and methods. They charged that his emphasis on industrial education over academics limited blacks to low-paying jobs. They also accused Washington of giving the nod to segregation and the disenfranchisement of blacks. In fact, recent research has shown that although in public Washington was an accommodationist, in private he worked against disfranchisement and other forms of discrimination. Finally, Washington's critics attacked what they called the Tuskegee Machine, by which Washington maintained his power and sought to silence his opponents.

Washington used his influence in the white community and with African American editors to defend himself and his policies. He tried to weaken both the Niagara movement, started in 1905 by African Americans who disagreed with him, and the biracial National Association for the Advancement of Colored People (NAACP; see JOEL E. SPINGARN), founded in 1909. By the time of his death from overwork at the age of fifty-nine, his philosophy of race relations had fallen out of favor. Nevertheless, Washington's ideas on economic self-reliance remained his lasting legacy.

**BIBLIOGRAPHY**

Harlan, Louis R., *Booker T. Washington: The Making of a Black Leader,* 1972, and *Booker T. Washington: The Wizard of Tuskegee, 1901–1915,* 1983; Thornbrough, Emma Lou (ed.), *Booker T. Washington,* 1969.

# Wattleton, Alyce Faye

(July 8, 1943–   )
Women's Rights Activist

Faye Wattleton, a former president of Planned Parenthood, the principal voluntary family planning organization in the country, has been a leader in the struggle to safeguard each woman's reproductive rights.

Wattleton was born in St. Louis, Missouri, the daughter of George Wattleton, a factory worker. Her mother, Ozie, was a seamstress as well as a minister of the Church of God, a branch of the Adventist denomination. As a child Faye was taught concern for others as well as a determination to achieve. At Ohio State University, where she got room and board working in a hospital for children, she studied nursing and earned a bachelor's degree in 1964. For two years she taught at a hospital school of nursing in Dayton, Ohio.

With a full scholarship, Wattleton entered a graduate program in infant and maternal nursing at Columbia University, in New York. In the course of training in midwifery at Harlem Hospital, she witnessed the danger and agony of poor women who resorted to illegal abortions, often performed by themselves. Wattleton earned a master's degree and in 1967 returned to Dayton as assistant director of the county public health district. Her work, particularly in reinforcing health care for pregnant women, led in 1970 to her appointment as executive director of the city's Planned Parenthood board.

During the years Wattleton was director in Dayton, the organization confronted increasing opposition from the "pro-life" forces, locally and in Congress. Planned Parenthood, furthermore, was criticized by some feminists, who viewed it as controlled by men in order to oversee women's reproductive activity, and by some black groups, who viewed it as run by white people intent on reducing the birth rate (and thus the population) of blacks—that is, as a form of genocide. Wattleton responded to such criticism in an interview, stating that her organization could scarcely be called "genocidal to minorities when only thirty per cent of the women we service are minorities. . . . The future and strength of the race is for women to be able to have kids when they want them and to love and provide them with the tools they'll need to get through a hostile world."

In January 1978 Wattleton became president of the Planned Parenthood Federation of America, Inc. (see ALAN GUTTMACHER). She was the first woman and the first black person to fill the post, as well as the youngest. She brought to the federation a talent for fund raising, outreach, and publicity. Wattleton defended controversial issues, notably legal abortion, always emphasizing that Planned Parenthood was not proabortion but pro-child and pro-choice. Her activism caused some corporate funding to be withdrawn, but contributions from individuals increased.

As opposition to family planning and abortion increased during the administration of President Ronald Reagan, Wattleton and Planned Parenthood were placed on the defensive. The administration cut 15 percent of the funds long awarded to Planned Parenthood's family planning clinics under Title X of the Public Health Service Act. In 1991 the United States Supreme Court ruled that Title X funding be withheld from clinics that mentioned abortion in the course of counseling. Antiabortion demonstrations have repeatedly tried to block the entrances to Planned Parenthood clinics and to harass Planned Parenthood doctors, counselors, and clients in any way possible. Wattleton reacted defiantly to such assaults. She assumed a far more public role than had her predecessors, demanding that the government protect the rights of Planned Parenthood to operate and to deliver its services. Under her direction, moreover, Planned Parenthood decided to give up the federal funding so that its freedom in coun seling would be preserved. Wattleton set up an Action Fund under Planned Parenthood to carry on the work of its clinics, as well as to underwrite stronger lobbying against restrictions on abortions. She proposed a Freedom of Choice Act, which has not yet reached the floor of Congress.

In early 1992, Wattleton announced her resignation from Planned Parenthood in order to conduct a television "talk show" that would enable her to broaden the areas of social action that interest her.

**BIBLIOGRAPHY**

Wattleton, Faye, *How to Talk with Your Child about Sexuality,* 1986.

# Webster, Noah

(October 16, 1758–May 28, 1843)
Journalist, Lexicographer

With his famous blue-backed speller, his elementary school grammar and reader, and his *An American Dictionary of the English Language,* Noah Webster established a uniform national language based on the unique way Americans wrote and spoke English. His work constituted the nation's social and cultural declaration of independence from England.

Born in West Hartford into a family whose ancestors had helped found the colony of Connecticut, Noah Webster graduated from Yale College in 1778. He spent the next two years teaching school while studying law. In 1781 Webster was admitted to the Connecticut bar, but instead of beginning active practice, he opened a school in Goshen, Connecticut, in 1782. Dismayed by the fact that elementary schoolbooks in use were based on British models and contained practically no information about the United States, Webster prepared his own speller to rectify these omissions. His spelling book, later known as the "blue-backed speller," included lists of American towns and cities and substituted American spellings for many English words. "Gaol," for example, became "jail," and "plough" became "plow." Appearing in 1783, the first edition of 5,000 copies of Webster's speller was sold out after a year. (By the end of the nineteenth century, it had sold an estimated 60 million copies.) He followed it with a grammar book in 1784 and a reader in 1785, the three books comprising *A Grammatical Institute of the English Language*. This work not only provided a complete system for teaching English in the elementary schools, but it did so using American examples instead of British ones to illustrate points made. For the first time, information about the European voyages to America and the history of the American Revolution appeared in a textbook.

Webster's concern with protecting his rights as an author led him to press for federal copyright laws. As a result of his efforts, an American copyright law was passed in 1790.

Interested in politics as well as education, Webster advocated a strong central government in a pamphlet entitled *Sketches of American Policy* (1785). Moving to New York in 1787, he edited the *American Magazine* and gained a reputation as one of the foremost essayists in the country. He also founded the first philological society in America. In 1789 Webster returned to Hartford, where he practiced law until he moved back to New York in 1793. Here he started publishing the *American Minerva*, later called the *Commercial Advertiser*, a daily newspaper that was an organ of the Federalist party, and later, *The Herald*, a semiweekly, subsequently renamed the *New York Spectator*. Webster wrote articles supporting the administrations of George Washington and John Adams. After 1798 he ran the papers from New Haven, then gave up journalism for good in 1803 because of his dislike of the Republican policies of Thomas Jefferson, who had been elected in 1800.

Now devoting himself wholeheartedly to lexicography, Webster in 1806 published *A Compendious Dictionary of the English Language*. Part language manual and part encyclopedia, the book dispensed with archaic meanings of words and updated vocabulary and spelling usage, while including over 5,000 new words. By working on it, Webster taught himself the art of lexicography. Thus the dictionary served as a dress rehearsal for the much larger and more comprehensive dictionary that he spent the next twenty years compiling.

Meanwhile, in 1812 Webster moved to Amherst, Massachusetts, where his interest in improving higher education made him one of the founders of Amherst Academy (later Amherst College). Webster served twice on Amherst's board of trustees between 1816 and 1821, and in 1820 he became president of the college's executive board.

All the while laboring on his dictionary, Webster in 1822 returned to New Haven, where he lived the life of a scholar. He spent the year of 1824 to 1825 abroad, studying in the best libraries of England and France, then returned to New Haven to complete his monumental work. Published in 1828 in two volumes, each containing more than 1,000 pages, *An American Dictionary of the English Language* was a first-rate scholarly achievement that won Webster an international reputation. As in his earlier dictionary, Webster continued the practice of recording nonliterary words, though unlike the modern dictionaries that bear his name, his did not include all spoken language. He based his definitions on American as well as British usage, starting with the primary meanings of words and deriving other meanings from these.

Following the publication of his magnum opus, Webster continued to write and do research. He revised his dictionary, wrote a history of the United States, and assembled his papers on various political and literary topics. He died at the age of eighty-four, having through his schoolbooks and dictionaries justly earned the nickname of America's First Schoolmaster.

**BIBLIOGRAPHY**

Morgan, J. S., *Noah Webster*, 1975; Rollins, R. M., *The Long Journey of Noah Webster*, 1980.

# Weld, Theodore Dwight

(November 23, 1803–February 3, 1895)
Abolitionist, Educator

Through patient effort and eloquent speeches that employed evangelical techniques, Theodore Weld and the band of followers he trained converted thousands in the North and the West to the abolitionist cause in the 1830s.

Born in Hampton, Connecticut, Theodore Weld came from a long line of New England ministers. He attended Hamilton College in Clinton, New York, but left in 1825 after coming under the influence of revivalist preacher CHARLES GRANDISON FINNEY. Weld spent two years preaching throughout western New York, while also studying for the ministry at the Oneida Institute in Whitesboro, New York.

He joined the antislavery cause and soon convinced two wealthy New York philanthropists, ARTHUR TAPPAN and LEWIS TAPPAN, also to become part of the abolitionist movement.

In 1831 Weld succeeded in convincing the Tappans to fund a theological seminary in the West where Finney might train his converts for the ministry. They sent Weld to find a site, and he chose the already established Lane Seminary in Cincinnati, Ohio. Weld studied at Lane to complete his preparations for the ministry, but he was forced out in 1834 when he led students in a series of debates on slavery that lasted for eighteen days. When the trustees called a halt to the debates, Weld and many of the students, the so-called Lane rebels, went to Oberlin College in Oberlin, Ohio, which then became a center of abolitionist activity.

As an agent of the newly formed American Anti-Slavery Society, Weld traveled throughout Ohio, Pennsylvania, and New York, lecturing and helping to organize antislavery societies. Tall and careless of his appearance, with piercing eyes and hair that stuck out like the quills of a porcupine, Weld was a powerful speaker who was undeterred by hostile audiences. In 1836 Weld organized a conference in New York to train agents for the American Anti-Slavery Society. Among the attendees were ANGELINA GRIMKÉ and SARAH GRIMKÉ, daughters of a South Carolina planter and slaveowner who had become Quakers and abolitionists. Two years later, Weld married Angelina Grimké and Sarah joined their household.

His voice failing, Weld, meanwhile, sought to advance the cause by writing pamphlets that were published anonymously. Of these, the most influential was *American Slavery As It Is* (1839), a compilation of items from southern newspapers detailing the horrors of slavery. The pamphlet was a major source of inspiration to HARRIET BEECHER STOWE, who drew upon the facts in it while writing her novel *Uncle Tom's Cabin*. From 1841 to 1843, Weld helped a group of antislavery congressmen, headed by John Quincy Adams, by providing research material on slavery. The group succeeded in getting the repeal of the gag rule, which had prevented debate in the House of Representatives of any antislavery petition.

The antislavery cause gradually moved away from Weld's brand of evangelical belief to take a more political approach. Left behind by this change, Weld retired from public life in 1843. However, his work was carried on by the many prominent people he had converted to the cause. They included the popular minister HENRY WARD BEECHER and James G. Birney, a former slaveowner from Alabama, who became the presidential candidate of the antislavery Liberty party in 1840.

Weld labored on the farm in Belleville, New Jersey, where he and his family had moved, and started a small school for young children. From 1854 to 1862 he served as the head of Eagleswood, a coeducational, integrated school near Perth Amboy, New Jersey, whose student body contained many of the children of his former abolitionist colleagues. Moving to Fairmont (later Hyde Park) near Boston in

1862, he taught English at a girls' school for several years. Weld also became active in the community, sitting on the school board and chairing the board of the public library. Weld died at the age of ninety-one, having outlived his wife, his sister in law, and all of his abolitionist associates.

**BIBLIOGRAPHY**

Abzug, Robert H., *Passionate Liberator: Theodore Dwight Weld and the Dilemma of Reform,* 1980; Thomas, B. P., *Theodore Weld: Crusader for Freedom,* 1950; Walters, R. G., *The Antislavery Appeal: American Abolitionism After 1830,* 1976.

# Wells-Barnett, Ida Bell

(July 16, 1862–March 25, 1931)
Reformer

As an antilynching crusader and the founder of the black women's club movement and other black rights organizations, Ida B. Wells-Barnett was one of the most influential African American women of her generation.

Born a slave in Holly Springs, Mississippi, Ida Wells was educated at Rust College, a school started by the Freedmen's Aid Society after the Civil War. Orphaned when she was fourteen, she lied about her age in order to obtain a teaching position

University of Chicago Library

in a rural one-room school. In 1884 Wells moved to Memphis, Tennessee, where she taught first in rural schools and then in the city schools, while continuing her own education in the summers at Fisk University. That year, Wells refused to leave her seat when a railroad conductor ordered her to move to the section meant for blacks. She was taken off the train, over which she sued the railroad and won, but in 1887 the Tennessee Supreme Court reversed the decision.

Describing the incident in an article for her church newspaper, Wells went on to contribute to other church papers and to weeklies aimed at African Americans. Because of her articles criticizing segregated education as inferior, Wells was dismissed from her teaching position in 1891. She then bought a one-third interest in the Memphis *Free Speech and Headlight,* later becoming the paper's editor.

In 1892 Well's life took a dramatic turn when three Memphis men whom she knew were lynched. Wells wrote a blistering editorial attacking the lynchings. While Wells was away on a visit to Philadelphia and New York, a mob attacked and destroyed the offices of the paper, and Wells was warned not to return.

Remaining in the Northeast, Wells began to campaign against lynching. She lectured extensively and helped found antilynching societies like the Women's Loyal Union in New York in 1892. She also aided in the establishment of an antilynching and antisegregation society in

Great Britain, where she lectured in 1893 and 1894. The following year, Wells published *A Red Record*, a statistical record of lynchings over a three-year period from 1893 to 1895 and a history of lynching since the freeing of the slaves thirty years earlier.

Making Chicago her home, Wells objected to the fact that the contributions of African Americans were not represented at the World Columbian Exposition in Chicago in 1893. Having earlier founded the first black women's club in Boston, she organized a similar group in Chicago in 1893, which became known as the Ida B. Wells Club. In 1895 Wells married Ferdinand Lee Barnett, founder of the city's first black newspaper and an advocate of black rights. While rearing their four children, Wells-Barnett did less lecturing and traveling but remained active in the Ida B. Wells Club, serving as its president and helping create both a kindergarten and an orchestra. In 1910 she helped found the Negro Fellowship League, which provided meeting rooms, a social center, and a dormitory to newly arrived African American men from the South. In 1913 she became the first woman to serve in Chicago as an adult probation officer, a position she held for three years. In 1918 Wells-Barnett made a courageous visit to East St. Louis, Illinois, in the wake of race riots, in order to get legal aid for the African Americans who had been subject to mob attack.

Militant in her views, Wells-Barnett opposed the policy of compromise and accommodation with whites favored by the black leader BOOKER T. WASHINGTON. She often attacked this policy before the National Afro-American Council, of which she served as secretary from 1898 to 1902. Siding instead with W. E. B. Du Bois, Wells-Barnett joined with him and others in the founding of the National Association for the Advancement of Colored People (NAACP; see JOEL E. SPINGARN) in 1910. But even the NAACP proved too conservative for the outspoken Wells-Barnett, and she eventually distanced herself from the organization.

Wells-Barnett was also active in the suffrage and women's movements. She founded the first black woman suffrage association, the Alpha Club of Chicago, and joined in suffrage marches. In 1930 she sought a seat in the Illinois state senate on the independent ticket but came in third. Wells-Barnett died a year later in Chicago at the age of sixty-eight.

**BIBLIOGRAPHY**

Duster, Alfreda M. (ed.), *Crusade for Justice: The Autobiography of Ida B. Wells*, 1970; Meier, August, *Negro Thought in America, 1880–1915*, 1963; Mossell, N. F., *The Work of the Afro-American Woman*, 1908.

# White, Walter Francis

(July 1, 1893–March 21, 1955)
Civil Rights Leader

Walter F. White served the cause of African Americans as assistant and executive secretary of the National Association for the Advancement of Colored People (NAACP) for nearly forty years. He came to be the most devoted fighter in the effort to stamp out lynching in the United States after World War I.

Walter White was born in Atlanta, Georgia, to George W. White, a mail carrier, and Madeline Harrison, a school teacher. Five thirty-seconds of his ancestry was African American.

Walter was blond, blue-eyed, and of light complexion and could have passed for white. He chose, with the rest of his family, to identify with his black ancestry. He attended the preparatory school of Atlanta University, which had been founded in 1867 for the education of blacks, and went on to graduate from the university in 1916. He worked as a clerk, then as a cashier, for the Standard Life Insurance Company. White's first activist involvement was in a protest move against the Atlanta Board of Education, which had planned to eliminate the seventh grade from black schools in order to free funds for a new white high school. The protest succeeded.

In December 1916, White led in founding a local branch of the young NAACP (see JOEL E. SPINGARN) and was elected its secretary. When the writer James Weldon Johnson, the national secretary of the NAACP, visited and learned of White's activities, he hired him as his assistant secretary in the New York office. Upon Johnson's retirement in 1931, White was promoted to national executive secretary, a post he held until the end of his life.

During the 1920s White focused his attention on lynching and personally investigated forty-one lynchings and eight race riots. In southern towns, pretending to be a white reporter for a Northern newspaper, he circulated freely, interviewing white people about racial tensions. After a violent lynching and riot in an Arkansas town, White in his reporter pose interviewed imprisoned black men, lynchers, and even the state governor; he managed to escape on a train just ahead of a white crowd who had discovered his identity. He wrote a novel about lynching, *The Fire in the Flint* (1924), and another about passing as white, *Flight* (1926). In 1929 he published a study of lynching, *Rope and Faggot: A Biography of Judge Lynch*, written on a Guggenheim fellowship.

White led the NAACP's campaign to get antilynching legislation through the Congress. Two bills passed the House of Representatives in 1934 and 1937, but both failed in the Senate. For his work lobbying Congress and bringing

racial violence to public notice, White was awarded the Spingarn Medal in 1937.

The NAACP legal department, under White's direction, began a long campaign in the courts to have state-enforced segregation declared illegal. (The legal strategy, plotted by Thurgood Marshall—later a justice of the Supreme Court—led to the Supreme Court's decision in 1954 that overturned the "separate but equal" doctrine.) In 1941 White joined A. PHILIP RANDOLPH in persuading President Franklin D. Roosevelt to issue an executive order banning discrimination in defense plants and setting up the Fair Employment Practices Commission. During World War II, White toured every war theater as a *New York Post* correspondent, investigating discrimination against black service men and women. His book *A Rising Wind* (1945) reported his findings and strengthened the case for President Harry S Truman's executive order desegregating the armed forces in 1948.

When the Daughters of the American Revolution refused the singer Marian Anderson permission to sing in Constitution Hall, Washington, in 1939, White joined Eleanor Roosevelt in arranging for the concert to take place at the Lincoln Memorial before 75,000 people. He rendered a different kind of service in August 1943, at the height of a violent race riot in Harlem, when he toured the streets all night with Mayor Fiorello H. La Guardia, calming the excited crowds.

White was an adviser to the U.S. delegation at the San Francisco conference to found the United Nations in 1945. Later he traveled worldwide, lecturing on race relations, and developed a special interest in India and the West Indies. He wrote two weekly newspaper columns, one for the black *Chicago Defender* and another for a syndicate of white papers.

White's activities outside the NAACP and his autocratic manner of administering his staff caused him difficulties. He was criticized by W. E. B. Du Bois, one-time editor of the NAACP journal, *Crisis*, who charged that White's involvements compromised NAACP policy.

When Du Bois was abruptly discharged from his professorship at Atlanta University in 1944, however, White used his influence to have him reinstated. In the postwar years, the NAACP came under criticism from more radical African American activists for being too conservative, averse to direct action, even timid. Such criticism reflected on White's leadership.

White married Leah Powell, an NAACP employee, in 1922, and they had two children. After a divorce, in 1949 White married the writer Poppy Cannon, who was white. White died suddenly of a heart attack in 1955, having served as NAACP secretary until his death.

**BIBLIOGRAPHY**

Cannon, Poppy, *A Gentle Knight: My Husband, Walter White*, 1956; White, Walter, *A Man Called White*, 1948, and *How Far the Promised Land?* 1955.

# White, William Allen

(February 10, 1868–January 29, 1944)
Journalist

Kansas editor and author William Allen White was one of the most respected and beloved figures of his day, serving as the mouthpiece of small-town, Main Street America for almost half a century.

Born in Emporia, Kansas, William Allen White moved with his family to El Dorado, Kansas, when he was ten. He attended the College of Emporia and the University of Kansas (1886–1890) while working for various local newspapers. Leaving college without his degree to serve as business manager of the El Dorado *Republican*, White later became an editorial writer for the Kansas City *Star*. In 1895 White borrowed $3,000 to purchase the Emporia *Gazette*, of which he was editor and publisher for the remainder of his life.

Thanks to the lively, genial editorials he wrote for this hitherto unknown newspaper, White became known throughout the country as the Sage of Emporia and the spokesperson of middle-class midwestern America. His writings reflected many of the values of his readers. White extolled the school and the church as cornerstones of democracy and contrasted the neighborliness of small communities with the impersonality of the big city. He believed public officials ought to be upright and called for fair play in politics.

White was a conservative Republican until converted to a more liberal outlook by his friendship with Theodore Roosevelt, whom he first met in 1897. From then on White began to express progressive ideas in his articles, supporting such measures as the initiative and the referendum, government regulation of business, and workers' compensation. In 1911 White helped found the National Progressive Republican League, and a year later, he backed Roosevelt's Progressive party bid for the presidency. Summing up the excitement of the campaign, he wrote, "Roosevelt bit me and I went mad." After Roosevelt's defeat, White returned to the Republican party, working without much success to get it to adopt more progressive policies.

White's first editorial to attract national attention was a biting attack on the Populist movement, entitled "What's the Matter with Kansas?" Appearing at the time of the election of 1896, the editorial was widely reprinted by Republican editors and party leaders. It helped White get a publisher for his first book of fiction, *The Real Issue* (1896), a collection of stories about Kansas life, and he soon began contributing stories and articles to magazines like *McClure's* and *Harper's Weekly.* A novel called *A Certain Rich Man* (1909) sold 125,000 copies.

In 1917 White was a member of a Red Cross mission to Europe, and two years later, he reported on the Paris Peace Conference. White took the side of the unions during the 1922 railroad strike and was arrested for displaying a prounion poster in the window of his newspaper office. The incident spawned an editorial on freedom of speech, "To an Anxious Friend," which won him a Pulitzer Prize. In a different vein, White's moving editorial tribute (May 1921) to his daughter Mary Katherine, who died in a riding accident, was widely reprinted and is still regarded as a classic.

During the 1920s White took a strong stand against the intolerance of the Ku Klux Klan. Unable to persuade either candidate for governor of the state to oppose the Klan, White in 1924 ran himself as an independent on an anti-Klan plank. He was defeated, but his campaign helped discredit the Klan nationally as well as within Kansas.

While often critical of the probusiness stance of the Republican party during the 1920s, White could not give his wholehearted endorsement to the New Deal of Franklin D. Roosevelt. He worried that it favored special-interest groups too much and was leery of what he saw as its tendencies toward collective control of the economy.

As World War II began, White was a major proponent of shipping supplies to Britain and France, despite the United States' neutrality. In 1940 he founded and chaired the Committee to Defend America by Aiding the Allies.

A prolific author, White produced a biography of Woodrow Wilson (1924) and two of Calvin Coolidge (1925, 1938) in addition to his many editorials, magazine articles, and fictional works. His newspaper writings were gathered into two collections, *The Editor and His People* (1924) and *Forty Years on Main Street* (1937). In 1943, while hard at work on his *Autobiography,* White was stricken with cancer. He died in Emporia at the age of seventy-five. Published posthumously, White's *Autobiography* won him a second Pulitzer Prize.

**BIBLIOGRAPHY**

Clough, Frank C., *William Allen White of Emporia,* 1941, rep., 1970; Emery, Edwin, *The Press and America,* 1962; Hinshaw, David, *A Man From Kansas,* 1945; White, William Allen, *Autobiography,* 1946.

# Wiener, Norbert

(November 26, 1894–March 18, 1964)
Inventor, Philosopher

A renowned scientist and mathematician, Norbert Wiener invented the new science of cybernetics. His practical and theoretical contributions in the fields of computer science and machine automation profoundly shaped the late–twentieth-century world.

Wiener was born in Columbia, Missouri, in 1894, the son of Leo Wiener, a professor of Slavic languages at Harvard University, and Bertha Kahn Wiener. A child prodigy, he knew the alphabet at eighteen months and algebra and geometry at age six. He graduated from high school in Ayer, Massachusetts, at eleven and received his B.A. from Tufts College at fourteen. He earned his Ph.D. from Harvard at age nineteen for a dissertation in mathematical logic and went on to study at Cambridge

University (England) with Bertrand Russell, Göttingen University (Germany), and Columbia University (New York).

Wiener began his forty-year teaching career at the Massachusetts Institute of Technology, in Cambridge, as an instructor in 1919, becoming a full professor in 1932. During World War II he made important contributions to the development of radar and guided missiles and made comparisons between the working of automatic machines (in particular, electronic computers) and the human nervous system. His book *Cybernetics: or Control and Communication in the Animal and the Machine,* introducing the science he had founded, appeared in France in 1947 and in the United States in 1948. He coined the word "cybernetics" from the Greek *kybernetes,* meaning "steersman" or "pilot." Bringing together physiology and engineering, the revolutionary new science of cybernetics became enormously influential.

Envisaging giant computers replacing the human brain in a great second industrial revolution, Wiener was concerned about the devaluation of the brain and the possibility of huge destruction by military devices. In 1947 he refused to do any further research for the American military.

Wiener's books included *The Human Use of Human Beings* (1950) and *God and Golem, Inc.* (published posthumously, in 1964). He received many science awards and was elected to the National Academy of Sciences. In early 1964 he received the National Medal of Science from President Lyndon B. Johnson and soon after, with his wife, the former Marguerite Engemann, left for the University of Amsterdam, where he was to be a visiting scholar. Invited to lecture at the Royal Academy of Sweden, Wiener died suddenly in Stockholm.

**BIBLIOGRAPHY**

Wiener, Norbert, *Ex-Prodigy,* 1953, and *I Am a Mathematician,* 1956.

# Wilkins, Roy

(August 30, 1901–September 8, 1981)
Civil Rights Leader

Roy Wilkins was a lifelong activist in the civil rights movement and a leader of the National Association for the Advancement of Colored People (NAACP) for nearly fifty years. He was criticized by more militant African Americans for working with white groups and within the legal structure.

Wilkins was born in St. Louis, Missouri, to college-educated parents from Mississippi. His father was a Methodist clergyman but had to take a job in a brickworks to support the family. His mother died of tuberculosis when he was four, and he and his younger sister and brother were sent to an aunt and uncle in Minnesota. After high school, Wilkins worked his way through the University of Minnesota as a cleanup man in a slaughterhouse and, during summers, as a redcap (porter) and waiter. At the university he was an editor of the student newspaper and of a black weekly. While a student he joined the NAACP (see JOEL E. SPINGARN) and vowed to devote his life to working for justice for African Americans.

Having grown up in a city where there was no segregation and little discrimination, Wilkins found life different when he moved to Kansas City, Missouri, which he called "a Jim Crow town through and through." ("Jim Crow" is a term used for discriminatory practices against blacks.) He had gone there to work as an editor of a weekly, *The Call*, which addressed a black audience. Wilkins became secretary of the local chapter of the NAACP and in his articles in *The Call* urged Missouri blacks to go to the polls and vote against racist candidates. His efforts paid off in 1930 when a senator who was an outspoken racist was defeated for reelection. The executive secretary of the NAACP, WALTER F. WHITE, took note of Wilkins's campaign and invited him to join the New York office as his assistant.

Wilkins's first important assignment took him into the heart of Jim Crow country. He was sent to investigate conditions among black workers rebuilding the Mississippi River levees on a federally sponsored flood-control project. Concealing his NAACP connection, which if discovered could have meant his being beaten, he worked in the labor camps at the wage of 10 cents an hour. His report, *Mississippi Slave Labor* (1932), helped influence Congressional legislation to improve working conditions and wages for workers on federal projects.

In 1934 Wilkins succeeded W. E. B. Du Bois as editor of the official NAACP journal, *The Crisis.* At the time he was lobbying actively for federal legislation against lynching and joined in picketing the U.S. attorney general's office because the agenda of a national conference on crime did not include lynching. On the picket line in Washington he experienced his first arrest. Though antilynching legislation was never enacted, Wilkins's and the NAACP's work in education and propaganda contributed to a

National Archives

marked decrease in the crime of lynching (see JESSIE DANIEL AMES).

During World War II, while continuing his work with the NAACP, Wilkins was an adviser to the War Department and, in 1945, together with Walter White, a consultant to the U.S. delegation at the United Nations charter conference in San Francisco.

Thereafter, Wilkins led in urging a constitutional approach to securing rights for African Americans. A confirmed integrationist, he urged blacks to focus on being American. "This is our nation. We helped build it," he declared. He pushed the legal campaign to end segregation in schools, which led in 1954 to the U.S. Supreme Court's decision in the critical *Brown* v. *Board of Education* case outlawing the "separate but equal" doctrine. The case was argued by the NAACP's special counsel, Thurgood Marshall, who later was appointed an associate justice of the Supreme Court.

Wilkins was acting executive secretary of the NAACP in 1949 and 1950, while Walter White was away, and also chairman of the National Emergency Civil Rights Mobilization, an influential Washington lobby. Upon White's death in 1955, Wilkins became executive secretary and served in that post (later called the executive directorship) until he retired in 1977. The NAACP membership had increased from about 25,000 in 1931 to more than 400,000.

During the civil rights movement, Wilkins played a forceful role, joining the marches and demonstrations in the South while working for success in Washington by legal means. Under his direction, the NAACP lobbied actively for the passage of the Civil Rights Act (1964) and the Voting Rights Act (1965). He praised the sit-ins by students and sent NAACP lawyers to defend any who were arrested. His willingness to work with whites and his insistence that the struggle for black equality be fought through existing legal channels alienated more radical blacks, who called him an Uncle Tom. He bitterly criticized the partisans of black power and black separatism (see MALCOLM X) and argued for full integration. In the 1970s, Wilkins attacked the Republican administrations for weakening civil rights enforcement. In his last years, many younger African Americans began to recognize what the NAACP had accom-

plished under his leadership. In the words of JESSE JACKSON, the black movement needed both the vitality of the Black Panthers and the wisdom of Wilkins.

Roy Wilkins died shortly after his eightieth birthday, leaving his wife of fifty-two years, Aminda. They had no children. President Ronald Reagan ordered the American flag flown at half staff at all government buildings.

**BIBLIOGRAPHY**

Solomon, H., and A. Wilkins (eds.), *Talking with Roy Wilkins: Selected Speeches and Writings*, 1977; Wilkins, Roy, with Tom Mathews, *Stand Fast: The Autobiography of Roy Wilkins*, 1982.

## Willard, Emma Hart

(February 23, 1787–April 15, 1870)
Educator

Emma Willard was a pioneer in education for women. She founded the highly successful Troy Female Seminary, which offered a collegiate curriculum to women; brought up for the first time the issue of privately endowed educational institutions for women; and publicized the need for trained women teachers.

Born on a farm in Berlin, Connecticut, the sixteenth of her father's seventeen children, Emma Hart grew up in an atmosphere that encouraged learning. Her well-educated, open-minded father discussed current events and philosophy with her, and she learned geometry on her own. In 1802 she enrolled in the Berlin Academy and in 1804 began teaching young children in the village school. The next year she began teaching older children in the family house, while continuing her own education at a school in Hartford, Connecticut.

In 1807 she became the head of the Female Academy in Middlebury, Vermont. Here she

met and married Dr. John Willard, a physician who shared her commitment to education for women. A visit by her husband's nephew strengthened her conviction that women's education was deficient when compared to men's. In 1814 she opened a school in the Willard home to equalize women's education. Her Middlebury Female Seminary offered academic subjects like math and philosophy instead of the usual female program of sewing, singing, and painting.

Encouraged by her success at Middlebury, Willard petitioned Governor DeWitt Clinton of New York and the state legislature in behalf of a program of state-financed schools for girls. In her influential *Plan for Improving Female Education*, published at her own expense in 1819, she skillfully argued the benefits of such a program, pointing out that educated women would make better wives, mothers, and elementary schoolteachers. She was also the first to call for private funding of schools that could teach women of limited means.

Willard's plan so impressed Governor Clinton that he invited her to move her school to Waterford, New York, that same year. Though chartered by the legislature, the school received no state funds. So when the small industrial town of Troy, New York, offered her $4,000 to start a school for girls there, Willard readily accepted. Founded in 1821, the Troy Female Seminary was unique in offering a college-level curriculum that stressed history, philosophy, the sciences, modern languages, and gymnastics. It quickly gained a national reputation, particularly for turning out qualified schoolteachers, who, in turn, spread Willard's educational ideas throughout the country.

An innovative teacher who was one of the first to use maps in teaching history and geography, Willard was also an able administrator. Under her direction, the Troy Female Seminary prospered. In addition to her work as a teacher and administrator, Willard wrote a number of textbooks. Based on her methods, the textbooks sold well and earned her substantial royalties.

After the death, in 1825, of her husband, who had served as school physician and business manager, Willard took full charge of the Troy Female Seminary. Besides her work for her own school, she campaigned and raised money for a girls' teacher training school that was established in Athens, Greece, in 1832. To further publicize the need for trained teachers in the United States, Willard in 1837 formed the Willard Association for the Mutual Improvement of Female Teachers, the first organization of its kind in the country.

Retiring from the Troy Female Seminary the following year, Willard turned its administration over to her son and daughter-in-law. Following a disastrous and short-lived second marriage, she returned to Troy, where she spent the rest of her life supporting education and other reform causes through writings and lectures. Willard worked to improve the public schools in New York and Connecticut and from 1845 to 1847 traveled throughout the South and the West, campaigning for more women teachers, higher salaries, and better school buildings. In 1854 she represented the United States, along with Connecticut educator HENRY BARNARD, at the World's Educational Convention in London. Though no suffragist, Willard did advocate financial independence for women and an extension of married women's property and legal rights. She died in Troy at the age of eighty-four.

**BIBLIOGRAPHY**

Flexner, E., *Century of Struggle: The Woman's Rights Movement in America*, 1959, rev., 1975; Lutz, Alma, *Emma Willard: Pioneer Educator of American Women*, 1964.

# Willard, Frances Elizabeth Caroline

(September 28, 1839–February 17, 1898)
Reformer

A founder of the National Woman's Christian Temperance Union and president until her death, Frances Willard was a dynamic and influential figure in late-nineteenth-century American reform.

Born in Churchville, New York, Frances Willard grew up on a farm on the Wisconsin frontier. Educated largely at home by her mother, she studied for a year at the Milwaukee Female College, then transferred to Northwestern Female College in Evanston, Illinois, graduating in 1859. She became an educator, teaching at many schools in six different states. In 1861 Willard was briefly engaged to Charles

Henry Fowler, a Chicago clergyman who later became president of Northwestern University, but Willard ended the engagement. After two years spent traveling in Europe with a wealthy friend, Willard in 1870 accepted the presidency of the newly formed Evanston College for Ladies. When the college merged with Northwestern University in 1873, she became dean of women, but disagreements with Fowler led her to resign.

Library of Congress

Willard had, meanwhile, helped organize the Association for the Advancement of Women, a movement of moderate feminism for those women who considered suffrage too extreme a demand. In 1874, not long after leaving Northwestern, she became president of the newly established Chicago Woman's Temperance Union and then secretary of the Illinois temperance association. She joined with other midwestern temperance leaders late in 1874 in forming the National Woman's Christian Temperance Union (WCTU), of which she was chosen recording secretary.

In temperance Willard found her life's work, but she was soon at odds with conservatives within the movement. While they emphasized peaceful protests as a means of achieving their goal, Willard believed that a broad program of reform, including woman suffrage and the eight-hour day for workers, was necessary. In 1876 she was sharply criticized for trying to introduce a prosuffrage resolution at the national WCTU convention. In 1877 Willard resigned as recording secretary, and after a brief stint working for the evangelist DWIGHT MOODY, she spent a year lecturing on suffrage throughout the country. Staying on as head of the WCTU's publications committee, she also promoted suffrage through the WCTU journal.

In 1879 the more liberal element of the WCTU gained control of the organization and elected Willard president.

Under Willard's leadership, the WCTU began to promote a variety of other reform causes, for which separate departments were organized. By 1889 thirty-nine such departments had been organized, including ones for suffrage; labor reform; female health and hygiene; and "society purity," focusing on the evils of rape and prostitution. There was also a mother's department, a department of peace and arbitration, and departments concerned with the welfare of immigrants, African Americans, and prisoners. Each department served an educational purpose, while at the same time working for reform legislation.

Thanks to Willard's influence, the WCTU's annual conventions became rousing spectacles, complete with banners, music, and flowers. Between conventions she embarked on long speaking tours, which drew huge crowds and made headlines, earning her a national reputation. Willard further sought through her activities to link the WCTU with other women's rights and reform organizations. In 1887 she and four other women were elected by local church conferences as delegates to the Methodist General Conference—the first women to be so named—but they were denied their seats, as a result of intervention by Charles Henry Fowler, now a bishop in the Methodist church. The following year, Willard played a leading role at the International Council of Women, which aimed at linking a number of women's organizations. She served as first president of the National Council of Women (1888–1890) and as vice president of the Universal Peace Union. In 1889 Willard helped found the General Federation of Women's Clubs, which became a strong middle-class instrument for women's issues and reform.

Willard also worked to make the WCTU a force in national politics. With both major political parties refusing to endorse prohibition, she founded the Home Protection party in 1880. Through this group she was able to get the Prohibition party to endorse woman suffrage and unite with it as the Home Protection Prohibition party. In 1884 this party was probably responsible for the Republicans' losing the presidential election, but the alliance between the WCTU and the Prohibition party fell apart soon afterward. Willard then sought unsuccessfully to get the Populist party to endorse a prohibition plank in 1892 and again in 1895.

Willard had, meanwhile, begun to extend her activities to the international scene. After an 1883 visit to San Francisco's Chinatown, she vowed to fight opium addiction as well as alcoholism and sent temperance missionaries abroad to set up temperance unions and circulate a petition calling on world leaders to act against alcohol and narcotic drugs. These efforts resulted in the founding of the World WCTU, which elected Willard president in 1891.

Beginning in 1892, Willard spent much of her time in England, trying to persuade British temperance leaders to adopt her broad-based reform approach. While there, she came under the influence of British socialism and joined Beatrice and Sidney Webb's Fabian society, a British group favoring a gradual rather than a revolutionary shift to socialism. Willard's long absences, combined with longstanding dissatisfaction with the thrust of her leadership, produced trouble at the 1897 WCTU convention in the United States. It took a major effort on Willard's part to regain the support of the majority and win all the key votes. Her health already on the decline, Willard died a year later at the age of fifty-eight. Thousands attended her funeral, and tens of thousands more took part in memorial processions throughout the country. Famous for her reform efforts, she was honored by the state of Illinois in 1905, when it placed a statue of her in the U.S. Capitol.

After Willard's death, the WCTU reverted to its old emphasis on prohibition, while glorifying her memory. In fact, Willard's legacy to nineteenth-century reform was significant. By joining together home, family, religion, temperance, suffrage, and social reform under the banner of "home protection," Willard succeeded in bringing an entire generation of conservative, middle-class women into new areas of public endeavor.

**BIBLIOGRAPHY**

Bordin, Ruth, *Women and Temperance*, 1981; Earhart, Mary, *Frances Willard: From Prayer to Politics*, 1944.

# Williams, Roger

(January 16, 1603–March 15, 1683)
Colonial Founder, Religious Leader

Puritan leader Roger Williams was an early advocate of religious liberty and the complete separation of church and state. He put these revolutionary ideas into practice when he founded the colony of Rhode Island.

Born in London into a well-to-do merchant family, Williams was converted to the Puritan faith while still a boy, against his family's wishes. He served as a stenographer to the prominent jurist Sir Edward Coke, who, impressed with the boy's capacity to learn, arranged for him to attend the Charterhouse School in 1621. Three years later, Williams entered Pembroke College, Cambridge, earning his B.A. in 1627. While at Cambridge, Williams became a Separatist—that is, he believed that Puritans must separate themselves completely from the Church of England to obtain salvation. After being ordained as a minister in 1629, Williams served as chaplain to Sir William Masham of Otes at Essex and through Masham became acquainted with many leading Puritan families. Facing increased persecution for his Puritan beliefs, Williams attended a conference at Sempringham, Lincolnshire, that was called by the founders of the Massachusetts Bay Colony to discuss plans for immigrating to America. Williams and his wife, the former Mary Barnard, sailed from Bristol on the *Lyon* on December 1, 1630, arriving at Nantasket, Massachusetts, on February 5, 1631.

Williams got into trouble almost immediately because of his Separatist views. He rejected a call from the Boston Church, charging that the congregation had not separated from the Church of England. He further angered the Puritan clergy by maintaining that civil magistrates had no authority to enforce the religious precepts of the Ten Commandments. Williams accepted a position at Salem, but after the interference of the civil authorities he was forced to move on to Plymouth. There Williams again raised hackles by asserting that the Plymouth land grant was invalid—the English king, he argued, had no authority to grant land belonging to American Indians. After two years, Williams returned to Salem as a minister over the opposition of the General Court. Under Williams's leadership the Salem Church became more democratic. Alarmed at the erosion of their authority, the Boston magistrates called him before the General Court, accused him of spreading "newe & dangerous opinions," and ordered him banished from the colony.

In April 1636 Williams and several followers from Salem founded the settlement of Providence on land purchased from the Narragansett Indians, with whom Williams maintained friendly relations. He learned their language, and during the Pequot War of 1637 he served all New England as a negotiator. Williams did not try to convert the Indians to Christianity, because he believed that Christ's true church had yet to come. He became a Baptist briefly in 1639, then a Seeker—someone who adheres to the basic tenets of Christianity without accepting any particular creed.

Williams founded his new community on the radical principle that "none bee accounted Delinquent for *Doctrine.*" In 1639 the settlers drew up a document that guaranteed freedom of conscience by limiting the authority of the town government to civil matters. This was the first time in America that church and state had been declared separate in writing. Williams also sought to ensure political democracy by following a liberal land policy, whereby later arrivals were to have the same rights as the first settlers, and by granting the vote not just to property owners but to the male heads of all families. Besides Providence, three other settlements were established in the area, which also provided asylum to members of religious groups fleeing persecution, among them, the Jews, the Quakers, and the Baptists.

Alarmed by these developments, the leaders of the Massachusetts Bay Colony formed the New England Confederation with the aim of destroying the independent settlements in Rhode Island, as the area came to be called. To protect his colony, Williams sailed to England in 1643 and was able to secure a charter that authorized the colony to create its own form of government and provided for the separation of church and state. While there, he wrote his most famous work, *The Bloudy Tenent of Persecution* (1644), in which he held that all people had a basic right to religious liberty and attacked the current governments for being undemocratic.

Upon his return to Rhode Island, Williams was prevented from uniting the various settlements by another claimant to a charter. In 1652 Williams again sailed for England, where he successfully defended the validity of his charter, wrote more treatises in defense of religious liberty and political democracy, including *The Bloudy Tenent Yet More Bloudy* (1652), and met with such Puritan leaders as Oliver Cromwell and John Milton.

Returning to Rhode Island, Williams served three successive terms as colonial president. His last years were darkened by bitter controversy with the Quakers and a destructive war with the American Indians. The conflict with the Quakers arose over a three-day debate between Williams and some Quakers in 1672. It was so acrimonious that Williams's reputation as a champion of religious liberty became diminished.

In the American Indian uprising of 1675 and 1676, known as King Philip's War, the Narragansetts sided with other New England tribes against their former friends, the Rhode Island colonists, who in turn were forced to ally themselves with their old enemy, the Massachusetts Bay Colony. Though now seventy years old, Williams served as one of two captains in command of the Providence forces. During the war, Providence was burned and the Narragansetts were virtually destroyed. Williams lived on for a half dozen years afterward, still active in public affairs until the end.

Reviled during his lifetime as a "Fire-brand" and a windmill gone mad, Williams has been hailed by nineteenth- and twentieth-century Americans as an early exponent of modern, secular ideas because of his advocacy of religious freedom and political democracy. Yet as a deeply religious man, who viewed the world in terms of the Bible, he was very much of his own century. Believing that his own time was one of error and apostasy, Williams looked forward to the coming of Christ's true church. He insisted upon religious liberty and the separation of church and state not to protect this true church, but to let error and false churches play their parts.

**BIBLIOGRAPHY**

Easton, Emily, *Roger Williams: Prophet and Pioneer*, 1976; Garrett, John, *Roger Williams: Witness Beyond Christendom, 1603–1683*, 1970; Miller, Perry, *Roger Williams: His Contribution to the American Tradition*, 1974.

# Wills, Garry

(May 22, 1934– )
Author, Journalist

The author of numerous works on politics, history, and philosophy and religion, Garry Wills is one of the country's foremost scholarly political commentators. Although he accepts the label "conservative," Wills has emerged as a provocative critic of both the conservative and liberal establishments in America.

Born in Atlanta, Georgia, Garry Wills grew up in various cities in Michigan and Wisconsin. As a Jesuit seminarian, he studied philosophy at St. Louis University, graduating in 1957. He left the Society of Jesus but continued his education within the Jesuit educational system, earning an M.A. in philosophy from Xavier University in Cincinnati in 1958. During this time, an essay sent to the conservative journal the *National Review* so impressed its editor, WILLIAM F. BUCKLEY, JR., that Buckley invited Wills to join his staff. Wills became a regular contributor to the magazine for many years.

Meanwhile, Wills earned a Ph.D. in classics at Yale University in 1961. While writing his dissertation he worked as an associate editor for the Richmond, Virginia, *News Leader*. He then spent a year (1961–1962) as a charter fellow at the Center for Hellenic Studies in Washington, D.C., after which he became an assistant professor of classics at the Johns Hopkins University (1962–1967), and later adjunct professor of humanities (1968–1980).

Wills's first book was *Chesterton: Man and Mask* (1961), an intellectual biography of Gilbert Keith Chesterton, an English Catholic man of letters. He followed it with *Politics and Catholic Freedom* (1964), which led to his being asked to become a columnist for the *National Catholic Reporter*. Out of assignments for *Esquire* magazine came two more books: *Jack Ruby* (1968), about the murderer of Lee Harvey Oswald, the alleged assassin of President John F. Kennedy; and *The Second Civil War for Armageddon* (1968), a book about contemporary race relations containing a plea for vast improvement.

In 1970 Wills published the first of his acclaimed, but highly controversial, political commentaries, *Nixon Agonistes: The Crisis of the Self-Made Man*, a scathing study of both the conservatism of President Richard Nixon and the American liberal tradition. His next book, *Bare Ruined Choirs: Doubt, Prophecy, and Radical Religion* (1972), was a collection of his essays about crises within the contemporary Catholic church.

Returning to politics in his next book, Wills wrote *Inventing America: Jefferson's Declaration of Independence* (1978). In this revisionist work, he argued that Jefferson was influenced mainly by the philosophers of the Scottish Enlightenment, for whom sociability and community were all-important, rather than by the English philosopher John Locke, who saw society as being composed of very separate individuals, each pursuing his or her self-interest. Thus, according to Wills, our tendency to interpret the Declaration of Independence in Lockean terms is not in keeping with what the founders intended. The book won the Organization of American Historians Merle Curti Award of 1978, the National Book Critics Circle Award for 1979, and a John D. Rockefeller III Award, also in 1979.

Throughout the 1980s and into the 1990s, Wills has continued to produce incisive commentary on politics and religion in such books as *Explaining America: The Federalist* (1981); *The Kennedy Imprisonment: A Meditation on Power* (1982), a demystification of both the president and the politics of "Camelot"; *Reagan's America: Innocents at Home* (1987); *Under God: Religion and American Politics* (1990); and *Lincoln at Gettysburg: The Words that Remade America* (1992). From 1980 to 1988 Wills also served as Henry R. Luce Professor of American Culture and Public Policy at Northwestern University and since 1988 has been an adjunct professor at the university.

**BIBLIOGRAPHY**

Wills, Garry, *Confessions of a Conservative*, 1979.

# Wilson, William Griffith

(November 26, 1895–January 24, 1971)
Cofounder of Alcoholics Anonymous

Bill W., as he was universally known, was the major force in the Alcoholics Anonymous (A.A.) movement, which enabled countless alcoholics the world over to overcome their addiction to drink and lead constructive lives.

In the fall of 1934, William Griffith Wilson, a failed Wall Street stockbroker and a hopeless drunk, was visited by an old drinking pal, Ebby T., who told him how he had been freed from his compulsive drinking with help from the Oxford Group, a religious movement. Between drinks Wilson was impressed; he desperately wanted to be rid of his alcoholic obsession, seemingly an impossible hope. In the aftermath of his next binge, Wilson landed in the Charles B. Towns Hospital, a New York "drying out" facility. Recalling what Ebby T. had told him, Bill Wilson experienced a spiritual awakening, a sudden release from his compulsion. From Dr. William D. Silkworth, a friend who specialized in treating addiction, he learned that alcoholism is, medically, an allergy tied to a psychological obsession.

Over the next months Wilson also learned that helping other alcoholics strengthened his own sobriety. During a crisis when he craved a drink, he sought out another alcoholic—Dr. Robert H. Smith, with whom he shared his "experience, strength, and hope." On the day of their meeting, when Smith downed his last drink, June 10, 1935, the movement they called Alcoholics Anonymous was born. Bill W. and Dr. Bob—as they always were known, anonymity being a principle of A.A.—continued to lead the movement, as it grew to more than half a million recovering alcoholics throughout the world. (Smith died of cancer in 1950, after fifteen years of sobriety.)

Wilson learned that Ebby T. had been influenced by a friend in the Oxford movement, Rowland H. In despair over his self-destructive drinking, Rowland H. had gone to Zurich, Switzerland, in 1931 to work with the analytical psychologist C. G. Jung. Jung had told him that, from a medical and psychiatric viewpoint, his case was hopeless. When Rowland anxiously asked if there might be any other help, Jung spoke of a rare possibility—"a spiritual or religious experience—in short, a genuine conversion." Wilson wrote to Jung in 1961 that his statement to Rowland H. was "beyond doubt the first foundation stone upon which [Alcoholics Anonymous] has since been built." Ironically, both Rowland H. and Ebby T. returned to drinking and played no part in Alcoholics Anonymous.

Wilson was born in East Dorset, Vermont, one of two children in an unhappy marriage. After his parents divorced, he was brought up by his maternal grandparents in the town of Rutland. In 1917 he was commissioned a second lieutenant in the U.S. Army and, at a party in honor of "our brave boys in uniform," had his first drink, a Bronx cocktail. In that year he also married Lois Burnham. He and his wife moved to New York, and Wilson worked in Wall Street with considerable success, until his drinking took over his life. After founding A.A., Bill W. devoted the rest of his career to A.A., with the constant support of Lois Wilson, and he lived to see the diagnosis of alcoholism as a disease accepted by the American Medical Association and the World Health Organization. In July 1970, disabled by emphysema and heart trouble, Bill W. rose from his wheelchair to address the international convention of A.A. in Miami, attended by 11,000 people. He died six months later at the age of seventy-five.

**BIBLIOGRAPHY**

Kurtz, Ernest, *A.A.: The Story,* 1988; Robertson, Nan, *Getting Better: Inside Alcoholics Anonymous,* 1988; Wilson, William Griffith [Bill W.], *Alcoholics Anonymous: The Story of How Many Thousands of Men and Women Have Recovered from Alcoholism,* 3d ed., 1976.

# Wise, Isaac Mayer

(March 29, 1819–March 26, 1900)
Rabbi, Religious Reformer

Rabbi Isaac Mayer Wise was the chief architect of Reform Judaism in nineteenth-century America.

Isaac Mayer Wise was born in Steingrub, Bohemia (now part of Czechoslovakia). At the age of twelve he went to Prague (Czechoslovakia) to study the Talmud and Jewish law at various religious academies, or yeshivas. Educated at the Universities of Prague and Vienna, Austria, he became a rabbi in 1842, moving to a congregation in Radnitz, Bohemia, the following year. Learning of the movement in Germany to reform traditional Judaism, Wise in 1845 attended the conference of Reform rabbis in Frankfurt, Germany. A year later, he decided to immigrate to the United States in order to escape from the government restrictions on Jews and also to advance the new religious ideas in the freer atmosphere of America.

Becoming rabbi of a synagogue in Albany, New York, in 1846, Wise immediately set to work to reform his congregation. This was no easy task because most of the nearly 60,000 Jews living in the United States still followed traditional practices. Among the reforms suggested at the Frankfurt conference and now proposed by Wise were limiting the use of Hebrew in favor of the native language at services, using choirs and organs, seating men and women together, and eliminating the prayer for the return of the Jewish people to Palestine. These reforms so divided Wise's congregation that it split into two factions. In 1851 the faction favoring reform broke away to establish a separate congregation with Wise as its rabbi.

In the next three years Wise worked to spread the ideas of Reform Judaism by contributing columns to two national Jewish periodicals, the *Occident* and the *Asmonean;* writing books and scholarly articles; and preparing *Minhag America,* a prayerbook of American Reform rites. He also made several trips to Washington, D.C., where he was warmly received at the White House and by members of Congress.

In 1854 Wise was elected rabbi for life of a large, wealthy, pro-reform congregation in Cincinnati, Ohio. Soon after his arrival in the city, he began publishing a weekly newspaper, the *Israelite* (later the *American Israelite*). Under his leadership, Cincinnati became the center of Reform Judaism in America. Eager to bring about unity among the various Jewish groups in America, Wise in 1873 founded the Union of American Hebrew Congregations (UAHC). He hoped this organization would include Orthodox Jews, now arriving from Eastern Europe, and Sephardic Jews, who had been in America since pre-revolutionary days, as well as the Reform element of mostly German background. But the UAHC drew only Reform congregations.

Wise's second major project was to start a seminary to train rabbis for the American Reform movement. In 1875 the Hebrew Union College was established in Cincinnati with Wise as president, a position he held for the rest of his life. As a teacher, Wise influenced a generation of graduates who carried his ideas to congregations throughout the country.

The third part of Wise's agenda involved establishing a rabbinical organization, which he accomplished in 1889 with the founding of the Central Conference of American Rabbis (CCAR). Wise served as president of the CCAR for the remainder of his life.

Wise defended the rights of Jewish people in America and encouraged immigrant Jews to become Americanized. He was sharply critical of Ohio governor Salmon P. Chase for calling the United States a "Christian nation," and he protested vigorously when General Ulysses S. Grant banned Jews from the military district he controlled in the Civil War. Before the war, Wise had frequently locked horns with abolitionists because of his willingness to accept slavery as the price of keeping the Union together. He was also outspoken in his opposition to the Zionist movement which sought to establish a Jewish homeland in Palestine.

Steadfast in his efforts to modernize Judaism, Wise toward the end of his life instituted various other reforms.

**BIBLIOGRAPHY**

Gumbinder, J. H., *Isaac Mayer Wise: Pioneer of American Judaism*, 1959; Heller, James G., *Isaac M. Wise*, 1965; Knox, I., *Rabbi in America: The Story of Isaac M. Wise*, 1957.

# Witherspoon, John

(February 5, 1723–November 15, 1794)
Educator, Patriot, Religious Leader

As a religious leader, John Witherspoon helped spur the rapid growth of Presbyterianism in the colonies and later the new nation. As president of the College of New Jersey (now Princeton University), he worked hard to enlarge and improve what was then a small, struggling institution.

Born in Yester, near Edinburgh, Scotland, Witherspoon was educated at the Haddington grammar school and at the University of Edinburgh, receiving his M.A. in 1739 and his divinity degree in 1743. Two years later, he was ordained a Presbyterian minister at Beith. He remained there until 1757, when he became pastor of the congregation in the town of Paisley. During these years, Witherspoon earned a reputation as a conservative clergyman who upheld orthodoxy. He attacked what he saw as the decadence of the church in sermons, debates, and often satirical writings, including *Ecclesiastical Characteristics* (1753) and *Essay on Justification* (1756).

In 1768 Witherspoon accepted a call to become president of the College of New Jersey, a post he held for the rest of his life. He proved an able administrator and succeeded in resuscitating the faltering institution during the first eight years of his tenure. Determined to make the college much more than a training school for ministers, Witherspoon introduced into the curriculum the study of philosophy, French, history, and oratory, and he required that stu-

dents master the English language. He also added graduate courses and provided for scientific equipment. Witherspoon believed that education should fit a man for public service. Students during his presidency included James Madison, William Bradford, Philip Freneau, and Henry Lee.

Also during these years, Witherspoon emerged as a leader among American Presbyterians. Witherspoon helped to heal the breach between the "Old" and the "New" factions and to strengthen church organization with the result that Presbyterianism grew rapidly in the colonies and on the frontier.

Although Witherspoon disapproved of ministers taking part in politics, he took the side of the colonists in the growing controversy between them and the British authorities. By 1776, when the outbreak of the Revolution forced the closing of the college, Witherspoon had already served on a number of provincial committees of correspondence and conventions. As a delegate to the Continental Congress that year, he urged the immediate adoption of a resolution of independence and the drafting of a declaration. When the Declaration of Independence was drafted, Witherspoon was the only clergyman to sign it.

Witherspoon served in Congress until late 1779, and again from December 1780 until November 1782, figuring prominently in more than 100 committees. He then returned to

Princeton to reopen the college and attempt to rebuild it after the setbacks of the war. Despite strenuous efforts on Witherspoon's part, however, the college did not fully recover from the effects of the Revolution during his lifetime.

Witherspoon also took up the work of organizing the Presbyterian Church along national lines. In 1789, at his suggestion, the first General Assembly of the Presbyterian Church was held, with Witherspoon as moderator.

Remaining active in public affairs as well, Witherspoon served two terms in the state legislature and in 1787 was a member of the state's constitutional ratifying convention. He died at his farm near Princeton, New Jersey, at the age of seventy-one.

In 1800 and 1801, *The Works of John Witherspoon*, in four volumes, were published posthumously, and a nine-volume edition of his works appeared fifteen years later. In an article in the *Pennsylvania Journal* in 1781, Witherspoon pointed out the difference in the language spoken in America from that in England, coining the term "Americanism."

**BIBLIOGRAPHY**

Collins, V. L., *President Witherspoon*, 1925; Woods, D. W., *John Witherspoon*, 1906.

# Wolfe, Thomas Kennerly, Jr.

(March 2, 1931– )
Writer

As a journalist, essayist, novelist, and commentator on contemporary American trends, Tom Wolfe is a leader of the mode of writing known as New Journalism, which combines detailed, objective reporting with the subjective techniques used in writing fiction.

Thomas Kennerly Wolfe was born in Richmond, Virginia, attended local schools there, and graduated cum laude from Washington and Lee University in 1951. At Yale he did graduate work in American studies, earning his Ph.D. in 1957. Seeking a change from academia, he entered upon a career in journalism, serving as a reporter for the *Springfield Union* from 1956 to 1959, as a reporter and Latin American correspondent for the *Washington Post* from 1959 to 1962, and as a reporter and writer for *New York* Sunday magazine of the *New York Herald Tribune* (now *New York* magazine) from 1962 to 1966.

In 1963 when Wolfe decided to do an article on custom automobiles in California for *Esquire* magazine, he discovered he could not write the piece in the usual journalistic manner and instead turned in detailed notes written in a stream-of-consciousness style using unconventional punctuation and slang. In this new style, which some reviewers called "aural" to describe Wolfe's attempt to bring his readers as close as possible to the experience he was evoking, Wolfe wrote articles for magazines on such popular phenomena of the sixties as heavyweight champion Muhammad Ali (then Cassius Clay), gangster society in Las Vegas, stock car racing, and disc jockey "Murray the K." These articles were collected and illustrated with drawings by Wolfe in his first book, *The Kandy-Kolored Tangerine-Flake Streamline Baby* (1965). A second collection of Wolfe's short pieces, entitled *The Pump House Gang*, appeared in 1968.

Also that year, Wolfe published *The Electric Kool-Aid Acid Test*, an account of his travels with the Merry Pranksters, Ken Kesey's West Coast group of hippies on LSD. Reviewers hailed the book as a profound look into psychedelic life.

Three of Wolfe's other books generated much controversy. *Radical Chic and Mau*

*Mauing the Flak Catchers* (1970) consisted of two long essays, the first of which dealt with a party given by composer Leonard Bernstein to raise money for the radical black organization, the Black Panthers. In it, Wolfe made fun of white liberals like Bernstein for slumming with black revolutionaries. Wolfe also made waves when he took on the New York art world in *The Painted Word* (1975) and modern architecture in *From Bauhaus to Our House* (1981).

In 1979 Wolfe published *The Right Stuff*, a book about the selection, training, and daily lives of the first seven American astronauts. Reviewers praised it for its vividness of detail and literary merit. *The Right Stuff* won an American Book Award in 1980 and was made into a popular movie. Wolfe's more recent books include *The Purple Decades. A Reader* (1982) and *The Bonfire of the Vanities*, a best-selling novel satirizing life in New York City in the 1980s and dealing with both the very rich and the very poor.

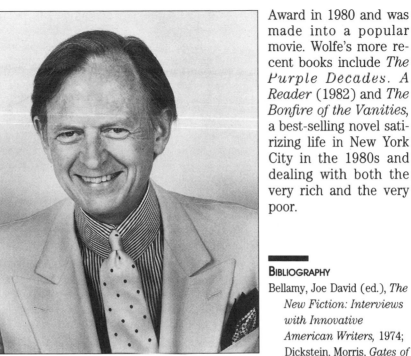

Copyright 1987 by Thomas Victor; Reprinted by permission of Harriet Spurlin

**BIBLIOGRAPHY**

Bellamy, Joe David (ed.), *The New Fiction: Interviews with Innovative American Writers*, 1974; Dickstein, Morris, *Gates of Eden: American Culture in the Sixties*, 1977; Hellman, John, *Fables of Fact: The New Journalism as New Fiction*, 1981; Klinkowitz, Jerome, *The Life of Fiction*, 1977.

# Woodhull, Victoria Claflin

(September 23, 1838–June 10, 1927)

# Claflin, Tennessee Celeste

(October 26, 1845–January 18, 1923)
Reformers

Colorful and thoroughly unconventional, Victoria Woodhull and her sister, Tennessee Celeste Claflin, challenged the domestic and public conventions of Victorian America with bold forays into high finance, journalism, politics, and sexual reform.

Victoria and Tennessee Celeste Claflin were born in Homer, Ohio, into a large family, which had to leave town following a fire of suspicious origins. Wandering from place to place and coming under the influence of spiritualism, then much in vogue in the Midwest, Victoria began to have trances at an early age, while Tennessee became skilled at conducting seances. For a while the family traveled as a medicine show selling an elixir of life with

Tennessee's picture on the bottle and with one of her brothers posing as a cancer doctor.

At age fifteen, Victoria Claflin married Canning Woodhull, an alcoholic physician, by whom she had two children. Divorcing Woodhull in 1864, she joined her sister Tennessee and they traveled throughout the Midwest as healers and clairvoyants. That same year, Tennessee Claflin was indicted in Illinois for manslaughter following the death of a woman from cancer. Fleeing town, the sisters continued to ply their trade elsewhere. In 1866 Claflin married a gambler, John Bartels, who left her almost immediately. Also that year, Woodhull married (without changing her name) Civil War veteran Colonel James Harvey Blood, who awakened her to ideas of socialism and free love. In 1868 the couple and all the Claflin relatives moved to New York City. Woodhull said she had received instructions for the move from Demosthenes in a visionary visitation.

Soon after their arrival in Manhattan, Woodhull and Claflin engaged in financial speculations with tips from the aging, widowed financier, Cornelius Vanderbilt, whom Claflin had bewitched while giving him a healing massage. Their success enabled them to open in January 1870 their own brokerage firm, Woodhull, Claflin & Company, in the city's financial district, which was then an all-male preserve. Prospering, the Woodhull-Claflin clan moved into a mansion in a fashionable neighborhood.

Around this time, Woodhull found another male mentor in Stephen Pearl Andrews, a physician and reformer who envisioned a utopia based on free love, where children and property were held in common. Imbued with feminist ideas, in 1870 Woodhull announced her candidacy for the presidency of the United States in the election of 1872. She was the first woman to run for the presidency. The sisters, together with Andrews and Blood, published the first issue of *Woodhull & Claflin's Weekly* on May 14, 1870. The paper advocated woman suffrage, free love, legalized prostitution, and birth control, and offered exposés of political and financial scandals. The weekly's 1871 publication in English of Karl Marx and Frederick Engels's *Communist Manifesto* marked its first appearance in America.

On December 21, 1870, Victoria Woodhull spoke to Congress on woman suffrage, becoming the first woman to address Congress on this or any other subject. The next month she addressed the House Judiciary Committee, urging Congress to legalize woman suffrage under the Fourteenth Amendment. Although the committee tabled her resolution, she so impressed leaders of the National Woman Suffrage Association (NWSA) with her eloquence and beauty that they invited her to speak at their meeting as well. Woodhull's appearance at the association's May meeting in New York City led the movement's opponents to claim that woman suffrage would lead to free love and destroy marriage and the family. In a move to deny such criticisms of woman suffrage and to prevent the assertive Woodhull from taking control of the movement, SUSAN B. ANTHONY stopped NWSA from backing Woodhull's presidential candidacy. Woodhull's supporters then formed the Equal Rights party and selected the black abolitionist FREDERICK DOUGLASS as her running mate, without his knowledge or approval.

By the time of the election, however, Woodhull was deep in scandal. In response to mounting criticism of her own irregular domestic arrangements (her first husband, Canning Woodhull, had joined the family in New York), she exposed the details of an affair between the popular minister HENRY WARD BEECHER and the wife of his colleague and fellow reformer, Theodore Tilton. When a full account of the affair was published in *Woodhull & Claflin's Weekly,* a self-appointed guardian of public morals, ANTHONY COMSTOCK, had the sisters jailed for sending obscene material through the mails. They were released and acquitted, but the incident effectively ended their careers. In 1876 Woodhull divorced Colonel Blood on grounds of adultery and ceased publication of the weekly. The following year, she and her sister left for England, where they both married wealthy men and continued to write and lecture in behalf of women's emancipation, though less in the public eye than previously. Victoria died at her husband's English estate at the age of eighty-eight; her sister died in London at the age of seventy-seven.

**BIBLIOGRAPHY**

Johnston, Johanna, *Mrs. Satan: The Incredible Saga of Victoria C. Woodhull,* 1967; Marbury, M. M., *Vicky: A Biography of Victoria C. Woodhull,* 1967.

# Woodson, Carter Godwin

(December 19, 1875–April 3, 1950)
African American Historian

C arter Woodson established a model for African American history through the Association for the Study of Negro Life and History and its publications, which helped to correct the biased views of historians and the general public.

Carter G. Woodson was born on a farm in Buckingham County, in a poor region of central Virginia, the eldest of nine children. Both parents had been born in slavery. Woodson had little schooling and, for the most part, saw to his own education. In his teens he went to West Virginia and for several years worked in the coal mines, then attended a segregated high school in Huntington. At twenty-one he graduated and enrolled in Berea College, in Kentucky, an institution that enabled students to work their way through school. Woodson interrupted his studies to teach school in West Virginia and returned to Berea for a B.Litt. degree in 1903.

In the summer of 1902 Woodson had gone north for the first time and taken courses at the University of Chicago. In 1903, after Berea, he returned to the university for the fall term, but he broke off his studies when he was offered a teaching post in the Philippine Islands, which had been under U.S. rule for only five years. During three years in the Philippines, Woodson learned Spanish and French. In 1906 he traveled westward, bound for home, and paused for a semester at the Sorbonne, part of the University of Paris. By fall 1907 Woodson was back at the University of Chicago, where he received

a B.A. degree the following spring and in August an M.A. in history. A year of graduate study at Harvard University followed.

While teaching in Washington, D.C., schools, Woodson completed a dissertation in American history for a Ph.D. from Harvard, awarded in 1912. He became dean of liberal arts and professor of history at Howard University but left in 1920 to spend two years as dean of West Virginia State College, near Charleston.

In 1915, while still in Washington, Woodson had founded the Association for the Study of Negro Life and History. Its title stated the dominant interest of his career—to record the contributions of African Americans in the development of American society. In 1916 he established and edited the *Journal of Negro History;* in 1921, a firm, Associated Publishers Inc., which brought out books by and about African Americans; and in 1937, the *Negro History Bulletin.* To give full time to these concerns Woodson left college work and moved back to Washington, where the association's headquarters were set up. He devoted his time to leading the association and editing the *Journal of Negro History,* relying on income from Associated Publishers and other financial support from foundations, individuals, and organizations. In 1926 he introduced Negro History Week, observed in February around the birthdays of Frederick Douglass and Abraham Lincoln; later it was expanded to Negro History Month. He continued to write articles and scholarly books, including *A*

*Century of Negro Migration* (1918), *The History of the Negro Church* (1921), and *The Works of Francis J. Grimké* (1942) (see FRANCIS GRIMKÉ).

Woodson never married. He dedicated himself to his work, except for regular summer visits to Paris. He was a ready source of help for young African American historians. It has been said that Woodson has contributed more to the development of Negro history than anyone except W. E. B. Du Bois. He died of a heart attack in his Washington house, which in 1976 was designated a National Historic Landmark. The *Journal of Negro History* was taken over by Morehouse College, in Atlanta.

**BIBLIOGRAPHY**

Grene, Lorenzo J., *Working with Carter G. Woodson, the Father of Black History, A Diary, 1928–1930,* 1989; Scally, Mary Anthony, *Carter G. Woodson: A Bio-Bibliography,* 1985; Woodson, C. G., *The Negro in Our History,* 1922.

# Woodward, Comer Vann

(November 13, 1908–   )
Historian

One of the foremost scholars of the American South, C. Vann Woodward offered in his books a revisionist interpretation of the South since the Civil War that included new insights into race relations.

C. Vann Woodward was born in Vanndale, Arkansas, and grew up in Morrilton. In 1928 he enrolled at Emory University and, after graduating two years later, studied at Columbia University, earning his M.A. there in 1932. After teaching briefly at Georgia Institute of Technology, Woodward began work on his doctorate at the University of North Carolina.

In 1938 Woodward published the first of a number of important books: *Tom Watson: Agrarian Rebel,* which was his Ph.D. dissertation. In it, Woodward broke new ground by stating that economic conflict following the Civil War occurred not only between the South and the North but also within the confines of the South, where southern whites differed among themselves about what the status of African Americans should be.

In the late 1930s and early 1940s Woodward taught history at the University of Florida, the University of Virginia, and Scripps College; he then served in the navy during World War II. His second book, *The Battle of Leyte Gulf* (1947), was based on this experience. Also that year, Woodward joined the faculty of the Johns Hopkins University, remaining there until 1961 when he became a Sterling Professor at Yale University. During these years Woodward continued with the task of reinterpreting southern history in *Origins of the New South 1877–1913* (1951), which won the Bancroft prize for 1952, and *Reunion and Reaction* (1951). In these books, he further explored the important political role that African Americans continued to play after Reconstruction.

Woodward followed these volumes with his widely acclaimed *The Strange Career of Jim Crow* (1955), in which he sought to demonstrate that the legal segregation of African Americans had originated later than Reconstruction. Some of the material for the book came from his civil rights work. Woodward consulted with the NAACP (National Association for the Advancement of Colored People; see JOEL E. SPINGARN) lawyers as they prepared their briefs for the landmark school desegregation case, *Brown* v. *Board of Education* in 1954. An activist as well as a scholar, Woodward later took part in the civil rights march to Selma, Alabama, in 1965.

In the late 1950s and 1960s Woodward continued to write about racial issues and the lessons of southern history in essays and magazine articles, some of which were collected and published in *The Burden of Southern History* (1961). Woodward hoped that the nation would finally implement the racial equality promised during Reconstruction. He also hoped that the country could learn from the South's heritage of defeat and adversity, a view he later came to doubt. A second collection of his essays, *American Counterpoint: Slavery and Racism in the North-South Dialogue*, appeared in 1971. In 1969 he was president of both the Organization of American Historians and the American Historical Association, the mark of singular recognition by his fellow historians.

After his retirement from Yale in 1977, Woodward devoted himself to editing the *Oxford History of the United States* and the work of the Civil War diarist, Mary Chesnut. Published in 1981, *Mary Chesnut's Civil War* won the 1982 Pulitzer Prize in history. Woodward's most recent books are the semiautobiographical *Thinking Back: The Perils of Writing History* (1986); *The Future of the Past* (1989), a book of essays; and a historical survey of foreign views of the United States, *The Old World's New World* (1992).

**BIBLIOGRAPHY**

Cunliffe, Marcus, and Robin W. Winks (eds.), *Pastmasters: Some Essays on American Historians*, 1969; King, Richard H., *A Southern Renaissance: The Cultural Awakening of the American South, 1930–1955*, 1980; Roper, Herbert, *C. Vann Woodward, Southerner*, 1987.

# Wright, Carroll Davidson

(July 25, 1840–February 20, 1909)
Public Official, Statistician

As chief of the Massachusetts Bureau of Labor Statistics and later first commissioner of the U.S. Bureau of Labor, Carroll Wright was a strong advocate of objective research on labor problems and the use of collective bargaining to settle disputes.

Born the son of a Universalist minister in Dunbarton, New Hampshire, Carroll Wright grew up in Washington, New Hampshire, where he attended the local schools and worked on his father's farm. After further study at academies in Massachusetts, New Hampshire, and Vermont, he began reading law in Keene, New Hampshire, supporting himself by teaching in the local schools. Wright moved to Boston to continue his legal studies, then in 1862 enlisted for service in the Civil War as a private in a New Hampshire volunteer regiment. Serving both around Washington, D.C., and on the staff of General Philip Sheridan in the Shenandoah Campaign of 1864, he rose to the rank of colonel.

Back in New Hampshire at war's end, Wright was admitted to its state bar in 1865 and the Massachusetts bar in 1867. Settling in Reading, Massachusetts, he established a successful practice.

Wright's life changed in 1873 when he was appointed chief of the Massachusetts Bureau of Labor Statistics. The four-year-old bureau—the first of its kind in the United States—was already so controversial that it had nearly been abolished. During Wright's fifteen-year tenure, both the state and the nation as a whole underwent a crucial period of economic growth. At the outset, Wright came under attack from all sides in his efforts to gather labor statistics. Employers feared he was on the side of labor, while workers were critical of Wright for not allying himself with them. Wright persevered, determined that such statistics ought to be gathered and published in a completely objective manner. His example helped the growing number of young officials in the field. In 1883 Wright organized the National Convention of Chiefs and Commissioners of Bureaus of Statistics of Labor, serving as president for nearly twenty years.

Wright recorded wage rate, the cost of living, occurrences of strikes and lockouts, and social statistics on poverty, crime, divorce, and other problems. In an essay titled "The Relation of Political Economy to the Labor Question" (1882) and in lectures delivered in Boston and elsewhere, Wright set forth his social philosophy. Abhorring class conflict, Wright believed that employers and workers ought to be able to resolve their differences through collective bargaining, with each side making concessions. He also favored the sliding scale in wage adjustment.

Having used his influence to help establish the U.S. Bureau of Labor in the Department of the Interior, Wright was appointed the new bureau's first commissioner by President Chester A. Arthur in 1885. To this post, which he held for the next twenty years, Wright brought a concern for fairness in industrial relations. In 1894 he was chairman of the commission investigating the Pullman strike of that year. Wright's commission revealed the abuse of the strikers by the federal courts, which had issued an injunction aimed at ending the strike. Later, during the prolonged and bitter anthracite coal strike of 1902, Wright served as recorder of the commission that was appointed by President Theodore Roosevelt to mediate the strike. The commission awarded the mine workers a 10 percent wage increase, although it denied recognition to the union.

Beginning in 1895, Wright combined work for the bureau with teaching. From that year until 1904, he was honorary professor of social economics at The Catholic University of America in Washington, D.C., and from 1900 he was also professor of statistics and social economics at Columbian (later George Washington) University. Wright also planned and supervised the first volumes of the economic history of the United States that were funded by the Carnegie Institution of Washington, D.C. His own works included *The Industrial Evolution of the United States* (1895) and the *Outline of Practical Sociology* (1899).

Wright was president of the American Statistical Association from 1897 until his death. He received numerous honors from foreign governments, among them the Cross of the French Legion of Honor. Chosen first president of Clark College in Worcester, Massachusetts (the undergraduate men's college of Clark University; see G. STANLEY HALL), in 1902, Wright also taught there. He resigned from the Bureau of Labor in 1905 and died several years later in Worcester.

**BIBLIOGRAPHY**

Leiby, James R., *Carroll Wright and Labor Reform*, 1960; North, S. N. D., "The Life and Work of Carroll Davidson Wright," *Quarterly Publications American Statistical Association*, June 1909.

# Wright, Frances

(September 6, 1795–December 13, 1852)
Reformer, Writer

Frances Wright was an early nineteenth-century freethinker, whose ideas on slavery, the relations between the sexes, and a national public education system were too radical for most of her contemporaries but had a profound influence on later generations of American reformers.

Born in Dundee, Scotland, Fanny Wright, as she was known, was orphaned at the age of two and raised first by maternal relatives in London and then in Dawlish, Devonshire. At age twenty-one, she and her younger sister, Camilla, went to live with a great-uncle who taught philosophy at Glasgow College. Wright read widely in the college library, becoming particularly fascinated with books about the United States. In 1818 she and her sister made their first visit to the United States, where Wright had *Altorf,* her play about the Swiss independence movement, produced in New York City. She mingled with local intellectuals and traveled throughout the Northeast. Upon her return to London in 1820, she published *Views of Society and Manners in America,* one of the most important early nineteenth-century travel diaries.

Wright's book attracted the attention of another lover of America, the Marquis de Lafayette, and the two became good friends. When Lafayette made his farewell visit to the United States in 1824, he invited Wright and her sister to accompany him. Since her relationship with Lafayette had become the subject of scandal, Wright and her sister traveled to America apart

Library of Congress

from him, deciding in 1825 to settle permanently in the United States.

Having attacked slavery in her book and later viewed its evils firsthand during a voyage up the Mississippi, Wright in 1825 published *A Plan for the Gradual Abolition of Slavery in the United States without Danger of Loss to the Citizens of the South.* In this pamphlet she called on Congress to set aside public land for slaves to farm, thereby earning their freedom. After a visit to the utopian community established by Robert Owen at New Harmony, Indiana, Wright decided to act on her own plan. That same year she purchased 640 acres near what is now Memphis, Tennessee. She also purchased a number of slaves, brought them to the plantation, which she called Nashoba, and promised them their freedom after five years' work.

Nashoba did not thrive—in part because Wright was frequently absent on extended visits to New Harmony and in part because of the controversy sparked by its interracial makeup, combined with the fact that members practiced free love, or the taking of multiple sexual partners. In 1829, after sinking half her inheritance into the failing plantation, Wright closed it down. She did, however, make good her promise to free the slaves who had worked there, transporting them to Haiti and arranging jobs for them.

Already in 1828 Wright had begun to advance her reformist ideas as part owner and editor, with Robert Owen's son, ROBERT DALE

OWEN, of the *New Harmony Gazette*. Now she embarked on lecture tours of the East and the Midwest, attacking both organized religion, as an obstacle to human happiness, and the institution of marriage, which she hoped to replace with free unions based on moral rather than legal ties. Wright also called for birth control and a system of free public education.

In 1829 Wright decided to make New York her base, settling on a farm six miles from the city. She purchased an old church on the Bowery in Manhattan and converted it into a "Hall of Science," where she lectured to workers, while editing another periodical, *The Free Enquirer*. Wright quickly emerged as a leader of the city's working-class reform movement, which had as its goals the political organization of workers and the establishment of a system of free education. Wright's own plan was for a national system of public-supported boarding schools, teaching industrial skills as well as academic subjects. In 1829 she helped start the Association for the Protection of Industry and for the Promotion of National Education. Joining forces with the Workingmen's party, this group was able to seat its candidate in the state legislature.

In 1830 Wright left the United States for Europe, where she remained for the next five years. During her absence, *The Free Enquirer* and the national education movement dissolved, and the Hall of Science was converted into a Methodist chapel. Upon her return, Wright settled in Cincinnati, Ohio, continuing to lecture and write. She campaigned for the Democratic party in the elections of 1836 and 1838, departing for Europe a year later. In the next decade, she led a peripatetic existence between the United States and Europe. By the time of her death in Cincinnati at the age of fifty-seven, Wright had become largely discredited and forgotten. It remained for future generations to appreciate her forward-looking ideas on education and equal rights.

**BIBLIOGRAPHY**

Eckhardt, C. M., *Fanny Wright: Rebel in America*, 1984; Lane, M., *Frances Wright and the Great Experiment*, 1972.

# Young, Brigham

(June 1, 1801–August 29, 1877)
Religious Leader

As second president of the Church of Jesus Christ of the Latter-Day Saints, Brigham Young led the remarkable modern exodus of the Mormons to Utah, where, in one of the most successful colonizing efforts in U.S. history, he established a strong religious, social, and economic base.

Born in Whitingham, Vermont, Young moved with his family to western New York when he was three. He had very little formal schooling—only eleven days—and as a young man worked as a journeyman painter and glazier. In 1830 Young read JOSEPH SMITH's *The Book of Mormon;* after two years of reflection he joined the church. In 1833 he led a band of converts to Kirtland, Ohio, and began his rise in the church. By 1835 Young had become third in seniority on the Quorum of the Twelve Apostles, the governing body of the church that ranked just below Joseph Smith, the founder of the Mormon church. Three years later, he became senior member of the Quorum and the following year directed the Mormons' removal to Nauvoo, Illinois. After a yearlong missionary trip in England, Young became the church's chief financial officer. When Joseph Smith was murdered in 1844, Young rallied the panic-stricken Mormons, and, winning over his rivals, asserted his leadership of the Mormon church. He became president of the church three years later.

Convinced that the Mormons could not live peacefully within the boundaries of the United States, Smith determined to lead them westward. In 1846 he brought them across Iowa to Winter Quarters, Nebraska, near what is now Omaha, and began preparations for a move further west. Young studied government publications and other sources, and talked with explorers, military men, and fur traders to locate a place of settlement. He also obtained assistance from foreign missions and from the United States government. In 1847 Young brought 148 Mormon settlers to the valley of the Great Salt Lake in present-day Utah.

At the time, the area around the Great Salt Lake belonged to Mexico and was thus beyond the jurisdiction of the U.S. government. Because of its arid barrenness, the valley seemed unlikely to attract other settlers. But the California Gold Rush of 1849 and the completion of the transcontinental railway twenty years later ended whatever hopes Young might have had that the Mormons could live for very long in isolation.

Meanwhile, thanks to Young's superb administrative abilities, the Mormons established a solid economic, political, religious, and social organization in Utah. Young launched public works and irrigation projects to make the desert bloom. He encouraged the development of local cooperative industries as well as farming and helped found many educational institutions, including the University of Deseret (1850), now the University of Utah. Young also promoted extensive immigration from the eastern United States and from Europe, which was supported through a Perpetual Emigration Fund.

Once they had arrived in the Salt Lake Valley, settlers were sent to outlying areas. By 1860 more than 150 self-supporting irrigated settlements had been established with a total population of 40,000. Colonists were selected according to their abilities, and after the settlements had been started, their work was carefully organized, enabling the Mormons to avoid many of the problems that beset other settlers in arid places.

Young maintained strict control over this ever-expanding empire. With the establishment of the Mormon state of Deseret in 1849, he served as governor and was later appointed to this position when Deseret became a U.S. territory a year later. President James Buchanan asked Young to leave that position in 1857 because of rumors of treason, but Young refused. He did not step down until federal troops under the command of Albert Sidney Johnston arrived, and even then, as president of the Mormon church, he continued to be the real authority in Utah.

An extremely practical man who had little interest in theology, Young added nothing new to church doctrine. At the same time, he refused to tolerate dissent. Beginning with his regime, expressing doubts about church doctrine became a sin punishable by excommunication. Much criticized for his dictatorial rule, Young also came under attack for his practice of polygamy. Young had as many as twenty-seven wives and fifty-six children.

Young remained head of the Mormon church until his death, leaving behind a unique and widespread community of some 140,000 Mormons that had successfully withstood the hardships of settlement as well as threats of destruction from without.

**BIBLIOGRAPHY**

Arrington, Leonard, *Brigham Young: American Moses,* 1985; Gates, Susa Y., and Leah Widstoe, *The Life Story of Brigham Young,* 1971; Hirshson, Stanley P., *The Lion of the Lord: A Biography of Brigham Young,* 1969.

# Young, Whitney Moore, Jr.

(July 31, 1921–March 11, 1971)
Civil Rights Activist

D.C. Public Library

As a civil rights partisan and the director of the National Urban League, Whitney Young was sometimes criticized by more militant black leaders as being too conservative and in the pay of the white establishment.

Whitney Young's background distinguished him from many other black leaders in the civil rights movement of the 1950s and 1960s. Born to educated middle-class parents in Lincoln Ridge, near Louisville, Kentucky, Young attended the Lincoln Institute, where his father, a former electrical engineer, was headmaster. As president of the senior class, he graduated with a B.S. from Kentucky State College (then a segregated institution) in Frankfort.

Hoping to study medicine, Young joined the Army Specialist Training Program in 1941 but found that all the places open to blacks in medical schools were taken. Instead, the army sent him to the Massachusetts Institute of Technology to study engineering. Soon, however, the army's specialist program ended, and Young was sent to Europe in a black antiaircraft artillery company. His attempt to resolve a dispute between resentful black enlisted men and their white officers was an important experience that helped him define his future role as a mediator between white elites and poor urban blacks.

Upon his discharge from the army, Young went to the University of Minnesota, where he earned a master's degree in social work. After graduating, he went to work for the National Urban League in St. Paul, Minnesota, and then in Omaha, Nebraska. In 1944 he married Margaret Buckner, who wrote books on black history and civil rights for children. They had two daughters.

From 1954 to 1960, Young served as dean of the School of Social Work at Atlanta University and also became president of the Georgia branch of the National Association for the Advancement of Colored People (NAACP; see JOEL E. SPINGARN).

In 1960 Young received a Rockefeller Fellowship for study at Harvard University, and the next year he became executive director of the National Urban League. It was a time of increasing black activism. The league, founded in 1910 by both blacks and whites to help southern blacks who had moved north, was considered a conservative organization. It worked quietly to find jobs for blacks, often in areas that traditionally were for whites only. It did not engage in political activity.

Over the next ten years Young carried on the traditional National Urban League approach, but he aggressively increased the budget and met with executives of the country's largest corporations. The league obtained jobs for tens of thousands of blacks during these years. An effective speaker and fund-raiser, Young believed it was important to keep in touch with America's centers of power and was well received by political and financial leaders. This caused civil rights leaders and young black militants to distrust him, especially when he was slow to join the movement opposed to the Vietnam War and to criticize military spending at the expense of the poor. He spoke out forcefully, however, against the slow pace at which business and government were fulfilling their promises to blacks.

A founder of the Urban Coalition, which focused attention on the plight of cities in the United States, Young served as president of the National Association of Social Workers and the National Conference on Social Welfare and was on the boards of the Rockefeller Foundation and the Urban Institute. He wrote two books: *To Be Equal* (1964) and *Beyond*

*Racism* (1969). In 1969 President Lyndon B. Johnson bestowed upon Young the Medal of Freedom, the nation's highest civilian award.

Whitney Young died suddenly of a heart attack while visiting Nigeria in 1971. He was forty-nine.

**BIBLIOGRAPHY**

Weiss, Nancy J., *Whitney M. Young, Jr. and the Struggle for Civil Rights*, 1989.

# Zenger, John Peter

(ca. 1697–July 28, 1746)
Printer

John Peter Zenger was a colonial printer, whose trial for seditious libel and subsequent acquittal marked a significant victory for the freedom of the press.

Born in Germany, Zenger was brought to New York City as one of a number of indentured immigrant children. Apprenticed to the colonial printer William Bradford from 1711 to 1719, Zenger sought employment elsewhere before returning to New York as a freeman of the city in 1723. He rejoined Bradford in a brief partnership, then in 1726 set up his own printing shop. His business consisted mostly of Dutch-language work and controversial material that Bradford, as the official government printer, could not afford to take.

In the early 1730s leaders of a new political party, formed in opposition to the arbitrary policies of Governor William Cosby, engaged Zenger to publish the *New-York Weekly Journal* as a counter to Bradford's *New York Gazette*, which Cosby was able to control. The first issue of the *Weekly Journal* appeared on November 5, 1733. Zenger assumed full responsibility for the paper's contents. Although its contributors remained anonymous, the brilliant lawyer and

journalist James Alexander apparently wrote and edited most of the articles.

Infuriated by the paper's attacks on him, Governor Cosby had Zenger arrested and imprisoned on November 17, 1734, on charges of seditious libel. Although held under excessive bail for nearly ten months, Zenger saw that his paper continued to be printed by passing instructions to his wife.

When Zenger's case was brought before the court in April 1735, his lawyers, James Alexander and William Smith, questioned the right of the Cosby-appointed chief justice to preside over the case. They were disbarred as a result, and John Chambers was named counsel for the defense. At the trial on August 4, 1735, the governor's supporters were taken by surprise when Andrew Hamilton, a Philadelphia attorney, presented himself as Zenger's lawyer.

In another surprise move, Hamilton admitted that Zenger had published the alleged libels; however, Hamilton denied that they were, in fact, libels and argued for the right to publish matters "supported with truth." This was the first time the question of truthfulness had been used as a defense in a criminal libel case. The chief justice, however, insisted that the jury determine only the fact of publication, leaving the question of libel to the court. Hamilton, in turn, urged the jury to "determine both the law and the fact," arguing that the "liberties of their country" were at stake in the case.

The jury found Zanger "not guilty," and he was released the next day. The next year, Zenger published *A Brief Narrative of the Case and Tryal of John Peter Zenger,* prepared by James Alexander. The precedent-setting case aroused great interest in the colonies and in Great Britain. Zenger was made public printer in 1737 for the colony of New York and was appointed to the same office in New Jersey the following year. After his death, his widow continued to publish the *Journal* until 1748 when it was taken over by one of Zenger's sons, who continued it until 1751.

**BIBLIOGRAPHY**

Buranelli, Vincent (ed.), *The Trial of Peter Zenger,* 1957; Rutherfurd, Livingston, *John Peter Zenger: His Press, His Trial and a Bibliography of Zenger Imprints,* 1904.

no update
9/05
DP